D1796806

THE LIBRARY
NATIONAL FOUNDATION FOR
EDUCATIONAL RESEARCH
IN ENGLAND & WALES
THE MERE, UPTON PARK
SLOUGH, BERKS, SL1 2DQ

DATE:
27/5/2011

CLASS
R/J11 NIL

STAR No:
50543

AUTHOR:
WILSON, J

B 1 499049 0

The Routledge Encyclopaedia of UK Education, Training and Employment

A comprehensive guide to all the main labour market initiatives and agencies combining education and employment in the UK, this encyclopaedia presents an historical progression from the Guilds and Statute of Artifices in 1563 through to present-day initiatives and changes. Fully cross-referenced throughout, with a full list of acronyms, bibliographic and internet resources, the encyclopaedia includes:

- detailed descriptions of all major government initiatives connecting education, training and employment;
- documentation covering England, Northern Ireland, Scotland and Wales, and initiatives in Ireland up to Irish independence;
- a brief history of education and employment in the UK;
- chronological history of government departments;
- outlines of all major public agencies and qualifications;
- information on rarely recorded and inaccessible historical documents.

With over 1,500 entries, this encyclopaedia crosses knowledge boundaries providing for the first time an integrated map of national human capital development. It addresses: preschool initiatives, primary, secondary, further and higher education; vocational education and training; labour market interventions, including those designed to return people to employment; and, government strategies designed to enhance economic and technological competitiveness. The cross-referenced structure provides connections to associated items and a chronological tracing of agencies and initiatives. This encyclopaedia will appeal to those involved in all aspects of education, training, employment, careers information, and policy making.

John P. Wilson has more than thirty years experience working in international education and training environments ranging from nursery teaching to PhD supervision. He works at Continuing Professional Development, University of Oxford, UK and at the Institute of Work Psychology, University of Sheffield, UK.

The Routledge Encyclopaedia of UK Education, Training and Employment

From the earliest statutes to the present day

John P. Wilson

Routledge
Taylor & Francis Group

LONDON AND NEW YORK

First edition published 2011
by Routledge
2 Park Square, Milton Park, Abingdon, Oxon OX14 4RN

Simultaneously published in the USA and Canada
by Routledge
270 Madison Avenue, New York, NY 10016

Routledge is an imprint of the Taylor & Francis Group, an informa business

© 2011 John P. Wilson

Typeset in Bembo and Helvetica by
Taylor & Francis Books
Printed and bound in Great Britain by
CPI Antony Rowe, Chippenham, Wiltshire

All rights reserved. No part of this book may be reprinted or reproduced or utilised in any form or by any electronic, mechanical, or other means, now known or hereafter invented, including photocopying and recording, or in any information storage or retrieval system, without permission in writing from the publishers.

British Library Cataloguing in Publication Data
A catalogue record for this book is available from the British Library

Library of Congress Cataloging-in-Publication Data
A catalog record has been requested for this book

ISBN 978-0-415-55822-8 (hbk)

Contents

Alphabetical List of Entries

Glossary of Acronyms

A2	Second Year of GCE Advanced Level	AEA	Advanced Extension Award	
AA	Advanced Apprenticeship	AEF	Aggregate External Finance	
AAU	Academic Audit Unit	AES	Adult Employment Subsidy	
AB	Awarding Body	AGCAS	Association of Graduate Careers Advisory Services	
ABSSU	Adult Basic Skills Strategy Unit	AHRB	Arts and Humanities Research Board	
ABCC	Association of British Chambers of Commerce	AHRC	Arts and Humanities Research Council	
ABE	Adult Basic Education	AIIS	Analogous Industrial Injuries Scheme	
ACAB	Association of Citizens Advice Bureaux	AIT	Access to Information Technology	
ACAS	Advisory Conciliation and Arbitration Service	ALBSU	Adult Literacy and Basic Skills Unit	
ACC	Association of County Councils	ALG	Assembly Learning Grant	
ACCAC	Qualifications Curriculum and Assessment Authority for Wales	ALI	Adult Learning Inspectorate	
		ALMP	Active Labour Market Policies	
ACDET	Advisory Committee for Disabled People in Employment and Training	ALN	Adult Literacy and Numeracy	
		ALP	Association of Learning Providers	
ACDP	Advanced Courses Development Programme (Scotland)	ALT	Association of Learning Technologies	
ACE	Adult Continuing Education	AMA	Association of Metropolitan Authorities	
ACE	Action for Community Employment (Northern Ireland)	AMA	Association of Municipal Authorities	
ACEO	Association of Chief Education Officers	AMA	Advanced Modern Apprenticeship	
ACL	Adult and Community Learning	AMA	Accelerated Modern Apprenticeship	
ACLF	Adult and Community Learning Fund	AMA	Advanced Modern Apprenticeship	
ACM	Association of College Management	AMB	Area Manpower Board	
		AMBIT	American Management and Business Internships (Northern Ireland)	
ACVT	Advisory Committee for Vocational Training (EU)			
ADC	Ability Development Centres	AME	Annually Managed Expenditure	
ADES	Association of Directors of Education in Scotland	AMG	Annual Maintenance Grant	
		AMP	Asset Management Plans	
AD(H)D	Attention Deficit (Hyperactivity) Disorder	ANIC	Association of Northern Ireland Colleges	
AE	Adult Education	AO	Adjudication Officer	

AO	Awarding Organisation		BET	Business Enterprise Training
AoC	Association of Colleges		BGT	Business Growth Training
APA	Annual Performance Agreement		BIG	Better Information Age
APE	Adaptations to Premises and Equipment			Government programme
			BIM	British Institute of Management
APEL	Assessment of Prior Experiential Learning		BIS	Department for Business, Innovation and Skills
APL	Accreditation of Prior Learning		BITC	Business in the Community
APS	Assisted Places Scheme		BLA	Business Learning Account
AQA	Assessment and Qualifications Alliance		BMRB	British Market Research Bureau
			BOA	Business on Own Account
AS	Advanced Subsidiary Level		BPRO	Blind Person's Resettlement Officer
AS	Advanced Supplementary Level			
ASC	Association of Scottish Colleges		BPTO	Blind Person's Training Officer
ASCETT	Advisory Scottish Council for Education and Training Targets		BSA	Basic Skills Agency (formerly ALBSU)
ASCOL	Association of Scottish Colleges		BSUS	Business Start-Up Scheme
ASDAN	Award Scheme Development and Accreditation Network		BTEC	Business and Technology Education Council
ASL	Additional and Specialist Learning		BTI	British Training International
AST	Advanced Skills Trainer		C2K	Curriculum 2000
AT	Adult Training		CA	Compensation Agency
ATA	Adult Training Agencies		CA	Contributions Agency
ATC	Accredited Training Centres		CA	Countryside Agency
ATLS	Associate Teacher, Learning and Skills		CAA	Computer Aided Assessment
			CAL	Computer Aided Learning
ATOs	Approved Training Organisations		CAL	Computer Assisted Learning
ATS	Adult Training Strategy		CALLMI	Computer Assisted Local Labour Market Intelligence
ATTITB	Air Transport and Travel Industry Training Board		CAO	Chief Adjudication Officer
AUA	Association of University Administrators		CAP	Career Action Plan
			CATITB	Cotton and Allied Textiles Industry Training Board
AVCE	Advanced Vocational Certificate of Education		CATS	Credit Accumulation and Transfer Scheme
AWBL	Assessment of Work Based Learning		CBA	Cost Benefit Analysis
BA	British Academy		CBAL	Community Based Adult Learning
BA	Benefits Agency		CBL	Computer Based Learning
BA	Bachelor of Arts		CBEVE	Cultural Bureau for Educational Visits and Exchanges
BACIE	British Association for Commercial and Industrial Education		CBI	Confederation of British Industry
			CBT	Computer Based Training
BBSRC	Biotechnology and Biological Sciences Research Council		CCEA	Council for the Curriculum, Examinations and Assessment (N. Ireland)
BCS	Business Consultancy Scheme			
BEC	British Employers Confederation		CCETSW	Central Council for Education and Training in Social Work
BECTA	British Educational Communications and Technology Agency		CCTE	Chambers of Commerce Training and Enterprise
BEM	Business Excellence Model		CDL	Career Development Loan (1988)
BEP	Business Enterprise Programme		CDLP	Career Development Loan Plus (1995)
BES	Business Enterprise Support			

CEDEFOP	European Centre for the Development of Vocational Training	COSHEP	Committee of Scottish Higher Education Principals
CEECs	Central Eastern European Countries	CoSLA	Convention of Scottish Local Authorities
CEG	Careers Education and Guidance	CoSLA	Council of Scottish Local Authorities
CEO	Chief Education Officer	CoVE	Centres of Vocational Excellence
CEO	Chief Executive Officer	CP	Community Programme
CEP	Community Enterprise Programme	CPA	Community Programme Agents
CES	Centre for Educational Sociology	CPD	Continuing Professional Development
CES	Community Education Services	CPRS	Central Policy Review Staff
CET	Continuing Education and Training	CPVE	Certificate of Pre-Vocational Education
CET	Council for Educational Technology	CQFW	Credit and Qualifications Framework for Wales
CETL	Centre for Excellence in Teaching and Learning	CRAC	Careers Research and Advisory Centre
CETW	Council for Education and Training for Wales	CSD	Civil Service Department
CFE	Colleges of Further Education	CSE	Certificate of Secondary Education
CGLI	City and Guilds of London Institute	CSNA	Careers Service National Association
CI	Central Institution	CSOF	Careers Service Operational Forum
CI	Community Industry	CSR	Comprehensive Spending Review
CIE	Cambridge International Examinations	CSYS	Certificate of Sixth-Year Studies (Scotland)
CIF	Common Inspection Framework	CTC	Central Training Council (1964)
CIHE	Council for Industry and Higher Education	CTC	City Technology Colleges
CILT	Centre for Information on Language Teaching and Research	CTLLS	Certificate in Teaching in the Lifelong Learning Sector
CITB	Construction Industry Training Board	CUB	Central Unemployed Body
CLAIT	Computer Literacy and Information Technology	CUP	Cambridge University Press
		CVCP	Committee of Vice Chancellors and Principals
CLC	City Learning Centre	CVET	Continuing Vocational Education and Training
CMED	Council for Management Education and Development	CVPE	Certificate in Vocational Preparation and Education
CNAA	Council for National Academic Awards	CYEE	Central Youth Employment Executive
CNAA	Council for National Accreditation and Awards	DARAS	Disability Access Rights Advisory Service
COGS	Confederation of Group Training Schemes	DAS	Disablement Advisory Service
COI	Central Office of Information	DBIS	Department for Business, Innovation and Skills
COIC	Careers and Occupational Information Centre	DCELLS	Department for Children, Education, Lifelong Learning and Skills
COLEG	Colleges Open Learning Exchange Group (Scotland)		
COP	Community Opportunities Programme	DCSF	Department for Children, Schools and Families

DCU	Development Co-ordination Unit		DWA	Disability Working Allowance
DDA	Disability Discrimination Act (1995)		E2E	Entry to Employment
			EA	Employment Action
DE	Department of Employment		EAB	Education Assets Board
DEA	Disability Employment Advisor		EAL	English as an Additional Language
DEFRA	Department of the Environment Food and Rural Affairs		EAP	English for Academic Purposes
			EAS	Enterprise Allowance Scheme
DELNI	Department of Education and Learning Northern Ireland		EAZ	Education Action Zone
			EBD	Emotional and Behavioural Difficulties
DENI	Department of Education Northern Ireland		EBP	Education Business Partnership
DEP	Department of Employment and Pensions		ECCTIS	Educational Counselling and Credit Transfer Information Service
DEP	Department of Employment and Productivity		ECCTS	European Course Credit Transfer System
DES	Department of Education and Science		ECITB	Engineering and Construction Industry Training Board
DETR	Department of the Environment, Transport and the Regions		ECITC	Engineering and Construction Industry Training Committee
DfEE	Department for Education and Employment		ECVET	European Credit System for Vocational Education and Training
DfES	Department for Education and Skills		ED	Education Department
DGVT	Director General for Vocational Training (EU)		EDAP	Education Data Advisory Panel
			EDAP	Employee Development and Assistance Programme
DHSS	Department of Health and Social Security		EDC	Economic Development Council
DISC	Drop-in Skills Centre		EEA	European Economic Area
DIUS	Department for Innovation, Universities and Skills		EECs	Early Excellence Centres
			EEF	Engineering Employers Federation
DL	Distance Learning		EEG	Employment and Enterprise Group
DLO	Desirable Learning Outcome		EEMTEB	Electrical and Electronic Manufacturers Training and Education Board
DLO	Direct Labour Organisation			
DMC	District Manpower Committees (In 1983 were replaced by AMBs)		EEP	European Employment Pact
DMS	Department of Manpower Services		EFL	English as a Foreign Language
			EFTA	European Free Trade Area
DoE	Department of Employment		EHE	Enterprise in Higher Education
DOORS	Data On Occupations Retrieval System		EHRC	Equality and Human Rights Commission
DoVE	Diploma of Vocational Education		EIC	European Information Centre
DPA	Directory Publishers Association		EiC	Excellence in Cities
DPR	Data Protection Registry		EIP	Employer Investment in People
DRC	Disability Rights Commission		EIS	Education Institute of Scotland
DRO	Disablement Resettlement Officer		EITB	Engineering Industry Training Board
DRTF	Disability Rights Task Force			
DSA	Disabled Students Allowance		ELLD	Enterprise and Lifelong Learning Department (Scotland)
DSS	Department of Social Security			
DTI	Department of Trade and Industry		ELMC	Employment and Labour Market Committee
DTLLS	Diploma in Teaching in the Lifelong Learning Sector		ELSA	Education, Labour and Social Affairs Committee
DTS	Direct Training Services			

ELWa	Education and Learning Wales	EYFS	Early Years Foundation Stage
EMA	Education Maintenance Allowance	EZ	Employment Zone
		FAB	Federation of Awarding Bodies
EMS	Environment Management Systems	FAM	Financial Appraisal and Monitoring
EMS	European Monetary System	FAS	Funding Agency for Schools
ENTO	Employment National Training Organisation	FCI	Financial Control Initiative
		FCO	Foreign and Commonwealth Office
EO	Equal Opportunities		
EO	Establishment Officer	FD	Foundation Degree
EO	Executive Officer	FDTL	Fund for the Development of Teaching and Learning
EOC	Equal Opportunities Commission		
EP	European Parliament	FE	Further Education
ERASMUS	European Action Scheme for the Mobility of University Students	FECs	Further Education Colleges
		FECDF	Further Education Competitiveness and Development Fund
ERC	Employment Rehabilitation Centre		
ERDF	European Regional Development Fund	FECF	Further Education Collaboration Fund
EREN	European Regions Educational Network	FEDA	Further Education Development Agency
ERM	Exchange Rate Mechanism		
ES	Employment Service	FEFC	Further Education Funding Council
ESA	Employment Services Agency		
ESD	Employment Services Division (MSC)	FEFC(W)	Further Education Funding Council for Wales
ESF	European Social Fund	FENTO	Further Education National Training Organisation
ESL	English as a Second Language		
ESOL	English for Speakers of Other Languages	FERL	Further Education Resources for Learning
ESRC	Economic and Social Research Council	FEU	Further Education Unit
		FfE	Framework for Excellence
ESREB	Employment Service Research and Evaluation Branch	FFEP	Family Friendly Employment Project
ESS	Education Standard Spending	FFF	Free Forward Fares
ESS	Employers Skills Survey	fforwm	The Forum of the National Association for Further Education Colleges and Associations in Wales (now Colleges Wales)
ET	Employment Training		
ETDA	Education and Training Development Agenda		
ERF	Employer Training Forums	FHE	Further and Higher Education
ETF	Environmental Task Force	FJDP	Forward Job and Development Plan
ETF	European Training Fund		
ETF	European Training Foundation	FIS	Financial Information Systems
ETI	Education and Training Inspectorate – Northern Ireland	FLT	Foundation Learning Tier
		FMA	Foundation Modern Apprenticeship
EU	European Union		
EUI	European University Institute	FMI	Financial Management Information
EURES	European Employment Service		
EV	External Verifier	FMS	Financial Management Strategy
EVS	European Voluntary Service	FPS	Federation of Personnel Services
EYDCP	Early Years Development and Childcare Partnership	FRESA	Framework for Regional Employment and Skills Action
EYDP	Early Years Development Plans	FS	Functional Skills

FSM	Free School Meals	HEA	Higher Education Academy
FSW	Future Skills Wales	HEADLAMP	Head Teachers Leadership and
FT	Full Time		Management Programme
FTE	Full Time Equivalent	HEFCE	Higher Education Funding Council
FTET	Full Time Education and Training		for England
FTW	Fares To Work	HEFCNI	Higher Education Funding Council
GA	Graduate Apprenticeship		for Northern Ireland
GAD	Government Actuary's	HEFCS	Higher Education Funding Council
	Department		for Scotland
GATT	General Agreement on Tariffs and	HEFCW	Higher Education Funding Council
	Trade		for Wales
GBO	General Building Operative	HEI	Higher Education Institution
	(Scotland)	HEIF	Higher Education Innovation Fund
GCE	General Certificate of Education	HEQC	Higher Education Qualifications
GCSE	General Certificate of Secondary		Council
	Education	HERDF	Higher Education Regional
GDN	Government Data Network		Development Fund
GDP	Gross Domestic Product	HERO	Higher Education Reach Out Fund
GEP	Graduate Enterprise Programme	HEROBaC	Higher Education Reach Out Fund
GEST	Grants for Education, Support and		to Business and the Community
	Training	HESA	Higher Education Statistics
GGP	Graduate Gateway Programme		Agency
GLH	Guided Learning Hours	HESDA	Higher Education Staff
GM	Grant Maintained (School)		Development Agency
GMSAC	Grant Maintained School Advisory	HEW	Higher Education Wales
	Council	HIE	Highlands and Islands Enterprise
GMSF	Grant Maintained Schools	HMCI	Her Majesty's Chief Inspector (of
	Foundation		Schools)
GNP	Gross National Product	HMI	Her Majesty's Inspector
GNVQ	General National Vocational		(Education)
	Qualification	HMIE	Her Majesty's Inspectorate of
GO	Government Office		Education (Scotland)
GSS	Government Statistical Service	HMSO	His/Her Majesty's Stationery
GSVQ	General Scottish Vocational		Office
	Qualification	HMT	Her Majesty's Treasury
GTA	Group Training Association	HNC	Higher National Certificate
GTC	General Teaching Council	HND	Higher National Diploma
GTC	Government Training Centre	HO	Home Office
GTCS	General Teaching Council for	HPD	Higher Professional Diploma
	Scotland	HRD	Human Resource Development
GTN	Government Telecommunications	HRM	Human Resource Management
	Network	HSC	Health and Safety Commission
GTP	Graduate Teacher Programme	HSDU	Higher Still Development Unit
GTP	Graduate Training Programme	HSE	Health and Safety Executive
GTS	Group Training Schemes	HSW	Health and Safety at Work
GTTR	Graduate Teacher Training	HTNT	Higher Technical National Training
	Registry	IAC	Internal Audit Commission
HC	House of Commons	IAD	Internal Audit Division
HCITB	Hotel and Catering Industry	IAG	Information, Advice and Guidance
	Training Board	IAS	Interrupted Apprenticeship
HCTB	Hotel and Catering Training Board		Scheme
HE	Higher Education	IB	Invalidity Benefit

ICG	Institute of Career Guidance	IT	Industrial Tribunal
ICT	Information and Communications Technology	IT	Information Technology
		ITB	Industrial Training Board
IDA	Information and Development Agency	ITC	Industrial Training Council
		ITE	Initial Teacher Education
IDGD	Inter-Departmental Group on Disability	ITeC	Information Technology Centre
		ITM	Improving the Training Market
IDS	Incomes Data Services	ITNTO	IT National Training Organisation
IDS	Industry Department for Scotland	ITO	Industrial Training Organisation
IEA	Institute for Economic Affairs	ITT	Initial Teacher Training
IER	Individual Employment Rights	IV	Internal Verifier
IER	Institute for Employment Research	ITTWE	Individual Training Throughout With an Employer
IES	Institute for Employment Studies	JACQA	Joint Advisory Committee for Qualifications Approval
IFP	Increased Flexibility Programme		
IGCSE	International General Certificate of Secondary Education	JANET	Joint Academic Network
		JC	Jobcentre
IIAC	Industrial Injuries Advisory Council	JC+	Jobcentre Plus
IiP	Investors in People	JCC	Joint Consultative Committee
IiYP	Investors in Young People	JCP	Job Creation Programme
ILAs	Individual Learning Accounts	JEB	Joint Examining Board
ILO	International Labour Organisation	JEG	Job Evaluation and Grading
ILP	Individual Learning Plan	JESP	Job Evaluation for Senior Posts
ILP	Individual Learning Programme	JFG	Job Finders' Grant
ILT	Information and Learning Technology	JICs	Junior Instructional Centres
		JIG	Job Interview Guarantee
ILT	Institute for Learning and Teaching	JIS	Job Introduction Scheme
		JISC	Joint Information Systems Committee
ILTHE	Institute for Learning and Teaching in Higher Education	JIU	Joint International Unit
ILTU	Industrial Language Training Unit	JRS	Job Rehearsal Scheme
IMF	International Monetary Fund	JRS	Job Release Scheme
IMSG	Information Management Sub-Group	JRW	Job Review Workshops
		JSA	Job Seekers Allowance
INSET	In-Service Education and Training	JSG	Job Seekers Grant
IoD	Institute of Directors	JSP	Job Search Plus
IPD	Institute for Personnel Development	JSS	Job Search Scheme
		JSS	Job Splitting Scheme
IPPR	Institute for Public Policy Research	JTP	Job Training Programme
		JTS	Job Training Scheme
IR	Inland Revenue	KPA	Key Performance Area
IRED	Industrial Relations and Europe Directorate	KPI	Key Performance Indicator
		KS	Key Stage (in education)
ISC	Independent Schools Council	KTP	Knowledge Transfer Partnership
ISCED	International Standard Classification of Education	L2L	Learning to Learn
		LAA	Local Area Agreement
ISO	International Standards Organisation	LABs	Labour Advisory Bodies
		LAMS	Learning Activity Management System
ISP	Individual Support Plan		
ISR	Individual Student Record	LCB	Local Competitiveness Budget
ISWP	Information Systems Work Programme	LCGs	Local Consultancy Grants
		LCP	Local Collaborative Project

LCU	Large Companies Unit (MSC)	MAs	Managing Agents
LDP	Local Development Project	MACE	Managing Company Expansion
LEA	Local Education Authority	MAFF	Ministry of Agriculture, Fisheries and Food
LEAPS	Lothian Equal Access Programme for Schools	MAIG	Modern Apprenticeships Implementation Group
LEC	Local Enterprise Company (Scotland)	MANTRA	Modern Apprenticeships and National Traineeships Advisory Group
LECs	Local Employment Committees		
LECT	League for the Exchange of Commonwealth Teachers	MAP	Micro-Processor Application Project
LEN	Local Enterprise Networks	MARIS	Materials and Resources Information Service
LFS	Labour Force Survey		
LfW	Learning for Work	MBSS	Music and Ballet Schools Scheme
LGA	Local Government Association	MCI	Management Charter Initiative
LGN	Local Guidance Network (Scotland)	MEP	Management Extension Programme
LIAISE	Learning Initiatives for Adults in Scottish Education	MEP	Member of the European Parliament
LID	Local Improvement District	MEP	Micro-electronic Education Programme
LIF	Local Initiative Fund		
LLL	Lifelong Learning	MFL	Modern Foreign Language
LLMRU	Local Labour Market Research Unit	MIA	Manpower Intelligence Agency
LLP	Local Learning Partnership	MISEP	Mutual Information System on Employment Policies
LLSC	Local Learning and Skills Council		
LMI	Labour Market Information	MIPD	Manpower Intelligence and Planning Division (MSC)
LMI	Labour Market Intelligence		
LMIB	Labour Market Information Board	MLNS	Ministry of Labour and National Service
LMS	Labour Market Systems		
LMS	Local Management of Schools	MoD	Ministry of Defence
LOTT	Licensed and Overseas Trained Teachers	MoL	Ministry of Labour
		MoSS	Ministry of Social Security
LPSH	Leadership Programme for Serving Heads	MSC	Manpower Services Commission
		NAA	National Assessment Agency
LSAC	Language Sports and Art Colleges	NAB	National Advisory Body
LSC	Learning and Skills Council	NACCCE	National Advisory Committee on Creative and Cultural Education
LSDA	Leaning and Skills Development Agency	NACCEG	National Advisory Council for Careers and Educational Guidance
LSDA NI	Learning and Skills Development Agency – Northern Ireland		
LSF	Learner Support Funds	NACEPD	National Advisory Council on Employment of People with Disabilities
LSIS	Learning and Skills Improvement Service		
LSO	Learning and Skills Observatory for Wales	NACETT	National Advisory Council for Education and Training Targets
LSP	Local Strategic Partnership	NACRO	National Association for the Care and Resettlement of Offenders
LSRC	Learning and Skills Research Council		
		NAFE	Non-Advanced Further Education
LTU	Long Term Unemployed	NAGCELL	National Advisory Group on Continuing Education and Lifelong Learning
LTW	Learning and Training at Work		
Mapp	Modern Apprenticeships (1993)		
MA	Modern Apprenticeships (1995)	NALS	National Adult Learning Survey

NAO	National Audit Office	NESS	National Employer Skills Survey
NAS	National Apprenticeship Service	NESTA	National Endowment for Science, Technology and the Arts
NASEC	National Apprentice Scheme for Engineering Construction	NETT	National Education and Training Targets
NATFHE	National Association of Teachers in Further and Higher Education	NFER	National Foundation for Educational Research
NAW	National Assembly of Wales		
NC	National Curriculum	NGfL	National Grid for Learning
NCA	New Client Advisors	NGG	National Guidance Group
NCAS	National Commercial Apprenticeship Scheme	NGO	Non-Governmental Organisation
		NHSU	National Health Service University
NCET	National Council for Educational Technology	NIACE	National Institute of Adult Continuing Education
NCITO	National Council of Industry Training Organisations	NICEC	National Institute of Careers and Education Counselling
NCS	National Childcare Strategy	NIC	National Insurance Contributions
NCSL	National College for School Leadership	NICCEA	Northern Ireland Council for the Curriculum, Examinations and Assessment
NCVO	National Council of Voluntary Organisations	NIESR	National Institute for Economic and Social Research
NCVQ	National Council for Vocational Qualifications	NIHEC	Northern Ireland Higher Education Council
NCWE	National Council for Work Experience	NIHEFC	Northern Ireland Higher Education Funding Council
NDAQ	National Database of Accredited Qualifications	NILO	National Investment Loans Office
NDC	National Disability Council	NILTC	National Industrial Language Training Centre
NDDI	National Disability Development Initiative	NIO	Northern Ireland Office
NDP	National Development Programme	NISVQ	National Information System for Vocational Qualifications
NDPA	New Deal Personal Advisor	NJAB	National Joint Apprenticeship Board
NDPB	Non-Departmental Public Body		
NDS	New Deal for Schools	NJAC	National Joint Advisory Council (Ministry of Labour)
NDYP	New Deal for Young People		
NEB	National Enterprise Board	NJATC	National Joint Apprenticeship and Training Council
NEC	National Extension College		
NEDC	National Economic Development Council	NJEE	National Juvenile Employment Executive
NEDO	National Economic Development Office	NJTS	New Job Training Scheme (MSC)
		NLN	National Learning Network
NEET	Not in Employment, Education and Training	NOCN	National Open College Network
		NOF	New Opportunities Fund
NEOST	National Employers Organisation for School Teachers	NOMIS	National Online Manpower Information System
NEP	New Enterprise Programme	NOMS	National Offender Management Service
NERA	National Economic Research Associates		
		NOP	National Opinion Poll
NERC	Natural Environment Research Council	NOS	National Occupational Standard
		NOW	New Opportunities for Women
NERF	National Education Research Forum	NPQH	National Professional Qualification for Headship

NPSS	National Priority Skills Scheme	OJTS	Old Job Training Scheme
NQF	National Qualification Framework	OL	Open Learning
NQT	Newly Qualified Teacher	OLC	Open Learning Credits
NRA	National Record of Achievement	OLS	Overseas Labour Service
NROVA	National Record of Vocational Achievement	OLSU	Offenders Learning and Skills Unit
NSA	National Skills Academies	OMSC	Office of the Manpower Services Commission
NSAG	National Staff Advisory Group	ONS	Office for National Statistics
NSDS	National Skills Development Scheme	OPCA/HSC	Office of the Parliamentary Commissioner for Administration and Health Service Commissioners
NSTF	National Skills Task Force		
NT	National Trainee		
NTA	National Training Agency	OPCS	Office of Population, Censuses and Surveys
NTA	National Training Award		
NTACs	New Technology Access Centres	ORT	Organisation for Rehabilitation and Training
NTI	New Technology Institute		
NTDP	National Training Development Plan	OSCI	Out of School Childcare Initiative
NTFS	National Teaching Fellowship Scheme	OST	Office of Science and Technology
		OSVQ	Occupational Scottish Vocational Qualification
NTG	Network Training Group		
NTI	New Training Initiative	OT	Occupational Training
NTO	National Training Organisation	OTF	Occupational Training Families
NTONC	National Training Organisation National Council	OTP	Open Tech Programme
		OTU	Open Tech Unit
NUBS	National Unemployment Benefit System	OU	Open University
		P4P	Partnerships for Progression
NVQ	National Vocational Qualification	PAC	Public Accounts Committee
NVYO	National Voluntary Youth Organisation	PACT	Placing Assessment and Counselling Team
NWS	New Workers Scheme	PANDA	Performance AND Assessment Reports (OFSTED)
NYA	National Youth Agency		
NYR	National Year of Reading	PAR	Policy Analysis and Review
NYWS	New Young Workers Scheme	PAT	Personnel Advice Team
OC	Open College	PAT	Pensions Appeal Tribunal
OCA	OFSTED Complaints Adjudicator	PAT	Policy Action Teams
OCR	Oxford, Cambridge and RSA Examinations	PAYP	Positive Activities for Young People
OCSC	Office of the Civil Service Commission	PBWE	Project Based Work Experience
		PCET	Post-Compulsory Education and Training
ODA	Overseas Development Administration		
		PCFC	Polytechnics and Colleges Funding Council
ODL	Open and Distance Learning		
OECD	Organisation for Economic Co-operation and Development	PDA	Professional Development Award (Scotland)
OFFA	Office for Fair Access	PECG	Public Expenditure Co-ordination Group
Ofqual	Office of the Qualifications and Examinations Regulator		
		PEP	Private Enterprise Programme
OFSTED	Office for Standards in Education	PER	Professional and Executive Recruitment (MSC agency)
OfV	Opportunities for Volunteering		
OGD	Other Government Department	PER	Professional and Executive Register
OIDB	Occupational Information Database		
		PES	Public Expenditure Survey

PEU	Public Enquiry Unit	QTLS	Qualified Teacher, Learning and
PFI	Public Finance Initiative		Skills
PGCE	Postgraduate Certificate in	QTS	Qualified Teacher Status
	Education	QUANGO	Quasi-Autonomous Non-
PGD	Programmes Division		Governmental Organisation
PI	Performance Indicator	QUIET	Quality in Education and Training
PICs	Private Industry Councils		Associates
	(American model for TECs)	RADAR	Royal Association for Disability
PICKUP	Professional Industrial and		and Rehabilitation
	Commercial Updating	RAE	Research Assessment Exercise
PLTS	Personal, Learning and Thinking	RAWG	Regional Allocation Working
	Skills		Group
PMLD	Profound and Multiple Learning	RDA	Regional Development Agency
	Difficulties	RDA	Rural Development Area
PPP	Public Private Partnerships	RDO	Regional Development Officer
PPS	Parliamentary Private Secretary	RDP	Registered Disabled People
PQ	Parliamentary Question	REE	Register of Educational
PRF	Performance-Related Funding		Establishments
PRINCE	Projects in Controlled	REEF	Race Employment and
	Environment		Educational Forum
PRO	Public Records Office	RFEA	Regular Forces Employment
PRP	Performance Related Pay		Association
PRT	Programme Review Team	RHOMIS	Regional and Head Office
PRU	People Referral Unit		Management Information System
PSA	Public Service Agency	RIC	Residential Instruction Centres
PSA	Public Service Agreement	RIDDOR	Reporting of Injuries Diseases and
PSAG	Projects and Standards Approval		Dangerous Occurrences
	Group		Regulations
PSB	Potential Schools Budget	RIS	Register of Independent Schools
PSBR	Public Sector Borrowing	RMIU	Regional Manpower Intelligence
	Requirement		Unit (MSC)
PSHE	Personal, Social and Health	RMSDs	Regional Manpower Service
	Education		Directors
PSI	Policy Studies Institute	RPI	Retail Price Index
PT	Part-Time	RREAS	Race Relations Employment
PTE	Permanent Transfer Expenses		Advisory Service
PTF	Practical Training Facilities	RSA	Royal Society for the
PTLLS	Preparation for Teaching in the		encouragement of Arts,
	Lifelong Learning Sector		Manufactures and Commerce
PTR	Pupil-Teacher Ratio	RSP	Regional Skills Partnerships
PYBT	Prince's Youth Business Trust	RSSL	Recruitment Subsidy for School
QAA	Quality Assurance Agency (for		Leavers
	Higher Education)	RTC	Residential Training Centres
QCA	Qualifications and Curriculum	RTS	Residential Training Service
	Authority	SAC	Social Affairs Council
QCDA	Qualifications and Curriculum	SAE	Special Aids to Employment
	Development Agency	SAS	Special Agreement School
QCF	Qualifications and Credit	SBATC	Scottish Building Apprenticeship
	Framework		and Training Council
QDC	Qualifications Data Collection	SBC	Small Business Courses
	Steering Group	SBR	Stricter Benefit Regime
QIA	Quality Improvement Agency	SBS	Small Business Service

SBU	Special Buying Unit	SEU	Standards and Effectiveness Unit
SCAA	School Curriculum and Assessment Authority	SfB	Skills for Business
		SfBN	Skills for Business Network
SCCC	Scottish Consultative Council on the Curriculum	SFEFC	Scottish Further Education Funding Council
SCE	Scottish Certificate of Education	SFES	Small Firms Employment Subsidy
SCEC	Scottish Community Education Council	SFEU	Scottish Further Education Unit
		SFHEA	Scottish Further and Higher Education Association
SCET	Scottish Council for Educational Technology	SfL	Skills for Life
SCONTO	Scottish Council of National Training Organisations	SfSB	Skills for Small Businesses
		SFTI	Small Firms Training Initiative
SCOP	Standing Conference of Principals	SFTL	Small Firms Training Loan
SCOTBEC	Scottish Business Education Council	SHEFC	Scottish Higher Education Funding Council
SCOTCATS	Scottish Credit Accumulation and Transfer Scheme	SIC	Standard Industrial Classification
		SLA	Service Level Agreement
SCOTEC	Scottish Technical Education Council	SLC	Student Loan Company
		SLD	Severe Learning Difficulties
SCOTTSU	Scottish Open Tech Training and Support Unit	SLDD	Students with Learning Difficulty
		SLDD	Students with Learning Disability
SCOTVEC	Scottish Vocational Education Council	SME	Small and Medium-sized Enterprise
SCPR	Social and Community Planning Research	SMU	Superhighways and Multimedia Unit
SCQF	Scottish Credit and Qualifications Framework	SNVQ	Scottish National Vocational Qualification
SCRAN	Scottish Cultural Resources Access Network	SO	Scottish Office
		SOC	Standard Occupational Classification
SCRE	Scottish Council for Research in Education	SOEID	Scottish Office Education and Industry Department
SCS	Senior Civil Servant	SOLACE	Society of Local Authority Chief Executives and Senior Managers
SCS	Senior Civil Service		
SCVS	Scottish Certificate of Vocational Studies	SOSR	Statement of Service Requirement
		SPAB	Special Programme Area Boards (Scotland)
SDF	Skills Development Fund		
SE	Scottish Enterprise	SPD	Special Programmes Division (MSC)
SE	Scottish Executive		
SEAM	Schools Environmental Audit Methodology	SPG	Special Purpose Grant
SEB	Scottish Examination Board	SQA	Scottish Qualifications Agency
SEC	Self-Employment Courses	SQMS	Scottish Quality Management System
SEELLD	Scottish Executive Enterprise and Lifelong Learning Department		
		SRB	Single Regeneration Budget
SELTIC	Scottish English Language Teaching in Consortium	SSA	Sector Skills Agreement
		SSA	Standard Spending Assessment
SEN	Special Educational Needs	SSC	Sector Skills Council
SEO	Senior Executive Officer	SSDA	Sector Skills Development Agency
SEO	Society of Education Officers	SSFE	Scottish School of Further Education
SEPACS	Sheltered Employment Procurement and Consultancy Unit		
		ST	Sector Training
SET	Scottish Education and Training	STA	Skillcentre Training Agency

STC	Sector Training Council	TFE	Training For Enterprise
STC	Staff Training Co-ordinator	TFW	Training for Work
STEP	Special Temporary Employment Programme	TGWU	Transport and General Workers Union
STRB	School Teachers' Review Body	THES	Times Higher Educational Supplement
STUC	Scottish Trades Union Congress		
STWCS	Short-Time Working Compensation Scheme	TI	Training Inspectorate
		TIF	Training Information Framework
SUfI	Scottish University for Industry	TIS	Travel to Interview Scheme
SUPERVACS	Super Vacancy Circulation System	TM	Training Managers
SVQ	Scottish Vocational Qualification	TME	Total Managed Expenditure
SVUK	Standards Verification UK	TNA	Training Needs Analysis
SWAP	Scottish Wider Access Programme	TO	Treat Official
		TOs	Training Officers
SWDP	Sector Workforce Development Plans	TOPs	Training Opportunities Programmes
SWE	Supervised Work Experience	TOPS	Training Opportunities Scheme
SWFG	Single Work-Focused Gateway	TPS	Teachers' Pension Scheme
SWOT	Strengths, Weaknesses, Opportunities, Threats (Analysis of)	TQA	Teaching Quality Assessment
		TQEF	Teaching Quality Enhancement Fund
TA	Training Agency		
TA	Training Agents	TQFE	Teaching Qualification for Further Education (Scotland)
TAP	Training Access Point		
TAS	Training Advisory Service	TQS	Training Quality Standard
TASSC	The Alliance of Sector Skills Councils	TSA	Training Services Agency
		TSAS	Training Standards Advisory Service
TC	Technology Colleges		
TC	Training Commission	TSC	Training Standards Council
TCR	Trainee-Centred Reviewing	TSD	Training Services Division (MSC)
TCS	Teaching Company Scheme	TSH	Transfer Scheme Handbook
TDA	Training and Development Agency for Schools	TSO	The Stationery Office
		TSPA	Training for Skills-Programme for Action
TDF	TEC Discretionary Fund		
TDLB	Training and Development Lead Body	TSS	Total Standard Spending
		TSTWCS	Temporary Short-Time Working Compensation Scheme
TEA	Training and Employment Agency in Northern Ireland		
		TTA	Teacher Training Agency
TEC	Training and Enterprise Council	TTWA	Travel To Work Area
TEED	Training, Enterprise and Education Directorate (DfEE)	TUC	Trades Union Congress
		TUPE	Transfer of Undertakings Protection of Employment
TEED	Training, Enterprise and Employment Directorate (DE)		
		TVEI	Technical and Vocational Education Initiative
TEFL	Teaching English as a Foreign Language		
		TWES	Training and Work Experience Scheme
TEGS	Training and Employment Grants Scheme		
		TWI	Training Within Industry
TES	Times Educational Supplement	TWIAS	Training Within Industry Advisory Service
TES	Temporary Employment Subsidy		
TESL	Teaching English as a Second Language	UATP	Unified Adult Training Programme
		UBO	Unemployment Benefit Office
TESOL	Teaching English to Speakers of Other Languages	UCAS	Universities and Colleges Admissions Scheme

UCET	Universities Council for the Education of Teachers		VS	Voluntary Sector
UCLES	University of Cambridge Local Examinations Syndicate		VTS	Vocational Training Scheme
			WBA	Work Based Assessment
			WBL	Work Based Learning
UFC	Universities Funding Council		WBLA	Work Based Learning for Adults
UfI	University for Industry		WCL	World Class Skills
UKCOSA	UK Council for Overseas Student Affairs		WEA	Workers Educational Association
			WEEP	Work Experience on Employers Premises
UKeU	UK e-University			
ULR	Union Learning Representative		WEP	Work Experience Programme
UNCED	United Nations Commission on Economic Development		WESB	Wales Employment and Skills Board
UNESCO	United Nations Educational, Scientific and Cultural Organisation		WISE	Women Into Science and Engineering
			WJEC	Welsh Joint Education Committee
URO	Unemployment Review Officer		WO	Welsh Office
UTP	Unified Training Programme		WOC	Wider Opportunities Course
UUK	Universities UK		WOTP	Wider Opportunities Training Programme
UVP	Unified Vocational Preparation			
VA	Voluntary Aided		WOW	Wider Opportunities for Women
VACS	Vacancy Circulation System		WRFE	Work Related Further Education
VAS	Voluntary Aided Schools		WSSD	World Summit on Social Development
VC	Vice Chancellor			
VCE	Vocational Certificate of Education		YA	Young Apprenticeship
			YC	Youth Credits
VDU	Visual Display Unit		YCS	Youth Cohort Study
VET	Vocational Education and Training		YEC	Youth Exchange Centre
			YEI	Youth Enterprise Initiative
VETG	Vocational Education and Training Group		YES	Youth Employment Service
			YOP	Youth Opportunities Programme
VFM	Value for Money		YOPS	Youth Opportunities Scheme
VLE	Virtual Learning Environment		YP	Young People
VOTEC	Vocational and Technical Education and Training		YT	Youth Training
			YTB	Youth Training Board
VPP	Voluntary Projects Programme		YTS	Youth Training Scheme
VRQ	Vocationally Related Qualification		YWS	Young Workers Scheme

Introduction

Without wealth there would be little education and without education there would be little wealth. The integrated nature of society creates a symbiotic relationship between the generation of economic wealth through productive activities such as the exchange of goods, services and labour, and education, which develops the capabilities to deliver these higher levels of productivity. The impact of this can be seen in the intellectual arms race in most countries to develop human capital, i.e. people with the knowledge, skills and motivation to be more productive – thus providing the economic wherewithal to finance health care systems, transportation, defence, housing, education, etc.

The development of UK human capital has evolved gradually, with a range of systems operating in the fields of education, training and employment, and there is an increasing recognition of their overlapping purposes and the need to coordinate and join up these activities. However, the changing range and variety of initiatives and agencies tends to make the area almost impenetrable to lay people and frequently to professionals. The challenge for employers, policy makers, government agencies, teachers, academics, students and individuals is to make sense of these areas.

Education, for example, can be divided into early years and nursery; primary school; secondary school; special needs; further education; higher education; vocational education and training; human resource development; human capital development, etc. To thoroughly understand any one of these areas requires people to specialise – thus narrowing the potential to understand the broader terrain; and if people do not understand the wider terminology and responsibilities of the other agencies and initiatives, they cannot effectively engage with them.

Similarly, labour market initiatives are widely encompassing and involve information, advice and guidance services; training for the unemployed; local, regional and national interventions to stimulate the economy or to address market limitations; and a large array of agencies and overseeing bodies to ensure quality and consistency. The result of this complexity is that labour market initiatives become incomprehensible to those in education and vice versa.

Understanding education, training and employment, therefore, is essential; yet the knowledge management policies of various government departments have led to the closure of a number of government libraries, including the Moorfoot Library, and the dispersal and disposal of their contents. Many of the documents that these libraries held were available only as hard copies and are thus not available online. Undoubtedly, the increased scope of the Internet has made access to information about initiatives and agencies much easier to collect. On the other hand, content changes frequently and documentation and even websites themselves disappear. This ephemeral nature of the virtual world has the potential to limit accessibility to information and thus reduce understanding.

This encyclopaedia has attempted to capture information about the various bodies and initiatives that have developed over time through a detailed examination of publications from the Department of Work and Pensions; papers from the Department for Business Innovation and Skills, and their predecessors; and every annual report produced by the numerous education departments from 1839. With over 1,500 entries it crosses knowledge boundaries, providing for the first time an integrated map of national human capital development, and of the history, development and relationships between education, training and employment.

A brief history of education, training and employment

The church and learning

The early history of formalised education and training is closely associated with the church, and the main centres of learning throughout the British Isles were located predominantly in the monasteries and ecclesiastical centres. For example, in Wales, the monastery and school in Cor Tewdws, in what is now Llantwit Major, were founded by the Roman Emperor Theodosius I in the fourth century and were re-established in the sixth century by Illtud, who created a large centre of learning (Jones and Roderick, 2003). In Scotland, the work of St Ninian in the fourth century was built upon by St Colomba, who travelled from Ireland in AD 563 and is credited with starting Scottish education. In addition, around AD 700, in the north-east of England, St Bede wrote books on many subjects including history, science and theology, some of which were for use in the classroom. Many of these activities were later built upon and extended by St Augustine.

Also associated with the church were the grammar schools, among the earliest being the King's School, Canterbury (AD 597) and the King's School, Rochester (AD 604). These scholae grammaticales taught Latin and were, unsurprisingly, often called Latin schools. Gradually, other languages such as Greek and English were introduced but the grammar school curriculum remained relatively narrow and restricted until the Grammar School Act 1840 enabled the use of bequests and fees to teach other subjects.

The powerful influence and control of education by the church diminished only slowly and the first indication of state policy regarding education was illustrated in the writings of King Alfred in the ninth century, who argued 'that every youth now in England that is free-born and has wealth enough, be set to learn, as long as he is not fit for any other occupation, till they know well how to read English writing; and let them be afterwards taught in the Latin tongue, who are to continue learning, and to be promoted to a higher rank' (Green 1883 p. 160). Much later, state sovereignty over some aspects of education was incorporated within Henry II's Articles of Clarendon 1164, which stated that 'The sons of tenants in villianage, ought not to be ordained without consent of the lord on whose lands they were born' (De Montmorency 1902 p. 32).

The establishment of the first universities, Oxford and Cambridge, in the twelfth and thirteenth centuries was also predominantly associated with the church. They were followed by Aberdeen, Glasgow and St Andrew's in the fifteenth century. Local initiatives and the university extension movement in the late 1800s encouraged a wave of civic universities to be established, including Birmingham, Bristol, Liverpool, Manchester, Nottingham and Sheffield. In the 1960s two more groups of universities came into existence, for example East Anglia, Kent, Sussex, Warwick and York, and the Colleges of Advanced Technology, which were given university status. A further wave saw more than 30 universities established in 1992 when the polytechnics' status changed.

Independent provision of education and training

The dissolution of the monasteries in the sixteenth century had a dramatic impact with the closure of their schools and the end of monastic scholasticism. In addition, the charitable works that the monasteries had provided were also discontinued, leaving a large number of impoverished people with little support. A number of Poor Law Acts beginning in 1601 introduced a variety of measures, for example workhouses, to support the poor and destitute and these were complemented by individuals and voluntary groups that began to provide charitable support in the form of asylums and houses of refuge.

It was soon recognised that providing shelter and accommodation for the poor was insufficient because this only created a dependency culture. The workhouses required people to undertake activities that were often menial, but these rarely developed the necessary skills to enable people to support themselves over the longer term. In addition, the dependent children became institutionalised, thus creating the potential for poverty to be transmitted to future generations. For this reason, many of the institutions began to educate and train the children and adults in their care, and also taught skills by creating hospital schools, houses of industry, houses of occupations, and industrial schools.

Around this time there was virtually no state provision of education for adults and so many voluntary organisations and societies emerged in the latter part of the 1700s and during the 1800s driven by curiosity and a desire for self-improvement. Among the groups that filled this vacuum was the Society for the Diffusion of Useful Knowledge, mechanics institutes, and library societies. This thirst for knowledge encouraged numerous other societies including the British Association for the Advancement of Science (1831 - now the British Science Association) and the Royal Society for the encouragement of the Arts, Manufactures, and Commerce (RSA), which was founded in 1754. The RSA supported the Great Exhibition of 1851, which provided a financial legacy helping to endow the museums in South Kensington and leading to the establishment of the Department of Practical Art a year later.

In *An Inquiry into the Nature and Causes of the Wealth of Nations* (1760), Adam Smith argued that children should be encouraged to 'read', 'write' and 'account' in order to support economic progress. Smith's ideas also entered into education and Sir Thomas Bernard, a founder of the Society for Bettering the Condition of the Poor described mass schooling as 'the division of labour applied to intellectual purposes' and argued that 'the principle in schools and manufactories is the same' (Armytage 1964 p. 90). This large scale teaching of the poor was achieved through the monitorial systems of Lancaster and Bell, in which a schoolmaster instructed the whole school in one large hall and this was then repeated through monitors supervising smaller groups of children.

The most common schools in the early 1800s were adventure schools and dame schools, which were established in order to provide a living for their owners through the school fees. The quality of many of these establishments, which often held the class in the living room of the dame's house, was poor and many of the teachers were barely literate.

State intervention

The unsatisfactory nature of educational provision and the severe shortage of schools led, in 1833, to the Lords of the Treasury making grants towards the cost of building schools, with the funds being distributed through the British and Foreign School Society and the National School Society. The subsequent establishment of the Committee of the Privy Council on Education in 1839 provided a clear acknowledgement of the increasing importance of education and the need for an administrative structure to coordinate and inspect the growing number of schools.

Many of the early schools not only taught the elementary subjects of reading, writing and arithmetic, but also included housekeeping and laundries for the girls and cottage gardening and animal husbandry for the boys on adjacent land. The latter subjects tended to diminish, particularly after the Education Department's 1862 Code of Regulations introduced 'payment by results' with HM Inspectors testing the performance of children only in the required elementary subjects. These restrictions were somewhat relaxed with the 1880 Code, which allowed school managers to extend the curriculum for older children to include mechanics, animal physiology, physical geography, botany and domestic economy.

While the Education Department was focusing its attention on the elementary subjects, the Department of Practical Art was established in 1852 under the Department of the Privy Council for Trade to provide skilled artisans to support industry and commerce. The Department of Practical Art became the Science and Art Department in 1853 and, until its full merger with the Education Department in 1899, provided encouragement and financial assistance to support the teaching of art and design related to manufacturing, and the teaching of science, technology and other practical subjects.

Although the British Isles were physically separated from mainland Europe, nineteenth century educationalists such as Fellenburg demonstrated the value of industrial schools. Similarly, Froebel, Pestallozi, and Montessori established schools and wrote about elementary and early-years education, influencing developments in Britain. Around the same time, industrialists, fearing the increasing economic competition from overseas, began to express a greater desire for an educated workforce. Moreover, the discipline of German conscripts in the Franco-German war was attributed to prior schooling and, thus, provided further encouragement for wider education.

The increasing arguments in favour of education for social, economic and military purposes gathered weight and eventually resulted in the Elementary Education Act 1870, which introduced universal education and a conscience clause allowing freedom of worship. In spite of this increased provision there were still school fees and many children

were so impoverished and threadbare that they attended 'ragged schools'. To address these inequalities and make school accessible to all children, free schooling was increasingly made available following the Free Education Act 1891.

Although school provision increased and was often free it was not attractive to all parents, with many preferring to send out their children at the earliest age to earn a living. To address this, schooling was made compulsory in 1880 and the school leaving age has been progressively increased with the Education and Skills Act 2008 extending this to 18 years from 2015.

Apprenticeships

During medieval times guilds of merchants, landowners and skilled tradesmen were established to provide benevolent works within their communities. As time passed, these guilds became increasingly specialised and concentrated on specific occupations, with the master passing on skills to apprentices, for example the Cutlers' Company. These guilds were the first to systematically organise and manage the roles and relationships between employer and employee.

Gradually, the state became more involved and the Statute of Artificers 1406 (an artificer was a person who made artefacts) stated that 'every man or woman of what state or condition that he be, shall be free to set their son or daughter to take learning at any school that pleaseth them within the realm' (De Montmorency 1902 pp. 28–29). Later the Statute of Artificers 1563 legislated that young people were 'to be enstructed or tought in any of the Artes Occupacions Craftes or Misteries which they or any of them [the masters] doo use or exercise' (De Montmorency 1902 p. 71). This Act was partially repealed by the Apprentices Act 1814, which ended the previously illegal nature of practising and learning a skill – thus opening up wider employment opportunities.

In the workplace, too, some enlightened employers provided factory schools for their employees and their children. Also, many areas that had developed a particular industry responded by providing specific education and training, for example a mining school in Wigan; an agricultural college in Cirencester; a shoe school in Northampton; spinning schools in Stornaway; and straw plaiting schools in Hertfordshire. In addition, the armed forces provided education and training both for orphans and children, for example the Royal Military Asylum, Chelsea, and for service personnel at naval dockyards, barracks, etc. The Council of Military Education specified the need for soldiers to be able to read and write and for these subjects to be included in regular military instruction.

A variety of Factory acts were introduced to regulate working conditions and employment including that of children in mills, factories and agriculture. The first of these was the Factory Health and Morals Act 1802 relating to apprentices. Also, the Factory Act of 1845 specified that all children under the age of 13 employed in mills should attend school for three hours per day. Where the Act was enforced these children then alternated between factory and school and were known as 'half-time children'.

During the nineteenth century apprenticeships spread more widely to new industries such as engineering, electrical activities and shipbuilding. By the 1960s there were a quarter of a million apprentices, but this figure had collapsed to 50,000 by the early 1990s due to economic recessions; declining manufacturing; young people staying in education longer; and the fact that many apprenticeships were often about time-serving (a traditional apprenticeship was normally five years) and not always about the quality of learning. This market failure encouraged government intervention with the introduction of Modern Apprenticeships, which raised numbers to 180,000 by 2010. To support these developments, the National Apprenticeship Service was launched in 2009 to support the whole range of activities and stakeholders involving apprenticeships.

Technical and further education

Around the turn of the twentieth century, there was considerable reorganisation of the educational structure at a national level with the Board of Education Act 1899 merging the Education Department, the Science and Art Department, and the Endowed Schools Commissioners into one Board of Education. At a local level, the Education Act 1902 transferred responsibility for schools from school boards to local education authorities and greater emphasis was given to continuation schools and the growing number of secondary schools. These offered an increased range of subjects, often in vocational areas, and an embryonic examination and certification system was established that motivated pupils and demonstrated potential to employers.

Further education was formally recognised with a change in title from 'Regulations for Evening Schools, Technical Institutions, and Schools of Art and Art Classes' to 'Regulations for Technical Schools, Schools of Art, and other Schools and Classes (Day and Evening) for Further Education' in 1905–06, and the early years of the 1900s showed a marked increase in courses of instruction offering special technical training.

In the First World War, the Ministry of Munitions established Instructional Factories to provide specialised training courses for munitions workers, many of whom had received their preliminary training in technical schools. After the war, these Government Instruction Centres assumed responsibility for the training of people disabled in the war and were later renamed Government Training Centres.

During the inter-war years there was increasing provision of secondary and vocational education, but it was not until the Education Act 1944 that a more coherent structure emerged with the tripartite system of grammar, secondary modern and secondary technical schools. The 11+ examination was taken by children and the higher performers went to grammar schools and most of the others to secondary modern schools.

Some children went to technical schools but an insufficient number were built and their impact was thus less than originally intended. This selection of children at an early age and the division it caused was often unpopular and the Education Act 1976 enabled local education authorities to introduce non-selective comprehensive education, although this was repealed in 1979 with the result that some areas still have grammar schools.

Developing the unemployed

The beginning of the twentieth century was marked by increased unemployment and various voluntary schemes were introduced to help the unemployed and their families. These initiatives were formalised through the Unemployed Workmen Act 1905, which provided statutory powers for the formal provision of Distress Committees, and the Labour Exchange Act 1909 introduced offices for keeping registers of available jobs and people seeking work.

The number of initiatives in both the training and employment arenas accelerated from the 1960s onwards and their degree of sophistication and focus increased as a greater understanding of the labour market developed. Provision for the unemployed can be seen in the progression of related initiatives: Vocational Training Scheme (1945–1972); Training Opportunities Scheme (1972–1985); Job Training Scheme (1985–1987); New Job Training Scheme (1987–1988); Employment Training (1988–1993); Training For Work (1993–1998); Work Based Learning for Adults (1998); and New Deal from 1998 onwards.

Labour market interventions

The successful reindustrialisation of Germany and Japan after the Second World War contrasted strongly with the relatively poor economic performance in the UK. The laissez-faire approach adopted by government towards training and education in industry and commerce was considered to be inadequate and an increasing emphasis was given to a range of initiatives from the late 1950s onwards. Indeed, a clear progression of agencies can be seen through the years to the present day: for example, Industrial Training Council (1958– 1964); Industrial Training Boards (1964–c1982), Industry Training Organisations (1984-1998), National Training Organisations (1998-2002); and the Sector Skills Councils (2002-).

The Industrial Training Act 1964 marked an increase in state intervention through the introduction of a levy designed to encourage employers to invest in training. The subsequent Employment and Training Act 1973 allowed some larger employers to disengage from this process and this indicated a reversal from overt compulsion to one that operated indirectly through employer representation on boards. The Manpower Services Commission operated from 1974 to 1988 and represented the interests of employers, unions, local authorities and education, and some of its objectives can now be seen operating through the UK Commission for Employment and Skills.

Developing human capital

Investment in all levels of education was increasingly acknowledged to be important for social and economic reasons; however, there was also a recognition that if this happened very early in a person's life, it might have a greater impact and also produce a greater return on investment. For this reason, as well as social ones, Sure Start was introduced in 1998, which had the objective of providing children with the best start in life by integrating early-years education, child care and family support in disadvantaged areas.

The increased investments in education, training for the unemployed and other measures testify to an increased recognition that learning in all its shapes is closely connected and contributes to social and economic progress. Unfortunately, this investment is less evident in the provision of continuing education and training for adults and for the growing number of retired people who make many social contributions.

Open and flexible learning

The delivery of education and training has changed progressively from a supply-driven model to a demand-led one in which the range of courses and options are more closely tailored to the needs of the person or customer. The founding of the Open University in 1969 increased accessibility for a wider group of people seeking education.

University courses were divided into modules that enabled the accumulation and transfer of study credits, and accreditation of prior experiential learning was accepted as a means of validating learning gained in the workplace. In particular, the development of national occupational standards and their associated Scottish/national vocational qualifications created a focus on the demonstration of competence and outcomes rather than time-served inputs.

This increased flexibility and articulation between systems were also illustrated with the development of a number of qualifications and credit frameworks that gradually converged into more encompassing frameworks, including the European Credit Transfer Scheme. Making study more transparent enabled learners to see a progression pathway, or ladder of small steps, which they could embark upon, exit and re-enter.

Another direction that this flexibility took was the development of vocational awards such as the General National Vocation Qualifications and later Diplomas and the Welsh Baccalaureate, which provided a broader provision and alternative to more academic qualifications such as GCSEs and A levels.

In addition, the variety of school provision and the scope of schooling would appear to have been increasing with city technology schools, academies, specialist schools and most recently studio schools.

Devolution

Devolution in the UK has led to an increasingly varied and sometimes divergent education and training system with the number of initiatives and bodies increasing as each country attempts to find its own way in the global economy. Although many of these agencies and initiatives differ in name only, in order to maintain independence and identity, there are bodies that are providing coordination, for example the UK Commission for Employment and Skills. The challenge will be to provide local responsiveness combined with national and cross-national coordination.

Conclusion

The achievements and progress of the Industrial Revolution were clearly in evidence at the 1851 Great Exhibition, where British products received excellence awards in nearly all the 100 different display areas. Unfortunately, this euphoria was dispelled at the 1867 Paris Exhibition where Britain was only successful in 10 of the 90 areas. The impact of this was to cause the 1867 Schools Inquiry Commission to examine 'the inferior rate of progress recently made in manufacturing and mechanical industry'. Furthermore, Lyon Playfair, a juror in Paris, wrote, 'The one cause of this inferiority upon which there was most unanimity is that France, Prussia, Austria, Belgium, and Switzerland possess good systems of industrial education for the masters and managers of factories and workshops and that England possesses none'. This apprehension resulted in the introduction of universal education provision in 1870.

More than 150 years later that anxiety has not receded and the 2006 Leitch Report stated, 'Our nation's skills are not world class and we run the risk that this will undermine the UK's long term prosperity'. Comparisons were drawn with the relatively poor levels of skills training in comparison to other OECD countries and numerous recommendations were made, including the establishment of the UK Commission for Employment and Skills, and the introduction of diplomas for young people. Times may change but many of the issues and strategies remain the same as, hopefully, the encyclopaedia illustrates.

An invitation

Great efforts have been made to ensure the encyclopaedia is as comprehensive and accurate as possible; however, not everything will have been identified and some errors may have crept into the text. You are warmly encouraged to contact me if you notice anything or wish to recommend an item: j.p.wilson @sheffield.ac.uk

Navigating the Encyclopaedia

Entry name is listed alphabetically. Merged names, e.g. 'jobcentre', are placed alphabetically, not as job centre.

Dates are included where available, e.g. 2002 or 2001/2002 indicates the start date; 1998–2000 the duration. Launch dates are generally more available because of official announcements while closures are conducted more quietly.

Complete references are noted in the bibliography.

SECTOR SKILLS COUNCILS

(Announced 16 October 2001, some operational from April 2002) Designed to replace the 73 **national training organisations** in April 2002 when the NTOs were no longer funded or recognised by the Government. They are independent organisations developed by groups of employers in sectors that have an employment base of economic or strategic significance. Their purpose is to lead the enhancement of skills and workforce development and their targets are based on four key goals: 'reducing skills gaps and shortages; improving productivity, business and public service performance; increasing opportunities to boost the skills and productivity of everyone in the sector's workforce, including action on equal opportunities; and improving learning supply, including **apprenticeships**, **higher education** and **national occupational standards**'. The Sector Skills Council Standard will set out the minimum requirements for a Sector Skills Council, which will then be licensed for five years. There are 25 SSCs that are overseen by the **UK Commission for Employment and Skills**, and represented by the Alliance of Sector Skills Councils.

Further reading: Sector Skills Development Agency (2001); www.sscalliance.org/ (accessed 01 June 2010)

Bold text indicates that there is a reference to this entry elsewhere in the encyclopaedia

See acronym list for full text.

Internet addresses have been included where available.

References using the term 'Minutes' refer to the Minutes of the Committee of the Privy Council on Education (1839–1857/58). References using the term 'Report' refer to the Report of the Committee of Council on Education (1858/59–1899), and subsequently to the Report of the Board of Education (1900–38).

References for annual reports state the year/s they address (e.g. Ministry of Labour and National Service Report 1953) not the publication date, which may be the following year.

Acknowledgements

This encyclopaedia would probably never have materialised but for the foresight of John Gibson, formerly of the Young People's Policy Division, Department for Education and Employment, who commissioned the predecessor of this encyclopaedia. Appreciation also is due to the Department for Children, Schools and Families, which gave permission for the findings to be incorporated within the encyclopaedia.

Both Ron Chapman and Joan Keogh were part of the team that conducted the original research that produced the A – Z of UK Labour Market Initiatives and I am very grateful for their contributions and friendship.

A major thank you to the library staff who helped my navigation through the various resources and databases, particularly those of the Sheffield Moorfoot office (a great resource sadly no longer in operation), the Department for Children, Schools and Families library at Sanctuary Buildings; the British Library at St Pancras; and the University of Sheffield.

The insight to deliver this overview has come from educational experiences at St Catherine's and St Patrick's primary schools and De La Salle College, Sheffield; Newman University College, University of Birmingham; Florida State University; and the University of Sheffield. In addition, support has also come from an extended family of educationalists: Joseph, Agnes, Mary, Chris, Paul, Stella, Anne-Marie, Marie, Frances and Catherine Wilson; Matthew, Maria, Norah, Kathleen, Eileen and Anne Connelly; and Dorothy Willens.

Finally, many thanks to the Routledge team of: Philip Mudd, Charles Haynes, Andrew Willis, Ulrike Swientek, Christopher Hook and Cara Trevor.

1-9

1-2-1 SUPPORTIVE CASE LOADING

(Piloted April 1994, National 1995) Piloted at the same time as **Workwise** with some regions evaluating 1-2-1 and others Workwise. It was originally introduced for 18- to 24-year olds and later extended for those 25+. It was designed for people who had been unemployed for more than a year and consisted of a series of six interviews with an **employment service** advisor. The interviews were provided over a period during which the person undertook guided job search activity. The extended contact allowed the advisor to establish realistic job goals and achieve them, and 239,000 opportunities were provided in 1996–97. It was replaced in 1998 by **Jobfinder**.

Further reading: DfEE Annual Report 1996, Cm3210, p. 108; Kay et al. (1995b)

8 WEEK REVIEW

(Piloted May 1989 – Mar 1990) This was a short lived experiment that never got beyond the pilot stage. In essence, new claimants were targeted to be followed up at the eight week stage. There were two main targets: those who were potentially long-term unemployed and those who should have found employment based on the assumption that they had undertaken a satisfactory job search.

Further reading: Crook (1991)

11+ EXAMINATION

This examination, used by **local education authorities,** was taken by pupils in the final year of primary school to select children for entry into **grammar schools**, secondary **technical schools** or **secondary modern schools**. A similar examination, the **Free Place Examination**, delivered at the approximate age of eleven, had existed since the early years of the twentieth century to select children for entry to the small number of secondary schools, many of which also charged for schooling. A system of scholarships was introduced and gradually the number of places increased and progressively became free. The Education Act 1944 introduced the **tripartite system** and used the 11+ examination that continues to be used in a small number of areas.

See also: Qualifying Examination

13 WEEK REVIEW

(1990) Claimants for unemployment benefit were interviewed after 13 weeks to evaluate what they were doing to seek employment. Interviewees had to prove that they were actively seeking work, by showing letters and dates of interviews with prospective employers etc. At the same time, the interviewer could recommend that the interviewee should take up one of the schemes in operation.

Further reading: Birtwhistle et al. (1993)

1

14–19: EXTENDING OPPORTUNITIES, RAISING STANDARDS

This Green Paper presented proposals for a new 14–19 phase that would improve economic competitiveness, promote social justice and help achieve 'a world-class education service with standards that match the best in the world, and where all our young people develop the confidence, skills and knowledge that they will need as adults' (DfES 2002a p. 3). It recognised four challenges:

'1. to build an education system in which every young person and every parent has confidence;
2. to ensure that no young person is denied the chance of a decent education;
3. to reap the skills benefits of an education system that matches the needs of the knowledge economy;
4. to promote education with character'.

(DfES 2002a pp. 4–5)

14–19 PARTNERSHIPS

The 2005 '*14–19 Implementation Plan*' specified the need to establish 14–19 partnerships to ensure that the national entitlement for young people to the right learning opportunities and right support would be achieved. A precise definition of a partnership was not given by the DCSF to enable local responses; however, it did describe their strategic roles: 'agreeing the local vision for 14–19 that is consistent with the wider Sustainable Community Strategy, Children and Young People's Plan and Local Area Agreement; developing and articulating strategies for the full range of 14–19 priorities; and, supporting diploma consortia so that they are ready to deliver' (DCSF 2007b p. 4).

16+ ACTION PLAN

(January 1983) This plan was launched in Scotland and a quarter of college students registered with SCOTVEC were from the **Youth Training Scheme**. In essence the programme was of a modular construction and in 1985 just over 12,000 students were registered for around 61,500 modules as part of their 'off the job' training. It integrated on-the-job and off-the-job training and provided a nationally recognised qualification to support trainees in jobseeking and in further education and training.

Further reading: MSC Annual Report 1985–86 p. 48; Roebuck (1985)

16+ EXAMINATION

This was developed by the Joint Matriculation Board and was designed to provide the basis for common assessment within schools rather than having the separate examinations of **O levels** and **Certificates of Secondary Education**. It led to the development of the **General Certificate of Secondary Education**.

21st CENTURY SKILLS: REALISING OUR POTENTIAL

Published in July 2003, this White Paper described the Government's plans to develop skills in order to encourage productivity, innovation and profitability in businesses; improve public services; and enable individuals to increase their employability. It identified five key areas for action: prioritising the skills needs of employers and helping to match demand with supply; increasing the ambitions of people to raise their skills (this included working with the **Learning and Skills Council**, and the **National Institute of Adult Continuing Education**); encouraging people to re-engage with learning; making colleges and training providers to be responsive to the needs of employers and learners; and increasing joint working across government and the public services – this included the **Department for Education and Skills**, the **Department of Trade and Industry**, the **Department for Work and Pensions**, the Treasury and other agencies involved with training, skills, business support and productivity.

Further reading: Department for Education and Skills (2003)

2

A

ABILITY DEVELOPMENT CENTRE

See: Placing, Assessment and Counselling Teams

ACADEMIES

Announced in March 2000, the first academies opened in September 2002 under the Learning and Skills Act 2000. Originally called city academies, 'Academies are all ability schools established by sponsors from business, faith or voluntary groups working with partners from the local community. Sponsors and the **Department for Education and Skills** provide the capital costs for the Academy' (DfES 2002e p. 6). They were either new secondary schools or they replace failing secondary schools. The academies were located in areas of disadvantage, whether urban or rural, and were designed to offer local solutions to local problems. Each academy was different and drew upon the expertise of its sponsors to develop a specific ethos and mission. The age range of pupils varied depending on local provision and the 2002 Education Act allowed for 'all age' academies. They were set up as companies limited by guarantee with charitable status and running costs were met in full by the state. Influenced by the Swedish free school system, the Academies Act 2010 enabled the establishment of academies by interested groups and for public funded schools to apply to became academies.

See also: City Technology Colleges

Further reading: DfES (2002e)

ACCELERATED MODERN APPRENTICESHIPS

See: Modern Apprenticeships – Accelerated (aMA)

ACCESS FUNDS

Further education institutions administered access funds, which provided support for individuals where access to education might have been inhibited by financial considerations, or where students faced financial difficulties. The Government allocated approximately £6m per annum during the period 1994–1997.

See also: Education Maintenance Allowance

Further reading: Further Education Funding Council (1993)

ACCESS TO ASSESSMENT

The Access to Assessment programme provided funds to support **training and enterprise councils** to increase access to **National Vocational Qualification** assessment and involved 2,800 employers and assisted 9,000 individuals to gain qualifications mainly at NVQ Level 2.

Further reading: DfEE Annual Report 1996, Cm 3210, p. 95; Employment Department (1993b)

ACCESS TO INFORMATION TECHNOLOGY

(Piloted in 1984, went national in July 1985, and ran until April 1988) Encouraged flexible accessible training and promoted greater awareness of the uses of IT. Both private and public sector training providers were set up in 1984 offering modular AIT courses at evenings and at weekends lasting from 20 to 30 hours. Following the 1984 pilot year, there was an increase in provision in 1985/86. Courses were open to both employed and unemployed people, but not to those in full time education. £1m was set aside in 1985/86 and approximately 80,000 participated.

Further reading: MSC Annual Reports 1984/85 p. 22, and 1985/86 p. 20; MSC (1985h)

ACCESS TO WORK

(6 June 1994) This initiative was designed to provide technical and personal support tailored to the individual needs of disabled clients. Support included: communicators for deaf people; support workers for people with physical and learning disabilities, and those with mental problems; and help towards adapting vehicles. It was one of three elements of the **Workpath** initiative, the other two being **Workstep** and **Work Preparation**. It was a successor to **Adaptations to Premises and Equipment**.

Further reading: DfEE Annual Report 1996, Cm 3210, p. 115; Beinart (1996)

ACCREDITED TRAINING CENTRES

The **Youth Training Scheme** was dependent on the quality of the managing agencies, the firms providing work experience, the colleges and everyone involved with the YTS partnership. Therefore, staff training was crucial and to help in this task a network of 55 accredited centres – one for each **Manpower Services Commission** area – was set up. The centres provided a range of advisory services, resource banks and training.

See also: Approved Training Organisations

Further reading: Youth Training Scheme (1984)

ACTION CREDIT

(Announced and piloted in 1989) This initiative enabled people to leave **employment training** and work part-time for up to six months while receiving benefit. It provided a means for people to store their earnings for access at a later date, but the take-up was very low, due possibly to mistrust of the scheme by those who were on the margins of employment and had limited understanding of what was being offered.

See also: Back to Work Bonus

Further reading: Fairclough (1992)

ACTION FOR CITIES

(Launched in March 1988) This was an interdepartmental government initiative. The **Employment Department Group** focused help on inner-city problems and on the long-term unemployed or those with special needs. The 1991/92 Employment Service Annual Performance Agreement specified that 34 per cent of placings be made for inner-city residents. There were specialist outreach staff working with communities and individuals, and other work included research, demonstration projects and some contracts with voluntary organisations working in inner cities.

Further reading: Rebello (1991); Training Agency (1989a)

ACTION FOR COMMUNITY EMPLOYMENT

(1981/82–1999/2000) This programme superseded the **Management Action Programme** in Northern Ireland and was targeted at the long-term unemployed. It was the equivalent of the **Community Programme** and enabled people to undertake work for a period of one year that was of benefit to the local community while acquiring experience and training. During the first ten years of operation more than 62,000 people participated on the programme. This programme was succeeded by **Worktrack.**

Further reading: Training and Employment Agency Annual Report (1992)

ACTION FOR JOBS

(1986) Action for Jobs was introduced to provide the unemployed, employers and employees with information about what was available to them and to address the high levels of unemployment that occurred during the recession.

ACTION RESEARCH

While also being a specific form of research involving the evaluation of an intervention (often in the social sciences), this was a scheme introduced in 1999 that was designed to encourage research into locally derived and locally delivered work-related learning projects for those 14–16 years of age. It was also tied into the **Key Stage 4** demonstration projects programme. The research was aimed at providing more productive evidence about the wider use of vocational and work-related approaches at Key Stage 4, which was designed to be fed back into the development of the curriculum for 14–16 year olds. £4m was allocated to this programme and 100 LEAs participated.

See also: Standards Fund

Further reading: DfEE Departmental Report 1999–00 to 2001–02, Cm 4202, p. 54; DfEE (2000f)

ACTION TEAMS FOR JOBS

(Announced in 1999) This initiative enabled local action teams to be set up to look at local needs and to take action or remedial action to either create work or discourage unemployment.

Further reading: DfEE (2000b)

ACTION ZONES

See: Education Action Zones

ACTIVITY AGREEMENTS

(April 2006) These were designed for 16- to 17-year-olds not in **education, employment or training** (NEET) and who were unlikely to be receiving benefit. The purpose was to re-engage these young people by providing a financial incentive alongside their agreement to commit to education or training.

See also: Activity Allowance; Education Maintenance Allowance

Further reading: HM Treasury (2007)

ACTIVITY ALLOWANCE

(April 2006) This was an allowance, usually £30 per week, provided to young people of 16–17 who committed themselves through an **activity agreement** to be involved with some form of education or training.

See also: Education Maintenance Allowance; Care to Learn

Further reading: HM Treasury (2007)

ADAPTATIONS TO PREMISES AND EQUIPMENT

(1977) This initiative offered grants to employers to modify equipment and premises to allow access and work for those with disabilities. At the outset, the scheme allowed an employer to claim up to £6,000 for such adaptation work to be completed.

See also: Disablement Advisory Service

Further reading: Parker (1990); Beattie (1990)

ADDITIONAL AND/OR SPECIALIST LEARNING

(2008) This was one component of the **diploma**, the other two being **generic** learning and **principal learning**. 'Additional learning' meant a broadening of the learning experience, and 'specialist learning' meant a deepening of the learning experience.

ADMIRALTY SCHOOLS

The Admiralty had responsibility for a number of schools and the Privy Council, in 1856, charged the Education Department to inspect the Greenwich **Hospital Schools**, the **royal dockyard schools** and **royal marines schools** (Report 1858–59 p. 423). Schools were also to be found on the flagships at Portsmouth, Devonport, and on harbour ships.

See also: Floating Engineer College; Merchant Marine Training Ships; Navigation School

Further reading: McClean (1999)

ADOPTION GRANTS

(1975) These grants were brought in to encourage employers to take on an otherwise redundant apprentice from elsewhere. Equally, they were made to **Industrial Training Boards** who could also undertake to ensure that the apprentice completed training.

Further reading: MSC Annual Report 1975–76 p. 25

ADULT AND COMMUNITY LEARNING

See: Adult and Community Learning Fund

ADULT AND COMMUNITY LEARNING FUND

(1999) A £5m fund was set up to support innovative community-based activities that offered opportunities for learning. The aim was to strengthen neighbourhood 'self-help' groups to provide services for local people. The plan was based on the redevelopment and regeneration of disadvantaged areas. In 1999, a total of 160 projects were started, and it was intended to look for 'co-sponsors' from trusts, charities and companies.

Further reading: DfEE (1999a)

ADULT BASIC SKILLS

Closely connected with the Adult Literacy and Basic Skills Unit. It was recognised that there was a core of people whose basic skills in reading and writing could be improved. It was to that end that ALBSUs were set up to ensure that those that had 'fallen through the net', for whatever reason, should have the chance to catch up. It was subsequently renamed the Adult Basic Skills Strategy Unit from 1 November 2000.

Further reading: Adult Literacy and Basic Skills Unit (1989)

ADULT BASIC SKILLS STRATEGY UNIT

(Operational from 1 November 2000) Formerly the **Adult Literacy and Basic Skills Unit**, it has members from partner organisations including the Prison Service, the **Qualifications and Curriculum Authority** and the **Learning and Skills Council**. The unit has responsibility for leading the strategy for literacy and numeracy at national and local levels.

Further reading: DfES Departmental Report 2002 Cm 5402 p. 115; http://rwp.excellence gateway.org.uk/readwriteplus/

ADULT COMMUNITY LEARNING

Adult Community Learning was provided by local authorities to support learning among young people and adults. For example, 'Community Learning Wales aims to provide innovative, affordable and accessible learning opportunities for all members of our communities – at a time, in a place, at a pace and through a curriculum that meets the needs of both individuals and local communities' (accessed 31 March 2010).

See also: Adult Education

Further reading: http://www.clwales.net/ Introducing%20CLW.htm

ADULT EDUCATION

'From 1 August 1924 the liberal education of adults in extra-mural classes promoted by such bodies as the Workers' Educational Association has been aided under a separate body of Adult Education regulations' (Report 1925–26 p. 56). The Regulations for Adult Education were confirmed on 7 January 1925 and prior to this the board had paid grants for local classes and vacations under the Regulations for Technical Schools, while residential colleges were aided separately. 'The new regulations continue, with small changes, the existing provision for residential colleges and vacation courses, and provide higher rates of grant for local classes. Local classes fall into two groups; the first includes those conducted under the control of Universities or University Colleges (University Tutorial Classes, Preparatory Classes and **University Extension** Courses), the second those conducted under the control of approved associations (One-Year and Terminal Courses). The **Workers' Educational Association** Districts control the majority of classes in the second group' (Report 1924–25 p. 126). As a result of the **Education Act 1902** the Board and LEAs supported voluntary organisations providing adult education (Report 1922–23 p. 102).

ADULT EMPLOYMENT SUBSIDY

(August 1978 – June 1979) This was a subsidy of £20 per week for 26 weeks for each unemployed person who was taken on by the employer. It never became a national project, and was only piloted on Merseyside, Tyneside and in Leeds. The scheme lacked promotion, and the take-up in total numbered only 1,400 participants.

Further reading: IFF Research Ltd (1979)

ADULT GUIDANCE CENTRES

By 3 April 1995, 24 centres had been established in Northern Ireland. Their purpose was to deliver pre-entry guidance to all potential adult entrants to **Jobskills**.

Further reading: Training and Employment Agency Annual Report (1996)

ADULT LEARNER ACCOUNTS

Piloted from August 2007 in the South-East and East Midlands **Learning and Skills Council** regions, Adult learner accounts were aimed at providing a wider range of providers delivering Level 3 education and training; offering information, advice and guidance (IAG) to help learners make appropriate choices; and, increasing awareness and making transparent the availability of state support, costs and contributions. Learners were required to register and receive regular IAG.

Further reading: Learning and Skills Council 2009

See also: Skills Accounts

ADULT LEARNERS WEEK

The **National Institute of Adult Continuing Education** established Adult Learners Week in 1992 to encourage participation in adult learning.

See also: Learning at Work Day

ADULT LEARNING GRANT

(piloted from September 2003 and phased in from autumn 2004, this grant became national from 2007) Normally, it provided weekly support to adults who were studying for Level 2 qualifications and for young adults studying for their first Level 3 qualification. Participants needed to study for at least 12 hours per week. It provided support up to £30 per week in addition to current earnings, plus help with course fees, childcare, bus fares and materials.

See also: Activity Allowance, Care to Learn

7

Further reading: DfES Departmental Report 2004, Cm 6202, p. 84

ADULT LEARNING INSPECTORATE

(April 2001 – 31 March 2007) The ALI was established to inspect all post-16 work based learning; adult learning in colleges; learning in **New Deals**, **UfI (learndirect)**; adult and community learning; and training and education in prisons. Self-assessment and inspection used the **Common Inspection Framework**, which asked the question, 'How effective and efficient is the provision of education and training in meeting the needs of learners, and why?' The operations of the ALI were incorporated into **OFSTED**.

Further reading: Adult Learning Inspectorate (2001); FEFC (April 2000)

ADULT LITERACY AND BASIC SKILLS UNIT

(1979) The unit was established at the National Extension College and set out to provide a range of materials to teach literacy, numeracy and social life skills. By 1981 the unit had run 46 courses for **Youth Opportunities Programme** tutors and supervisors. Clients could be assessed in the basic skills of reading and writing, such that they could be trained to the minimum standards of literacy and numeracy. ALBSUs received funding to enable the qualified staff to aid the recipient in attaining these skills. It was superseded by the **Basic Skills Agency**.

See also: Adult Basic Skills

Further reading: Adult Literacy and Basic Skills Unit Annual Reports; Adult Literacy and Basic Skills Unit (1985) (1989)

ADULT SCHOOLS

(1798) Many schools for the education of adults had their origins in the Sunday School movement. It is believed that the first independent adult school was established in Nottingham in 1798 to provide for instruction of women who were employed in local lace and hosiery factories. It subsequently included a men's class.

Further reading: Rowntree & Binns (1903)

ADULT TRAINING CAMPAIGN

(February 1985) The main purpose was to raise people's awareness of the importance of training and encourage them to take remedial action. It was designed to focus on alternative educational and training arrangements in Scotland. This campaign was primarily a Scottish initiative, although it was looked at by English counterparts.

Further reading: MSC (1985e); MSC Annual Report 1984–85 p. 47

ADULT TRAINING PROGRAMMES

See: Adult Training Strategy

ADULT TRAINING STRATEGY

(1984) This strategy in Scotland was designed to match skills with skills needs. It was launched in response to concerns about the effect of Britain's approach to adult training on competitiveness. It aimed to change the attitudes and behaviour of employers, individuals and training providers, and progressed in three ways: **Adult Training Campaign; Measures to make the training market work better**; and **adult training programmes**.

Further reading: MSC (1983a); (1985b); MSC Annual Report 1984–85 p. 47

ADVANCED COURSES

In 1917–18, Advanced Courses in classics, and science and mathematics were recognised under the Regulations for Secondary Schools (Wales) at seven Welsh schools (Report

1917–18 pp. 31–32). They were also conducted in English grant-aided secondary schools in 1919–20 (Report 1919–20 p. 27) and were designed to help secure employment or as a bridge to university education, and were a precursor to **advanced levels**.

See also: Second Examination

ADVANCED EXTENSION AWARDS

(2005) Designed to 'stretch and challenge' students by incorporating more demanding questions into **advanced levels** and other Level three programmes. The AEAs addressed the challenge of the increasing number of students who achieved high grades at advanced level, and thereby enabled enhanced differentiation and selection by universities and employers.

Further reading: DfES Departmental Report 2005, CM 7092, p. 53

ADVANCED LEVEL

(1951) The General Certificate of Education advanced level (A level) replaced the **Higher School Certificate** in 1951 and was awarded to those passing the examinations following, normally, two years of study. It was taken by those who had completed their required GCSE course work and successfully gained the required grades, and who wanted to seek access into further and higher education, or into schemes where further study was offered. It was subsequently titled the Advanced General Certificate of Education (AGCE) to differentiate it from the **Advanced Vocational Certificate of Education** (AVCE).

See also: Advanced Subsidiary Levels; Second Examination

Further reading: Barlow (1995); Ministry of Education Circular 168, Examinations in Secondary Schools, April 1948

ADVANCED LEVELS – VOCATIONAL

See: Advanced Vocational Certificate of Education

ADVANCED MODERN APPRENTICESHIPS

See: Modern Apprenticeships – Advanced

ADVANCED NATIONAL SCHOOLS

(1856) In a letter to the Committee of Council, the Reverend Henry Moseley, an HMI, described trade schools as advanced national schools (Minutes 1855–56 p. 23).

ADVANCED SKILLS TEACHERS

(1999) 'An Advanced Skills Teacher (AST) is a teacher who has passed a national assessment and been appointed to an AST post. ASTs concentrate on sharing their skills, through outreach work, with teachers in their own and other schools'. The AST grade was designed to enable good teachers to enhance their skills and share them with others without advancing and moving away from the classroom. Some 80 per cent of their time was spent in the classroom and 20 per cent was spent sharing good practice in other schools.

See also: New Qualified Teacher; Qualified Teacher Status

Further reading: http://www.teachernet.gov. uk/professionaldevelopment/ast/

ADVANCED SUBSIDIARY LEVELS

(September 1999) Advanced subsidiary levels were introduced as a means of examining students in Year 12 (formerly the first year of the 'sixth Form') and partly to counter what was perceived as a considerable drop out of students between completing the GCSE syllabus and taking A level examinations. The first examinations were taken in 2000. An A level counted as 6 units and an additional subsidiary level as 3 units; for example,

9

a student studying 4 advanced subsidiary levels in Year 12 and taking 3 units forward to A level (in Year Thirteen) would get 21 units of study. The advanced subsidiary levels could be studied in linear or modular form. They were not the same as **advanced supplementary levels** introduced in 1990.

Further reading: Qualifications and Curriculum Authority (1999)

ADVANCED SUPPLEMENTARY LEVELS

Advanced supplementary levels were introduced in 1990 to broaden the range of subjects that a student might study at A level. They required study to the same academic level as full A level courses but were intended to need only half the time and were worth only half a full A level qualification. They were later discontinued and were not the same as subsequent **advanced subsidiary levels**.

Further reading: FEFC (December 1994)

ADVANCED VOCATIONAL CERTIFICATE OF EDUCATION

(September 2000) This qualification was introduced to replace the Advanced **General National Vocational Qualification**. Its purpose was to provide enhanced rigour and flexibility to vocational courses and to ensure that vocational tests achieved the same respect as A levels. The AVCE had three levels: the Double Award was a 12-unit course equivalent to two A levels; the Advanced Award was a six-unit course equivalent to one A level; and the Advanced Subsidiary Award consisted of 3 units equal to an Advanced Subsidiary level. They were known as Vocational A levels and were described in *Colleges for Excellence and Innovation* (DfEE 2000g) and in the DfES *Green Paper 14–19 Extending Opportunities, Raising Standards*, Cm5342 (DfES 2002a). The **Qualifications and Curriculum Authority** decided to withdraw the AVCE in 2004 and it was finally discontinued in 2007.

Further reading: DfEE Annual Report 2001–02 to 2003–04, Cm 5102, p. 13; http://www.qcda.gov.uk

ADVENTURE SCHOOLS

During the early 1800s, these schools were the most common form of school and were founded by 'adventurers' or entrepreneurs who sought to make a living from running a school. 'The adventure-school is maintained wholly upon the wages paid by pupils, at the stated terms, weekly, monthly or quarterly. It presents a simple case of the exchange of labour for its value. The rate of wages is what the one party chooses to ask, and the other to give. The teacher undergoes no trial of his qualifications, and generally receives no express appointment, perhaps no invitation to the office. His teaching embraces such branches of knowledge as he may himself think fit to offer, and as he may be asked to teach; it matters nothing to his right to exercise the calling of what skill he may be able to conduct it' (Minutes 1844 Vol. 2, p. 351). These schools were not always located where there was a need. Also, the income from these schools was uncertain with the consequence that teachers were not always so devoted to their task and sometimes took other occupations to supplement their income. The Code of 1883 stipulated, with regard to adventure schools, that 'The school must not be conducted for private profit' (Report 1882–83 p. 120). Schools at this time in Scotland were categorised according to the means by which they were supported. In addition to adventure schools, there were also: **Burgh, parochial, privately endowed** and **subscription** schools.

See also: Commercial Schools; Dame Schools

ADVISORY COMMITTEE ON YOUTH EMPLOYMENT FOR SCOTLAND

(1973) The purpose of this committee was to run in parallel with the **Youth Employment Service** operating in England, but was designed to take into account the differences in the education system for Scotland.

Further reading: Department of Employment Gazette March 1973 p. 243

ADVISORY COMMITTEE ON YOUTH EMPLOYMENT FOR WALES

As above for Scotland, but not so much concerned with education (the system in Wales was similar that in England).

Further reading: Department of Employment Gazette March 1973 p. 243

ADVISORY, CONCILIATION AND ARBITRATION SERVICE

(October 1974) Formerly the **Conciliation and Arbitration Service**, ACAS is an independent statutory body, not subject to direction from any minister as to how it exercises its functions. It is directed by a council, consisting of the ACAS chairman, and employer, trade union and independent members. The service publishes an annual report to Parliament and states that: 'We aim to improve organisations and working life through better employment relations. We help with employment relations by supplying up-to-date information, independent advice and high quality training, and working with employers and employees to solve problems and improve performance'.

www.acas.org.uk/index.aspx?articleid=1342 (accessed 02 April 2010)

ADVISORY SCOTTISH COUNCIL FOR EDUCATION AND TRAINING TARGETS

(1994) ASCETT was responsible for setting competitiveness targets and monitoring progress towards them. The council also promoted awareness throughout Scotland about the importance of targets and for the sustained need to improve skills levels.

Further reading: ASCETT (1995)

AFTER-CARE COMMITTEES

(1905) Following the establishment of special schools, after-care committees, composed of education committees, managers and other interested parties, were established to support the interests of disabled children. The **Board of Education** described them in this way: 'and they exist for the purpose of obtaining work, further education and apprenticeship for those children who reach the limit of elementary school age. These Committees which exist in London, Birmingham, Nottingham and Leicester ought to be an essential part of the "Special School" organisation. Without them there is a certain risk that the child will on leaving school find himself without outlook or any chance of career. The Committees step in to prevent the waste of years of educational effort, to rescue the child from falling at once into the ranks of pauperism, by guiding him and keeping him in a career of usefulness where he may, if only in part, contribute to his own welfare and become a self-respecting citizen instead of a hopeless and perhaps harmful dependent' (Board of Education 1904–05 p. 35). After-care committees were also used to support the welfare of ordinary-abled young people (Report 1918–19 p. 7).

AGRICULTURAL AND TECHNICAL INSTRUCTION (IRELAND) ACT 1899

This act established the Department of Agriculture and Technical Instruction and enabled some of the responsibilities of the **Department of Science and Art** to be transferred together with some grants. The act defined technical instruction as 'instruction in the principles of science and art applicable to industries and in the application of special branches of science and art to specific industries or employment' (Coolahan 1981 p. 87). In line with the understanding of technical education at the time it did not apply to 'teaching the practice of any trade or industry'.

(THE) AGRICULTURAL CHILDREN ACT 1873

This act, which came into operation on 1 January 1875, prohibited children under the age of eight years from working in agriculture. Between the ages of eight and twelve, a specific number of school attendances were required in order that they be allowed to work. 'It shall not be lawful for any employer or his agent to employ any child under the age of eight years in the execution of any agricultural work, unless he be the parent of such child, and the child be so employed by him on land in his own occupation' (Minutes 1873–74 p. xxxv). From the age of eight until ten years old a child had to present a certificate that stated that they had completed 250 attendances (a half day was considered one attendance). Between ten and twelve, the child had to have 150 attendances in the previous twelve months before employment.

See also: Factory Acts

AGRICULTURAL COLLEGES

(1845) In 1842, a meeting was held at the Fairford and Cirencester Farmers Club where Robert Jeffreys-Brown spoke on the 'Advantages of Specific Education for Agricultural Pursuits'. Following this, public subscription led to the establishment of the first agricultural college (construction began in 1845) and in the same year it received its Royal Charter becoming the Royal Agricultural College. The Technical Instruction Act (1889) encouraged the organised provision of agricultural colleges, which subsequently received support from the Board of Agriculture and Fisheries, and County Councils (Report 1908–09 p. 81).

See also: Agricultural Schools; Farm Schools

(COUNTY) AGRICULTURAL INSTITUTES

County agricultural institutes, while small in number during the early 1900s, provided an important source of what was considered 'technical education' in rural areas. 'A County Institute, besides being the headquarters of the County Staff, and thus the centre for the whole area, provides winter courses of two to five months for men, and summer courses of one to three months for women. ... For the training of the man whom circumstances prevent from rising above the rank of agricultural labourer or at the most cultivator of an allotment there are available in the first place the rural **evening school** and the county horticultural lectures. One county is developing a system of model allotments for the benefit of the labouring classes. ... They are valued by the farmers as supplying them with more highly skilled workers and by the labourers as tending to reduce the duration of periods of unemployment. There can be no doubt, too, that the public interest aroused in the localities by such classes restores to the labourers the old time pride and interest in skilled farm work' (Report 1908–09 pp. 83–84).

See also: Agricultural Colleges

AGRICULTURAL SCHOOLS

These schools combined education with industrial work in agriculture. Many schools had an area of land that the pupils tended and some schools placed greater emphasis on the agriculture (Minutes 1854–55 p. 546).

See also: Agricultural Colleges; Cottage Garden; Farm Schools; Industrial Garden

AGRICULTURE

(1883) This subject was introduced into a number of training colleges and was supported by grants from the **Science and Art Department**. The principles of agriculture were also introduced as one of the **specific subjects** under the 1883 Code enabling its study by elementary school scholars, older scholars, pupil-teachers and assistant teachers, and teacher training students (Report 1882–83 p. xxv/p. 139).

From 1912 'the Board ceased to supervise technical instruction for agriculturalists or intending agriculturalists, whether given in university departments of agriculture, in other **agricultural colleges**, in farm institutes and **farm schools** or in part-time courses under the local education authorities' (Report 1924–25 p. 24) and these came under the responsibility of the Department of Agriculture and Fisheries.

AIMHIGHER

(1 August 2004) This programme was established to widen participation in higher education by young people who came from under-represented communities. Its intention was to develop understanding, raise aspirations and reduce barriers to higher education among young people, with the intention of increasing entry to higher education to 50 per cent of school leavers by 2010. The programme was funded by the **Department for Education and Skills** and the **Higher Education Funding Council for England**.

Further reading: http://www.hefce.ac.uk/ Widen/aimhigh/

ALL-AGE SCHOOLS

These are schools that provide education for children all the way through their primary and secondary education. Two models tend to exist: '(i) All age school federation – this comprises two or more schools which share a degree of governance and pedagogical programmes, but remain funded as separate institutions. They may or may not share one site/campus. (ii) All-age school – this is one school comprising all or multiple phases with one governing body and is funded as a single institution. It often occupies a single site/campus or is combining its previously separate institutional sites into a new build' (DfES Innovation Unit, undated p. 3).

The benefits of these schools were considered to overcome the dip in performance that occurs when children change school; increase the transfer of skills and knowledge within the school; increase available resources; and provide increased career opportunities.

See also: Middle Schools

ALLIANCE OF SECTOR SKILLS COUNCILS

(1 April 2008) It replaced the **Skills for Business Network** and consisted of representatives from all 25 sector skills councils that operate across the UK. Its core purpose is to:

- 'Act as the collective voice of the SSCs
- Promote understanding of the role of SSCs within the skills system across England, Scotland, Wales and Northern Ireland
- Co-ordinate policy positions and strategic work on skills with stakeholders across the four home nations
- Help build the performance capability of the SSCs to ensure they continue to work effectively on the employer-driven skills agenda'

(www.sscalliance.org/ (accessed 02 April 2010)

AMERICAN MANAGEMENT AND BUSINESS INTERNSHIP

This programme offered managers and technical experts in Northern Ireland and the six border counties in the Irish Republic placements in American companies so that they might get first hand experience in management and production techniques. AMBIT was funded by the International Fund for Ireland and the US Department of Commerce.

See also: Overseas Export Marketing Programme – Explorers; Overseas Career Development Programme; Business Education Initiative

Further reading: Training and Employment Agency Annual Report (1995)

ANDERSON'S COLLEGE

(1796) This was a technical school funded by John Anderson, a professor at Glasgow University. He bequeathed monies for 'an institution to be nominated Anderson's University' to teach industrial and scientific subjects. It amalgamated with the College of Science and Arts in 1887 and subsequently become the University of Strathclyde.

Further reading: Sexton (1994)

ANNUAL GRANT SCHOOLS

(c.1858) The initial grants provided by the Committee of Council on Education in the 1840s and 1850s were generally a contribution to the construction of school buildings, following requests from school trustees. Gradually, funding was also provided to schools to pay for schoolmasters and mistresses and this was often based on the number of attending children. This **capitation grant** began to be provided on a regular basis and state funded schools were sometimes known as annual grant schools (Report 1858–59 p. 99). 'The aid given to maintain schools is known as "Annual Grants" being annually payable, at a fixed time, to each school allowed to receive them' (Revised **Code of Regulations**, Report 1861–62 p. xvi). The amount of award was dependent on the pupils' performance at the annual inspection, which continued until withdrawn in stages from 1895.

ANNUAL REGISTER OF TRAINING RESEARCH

(Operational in 1971) This register listed some of the main research that was carried out by the **Department of Employment** and 300 then current and recently completed projects related to training were described. The purpose of the register was to keep training specialists informed of research activities, avoid duplication of effort, and highlight neglected areas that merited more investigation.

This was part of a concerted action to provide information about training.

See also: Training Information Paper; Training Abstracts Service; Glossary of Training Terms; National Apprenticeship Service

Further reading: Training Agency (1990)

APPLIED GCSE

See: (Applied) General Certificate of Secondary Education

APPOINTMENTS SERVICE

(Closed 1956) The appointments service was set up to deal with people seeking managerial and professional jobs and dealt in particular with ex-HMS officers and graduates in technical and scientific subjects. The three offices based in London, Manchester, and Glasgow were closed in 1956 and the services of the **employment exchanges** were developed to cater for persons seeking, and employers notifying, vacancies of the type formerly dealt with by this service. Occupations of Appointments Register Standard were classified according to the extent to which they were concerned with people, things and ideas. Candidates' personal qualities were assessed on the same basis.

See also: Professional and Executive Register

Further reading: Ministry of Labour and National Service Annual Report 1956 Cmnd 9791, p. vi

APPRENTICE OF THE YEAR

(Northern Ireland) This was awarded to the best apprentice on the basis of overall occupational progress, practical and theoretical ability, positive approach to employment and outstanding personal qualities. The awards were presented for: Apprentice of the Year; Most Promising 1st Year Apprentice; Personal Achievement; Training Organisation; and Employer.

APPRENTICE TEACHERS

(1856) This was another name for **pupil-teachers** who worked in schools and who, if satisfactory at the end of the required period, became certified teachers. The schools needed to have a registered/certified teacher in order for there to be apprentice or pupil-teachers (Minutes 1855–56 p. 221).

APPRENTICESHIP

A means of formalised training for those who wished to follow a particular career path. Three main features of apprenticeships are that they involve on-the-job training; the person earns while they learn; and, thirdly, they allow employers to shape training to their requirements. The period for a traditional apprenticeship used to be up to five years (before the Second World War it was seven years), but with the high unemployment and economic downturns of the 1970s and 1980s the number of opportunities were severely reduced. Apprenticeships were offered in industries with a craft-based discipline, though it is now possible to study as an apprentice to be an hairdresser for example. The period for apprenticeships has now been shortened - normally to two-three years.

See also: Accelerated Modern Apprenticeships, Advanced Modern Apprenticeships; Foundation Modern Apprenticeships; Health and Morals of Apprentices Act 1802

Further reading: DfES (September 2001)

APPRENTICESHIP AMBASSADOR SCHEME

(19 April 2006) The scheme was designed to promote apprenticeships to businesses and to increase the number of apprenticeships, particularly in areas of low penetration. It was sponsored by the **Department for Education and Skills**, the **Department of Trade and Industry**, HM Treasury, The **Learning and Skills Council**, and the **Sector Skills Development Agency**.

Further reading: Department for Education and Skills (2007) Departmental Report 2007, Cm 7092, p. 58

APPRENTICESHIP COMMITTEES

(1906) These were voluntary organisations that operated to coordinate apprenticeships in their areas. They were established in a number of places and include the London Apprenticeship and Skilled Employment Committees, and committees that met under the auspices of the Victoria Settlement in Liverpool.

Further reading: Gordon (1911)

APPROVED CENTRES

This is an organisation that is approved by an **Awarding Body** to assess and verify qualifications. Centres are normally educational institutions, training organisations or employers that use trainers, supervisors or managers and assessors.

Further reading: The Monitor (1997)

APPROVED SCHOOLS

(1933) These were schools to which young offenders could be sent by the courts. They were formed from the earlier **industrial schools** and **reformatory schools**. The Children and Young Persons Act 1969 removed the term 'approved school' and they subsequently became known as community homes under the responsibility of local authorities.

APPROVED TRAINING ORGANISATION

(1986) ATOs were linked to the **New Job Training Scheme (NJTS)**. Approved external organisations offering appropriate training were awarded JTS status and were monitored and evaluated (see also **accredited training centres**). They were linked to the two-year **Youth Training Scheme**.

Further reading: MSC (1986b)

AREA INSPECTIONS

(October 1999) Also known as area-wide inspections, these were investigations of **further education** and educational provision for 16- to 19-year-olds. They were carried out jointly by **OFSTED** and the Adult Learning Inspectorate in order to provide coordination for their separate areas of responsibility. The framework for inspections met the requirements of the Learning and Skills Act 2000 as amended by the Education Act 2002. The first inspection was of Hackney LEA.

Further reading: OFSTED (2003)

AREA MANPOWER BOARDS

(January 1983) Established to replace district manpower committees (which had superseded **local employment committees**). The **Manpower Services Commission** set up 28 area boards with responsibility for the planning and operation of programmes in their area (5 boards in Wales). AMBs in England, Scotland and Wales were set up to provide the MSC, and later the **Training Commission,** with advice and assistance in the delivery of employment and training initiatives. They were constituted with a membership of 5 persons from the TUC, 5 persons from the CBI, 1 from the local education service, 1 from professional education services (normally a college principal), 1 from the voluntary sector and 1 from the disabled sector. The boards were reconstituted in 1986 with an increase in representation by women and ethnic minorities. Members were nominated from industry and commerce.

Further reading: MSC (March 1983); MSC Annual Report 1983–84, p. 43

AREA OFFICE

The **Manpower Services Commission** set up 28 area boards, each of which was supported by an area office to aid the **Special Temporary Employment Programme**

and **Youth Opportunities Programme**, where the programmes would be put into operation, to ensure that there was maximised community involvement.

Further reading: Ainley & Corney (1990)

AREA TRAINING OFFICE

(1947–75) These organisations were established as a result of the 1944 McNair Report into the provision of teachers and youth leaders to coordinate and validate teacher training.

ARMED FORCES RECRUITMENT

(1990) Piloted in 6 **Jobcentres** in England for one year. Applicants saw service careers details at Jobcentres, and then were referred to an armed forces careers office nearest to the centre. The scheme was closed at the end of the year as the take-up was considered no greater than conventional and previous calls to recruitment offices for the armed forces.

See also: Regular Forces Employment Association

Further reading: Employment Gazette (1990 pp. 20–24)

(JUNIOR) ART DEPARTMENTS IN ART SCHOOLS

During the 1920s junior art departments in art schools provided 'Drawing, Artistic Handicraft, and (at least for those under exemption age) General [education], in full-time, courses' to those 'under 16' (Report 1925–26 p. 57).

See also: Art Schools

ART SCHOOLS

During the 1920s, art schools provided 'Drawing, Artistic Handicraft and [design] (and in special circumstances literary and pedagogic subjects) in full-time or part-time courses planned for students who [had] already received at least elementary instruction in drawing'. This provision was for those students 'over exemption age' (Report 1925–26 p. 57).

By the 1930s the system of art schools was recognised to have developed in a 'haphazard' way and needed reorganisation and a Report on Art and Industry by Lord Gorell resulted in Circular 1432 recommending an hierarchical reorganisation into art classes, art schools and art colleges (Report 1933 p. 56).

See also: Schools of Art

ASSEMBLY LEARNING GRANT

(2002) Replacing discretionary Hardship and Access Funds, the Assembly Learning Grant was introduced by the Welsh Assembly to support those who were financially disadvantaged from continuing their further or higher education. This was in addition to **student loans** and was means tested and eligible for those who had lived in Wales for at least three years. The Assembly Learning Grant Further Education Scheme was designed to encourage those people over 19 years old to continue their education and study for qualifications such as GCSEs or NVQs. Up to £1,500 was available for full-time study and £750 for part-time study with a minimum of 275 study hours required to receive the grant.

See also: Education Maintenance Allowance

Further reading: http://new.wales.gov.uk/about/cabinet/cabinetstatements/2002/120202JDStudentsupport;jsessionid=PMH6LvQYvZLhdGkrd41wvrh211JQP1prbfhJ0vJFLgn8sMmTkl9W!-875933534?lang=en (accessed 11 February 2010)

ASSEMBLY SCHOOLS

(1850s) These were schools provided by the General Assembly of the Church of Scotland The final two schools in Shetland closed in 1879 (Minutes 1855–56, p. 576).

Further reading: Scotland (1969)

ASSESSMENT AND EMPLOYMENT INDUCTION COURSES

These were part of the **Youth Opportunities Programme** designed to improve the employability of young people by assessing what work they were most suitable for and interested in. There was also a large element in these courses that aimed to improve their knowledge of the world of work, and to improve their basic social skills. All of this was covered in a two-week period.

Further reading: MSC (1982d)

ASSESSMENT AND QUALIFICATIONS ALLIANCE

The AQA examination board was formed as a result of the alliance of the Associated Examining Board/Southern Examining Group, and the Northern Examinations and Assessment Board in 1997 and their full merger in April 2000. It is a company limited by guarantee and a charity. It offers a number of services and qualifications including **GCSE**, **a-level**, and vocational qualifications.

Further reading: www.aqa.org.uk/

ASSESSOR

This is a person who was appointed by an **approved centre** to assess a candidate's evidence for a **Scottish/National Vocational Qualification** or other vocational qualification. The assessor worked in direct contact with the candidate.

See also: Internal Verifier and External Verifier

Further reading: The Monitor (1997)

ASSISTANCE TOWARDS EMPLOYMENT

(April 1984) ASSET Centres were involved with the provision of a range of services for the disabled under the **Employment Rehabilitation Service (ERS)**. In 1991, £11.7m was set aside to cater for the special needs of some 8,900 people who fell within the terms of disability. Three teams were set up. Disabled people who were seeking employment could go to ASSET centres where they could be assessed and could seek out employers who were prepared to have their premises adapted to suit the disabled employee. The assistance was mainly given in areas of large conurbations.

See also: Disablement Advisory Service

Further reading: MSC (1987a)

ASSISTANT TEACHER

This was an assistant to the schoolmaster or head teacher during the 1800s. Assistant teachers were often **pupil-teachers** who had completed their five-year apprenticeship and were certified (Report 1860–61 p. 47). They could also teach because they had qualified through attending a two-year course at a **training college**. There were three types of recognised teachers in the 1860s: certificated teachers (**teaching certificate**); **pupil-teachers** and assistant teachers (Report 1863–64 p. xxxix). In the revised **Code of Regulations**, assistant teachers were defined as, 'Pupil-teachers who can be certified, pursuant to Article 90, to have completed their apprenticeship with credit, [and who] may serve as assistants in schools in place of pupil-teachers without being required to be annually examined. But such assistants cease to fulfil the conditions of Article 52 (b), if at any time the inspector reports them to be inefficient teachers' (Report 1863–64 p. xlviii).

ASSISTED PLACES SCHEME

(1980–97) The Education Act 1980 enabled academically talented children who scored in the top 10 to 15 per cent of the school's entrance examination to receive free or subsidised education at independent schools. This scheme was ended by the Labour Government in 1997, who claimed that it was elitist.

Further reading: Edwards et al. 1990

ASSOCIATION FOR DISCOUNTENANCING VICE AND PROMOTING THE KNOWLEDGE AND PRACTICE OF THE CHRISTIAN RELIGION

(1792) Founded by William Watson, this association was incorporated by an Act of Parliament in 1800 and founded a number of schools across Ireland.

Further reading: Durcan (1972)

ASSOCIATION OF COLLEGES

(1996) It was founded to promote the interests of **further education** colleges in England and Wales. In particular it is involved with:

- 'representing and promoting the interests of colleges and providing members with professional support services;
- influencing DCSF, BIS and agencies to maximise funding for colleges, their students and staff;
- securing a strong Parliamentary and media reputation for the sector;
- providing professional support services for member practitioners in HR, health and safety, IT, curriculum, quality, PR, estates;
- advocating for colleges at all levels on inspection, curriculum, examinations, best practice and more;
- delivering key events in the education calendar and providing business solutions to colleges and partners in consultancy, training, recruitment and conferencing; and,
- representing the view and interests of members to regional policy-making, strategic and funding bodies and providing professional support services to regional members.'

www.aoc.co.uk/en/about_us/what_ we_do/ (accessed 02 April 2010)

See also: CollegesWales

ASSOCIATION OF TEACHERS OF DOMESTIC SCIENCE

(1897) When cookery and laundry work were introduced into the school syllabus, they were often taught by specialist teachers who did not have full teaching status. The association was established to represent them and achieve equality with certified teachers and it obtained a compulsory three-year training course. It became the Association of Teachers of Domestic Subjects in 1909 and reverted to its original name in 1962. Around 1983, it became the National Association of Teachers of Home Economics Ltd and in 1991 the National Association of Teachers of Home Economics and Technology.

Further reading: Durcan (1972)

ASYLUM SCHOOLS

An asylum was a place of shelter and asylum schools were provided for many orphans and destitute children during the seventeenth and eighteenth centuries. They also provided accommodation for children who were blind, deaf and suffering other disabilities. To support the children, they were given schooling and training in various skills and crafts in order that they might support themselves in the future.

See also: House of Occupations; Houses of Refuge; Industrial Schools

ATHENAEUM

Many of these societies were established in towns and cities during the 1800s to encourage learning and to deliver classes and talks in the arts, sciences and humanities. They were alternative sources of learning and adult education to the **mechanics institutes**, although they sometimes shared premises, for example in Sheffield. The Athenaeum periodical was published from 1828–1923, producing articles on a similar range of subjects; it subsequently became *The New Statesman*.

Further reading: Tylecote (1957)

ATTENDANCE ALLOWANCE

(1855) The HMI, Reverend H. W. Bellairs, reported that a school at Forthampton, Gloucester, had raised attendance from one-third to two-thirds. 'Each child at the end of every week, who has attended regularly and conducted himself well, receives a ticket representing attendance and conduct. These tickets are exchanged at the end of every month for tickets representing higher merits. At the end of every year the value of the marks is summed up, and every child possessing tickets representing an attendance of 200 days and the requisite amount of good conduct receives a sum of money graduated according to class; in the first class, six shillings; in the second, four shillings; in the lower classes, two shillings' (Minutes 1855–56, p. 241).

See also: Education Maintenance Allowance

ATTENDANCE OFFICERS

These were officials who reported to the **School Attendance Committee** and whose duty was to ensure that children attended school, in accordance with the **Elementary Education Act 1876** (Report 1889–90 p. 281).

ATTENDANCE REGISTER

Accurate statistics regarding attendance in schools were limited because of poor record keeping and the turnover of staff. A Scottish HMI stated, 'I am much inclined to urge that, in all schools subject to government inspection, well planned and uniform registers should be required and perhaps provided by government. The registers should not be too complicated, that the time may not be spent in taking statistics which should be employed in instruction' (Minutes, 1853–54, p. 990).

In order to receive a capitation grant, schools were required to keep a register of pupils' attendance. A specimen provided in the Minutes (1856–57, p. 533) also allowed for other information regarding reading, writing, arithmetic, etc. to be recorded.

See also: Log Book of School

AWARDING BODY

Awarding bodies were originally accredited by the **Qualifications and Curriculum Authority** to monitor the assessment process and award vocational qualifications. With the **lead bodies and national training organisations** they were jointly responsible for the development of **Scottish/national vocational qualifications**. Bodies in England and Wales that certified qualifications included Educational Excellence (**Edexcel**), **Royal Society of Arts** (RSA), Engineers Training Association (ENTRA), **City and Guilds of London Institute** (CGLI), and the London Chamber of Commerce and Industry (LCCI).

See also: Examination Board; Awarding Organisations

Further reading: The Monitor (1997)

AWARDING ORGANISATIONS

(*c.*2008) The term was used to describe those organisations that awarded qualifications. Originally titled **awarding body**, the term was changed to take into account the ability of other organisations to have their internal qualifications acknowledged.

AWDURDOD CYMWYSTERAU, CWRICWLWM AC ASESU CYMRU

Established on 1 October 1997 to replace the Curriculum and Assessment Authority for Wales, ACCAC – the Qualifications, Curriculum and Assessment Authority for Wales – was an assembly sponsored public body within the National Assembly for Wales. ACCAC advised on education and qualifications and it regulated all external qualifications except NVQs, which were the responsibility of the **Qualifications and Curriculum Authority**. In March 2006, ACCAC merged with the Education Department of the Welsh Assembly and, on 1 April 2006, became the **Department for Children, Education, Lifelong Learning and Skills**.

B

BACCALAUREATE

The Baccalaureate qualification was originally introduced in early nineteenth century France by Napoleon I. It is taken at the end of secondary school by students aged approximately eighteen years and consists of a range of subjects within three main areas: general, professional and technological. There is also a European Baccalaureate taken in European schools and an International Baccalaureate, which is a two-year course of study in six main subject areas, for 16- to 19-year-olds. To deepen the educational experience, students are required to write an extended essay, reflect on the theory of knowledge, and learn actively and creatively. **Advanced levels** have been considered too specialised and narrow, focusing (typically) on only three subjects and pupils have been required to make a decision on subjects at the early age of sixteen that potentially limits their educational and career prospects. For this reason a growing number of schools have adopted the International Baccalaureate. A **Welsh Baccalaureate** was introduced in 2003.

BACHELOR OF EDUCATION

The Robbins Report on higher education recommended that teachers should be graduates and the three-year Certificate in Education provided at **colleges of education** became a four-year Bachelor of Education.

BACK TO WORK BONUS

(1995) This was a social security scheme that was described in the Jobseeker's Act 1995; it allowed unemployed people who worked part-time to be credited with up to half of their earnings to a maximum of £1,000.

Further reading: Lourie (1998)

BACK TO WORK PLANS

(Announced in 1990) These plans outlined the action that a claimant agreed to take in order to find work or training. By 1994/95 **Employment Service** advisors had given 4.4 million interviews to new claimants, and presented them with this scheme.

Further reading: Loy (1990)

BACKING YOUNG BRITAIN

(2009) During the recession of 2008–09 it was recognised that young people were disproportionately affected by the lack of jobs and the Backing Young Britain campaign was designed to ameliorate this. The campaign encouraged businesses, government bodies and charities to support young people by committing to one or more of the following initiatives: 'To become a volunteer mentor for school or university leavers to help them find their feet in the jobs market. Provide work experience places, volunteering places or a work trial to help young people learn about work, make contacts and fill their CV. Offer an internship for a graduate. Create a new internship for 18-year-olds and non-graduates to give them a chance to prove themselves. Provide an apprenticeship for 16- to 24-year-olds. Joining a **local employment partnership** to make sure job vacancies are advertised to local unemployed people. Bid for one of the 100,000 jobs for young people in the Government's **Future Jobs Fund**'.

Further reading: http://interactive.bis.gov.uk/backingyoung britain/ (accessed 02 February 2010)

BACKWARD CHILDREN

(1897) The **Education Department** recognised in Circular 395 that there were a considerable number of children who were 'ignorant and quite without school habits', which was a result of neglect; irregularity of attendance; the migratory nature of their families; and slow intellectual development. The department also noted that these older children 'cannot generally be taught with ordinary scholars capable of passing the First **Standard** in the course of the year, except at the cost of very great anxiety on the part of the teachers and some strain upon the school organisation; whenever this is attempted, educational progress is imperfect and slow; and, not seldom, the habit of truancy is the result' (Report 1896–97 p. 658). These children were considered to be of a mental type above defective children and it was recommended that a 'separate organisation, therefore, is required for their instruction and training' (ibid). Where numbers did not justify separate provision these children might be provided for in the infant school with the mistress having the right 'to refuse any boys whom she felt were unsuitable companions for her infants' (ibid).

See also: Elementary Education (Defective and Epileptic Children) Act 1899

BANDING

This is the categorisation of children in schools according to ability and their placement in separate classes within a year group.

BANDS – DRUM AND FIFE

(*c.*1858) Drum and fife bands, together with **drilling**, were introduced to many schools and served a range of purposes, including increased interest in school and pleasure. There was also a military dimension: 'Musical instruction on wind instruments had been introduced into some of the large pauper schools, with the view of preparing the children for enlistment in military bands' (Report 1858–59 p. 469). Also, 'the children are rendered more fit for defenders of their country as volunteers if circumstances should call them to it' (Report 1861–62 p. 27).

BASIC SKILLS AGENCY

This is the national agency for basic skills in England and Wales and it receives support from the Government. It defined basic skills as 'the ability to read, write, and speak in English (or Welsh), and to use mathematics at a level necessary to function at work and in society in general'. It was estimated that one in five people might have poor literacy and numeracy. Around a quarter of a million adults were being helped in this area, and the plan was to double this figure to half a million or more by 2002. This was given added impetus by the Green Paper *The Learning Age*.

See also: Adult Literacy and Basic Skills Unit; Adult Basic Skills Strategy Unit; Family Learning Skills for Life

Further reading: Basic Skills Agency (2001); http://www.skillsforlifenetwork.com (accessed 01 June 2010)

BASIC SKILLS AT WORK

(Announced in January 1991) BSAW was sponsored by the **Employment Department**, the **Department of Education and Science**, and the Welsh Office Education Department and administered through the **Adult Literacy and Basic Skills Unit (ALBSU)**. It provided funding for **Training and Enterprise Councils** and LEAs to develop new approaches to literacy and numeracy in local areas. The sum of £3m was made available for the period of three years 1991–94 to increase the quantity and quality of basic skills training. It was targeted at unemployed people who needed to improve their literacy, numeracy and basic skills, and those in employment who were not able to progress any further without higher level skills. There were three elements to the programme:

- a basic skills needs survey, which provided information to TECs and LEAs about work-related needs among adults in the local area;
- a free consultancy by ALBSU, which included an audit of existing provision and an assessment of the extent to which it catered for existing needs; and
- pilot projects, which explored new methods of providing basic skills training.

See also: Skills for Life

Further reading: Institute of Manpower Studies (1991)

BASIC SKILLS EMPLOYERS PLEDGE

Introduced in Wales in 2007, the Basic Skills Employers Pledge was an initiative to encourage employers to demonstrate commitment to 'help employees with poor basic skills to improve these basic skills' (Department for Children, Education, Lifelong Learning and Skills 2008 p. 38). To enter the pledge scheme, employers were expected to make a public commitment; and to achieve a pledge award, they had to introduce an action plan to address limitations in basic skills among their employees. A grant of up to £10,000 was made available to support the action plan.

See also: Skills Pledge

BEACON COLLEGES

Colleges with excellent inspection reports, and which took account of those serving deprived areas, received Beacon status. Beacon colleges receive monies from the **Standards Fund** to enable them to share good practice with other colleges.

Further reading: DfEE Departmental Report Plans 2001–02 to 2003–04 Cm 5102, p. 88

BEACON SCHOOLS

(announced summer 1998) The purpose of these schools was to recognise a cross-section of educational best practice and spread it to other schools. Additional funding was made available to encourage dissemination and promotional activities, including the development of curriculum materials, and in-service education and training (INSET).

See also: Excellence in Cities

Further reading: Rudd et al. (2000)

BEACON STATUS

See: Learning and Skills Beacon Status

BELL, ANDREW

See: Madras System

BILATERAL SCHOOLS

These were secondary schools that provided separate and distinct courses in two of the types of education provided by **grammar**, **secondary modern** and **technical schools**.

See also: Triple School

BINARY SYSTEM

The 1966 White Paper *A Plan for Polytechnics and Other Colleges: Higher Education in the Further Education System* described a higher education system for polytechnics and colleges that was funded by the Polytechnics and Colleges Funding Council, which was separate from universities: hence the term binary.

BIRKBECK SCHOOLS

(1830s) These were **secular schools** established by George Birkbeck, who was a Quaker. They were to be found in Peckham, Manchester, Glasgow and Leith (Minutes 1853–54, Vol. 1, p. 44).

BIRMINGHAM EDUCATIONAL ASSOCIATION

(1856) The HMI Reverend H. W. Bellairs' report (Minutes 1857–58, pp. 280–281) described how he went to the Committee of Oxford University, and jointly with members of the Birmingham Association to the Committee of the Senate of Cambridge University, to invite them to examine in Birmingham. 'This Committee [Birmingham], having heard the remarks of Mr Bellairs and Mr Temple's letter, beg leave to apply through these gentlemen, to the University of Oxford, to consider the subject of middle-class education, with the view of providing remedies for existing defects; and, in case the University should see fit to adopt the suggestions made by Mr Temple in his letter to Mr Bellairs, dated 11 April 1857, and to send an examiner to Birmingham, this Committee pledges itself to use its best exertions to secure candidates and to provide the necessary accommodation'. The significant impact of this initiative was recognised by Reverend Bellairs, who stated: 'To the Birmingham Association, also, belongs the merit of taking the first step in a movement which, I believe, will prove to be a most important one in improving the general education of the kingdom'.

See also: Oxford and Cambridge Schools Examination Board; Prize Schemes

BLIND AND DEAF SCHOOLS

(1893) The Elementary Education (Blind and Deaf Children) Act 1893 required blind and deaf children to compulsorily attend schools and established special schools for this purpose. Additional provision was also made within the **Elementary Education (Defective and Epileptic Children) Act 1899** for pupils with these conditions. **Technical schools** were also established for blind, deaf, and dumb people (Report 1908–09 p. 93).

See also: Special Schools

BLOCK RELEASE

In many forms of vocational education and training, employees were given a period of time away from the place of work to study and, often, to take examinations. This approach was more concentrated than in apprenticeships, for example, where leave was taken weekly. Block release occurred one or more times during a course of study.

See also: Sandwich Course

BLOCK RESERVATION

This exempted men from military service on the basis of age and occupation. The Schedule of Reserved Occupations listed exemptions and changed according to the needs of the forces and essential industries: for example, munitions was called a 'Protected Establishment'. It was replaced by **individual deferment**.

See also: National Service; Deferred Call-up

Further reading: Slack (1942)

BLUE COAT SCHOOLS

(1553) The Reformation dissolved the monasteries with the result that many of the public services they provided ended, for example, health and education. To address this poverty, Edward VI encouraged the establishment of three royal hospitals: Bridewell Hospital (now King Edward's School, Witley, Surrey); St Thomas Hospital; and, Christ's Hospital. The colour 'blue' was the colour of almsgiving and charity and it led to the pupils wearing blue Tudor frock coats. The first Blue Coat School was Christ's Hospital, originally in the City of London, but which subsequently moved to Horsham, Sussex. At Bridewell Royal Hospital the children were trained by craftsmen and tradesmen instead of school-masters. A schoolmaster was appointed in 1632 to teach reading and writing to the apprentices. In 1830 a **house of occupations** was estab-lished to house the apprentices away from the negative influence of prisoners. Other blue coat schools were founded on similar princi-ples by local benefactors and included: Ban-bury (1705); Birmingham (1724); Coventry (1714); Dublin (The King's Hospital, 1669); Dudley (1869); Hereford (1973); Liverpool (1708); Nottingham (1706); Oldham (1834); Reading (1646); Sheffield (1911).

BOARD OF EDUCATION

(1899–1944) The Board of Education was established through the **Board of Education Act 1899** and combined the responsibilities of the **Education Department** and the **Science and Art Department**. The Board was divided into two branches, one for elementary educa-tion and the other for secondary education. It was succeeded by the **Ministry of Education**.

BOARD OF EDUCATION ACT 1899

Following recommendations by the Bryce Commission, this act created a single educa-tion authority uniting the **Education Depart-ment** and the **Science and Art Department** and creating the **Board of Education**, which had three branches with responsibility for elementary, secondary and technological education. The act, which became law on 9 August 1899, came into force on 1 January 1900 and specified that 'There shall be estab-lished a Board of Education charged with the superintendence of matters relating to Educa-tion in England and Wales' (Report 1898–99 p. 505).

BOARD OF TECHNICAL INSTRUCTION

(1899) In Ireland, a Council of Agriculture, an Agricultural Board and a Board of Tech-nical Instruction were established as a result of the Technical Instruction Act 1899.

BOARD OF TRADE

In 1621 the Privy Council was directed by King James I to establish 'The Lords of the Committee of Privy Council appointed for the consideration of all matters relating to Trade and Foreign Plantations', which exam-ined trading difficulties and their financial implications. The committee became known as the Board of Trade and it began to provide advice and direction. On 20 January 1893 a separate branch of the Board of Trade was formed and titled the 'Commercial, Labour and Statistical Department' – later renamed as the **Labour Department**.

BOARD SCHOOLS

Board schools and board day schools were schools provided by the **school boards** that were established by the **Elementary Educa-tion Act 1870**. The term 'board day schools' was to distinguish schools that operated during the day from **night schools** and **evening schools**.

BOARDING SCHOOLS

These are schools at which pupils live and receive both education and accommodation. Schools that make this provision are repre-sented by the Boarding Schools' Association.

BOLTON COMMITTEE

(1971) This was a committee set up by gov-ernment to look at the needs of small firms with respect to training. The basic problem was that small firms were concerned that per capita, the cost of training was higher for them than for larger enterprises; as a result, therefore, they were not making the best of the training that was on offer. There was also concern about the limitations of the training levy system. A report of committee's findings was published, along with recommendations.

Further reading: Bolton (1971)

BOOKKEEPING

This was described as a **specific subject** in the 1890 **Code** (Report 1889–90 p. 119) and details of the syllabus were described in Report 1891–92 p. 205. It was introduced as a subject in the 1897 **Evening Continuation School Code**, which specified that 'The Elementary course is specially designed to meet the needs of boys entering an office directly on leaving school, the Intermediate Stage for junior clerks in merchants' and other offices, and the Advanced Stage to enable bookkeepers and others in somewhat more responsible office positions to qualify for undertaking special branches of the higher work usually occurring in the offices of societies, companies, and accountants' (Report 1896–97 p. 617).

BOYS INSTITUTE

During the 1800s and 1900s these were **night schools** established generally for boys older than those attending **elementary schools**. 'There is something too in the name of school which grates upon the feelings of young people, whose manly independence of self-maintenance begins at the age of 16, and who are often husbands at the age of 18 or 19. The names "Boys Institute" and "**Working Men's College**" have been found more attractive than the name of school' (Report 1863–64 p. 142).

BRANCH SCHOOLS

This term describes outlying schools and ones that weres normally connected to a main institution; for example, Ramsey, Cambridgeshire had a branch school – the Peterborough School of Art. In the early 1900s, the **Board of Education** described 'Branch **Technical**, **Commercial**, and **Domestic Schools**' (Report 1908–09 pp. 68 & 71).

See also: School of Ease

BRIDGE TO EMPLOYMENT

(May 1997) In Northern Ireland this was originally an EU-funded peace and reconciliation initiative. It was designed to meet the recruitment needs of inward investors and expanding companies by recruiting long-term unemployed people and helping the long-term unemployed compete more successfully with those in employment.

Further reading: Training and Employment Agency Annual Report (1997)

BRISTOL DIOCESAN TRADE SCHOOL

(1 January 1856) The Committee of the Bristol Diocesan School Society established a day and evening trade school to support tradespeople in Bristol. In a letter asking for financial support the Reverend Henry Moseley reported that there were 1,708 manufacturers, tradesmen, and master-workmen who would benefit from an understanding of the principles of manufacturing, mechanical pursuits and elementary principles of science. Three groups of trades were identified and listed: 18 trades were identified connected with building; 72 trades were connected with manufactures; 62 trades were dependent on experimental sciences, particularly chemistry. It was also proposed that the school should include a navigation school for boys destined for sea-service based on the Royal Naval Schools at Greenwich Hospital. The recommended name for the school was The Bristol

Trade and Navigation School. It was also supported by the Society of Merchant Venturers.

Further reading: Minutes 1855–56 pp. 21–29; Report of the Bristol Diocesan School Society (1855)

BRITISH ACCREDITATION COUNCIL

(1984) A registered charity, the British Accreditation Council provides accreditation for private post-16 education in Britain.

BRITISH AND FOREIGN SCHOOL SOCIETY

(1808) Originally established by evangelical and non-conformist Christians in 1808, and called the 'Royal Lancasterian Institution for Promoting the Education of the Children of the Poor', it subsequently was called, 'the Institution for Promoting the Education of the Labouring and Manufacturing Classes of Society of every Religious Persuasion', and then the British and Foreign School Society in 1814. The schools followed the approach of Joseph Lancaster and the principles of this society were:

I.   That in all schools established in connection with, or assisted by, the British or Foreign School Society, the Sacred Scriptures in the authorized version, or extracts therefrom, shall be read and taught daily.
II. That no catechism, or other formulary peculiar to any religious denomination, shall be introduced or taught during the usual hours of school instruction.
III. That every child attending the day-school shall be expected to attend the particular Sabbath-school or place of worship which its parents prefer.
     (Minutes of 1844, Volume 2, 1845, p. 427)

The titles 'national school' and 'British school' were removed in 1906 because of the potential confusion with the provision of state education nationally that was in union with the National [School] Society. 'The epithet "National" in the names of Schools was frequently misapplied. In its strict meaning the term indicated that the School to which it applied was in union with the **National [School] Society**. It had, however, gradually come to be used loosely as synonymous with "Church of England", and it appeared to the Board that this was in any case somewhat misleading now that the maintenance of all Public Elementary schools has become a national charge. The epithet "British" originally applied to Schools in union with the British and Foreign School Society is open to similar objections' (Report 1906–07 p. 28).

See also: Central Society of Education; Lancasterian School

BRITISH ASSOCIATION FOR THE ADVANCEMENT OF SCIENCE

See: British Science Association

BRITISH COUNCIL

(1934) Formally titled 'The British Council for Relations with Other Countries', this council was established to promote cultural relations with other countries and encourage a wider understanding of Britain.

BRITISH EDUCATIONAL COMMUNICATIONS AND TECHNOLOGY AGENCY

(April 1998–2010) BECTA replaced the **National Council for Educational Technology**. The Agency had a specific remit to ensure:

● that technology supports closely the aim to drive up standards in core curriculum subjects, and in the development of lifelong learning;
● that young people leave school and college with the skills in ICT for the twenty-first century; and

- that it is inclusive of those with special educational needs.

To that end, in 1999–2000 the sum of £5m was made available to BECTA such that:

- it could develop and support the **National Grid for Learning**;
- it could support the effective use of ICT in primary and secondary curriculum subjects, school management and special educational needs;
- it could support the development of information and learning technologies in the further education sector; and
- it could keep abreast of developments in educational technologies used overseas to inform development in the UK.

Further reading: British Educational Communications and Technology Agency (1999)

BRITISH SCHOOLS

This was a term used to distinguish the schools of the **British and Foreign School Society** operating in the late 1840s using the 'old' system of **monitorial** instruction. The 'new' British Schools were ones that had a trained or qualified teacher who understood pedagogy and conducted lessons using the **simultaneous method** and other methods of instruction.

Further reading: Minutes 1847–48, Volume II, p. 330

BRITISH SCIENCE ASSOCIATION

(27 September 1831) Originally founded in York in 1831, its purposes were 'to give a stronger impulse and a more systematic direction to scientific inquiry; to promote the intercourse of those who cultivate Science in different parts of the British Empire with one another and with foreign philosophers; to obtain more general attention for the objects of Science and the removal of any disadvantages of a public kind that may impede its progress'

(British Science Association, accessed 2010). It organises the British Science Festival, and the National Science and Engineering Week. Formerly the British Association for the Advancement of Science, it was renamed as the British Science Association in January 2010.

Further reading: MacLeod and Collins (1981); www.britishscienceassociation.org/

BRITISH TRAINING INTERNATIONAL

Following the recommendations of the Beaumont Report, in which it was proposed that there should be an export strategy for **Scottish/national vocational qualifications**, it was suggested that a new company should be set up to act as this export centre: BTI. At the time it held the only database of all UK training.

The **British Council** absorbed BTI in November 2000 and it was renamed Vocational Partnerships.

See also: UK Vocational Education and Training Export Centre

Further reading: Beaumont (1996); www.bti.org.uk

BUG BUSTER TRAINING

(1998–99) This was a specific programme for SMEs to ensure that the 'millennium bug' would not affect IT facilities within small businesses. In 1998, **training and enterprise councils** were charged with the responsibility to train 20,000 employees from small and medium-sized business via 180 training providers. The take-up was such that the 20,000 places were enrolled by March of that year.

Further reading: DfEE Departmental Report 1999–2000 to 2001–02, Cm 4202, p. 164

BUILDING CONSTRUCTION

An examination for this subject was described in the Report of the Board of Education 1899–1900 (Vol.1, p. 22).

BUILDING GRANTS

Grants for the building of schools were first offered by the Committee of Council on Education in 1839 (Report 1863–64 p. 244). These schools were for the children of the labouring poor.

See also: Capitation Grants; School for Labouring Poor

BUILDING SCHOOLS FOR THE FUTURE

Building Schools for the Future was launched in February 2004 with the aim of rebuilding or remodelling 3,500 state secondary schools in England with much of it funded by a private finance initiative. Partnership for Schools, a non-departmental public body, was given responsibility for managing and delivering this provision.

Further reading: www.partnershipsforschools. org.uk/ (accessed 01 June 2010)

BURGH SCHOOLS

In Scotland, the Act of 1696 provided for schools to be established in every parish, without exception. However, the Act of 1803 amended this so that there was no requirement to establish a school in parishes that 'consist only of a Royal Burgh'. The reason for this was that in these areas it was assumed that there was a lesser need since support for these schools came from Burgh funds, endowments and voluntary subscriptions.

Further reading: Minutes 1844, Volume 2, p. 354

BURNHAM COMMITTEE

The committee was named after the first chairman, Lord Burnham, who, in August 1919, convened representatives from the Associations of Local Education Authorities and the National Union of Teachers to address the issue of teachers' salaries in public elementary schools. On 21 November 1919 the Standing Joint Committee reported a unanimous recommendation of a 'provisional minimum scale' of salaries. In May and December 1920 committees, also under the chair of Lord Burnham, were respectively established to consider the salaries of secondary school teachers, and teachers in technical schools etc. See Table 1.

BURSARS

(1907–18) To provide a new route for the supply of teachers, the **Board of Education** provided grants to **local education authorities** that enabled young people who intended to become teachers to continue their education for an additional year, and they were called 'bursars'. Bursars who had

Table 1 Salaries of teachers

Areas	Assistant Masters			Assistant Mistresses		
Graduates	Minimum £	Annual Increment £	Maximum £	Minimum £	Annual Increment £	Maximum £
England and Wales (except London)	240	15	500	225	15	400
London	290	15	550	275	15	440
Non-graduates	£	£ s.	£	£ s.	£ s.	£
England and Wales (except London)	190	12 10	400	177 10	12 10	320
London	210	12 10	450	197 10	12 10	360

satisfactorily completed their leaving examination were entitled to enter training colleges one year earlier (at the age of 17) than ex-pupil teachers. If an ex-bursar wished to get practical teaching experience before entering training college they were called '**student teachers**' (Report 1906–07 p. 53). This system of grants to LEAs for individual bursars was discontinued after the Act of 1918 although, for a period, the term continued to be used by LEAs to describe secondary school pupils aged 16 years and over who had a free place and received a maintenance allowance and were intending to attend training college.

Further reading: Report on the Training of Teachers for Public Elementary Schools 1925 p. 15

BUSINESS AND TECHNOLOGY EDUCATION COUNCIL

(1983–96) BTEC was an awarding body and became **Edexcel** on the merger of BTEC and the University of London's Examinations and Assessments Council in 1996. The Business and Technician Education Council (subsequently renamed the Business and Technology Education Council) was originally formed in 1983 by the merger of the Technician Education Council (TEC had been established in 1973 to develop a unified system for technical education and subsequently validated courses in further and higher education) and the Business Education Council (BEC was established in 1974 to rationalise, and link to the requirements of employment, sub-degree vocational education in FE, HE colleges and polytechnics). The TEC unified courses led to the development of Ordinary National Diplomas (ONDs) and **Higher National Certificates** and **Diplomas** (HNCs/HNDs). Prior to this the qualifications had been the responsibility of professional bodies including **City and Guilds of London Institute**. Similarly BEC took over responsibility for ONCs/ONDs and HNCs/HNDs, which had been administered by various joint committees. In 1978 it introduced BEC Nationals and Highers as replacements.

See also: Awarding Bodies

Further reading: Business and Technician Education Council (1985); www.edexcel.org.uk

BUSINESS EDUCATION INITIATIVE

(1994) Northern Ireland scheme aimed at providing young graduates with international perspectives by studying business-related subjects during placements at colleges and universities in the USA for a year.

See also: Overseas Export Marketing Programme – Explorers; Overseas Career Development Programme; the American Management and Business Internship

Further reading: Training and Employment Agency Annual Report (1995)

BUSINESS ENTERPRISE PROGRAMME

(April 1987–March 1991) This programme took over from the **Training for Enterprise** and the **Job Training Programme** (Northern Ireland) after September 1988 in order to provide business start-up training for people not eligible for ET. It was then taken into the Business Enterprise Support programme in 1991.

See also: Business Enterprise Training

Further reading: RSGB (1991)

BUSINESS ENTERPRISE TRAINING

(1991/92) The intention of BET was to encourage employers to consider training as a strategic investment. The Employment Department, while recognising that the primary responsibility for training was with the employers, used BET to improve support for training. It had formerly been called **Business Growth Training**. From April 1991 BET and the **Enterprise Allowance Scheme** budgets were merged.

See also: Business Enterprise Programme

Further reading: MSC (1987b)

BUSINESS GATEWAY

Business Gateway in Scotland provides information services to businesses including: business news and events; financial support information; free business workshops; information resources; link directories; information on tendering; and training. It is the equivalent of England's **Business Link** and Wales' **Flexible Support for Business**.

Further reading: www.bgateway.com (accessed 01 June 2010)

BUSINESS GROWTH TRAINING

(1 April 1988 – March 1994) BGT had a budget of £55m and had three main objectives:

- to encourage employers in the community to plan and deliver systematic training and staff development to achieve business goals;
- to promote improvements in the efficiency, methods, quality, standards and scope of employers training; and
- to increase the awareness of employers about the benefits of effective training.

BGT also complemented and reinforced the **Department of Trade and Industry**'s Enterprise Initiative. BGT provided five support options:

- Option 1: kits for better business and training plans;
- Option 2: better business skills for owner managers;
- Option 3: using consultants to manage business change;
- Option 4: tackling your skill needs jointly with other companies; and,
- Option 5: how to implement your own innovative training solution).

This initiative superseded and brought together the range of **Training Agency**'s grant support that previously had been available to employers including **local grants to employers**; the **Managing Company Expansion** Scheme; **local collaborative projects**; **national priority skills scheme**, grants to promote open and flexible learning, and a number of Training for Enterprise Schemes. Renamed **Business Enterprise Training (BET)** in 1990, it became part of Business Enterprise Support in 1991. The budget for this programme became part of the **single regeneration budget** (SRB). It ceased to be a programme when responsibility was transferred to **TECs.**

Further reading: Marshall et al. (1993)

BUSINESS IN THE COMMUNITY SCHEME

Business in the Community was an association of 400 major companies and government departments committed to the promotion of corporate community involvement. The companies provided cash, people and other resources to support economic and social regeneration. Scottish Business in the Community (SCOTBIC) provided a similar service for Scottish Enterprise Trusts.

Further reading: Business in the Community (1989); http://www.bitc.org.uk

BUSINESS INITIATIVE FOR SMALLER FIRMS

(March 1986) Set up to help improve performance in smaller firms and involve relevant agencies. SMEs could call upon skilled help to review their whole operation and make suggestions as to how they could improve their skills and markets.

Further reading: COIC (1988)

BUSINESS INTERCHANGE

(April 2007 – March 2010) This was a life-long learning UK initiative designed to support teachers, trainers and tutors in all industry sectors to update their industrial knowledge and experience within their continuing professional development programme. It was one of four programmes set out in the 2006 White Paper *Further Education: Raising Skills, Improving Life Chances*; the other programmes were **Give Something Back**; **Business Talent**, and **Make a Difference**.

Further reading: www.lluk.org.uk (accessed 01 June 2010)

BUSINESS LINK

(1992) Originally this was a national network of approximately 240 one-stop shops that provided advice and business support services for SMEs in England. This network was intended to overcome the market failures of SMEs: the cost of gathering information; the need to be a jack-of-all-trades; and the potential to take a short-term view. Business link were companies that were a partnership between the **Training and Enterprise Council** Chambers of Commerce and the Local Authority. They provided five core services: diagnostic services; an enquiry and information service; personal business advisors; a programme for management development; and support for start-ups. Later, they were organised on a regional basis.

See also: Flexible Support for Business (Wales); Business Gateway (Scotland); Small Business Service

Further reading: Bryson et al. (1999); www.businesslink.org.uk (accessed 01 June 2010)

BUSINESS ON OWN ACCOUNT

(1944–94) A special scheme whereby those who were disabled and thus unable to work within an employer's premises could set themselves up in business and work from their home.

Further reading: Ministry of Labour and National Service Report for 1939–46 Cmd 7225 pp. 232–243

BUSINESS START-UP SCHEME

(April 1991 – March 1995: BSUS continued in Scotland until 2000) BSUS came into being to replace the **Enterprise Allowance Scheme**. It provided an allowance (£40 per week) and an introductory briefing for unemployed people who wished to become self-employed or start up a business. It was administered by **Training and Enterprise Council**s and allowed greater diversity; the weekly amount and duration of payments varied between TECs to suit local needs. However, due to the economic downturn, this scheme placed a greater stress on the survival of businesses, and hence non-viable enterprises were being 'kept alive', rather than dying naturally. The resource became part of the **single regeneration budget** in 1994. This was then transferred to the Department of the Environment in 1995 and BSUS was closed.

Further reading: Tremlett (1995); Tremlett et al. (1995)

BUSINESS TALENT

(April 2007 – March 2010) This was a life-long learning UK management recruitment programme designed to help colleges and providers to attract exceptional talent from public and private organisations into senior management roles. It was one of the four programmes set out in the 2006 White Paper *Further Education: Raising Skills, Improving Life Chances*; the others were **Give Something Back**; **Business Interchange**; and **Make a Difference**.

Further reading: www.lluk.org.uk (accessed 01 June 2010)

BUSINESS TRAINING SCHEME

(Planned from Sept 1945, it ran from 1946 – June 1950) This was a three-month course at a Technical College in the field of business administration – for released military personnel. A second scheme called 'Permanent Courses in Business Administration' operated as a three-term course in October 1947.

Further reading: Ministry of Labour and National Service Report for 1939–46 Cmd 7225 pp. 162–63; Ministry of Labour and National Service (1948)

C

CAMPAIGN FOR LEARNING

The Campaign for Learning originated in a **Royal Society for the Encouragement of Arts, Manufactures and Commerce** initiative in 1996 and became an independent charity in 1997. Its purpose was to encourage learning throughout society and among its initiatives were Family Learning Day (1998); **Learning at Work Day** (1999); and National Workplace Learning Network (2007).

Further reading: www.campaign-for-learning. org.uk (accessed 01 June 2010)

CANAL BOATS ACT 1877

Section 7 of this act provided for the Registration Authority to register the place where a canal boat belonged, in order to ensure that children of school age were included in the returns of the school boards under the objectives of the Elementary Education Acts. Section 6 stipulated that 'A child in a canal boat registered in pursuance of this Act, and his parent shall, for the purposes of the Elementary Education Acts, 1870, 1873, 1876, be deemed, subject as herein-after mentioned, to be resident in the place to which the boat is registered as belonging, and shall be subject accordingly to any byelaw in force under the said Acts in that place' (Report 1881–82 p. 106). Not surprisingly, the boat owners were reluctant to comply with these laws and the powers to act that were held by the authorities were limited, making their implementation

relatively ineffective. The 1884 Canal Boats (1877) Amendment Act provided for inspectors, which brought an improvement for the estimated 9–10,000 children who lived onboard.

CAPITAL

(1977) Capital stood for 'Computer Assisted Placing In The Areas of London'. It was the forerunner of the national database and operated in 15 Jobcentres in north-east London. It handled over 4,000 vacancies and 9,000 registrations each month, which was about 10 per cent of the London total.

See also: Worktrain

Further reading: Glazier (1979)

CAPITATION GRANTS

(*c.*1855) 'The capitation grant is the direct subscription which the public [through the Education Department] make to the funds of a school, in consideration of, as well as in order to omission, its efficiency' (Minutes 1859–60 p. 24). These were originally applied to country parishes and payment was made to the schools based on the attendance of pupils (Minutes 1855–56, p. 241). 'By the original Minute of 2 April 1853 "the children attending factories and printworks under any Statute were to be counted as fulfilling the condition of capitation grants, if they complied with the requirements of the particular Acts" and the

Minute of 29 April 1854 must now be taken to be supplementary to those acts, not only as heretofore, in the rural districts, but, in all parts of Great Britain whatever' (Minutes 1856–57, p. 36).

See also: Annual Grant Schools

CARE TO LEARN

(1 August 2003) The purpose of Care to Learn was to provide financial support to teenage parents, including fathers, and would enable them to continue or return to education or training. There were no specific hours and the courses could be full- or part-time and last from a few weeks to over two years. The only requirement was that it was a course, or non-employed status programme, with a work-based learning provider that was publicly funded and based in England; it didn't apply to higher education. To be eligible for childcare support they had to be aged 16 or over and under 19; or they had to have started a course before they were 19. Payment for childcare was made direct to the parent(s) and travel expenses were reimbursed through the education or training provider. From September 2004 the scheme was valid for all young parents under the age of 19.

See also: Activity Agreements; Learning Agreements; Education Maintenance Allowance

Further reading: *HM Treasury (2007) Supporting Young People to Achieve: The Government's Response to the Consultation, March, HM Treasury*; http://www.direct.gov.uk/en/EducationAnd Learning/14To19/MoneyToLearn/Caretolea rn/DG_066556 (accessed 01 June 2010)

CAREER DEVELOPMENT LOAN

(Piloted in 1986 and went national in July 1988) The aim was to encourage individuals to take personal responsibility for their careers and to be willing to finance it themselves. Three banks provided the service: Barclays,

Clydesdale and Co-operative. The **Employment Department** paid the interest on the loan for the training period and for up to three months afterwards and also guaranteed a proportion of each bank's CDL portfolio. By 1998, up to £336m had been advanced to 105,000 applicants since the programme began. Of those setting out, 82 per cent completed their courses, 71 per cent achieved jobs on completion of their courses, and 74 per cent of trainees felt that the CDL was a worthwhile investment in terms of their future careers.

See also: Career Development Loans Plus

Further reading: DfEE (1995); Employment Department (1993a); www.lifelonglearning. co.uk/cdl/

CAREER DEVELOPMENT LOANS PLUS

(1995) This was a pilot scheme in which the **Employment Department** paid interest on loans from banks to individuals to finance training. Borrowers who had completed training might delay repayments for up to 18 months. It applied more to graduates to enable them to set up in business after qualifying.

See also: Career Development Loans

Further reading: Employment Department (1995)

CAREERS ADVISORY OFFICERS

The **Youth Employment Service** provided advice to school leavers on career options. Careers advisory officers specialised in selected areas of youth employment and provided careers advice to children in the Channel Islands. They also made tours to advise the children of servicemen in Germany and the Middle East.

Further reading: Central Youth Employment Executive (1953)

CAREERS AND OCCUPATIONAL INFORMATION CENTRE

(1980) COIC was set up to provide details of work options, predominantly to school leavers, with details of career paths; it was planned primarily as a publishing house to specialise in literature, information and software. By 1993/94 expenditure was £2.4m, with income from sales at £1.3m. The centre's sales, invoicing and distribution were contracted out as a way of reducing costs in 1993/94.

Further reading: COIC (1988)

CAREERS SCOTLAND

In 2002, Careers Scotland was formed by taking over the responsibilities of 67 different organisations. This national agency provided careers information, advice and guidance to young people in colleges and school, and those who had finished compulsory schooling. It gained independence from the Scottish Executive in 2006.

Further reading: www.careers-scotland.org.uk/ (accessed 01 June 2010)

CAREERS SERVICE

(1973) Previously the **Youth Employment Service**, it was established at the same time as the reform in placing services and advisory services of adults with the creation of the **Professional and Executive Register** and **Jobcentres**. It existed to provide vocational guidance for people in schools and colleges. It was originally under the responsibility of LEAs, where the 1973 Employment and Training Act gave local authorities a statutory duty to provide the service, with the education department coordinating it across England and Wales. The Trade Union and Employment Rights Act 1993 transferred the duty to provide a careers service to the Secretary of State for Employment. In 1994 the responsibility to provide the service rested with the Secretary of State for Employment. However, in 1994, the service was contracted out to private enterprise, with a view to improving efficiency and management. It was replaced by the **Connexions Service**.

Further reading: Hillage and Wilson (1992); Institute for Manpower Studies (1992); www.careers-uk.com

CAREERS SERVICE INSPECTORATE

The Careers Service Inspectorate of the **Employment Department** monitored and evaluated the performance of the **Careers Service** that was delivered by **local education authorities**. In 1991/92, 20 per cent of the cost of the careers service was provided by the **Employment Department**.

Further reading: Bedford (1982)

CAREERS SERVICE STRENGTHENING SCHEME

Specific grants were made available by the **Employment Department** to the **Careers Service** to encourage certain objectives and output targets: for example, placings into jobs, **youth training** and visits to employers and training providers. In 1989/90 the Strengthening Scheme was revised and the grant was variable and was based on relative shares of youth unemployment.

CAREERS WALES

(April 2001) Careers Wales (Gyrfa Cymru) was a statutory body funded by the Welsh Assembly to provide impartial information, advice and guidance to people of all ages in Wales. It brought together six careers organisations and managed a number of services, including **learndirect** telephone helpline; **education business partnerships**; Youth Gateway; and CLIC information and advice for young people.

Further reading: www.careerswales.com

CARR REPORT

(1958) The National Joint Advisory Council instructed the committee under the chair of Robert Carr MP 'to consider the arrangement for the training of young workers in industry, with particular reference to the adequacy of intake into apprenticeship and other forms of training, in the light of the expected increase in the number of young persons entering employment and the need to ensure an adequate supply of trained workers for future needs'. The report made a number of recommendations including the setting up of the **Industrial Training Council**.

Further reading: Carr Report (1958)

CATEGORIES OF SCHOOL

Three main categories of school were specified in Section 20 of the School Standards and Framework Act 1998: **community schools** and community special schools; **foundation schools** and foundation special schools; and, **voluntary schools**, which were either voluntary aided or voluntary controlled.

CATHOLIC POOR SCHOOL COMMITTEE

(1847) The committee was established in 1847 and was responsible for the establishment of schools. A Secondary Education Council was later established and in 1905 the Catholic Education Council for England and Wales was established. It subsequently became the Catholic Education Service. In 1850 the Poor School Committee established a Roman Catholic Training School for males at Hammersmith, called St Mary's, under the Brothers of Christian Instruction. The training was based upon that of the Abbé de Lamennais, in north-west France. In 1925 the training school was transferred to Strawberry Hill, Twickenham (Minutes 1852–53, p. 473). A training school for female students was opened in Nottingham in 1855, but for reasons of cost was transferred to All Souls, St Leonard's-on-Sea, on 7 February 1856, with support and teachers from the Society of the Holy Child Jesus (Minutes 1856–57, p. 789). A northern training school for females was established at Mount Pleasant in Liverpool on 19 January 1856 (Minutes 1856–57, p. 797).

CEDEFOP

(February 1975) The European Centre for the Development of Vocational Training is a community body whose task is to promote the development of vocational training at community level. The Council of ministers took the decision to establish the centre in February 1975 and it was formerly established by Council Regulation 337/75. The CEDEFOP Management Board consists of representatives of the commission, workers organisations, employers and governments. It was originally located in Berlin and was later transferred to Thessaloniki. The European Training Village website provides a wide range of information on European training issues.

Further reading: www.trainingvillage.gr

CEDEFOP STUDY VISIT PROGRAMME

This programme was funded under the auspices of the European Commission, and allowed students within the European Union to make study visits. The usual system was for a group of universities or colleges to set up interchanges within a discipline, such that the student could improve their language skills and share in something of the culture of the country they were studying/working in. The study visit programme was later taken over by the **Leonardo da Vinci** programme.

See also: CEDEFOP; Erasmus; Petra

Further reading: www.trainingvillage.gr

CENSUS OF EMPLOYMENT

(Piloted 1970, began 1971) Conducted by the **Statistical Services Division**. The census was carried out by the SSD to recognise skills shortages and provide statistical advice as to training, education and enterprise functions. The first census was carried out in 1971 following a trial in 1970, and was conducted annually until 1978. These figures were monthly, quarterly or annual depending on need, and covered employment, unemployment, vacancies, redundancies, industrial disputes, earnings, skills shortages, training and tourism. SSD also conducted the New Earnings Survey. Responsibility for producing the census was subsequently taken over by the Office for National Statistics.

See also: Labour Force Survey

Further reading: Office for National Statistics (1993)

CENTRAL CLASSES

See: Centre System

CENTRAL INSTITUTION (SCOTLAND)

This was a Scottish higher education institution that provided instruction in commerce, agriculture, art, domestic science, music, technology. These institutions were an approximate equivalent of the polytechnics and the Further and Higher Education Act 1992 allowed higher education institutions such as the central institutions and polytechnics to award their own degrees, thus leading to many of them becoming universities in their own right. In 2008, the Scottish Agricultural College was the last central institution to enter the university sector.

CENTRAL SCHOOLS

In the 1850s the name 'central schools' also meant '**model schools**'; however, this term declined and was more commonly associated with the schools that were first established during the early 1900s to cater for the increasing demand for higher levels of education. Frequently, they were centrally located to enable access (hence their name) and in

some cases represented a change in name from **higher elementary school**. The central schools of the London Education Authority were described by a Board of Education report (Report 1911–12 p. 42): 'The object of these central Schools is to continue the general education of their pupils while giving them at the same time a definite bias towards some kind of industrial or commercial work. Boys and girls are prepared for permanent employment on leaving school, and the instruction is, therefore, to be such that children will be ready to go directly into business houses or workshops at the completion of the course without any special training. This object, however, is not to be interpreted so as to prevent the pupil proceeding by scholarship or otherwise to a place of higher education'

CENTRAL SOCIETY OF EDUCATION

(1836) This society was established to promote education but without any religious involvement.

See also: National School Society; British and Foreign School Society

Further reading: Ely (1982)

CENTRAL TECHNICAL SCHOOLS

These schools were encouraged by the **Technical Instruction Act 1889** and, as the names suggests, were often centrally located in a town to enable greater access. They were sometimes known as **municipal technical schools** and might contain, within one building, **technical schools, commercial schools, domestic schools** and **art schools** provision (Report 1908–09 p. 68).

CENTRAL TRAINING COUNCIL

(1964–73) The CTC was set up under Section II(1) of the **Industrial Training Act (1964)** and comprised six employer and six trade union representatives – advisory and consultative function only. Its purpose was to advise the Minister 'on the exercise of his functions under the act and on any other matter relating to industrial or commercial training which he may refer to it [CTC]' (Ministry of Labour Gazette 1965 p. 487). It was wound up at the end of 1973.

CENTRAL WELSH BOARD

See: Welsh Central Board

CENTRAL YOUTH EMPLOYMENT EXECUTIVE

(1965) This body was brought into operation to train **youth employment officers**, whose remit was to visit schools and act as the fore-runner of the careers guidance teachers advising those in the last year of secondary education about their options. The executive developed careers activities in schools and supported the **Youth Employment Service** activities in the field of career options and work placement. The executive reported to **National Youth Employment Council.**

Further reading: Ministry of Labour Gazette 1965 p. 298

CENTRE FOR EXCELLENCE IN LEADERSHIP

(October 2003–30 September 2008) Described in Success for All (DfES November 2002), the objective of CEL (a charitable trust) was to work alongside sector partners to support world-class leadership in the learning and skills sector. In 2008, the responsibilities of the Centre for Excellence in Leadership and the **Quality Improvement Agency for Lifelong Learning** were combined within a new body, the **Learning and Skills Improvement Service**.

See also: Leadership Foundation for Higher Education; National College for School Leadership

Further reading: DfES (November 2002)

CENTRE SYSTEM

The centre system of teaching was used to support the education of **pupil–teachers** who were brought together in apprentice year groups to be instructed in subjects where their knowledge was limited (Report 1889–90 p. 322). These were also known as central classes (Report 1898–99 p. 626).

CENTRES FOR EXCELLENCE IN TEACHER TRAINING

(September 2007) This network was designed to enhance the quality of further education teacher training. It was intended that there would be at least one CETT in each English region.

See also: Training and Development Agency for Schools

Further reading: Department for Education and Skills (2007) Departmental Report 2007, Cm 7092, London, The Stationery Office, p. 96

CENTRES FOR EXCELLENCE IN TEACHING AND LEARNING

CETLS were originally described in the **Higher Education Funding Council for England** strategic plan 2003–08. The two main aims were to reward excellent teaching practice and to invest in that practice to sti-mulate improvements for the benefit of stu-dents, teachers and institutions. In January 2005, 74 CETLs were awarded funding.

Further reading: www.heacademy.ac.uk/our work/networks/cetls

CENTRES OF EXCELLENCE

(2000) Northern Ireland initiative for recog-nition of good practice in further education colleges. The focus was on six skills areas of particular relevance to the Northern Ireland economy: ICT and computing; elec-tronics; software engineering; manufacturing engineering; construction and the built environment; and, tourism and hospitality.

CENTRES OF VOCATIONAL EXCELLENCE

(July 2001 – 31 July 2008) In July 2001, 16 pathfinder centres of vocational excellence were established by the **Learning and Skills Council**. The centres were planned to enhance the existing provision that met Level 3 craft and technical needs of employers. Among the objectives were the aims to increase active employer/college engagement; secure enhanced vocational learning opportunities for all learners in further education; and encourage collaboration amongst providers and advance the nature of excellence in economically important vocational specialisms. By 2006, there were more than 400 CoVEs, taking into account local, regional and sectoral needs. The CoVE recognition was replaced by the **Training Quality Standard**.

Further reading: DfEE (2000g); DfEE (2001b); DfES Departmental Report 2002–03 to 2003–04 Cm 5402 p. 141

CERTIFICATE OF EXTENDED EDUCATION

(1976–83) This certificate was introduced by a number of examination boards to cater for those of lower ability. Those pupils who achieved **ordinary levels** often went on to take **advanced levels** and the Certificate of Extended Learning was a qualification designed to encourage the lower ability children to stay on at school. Grades I, II, III were considered equivalent to a C grade at O level. The CEE was not considered successful and was abolished to be replaced by the **Certificate of Pre-Vocational Education**.

CERTIFICATE OF PRE-VOCATIONAL EDUCATION

(Launched nationally in September 1985) CPVE was a DES initiative arising from pressures to provide more relevant vocational courses. It was a one-year, full-time course for general and vocational education for those pupils over the age of 16 in colleges and schools. Its main purposes were the following: to provide a transition from school to adulthood; to supply individually relevant educational experience; to recognise young people's attainment; and to provide progression opportunities to continuing education, training and work. It was succeeded by the **Diploma of Vocational Education**.

Further reading: Hitchcock (1988); Morning (1988)

CERTIFICATE OF SECONDARY EDUCATION

(1965–87) The CSE was recommended by the Beloe Committee and was designed for pupils who had successfully completed examinations at the ages of 15 or 16. It ran in parallel with GCE O levels (**General Certificate of Education** ordinary levels) and was more commonly used in secondary modern schools, while the O levels were more frequently found in grammar schools. CSEs were sometimes interpreted as being inferior to O levels and there was also no natural division between GCEs and CSEs; thus to address this inconsistency the two examinations were replaced by the **General Certificate of Secondary Education** (GCSE), which began in September 1986 with examinations in 1988.

Further reading: DES (1990)

CERTIFICATES OF AGE

Local authorities were given the power under the Elementary Education Act 1876 to obtain from the registrar of births and deaths a return of the births of children in their district. This allowed them to issue an age certificate to parents or others concerned with the education or employment of a child (Report 1878–79 p. 358). 'In most instances, the births were certified by the registrar's or baptismal certificate, but not unfrequently by a record in a family bible, or some other book, and occasionally by the word of the parent only' (Report 1878–79 p. 589). This certificate was also combined with a **certificate of proficiency**, and **certificate of school attendance** in the **child's school book**.

CERTIFICATES OF PROFICIENCY

Under the Elementary Education Act 1876, Certificates of Proficiency were issued by **Her Majesty's Inspectors** to those scholars who had achieved the required standard in reading, writing and arithmetic (Report 1878–79 p. 359). This certificate was also combined with a **certificate of age**, and **certificate of school attendance** in the **child's school book**. A certificate of proficiency was also called a **labour certificate**.

CERTIFICATES OF SCHOOL ATTENDANCE

Under the Elementary Education Act 1876 'any local authority, parent, or other person interested in the employment or education of a child under 14, may require the principal teacher for the time being of any certified efficient school which such child has attended to furnish a certificate specifying the number of school attendances made by the child in the school during each year, since the age of five, for which the school registers are preserved' (Report 1878–79 p. 359). This certificate was also combined with a **certificate of age**, and **certificate of proficiency** in the **child's school book**.

See also: Leaving Certificate

CERTIFIED EFFICIENT SCHOOL

A certified efficient school was one that satisfied the criteria specified in the Education Act 1876 and in the **Code of Regulations**.

CHANNEL ISLAND SCHOOLS

From 1842 until 1872 Channel Island schools received grants from the Committee of Council; however, in 1871 the Treasury noted that they were not under imperial taxation and the Education Office informed the schools' managers that grants would not continue to be dispersed. The Secretary of State for the Home Department communicated to the governors of the islands that other arrangements should be made. Schools in receipt of annual grants would be continued and inspected, while teachers were under probation and **pupil-teachers** were still indentured. Following a report, Guernsey (and Alderney) 'declined all future connexion with the English system, and undertook the whole burden of the maintenance, organisation, and inspection of public elementary education in the island' (Minutes 1872–73 p. 206). Jersey decided to maintain links with the mainland and used island funds to apply the New **Code** and defray the costs of **Her Majesty's Inspectorate of schools**. This would then more closely align the situation to that which operated in the **Isle of Man schools**.

CHARITY SCHOOLS

During the 1700s and 1800s many charity schools were erected by parishes and other benefactors to educate the poor and needy who were not catered for by the grammar schools. Charity schools were sometimes, but not exclusively, known as Blue Coat schools.

Further reading: Jones (1938)

CHARTER FOR JOBSEEKERS

(1991) The charter was developed as a result of the Citizen's Charter. Its purpose was to provide a clear statement of the standards of service that could be expected by the public. The employment service published its Charter for Jobseekers in 1991 describing the standards of service that unemployed people were entitled to expect. The following would be displayed in all offices: 'details of all services offered; local targets for the level of service offered, covering waiting times for services such as interviews, how quickly the telephone would be answered, and standards for promptness and accuracy in benefit payments; information relevant to the local labour market on progress made in meeting targets'.

Further reading: Employment Gazette 1991 p. 420

CHARTER FOR LEARNING

The original Charter for Learning laid down parameters for the standard that the school leaver should have achieved when they presented themselves to an employer. From 1998 the new Charter for Learning took into account not only academic achievement, but also training aspects as well. This enabled all the past schemes to be rolled into one and it preceded the **New Deal**.

Further reading: DfEE Departmental Report March 1997 Cm 3610, p. 15

CHARTER SCHOOLS

See: (The) Incorporated Society

CHARTERED INSTITUTE OF PERSONNEL AND DEVELOPMENT

In 1913, the Welfare Workers Association was founded in York by a number of people including Seebohm Rowntree. It later became the Central Association of Welfare Workers (1917); Central Association of Welfare workers (Industrial) (1918); Welfare Workers Institute (1919); Institute of Industrial Welfare Workers (1924); Institute of Labour Management (Industrial Welfare, Staff Management and Employment Administration) (1931); Institute of Personnel Management (1946). In 1994 the Institute of Personnel and Development merged with the **Institute of Training and Development**

to become the Institute of Personnel and Development and the Chartered Institute of Personnel and Development from 2000.

Further reading: www.cipd.co.uk

CHARTERED TEACHERS

In Scotland, the chartered teacher grade was introduced in 2002 to encourage teachers to advance their career without leaving the classroom. The Standard for Chartered Teachers consisted of four main components: professional values and personal commitments; professional knowledge and understanding; professional and personal attributes; and, professional action. The chartered teacher was characterised by four professional values '(a) effectiveness in promoting learning in the classroom; (b) critical self-evaluation and development; (c) collaboration and influence; and, (d) educational and social values' (Scottish Executive 2002 p. 1). Chartered teachers received, in 2009, a salary enhancement of £6,500 per year. In the same year an Association of Chartered Teachers was established to further promote the profession of teaching.

Further reading: www.scotland.gov.uk/Public ations/2002/12/15833/14074 (accessed 01 April 2010)

CHILDREN'S EMPLOYMENT COMMISSIONERS

During 1840–42, a Royal Commission of Enquiry was undertaken into the employment of children in mines in Great Britain and Ireland. The commission then reported annually.

CHILD'S SCHOOL BOOK

(1877) This was a form titled 'Child's School Book', which provided details about a child and which required much extra clerical work by the school teacher. 'It will thus show the child's date of birth, attendances at school, and the standards which it may successively pass during its school life. The form with its certified entries will also serve as a pass to work, which can be shown to any person who may wish to take the child into his employment' (Report 1876–77 p. 256).

See also: Certificate of Age; Certificate of Proficiency; and Certificate of School Attendance

CHOICE OF CAREERS

(1953–59) A series of booklets produced by the **Ministry of Labour and National Service** aimed at school leavers. The series was listed in **Ministry of Labour** Annual Reports as they were developed and included: Furniture Manufacture; The Coal Mining Industry; The Radiographer, The Coppersmith and The Mastic Asphalt Spreader.

Further reading: Ministry of Labour and National Service 1953 Report p. 65

CHWARAE TEG

This was a Welsh initiative for women to support them to realise their full potential. It led to the **Fair Play for Women** initiative.

Further reading: Employment Department (1994a)

CIRCULATING SCHOOLS

(1731) The Reverend Griffith Jones, a member of the **Society for Promoting of Christian Knowledge**, began the first circulating schools in Carmarthenshire to encourage people to read in Welsh with the use of the Bible. These schools spread throughout Wales and were known as circulating schools because they were held for a period of about three months before moving to another location.

CITIZENSHIP EDUCATION

In 1999, a report chaired by Bernard Crick recommended the inclusion of citizenship education within the national curriculum and this was implemented at **Key Stages** 3 and 4 in 2002.

See also: Life and Duties of the Citizen

Further reading: Qualifications and Curriculum Authority (September 1998)

CITY ACADEMIES

See: Academies

CITY ACTION TEAMS

(April 1985) Set up in seven Inner City Partnership Areas (ICPAs) in Newcastle, Manchester, Liverpool and London. In 1985/86, £138m was spent helping 138,000 people. These teams looked at employment needs in those areas with innovative schemes such as 'incubator units' for small firms or self-employed people to try out business ideas; for example, in Gateshead a communal workshop and thirteen small factory units were provided.

Further reading: Employment Department (1991a)

CITY AND GUILDS OF LONDON INSTITUTE

(1878) This was established by 16 of the City of London's livery companies and was also known in its earlier years as the City and Guilds of London Technical Institute. On 15 November 1900 the **Board of Education** recognised, for the first time, the examination of the Institute. It is an **awarding body**.

Further reading: www.cityandguilds.com

CITY CHALLENGE

(1992/93 – 1996/97) City Challenge was implemented by the Department of the Environment with support from the **Employment Department Group**. It was part of the Government's interdepartmental initiative '**Action for Cities**'. Work by the

ED Group included research, demonstration projects, evaluation, dissemination of good practice and contracts with voluntary organisations working in inner cities. It was recognised that developing effective partnerships and community involvement requires the provision of training and other resources.

Further reading: Powell (1995); Hall and Mawson (1999)

CITY LEARNING CENTRES

City learning centres were part of the **Excellence in Cities** programme and were designed to provide learning opportunities using ICT for pupils, teachers and the wider community. Up to £1.2m was made available for capital and initial start-up costs with recurrent funding of £220,000 per year. The CLC did not belong to the school organisation in which it was based, but came under the control of a centre management board and was a shared resource for all of its partnership schools.

Further reading: HMI (2003)

CITY STRATEGY

Beginning in 2007 with 15 pathfinder city strategy partnerships, this initiative targeted disadvantaged communities with the target of achieving 80 per cent employment in these areas. The principle underlying this initiative was that local partners would be more effective because of local knowledge of employers' needs and the combining of resources. In March 2009 the **Department for Work and Pensions** extended the initiative for two further years.

Further reading: www.dwp.gov.uk/policy/welfare-reform/city-strategy/

CITY TECHNOLOGY COLLEGES

Between 1988 and 1993, 14 CTCs and one City College for the Technology of Arts (BRIT School) were established under the Education Reform Act 1988. They were secondary schools, independent of the local authority control, and were mainly set up in the major cities to concentrate on science and technology with strong links to business and industry that provided some funding. Many of the CTCs converted to **city academies**.

Further reading: Esp (1990)

CLASS SUBJECTS

These were subjects for which a school received grants depending on the proficiency of the whole class that was often examined together by Her Majesty's Inspectors. 'The choice of *Class Subjects* (Article 19 C.), the grants for which depend upon the general proficiency of the classes, and not individual scholars, has not, of late, been in any way restricted' (Report 1882–83 p. xvii). Originally, schools received grants for performance in the elementary subjects of reading, writing and arithmetic; these subjects were then increased to include English, geography, grammar, history and needlework. In 1880 these restrictions were removed and other subjects were allowed, although adoption of new subjects was relatively slow e.g. 'natural history in 11 instances; domestic economy in 8; chemistry in 2; agriculture in 1; and mensuration in 1: while of the subjects to which the grants were previously confined, geography has been taken in 14,205 instances; grammar in 17,510; history in 1,315; and needlework in 7,999' (Report 1882–83 p. xvii). Initially, class subjects differed from **specific subjects** in that grants were paid with regard to the proficiency of pupils tested by individual examination; later, however, specific subjects received grants too. In 1900, 'The old classification of subjects as "obligatory", "class," "specific", was replaced by a twofold division into – (a) Subjects to be taken "as a rule" in all schools though not necessarily in every class – English; Arithmetic; Drawing (for boys); Needlework (for girls); Lessons,

45

including Object Lessons, on Geography, History, Common Things; Singing and Physical Exercises. (b) A list of subjects, one or more of which was to be taken when circumstances in the opinion of the Inspector made it desirable. These were the old "specific" subjects' (Report 1910–11 p. 20). This degree of flexibility was largely removed by the **national curriculum**.

COAL MINES REGULATION ACT

(1872) This act required boys between the ages of 10 and 12 to attend school for 20 hours every fortnight and made it a statutory duty for pit managers to be trained and certified. A board of examinations was established, which appointed examiners, organised examinations and supervised applications for certificates of competency that were awarded by the Secretary of State. The Coal Mines Regulation Act 1887 extended the certification to under-managers. The Coal Mines Act 1911 included the specifications of the operations of the Board of Mining Operations.

See also: Colliery Schools; Mines – Regulation and Inspection Act

CODE OF GOOD PRACTICE ON THE EMPLOYMENT OF DISABLED PEOPLE

(1990) Employers who adopted the Code of Good Practice committed themselves to offer effective induction, including the provision of special equipment if necessary, and to retain in suitable jobs existing employees who became disabled. Employers were then able to display a **disability symbol** (resembling a tick mark) demonstrating their commitment on letterheads, recruitment literature, employment application forms, publicity materials and exhibitions. The symbol indicated to disabled job seekers and employees that they would be considered for vacancies, training, career development and promotion on the basis of ability. Following the **Disability Discrimination Act** 1995 a revised code was issued to underpin the changes.

Further reading: Employment Service (1988a)

CODE OF PRACTICE FOR AGE DIVERSITY IN EMPLOYMENT

(1999) A voluntary Code of Practice issued in 1999 following the Cabinet Office's 1997 document *Winning the Generation Game*. The code provided advice to employers on how to avoid 'ageism' in recruitment, promotion and training, etc.

CODE OF REGULATIONS

From 1839, the Minutes of the Committee of the Privy Council on Education detailed the minutes and regulations of the committee with regard to operations, grants, inspection etc. These specifications were consolidated into a reduced form or code in 1860 (Alphabetical Index of the House of Commons 1852–99 p. 449). A royal commission, chaired by the Duke of Newcastle, was established in 1858 to investigate the rising level of funding provided to schools. It reported in 1861 and recommended the continuation of funding linked to '**payment by results**'. The Committee of the Privy Council on Education issued a 'New Code' of Regulations on 29th July 1861. This code was subsequently amended, following criticism, and announced in Parliament on 13 February and 28 March 1862—it was called the 'Revised Code'. It described the conditions under which annual grants would be provided to schools, the qualifications required of teachers, the **standards** to be achieved by the pupils, and the inspections that would continue to be conducted by HMIs, etc. (Report 1861–62 pp. xv–xliv). The Revised Code 'was not put into general operation before the latter part of 1863' (Report 1865–66 p. viii). In effect, this was the commencement of direct central control of the curriculum. The code subsequently was updated in January of each year (Article 150: Report 1863–64 p. lv). The Reverend Bellairs, HMI, submitted his report: 'Again, under the Revised Code I feel strongly the advantage of being able to recommend grants in exact proportion to work done. Hitherto the question was all or none, and under a sense of the really tremendous penalty of refusing grants to a school, perhaps struggling for existence from low funds, I have frequently refrained from recommending a course which would have ruined the teacher and closed the school. The mischief of this was very great' (Report 1864–65 p. 14). Codes were issued for different forms of education, for example the **Evening Continuation School Code**. In 1926, largely as a result of the general strike and financial austerity, the Board of Education revised grant regulations and renumbered the regulations of the various codes. The revision 'covered the Code (now Grant Regulations No 8), The Secondary School Regulations (now Grant Regulations No 10), the Regulations for Further Education (technical schools, etc) (now Grant regulations No 6), and for the training of teachers (now grant regulations No. 7)' (Report 1925–26 p. 4).

(ROYAL) COLLEGE OF PRECEPTORS

(20 June 1846) Recognising that many teachers did not hold accredited qualifications, thus lowering the status of teachers in comparison with other professions, John Parker, the principal of Trafalgar House, a small school in Brighton, championed the establishment of colleges for teachers. In 1845 he presented a paper, 'The Elevation of the Scholastic Profession and consequent advancement of Education, by the establishment of a Royal Incorporated College of Schoolmasters'. A committee was subsequently convened and met in 1846 at the Freemason's Tavern to announce the establishment of the College of Preceptors. In 1848 it received its Royal Charter from the **Board of Trade**. The College promoted the registration of teachers

and this was loosely described in Section 4 of the Board of Education Act 1899, which established a Teachers Registration Council. This initiative was abandoned in 1906 due to problems in framing a register. It was relaunched in 1998 as The College of Teachers.

Further reading: Report 1905–06 p. 17; Willis (2005)

(THE) COLLEGE OF TEACHERS

See: (Royal) College of Preceptors

COLLEGES OF ADVANCED TECHNOLOGY

In 1956 the White Paper *Technical Education* recommended an increase in the provision of advanced courses in technical colleges and the creation of colleges of advanced technology for eight technical colleges that provided high levels of study. In 1963, the Robbins Report on higher education provided for CATs to be granted university status and receive a Royal Charter.

COLLEGES OF EDUCATION

The Robbins Report (1963) into higher education recommended that teaching should be made a graduate profession and that **training colleges** should be called colleges of education and develop closer links with universities. Many colleges of education subsequently became **colleges of higher education:** for example, Newman College, Birmingham, and, later still, Newman University College.

See also: Model School; Normal School

COLLEGES OF FURTHER EDUCATION

During the 1920s colleges for further education delivered '[p]reparation for specific occupations or (in the case of a course confined to students who have satisfied matriculation requirements) for University

Intermediate or Final Degree Examinations, by means of full-time courses of at least a year planned for students who have reached the standard of an approved First Examination; and/or Vocational, domestic, Art or General instruction in evening courses' to 'Students over 16 who have attended Evening Institutes up to that age or have received advanced instruction at Public Elementary Schools or elsewhere up to 15 at least' (Report 1925–26 p. 57). During this period, colleges for **further education** might also include **(day) continuation schools**, **(junior) technical schools**, **(junior) housewifery schools** and **technical day classes**. In more recent decades colleges *for* further education have mostly become known as colleges *of* further education and were funded by the **Learning and Skills Council** until April 2010 when responsibility was transferred to **local education authorities**.

See also: Further Education

COLLEGES OF HIGHER EDUCATION

In the 1970s, colleges of higher education were formed as a result of the reorganisation within higher education. The majority of colleges of education merged with polytechnics or universities with the remainder becoming colleges of higher education.

COLLEGESWALES

In November 2009, the Forum of the National Association for Further Education Colleges and Associations in Wales (fforwm) was replaced by CollegesWales/Colegau-Cymru, an educational charity and company limited by guarantee. Its purpose was to represent further education and colleges in Wales to influence education, training and lifelong learning.

See also: Association of Colleges

Further reading: www.collegeswales.ac.uk; www.colegaucymru.ac.uk

COLLIERY SCHOOLS

(*c.*1860) Night schools or evening schools for colliers were introduced by the Earl of Ellesmere, who employed teachers of general subjects. In addition, he also employed a 'Mr Traice, who devotes himself to teaching, to all the evening schools in rotation, those branches of knowledge which are most essential to miners. Mr Traice imparts instruction on ventilation, on the gases which are explosive and injurious to health, on machinery, and similar subjects; I have no doubt whatever, that if the mining population generally had similar teaching, and were thus regularly impressed with the importance of these subjects, the terrific accidents which occur so often, and which nearly always arise from ignorance or carelessness, would be very considerably diminished in frequency' (Report 1860–61 p. 94).

See also: Government School of Mines; Mining Schools

COMENIUS

Named after Jan Amos Comenius, this programme is designed to extend knowledge and understanding about Europe among children and teachers, and develop life-skills for life within Europe. The other European lifelong learning programmes include **Erasmus**, **Gruntvig, Leonardo da Vinci** and **Transversal**.

Further reading: www.britishcouncil.org/comenius; http://ec.europa.eu/education/life long-learning-programme/doc78_en.htm

COMETT

(1986–90) The 'Community Programme in Education and Training for Technology' aimed to strengthen and stimulate community wide cooperation between higher education establishments and industrial or other enterprises in respect of technological training. Comett involved the following activities:

- It involved the setting up or developing University-Enterprise Training Partnerships. These were partnerships between Higher Education and industry in the framework of a European network. They were based on a geographical region or a sector of technology.
- It included support for students, new graduates and lecturers to gain relevant work experience in companies in the member states; it supported fellowships and industrial personnel in higher education institutions in other member states.
- It established support or joint projects to develop advanced technology training courses with a European dimension and to encourage the development of distance learning using new training technologies.
- It helped to support activities such as information exchange, establishment of data bases, and a programme of conferences and evaluation to support and monitor Comett development.

Comett student grants could last between 3 and 12 months. In 1990, the total number of undergraduate student placements throughout the EC was 3,777, of which 666 grants were awarded to UK HEIs.

See also: Comett II

Further reading: Commission of the European Communities Task Force (1992)

COMETT II

(January 1990 – December 1994) A European Community action programme for education and training for technology.

See also: Comett

Further reading: Commission of the European Communities Task Force (1992)

(PRELIMINARY) COMMERCIAL CERTIFICATES

(early 1900s) Educational institutions awarded these certificates following examinations by pupils who had studied for two years. The syllabus for this course in the Lancashire and Cheshire Union of Institutes was: 'First year: obligatory – commercial arithmetic, English, geography; optional – commercial correspondence and business routine. Second year: obligatory – commercial arithmetic, English, commercial correspondence and business routine; optional – bookkeeping, geography, shorthand, modern language (elementary grade)' (Laurie 1912a p. 97).

COMMERCIAL EVENING SCHOOLS

These were a form of **evening continuation school**, which taught the commercial subjects described in the Code (for example, commercial bookkeeping, shorthand, commercial geography) and were taught by specialists. The Leeds Board supported these schools (Board of Education 1900–01 Vol. 2, p. 115).

COMMERCIAL SCHOOLS

Established largely in the 1800s, these were schools that charged for the attendance of pupils (Report 1858–59 p. 505), for example Bedford Commercial School (Minutes 1844 vol 2 p. 39). These schools were not the same as the commercial schools of the twentieth century listed below.

See also: Dame Schools; Adventure Schools; Proprietary School; Farmed Schools

COMMERCIAL SCHOOLS

This term was sometimes associated with **trade school** and around 1900 these schools were established to provide education in commercial subjects (Report 1906–07 pp. 74 and 75). By the 1920s, many large towns had a junior commercial school that provided full-time instruction for pupils who had left public elementary school. They were admitted at the age of 13 or 14 and the course had a duration of two or three years. The subjects included English, French, arithmetic, bookkeeping, shorthand, typewriting, commercial knowledge and physical exercises, and often science. In some towns there were full-time courses of one or two years for pupils who had completed secondary education and the curriculum generally included: English, economic history, geography, business economics, bookkeeping, commercial arithmetic, foreign languages, shorthand and typewriting, and sometimes economic theory and commercial law. Evening commercial institutes (Report 1922–23 p. 93) were held in the premises of public elementary schools and some of the advanced courses prepared students for professional examinations: Chartered Institute of Secretaries, the bodies of Accountants, Chartered Insurance Institute, Corporation of Insurance Brokers, Institute of Bankers, and Institute of Transport (Report 1924–25 p. 74). The commercial schools were the equivalent, at the time, of **technical schools**. These schools were not the same as the commercial schools of the nineteenth century, mentioned above.

COMMERCIAL SUBJECTS

(1897) Commercial arithmetic, commercial geography and commercial history were introduced as new subjects in the 1897 **Evening Continuation School Code**, acknowledging the importance of trade and commerce to Britain. Commercial arithmetic was divided into three stages: the elementary one addressed multiplication and division of decimals, long tots and cross tots (balancing of accounts tables), interest, discounts; the intermediate stage dealt with stocks and shares, profit and loss, discount, insurance annuities, etc.; the advanced stage considered freights, bills of lading, rates of exchange, debentures, stocks, bankers interest and compound interest (Report 1896–97 p. 616). 'Commercial Geography deals with the geographical distribution of commercial commodities, chiefly food, with raw and manufactured products, and minerals, and with various facilities and hindrances to trade' (Report 1896–97 p. 619).

This course also was divided into three stages: the elementary stage addressed the British Isles and trade routes; the intermediate stage studied the commercial relations with one British Colony and one foreign country; the advanced stage involved a detailed study of one branch of British trade. 'Commerce is a great factor in all civilisation. Commercial history tells how mankind has progressed from small isolated communities to the great organised nations of the modern world, which depend for their existence on mutual trade and intercourse. All trade is dependent on easy means of intercourse. In the beginning all trade had to pass by the natural routes afforded by the waterways of the world. Even at the present day the lines of the great roads and railways often follow the courses of rivers' (Report 1896–97 p. 621). The 1899 Code introduced commercial correspondence and office routine and stated that, 'The First Year's Course is planned to give boys and girls, on leaving the day school, an intelligent knowledge of the details and minor duties which are expected from them on entering business life. Pains should be taken to impress on the pupil the importance of a satisfactory discharge of his duties and the value of habits of obedience, accuracy, promptitude, and dispatch. The Second Year's Course is intended for Junior Clerks and those engaged in subordinate positions in offices, warehouses, and other establishments' (Report 1898–99 p. 775).

COMMISSION FOR RACIAL EQUALITY

(1976 – 30 September 2007) The CRE was set up under the **Race Relations Act 1976** and was a publicly funded non-governmental body that promoted racial equality and challenged racial discrimination. The Commission for Racial Equality was a successor body to a number of previous bodies: National Advisory Committee for Commonwealth Immigrants (1964–65); National Committee for Commonwealth Immigrants (1965–68); Community Relations Commission (1968–76); Race

Relations Board (1965–76). Its responsibilities were taken over by the **Equality and Human Rights Commission**.

COMMISSIONERS OF NATIONAL EDUCATION IN IRELAND

Established in 1832, the commissioners of national education in Ireland oversaw the National Education Board, which had responsibility for some schools. Prior to the establishment of the board, many schools already existed, including Templemoyle Agricultural Seminary (1827–66), an **industrial school** that originated from the North-West of Ireland Society. The school teaching was predominantly agricultural-based with education alternating between classes in the morning and outdoor work in the afternoon and vice versa. The commissioners, in a report in 1837, stated their intention to divide Ireland into 25 school districts and put a model agricultural school at the centre. Each model school would have two departments: one with elementary teaching, and the other with secondary teaching for scientific subjects and instruction in manual occupations. They would have '[a] work-room annexed to each, and also a portion of land, which those children, whose parents may so direct, shall be taught to cultivate' (Minutes of Council on Education 1842–43, pp. 542–65).

See also: Incorporated Society; Education and Training Inspectorate; Ireland – National Schools

COMMITTEE FOR THE EMPLOYMENT OF DISABLED PEOPLE

(1980) The CEDP committee replaced the **National Advisory Council on Employment of People with Disabilities** in 1980. It went from a national organisation to a series of local area project teams in which local community members were recruited and the committee's resettlement staff became known as 'recognised local contacts' to enable the disabled seeking work to have a named helper.

Further reading: MSC Annual Report 1980–81 p. 6

COMMITTEE OF MINISTERS OF THE REFORMED CHURCH

Shortly after the Reformation, the Committee of Ministers of the Reformed Church in Scotland prepared a scheme of ecclesiastical government under the direction of the Privy Council. They judged that 'every several kirk should have one schoolmaster appointed' (First Book of Discipline, cap.7). They also proposed that 'colleges or academies, where logic, rhetoric, and the languages might be taught, should be erected in every considerable town; the stipends of the masters to be drawn from the Patrimony of the Church'. This eventually led to the development of **parochial schools**.

Further reading: Minutes 1844, Volume 2, p. 351

COMMITTEE OF THE COUNCIL ON EDUCATION

(10 April 1839 – 1981) The committee was formed as part of the Privy Council to distribute any sums voted by Parliament for the purpose of promoting public education. It took over this responsibility from the **Lords of the Treasury** in 1839. It was insisted '[t]hat for every 10s [50 pence] to be granted by the Committee, the means of educating one child (at least) shall be provided'. It was calculated that a minimum of 6 square feet be allowed for each child when building a school (Minutes 1839–40 p. 2). From 1839 until 1857/58 the 'Minutes of the Committee of the Privy Council' were published annually and then from this date until 1938 the proceedings were published as the 'Report of Committee of Council on Education'. The duties of the committee were taken over in 1899 by the **Board of Education**. Finally, in

December 1981, the residual functions of the committee were transferred to the Treasury and a Management and Personnel Department.

Further reading: Argles and Vaughan (1982)

COMMITTEE OF VICE-CHANCELLORS AND PRINCIPALS

See: Universities UK

COMMON ENTRANCE EXAMINATION

(1904) This examination was introduced to standardise the entry requirements to senior or secondary independent schools, although some schools continued to set their own examinations. The examination is set by the Independent Schools Examination Board consisting of representatives from the Headmasters' and Headmistresses' Conference, Girls' Schools Association and the Incorporated Association of Preparatory Schools. Test papers, taken by pupils who wish to enter an independent secondary school at the ages of 11+ or 13+, are marked by the first choice school, which sets a specific standard or pass mark - this may vary from school to school.

COMMON INSPECTION FRAMEWORK

(2000/01) Was developed in 2000/01 as a basis to examine colleges. The main purposes were to:

- 'give an independent public account of the quality of education and training, the standards achieved and the efficiency with which resources are managed by individual organisations, across areas or in particular aspects of post-16 education and training;
- help bring about improvement by identifying strengths and weaknesses;
- keep the Secretary of State informed about the quality and standards of education and training'.

OFSTED (2001b p. 3)

See also: Adult Learning Inspectorate

Further reading: DfEE (2000i)

COMMON SCHOOLS

(*c.*1850s) Common schools were those established by various bodies including many church groups. 'The characteristic difference between **ragged** and common schools for the poor seems to be this: – the former are attended by a class of children who, without special provision, will never learn to work for their living; while the latter are attended by a class who will, in the common course of things, learn to work, but will fail to obtain any due measure of moral and intellectual preparation for life. In the former, therefore, *labour*, in the latter, *learning*, is the staple of instruction; not, of course exclusively, but in the main' (Minutes 1852–53, Vol. 1, p. 54). This term was more generally used in Scotland and referred to the 'common elementary school' (Report 1863–64 p. 254). The status of schools was evident from HMI Doctor Cumming's remarks: 'According to our old parochial system, the teacher was often brought from the university to the common school, and had the prospect of rising, through the **burgh school** and the high school to the professor's chair' (Report 1860–61 p. 252).

COMMON THINGS

Lessons on common things involved the teaching and discussion of subjects and items such as a chair, a penknife, water, tree bark, or the senses, which were often an elementary form of **science class**. In many circumstances these classes were a form of **object teaching** in which an item or perhaps a picture was introduced, discussed, examined and written about. The subject dates from at least 1857 (Frost 1857) when an earlier book on object lessons was published (Mayo 1831) and in 1902 there were 23,295 departments for older children most of which had common things as a subject (Report 1910–11 p. 20).

COMMUNITY ACTION

(July 1993) The objective of Community Action, which replaced **Employment Action**, was to help people back into employment by providing recent work experience and help with job search while undertaking activities of benefit to the community. It was contracted out and delivered mainly by organisations from the voluntary/ charitable sector, with participants receiving benefit payments and an allowance. It was a temporary four-month employment in the voluntary sector for those who had been unemployed for over 12 months and was linked to **Job Search**. It was due to end in 1995, but was extended with the aim of providing 40,000 opportunities per annum for the following three years.

Further reading: Employment Service (1994); Employment Department Group Departmental Report 1995, Cm 2805, p. 15

COMMUNITY DEVELOPMENT PROGRAMME

(1991/92) This programme in Northern Ireland replaced the Manpower Training Scheme during 1991/92. The CDP emphasised the importance of planning and provided a framework to carry out a management development review, and to assess the training and development needs of other workers that were linked to key business needs and objectives.

Further reading: Training and Employment Agency Annual Report (1992)

COMMUNITY ENTERPRISE PROGRAMME

(April 1981–September 1982) This programme replaced the **Special Temporary Employment Programme** and provided temporary employment on schemes of com-

munity benefit at an appropriate local wage. These schemes were either of environmental improvement or energy conservation in nature. They were designed especially for those in the 18–24 age range who had been out of work for 6 months, and for those over 25 who had been unemployed for over one year. During their period of operation, 74,000 people started on the programme. It was superseded by the **Community Programme**.

Further reading: Short et al. (1982); Tucker (1993)

COMMUNITY INDUSTRY

(1971–91) Community Industry Limited began in six areas in 1971 (it was restructured in 1972) and was a company with charitable status set up to provide community industry places designed for young people with personal or learning problems who fell outside the scope of the **Youth Training Scheme**. In 1985/86 there were 7,000 schemes, of which 1,440 were in Scotland and 825 in Wales. From May 1990 community industry became a **youth training** provider. The special provision for disadvantaged young people provided by CI was incorporated into the general framework of YT in 1991.

Further reading: Shanks and Courtenay (1982)

COMMUNITY PROGRAMME

(October 1982 – September 1988) It was formerly the **Community Enterprise Programme** and was intended to provide 120,000 temporary employment opportunities. From June 1985 the programme was expanded from its initial target to 230,000 places. The Community Programme was the largest programme operated by the **Manpower Services Commission** to help people who had been out of work for a long period. Around 80 per cent of the jobs were part-time; 75 per cent of the participants were male; 33 per cent were in the 18–20 age range; 75 per cent were single; and 65 per cent were long-term unemployed. The programme provided full- or part-time jobs of up to a year's duration on work of practical benefit to the community. Although not primarily a training programme, some job related training was provided. CP workers also attended courses outside working hours organised through the **Wider Opportunities Training Programme**. The programme was replaced by **employment training**.

See also: Community Action

Further reading: Normington et al. (1986); Turner (1985); Unemployment Unit (1988)

COMMUNITY SCHOOLS

Sometimes known as community colleges, many of these schools were preceded by county secondary schools and were renamed following the School Standards and Framework Act 1998. They were wholly owned and run by the local education authority.

(NEW) COMMUNITY SCHOOLS

The pilot programme for these schools began in Scotland in April 1999 and was based upon the Full Service Schools initiative in the USA, which integrated school-based health and social services to help individuals and families address educational under-achievement in disadvantaged areas. The objectives were to ensure that 'each child has the fullest opportunity to maximise his or her potential – achievements in all areas must be celebrated, basic skills must be nurtured and developed, self-esteem must be enhanced and high expectations maintained; full attention is paid to identifying and addressing the child's needs – social, developmental, emotional and health – and their impact on the ability of the child to realise his or her potential; particular focus is given to the role of the family and parents/guardians and the contribution they can make; and teachers, social workers, community education and health professionals operate in an integrated framework to achieve these objectives'. The new community schools had a number of characteristics: 'A focus on all the needs of all the pupils at the school. Engagement with families. Engagement with the wider community. Integrated provision of school education, informal as well as formal education, social work and health education and promotion services. Integrated management. Arrangements for the delivery of these services according to a set of integrated objectives and measurable outcomes. Commitment and leadership. Multi-disciplinary training and staff development' (Scottish Office 1999).

See also: Extended Schools

COMMUNITY TASK FORCE

(January 2010) Within six months of a job-seeker's allowance claim, 18- to 24-year-olds were guaranteed either a job, a work placement, work-related skills, or training. The main impetus for this scheme was the disproportionate impact of the recession on youth unemployment and the intention that none of them would be permanently disadvantaged. The aims were to increase employability and work-related skills, benefit the community and find work with local employers; in addition, it was mandatory. It involved 25 hours per week work-based activity and 5 hours job-search activity.

COMMUNITY WORK PROGRAMME

(Piloted in 1995 and ended 1997) Northern Ireland scheme sponsored by the **Training and Employment Agency**, managed by the Regional Partnership and delivered by local providers in Fermanagh and Strabane District Council areas. Its main purpose was to enable communities to break the cycle of long-term unemployment. Recruitment to the programme ceased from 1 April 1997. This programme was replaced by **New Deal** and **Worktrack**.

Further reading: Training and Employment Agency Annual Report (1996)

COMMUNITY WORKSHOPS

(1978) Originally called **work preparation** units, community workshops were first developed in Northern Ireland in 1978. By 1985 there were 45 Workshops, which were organised by local groups representing industrial, educational, youth and other community interests. A management committee employed the staff and oversaw training, and the Department of Economic Development provided funding, advice and technical support. The community workshops were particularly targeted at young people who were reluctant to travel far from home or who did not feel comfortable learning within institutions such as **further education colleges** or **government training centres**.

Further reading: Department of Manpower Services (1985)

COMPACTS

Local partnerships between employers, young people, schools, colleges, and training providers. Young people worked towards agreed goals including levels of attendance, punctuality and attainment, and if they were successful, employers guaranteed them a suitable job with training or training leading to a job. The main aim of compacts was to raise the motivation and achievement of children in inner-city schools. Pump priming of up to £100,000 was available towards the cost of setting up and running the compact. Public funds were committed for four years and after that the compacts were expected to be self-sufficient and self-financing. In 1991 there were approximately 50 compacts with over 5,000 employers involved committing 25,000 jobs with training.

Further reading: Morris, Saunders and Schagen (1992)

COMPANIES' SCHOOLS

In 1905, **secondary schools** that belonged to or were provided under the Companies Acts 1862 to 1900 were eligible for recognition under the Regulations for Secondary Schools. The Treasury issued a Regulation stating: 'A school owned or conducted by a Company will be eligible for recognition if the property of the Company is secured on trust for the purposes of secondary education. The amount of share capital, so far as actually expended on site, buildings, or equipment of the school, can in such cases be treated as a charge on the property, subject to repayment of principal with interest at the rate of not more than 4 per cent, within such period, not exceeding 50 years from the winding-up, or the date of recognition, as the Board may approve'. The company became eligible if the Articles of Association confirmed '[t]hat the income and property of the Company shall be applied solely to objects, and that no portion thereof shall be paid to members by way of dividends or otherwise, with an exception as to salaries for services rendered. That on winding-up or dissolution of the Company any surplus property shall be applied solely to educational objects' (Board of Education 1904–05 p. 48).

COMPETENCE

See: Occupational Standards

COMPREHENSIVE EDUCATION

Arguably, the first form of comprehensive education was provided as a result of the **Elementary Education Act 1870**, which was designed to provide universal education for children aged between 5 and 12 years of age. The term has subsequently come to mean a non-selective secondary school and the first was Holyhead County School in 1949. Circular 10/65 encouraged **local education authorities** to plan for comprehensive education, and legislation was introduced with the Education Act 1976. This was repealed by the Education Act 1979, which enabled LEAs to continue with a system of selective education and **grammar schools**.

COMPULSORY ATTENDANCE

The Education Act 1870 made provision for school boards to seek approval from the Education Department to enact a byelaw '[r]equiring the parents of children of such age, not less than five years nor more than thirteen years, as may be fixed by byelaws, to cause such children (unless there is some reasonable excuse) to attend school' (1870, p. 62). The Education (Scotland) Act 1872 made attendance at Scottish schools compulsory. Compulsory attendance in English and Welsh schools was not made mandatory at a national level until the Education Act 1880, which required children to attend from the age of 5 until they reached 10 although children were encouraged to stay if they had not reached a certain standard. The leaving age was extended to 11 years by the **Elementary Education (School Attendance) Act 1893**, and the **Elementary Education (School Attendance) Act (1893) Amendment Act 1899** increased this to 12 years of age. Following both World Wars the leaving age was extended; The Fisher Education Act 1918 required all children to remain at school until the end of the term in which they reached the age of 14, thus ending the half-time scholars, and made provision for local byelaws to increase this to 15. The **Education Act 1944** increased this nationally to 15 and in September 1972, the Raising of the School Leaving Age (ROSLA) further increased this to 16. The Education and Skills Act 2008 increased compulsory education or training from 16 to 18 years, with the age limit of 17 being achieved by 2013 and that of 18 by 2015, with an exemption if a person had reached a Level 3 standard. Children must attend school in the term after they reach five years of age and are known as 'rising fives'.

See also: Truants' Schools

COMPUTER SCIENCE SANDWICH STUDENT GRANT SCHEME

(1981–84) Introduced to counteract the shortage of industrial placements available to students, with 250 grants of £45 per week being made. The project could last for up to one year on the employer's premises. The scheme ceased in 1984 when it was recognised that ICT skills were to become part of the **national curriculum**. It was part of three schemes run under the **Training for Skills Programme for Action**; the other two were the **Grants to Employers Scheme** that allowed staff to be sent on programming and systems analysis courses and the Threshold Scheme that was delivered by the national computing centre to increase the supply of workers trained in computer skills.

Further reading: MSC Annual Report 1981/82, p. 19

CONCILIATION AND ARBITRATION SERVICE

(1968) Part of the Manpower and Productivity Service, which was set up in 1968, and was later to become **Advisory Conciliation and Arbitration Service**. By 1972 it had been separated from MPS to have autonomy. It operated under the framework of the Code of Industrial Relations Practice. Initially, it consisted of a small headquarters staff with regional teams of manpower advisors to assist in the general conciliation of industrial disputes.

Further reading: See ACAS Annual Reports

CONDITION MANAGEMENT PROGRAMME

(2007) This rehabilitation programme was part of the **Pathways to Work** initiative that addressed those people receiving incapacity benefits and was designed to: 'understand and manage their health condition better, particularly in a working context; reduce unnecessary fears about health and work and to enable participants to feel more confident and better able to cope, especially with returning to work; and, enable participants who return to work to be more "expert" in managing their health condition and more confident in negotiating adjustments where needed with their employer' (Jobcentre Plus undated p. 5).

Further reading: www.jobcentreplus.gov.uk/ JCP/stellent/groups/jcp/documents/website content/dev_012591.doc

CONNEXIONS CARD

This smart card was tested in Newcastle and Gateshead and was formerly called the **learning card**. Around 2.4 million young people aged 16–19 who were in some form of learning were eligible for this card. The card recorded attendance and was used as a basis for a rewards system. With good attendance young people could earn reward points to obtain discounts in high street stores, leisure centres and cinemas.

Further reading: DfES (2001a); www.connex ions.gov.uk

CONNEXIONS SERVICE

(2 April 2001) Designed to offer coherent and coordinated advice to all teenagers, especially those who are at most risk of disaffection or failure. It takes in careers, youth and other voluntary services and its key objective is to encourage more young people to stay in education or training. It was piloted in 13 areas in 2000. In October 2000, funding for the first 16 Connexions partnerships was announced. Connexions replaced the **Careers Service**.

Further reading: Making Connexions March 2001 Issue 1; DfEE (2000c); www.con-nexions.gov.uk

CONTINUATION SCHOOLS

'Evening and continuation schools' were mentioned in the Report 1889–90 p. 185. On 18 May 1893 a Code of Regulations concerning evening continuation schools was issued and it stated, 'The new regulations are designed generally to meet the requirements of scholars who are no longer subject to the law of compulsory attendance at school, and who desire to prolong their education, either in the ordinary school subjects or in some **special subjects** in order to fit themselves for some industrial career'. Among the main changes were: 'The attendance of persons over 21 years of age will henceforth be recognised. No scholar will henceforth be compelled to take the elementary subjects. Grants will be paid as in Day Schools for the instruction of the school as a whole instead of, as formerly, for the attainments of individual scholars. The Fixed Grant is no longer paid on the average attendance, but on the aggregate number of hours' instruction received by the scholars. This will give direct encouragement to the prolongation of Evening School sessions, and the lengthening of meetings' (Report 1892–93 p. 386).

'There seems to be a sort of interregnum just now between the old **night school** and the new continuation school. According to the evidence, the old night schools are rather dwindling, but the new continuation schools are being gradually taken in hand by county councils here and there, and it is likely that there will be before long a development of these institutions in connexion with higher schools' (Report 1892–93 p. 35). There were evening continuation schools and day continuation schools. The education provided by continuation schools was of a lower standard than that provided by **technical schools** and **higher commercial schools**. 'It was assumed in 1918 that the distinctive purpose of a day continuation school would be the further education, on non-vocational lines at least for students under 16, of young people in employment' (Report 1924–25 p. 49).

'Before 1918 there were a few day con-tinuation schools, the best known being those at Birmingham and York maintained for the benefit of the younger employees of Messrs. Cadbury and Messrs. Rowntree' (Report 1924–25 p. 48). In the 1920s day continua-tion schools were described in the regulations as 'General, with or without Vocational, Domestic or Art Instruction, in part-time course, between 8am and 6pm' for those stu-dents '[f]rom exemption age to 18') (Report 1925–26 p. 57).

Further reading: Sadler (1907)

CONTRACT SCHOOL

This was a secondary school, which, because it was failing, was taken over by a private organi-sation; for example, Nord Anglia Education was selected by Surrey County Council to take over the running of Abbeylands School, Addlestone, Surrey in 2001.

COOKERY – TRAINING SCHOOL OF

The importance of cookery and nutrition to the health and economic well-being of the nation were generally recognised and training schools of cookery were established in the 1870s; for example, the Glasgow School of Cookery, which was a teacher training school, later amalgamated with the West End School of Cookery, Glasgow to form the Glasgow and West of Scotland College of Domestic Science. To coordinate provision and support the objective of teaching cookery in all schools, the Committee of the National Training Schools of Cookery and the North-ern Union Training Schools of Cookery were established. In a letter to Canon Warburton, HMI, concerning training colleges of school-mistresses, the Secretary of the Liverpool Training School of Cookery stated, 'We think no subject can be more useful in after life to the girls educated in our elementary schools' (Report 1882–83 p. 589). Training schools of cookery and laundry issued a local diploma or school teacher's Licence to those

who had undertaken a minimum period of 20 hours per week for six months for a cookery certificate, and 20 hours per week for three months for a **laundry work** Certificate (Report 1892–93 p. 480).

See also: Domestic School

CORE SKILLS

These were the Scottish equivalent of **key skills**. They were the skills required by peo-ple to underpin performance in work and life. They were used, for example, within modern apprenticeships provided by **Skillseekers** in Scotland. The term 'core skills' had also been an earlier term for **key skills**, which did not help clarity. The Core Skills Project, funded jointly by the European Social Fund and the **Manpower Services Commission**, identified 103 core transferable skills under the four main headings of number, communication, problem-solving and practical. These were then considered in relation to work-based learning and the **Youth Training Scheme**.

Further reading: DfEE (1999h); Levy (1987)

COTTAGE GARDEN

Many schools and **industrial schools** in the mid-1800s had a plot of land on which the boys cultivated vegetables and sometimes reared animals such as chickens and pigs. This land was sometimes called a school field-garden and produce was sometimes used for school meals produced in the school kitchens where the girls worked; some of it was sold and the income distributed to the boys; some produce was used to reduce school fees. The **Lords of the Treasury** would sometimes consider pro-viding grants for one half of the rent and for the purchase of tools (Minutes 1846 Vol. 1, p. 12).

COUNCIL FOR NATIONAL ACADEMIC AWARDS

(1964–92) The CNAA awarded degrees to those who had graduated from Scottish

central institutions and polytechnics that could not award their own degrees. It maintained a standard across the institutions and allowed comparability with universities. The Further and Higher Education Act 1992 led to the abolition of the CNAA as a result of the difference between universities (**university**) and **polytechnics** being dissolved. The CNAA was preceded by the **National Council of Technological Awards.**

See also: National Council of Technological Awards

COUNCIL FOR THE CURRICULUM, EXAMINATIONS AND ASSESSMENT

(1 April 1994) The duties of the CCEA in Northern Ireland were set out in The Education (Northern Ireland) Order 1998. Its responsibilities are to provide advice and support for what is taught and assessed in schools and colleges. It is a non-departmental public body that reports to the Department of Education Northern Ireland.

See also: Office of the Qualifications and Examinations Regulator

Further reading: www.ccea.org.uk

COUNCIL OF MILITARY EDUCATION

(1860) In 1849, the Duke of Wellington stated that 'all recruits until dismissed drill, should attend the garrison or regimental schoolmaster daily for two hours' (Council for Military Education 1860 p. iv). However, later research discovered that 19 per cent of the ranks could neither read nor write and almost 20 per cent could read but not write and the, then, newly established Council of Military education (Council of Military Education 1860 p. v) concluded: 'The Council, therefore, cannot but think that primary education, meaning no more by this term than the ability to read and write, has become a matter of such importance as justly to claim its place in the regular course of military instruction, and to form an integral part of the discipline of the army'.

COUNCIL ON MANPOWER SERVICES

This was the original working title for the **Manpower Services Commission**.

Further reading: Ainley and Corney (1990)

COUNCIL SCHOOLS

Schools run by the local education authority of a borough or county council (Report 1908–09 p. 19).

COUNTER-CYCLICAL TRAINING MEASURES

During the period 1977–78, some 3,000 grants or awards were made through the **industrial training boards.** They were largely for young people and applied to Scotland. They were designed to offset the worst effects of the recession on training and to create more opportunities in industry, commerce and the public sector for occupations requiring long-term training.

Further reading: MSC Annual Report 1977–78 p. 38

COUNTY INTERMEDIATE SCHOOLS

These operated in Wales and taught a range of subjects including science and technology (Board of Education 1900–01 Vol. 2, p. 253).

COUNTY SCHOOLS

The Education Act 1902 dispensed with school boards and transferred responsibility to local education authorities within counties and boroughs, thereby leading to many **board schools** being renamed county schools or county secondary schools. They later became **community schools**.

CRAFT SCHOOLS

These were schools where crafts and forms of **manual instruction** were taught in particular to disabled children; for example, an invalid craft school was established in 1903 at Chailey, East Sussex, by the Guild of Poor Brave Things, which subsequently became Chailey Heritage School (Report 1906–07 p. 48).

CREDIT AND QUALIFICATIONS FRAMEWORK FOR WALES

The Credit and Qualifications Framework for Wales was established to integrate all education and learning within a single unifying structure. It was developed by Education and Learning Wales **ELWa**, the Higher Education Funding Council for Wales, and the **Qualifications, Curriculum and Assessment Authority for Wales**.

See also: Scottish Credit and Qualifications Framework; Qualifications and Credit Framework

Further reading: http://wales.gov.uk/topics/educationandskills/learningproviders/creditqualificationsframework/?lang=en

CRIPPLE SCHOOLS

These were **special schools** provided around 1900 for disabled children to encourage physical and educational development and provide them with practical skills (Report 1906–07 pp. 48–49).

See also: Craft Schools

CURRICULUM COUNCIL FOR WALES

See: Secondary Examinations Council

CUSTOMISED TRAINING

This was a tailor-made training programme for the unemployed, run by the **Business in the Community Scheme**. Customised training was part of **employment training** and was a scheme for unemployed people that led to a guaranteed job interview, and, if they met pre-set standards, a job. The **Training Agency** provided £120,000 to the **Business in the Community** customised training unit, which had small teams in London, Birmingham, the East Midlands and Durham.

Further reading: Business in the Community (1990)

D

DAIRY CLASS

The 1893 **Code** described dairy work as a specific subject and made provision for a grant to be made for the study of this subject (Report 1892–93 p. 320). Mr Tillard, HMI, described a school at Baconsthorpe where 'a dairy class has been started for the older girls in the day school ... the experiment of teaching butter making on scientific principles to country girls is, I think, one that deserves all possible encouragement' (Report 1892–93 p. 88).

DAME SCHOOLS

These were schools run by a woman or mistress with some teaching of reading, knitting or sewing. It was often a source of employment for the owners of these schools (Minutes 1840–41, p. 126). A proposed definition was given in the Minutes (1856–57, p. 281): 'a school of private adventure, kept in the teacher's own cottage'. As teaching became more professionalised with the apprenticeship of **pupil-teachers** and teachers attending training colleges, the number of Dame schools declined. 'Female schools have increased and are increasing. The *dame* is being gradually superseded by the certificated mistress, fully equipped to give girls a thorough education' (Report 1862–63 p. 160).

See also: Commercial Schools; Adventure Schools

DANGEROUS MACHINES (TRAINING OF YOUNG PERSONS) ORDER 1954

This order specified 18 machines that were listed as being dangerous and young persons were not allowed to work on them unless they had received proper training. The Factories Act 1961 prohibited the employment of young persons on such machines unless: 'he had been fully instructed as to the dangers arising in connection with the machinery and the precautions to be observed; and he has received sufficient training in work at the machine or is under adequate supervision by a person who has a thorough knowledge and experience of the machine' (Ministry of Labour Gazette 1962 p. 454).

See also: Factories Act 1961

DAY CONTINUATION SCHOOLS

See: Continuation School

DAY EXAMINATIONS

In June 1897, day examinations, at elementary and advanced stages, were begun in some science subjects in **day schools** and **training colleges** (Board of Education 1899–1900 Vol. 1, p. 18).

DAY RELEASE

The Minister of Education appointed a committee to increase the grant given to release young people under the age of 18 from employment to allow them to attend technical and other further education courses – Report of the Committee on the Development of Day Release. The committee recommended that all young people should be enabled to continue their education at least on a part-time basis. It recommended doubling the numbers of 209,000 boys and 52,000 girls.

See also: Right to Time Off for Study or Training

Further reading: Evans (1980)

DAY SCHOOLS

This was a term used in the late 1800s to distinguish elementary school provision from the increasing number of **evening schools** and **night schools**.

DAY SCHOOLS OF INDUSTRY

These were **industry schools** that were attended on a daily basis rather than being residential (Minutes 1853–54, Vol. 2, p. 101). 'A day industrial school within this Order [Applying the Provisions of the Industrial Schools Act, 1866, to Certified Day Industrial Schools] shall mean a school in which industrial training, elementary education, and one or more meals a day, but not lodgings, are provided for the children' (Report 1876–77, p. 274).

DAY TRAINING COLLEGE

See: (Day) Training College

DEFERRED CALL-UP

Call-up for national service was allowed to be deferred if people were apprenticed or articled pupils.

See also: Block Reservation; National Service

Further reading: Ministry of Labour and National Service Annual Report 1957, Cmnd 242, p. 12

DEMONSTRATION SCHOOLS

These were schools attached to a university department of education and were similar to those associated with early training colleges and normal schools: for example, the Fielden Schools connected with the University of Manchester.

See also: Practising School

Further reading: Findley 1908

DEPARTMENT FOR BUSINESS, INNOVATION AND SKILLS

In June 2009, the Department for Business, Innovation and Skills took over many of the responsibilities of the **Department for Innovation, Universities and Skills**, including higher education and skills. It was divided into 12 main areas of operations: Business, Economic and Policy Analysis, Fair Markets, Finance, Innovation and Enterprise (including the Better Regulation Executive), Legal Services, Operations and Change, Science and Research, Shareholder Executive, Strategy and Communications, UK Trade and Investment, and Universities and Skills.

Further reading: www.bis.gov.uk

DEPARTMENT FOR CHILDREN, EDUCATION, LIFELONG LEARNING AND SKILLS

An executive body of the Welsh Assembly, Mae'r Adran Blant, Addysg, Dysgu Gydol Oes a Sgiliau is responsible for education, training and children's services. 'The Department aims to improve children's services, education and training provision to secure better outcomes for learners, business, and employers as set out in our strategic document, "The Learning Country". It helps empower children, young people and adults through education and training to enjoy a better quality of life' (DCELLS 2010).

See also: Department for Education, Lifelong Learning and Skills

DEPARTMENT FOR CHILDREN, SCHOOLS AND FAMILIES

(28 June 2007) Replaced the **Department for Education and Skills**. 'The purpose of the Department for Children, Schools and Families is to make England the best place in the world for children and young people to grow up. We want to: make children and young people happy and healthy; keep them safe and sound; give them a top class education; and help them stay on track'.

www.dcsf.gov.uk (accessed 13 September 2009)

DEPARTMENT FOR EDUCATION

(1992–95) The **Department of Education and Science** was replaced by the Department for Education in 1992, with responsibility for science being given to the **Department of Trade and Industry**'s Office of Science and Technology, and the Cabinet Office's Office of Public Service. The Department for Education was replaced by the **Department for Education and Employment** in 1995.

DEPARTMENT FOR EDUCATION AND EMPLOYMENT

(5 July 1995 – June 2001) Established 5 July 1995, the DfEE was a merger of the **Department of Education and Science** and the **Employment Department**. Its aim was 'to give everyone the chance, through education, training and work, to realise their full potential, and thus build an inclusive and fair society and a competitive economy'. It was abolished in June 2001 with parts merged into the **Department for Education and Skills** (Smithers and Robinson 2000 p. 191)

DEPARTMENT FOR EDUCATION AND SKILLS

(8 June 2001 – 27 June 2007) Replaced the **Department for Education and Employment** and represented a concentration of education and training responsibilities with employment service functions going to the **Department for Work and Pensions** in October 2001. The aims of the DfES were: 'to help build a competitive economy and inclusive society by:

- 'Creating opportunities for everyone to develop their learning.
- Releasing potential in people to make the most of themselves.
- Achieving excellence in standards of education and levels of skills'.

The objectives of the department were to:

- 'Give children an excellent start in education so that they have a better foundation for future learning.
- Enable all young people to develop and to equip themselves with the skills, knowledge and personal qualities needed for life and work.
- Encourage and enable adults to learn, improve their skills and enrich their lives'.

DfES Departmental Report 2004 p. 7

It was superseded by the **Department for Children, Schools and Families**, and the **Department for Innovation, Universities and Skills**.

DEPARTMENT FOR EDUCATION, LIFELONG LEARNING AND SKILLS

(1 April 2006) This department was established within the Welsh Assembly Government and incorporated a number of functions including **ELWa** – Education and Learning Wales; **Dysg** the Welsh operation of the Learning and Skills Development Agency; ACCAC (**Awdurdod Cymwysterau,**

Cwricwlwm ac Asesu Cymru/the Qualifications, Curriculum and Assessment Authority for Wales) and the Education Department of the Welsh Assembly. The Department was later named the **Department for Children, Education, Lifelong Learning and Skills**.

DEPARTMENT FOR EMPLOYMENT AND LEARNING

(20 July 2001) Formerly the **Department of Higher and Further Education, Training and Employment**, the aim of the Department for Employment and Learning (Northern Ireland) was: 'To promote a culture of lifelong learning, and to equip people for work in a modern economy'. Its objectives were: 'to work with others to achieve wider access to education and training and to seek the highest standards of learning, research, training and scholarship, thereby contributing to economic development and social inclusion. To promote access to, and fairness in, employment, thereby contributing to economic development and social inclusion' (Department for Employment and Learning, Annual Report 2003/2004 p. 4).

It is responsible for Further and Higher Education and the **Department of Education Northern Ireland** has responsibility for primary and secondary education.

Further reading: www.delni.gov.uk

DEPARTMENT FOR INNOVATION, UNIVERSITIES AND SKILLS

(28 June 2007 – June 2009) The Department combined the science and innovation responsibilities from the **Department of Trade and Industry,** and the skills, further education and higher education functions from the **Department for Education and Skills**. With responsibility for all post-19 learning, ranging from basic literacy to post-doctoral research, its broad objectives were to:

- 'Accelerate the commercial exploitation of creativity and knowledge, through innovation and research, to create wealth, grow the economy, build successful businesses and improve quality of life.
- Improve the skills of the population throughout their working lives to create a workforce capable of sustaining economic competitiveness, and enable individuals to thrive in the global economy.
- Build social and community cohesion through improved social justice, civic participation and economic opportunity by raising aspirations and broadening participation, progression and achievement in learning and skills.
- Pursue global excellence in research and knowledge, promote the benefits of science in society, and deliver science, technology, engineering and mathematics skills in line with employer demand.
- Strengthen the capacity, quality and reputation of the Further and Higher Education systems and institutions to support national economic and social needs.
- Encourage better use of science in Government, foster public service innovation, and support other Government objectives which depend on the DIUS expertise and remit'.
  www.diusseniorrecruitment.com/sections/ about_org/mission_statement_and_depart mental_objectives (accessed 31 March 2010)

In June 2009 it became the **Department for Business, Innovation and Skills**.

DEPARTMENT FOR WORK AND PENSIONS

(2001) This department was formed by the merger of the Department for Social Security and parts of the **Department for Education and Employment**. It included the Pensions Service, **Jobcentre Plus**, and the Child Support Agency.

Further reading: www.dwp.gov.uk

DEPARTMENT OF AGRICULTURE AND TECHNICAL INSTRUCTION – IRELAND

The department was established as a result of the Board of Education Act 1899 and the institutions (National Library of Ireland, Royal Botanical Gardens, Glasnevin, Science and Art Museum Dublin) that came under the Science and Art Department were transferred to it on 1 April 1900 (Board of Education 1899–1900 Vol. 1, p. 9).

DEPARTMENT OF EDUCATION AND SCIENCE

(1964–92) The DES was formed from the integration of the Science Department into the **Ministry of Education**. It was subsequently replaced by the **Department for Education**.

DEPARTMENT OF EDUCATION NORTHERN IRELAND

Established in December 1999, the Department of Education Northern Ireland was responsible for the administration of education; providing advice to ministers; and managing resources. DENI had responsibility for the Education and Training Inspectorate, which evaluated and reported on the quality of teaching, learning and teacher education. It is complemented by the **Department for Employment and Learning**, which has responsibility for further and higher education.

Further reading: www.deni.gov.uk

DEPARTMENT OF EMPLOYMENT

(1970) The title was shortened from the **Department of Employment and Productivity** after a change of government. The title **Employment Department** was adopted as a familiar name in 1988 although it was still designated the Department of Employment for legal purposes.

Further reading: Crooks (1993); Price (2000)

DEPARTMENT OF EMPLOYMENT AND PRODUCTIVITY

(1968–70) This department absorbed the **Ministry of Labour**. The term 'Productivity' was dropped from the title after a change of government in 1970.

Further reading: Price (2000)

DEPARTMENT OF HIGHER AND FURTHER EDUCATION, TRAINING AND EMPLOYMENT

(2 December 1999 – 20 July 2001) In Northern Ireland, the Department of Economic Development's **Training and Employment Agency** was combined with the functions of the Further and Higher Education Division of the **Department of Education Northern Ireland**. The aim of the Department of Higher and Further Education, Training and Employment was: 'to promote a culture of lifelong learning and to equip people for work in a modern economy'. Its objectives were to:

- 'promote economic growth, improved living standards and an increased number of accessible employment opportunities.
- achieve the highest quality of education and training provision, and seek the highest standards of learning, research, training and scholarship.
- promote an inclusive society where citizens have equality of opportunity, and
- enhance North–South and East–West cooperation under the auspices of the North–South Ministerial Council and the British–Irish Council'.

Department of Higher and Further Education, Training and Employment, Business Plan 2000–2001 p. 5

In July 2001, under the Department for Employment and Learning Act (Northern Ireland) 2001, its responsibilities were transferred to the **Department for Employment and Learning** Northern Ireland.

DEPARTMENT OF PRACTICAL ART

(1852) A Department of Practical Art was established under the direction of the Lords of the Committee of the Privy Council for Trade to administer School[s] of Design. In 1853, a science division was added and it became the **Science and Art Department** for Britain and Ireland or the Department of Science and Art.

DEPARTMENT OF SCIENCE AND ART

See: Science and Art Department

DEPARTMENT OF TRADE AND INDUSTRY

The DTI was established in 1975 and combined many of the functions of the **Board of Trade** and the **Ministry of Technology**. In 1974 it was divided into Department of Trade, Department of Industry, and Department of Prices and Consumer Protection. In 1983 the Departments of Trade and Industry were merged and in 2007 it became the **Department for Innovation, Universities and Skills**, with responsibilities for business growth, company law, consumer law, employment law and Regional Development Agencies being transferred to the Department for Business, Enterprise and Regulatory Reform. The latter was merged into the **Department for Business, Innovation and Skills** in 2009.

DESIGNATED EMPLOYMENT

(1 September 1946) Occupations 'designated' by the minister as suitable for registered disabled people (RDP): car-park attendant and lift attendant. An expansion of the scheme was considered in 1947 but concluded that it was necessary to avoid the impression that certain low-grade jobs were only suitable for the disabled.

See also: Quota Scheme

Further reading: Ministry of Labour and National Service Report for 1947 Cmd 7559 p. 108

DEVELOPING EUROPEAN LEARNING THROUGH TECHNOLOGICAL ADVANCE

(1988) DELTA, which aimed to combat Europe's training problems through new technology, was organised in the UK by the **Training Commission**'s Learning Technology Unit. It was designed to run for two years and help trainers share and understand new technologies and use them to train workforces. This was to be achieved by: constructing a learning system reference model to plan and manage the programme; developing new hardware and software for learning; testing communication methods between countries including satellites; and helping to create favourable environments for learning.

Further reading: Employment Gazette 1988 p. 518

DEVELOPMENT AREAS

As part of the economic support for specific areas training initiatives were linked to the regeneration efforts.

See also: Development Districts

Further reading: Heriot-Watt University (1974)

DEVELOPMENT DISTRICTS

(1 July 1966) The **Ministry of Labour** provided direct training assistance free of charge to firms in development districts in addition to the already existing financial grants that were available towards the cost of training labour. This was available to those starting new establishments, those expanding their existing labour force, or those firms which required retraining to prevent a reduction in the labour force. These schemes were applied under the Industrial Development Act. The direct training assistance involved:

- the provision of a Ministry instructor teaching new workers semi-skilled engineering operations on the firm's premises;
- the training of instructors in the firm to continue the work;
- the assessment of the suitability of people from **industrial rehabilitation units**;
- the local provision of instructor training by staff from local colleges;
- the biasing of syllabuses of training for skilled workers at **government training centres**; and
- the provision of a new programme of **training within industry** for operator instructors.

In 1966 the financial assistance towards the cost of training in **development areas** per week was £5 for men, £3 10s (£3.50) for women, and for those under 18 years old it was £2 10s (£2.50) for men and £2 for women. Grants were not paid for courses lasting longer than 52 weeks or less than two weeks or where the total payable to a firm was less than £100. These development districts were superseded on 19 August 1966 by development areas under the Industrial Development Act 1966.

Further reading: Ministry of Labour Gazette 1966 pp. 316 and 568

DEVELOPMENT PROJECTS

In October 1997, 12 development projects were funded for 12 months – £0.4m was made available to provide information and advice. These projects were designed to combat the situation in which it was recognised that not everyone had access to a telephone, and hence making information available to disadvantaged people became harder. These 12 projects stretched across rural areas to inner-city areas and were aimed to test out different methods of delivering information and advice services. An external evaluator was commissioned to produce case studies of examples of effective methods.

Further reading: DfEE Departmental Report 1998–99 Cm 3910 p. 56

DIPLOMA

(September 2008) The diploma, generally, is an award for 14- to 19-year-olds in a range of vocationally related subjects and can be studied at three levels: Foundation Diploma = 5 GCSEs at grades D – G; Higher Diploma = 7 GCSEs at grades A★ – C; Advanced Diploma = 3.5 A-levels. The purpose of the diploma was to give young people an education that incorporated theoretical and applied learning to support skills and knowledge in a work-related context and they were designed to address all the major areas of the economy. A diploma included:

- **generic learning – functional skills**; personal, learning and thinking skills; a project; and, **work experience;**
- **principal learning** in the knowledge and skills related to the 'line of learning'; and
- **additional and/or specialist learning** that allowed a person to tailor their programme to their personal interests and aspirations.

In 2008, teaching began in five areas or 'lines of learning': Construction and Built Environment; Creative and Media; Engineering; Information Technology; and Society, Health and Development. In 2009, five more diplomas were added: business, administration and finance; environmental and land-based studies; hair and beauty studies; hospitality; and manufacturing and product design. In 2010, public services; retail business; sport and active leisure; and travel and tourism were added. These subjects were similar to those available in the **Welsh Baccalaureate**. Also, a statutory national entitlement was introduced to enable all 14- to 19-year-olds to study the diplomas from September 2013. Schools and colleges were not expected to provide all the subjects and access was provided through consortia.

See also: (Extended) Diploma; (Progression) Diploma

Further reading: DfES (2007); http://www. qcda.gov.uk/25217.aspx; http://www.diploma-support.org/system/files/practitioner-guide-diploma.pdf

(EXTENDED) DIPLOMA

(September 2011) The extended **diploma** was expected to contain extra maths and English. It could be studied at three levels: foundation level = 7 GCSEs at grades D – G; higher level = 9 GCSEs at grades A$\star$ – C; and advanced level = 4.5 A levels.

See also: Progression Diploma

(PROGRESSION) DIPLOMA

(2008) A progression diploma was introduced, which was equivalent to 2.5 A-Levels, and it consisted of two of the three components of a **diploma**—principal learning and generic learning—but did not include an additional or specialist learning component. The progression diploma required 720 guided learning hours compared to 1,028 for the diploma, which included all three components. It was studied at levels 2 and 3.

See also: Extended Diploma

DIPLOMA OF EDUCATION

(1974) This was a two-year programme of first degree level, which had the provision for students to continue to complete their three-year degree. As credit transfer became more common, the need for this form of study reduced.

See also: Foundation Degree

DIPLOMA OF VOCATIONAL EDUCATION

(1991) This was a successor to the **Certificate of Pre-Vocational Education**. It was introduced by CGLI and was more occupationally focused than its predecessor. It pro-vided opportunities to develop cores skills and there was a three-level framework: Foundation—14–16 years; Intermediate—one-year post-16 course; and National Level – a proposed two-year course that was never developed. It subsequently evolved into the **General National Vocational Qualification**.

DIRECT GRANT

Until 1922, secondary schools that were not provided by local education authorities could receive support from the **Board of Education** and/or the local education authority. This duplication was progressively removed and, from 1927, schools could choose either a direct grant from the board, thereby becoming direct grant schools, or to receive their funding from the authorities. Those schools that had previously received funding from the board and then from the local authorities were known as indirect grant schools (Report 1935 p. 12). This system ended in 1976 and direct grant schools either became independent or joined the maintained sector.

DIRECT TRAINING SERVICES

(1973–83) This programme was a collection of other programmes brought together under the umbrella title of Direct Training Services. In it were programmes from the **Training Services Agency**, **training within industry**, Sponsored Training, and the **mobile instructor service**. All **Manpower Services Commission** Direct Training Service programmes, except **training within industry**, transferred to the **Skills Training Agency** in 1983 and were renamed Skillcentre Services to Employers (SSE). In 1985 the mobile training service was expanded and Skillcentres were cut back.

Further reading: MSC (1981d)

DISABILITY DISCRIMINATION ACT 1995

It repealed the Disabled Persons (Employment) Act 1944 and was seen as a landmark in equal opportunities for people with disabilities. It provided a statutory right against discrimination in all aspects of employment. In education, the act provided for better information to be available about the arrangements that were in place for disabled people at schools, colleges and universities.

Further reading: www.disability.gov.uk

DISABILITY RIGHTS COMMISSION

(25 April 2000 – 30 September 2007) The Disability Rights Commission replaced the **National Disability Council** as a result of the Disability Rights Commission Act (1999). The DRC was an executive non-departmental public body independent of the Government. Its main duties were to: 'work towards the elimination of discrimination against disabled people; promote the equalisation of opportunities for disabled with those of non-disabled people; promote good practice; and, advise the Government on the operation of legislation and whether changes need to be made to it'. In 2007, it was combined with the **Commission for Racial Equality** and the **Equal Opportunities Commission** to create the **Equality and Human Rights Commission**.

Further reading: DfEE (1998g)

DISABILITY SYMBOL

(1990) This was a scheme to encourage employers to employ disabled workers. Employers signing up to the scheme committed themselves to a **Code of Good Practice on the Employment of Disabled People**. The symbol depicted two tick marks resembling people and said: 'Positive about Disabled People'. By 1994 there were 900 employers in the scheme.

Further reading: Employment Gazette 1990 p. 527

DISABLED – FIT FOR WORK PROGRAMME

(December 1979) This was a **Manpower Services Commission** initiative for the disabled under the banner 'Disabled Workers are Good Workers', which was launched in December 1979. The programme not only looked at the employee but also at the best practice of the employer to enable disabled workers to attain employment. By 1980 Disablement Resettlement Officers had placed some 60,000 disabled workers into employment and there were around 400 employer applicants for the **'Fit for Work' awards**.

Further reading: Rowley (1983)

(TRAINING OF) DISABLED MEN

Following the end of the First World War, men discharged from the forces as unfit were often trained in **technical schools**. Many of the disabled men were integrated with ordinary students; however, in some cases special training classes were established, with support from the **Ministry of Labour**, and were held in many subjects including engineering, boot making, painting and decorating, commercial work, dispensing, design, and architectural draughtsmanship (Report 1917–18 p. 35).

DISABLED PEOPLE SCHEME – EMPLOYMENT INITIATIVES FOR

(1985) The initiatives were designed to encourage and enable voluntary organisations to develop innovative employment services complementary to the **Manpower Services Commission**'s existing services by offering sliding-scale financial support during the first three years of a project.

Further reading: MSC Annual Report 1985/86 p. 30

DISABLED PERSONS (EMPLOYMENT) ACT 1944

Among its provisions the act empowered the **Ministry of Labour** to 'provide or make arrangements for the provision by other persons of … industrial rehabilitation courses for disabled persons … who, by reason of unfitness arising from injury, disease or deformity, are in need of such facilities in order to render them fit for undertaking employment, or work on their own account'. It was updated by the **Disability Discrimination Act 1995**.

See also: Quota Scheme

DISABLED PERSONS REGISTER

(1944–95) Linked to employers' quota liability under the 1944 **Disabled Persons Act**. A 'registered disabled person' was issued with an identifying card, commonly referred to as a 'green card'. Registration ended with the advent of the **Disability Discrimination Act 1995**.

Further reading: Ministry of Labour and National Service Report for 1947 Cmd 7559 p. 108

DISABLED – QUOTA SCHEME

See: Quota Scheme

DISABLED VOCATIONAL TRAINING SCHEME

(1960) Started to enable disabled people to return to the labour market.

Further reading: Ministry of Labour Gazette 1961 p. 195

DISABLEMENT ADVISORY COMMITTEES

Were voluntary bodies attached to **employment exchanges**. They were set up to supply local advice and knowledge that would assist in finding suitable employment and/or training for people registered as disabled. They were replaced in 1986 by the **Committee for the Employment of Disabled People** local projects.

70

Further reading: MSC Annual Report 1980–81 p. 6

DISABLEMENT ADVISORY SERVICE

(1984) DAS was designed to encourage employers to adopt progressive policies and practices in the retention, recruitment and career development of employees with disabilities. DAS used a number of programmes to provide support to disabled people including **special aids to employment, adaptations to premises and equipment**, and **Fares to Work**.

Further reading: Field (1985)

DISCIPLINE AND ORGANISATION GRANT

(1890) This was introduced '[t]o emphasise, by means of a special and graduated grant for discipline and organisation, the importance of conduct and moral training as essential factors of the success and usefulness of a **public elementary school**' (Report 1889–90 p. 171). Article 101a of the **Code** stated that '[t]o meet the requirements respecting discipline, the managers and teachers will be expected to satisfy the Inspector that all reasonable care is taken, in the ordinary management of the school, to bring up the children in habits of punctuality, of good manners and language, of cleanliness and neatness, and also to impress upon the children the importance of cheerful obedience to duty, of consideration and respect for others, and of honour and truthfulness in word and act' (Report 1889–90 p. 132).

DISSENTING ACADEMIES

The Act of Uniformity 1662 led to many clergymen, some of whom were from Oxford and Cambridge universities, leaving the established Church of England. These dissenters then established their own academies often with a wider curriculum lasting up to five years.

DISTRESS COMMITTEES

The **Unemployed Workmen Act 1905** provided statutory powers for the formal provision of Distress Committees to replace semi-official committees such as the London Unemployed Fund. The purpose of the committees was to investigate labour conditions in their area and to receive and consider applications for support. Funding for these committees was from voluntary contributions, for example from the Queens Unemployment Fund, and from rates. Within this provision a number of boroughs also instituted employment or **labour exchanges**.

DISTRICT SCHOOLS

(1860s) In many rural areas the number of pupils attending a school was too small to receive a grant and this discouraged regular attendance. To resolve this situation, a larger central school, or district school, was sometimes established that combined two or more parishes. A similar principle was applied in urban areas (Report 1867–68 p. 30). The term was also associated with **Poor Law schools**: 'District Schools (*i.e.* schools maintained by the managers of School Districts comprising more than one Poor Law Union)' (Report 1908–09 p. 111).

DIVISION – CHIEF INSPECTORS

HM Inspectors were given responsibility to inspect a geographical territory, which in the early years of the inspectorate was conducted by one person. As the number of schools increased, additional inspectors were employed to manage the responsibilities in districts. The geographical areas were known as divisions and in the 1880s there were ten divisions: North Eastern – Northumberland, Durham, York; North Western – Cumberland, Westmoreland, Lancaster, and Isle of Man; North Central – Chester, Derby, Nottingham, Stafford; West Central – Gloucester, Hereford, Salop, Somerset, Worcester; Welsh – Wales, Monmouth; Eastern – Bedford, Cambridge, Hertford, Huntingdon, Lincoln, Norfolk, Suffolk, Essex; East Central – Berkshire, Buckingham, Leicester, Northampton, Oxford, Rutland, Warwick; South Western – Hampshire, Wiltshire, Dorset, Devon, Cornwall, Channel Islands; South-Eastern – Surrey, Kent, Sussex; Metropolitan – District of the London School Board, Middlesex, Essex (Report 1885–86 p. 201).

DIVISION – SCHOOLS

(1850s) In the early days of education children were gathered into one large group in the school room and were taught together regardless of age and often ability: 'Age is not the principle on which children are classified in a school' (Minutes 1853–54, Vol. 1, p. 14). However, this system was limited and although there may have been a number of classes in the school it was proposed that children were classified into two divisions: those below the age of nine and those above. During the 1880s, guidance to HM Inspectors for examination in singing suggested four Divisions: '1st Division = Infants; 2nd Division = **Standards** I. and II.; 3rd Division = Standards III. and IV.; and 4th Division = Standard V. and upwards. This, of course, only applies to large schools; in small schools Inspectors may permit any grouping which they think justified by the circumstances' (Report 1885–86 p. 175). In 1903–04, five divisions of principal subjects were described in connection with evening schools (Board of Education 1903–04 p. 62).

See also: First Class

DOCKYARD SCHOOLS

(1843) The first School of Naval Architecture was founded in 1811 and closed in 1832. Subsequently dockyard schools were established by Order of Council in 1843 in

Chatham, Pembroke and Portsmouth to train apprentices within the navy.

See also: Admiralty Schools

DOMESTIC ECONOMY

(1880) Domestic Economy was introduced as a specific subject for girls in 1880. Schedule IV for **specific subjects** detailed the objectives in three stages:

1. 'Food; its composition and nutritive value. Clothing and washing.
2. Food; its functions. The dwelling; warming, cleaning and ventilation.
3. Food; its preparation and culinary treatment. Rules for health; the management of a sick room.'

Report 1883–84 p. 133

See also: Domestic Science

DOMESTIC SCHOOLS

Domestic schools, sometimes known as **housewifery schools**, provided training in the domestic subjects for use in the home and also for domestic employment. Although the term entered common usage in the early 1900s, the schools had developed from a long tradition of schooling that included domestic subjects.

See also: Domestic Economy; Domestic Science

Further reading: Report 1908–09 p. 68

DOMESTIC SCIENCE

'Domestic Science – the science underlying **domestic economy** and hygiene' was introduced in the 1897 **Evening Continuation School Code**. 'The object of the Course is to inculcate habits of accuracy in reasoning and manipulation, as well as to teach the rules governing domestic manage-

ment. … It is intended that the instruction in this subject should be based on experiments performed, as far as possible, by the children themselves. The applications to the home should be the results of the discoveries made in the course of the experiments, which should be undertaken in a spirit of inquiry or research' (Report 1896–97 p. 608).

DOMESTIC TRAINING

(1946–72) In this scheme the trainee was shown how to deal with all domestic chores, and on completion of the training was considered 'fit to go into service'.

See also: National Institute for Houseworkers

Further reading: Ministry of Labour Annual Report 1959 p. 49 and 1960 p. 33

DRAWING

Drawing became one of the **class subjects** in the 1885 **Code** and from 31 March 1887 all grants provided by the **Science and Art Department,** and conducted by a Local Superintendent of the Department, for the instruction of drawing in **public elementary school[s]** were ended and subsequently provided by the **Education Department** (Report 1884–85 pp. 119/147). In the 1890 **Code**, drawing was described as an **obligatory** or **elementary subject** (Report 1889–90 p. 118).

DRILL MASTER

(*c.*1850s) These staff were to be found in some schools, for example Greenwich Royal Hospital Schools, and were responsible for the military drilling and discipline of pupils outside the classroom.

See also: Training Master

DRILLING

See: Military Drill; School Drill

DULL CHILDREN

See: Exception Schedule

D-UNITS

The D-units were originally produced by the **Training and Development Lead Body** and represented the assessment stage of the training cycle: D31 – designing assessment systems; D32 – assessment of performance; D33 – assessment using diverse evidence; D34 – verifying the assessment procedures within an organisation; D35 – external verification of the assessment process; D36 – giving advice on accreditation of prior learning. They were subsequently amended and became the assessor and verifier standards/awards.

See also: Learning and Development & Assessment and Verification National Occupational Standards

Further reading: Ollin and Tucker (1994); Training and Development Lead Body (1995)

DYSG

This was the **Learning and Skills Development Agency**'s national operation in Wales. It supported the development of policy and its implementation across post-16 education and training. On 1 April 2006 it joined the Welsh Assembly Government and was incorporated within the **Department for Education, Lifelong Learning and Skills**.

E

E-UNIVERSITY

The e-university was announced on 15 February 2000, and the company was incorporated on 12 July 2001 with programmes going online in March 2003. This was a **Higher Education Funding Council for England** (HEFCE) project designed to enable graduate and post-graduate students to increase their knowledge of specific subjects through online learning and enable higher education to compete internationally. The e-university did not develop its own programmes but operated as a broker or facilitator working with universities and colleges to develop, assemble and deliver courses for individuals, companies and public organisations at home and overseas. The initial cost was estimated at £75m with annual running costs of £40m. It only recruited 900 students and was scrapped in 2004.

Further reading: House of Commons Education and Skills Committee (2005)

EARLY YEARS FOUNDATION STAGE

(September 2008) Replacing the earlier Foundation Stage, the Early Years Foundation Stage addressed the development of young children aged 0–5 years and it was enabled through the Childcare Act 2006. Four themes, each with an associated principle, were described: 'A unique child – Every child is a competent learner from birth who can be resilient, capable, confident and self-assured. Positive relationships – Children learn to be strong and independent from a base of loving and secure relationships with parents and/or a key person. Enabling environments – The environment plays a key role in supporting and extending children's development and learning. Learning and development – Children develop and learn in different ways and at different rates and all areas of Learning and Development are equally important and inter-connected'.

See also: Sure Start

Further reading: http://nationalstrategies. standards.dcsf.gov.uk/early years (accessed 20 February 2010)

EARNINGS RELATED SUPPLEMENTS

(October 1966) When a person had to retrain for another occupation it was recognised that there would be a large element of 'wage reduction' whilst they were in training. Hence, supplements to allowances paid to trainees were introduced to aid those who were faced with this drop in income. The trainee had to be over 18 and under 65 and have contributed PAYE on recognisable income of £450 per annum. The supplement was reckoned at one-third of their average weekly earnings between £9 and £30 per week.

ECONOMIC AND LABOUR MARKET REVIEW

(January 2007) *Labour Market Trends* was combined with *Economic Trends* and published as the *Economic and Labour Market Review*, providing a range of information about economic and labour issues.

See also: Labour Force Survey; Education and Training Statistics for the United Kingdom

EDEXCEL

(1996) Arising from the Stafford review of examination standards in 1995, Edexcel, an **awarding body**, was formed by the merger of the **Business and Technology Education Council** (BTEC), which provided vocational qualifications, and the University of London Examinations & Assessment Council (ULEAC), which provided GCSEs and A-levels. Edexcel derives from 'educational excellence'. It is one of the three English unitary awarding bodies, the other two being **Assessment and Qualifications Alliance**, and **Oxford, Cambridge and RSA Examinations**.

Further reading: www.edexcel.org.uk

(THE) EDUCATION (SCOTLAND) ACT 1872

This act established similar principles to those of the Education Act 1870 in England and Wales, but made attendance at school compulsory. Previous legislation that was inconsistent with the provisions of the 1872 Act was repealed, for example the Education Act 1696 (Act for Settling of Schools) enacted by the Scottish Parliament for the establishment of schools in every parish and which built on the Acts of 1633, 1646. The 1872 Act also established a **Scotch Education Department** and a Code of Regulations for Scotland known as the Scotch Code, which was an equivalent of the **Code of Regulations** (Minutes 1872–73, p. cxxv).

EDUCATION ACT 1902

The Royal Commission of 1894 led by Lord Bryce was tasked to address the mixed and confusing provision of secondary education.

The commission described the situation: 'It is full of resources, national grants given on the most varied conditions, distributed through all sorts of bodies, local rates applied under many names to many things, endowments ancient and modern, some more, others less restricted in their scope, some devoted to mixed, others purely to educational purposes; it is full of agents, agencies, institutions, authorities, local and national, provincial and special, almost all independent in origin, unconnected in working, often occasional in purpose' (Report 1923–24 p. 10). To address these issues the Education Act 1902, combined with the Education Act 1899, were to provide 'the machinery for setting up a general coordinated system of schools', which until that time had been considerably ad hoc. The 1902 Act abolished the **school boards** and replaced them with 333 **local education authorities** operating with borough or county councils. The purpose of the LEAs was to 'consider the educational needs of their area and take such steps as seem to them desirable, after consultation with the Board of Education, to supply or aid the supply of education other than Elementary, and to promote the general co-ordination of all forms of education' (Report 1923–24 p. 9). It also brought together control by local authorities of **continuation schools** and **technical schools** and their development. Denominational schools were integrated within the state system and were classified as 'non-provided schools'.

EDUCATION (PROVISION OF MEALS) ACT 1906

This act became operational from 21 December 1906 and provided statutory powers to **local education authorities** to provide meals for school children. It was instrumental in 'bringing the authorities into recognised relationship with the voluntary agencies which already exist for this purpose in many localities, and enabling them to aid such agencies by the provision of kitchens, dining rooms and plant, as well as of cooks, servers, and other necessary officers. The act further empowers the Authorities, where sufficient funds for the purchase of food from voluntary contributions and parents' payments are not forthcoming, to spend money from the rates for the provision of food within the limit of a ½d. rate' (Report 1906–07 p. 34).

See also: Penny Dinners; School Meals

EDUCATION (ADMINISTRATIVE PROVISIONS) ACT 1907

This act introduced a number of new requirements for **local education authorities**, the most important one being the **schools medical service**. A memorandum (Circular 576) was issued and the two main points were that (a) medical inspection 'must be periodical and include *not less than three* inspections during the School life of each child, and (b) the desirability of carrying out the work of medical inspection in intimate conjunction with the Public Health Authorities and under the direct supervision of the Medical Officer of Health. Only in this way can the hygiene aspect of public education be brought into effective and economical relation to the larger questions of public health of which it is but a part' (Report 1906–07 pp. 9–10). The Act (Section 13 (i) (a)), also gave powers to local authorities to make available, for children, **vacation schools** and classes, **play centres**, and other recreation during the holidays. LEAs were also empowered to provide scholarships and bursaries for scholars from the age of 12. The act also relieved LEAs from compiling a register of teachers, this being a responsibility of the **Teachers' Registration Council**.

See also: Lads' and Girls' Clubs

(THE) EDUCATION (CHOICE OF EMPLOYMENT) ACT 1910

This act gave **local education authorities** similar powers to those granted to Scottish

school boards in the Education (Scotland) Act 1908. In January 1911 a memorandum of cooperation was issued regarding **labour exchanges** and local education authorities. In Edinburgh the agreement with the **Board of Trade** stated that ' … the keeping of the Registers (1) of scholars and ex-scholars seeking employment, (2) of vacancies notified by employers, will be entrusted to an official supplied by the Board of Trade to the **Juvenile Employment Bureaux** in the School Board Offices, and paid by the Board of Trade. The furnishings and upkeep of the room occupied by this official, although in the School Board Offices, will be charged to the Board of Trade. And it is understood that the Director of the Bureau will confer with the Board of Trade official as to the vacancies, before that official takes any steps to place the boy or girl in employment' (Gordon 1911 pp. 158–89).

See also: School Employment Bureaux

EDUCATION ACT (NORTHERN IRELAND) 1923

This act addressed all aspects of education, with the exception of university education. It established an advisory council and an education authority reporting to the council of each county and county borough. The responsibilities of the technical instruction committees were transferred to the education authorities.

See also: Ireland – National Schools

EDUCATION ACT 1944

This act, sometimes called the Butler Act, declared in Section 7 that '[t]he statutory system of public education shall be organised in three progressive stages to be known as **primary education**, secondary education and further education; and it shall be the duty of the local education authority for every area, so far as their powers extend, to contribute towards the spiritual, moral, mental, and physical development of the community by securing that efficient education throughout those stages shall be available to meet the needs of the population of their area'. It also established free secondary education for all, delivered through three types of school: **grammar school**, **secondary modern school** and, on a smaller scale, **technical schools**, and replaced the **Board of Education** with a **Ministry of Education**. Within the Act provision was made for compulsory day-release to allow all young workers to attend County Colleges. Also, **voluntary school[s]** were divided into controlled schools, aided schools, and special agreement schools.

EDUCATION (SCOTLAND) ACT 1945

This act was similar to the Education Act 1944 (England and Wales), which raised the school leaving age and detailed further education.

EDUCATION ACTION ZONES

(1998) Introduced in the School Standards and Framework Act 1998, EAZs involved the bringing together in areas of new partnerships between schools and local partners including industrial and social researchers, such that levels of achievement could be raised in areas where social and economic deprivation had been recognised. Priority targets were underachievers and the disaffected as well as developing work related opportunities for 14–16-year-olds.

See also: Education Business Partnerships; Excellence in Cities

Further reading: DfEE (1997c)

EDUCATION AND TRAINING INSPECTORATE

This body was established to inspect the quality of education and training in Northern Ireland and provide information to the **Department for Employment and Learning**; the Department of Culture, Arts and Leisure; and, the **Department for**

Education. The role of the Education and Training Inspectorate can be traced back to the **commissioners of national education in Northern Ireland**. In January 1989, the work of the inspectorate was expanded to include training services in Northern Ireland, when it became known as the Education and Training Inspectorate.

See also: Estyn (Wales); Her Majesty's Inspectorate of Education Scotland; Office for Standards in Education Office (OFSTED), Children's Services and Skills (England)

Further reading: Department for Employment and Learning Annual Report 2002–2003; http://www.etini.gov.uk

EDUCATION AND TRAINING STATISTICS FOR THE UNITED KINGDOM

(1 November 1997) The first **education census** was conducted in 1851 and since then accessible, accurate and comparable figures for the numbers of people in education and training and their levels of performance have been a necessary requirement for effective administration and management. Education and training statistics have been published in this form since 1997 and they give details of numbers of pupils, examination performance etc.

Further reading: www.dcsf.gov.uk/rsgateway/DB/VOL/index.shtml

EDUCATION BUSINESS PARTNERSHIP

(Announced on 24 April 1990) Intended to build on the work of **Compacts,** the **Technical and Vocational Education Initiative** and **work related further education** by supporting formally constituted partnerships between education, business and wider local community. The partnerships were designed to encourage practical opportunities for businesses to influence education and training provision. Pump-priming funding was made available with £50,000 in the first year and £25,000 in the second year from the

Employment Department for **Training and Enterprise Councils** to encourage overarching partnerships. In the third year, self-sufficiency was expected. In June 2000 the Government requested them to reorganise into 47 areas matching **learning and skills councils**. It was coordinated through the National Education Business Partnership Network.

See also: Education Action Zones

Further reading: Bayliss (1991); Employment Department (1991c); Hackworth (1988); http://www.nebpn.org

EDUCATION CENSUS

(1851) Alongside the national census of 1851 a voluntary education census was conducted and a report presented by the Commissioners for Taking a Census of Great Britain on Education (Minutes 1852–53). This report provided information about the number of pupils, ages, attendance, type of school, etc. A detailed census was conducted under Section 67 of the Education Act 1870, which required, by 31 December 1870, all municipal boroughs, parishes, and the metropolitan district of London, to provide returns of the number of elementary schools and children needing elementary education for their district. The purpose of these returns was to determine the extent of school provision and any shortfall that needed to be provided by the then newly forming **school board**s. Many districts subsequently conducted educational censuses; for example, in Birmingham, School Attendance Officers conducted door-to-door enquiries and gathered details about the numbers of children, ages, schools attended and fathers' occupation, etc.

See also: Education and Training Statistics for the United Kingdom

EDUCATION CODE (1890) ACT 1890

Evening schools or night schools originally developed to provide an educational opportunity for young people who had left school for work and had not completed their education in the elementary subjects of reading, writing and arithmetic. With the provision of universal education and compulsory attendance, the demand for these subjects declined and this act broadened the range of subjects that could be taught and brought them in line with the widened provision in elementary schools. 'It shall not be required as a condition of a parliamentary grant to an evening school that elementary education shall be the principal part of the education there given' (Report 1891–92 p. 2).

EDUCATION DEPARTMENT

(25 February 1856) As the work of the Committee of the Privy Council on Education grew, the Education Department was formally constituted in 1856 and placed under the Lord President of the Privy Council, who led the Privy Council on Education. The Education Department combined a number of functions and included the 'Education Establishment of the Privy Council Office', and the 'Establishment for the encouragement of Science and Art now under the direction of the **Board of Trade** and called the **Science and Art Department**' (Minutes 1855–56, p. 2).

EDUCATION MAINTENANCE ALLOWANCE

(Piloted September 1999, national from September 2004) As part of the **New Deal for Skills** the purpose of EMAs was to allow young people aged 16–19 to achieve their potential, regardless of their financial circumstances. The scheme began in 1999 with 15 LEAs to support young people who remained in full-time non-advanced post-16 education and was extended by a further 41 pilots in 2000, and a further extension across England in 2004.

From 2006, EMA was extended to those **not in education, employment or**

training through **activity agreements** and Learning Agreement pilot schemes.

See also: Access Funds; Adult Learning Grant

Further reading: Ashworth (2001); DfES (2002c); HM Treasury (March 2004)

EDUCATIONAL DEVELOPMENT ASSOCIATION

This began life, in 1888, as the British Sloyd Association to foster manual skills, particularly in woodwork, as a result of many British teachers attending the Slöyd Seminarium in Nääs, Sweden, which was established by Otto Salomon and based on the ideas of Uno Cygnaeus in Finland in 1865. The Educational Handwork Union was established in 1892 in the north of England and the two merged in 1905 to form the Educational Handwork Association, which subsequently became the Educational Development Association in 1946.

See also: Manual Work

Further reading: Durcan (1972)

EDUCATIONAL EXHIBITION

(1854) The first educational exhibition held in Britain, at St Martin's Hall, London, was organised by the **Royal Society for the Encouragement of Arts, Manufactures and Commerce** (Minutes 1854–55, p. 473). Among the exhibits were **Froebel** gifts, designed to encourage child development.

EDUCATIONAL EXPERIMENTS

In the first decade of the 1900s, grants were first provided by the Board of Education to encourage experimental or pioneering forms of education. This grant was described under Article 39 of the **Code of Regulations** and two examples were: the Perse School, Cambridge, conducted a new oral teaching method for Latin and Greek; and Knaresborough Rural Secondary School produced a course of instruction designed to address the needs of children intending to follow rural or agricultural occupations (Report 1911–12 p. 75).

EDUCATIONAL INFORMATION AND EMPLOYMENT BUREAUX

See: School Employment Bureaux

EDUCATIONAL INSTITUTE OF SCOTLAND

(1847) This was originally founded in Edinburgh to 'promote sound learning' and it received a Royal Charter in 1851. It subsequently became involved with the negotiation of teachers' pay and is the oldest teaching union in the world.

Further reading: www.eis.org.uk

EDUCATIONAL MUSEUM

(1857) An educational museum was established in South Kensington to support education and 'especially those engaged in teaching'. It was intended to be a '[m]useum which will exhibit under a proper classification all important books, diagrams, illustrations, and apparatus connected with education, already in use or which may be published from time to time, either at home or abroad' (Minutes 1856–57, p. 43). It contained exhibits originally from the **educational exhibition** and donated by the Society of Arts to the Education Board. Educational museums were also encouraged in many training colleges and contained diagrams, objects, apparatus, etc. (Report 1893–94 p. 158).

EDUCATIONAL SOCIETIES

Many societies were established to encourage and support educational endeavours.

See also: British and Foreign School Society; Home and Colonial Infant School Society;

National School Society; Society for Promoting Christian Knowledge

ELEMENTARY DRAWING SCHOOLS

(1852/3) Correspondence between the **Board of Trade** and the **Committee of Council on Education** began in 1850–51 regarding the limited ability of Schools of Design, subsequently **Schools of Practical Art**, to adequately teach design when many of the students did not have sufficient drawing ability. The Board of Trade indicated that it wished to encourage, and would provide some funding for, the development of elementary drawing schools and classes 'to render elementary drawing a systematic part of the education of all classes of the community' (Minutes, 1852–53, Vol. 1, p. 21). It was envisaged that existing schools might use a peripatetic teacher of art. The intention was to improve art and design in manufactures and also raise general awareness so that the public would appreciate and buy more beautiful products. They were sometimes known as Schools of Elementary Art or Schools for Drawing and Modelling.

ELEMENTARY EDUCATION ACT 1870

This act was commonly known as the Forster Education Act, named after the Bradford industrialist and Liberal MP, W. E. Forster, who championed its cause. The act, which did not apply to Scotland or Ireland, introduced the provision of universal education for children aged between 5 and 12 years of age. Its objective was that 'It will place an elementary school wherever there is a child to be taught, whether of rich or poor parents, and it will compel every parent or guardian of a child to have it taught, at least, the rudiments of education, and that without reference to any religious creed or persuasion' (1870, p. iii). A conscience clause was also introduced that stated, 'No religious catechism or religious formulary which is distinctive of any particular denomination shall be taught in the school' (1870 p. 11) and it also allowed for parents to withdraw children from religious instruction. The act ended inspection based on religious denomination. It also enabled the establishment of **school boards**, with elected members, to supervise the provision of schools wherever there was a shortage of provision. The act allowed private, church or endowed schools to be transferred to school boards. Funding for the schools came from local taxation and, although school fees were not abolished, the fees of poor children were paid by the school board. The previous system of grants, which began in 1833 under the Lords of the Treasury, came to an end on 31 December 1870. Under the New **Code** of Regulations, **evening schools** did not have to be connected to **day schools** and a number of **mechanics institutes** allowed their elementary classes to be inspected. The maximum age limit allowed by the act was 13. The Education (Scotland) Act 1872 established similar principles to those in England and Wales but made attendance at school compulsory.

Further reading: Cunningham (1870)

ELEMENTARY EDUCATION ACT 1876

This act declared that it was the duty of every parent or guardian to ensure the education of their child(ren). Also, employers were prohibited from employing children below the age of ten years. To enable these stipulations, school attendance committees were formed. The act stated: '4. It shall be the duty of the parent of every child to cause such child to receive efficient instruction in reading, writing, and arithmetic, and if such parent fail to perform such duty, he shall be liable to such orders and penalties as are provided by this Act. 5. A person shall not, after the commencement of this Act, take into his employment (except as herein-after in this Act mentioned) any child – (1) Who is under the age of ten years; or (2) Who, being of the age of ten years or upwards, has not obtained such certificate either of his proficiency in reading, writing, and elementary arithmetic, or of previous due attendance at a certified efficient school, as is in this Act in that behalf mentioned, unless such a child, being of the age of ten years or upwards, is employed, and is attending school in accordance with the provisions of the **factory Acts**, or any bye-law of the local authority' (Report 1876–77 p. 1). **School attendance committees** were also enabled to 'exempt for certain periods from the restrictions contained in the act, children above the age of eight years for the necessary operations of husbandry and the ingathering of crops; but such periods are not to exceed in the whole six weeks between the 1st of January and the 31st of December in any year' (Minutes 1876–77 p. 231). The act (linked to the Industrial Schools Act 1866) also enabled the provision of day industrial schools, which allowed children to attend only during the day under the condition that they had satisfactory attendance and behaviour under a specified license.

ELEMENTARY EDUCATION (INDUSTRIAL SCHOOLS) ACT 1879

This act amended the law regarding the powers of school boards relating to **industrial schools** and brought them more closely in line with the provisions of the Elementary Education Acts of 1870, 1873 and 1876. Children who were frequently absent from school could be sent to an industrial school by the **school attendance committee** (Report 1879–80, p. 2).

ELEMENTARY EDUCATION ACT 1880

The **Elementary Education Act 1876** enabled school attendance committees to enact byelaws making school attendance compulsory. Not all applied this power, sometimes because of limitations of control over parishes. Therefore the 1880 Act made it the duty of the local authority (**school board** or **school attendance committee** as speci-

fied by the Elementary Education Act 1876) to enact byelaws to compel attendance at school. Among other stipulations, the act specified that '[e]very person who takes into his employment a child of the age of ten and under the age of thirteen years resident in a school district, before that child has obtained a certificate of having reached the standard of education fixed by a byelaw in force in the district for the total or partial exemption of children of the like age from the obligation to attend school, shall be deemed to take such child into his employment in contravention of the Elementary Education Act, 1876 and shall be liable to a penalty accordingly' (Report 1880–81 p. 2).

ELEMENTARY EDUCATION ACT 1891

In England and Wales, this act, sometimes called the Free Education Act or Assisted Education Act, made available to schools a grant of 10s (50p) per pupil per year, thereby enabling parents and guardians to cease their payment of **school pence**. It was applicable to schools operating within this provision but not for church or **voluntary schools**. 'In any school receiving the fee grant, where the average rate charged and received in respect of fees and books, and for other purposes, during the school year ended last before the first day of January one thousand eight hundred and ninety–one, was not in excess of ten shillings a year for each child of the number of children in average attendance at the school, no charge shall be made for any children over three and under fifteen years of age' (Report 1891–92 p. 4). A memorandum by the Education Department specified what free education meant: 'The free education to which parents have a right must be unconditional; that is to say, must not be free while the child is in certain standards only, or be given on the ground of poverty, or be subject to any inquiry as the means of the parent or the reasons the parent has for desiring it, or be free only on condition that the child attends regularly, or have any other condition attached to it. It must be wholly free, without charge for books, slates, or anything else; and it must be at a school within a reasonable distance of the child's home' (Report 1892–93 p. 478). The impact of the act was to increase attendance above the growth in population and to increase regularity of attendance. 'The number of scholars on the registers, which in 1893 was 5,126,373 as compared with 5,006,979 in the preceding year, has this year risen to 5,198,741, an increase of 72,368 (or 1.41 per cent); and the average attendance, which in 1893 was 4,100,030, has this year gone up to 4,225,834, showing an increase on the year of 3.07 per cent' (Report 1893–94 p. ix). The act also led to a steep decline in **dame schools** and **adventure schools**.

ELEMENTARY EDUCATION (BLIND AND DEAF CHILDREN) ACT 1893

The act stated, 'Under the **Elementary Education Act 1876**, a parent must cause his child to receive, shall in the case of a blind or deaf child, be construed as including instruction suitable to such a child, and the fact of a child being blind or deaf shall not of itself, except in the case of a deaf child under seven years of age, be a reasonable excuse for not causing the child to attend school, or for neglecting to provide efficient elementary instruction for the child … It shall be the duty of every school authority, as defined by this Act, to enable blind and deaf children resident in their district, for whose elementary education efficient and suitable provision is not otherwise made, to obtain such education in some school for the time being certified by the **Education Department** as suitable for providing such education, and for that purpose either to establish or acquire and to maintain a school so certified' (Report 1893–94 p. 302).

The statutory school age for blind and deaf children was five or seven until 16 years of age. In 1895–96 the Smith Training College, Upper Norwood, London, was recognised as a **normal college** for the training of blind teachers of the blind. A specific syllabus for blind candidates for teachers' certificates was published in 1897 (Report 1896–97 p. 363).

See also: Special School

ELEMENTARY EDUCATION (SCHOOL ATTENDANCE) ACT 1893

This act came into force on 1 January 1894 and required compulsory attendance until eleven years of age. Prior to this, children could leave school at the age of ten years on passing **Standard** IV. 'Be it enacted by the Queen's most Excellent Majesty, by and with the advice and consent of the Lords Spiritual and Temporal, and Commons, in this present Parliament assembled, and by the authority of the same as follows: 1. The age at which a child may in pursuance of any byelaws made under the Elementary Education Acts, 1870 to 1891, obtain a partial exemption from the obligation to attend school, on obtaining a certificate as to the standard of examination which he has reached shall be raised to eleven … 2. If any person takes a child into his employment in such manner as to prevent the child from attending school in accordance with the byelaws for the time being in force in the district in which the child resides, he shall be deemed to take the child into his employment in contravention of the **Elementary Education Act 1876**, and shall be liable to a penalty accordingly' (Report 1893–94 p. 307).

See also: Elementary Education (School Attendance) Act (1893) Amendment Act 1899; Compulsory Attendance

ELEMENTARY EDUCATION ACT 1897

This act provided an additional grant to support the school board expenses (Report 1896–97 p. 386).

ELEMENTARY EDUCATION (DEFECTIVE AND EPILEPTIC CHILDREN) ACT 1899

This act provided grants to school authorities to identify and make provision for these children in day classes or boarding schools. The term **'special school'** was used in connection with this act and it stated: 'Where a school authority have ascertained that there are in their district defective children, they may make provision for the education of such children by all or any of the following means: (a) By classes in public elementary schools certified by the **Education Department** as special classes; or (b) By boarding out, subject to the regulations of the Education Department, any such child in a house conveniently near to a certified special class or school; or (c) By establishing schools, certified by the Education Department, for defective children' (Report 1898–99 p. 509).

ELEMENTARY EDUCATION (SCHOOL ATTENDANCE) ACT (1893) AMENDMENT ACT 1899

This act raised the school leaving age from eleven to twelve years of age. 'On or after the first day of January one thousand nine hundred the **Elementary Education (School Attendance) Act 1893** shall have effect as if "twelve" were substituted therein for "eleven"' (Report 1898–99 p. 530). Provision was also made for local byelaws to 'fix thirteen as the minimum age for exemption from school attendance in the case of children employed in agriculture, and that in such parish such children over eleven and under thirteen years of age who have passed the **standard** fixed for partial exemption from school attendance by the byelaws of the local authority shall not be required to attend school more than two hundred and fifty times [half days] in any year' (Report 1898–99 p. 530).

See also: Compulsory Attendance

ELEMENTARY SCHOOL TEACHERS (SUPERANNUATION) ACT 1898

This act provided for the entitlement of schoolteachers at or over the age of 65 to

superannuation allowances subject to the terms of the act. Contributions to the deferred annuity funds were £3 for men and £2 for women. Those teachers who were of a special fitness were allowed to continue for a limited period (Board of Education 1899–1900 Vol. 1, p. 12).

ELEMENTARY SCHOOLS

Were so called because they concentrated on the 'elementary subjects' of instruction: reading, writing and arithmetic (Report 1861–62 p. 106). Children, generally from impoverished backgrounds, had the option of attending these schools funded up to the age of 14, although few in the mid-1800s did so. Elementary schools were distinct from **normal schools** in that they did not make provision for the training of schoolmasters and schoolmistresses (Report 1861–62 p. xvi). The Education Act 1870, Section 3 specified: 'The term "elementary school" means a school or department of a school at which elementary education is the principal part of the education there given, and does not include any school or department of a school at which the ordinary payments in respect of the instruction, from each scholar, exceed ninepence a week' (Report 1870–71, p. liii). Arising from Article 19 of the Code of 1875 some **specific subjects** were transferred to ordinary subjects. Mr Currey, HMI, stated: 'This amendment will, I feel sure, do an immense amount to improve the general character of the teaching throughout the country. The good schools will not have the least difficulty in conforming to the new rules, and a much needed pressure will be put upon the inferior ones. There will be a good deal of grumbling, but improvement will gradually take place, and that which has been called impossible will be found to be realised pretty generally' (Report 1875–76 p. 295). The **Elementary Education Act 1870** distinguished between elementary schools and **public elementary schools**, with the former being a broader term that included both state schools and denominational schools, while the latter specifically referred to state funded schools. The Hadow (1926: xxi) report recommended the removal of the term 'elementary' because it had become 'misleading' and included education that was not elementary, for example **central schools**; it recommended that the term 'elementary' be replaced by 'primary', which happened with the **Education Act 1944**.

ELEMENTARY SCIENCE

See: Science Classes

ELEMENTARY SUBJECTS

These were the subjects of reading, writing and arithmetic, which were the main subjects taught in elementary schools. The 1862 Revised **Code** set out the expected standards, or levels, in each discipline – see Table 2.

See also: Class Subjects; Specific Subjects

ELWA

(2000/01–2006) This name meaning 'to gain' or 'to profit by' in Welsh is also an acronym for Education and Learning Wales. It is an umbrella term combining the operations of the **National Council for Education and**

Table 2 Standards for reading, writing and arithmetic

	Reading	Writing	Arithmetic
Standard I	Narrative in mono-syllables	Form on blackboard or slate from dictation, letters, capital and small manuscript	Form on blackboard or slate from dictation figures up to 20 Name at sight figures up to 20 Add and subtract figures up to 10 orally from examples on blackboard
Standard II	One of the narratives next in order after mono-syllables in an elementary reading book used in the school.	Copy in manuscript character a line of print	A sum in simple addition or subtraction and the multiplication table
Standard III	A short paragraph from an elementary reading book used in the school	A sentence from the same paragraph slowly read once and then dictated in single words	A sum in any simple rule as far as short division (inclusive)
Standard IV	A short paragraph from a more advanced reading book used in the school	A sentence slowly dictated once by a few words at a time, from the same book but not from the paragraph read	A sum in compound rules (money)
Standard V	A few lines of poetry from a reading book used in the first class of the school	A sentence slowly dictated once by a few words at a time, from a reading book used in the first class of the school	A sum in compound rules (common weights and measures)
Standard VI	A short ordinary paragraph in a newspaper or other modern narrative	Another short ordinary paragraph in a newspaper or other modern narrative slowly dictated once by a few words at a time	A sum in Practice or Bills of Parcels

Training for Wales and the Higher Education Funding Council for Wales. In 2006, its functions were taken over by the **Department for Education, Lifelong Learning and Skills**.

EMPLOYED KEY WORKERS TRANSFER SCHEME

(1950) This operated under the powers arising! from the Distribution of Industry Act 1950. Its purpose was to enable workers employed in key jobs to transfer to new establishments set up by their employers in **development areas**. This support was contingent on employment being expanded in these areas.

See also: General Transfer Scheme; Resettlement Transfer Scheme

Further reading: Ministry of Labour and National Service Report 1953 p. 45

EMPLOYEE DEVELOPMENT SCHEME

(Piloted in 1995) Designed for large companies as a means of giving the employee a defined career path in learning. There were plans for the scheme to be adapted for small and medium-sized enterprises, although it was recognised that there would be complications in that an SME might not have 'staff cover' for a student who needed 'day release', especially if they were mature employees.

Further reading: Beattie (1997); DfEE Departmental Report 1996 Cm 3210 p. 95

EMPLOYER COALITIONS

(*c.* 1998) The New Deal Task Force set up Employer Coalitions in 10 UK regions to help disadvantaged people gain employment. They were previously directed by the **National Employment Panel** and **Working Ventures UK**. Employer Coalitions aimed to 'unlock employers' expertise, energy and resource to:

- meet employers' needs;
- up-skill and recruit individuals, particularly people disadvantaged in the labour market; and
- enhance employment and skills delivery systems'.

www.employercoalitions.co.uk/
index.php?page=home
(accessed 09 April 2010)

EMPLOYER TRAINING PILOTS

(September 2002) The purpose of the pilots was to increase training demand by reducing barriers that hindered people from training and targeting those with low skills; they were intended to address market failures. They were initially introduced in six Local Learning and Skills Council areas. The pilots assessed the impact on training demand, up to Level 2, of a number of elements: free training programmes; support given to employers to allow staff paid time off for training; the brokering of suitable training provision; information and training needs analysis. **Train to Gain** was based on the Employer Training Pilots.

Further reading: DfES (July 2003); Hillage and Mitchell (2003)

EMPLOYMENT ACT 2002

See: Learning Representatives

EMPLOYMENT ACTION

(October 1991–93) Temporary employment schemes were to cease in 1988 when **employment training** was introduced. However, when unemployment began to rise, EA was started to give temporary employment of up to 6 months for those who had been unemployed for six months or more. There were similar criteria to ET with a similar payment. It was delivered by **training and enterprise councils** and aimed to:

- provide temporary work to maintain work-related skills for those who did not want training;
- meet the local and national economic needs by helping long-term unemployed who were ready to re-enter the labour market;
- provide structured job searches to enable permanent jobs to be found.

It was replaced by **Community Action** and **Training for Work**.

Further reading: Payne et al. (1999); Pratten and Ryan (1995)

EMPLOYMENT ACTION FOR JOBS

This scheme ran across Britain and continued until March 2004. Employment Action Teams were tasked with assisting jobless people aged 16–65 through actions such as: childcare; grants for interview clothing; and training courses for personal development and interview techniques.

EMPLOYMENT AND TRAINING ACT 1948

Statutory provision for training able-bodied people (disabled people were provided for in the **Disabled Persons (Employment) Act 1944**). The aim of the act was to reduce post war shortages of labour in industries essential to national prosperity. It required the **Ministry of Labour and National Service** to assist people and employers to select, fit, and obtain suitable employment.

EMPLOYMENT AND TRAINING ACT 1973

The main purpose of this act was to establish three statutory bodies: the **Manpower Services Commission** and its two agencies – the **Employment Service Agency** (ESA), and the **Training Services Agency** (TSA).

EMPLOYMENT DEPARTMENT

The title Employment Department was adopted as a familiar name in 1988 although it was still designated **Department of Employment** for legal purposes.

Further reading: Crooks (1993); Price (2000)

EMPLOYMENT DEPARTMENT GROUP

(1989) The group's work was spread between: the **Employment Department**; the **Employment Service**; the **Health and Safety Commission** and **Executive (HSC/E)**; the **Advisory, Conciliation and Arbitration Service (ACAS)**. In 1995 its stated aim was to increase labour market efficiency, maximise individuals' chances in the labour market, and encourage investment in skills by improving the training infrastructure.

Further reading: Employment Department Group Report March 1995, Cm 2805, pp. 9–10

EMPLOYMENT EXCHANGES

(1916–73) In 1916 they became the successors to the original **labour exchanges** that were established in 1910 by the **Board of Trade**. EEs were local offices of the **Ministry of Labour** and subsequent departments responsible for paying unemployment benefit as well as holding a register of job vacancies notified by employers. Attempts were made to modernise their approach by 'New Look' (1954) and later they were replaced by **Jobcentres** in 1973 and subsequently by **Jobcentre Plus**.

Further reading: Price (2000 p. 97)

EMPLOYMENT GAZETTE

Originally called the *Labour Gazette*, which was established by the **Board of Trade** in 1893, it subsequently had differing titles. The *Employment Gazette* was published monthly and provided details about employment and labour market matters. It was later renamed *Labour Market Trends*.

EMPLOYMENT INDUCTION COURSES

See: Assessment and Employment Induction Courses

EMPLOYMENT NEWS

See: Labour Market Trends

EMPLOYMENT OF CHILDREN ACT 1903

This act regulated the employment of children both directly and through byelaws. 'Street trading may be regulated by local licenses, and is wholly forbidden for children under 11 years of age. Injurious employments are prohibited. Children not exempt from school attendance may not be employed more than 25 hours a week, and half-timers, employed under the **factory acts** may not be employed in any other occupation; and night employment of children is forbidden except under sanction of a special byelaw' (Board of Education 1902–03 pp. 45–46).

EMPLOYMENT OFFICES

Was a familiar name for employment exchanges.

EMPLOYMENT REHABILITATION CENTRES

(1973–92) Formerly **industrial rehabilitation units**, the ERCs were established for people above school leaving age who suffered illness or injury and who needed rehabilitation in order to improve their potential for employment. In 1986 there were 26 residential employment rehabilitation centres, which provided almost 2,800 places to assist the assessment and the employment rehabilitation of disabled people. In 1984, a number of Asset Centres were established in geographic locations that were not served by the ERCs. The Employment Rehabilitation Centres were closed in 1992.

EMPLOYMENT REHABILITATION PROGRAMME

This programme was contracted out on a competitive basis to over 400 agencies and was designed to help clients to address specific areas of work-related requirements including 'understanding the effects of disability on work related activities; building the confidence to pursue work opportunities effectively; making an effective occupational choice; improving interpersonal skills at work; developing the physical ability to cope with work; and, re-learning basic skills' (DfEE Annual Report 1996, Cm 3210, p. 115).

EMPLOYMENT REHABILITATION SERVICE

(February 1975–1992) With the arrival of the **Employment Service Agency** and also the **Manpower Services Commission**, the **industrial rehabilitation units** were renamed as Employment Rehabilitation Centres and at the same time they were separated from any associated skill centres and medical establishments. There were 27 centres in 1987 and there were about 17,000 people attending them annually. The service was designed to help clients understand and address specific areas of work related needs:

- understanding the effects of disability on work-related activities;
- building the confidence to pursue work opportunities effectively;
- making an effective occupational choice;
- improving interpersonal skills at work;
- developing the physical ability to cope with work: and relearning basic skills.

In 1990 the ERS became part of the **Employment Service** and by 1992 the role was taken over by **placing, assessment and counselling teams** and ability assessment centres.

Further reading: Cornes et al. (1982)

EMPLOYMENT SERVICE

ES was formed on 26 October 1987 and inherited two national networks: 1,100 **Unemployment Benefit Offices** and 1,000 **Jobcentres.** The two networks were physically merged within the **Department of Employment** to provide a more integrated service linking advice about benefits and available jobs. It was said at the time to be the start of a 'stricter benefit regime'. The Employment Service was given 'Agency' status in 1990. It was absorbed into the **Department for Work and Pensions** and renamed **Jobcentre Plus** and officially launched on 1 April 2002.

Further reading: Price (2000); www.employ mentservice.gov.uk

EMPLOYMENT SERVICE AGENCY

(October 1974) **Department of Employment**'s Employment Service renamed and brought under the **Manpower Services Commission.** The new structure freed the **Employment Service** from the responsibility of unemployment benefit delivery. The ESA was established under the **Employment and Training Act 1973**.

Further reading: MSC Annual Report 1974–75 p.19

EMPLOYMENT SERVICE DIRECT

This telephone help-line was to support clients in finding jobs and further information about employment.

Further reading: DfEE Departmental Report, Plans 2001–02 to 2003–04, Cm 5102, p. 102

EMPLOYMENT TRAINING

(September 1988–March 1993) Employment training was introduced following the 1988 White Paper *Training for Employment* and it replaced the **New Job Training Scheme** to provide structured training, preferably with employers or with a training organisation.

Anyone who had been unemployed for over six months was eligible and participants were paid benefits plus £10 weekly for the duration of the training period of up to 12 months maximum. The average training time was six months. Within 15 months of its inception, 150,000 people had registered for this initiative and data shows that those enrolled were a broad spectrum of the unemployed – 71 per cent male, 11 per cent from ethnic minorities and 12 per cent with disabilities. Nationwide, there were some 1,000 training managers and 170 training agents operating. Training set on employers' premises was intended to provide the opportunity to demonstrate capability in practice. The ET programme budget was initially £1,500m on inception, rising at the rate of inflation throughout its life. The programme was replaced by **Training for Work**.

Further reading: Clemens et al. (1991)

EMPLOYMENT TRANSFER SCHEME

(1972–86) ETS was designed to help unemployed (and also those threatened with redundancy) to move to other areas to take jobs that could not be filled locally. It was phased out due to rising unemployment coupled with poor take-up of the scheme.

See also: Job Search Scheme, Free Forward Fares Scheme

Further reading: England (1983); Hunn (1984)

EMPLOYMENT TRIBUNALS

Formerly called **industrial tribunals**.

See also: Advisory, Conciliation and Arbitration Service

EMPLOYMENT ZONES

In 1998, prototype zones were launched in five areas to help long-term unemployed over-25-year-old job seekers. The prototypes had three objectives:

- Neighbourhood Match – a scheme to assist transition from welfare into sustainable employment.
- **Learning for Work** – the chance to learn and gain qualifications and thus to improve chances of employability.
- Business Enterprise – training and assistance to move from welfare into self-employment.

This was a public–private partnership in the designated zones; the participants could remain on the scheme for up to 2 years, and came off **job seeker's allowance** when they started on this programme. The funding was set at £33m in the period 1997–99.

Further reading: DfEE (1997e)

ENDOWED SCHOOLS ACT (1869)

This act established an Endowed Schools Commission with three special commissioners who were to oversee endowed or charity schools, of which many were considered to be ineffectively run and failing to make full use of their endowments. The commission was abolished in 1874 as a result of the Endowed Schools Amendment Act 1873 and the responsibilities were taken over by the Charity Commission, which reported, on the matter of schools, to the **Education Department**.

ENGLAND AND WALES YOUTH COHORT STUDY

Beginning in 1984, the England and Wales Youth Cohort Study was a series of surveys that tracked the progress of young people during the first few years after compulsory education. It was the main source of information used by the government departments responsible for young people.

See also: Education Census

ENGLISH LANGUAGE TRAINING

(1975) Some 26 units were set up to train immigrants to the UK in not only the use of

the language, but also the technical use of language.

See also: National Centre for Industrial Language Training; Language Export Centres; ESOL for Work Qualifications

Further reading: Hedge et al. (1975)

ENTERPRISE ADVISOR PILOTS

These pilots are described in the DfES Departmental Report 2003, which proposed their establishment in deprived areas; they were accessed through the Education Business Partnership Consortia networks.

See also: National Council for Graduate Entrepreneurship

Further reading: DfES Departmental Report 2003, Cm5902, p. 27

ENTERPRISE ALLOWANCE SCHEME

(Piloted in January 1982 and operational August 1983–March 1991) Provided allowance of £40 per week for 52 weeks to eligible unemployed people who had been unemployed for any duration to enable them to set up their own business. Within this the **Graduate Enterprise Programme** provided EAS funding for a small number of graduates. The ceiling was originally set at 32,500 participants but in 1984/85 46,000 joined the scheme. Estimates showed that for every 100 businesses set up, 50 extra jobs were created. In April 1991 the EAS and **Business Enterprise Training** budgets were merged and it was succeeded by the **Business Start-up Scheme**.

Further reading: Lehmann (1993); Owens (1989)

ENTERPRISE AWARENESS IN TEACHER EDUCATION

(1991) EATE originated in the **Department of Trade and Industry** and transferred to the **Employment Department** on 1 April 1991. It was designed to provide an opportunity for students undertaking initial teacher training to increase their understanding of the needs of industry and commerce.

See also: Teacher Placement Service

Further reading: McCreath and Naylor (1992)

ENTERPRISE DIRECTORATE

In 2007, the Enterprise Directorate replaced the **Small Business Service** and operated within the Department for Business Innovation and Skills 'across Whitehall, the Regional Development Agencies and key delivery partners to ensure that Government – national, regional and local – understands and responds to the needs of entrepreneurs and small businesses'.

www.bis.gov.uk/Policies/enterprise-and-business-support (accessed 14 April 2010)

ENTERPRISE EDUCATION

(150 pathfinder projects approved September 2003) From 2005/06 all **Key Stage** 4 pupils experienced the equivalent of five days enterprise activity involving the development of enterprise capability, innovation, creativity, risk-management and risk-taking, financial capability, and economic and business understanding. The purpose of this £60m initiative was to encourage young people to understand the nature of business, enterprise and the economy in order 'to develop skills, knowledge, and attitudes essential in a changing labour market'.

Further reading: DfES Departmental Report 2004 p. 70

ENTERPRISE IN HIGHER EDUCATION

(1989) The **Employment Department** worked with higher education institutions (**universities**, **polytechnics**, and **colleges of higher education**) to provide funding support for development and demonstration projects. The main purpose was to improve undergraduate and graduate effectiveness, enterprise and understanding of work needs. It was also designed to develop links with business, its relevance to adult and work life, and awareness of the labour market. EHE was achieved through encouraging changes in the curriculum, new approaches to learning and increasing links with employers. Over 50 HE institutions were involved. In the first two years, 39,000 students in England and Wales were involved.

Further reading: DES (1992); Scottish Affairs Committee (1995)

ENTERPRISE, TRANSPORT AND LIFELONG LEARNING DEPARTMENT

(May 2003–2007) This department replaced the **Scottish Executive Enterprise and Lifelong Learning Department** and also incorporated transport. The departmental system was replaced by the Scottish National Party in 2007 with a system of directorates: **Scottish Government Directorate for Children, Young People and Social Care**; **Scottish Government Directorate for Education**; **Scottish Government Directorate for Lifelong Learning**.

ENTERPRISE ULSTER

Enterprise Ulster was funded by the **Training and Employment Agency** in Northern Ireland and included ' … creating project partnerships with organisations whose activities are of benefit to the community; recruiting trainees who will benefit from training and/ or participation in employment projects; providing placements within organisations willing to contribute to the development of trainees' (Training and Employment Agency Annual Report 1995).

ENTRY LEVEL CERTIFICATES

These are qualifications that approximate to Level 3 of the national curriculum. They are designed for those students who are at Key Stage 4 and who are unlikely to achieve a GCSE. The Entry Level certificates are graded Entry 1, Entry 2 and Entry 3 in a number of subjects.

Further reading: www.edexcel.org.uk

ENTRY TO EMPLOYMENT

(2002) E2E was run by the **Learning and Skills Council** and its purpose was to act as a stepping stone into **modern apprenticeships** for young people aged 16–19. It was aimed at young people who were disillusioned with education and training, and also those with learning difficulties or disabilities who needed support to prepare for modern apprenticeships or work. It was delivered through a partnership involving local **Learning and Skills Councils**, **Connexions**/careers services and learning providers. The **Learning and Skills Development Agency** was awarded the contract to run the support and development programme, which began in 10 pathfinder areas in August 2002. The full programme became national in August 2003. It was developed as a flexible entry/Level 1 programme on the work-based learning route to support young people. Attendance was normally 30–40 hours and attendees received a training allowance of £40 per week (in 2005) and travel expenses. The introduction of the **foundation learning tier** led to the progressive replacement of entry to employment beginning in 2009/10, with the rollout expected to be completed in 2013.

Further reading: DfES Departmental Report 2005, p. 60

EPIDEMIC GRANT

During the 1890s informal arrangements to take into account the absence of sick scholars during inspection were formalised in the **Code**. 'Where the Department are satisfied that by reason of a notice of the Sanitary Authority under Article 88 or any provision of an Act of Parliament requiring the exclusion of certain children, or by reason of the exclusion under medical advice of children from infected houses, the average attendance has been seriously diminished and that consequently a loss of **annual grant** would, but for this Article, be incurred, the Department have power to make a special grant not exceeding the amount of such loss in addition to the ordinary grant' (Report 1896–97 p. 418).

See also: Favus School

EQUAL OPPORTUNITIES COMMISSION

(1975 – 30 September 2007) The EOC was created under the **Sex Discrimination Act 1975** and had a statutory responsibility for promoting equality of opportunity between men and women, including discrimination on the grounds of married status, and reviewing sex discrimination and the Equal Pay Act 1970. Its duties were absorbed into the **Equality and Human Rights Commission**.

EQUAL OPPORTUNITIES POLICIES

The Northern Ireland **Training and Employment Agency** promoted equal opportunities through the principles of Policy Appraisal and Fair Treatment (PAFT) and Targeting Social Need (TSN). The **Disability Discrimination Act 1995** was introduced with all T & EA staff attending awareness seminars. The 1997 Race Relations (NI) Act was also incorporated within T & EA policies.

Further reading: Training and Employment Agency Annual Report (1997)

EQUALITY AND HUMAN RIGHTS COMMISSION

On 1 October 2007, the EHRC took over the responsibilities of the **Commission for Racial Equality**, the **Equal Opportunities**

Commission, and the **Disability Rights Commission** in England, Scotland and Wales with the **Equality Commission** having responsibilities in Northern Ireland. The EHRC was created as a result of the Equality Act 2006 and it stated: 'Our job is to promote equality and human rights, and to create a fairer Britain. We do this by providing advice and guidance, working to implement an effective legislative framework and raising awareness of your rights'.

Further reading: Equality and Human Rights Commission (2010); www.equalityhuman-rights.com/

EQUALITY COMMISSION FOR NORTHERN IRELAND

(1999) The Equality Commission was established under the Good Friday Agreement and it absorbed the responsibilities of: the Commission for Racial Equality (Northern Ireland); the Equal Opportunities Commission for Northern Ireland; the Fair Employment Commission for Northern Ireland; and the Northern Ireland Disability Council.

Further reading: www.equalityni.org

EQUALITY DIRECT

This service was designed to provide joined-up advice on a variety of equality issues. It has a number of partners including **Advisory, Conciliation and Arbitration Service, Commission for Racial Equality, Equal Opportunities Commission**, and **Race Relations Employment Advisory Service**.

Further reading: DfEE Departmental Report, Plans 2001–02 to 2003–04 p. 110; www.equalitydirect.org.uk

ERASMUS

(1987) Stands for 'European Action Scheme for the Mobility of University Students' and it began in 1987. It enabled students to gain wider knowledge of European culture in the setting of their studies and around 9,000 UK students took part in 1990 out of 44,500 from the whole of the EC.

Further reading: Baumgratz-Gangl and Deyson 1990; www.britishcouncil.org/erasmus.htm; http://ec.europa.eu/education/lifelong-learning-programme/doc78_en.htm

ESSENTIAL SKILLS FOR LIVING

This was an initiative launched in April 2002 by the **Department for Employment and Learning** Northern Ireland to improve adult literacy, numeracy and computer skills.

See also: Skills for Life Qualifications; Basic Skills Agency

ESOL FOR WORK QUALIFICATIONS

(16 October 2007) English for speakers of other languages qualifications were launched in 2007 to help migrant workers develop the English language skills needed to operate effectively in the workplace. These qualifications were shorter and more work targeted than traditional ESOL qualifications. The fee for the course was £880, which was to be funded by the Government with employers expected to contribute £330 where they benefit from the training.

See also: English Language Training; National Centre for Industrial Language Training

ESTATE SCHOOLS

These were schools established by large landowners generally for the children of their employees and those in the near vicinity: for example, The Lilleshall school in Shropshire supported by the Duke of Sutherland.

Further reading: Report 1863–64 p. 115

ESTYN

(12 February 1907) The office of Her Majesty's Inspectorate for Education and Training in

Wales is called Estyn and it is responsible for a wide range of inspections including: schools, further and adult education, and teacher education and training.

See also: Office for Standards in Education (OFSTED) Children's Services and Skills; Her Majesty's Inspectorate of Education Scotland; Education and Training Inspectorate

Further reading: www.estyn.gov.uk

EUROPASS

Europass was established by a European Parliament and Council decision on 15 December 2004. Its purpose was to improve cross-European mobility through making qualifications more understandable and transferable. It consisted of five documents: Europass Curriculum Vitae; Europass Language Passport; Europass Certificate Supplement; Europass Diploma Supplement; and, Europass Mobility. Mobility was improved by the **European Credit Transfer and Accumulation System**.

Further reading: http://europass.cedefop. europa.eu/europass/home/hornav/Introducti on.csp?loc=en_GB

EUROPEAN AGRICULTURAL GUARANTEE AND GUIDANCE FUND

(1970) This was a fund set up by the European Commission to guarantee the price of commodities that farmers produced. It also had an element of training in that farmers could apply for grants to aid in the training of employees in the fields of industrial equipment usage and safety.

Further reading: Department of Employment Gazette 1972 p. 969

EUROPEAN CREDIT SYSTEM FOR VOCATIONAL EDUCATION AND TRAINING

'The European Credit System for Vocational Education and Training (ECVET) is aimed to facilitate the accumulation, transfer and recognition of knowledge, skills and competences gained by individuals towards a qualification. ECVET is applicable to learning outcomes gained in different learning environments or through periods of vocational education and training abroad. It is intended to give people greater control over their individual learning experiences and make it more attractive to move between different countries and different learning environments'. It was the vocational equivalent of the **European Credit Transfer and Accumulation System**.

http://ec.europa.eu/education/lifelong-learning-policy/doc50_en.htm (accessed 20 February 2010)

See also: Qualifications and Credit Framework

EUROPEAN CREDIT TRANSFER AND ACCUMULATION SYSTEM

The ECTS was designed to provide transparency of learning and teaching across Europe by recognising studies for credit transfer and credit accumulation. It enabled people to study at different locations across Europe and build qualifications. It was complemented by the **European Credit System for Vocational Education and Training**.

See also: Europass; Qualifications and Credit Framework

EUROPEAN ECONOMIC COMMUNITY TREATY ARTICLE 128

Declaration of community-wide vocational training policy.

Further reading: Department of Employment Gazette 1972 p. 269

EUROPEAN EMPLOYMENT SERVICE

EURES is a European Union initiative involving the public employment services of the member states of the EU economic area.

It advertised both jobs and living and working conditions.

See also: European Employment Service Cross Border Partnership

Further reading: http://europa.eu.int/jobs/eures

EUROPEAN EMPLOYMENT SERVICE CROSS BORDER PARTNERSHIP

Northern Ireland initiative launched in October 1997. Its purpose was to help overcome obstacles facing those who lived close to the border and who wanted to work or train on the other side. The partnership also provided help to employers by giving them greater access to labour across the border from their operations. The partnership involved the **Training and Employment Agency** from Northern Ireland, FÁS from the Republic of Ireland, and employers and trade union organisations.

See also: European Employment Service; Wider Horizons Programme

Further reading: Training and Employment Agency Annual Report (1998)

EUROPEAN REGIONAL DEVELOPMENT FUND

(1975) The ERDF was established to reduce European regional and structural economic differences. Under-developed and declining regions were supported by the fund, which addresses a number of areas including: enhancing competitiveness; business infrastructure; development of employment initiatives; research and technological development; and the development of transportation, telecommunication and energy networks.

EUROPEAN SOCIAL FUND

From 1990, the ESF was primarily supporting vocational training and employment measures for young people and the long-term unem-ployed. Implementation of the Fund was overseen by national and regional committees such as **training and enterprise council**s, local authorities, higher and further education institutes, **national training organisations** and the voluntary sector. From 1998 the UK could pay ESF funds direct without having to wait for the monies to come through from Brussels, hence removing financial uncertainty for many organisations involved in training. In 1997–98 the ESF funded £234m to the UK of which £134m was for England.

Further reading: Employment Department (1992d)

EUROPEAN TRAINING FOUNDATION

(1995) Based in Turin, the ETF was set up as a European agency to encourage research into training initiatives within member states of the European Union. In addition it supports the development and dissemination of European best practice to other member states. It also provides support and advice on modernising and adapting training systems to partner countries and to countries of central and Eastern Europe and the former Soviet Union. It was proposed by the European Council of 8–9 December 1989.

See also: International Centre for Advanced Training

Further reading: Commission of the European Communities (1990b); www.etf.it

EUROPEAN UNION SPECIAL SUPPORT PROGRAMME FOR PEACE AND RECONCILIATION

This programme supported cooperation between the **Training and Employment Agency** (Northern Ireland) and FÁS, the Republic of Ireland's training authority. The two training authorities agreed a joint approach to improving economic development through improving the employability of trainees on both sides of the border.

Further reading: Training and Employment Agency Annual Report (1997)

EUROPEAN UNIVERSITY INSTITUTE

Based in Florence, this is a post-graduate research institute researching in the European perspectives in the human and social sciences, history, law, economics and political and social sciences. The UK provided bursary support for 26 students and also contributed to the costs of the Institute. The 1998–99 cost was £1.9m rising to £2.5m in 1999–2000.

Further reading: Foreign and Commonwealth Office (1992)

EUROTECNET

(1990–95) (European Technology Network for Training) A European Community initiative to develop a network to exchange experiences about the impact of new technology on training. Priority was given to SMEs. Projects were selected for inclusion on the basis that the scheme would network with other EC partners looking at technological changes and their impact on employment, qualifications and skill requirements. EC funded this training to the sum of £5.6m per annum.

Further reading: Commission of the European Communities (1990a)

EVENING CONTINUATION SCHOOL CODE

This was first introduced in 1893 to ' … meet the requirements of scholars who are no longer subject to the law of compulsory attendance at school, and who desire to prolong their education, either in the ordinary school subjects or in some special subjects in order to fit themselves for some industrial career' (Report 1892–93 p. 386). The code was similar to that issued for use in elementary schools and both were updated annually to accommodate regulations, curricula changes etc. In some areas, funding for these schools

was provided by the school board to enable higher level subjects to be delivered; however, a court case ruled this illegal and funding was discontinued for those schools that did not follow the Elementary Education Acts. The Report of the Board of Education 1900–01 (Vol. 1, p. 9) stated: 'The recent decision of the case of Rex v. Cockerton arising out of a surcharge made upon members of the London School Board for certain expenses incurred in conducting science and art classes, has shown that schools of the kind contemplated by the Evening Continuation Schools code cannot be legally carried on by School Boards at the expense of the rates'. To manage this situation and allow the schools to continue to operate an Act of 1901 was passed to allow Boards to fund such schools.

EVENING CONTINUATION SCHOOLS

See: Continuation Schools

EVENING PLAY CENTRES

In 1923–24 there were 251 centres. 'At the thirty-three centres organised by the London Evening Play Centres Committee nearly one-and-a-half million attendances were made during 1923–24. Two successful Holiday Play Centres were organised by the Committee during August 1923, which afforded opportunities for organised play to a large number of children. We should be very glad to see an increase in these admirable organisations' (Report 1923–24 pp. 137–38).

EVENING SCHOOLS

Evening schools, sometimes known as **night schools**, were originally introduced to provide education for those scholars who had left school early and had not completed their **elementary education**. The Code of 1890 regarding evening schools was changed to provide for a wider curriculum. 'The provisions relating to evening schools were materially altered by the Code of 1890, with a view to encourage more advanced and varied teaching in such schools, and to enable managers to adapt the course of study to the industrial and other requirements of particular districts. Art. 106 removes the condition which has hitherto obliged all evening scholars to be presented in the three elementary subjects; and permits those who are certified to have passed the examination in the Fifth Standard to be presented in any four special (class or specific) subjects which the managers may select. The requirement that the first of such special subjects shall always be English and the second geography or elementary science is withdrawn; and the freedom of choice offered by means of the alternative courses and other provisions applicable to special subjects in day schools is also fully available to the conductors of evening schools. By these means it is hoped that managers will be encouraged to frame in various districts such courses of instruction as are most likely to attract young people, and to induce them to continue their studies beyond the ordinary school age' (Report 1890–91 p. 199). The 1897 **Evening Continuation School Code** introduced the entitlement of people over the age of 21 to attend evening classes (Report 1896–97 p. 576).

See also: Evening Schools for the Labouring Classes

EVENING SCHOOLS FOR THE LABOURING CLASSES

(1851) Support was given for certified teachers to receive grants and exchange their daytime duties for evening duties in the teaching of 'young persons between the ages of 12–17 among the respectable and well-conducted portion of the labouring class' (Minutes 1851–52 p. 74). With the **New Code**, evening schools were allowed for the first time and were attached to day schools with the result that numerous mechanics institutes allowed their elementary classes to come under inspection (Minutes 1874–75

p. 211). Evening schools with an elementary curriculum initially grew in number to accommodate those young people who had not originally received a basic education. Gradually, however, attendance declined as the effects of compulsory education resulted in children receiving an education.

See also: Continuation School; Evening Continuation School; Night School

Further reading: Minutes 1851–52 Volume 1, p. 18

EXAMINATION BOARDS

Examination boards were originally administered by universities, for example the Joint Matriculation Board incorporated Birmingham, Leeds, Liverpool, Manchester and Sheffield universities. These have consolidated to six examination boards in the UK: **Assessment and Qualifications Alliance** (AQA); **Council for the Curriculum, Examinations and Assessment** (CCEA) (in Northern Ireland); **Edexcel**; **Oxford, Cambridge and RSA** (OCR); **Scottish Qualifications Authority** (SQA); and, **Welsh Joint Education Committee** (WJEC).

See also: Awarding Body

EXAMINATIONS

(1862) Under the **Revised Code of Regulations**, HMIs were required to inspect and examine the performance of the pupils in reading, writing and arithmetic, which often would be assessed on a scale using 'excellent, good, fair, moderate, imperfect, failure'. Examination often took the form of the class be examined as a group by **Her Majesty's Inspector[ate of Education]**. In the early years the level of grants to the school was partly dependent on the performance of the children. Instructions were given about conducting the examination and that 'four to six hours will suffice for examining and marking 150 children' (Report 1862–63 p. xxii).

EXAMINING BODIES

The external examination system began largely with the older universities and progressed to a more coherent examination system with the **Board of Education** recognising the examinations of **City and Guilds of London Institute**, the Institution of Mechanical Engineers etc. The term 'examining bodies' became more commonly used in the 1920s (Report 1922–23 p. 89) and local examining bodies included: the Union of Lancashire and Cheshire Institutes; the Union of Educational Institutes; East Midland Educational Union (1911); Northern Counties Technical Examinations Council (1921) (Report 1935 p. 18).

See also: Examinations; National Certificates; Secondary Schools Examination Council

EXCEPTION SCHEDULE

During the 1880s grants were awarded for the average performance of children during inspection by one of **Her Majesty's Inspectors** and no allowance was made for children with limited ability. The 1884 **Code** stated: 'All scholars whose names are on the registers of the school must, as a rule, be present at the inspection, unless there is a reasonable excuse for their absence' (Report 1883–84 p. 116). Debate then ensued about what was 'a reasonable excuse' between school managers and HMIs. Mr Waddington HMI stated: 'Downright "defective intellect" is pretty easily discovered, mere "irregularity of attendance" is not, as we are instructed, a valid reason for exemption, but to judge the cases where "obvious dulness" [sic] is pleaded is a difficult and thankless task. ... May I suggest that a small definite per-centage allowance of exemption (say, 5 per cent.) should be authorised, which must cover all excuses on the ground of defective intellect, obvious dullness, or previous neglect' (Report 1883–84 p. 433). The need for this exemption clause was largely removed with the 1890 Code, which discontinued the system of

average percentage passes in the elementary subjects (Report 1889–90 p. 171).

EXECUTIVE DEVELOPMENT PROGRAMME

Designed for existing managers by the **Training and Employment Agency** in Northern Ireland. Ten open access programmes were designed to deliver leading-edge development and exposure to best practice in generic management skills.

Further reading: Training and Employment Agency Annual Report (1997)

EXECUTIVE JOBCLUB

Similar to **job clubs** but with an emphasis on unemployed executive and professional people. The first was in Ferndown near Bournemouth and offered expert help and professional advice to support the clients return to work.

Further reading: Employment Service (1988a)

EXECUTIVE POST

See: Professional & Executive Register

EXCELLENCE IN CITIES

(March 1999) The initiative was designed to address the pressing issues in inner cities and specifically inner-city education. The emphasis was on developing the skills of all children in six conurbations: Inner London, Birmingham, Manchester/Salford, Liverpool/Knowsley, Leeds/Bradford, and Sheffield/Rotherham. The programme was developed to improve the performance of pupils and schools in city areas by encouraging the raising of expectations. EiC was based on the belief that schools working collaboratively would benefit pupils, parents and communities compared with working in isolation. This would be supported by government, local education authorities, and schools working in partnership. EiC is composed of seven key strands: Learning Mentors; Learning Support Units; extended opportunities for gifted and talented pupils; a network of new **city learning centres**; EiC **action zones**, more **Beacon schools**; and more **specialist schools**.

Further reading: DfES (2002d)

EXHIBITION

This was a term for a competition for which a financial or other reward was made; for example, they were made to **Queen's Scholars** who were successful in their examinations.

Further reading: Minutes 1852–53, Vol. 1, p. 370

EXPORT MARKETING PROGRAMME

During 1993/94 this Northern Ireland scheme provided the opportunity for 49 companies to undertake company specific marketing assignments into Europe and the west and east coasts of the USA.

Further reading: Training and Employment Agency Annual Report (1994)

EXPORT OFFICE PROCEDURE COURSE

(1969) Introduced as a means of training employees such that the United Kingdom could better participate in the field of exporting. The course was closed in 1973 when it was recognised that many companies in the field of exporting were doing their own in-house training.

Further reading: Department of Employment Gazette 1972 pp. 352–53

EXTENDED INTRODUCTION

(1990) This was an **Employment training** initiative that succeeded the **Voluntary Projects Programme**. This programme was designed to reach out to those on the very edge of the labour market, including lone parents, people with basic literacy and numeracy problems, and ex-offenders with a known drug-related problem.

See also: Initial Training

Further reading: Employment Gazette 1990 p. 304

EXTENDED SCHOOLS

These schools offer a wider than usual range of services to pupils, families, school staff, and the wider community. The provision varied depending on location and might include childcare, health and social care, adult and family learning, ICT access, study support, and arts and sports facilities. Some 25 pathfinder projects were initiated to investigate approaches and processes. Access was extended throughout the day, during weekends and holidays. A similar initiative, called **(new) community schools** was established in Scotland.

See also: Village Schools

Further reading: Wilkin et al. (2003)

EXTERNAL VERIFIERS

These people are appointed by an **approved centre** (which was approved by an **awarding organisation**) to monitor the work of the approved centres. They are the link between the awarding body and the centre.

Further reading: Mansfield and Mitchell (1996)

EXTINCT SCHOOLS

This was a term used to describe schools that had received a grant from the **Committee of Council on Education** that were no longer operating – e.g. Glossop-dale Universal School (Minutes 1844 Vol. 2, p. 470).

FACTORIES ACT 1961

Section 21 of the act prohibited the employment of young people using machines unless:

1 'he has been fully instructed as to the dangers arising in connection with the machinery and the precautions to be observed; and
2 he has received sufficient training in work at the machine or is under adequate supervision by a person who has a thorough knowledge and experience of the machine or is under adequate supervision by a person who has a thorough knowledge and experience of the machine.'

This act built on the **Dangerous Machines** (Training of Young Persons) Order 1954, which proscribed 18 machines as being of a dangerous character and stated that young people might not work with them unless the details above were applied.

FACTORY ACT 1874

This act required children to pass **Standard III** before they could begin half-time work. Children between 13 and 14 had to pass Standard IV before they could work full-time (Report 1882–83 p. 299).

FACTORY ACTS

These were a collection of acts that regulated working conditions and employment, particularly for children, in mills and factories. The Factory Act of 1845 specified that all children under the age of 13 employed in mills should attend school for three hours per day. The act also allowed for children to begin work at the age of three and this was subsequently raised to ten years in 1874. Three main types of factory schools developed: those founded and supported by the proprietor; those formed by a cooperation of mill owners; and, those developed by religious denominations although not always exclusively for factory children. This was the first instance of 'legislative compulsory education' (Minutes 1851–52 p. 565). Other factory acts made provision for children; for example, the Print Works Act 1845 stated that children were expected to attend school for 30 days per half-year; the Workshops Regulation Act 1867 specified 10 hours per week for those children permitted to work in factories employing less than 50 people. And, the Factory Act Extension Act 1867 extended the provision to all factories employing more than 50 people.

See also: Half-time Children; Factory Schools; Agricultural Children Act 1873; Health and Morals of Apprentices Act 1802

FACTORY BOOKS

These were registers kept by schools to record the attendance of **half-time children** (Report 1877–78 p. 537).

FACTORY SCHOOLS

The Factory Act 1833 required children under 13 years to have two hours of school per day and this was increased by the Factory Act 1844 and the regulations regarding attendance further changed over time. Although these schools were often attached to factories they were sometimes termed factory schools only because they were in close proximity to a factory from which children were required to attend for **half-time**. Unfortunately, the attainment of these children was much lower than those who attended on a regular basis, since the interests of many parents and factory owners were to keep the children working and earning rather than attend school. In 1848, Mr A. Thurtell, Inspector of schools, observing the conflict of interests regarding the employment of children in cotton factories wrote that 'something has to be done to diminish the evil, and avert the curse; but much more remains to be done; and against its being done, the supposed interests of both classes immediately concerned will, of course, not cease to create opposition' (Minutes 1847–48 Vol. 2, p. 17). The factory school established by the Llynvi Iron Company at Maesteg, South Wales made weekly deductions from wages to pay for the schooling of children (Minutes 1852–53 Vol. 2, p. 674).

See also: Factory Acts; Gartsherrie Schools

FAIR EMPLOYMENT COMMISSION – NORTHERN IRELAND

(1 Jan 1990) The Fair Employment Commission was established under the Fair Employment Act 1989 to combat religious discrimination. The commission replaced the Fair Employment Agency and was designed, among other elements, to combat relatively high unemployment among the Catholic population. Companies were obliged to monitor their employment practices including recruitment, promotion, and training policies. The commission was empowered to set goals and timetables for affirmative action and, if necessary, to bring cases to the Fair Employment Tribunal.

Further reading: Northern Ireland Office (1990)

FAIR PLAY FOR WOMEN

(April 1994) The objective of this initiative was to encourage women to realise their full potential in the community and create a fair society. **Training and enterprise councils** and other local organisations were encouraged to develop local initiatives to allow women to contribute fully in the labour market and elsewhere. It was based on the successful **Chwarae Teg** initiative in Wales.

Further reading: Employment Department (1994a)

FAITH SCHOOLS

This term incorporates the wide range of denominational schools that have increased in recent years (Department for Children, Schools and Families 2007).

See also: Catholic Poor School Committee; Charity Schools; Dissenting Academy; Home and Colonial Infant School Society; Hindu School; Jewish Schools; Muslim School; National School Society; Seventh-day Adventist School; Sikh School; Wesleyan Schools; Society of Friends Schools

FAMILY LEARNING

(1997) Started out in 1997 as the Family Literacy Initiative enabling parents with poor literacy skills to improve them whilst at the same time helping the development of their children's literacy. In 1997–98, there were 265 courses that were run by 63 LEAs; this was expanded and funded to the level of £4m, allowing 600 courses to be run by all LEAs in 2000.

See also: Basic Skills Agency

Further reading: OFSTED (2000)

FARES TO WORK

(1945) This scheme was provided for in the Disabled Persons Act 1944. It enabled those with disabilities to claim up to 75 per cent of the cost of a taxi from their home to their place of work, if they could show that their disability precluded them from using public transport.

Further reading: Parker (1990)

FARM SCHOOLS

These were schools attached to farms such as at Teddesley where boys were employed to work on Lord Hatherton's farm and attended night school in the winter and early morning school during the summer months. At Middle, near Shrewsbury, a **half-time** scheme was used with boys attending school during part of the day and then working under supervision during the other part of the day on neighbouring farms (Minutes 1854–55 p. 543).

See also: Agricultural Schools; Industrial Garden

FARM TRAINING SCHEME

This was an initiative to train people in agriculture and then support their emigration to Canada. It was relatively short-lived because the depression after the First World War also affected the colonies where the participants were to emigrate.

See also: Labour Colony

Further rerading: Crooks (1993)

FARMED SCHOOLS

In the latter part of the 1800s school managers sometimes deputed the responsibility of teaching to a teacher and received the **school pence** or fees themselves. This form of **adventure school** for private profit was proscribed in the **Code**, which stated, 'The school must not be conducted for private profit, and must not be farmed out by the manager to the teacher. The managers must be responsible for the payment of teachers and all other expenses of the school' (Report 1894–95 p. 325).

FAST TRACK BUSINESS PROGRAMME

This was designed to help people start up and run their own businesses in Northern Ireland. Training covered the areas of business knowledge, managerial skills and personal competences. It was intended to boost personal development of owner managers and the growth prospects of companies during the first three years of operation.

Further reading: Training and Employment Agency Annual Report (1994)

FAST TRACK TEACHING PROGRAMME

(2002) This programme was intended to identify the most talented serving teachers, new graduates and career changers, and provide support to enable them to progress quickly to become school leaders.

Further reading: DfES Departmental Report 2004, Cm 6202, p. 94

FAVUS SCHOOL

(1907) This school was established by the London County Council in Whitechapel for 'physically defective children'. 'Here are brought together about 100 children suffering from a very intractable scalp infection. It is to be hoped that under the new legislation [**Education (Administration Provisions) Act 1907** regarding medical inspection in schools] medical measures will be stringently enforced through the establishment of Schools of this type in order to stamp out diseases which, if neglected, cause such havoc and loss of school time, and which submit to treatment without great difficulty if properly handled' (Report 1906–07 p. 49).

FEDERATION SCHOOLS

There were two types of federation schools existing in 2010. The first involved an executive head who presided over two or more schools where the schools retained their governing body and individual budgets. The second type of federation involved an executive head overseeing a single governing body and integrated budget.

FEMALE IMPROVEMENT SOCIETY

(1848) This was a mutual instruction society, (see **mutual instruction societies**) founded in Keighley for factory women and had attendances of more than 100 women per week.

Further reading: Tylecote (1957 p. 231)

FEMALE SERVANTS' TRAINING SCHOOL

(c. 1852) This industrial school at Haley Castle, Worcestershire, trained young girls to be household servants. They were taught reading, writing, arithmetic, cooking, bread making, washing, ironing, etc. The pupils paid 4 shillings per week, which included clothing, lodging, boarding and education. The school was for pupils between the ages of 10 and 16 (Minutes Vol. 2, 1852–53, p. 104). Similar establishments were started in other places: for example, a training institution for female servants by Mrs Guthrie in Wiltshire (Report 1858–59, p. 116) and Miss Martineau's industrial school in Norwich (Report 1858–59 p. 180).

FIRST AID TO THE INJURED

See: Nursing

FIRST CLASS

During the 1840s and 1850s public (state) education was conducted with the children all taught together in one large school room. This proved relatively unsatisfactory and the room was often divided by means of curtains or more substantial walling. This then allowed for pupils to be divided based on their age and, often, ability. The first class consisted of children aged approximately 10–13, with the second, third classes etc. below them. Children in the first class were expected to have a higher standard of ability than those in the classes below them. If this was not the case, children did not advance even though their peers did. Sometimes parents insisted on their children advancing and these children were called 'interloping children' (Report 1860–61 p. 175). This counting from the top of the school was subsequently replaced by a numbering system beginning with the entry class.

See also: Division

FIRST EXAMINATION

(1918/19) This examination, established in 1917 and first taken in 1918 by pupils of about 16 years of age was a precursor to the **ordinary levels**. The subjects consisted of three groups: English subjects; languages other than English; and, science and mathematics. To pass, each pupil had to be successful in each of these three areas, although the precise regulations varied during their history. Pupils who passed this examination were awarded the **school certificate** and passing this examination coincided with the movement from the middle to the upper forms of the school. It was overseen by the **Secondary Schools Examination Council**, which was tasked with bringing order to a wide range of qualifications. The First Examination was followed, for those who wished to sit it, by the **Second Examination** for those of about 18 years of age (Report 1923–24 p. 30).

(SCHOOLS FOR) FISHERMEN

These were schools established to provide education for fishermen: for example, the School for Fishermen in Fleetwood was established in 1892 and was the origin for Blackpool and the Fylde College. Another school established in Hull *c.*1913 was known as the Municipal Technical School for Fishermen.

FIT FOR WORK AWARDS

(1980) Launched to make employers aware and proactive to the needs of the disabled in the workplace. The award scheme was set up to disseminate best practice for the disabled in mainstream employment, and the award was presented at an annual dinner. By 1990 there were 100 award-winning companies.

See also: Fit for Work Scheme; Disabled – Fit for Work

Further reading: Rowley (1983)

FIT FOR WORK SCHEME

(1979–1990) This initiative was established for those with physical and mental disabilities to enable them to enter the labour market. It began in 1979, and was extended annually through to 1990. Assessment of capability, suitability for work, and work availability within the area were all part of this scheme. See **Fit For Work awards** and **Disabled – Fit For Work Scheme**.

Further reading: Rowley (1983)

FLEXIBLE LEARNING FRAMEWORK

Launched as a national strategy for education and training at the beginning of the 1990s. It involved enabling pupils to 'learn how to learn' as well as learning specific subject knowledge by the pupils becoming actively involved with their own learning. It represented a radical departure from 'chalk and talk'. The framework helped teachers and training managers to organise learning so that it 'meets individual learning needs; helps pupils to take on more responsibility; makes

effective use of resources (materials, locations, machinery and teacher/pupil time); allows for differentiated learning; supports staff development and support' (Employment Department 1991b).

FLEXIBLE SUPPORT FOR BUSINESS

Formerly 'Business Eye', Flexible Support for Business was launched in April 2008 to expand the provision provided by the **Workforce Development Programme** in Wales. The main elements of the support are a single access telephone number and website; dedicated relationships managers; and a Single Investment Fund (Department for Children, Education, Lifelong Learning and Skills 2008 p. 57). Among the services it provides are: business news and events; financial support information; free business workshops; information resources; link directories; information on tendering; and training. It is the equivalent of England's **Business Link** and Scotland's **Business Gateway**.

Further reading: http://fs4b.wales.gov.uk/ bdotg/action/home?site=230&domain=fs4b. wales.gov.uk&target=http://fs4b.wales.gov.uk/ (accessed 20 February 2010)

FLOATING ENGINEER COLLEGE

(c1859) This was established by the Royal Navy onboard the Devonshire at Sheerness for the development of engineers (Minutes 1859–60 p. 499).

See also: Admiralty Schools

FLUCTUATING SCHOOLS

(1860s) These were schools which from time to time did not fulfil the stipulations of the **Revised Code of Regulations**; as a result, they did not always receive a grant and so were sometimes in the regulatory system and sometimes not (Report 1863–64 p. 104).

FLYING START

This programme was introduced in Wales in 2006 with the purpose of improving the prospects of children aged 0 to 3 in disadvantaged areas, through childcare and supporting child development and learning through play (Department for Children, Education, Lifelong Learning and Skills 2008 p. 26).

See also: Sure Start

FOCUS FOR WORK

(1 October 2001) This Northern Ireland initiative combined **Bridge to Employment**, **Worktrack**, **job clubs**, and a new **Training for Work** programme. It was designed for those unemployed for less than 18 months; working with providers, it aimed to provide a personal service to support job finding and planning; develop interview skills; and enable tailored vocational training leading to advanced vocational qualifications.

Further reading: www.delni.gov.uk

FORCE

(1 January 1991–31 December 1994) Formation Continue en Europe (FORCE) was a European Community programme designed to support and complement activities and policies developed in and by member states in continuing vocational training of workers in companies. Its objectives were to: encourage greater and more effective investment and returns from continuing vocational training; encourage continuing vocational training measures; encourage innovations in the management of continuing vocational training, methodology and equipment; take account of the internal market; and, contribute to greater effectiveness of continuing vocational training mechanisms.

Further reading: Task Force Human Resources Education, Training, Youth (1990)

FORCES RESETTLEMENT SERVICE

The aims of the Forces Resettlement Service were: 'to provide information and guidance for all ranks on their choice of civilian career; to provide servicemen and women with re-settlement training, both pre- and post-discharge; to give them the information they need to find themselves work or a new career; and to point them in the right direction for employment advice from outside agencies' (Williamson 1990 p. 20).

FOREST OF DEAN SCHOOLS

(1855) The HMI Reverend H. W. Bellairs' recommended that Her Majesty's Commissioners of Woods and Forests only award grants to schools in the Forest of Dean receiving a favourable report from HMIs (Minutes 1855–56, p. 247).

FORTY PLUS SERVICE

This initiative was developed to address the challenge of 'ageism' faced by unemployed managers over the age of 40 seeking to regain employment. Initially set up in London in 1980, it went nationwide in 1981.

Further reading: MSC Annual Report 1981/82 p. 21

FOUNDATION DEGREES

(Announced February 2000 and commenced autumn 2001) Arising from the Dearing Report, which advised on the development of a 'sub-degree' linked to the mid-skilled labour market, these qualifications were designed to be below the conventional university baccalaureate and represented 240 Credit Accumulation and Transfer Scheme points. They were intended to decrease the shortage of people with technician level qualifications. The core components comprised specialist knowledge that employers require, underpinned by rigorous broad-based academic knowledge; accredited key skills, credits for appropriate qualifications; active links with a student's work experience and academic study; and guaranteed arrangements for articulation and progression to honours degree courses, which would require an additional 1.3 years of academic study.

See also: Diploma of Education

Further reading: DfEE (2000d)

FOUNDATION FOR EDUCATION BUSINESS PARTNERSHIP

(1990) The FEBP was established to promote links between education and business. It was funded by the **Training Agency**, the **Department of Education and Science**, and a number of blue chip companies. Its target for 1991 was to create effective partnerships in half of the 104 local education authorities in England and Wales. The launch coincided with a MORI survey that showed employers were dissatisfied with schools' preparation of children for work.

Further reading: Employment Department (1991e)

FOUNDATION LEARNING TIER

Foundation learning had a phased implementation from September 2007 onwards, and all local authorities were required to provide some by September 2010. It was described in the Green Paper, *Raising Expectations: staying in education and training post-16*; it was designed to provide a more coherent approach to qualifications and training for young people and adults below Level 2 and to develop **progression pathways** to Level 2. Learning provision at Entry Level and Level 1 required rationalisation and coordination in order to increase the low levels of progression to Level 2. The **Qualifications and Curriculum Authority** and **Learning and Skills Council** oversaw a series of trials at 44 sites that were conducted during 2006/07. Foundation learning combined subject or vocational learning with **functional skills** and personal and social development. It was one of the four learning suites for students, the others being: **General Certificate of Secondary Education**; **apprenticeships**; and, **diploma[s]**. It replaced **Entry to Employment**.

Further reading: www.qcda.gov.uk/

FOUNDATION MODERN APPRENTICESHIPS

See: Modern Apprenticeships – Foundation

FOUNDATION SCHOOL

Established under the School Standards and Framework Act 1998 and replacing grant maintained schools, a foundation school is one that has charitable status, owns its own buildings, employs its own staff, decides admissions policy and receives funding from the **local education authority**. It has a greater degree of self-governance than a **community school** and has a governing body with representatives from five groups: parents, school staff, local education authority, the community, foundation or partnership governors; and, there is also a sixth optional group—its sponsors. It is different from an **academy** where the funding comes directly from central government.

FRAMEWORK FOR HIGHER EDUCATION QUALIFICATIONS

This was the higher education equivalent to the **Qualifications and Credit Framework**, and approximately aligned with levels 4–8 on the QCF. There were five levels: certificate level – certificates of higher education; intermediate level – foundation degrees, ordinary bachelor's degrees, diplomas; honours level – bachelor's degrees with honours, graduate certificates, graduate diplomas; masters level – taught and research master's degrees; doctorate level – PhD, DPhil, etc.

FRAMEWORK FOR REGIONAL EMPLOYMENT AND SKILLS ACTION

(2002) The framework was a joint initiative by the **Department of Trade and Industry**, the **Department for Education and Skills**, and the **Department for Work and Pensions**. It was based on a dependable labour market and good skills information, and it provided a single action plan to match skilled people to good quality jobs. Originally called Regional Employment Action Plans, work on the frameworks was carried out between October 2000 and February 2001. The frameworks were to be in place by October 2002 in order to link with the reviews of Regional Economic Strategies. To oversee the development, implementation and monitoring of the FRESAs, Regional Employment and Skills Forums were established by each Regional Development Agency. Each forum was chaired by the RDA and had core representation from the **Learning and Skills Council**, **Employment Service**, local authorities, the Government Office, TUC and CBI, together with other representatives as agreed locally. It built upon and replaced the Skills Action Plan and has a nationally agreed core and is flexible enough to match regional needs. Its emphasis is on outcomes, actions and impact, and it describes the contribution of all parties. It also addressed short-, medium-, and long-term issues to ensure that plans are coordinated and coherent.

Further reading: Regional Development Agency National Coordination Unit (2002)

FREE CHURCH SCHOOLS

Following the Disruption (1843) and the establishment of the Free Church of Scotland, the Free Church schools were established. They were supported by local subscriptions and the teachers were paid from the Teachers' Sustentation Fund provided by the Education Committee of the Assembly of the Free Church. Where a school was not connected with a Free Church of the district, for example Glasgow's 'East Gorbals Territorial' School, it was funded by general subscriptions.

See also: Burgh Schools; General Assembly Schools; Sessional Schools

FREE FEEDING SCHOOL

(*c*.1872) Mr Kennedy's HMI report described the need for a type of school that provided sustenance for poor children and that existed between free schools and the certified **industrial** or **reformatory schools**. He described how one such school was established in Manchester by Mr Charlewood, a benevolent solicitor (Minutes 1872–73 p. 104).

FREE FORWARD FARES SCHEME

(1981–95) Designed to help people who did not qualify for the **Employment Transfer Scheme (ETS)** with travel costs so that they were able to take up employment. The scheme was operated predominantly within the **Job Transfer Scheme** in areas of pit closure. It was replaced by the **Travel to Interview Scheme**.

Further reading: Bryson (1996)

FREE PLACE EXAMINATION

During the early twentieth century, many local authorities began to introduce free secondary school places, after compulsory educational attendance, based on the passing of an examination. This examination was normally a written examination in English and arithmetic, although some local authorities also had an oral examination and sometimes a reading examination (Hadow, 1926 p. 133). It subsequently became extended and the **Board of Education** reported (1926–27 p. 26): 'The successes in the first school examinations of free pupils, as compared with fee-paying pupils are very striking. Taking the pupils who had left secondary schools in England and Wales after the age of 12 in the year 1926–27, we find that, whereas only 19.8 per cent of the fee-paying pupils had obtained the **school certificate** before leaving, 48.1 per cent of the free pupils had done so'. This examination was a forerunner of the **11+ examination**.

FREE SCHOOLS

These were schools for which pupils paid no fees, although they might make a small contribution for expenses, for example to provide fuel for heating. The cost of the free school was frequently supported by bequests etc.: for example, the Free School for Boys, Banff, was established in 1815 by funds left by Mr Pirie, and 'intrusted [sic] to the management of the magistrates, minister, and kirk session of Banff' (Minutes 1841–42 p. 146). Free schools were also known as **ragged schools** (Minutes, 1851–52, p. 75). The statutory provision of free schooling was introduced by the Elementary Education Act 1891. In the autumn of 1918, Sheffield became the first authority to provide free secondary schools (Report 1926–27 p. 25).

FRESHSTART

This voluntary programme was designed to support ex-offenders to re-enter the community through a guarantee of a pre-arranged **jobseeker's allowance** interview within three days of release from custody and early entry to a **New Deal** programme.

FROEBEL SOCIETY

(1874) Friedrich Froebel (1782–1852) developed a number of practices and principles to encourage the development of young children and established a **kindergarten** for children in 1837. Previously he studied and worked at a school run on the **Pestalozzi** method in Yverdon, Switzerland, and was influenced by the practices used there. The Prussian Government closed the kindergartens in 1851, causing many teachers to leave

and establish kindergartens in other countries, for example in London. At the first **educational exhibition** in 1854, Froebel gifts (educational toys including blocks) were demonstrated by Herr Hoffman. 'The grand feature of the system is "occupation". The child is taught little; it simply produces for itself. It has toys given to it of the simplest sort; bits of sticks or peas soaked in water. It is shown how to use them, and becomes an architect and an inventor' (Minutes 1854–55 p. 473). Froebel gifts were sequenced for development: first gift (a ball on a string), second gift, etc. (Minutes 1855–56 p. 314). Froebel's philosophy was adopted widely and one of the first schools to use the principles was St Mark's, Lakenham (Minutes 1855–56 p. 314). The Froebel Society was established in 1874 and, subsequently, in 1892, the Froebel Educational Institute was founded following a proposal by Julia Salis Schwabe for a training college including a demonstration school. The 1892 **Code** allowed those with an Elementary or Advanced Certificate from the national Froebel Union to practice as assistant teachers in infant schools. The training college moved to Roehampton in 1922 and later became part of Roehampton University.

Further reading: Weston (2000); Weston (2002); http://www.froebel.org.uk/

FROM LEARNING TO EARNING

This scheme is designed to modernise education and training facilities for prisoners with the purpose of reducing re-offending and increasing employment opportunities.

See also: Prisoners Learning and Skills Unit

Further reading: DfES Departmental Report 2003 p. 40

FUNCTIONAL SKILLS

In autumn 2005 generic definitions of functional skills were agreed and the **Qualifications** and **Curriculum Authority** began consultations in February 2006. A pilot began in September 2007 and the revised GCSEs were scheduled for September 2010. The Tomlinson review of 14 to 19 learning in England concluded that new tests of 'functional' numeracy and literacy were needed because **key skills** had not achieved their purpose and this led to the White Paper *14–19 Education and Skills 2005*. A definition is: 'Functional skills are those core elements of English, maths and ICT that provide an individual with the essential knowledge, skills and understanding that will enable them to operate confidently, effectively and independently in life and at work. Individuals of whatever age who possess these skills will be able to participate and progress in education, training and employment as well as develop and secure the broader range of aptitudes, attitudes and behaviours that will enable them to make a positive contribution to the communities in which they live and work'. Functional skills were available as a stand alone qualification or as part of other qualifications such as GCSEs.

http://www.qcda.gov.uk (accessed 1 June 2010)

See also: Progression Pathways

FUNDING AGENCY FOR SCHOOLS

(1 April 1994–1 November 1999) This was established under the Education Act 1993 and its purpose was to monitor and provide funding to grant maintained schools in a similar way to the **Further Education Funding Council for England** and the **Higher Education Funding Council**. It was abolished as a result of the School Standards and Framework Act 1998.

FURTHER ASSESSMENT

This was an initiative within **Employment training**, which catered for the long-term unemployed who were unsure of what they wanted to do. It allowed them the opportunity

to 'taste' and experience different types of occupational training before making a firm commitment. It also allowed those who were reasonably clear about their employment aims but who were considering a radical change of career to discover, first, whether they had an aptitude for the desired occupation.

See also: Initial Training

Further reading: Clemens et al. (1991)

FURTHER EDUCATION

Further education was formally recognised with a change in title from 'Regulations for **Evening Schools**, Technical Institutions, and **Schools of Art** and Art Classes' to 'Regulations for Technical Schools, Schools of Art, and other Schools and Classes (Day and Evening) for Further Education' (Report 1905–06 p. 74). The **Board of Education** also reported that '[t]here has been marked activity in the establishment of courses of instruction affording special technical training, and the effective character of the many courses organised under varied conditions shows that local circumstances have received the consideration necessary for success in this kind of educational work. Technical institutions affording whole-time training for those who can give two or more years to study after completing a **secondary school** course, have improved and multiplied their courses of instruction, and many **local education authorities** have arranged corresponding courses of lower grade to meet the needs of those whose previous general school course, like their subsequent work in trades, manufactures or commerce, is of lower standard … The improved organisation of the very varied institutions engaged in supplementing the training which a youth receives in the office or workshop, has borne fruit in many practical developments, demonstrating the extent to which further education may become a recognised element in the lives of the younger members of the community' (Report 1905–06 p. 73). The Further and

Higher Education Act 1992 removed responsibility for FE colleges from local education authorities and transferred this to the **Further Education Funding Council**. The FEFC was replaced by the **Learning and Skills Council**, which was than replaced by **Skills Funding Agency**, **Young People's Learning Agency** and **National Apprenticeship Service**.

See also: Colleges of further Education

FURTHER EDUCATION ACCESS FUNDS

These were funds allocated by the **Department for Education and Employment** through the **Further Education Funding Council**. The funds were part of the Government's 'Widening Participation' agenda and were provided by colleges to individuals who had financial difficulties in entering or continuing further education. Payments were made for transport, equipment, accommodation, materials and childcare.

Further reading: DfEE Departmental Report 1998–99 p. 54

FURTHER EDUCATION AND TRAINING SCHEME

(April 1942) This initiative provided grants to men and women to enable them to obtain further education and training beyond secondary school standard, which war-time service, including civilian work of national importance, had interrupted or prevented. It was modified in 1947 to be more selective in terms of entry.

Further reading: Ministry of Labour and National Service Report 1947 Cmd 7559 p. 88

FURTHER EDUCATION CENTRE (SCOTLAND)

This was an institution that provided further education and was not a central institution, teachers' training college or university.

FURTHER EDUCATION COLLEGES

FE colleges provide a major proportion of post–16 education and skills.

Further reading: Ainley (1988)

FURTHER EDUCATION COMPETITIVENESS FUND

(1995/96) This fund was administered through the **Employment Department** and enabled **Training and Enterprise Councils** to equip FE colleges to help respond to the needs of the local labour market. A total of £31m was allocated to this and the **Further Education Development Fund**.

Further reading: Hughes (1996)

FURTHER EDUCATION DEVELOPMENT AGENCY

(1995–October 2000) FEDA was formed out of the **Further Education Unit** and the **Further Education Staff College**. It was replaced by the **Learning and Skills Development Agency** in November 2000.

FURTHER EDUCATION DEVELOPMENT FUND

(1995/96) Administered through the **Employment Department**, this fund enabled **Training and Enterprise Councils** to provide support for activities in the local area at FE level. It ran in parallel with the **Further Education Competitiveness Fund**.

Further reading: Hughes (1996)

FURTHER EDUCATION FUNDING COUNCIL FOR ENGLAND

(1992 – 31 March 2001) The FEFC was statutorily required to secure the provision of 'sufficient facilities for the full time education of 16–18 year olds; adequate facilities for the part-time education of those over 16, and for full time education of those over 18, where

111

such education falls within Schedule 2 of the Further and Higher Education Act 1992'. The FEFC took over this responsibility from the local education authorities, but it was disbanded on 31 March 2001 and its functions were incorporated within the **Learning and Skills Council**.

Further reading: Further Education Funding Council (1992)

FURTHER EDUCATION FUNDING COUNCIL FOR WALES

(1992–31 March 2001) This was established in 1992 as a non-departmental public body of the Welsh Office and on 1 July 1999 became an Assembly sponsored body. It was responsible for funding and overseeing further education in Wales and, following the Learning and Skills Act 2000, these responsibilities passed to the **National Council for Education and Training for Wales** on 1 April 2001.

FURTHER EDUCATION NATIONAL TRAINING ORGANISATION

This **national training organisation** promoted teaching and training standards for those involved with teaching in post-16 and **further education**. Competence-based standards were developed in 1999. In 2000, it was initially funded by the **Department for Education and Skills** and, subsequently, its responsibilities were transferred to the **Standards Verification Agency** in January 2005.

FURTHER EDUCATION STAFF COLLEGE

(1960–1995) Founded at Combe Lodge, Blagdon near Bristol, the FESC was responsible for the development of staff working in further education colleges. In 1995, it merged with the **Further Education Unit** to form the **Further Education Development Agency**.

FURTHER EDUCATION UNIT

(1977–95) The FEU was a development agency that addressed curriculum issues in further education. In 1995, it merged with the **Further Education Staff College** to form the **Further Education Development Agency** (FEDA).

FUTURE JOBS FUND

Announced in the 2009 Budget, the monies attached to this British challenge fund were to be spent between October 2009 and March 2011. The fund was managed by the **Department for Work and Pensions** in partnership with a number of other agencies and its objective was to create 170,000 new jobs among 18- to 24-year-olds who had been out of work for almost a year. It acknowledged that those people who had been out of work for this period or longer had a greater chance of remaining long-term unemployed unless there was some intervention. The Future Jobs Fund was part of the **Young Person's Guarantee**.

Further reading: http://campaigns.dwp.gov.uk/campaigns/futurejobsfund/index.asp

FUTURE SKILLS WALES

Future Skills Wales originally began as a research project in 1998 to identify and establish current and future generic skills. This work was continued when the Future Skills Wales Unit was established in June 2000 and was incorporated within the **Learning and Skills Observatory for Wales**.

Further reading: http://www.learningobservatory.com/future-skills-wales/

G

GALLERY LESSON

This was a lesson given by the schoolmaster and occasionally schoolmistress from a gallery overlooking all the children in the schoolroom. It was then repeated by monitors and **pupil-teachers** to smaller groups of children. It was considered by the inspector to be a test of a future teacher's ability.

See also: Simultaneous Method

Further reading: Report 1860–61 p. 279

GARDEN FESTIVAL

The garden festivals, for example in Liverpool, Gateshead, Ebbw Vale and the Potteries, were designed to help in the regeneration of areas arising from inner-city riots in the early 1980s. For example, in support of this, a £4m job training initiative was launched in Gateshead to enable people to receive training, achieve qualifications and obtain permanent work after the festival closed. Training occurred in areas ranging from gardening to steam engine maintenance. Assessment was carried out by City and Guilds, RSA and the Hotel and Catering Industry Training Board. Many of the people employed were on the **Community Programme** or in **employment training**.

See also: Heseltine Initiatives; Industrial Training Boards

Further reading: Employment Gazette June 1990 p. 325; Jessop (1989)

(COTTAGE) GARDENING

(1897) Gardening as a school subject was introduced in some schools during the 1840s and 1850s (Report 1870–71 p. 127) and many schools had an area of land in which vegetables were grown and, sometimes, on which livestock were raised. The produce was sometimes sold to support the school, while on other occasions the scholars kept the proceeds. Gradually, however, the practice declined until it once again became more popular in the 1890s and the practical instructions to HM Inspectors explained that '[c]ottage gardening is the practical or experimental side of agriculture or horticulture in small holdings, and may be taken with either of those subjects. The main object of a school garden is not putting boys as apprentices to the gardener's craft. There are two ways of setting boys to work at gardening. They may either cultivate a plot in common, or each boy may be provided with a plot of his own. Each plan has its special advantages. Some boys, no doubt, who learn gardening will become gardeners in a professional way when they grow older, but as a school subject it would be wholly out of place unless it served a general purpose as well as this merely technical aid. The lessons in elementary science which are given in the schoolroom may be illustrated by practical work in the garden beds, and then the science will escape being mere book learning, and the gardening will be far more than technical training' (Report 1896–97 p. 511). Grants were provided for the teaching of cottage gardening from 1897. During the First World War, school gardens, using vacant allotments and gardens near schools, were encouraged to increase the supply of food with 40 acres worked in County Durham and 349 new school gardens in the West Riding (Report 1916–17 p. 30).

See also: Farm School; Home Occupations and Industries; Horticulture; Industrial Garden

GARTSHERRIE SCHOOLS

These were schools established in Scotland by the Baird family for use by the communities where they had their iron mines and factories. The Gartsherrie School of Science, Coatbridge, was founded in 1867 as a technical school.

See also: Factory Schools

Further reading: Anderson (1995)

GATEWAYS TO LEARNING INITIATIVE

(1993–1995) The Gateways to Learning Initiative funded 58 **training and enterprise councils** to develop adult careers guidance networks and help 70,000 individuals to produce action plans for their future employment. In collaboration with other providers it aimed to improve: awareness, take-up of assessment, guidance, advice, learning opportunities and accessibility. A guidance voucher system was used to encourage the choice for the consumer.

Further reading: Employment Department (1992c)

GENERAL ASSEMBLY SCHOOLS

These were schools established and supervised by the General Assembly of the Church of Scotland during the mid-1800s. They were funded by parish collections, subscriptions, and individual donations (Report 1866–67 p. liii).

See also: Sessional Schools; Burgh Schools; Free Church Schools

GENERAL CERTIFICATE OF EDUCATION

(1951–1987) The **School Certificate** was replaced by the GCE ordinary level in 1951. It consisted of two levels of qualifications: **ordinary levels** (O levels) normally taken at 16 years old; and **advanced levels** (A levels) normally taken at 18 years old. The O levels were subsequently merged with the **Certificate of Secondary Education** and replaced by the **General Certificate of Secondary Education**, where the results gave more consideration towards course work counting as a percentage of the final result.

See also: Key Stages 4 and 5

Further reading: School Examinations and Assessment Council (1990)

GENERAL CERTIFICATE OF SECONDARY EDUCATION

(September 1986, first examinations summer 1988) The **Certificate of Secondary Education** and the **General Certificate of Education** were merged to form a single examination system at 16+. Compared to the GCE, the GCSE had a larger element of work throughout the period of study, representing a move away from memory and recall towards process skills and a more practically based examination.

See also: 16+ Examination; First Examination

Further reading: Hitchcock (1988); School Examinations and Assessment Council (1990)

(APPLIED) GENERAL CERTIFICATE OF SECONDARY EDUCATION

Dating from 2002, when they were originally called Vocational GCSEs, applied GCSEs were made available in: applied art and design; applied business; applied ICT; applied science; engineering; health and social care; leisure and tourism; and manufacturing, and were equivalent to two GCSEs. They were designed to relate to vocational areas and to be of a practical nature that enabled students to learn by doing. They were predominantly assessed through coursework.

See also: (Vocational) General Certificate of Secondary Education

(INTERNATIONAL) GENERAL CERTIFICATE OF SECONDARY EDUCATION

(1985) The IGCSE was established by the University of Cambridge Local Examinations Syndicate (from 1998 called Cambridge International Examinations and Oxford, Cambridge, RSA Examinations) to provide a secondary school examination for pupils overseas. It was examination based, in comparison to the examination and course work assessment provided with GCSEs. Also, it proved attractive to some UK independent schools because it was believed to extend the more able students and provide a more appropriate preparation for **advanced levels**.

(VOCATIONAL) GENERAL CERTIFICATE OF SECONDARY EDUCATION

(Announced in January 2001 and commenced in September 2002) There were eight Vocational GCSE subjects that were offered: art and design; applied business; engineering; health and social care; applied information and communication technology; leisure and tourism; manufacturing; and applied science. Students produced a portfolio of work that was internally assessed and externally moderated (70 per cent of the marks). Knowledge and understanding were tested through external examinations (30 per cent). They were assessed in the same manner as ordinary GCSEs using the A$\star$–G grading system. They consisted of three units and were the equivalent of two GCSEs (double

award). They also could be taken alongside traditional academic GCSEs. They were subsequently named 'Applied GCSEs'.

See also: (Applied) General Certificate of Secondary Education; Increased Flexibility for 14- to 16-year-Olds Programme

Further reading: Qualifications and Curriculum Authority (2002); www.edexcel.org.uk

GENERAL NATIONAL VOCATIONAL QUALIFICATION

(Announced 1991) They were originally announced in the White Paper *Education and Training in the 21st Century* in 1991 and described as an alternative to GCE/GCSE examinations and the job specific **national vocational qualifications (NVQs).** Their purpose was to develop skills and knowledge in vocational areas such as social care, leisure and tourism, and business. The standard was later raised to include three levels: Advanced (Level 3), Intermediate (Level 2), and Foundation (Level 1), with grades at distinction, merit and pass. The **Advanced Vocational Certificate of Education** replaced advanced GNVQs in September 2000. Foundation, Intermediate and Part One GNVQs were replaced by Vocational GCSEs from September 2002.

General National Vocational Qualification – Part One was piloted in 1995 and 1996 and was designed to broaden the choices available, and to provide clear routes for 14–16-year-olds to progress to further education, training or employment. It was piloted in a number of schools in the subjects of business, health and social care, and manufacturing. The last award for GNVQ Part 1 was 2004, after which it was superseded by an **applied GCSEs** double award. The last entry to GNVQs was in 2005 and it was discontinued from October 2007.

See also: Diploma of Vocational Education; (Vocational) General Certificate of Secondary Education

Further reading: Whitear (1995); DfEE (1996a)

GENERAL TEACHING COUNCIL FOR ENGLAND

(1 September 2000) Established following the Teaching and Higher Education Act 1998, the General Teaching Council for England was required:

- 'to contribute to improving standards of teaching and the quality of learning;
- [and] to maintain and improve standards of professional conduct among teachers, in the interests of the public'.
  www.gtce.org.uk/gtc/what_the_gtc_does/ history/ (accessed 04 April 2010)

It also maintained a register of teachers and provided advice to government and other agencies. The council consisted of 64 members drawn from the teaching profession; trades unions; organisations connected with teaching; and, public appointments.

See also: General Teaching Council for Northern Ireland / Scotland / Wales; (Royal) College of Preceptors

Further reading: Willis (2005); www.gtce.org. uk (accessed 01 June 2010)

GENERAL TEACHING COUNCIL FOR NORTHERN IRELAND

(October 2002) The GTCNI was established under the Education (Northern Ireland) Order 1998 and its purpose was to raise the status of teaching and maintain standards through a register of teachers. The council's stated objectives were:

- 'To build a broad "professional community" and enhance the status of teaching as a profession.
- To provide an independent and authoritative voice for the profession on matters pertaining to teaching.

- To promote and maintain the highest standards of professional conduct and practice in collaboration with key partners'.
  http://www.gtcni.org.uk

See also: General Teaching Council for England / Scotland / Wales; (Royal) College of Preceptors

GENERAL TEACHING COUNCIL FOR SCOTLAND

(1965) The GTCS was legislated by the Teaching Council (Scotland) Act 1965, which stipulated that it was '[a]n Act to provide for the establishment in Scotland of a Teaching Council; to provide for the registration of teachers, for regulating their professional training and for canceling registration in cases of misconduct'.

www.england-legislation.hmso.gov.uk/Revised Statutes/Acts/ukpga/1965/cukpga_19650019 _en_1 (accessed 04 April 2010)

This was amended by the Teaching and Higher Education Act 1998. The council was established to address concerns that standards had declined since the Second World War and that unqualified teachers were working in maintained schools. The council stated that its objectives were:

- 'to contribute to the development of a world-class educational system in Scotland;
- to maintain and [to] enhance professional standards in schools and colleges in collaboration with partners;
- to be recognised as an advocate for the teaching profession'.
  http://www.gtcs.org.uk/About_GTCS/ Council/co-option_role_commitment_ required.aspx (accessed 04 April 2010)

See also: General Teaching Council for England / Northern Ireland / Wales; (Royal) College of Preceptors; Teachers Associations

Further reading: Willis, (2005)

GENERAL TEACHING COUNCIL FOR WALES

(1 September 2000) The General Teaching Council for Wales (Cyngor Addysgu Cyffredinol Cymru) was established in 2000 and was statutorily empowered by the Teaching and Higher Education Act 1998, which required every qualified teacher in Welsh-maintained schools to register with the council. Its main aims were:

- 'to contribute to improving standards of teaching and the quality of learning;
- 'to maintain and improve standards of professional conduct amongst teachers'; and,
- 'to provide an independent voice for teachers'.
    www.gtcw.org.uk/gtcw/index.php/en/the-council/about-us (accessed 04 April 2010)

See also: General Teaching Council for England / Northern Ireland / Scotland; (Royal) College of Preceptors

GENERAL TRANSFER SCHEME

The purpose of this scheme was to enable the filling of important vacancies where there was no suitable local labour. Workers were encourage to transfer from one part of the country to another. In 1952, a total of 3,034 people were assisted.

See also: Employed Key Workers Transfer Scheme; Free Forward Fares Scheme; Resettlement Transfer Scheme

Further reading: Ministry of Labour and National Service Report 1953, Cmnd. 9207, p. 53

GENERIC LEARNING

(2008) Generic learning is one component of the **Diploma**, the other two being **principal learning**, and **additional and/or specialist learning**. It consists of: **functional skills**;

personal, learning and thinking skills; a project; and ten days work experience. Generic learning is closely linked to principal learning.

Further reading: www.diploma-support.org/system/files/diploma-guide-ch05_1.pdf

GET READY FOR WORK

The Scottish, Get Ready for Work initiative was developed to enable 16- to 19-year-olds to choose a job, further education or college. It provided training in a number of employment skills, arranged work placements and gave a training allowance.

Further reading: www.scottish-enterprise.com/sds-getreadyforwork

GETTING STARTED

The Getting Started workshops were designed for new employers wishing to participate in volunteering. They ran throughout 1996–97.

Further reading: DfEE Departmental Report 1996 Cm3210 p. 124

GIRLS PUBLIC DAY SCHOOL TRUST

Originally founded in 1872 as the Girls Public Day School Company, it became the Girls Public Day School Trust Ltd in 1906 and the Girls Public Day School Trust in 1950. In the early days of these schools, the daughters of the professional and middle classes filled the gap in educational provision between that for poorer girls, who attended public elementary schools, and the daughters of the upper classes, who had governesses, masters, and private boarding schools. They were called public schools because they were not to be owned by one individual nor conducted for private gain.

See also: Dame Schools; Adventure Schools; Common Entrance Examination

GIVE SOMETHING BACK

(April 2007–March 2010) This was a **Life-long Learning UK** recruitment campaign aimed at encouraging practitioners in the private and public sectors to train as teachers, trainers and tutors in their vocational areas. It was run in collaboration with **Skills for Business** and successful applicants had the opportunity to undertake a five-day training course that led to the Preparing to Teach in the Lifelong Learning Sector course. It was one of four programmes set out in the 2006 White Paper *Further Education: Raising Skills, Improving Life Chances*, the others being: **Make a Difference**; **Business Talent,** and **Business Interchange**.

Further reading: www.lluk.org.uk

GLASGOW EDUCATIONAL ASSOCIATION

(1834) The association was formed in 1834 and was later known as the Glasgow Educational Society. Among the objectives of the association were the aims to promote education; to seek aid from parliament; and to establish a normal seminary to provide intellectual and moral training for schoolmasters. The sessional school of the Tron parish in Edinburgh was acknowledged as a model elementary school and was the 'germ of the **Normal school** system in Scotland' (Minutes, 1856–57 p. 806). Teachers from the highlands were placed in the school for a few months by the Education Committee of the Church of Scotland from 1826–1834. The original intention of the Glasgow Educational Association was to have four schools: infant, juvenile, commercial and female school of industry, although no later mention was made of the commercial school. The association, including David Stow, established the first normal college in Scotland at Dundas Vale, Glasgow, which opened on 31 October 1837 and was the first building specifically constructed for the training of male and female teachers together with a **practising school**.

See also: Stow, David

GLASGOW PHILOSOPHICAL SOCIETY

(1802) This society was established to encompass a wide range of subjects in industry and science. It was one of many **philosophical societies** and mutual improvement societies/**mutual instruction societies** that were established during the 1800s. It became the Royal Philosophical Society of Glasgow in 1901.

Further reading: www.royalphil.org

GLASGOW TRAINING SYSTEM

This was an approach developed by David Stow, a Scottish educationalist, who established his first model infant school in 1827 in Glasgow and in 1831 a juvenile **model school** was established that led to the establishment of the **Glasgow Educational Association**. In 1836 he laid the foundation stone for a **normal school** for training teachers, which operated a system of collective teaching in comparison to the divided instruction of the **monitorial system**. It was considered to be superior to those who had trained at Borough Road, London (see **Lancasterian school**). This was because training took a longer time and instead of just learning the 'mechanical routine' of teaching, participants could absorb the spirit and atmosphere of the institution. Intellectual, physical and moral training were encouraged by Stow, who produced eleven editions of his training system.

See also: Wesleyan Schools

Further reading: Minutes, 1847–48, Volume II, p. 331

GLOSSARY OF TRAINING TERMS

(First published in 1967) The increased interest in industrial training highlighted the ambiguity and confusion over terminology that created problems in communication. To alleviate this problem the **Ministry of Labour** produced a glossary of training terms. The definitions of the terms were discussed with the industrial training boards. It was updated later by the MSC.

Further reading: MSC (1985f)

GOVERNMENT SCHOOL OF DESIGN

See: School of Design

GOVERNMENT SCHOOL OF MINES

(1851) The mining districts in Britain encouraged the Government to provide education support and in 1851 the Government School of Mines was established at the Museum of Practical Geology in London. With the establishment of the **Science and Art Department**, this school was made the Central School of Science. Two laboratories were attached to the school, one for chemistry and the other for metallurgy with the former being absorbed into the Royal College of Chemistry. One branch of the school was called the 'Working Men's Division', which provided lectures on general science and practical interest. It was also known as the Metropolitan School of Science applied to Mining and the Arts; and as the Government School of Mines and Science applied to the Arts (Department of Science and Art Report 1854 p. xliv). In 1863 it became the Royal School of Mines.

See also: Colliery Schools; Mining Schools

GOVERNMENT TRAINING CENTRES

(1925) These centres replaced government instruction centres and initially offered a voluntary scheme funded by the **Ministry of Labour** to enable, mainly, men aged from 18 to 32 in the craft industries and engineering to receive specialist training. In 1945, there were 17 government training centres and

they changed attention to the resettlement of men and women whose careers had been disrupted by the war, and to training labour for reconstruction. A number of centres were specifically added for construction and by 1947 there were 80 centres operating. However, later in that year cuts in capital expenditure resulted in construction trades being restricted to disabled people and by 1962 there were only 13 centres remaining. As a result of the **Industrial Training Act 1964**, the training centres were increased from 19 in 1964 to 30 and were situated in the main industrial areas. They offered courses in approximately 40 different trades and developed practical skills and related theoretical knowledge. Most of the courses lasted six months and in some trades there was continued training with an employer and the Ministry paid the employer a small training fee. The centres were designed to be like a factory with similar hours, time-keeping and other routines. Numbers in class varied from eight to 16 and size was based on the danger of the trade, technical content, complexity of machines, etc. Instructors were selected based on their experience, supervisory ability and skill of imparting knowledge. The syllabus involved a progressive range of exercises, lectures, informal talks etc. GTCs were subsequently renamed **skillcentres**.

See also: Instructional Factories

Further reading: Hall (1972)

GOVERNMENT VOCATIONAL TRAINING SCHEME

(July 1945–1972) Vocational training provided by the Government began in 1917 when disabled ex-servicemen of the 1914–1918 War were trained in Instructional Factories. From 1924 to 1938, these factories were used to support young unemployed men in areas of high unemployment to develop skills. In the crisis before the Second World War, the focus was placed on training men and women for the munitions industry, particularly engineering. When the war broke out, all training not of direct relevance to the war effort was ended. The number of **government training centres** was increased from 16 in 1938 to 38 by the end of 1941, and double and even triple shift working was introduced. From August 1939 to July 1945, 420,000 people (including 150,000 women) received training that included shorter refresher courses for coal miners and service tradesmen. It was also designed to train apprentices/employees in key skills within industry. Training was minimal in the war years.

See also: Industrial Training Boards; Vocational Training Scheme

Further reading: Hall (1972); Ministry of Labour Gazette 1964 p. 196; Ministry of Education (1953)

(SCHOOL) GOVERNORS

Many voluntary schools and charity schools founded in the ninetenth century had boards of governors and this form of control was extended by the **Education Act 1944** Section 17 (p. 15): 'For every county school and every voluntary school there shall be an instrument [of management or instrument of government] providing for the constitution of the body of managers or governors of the school in accordance with the provisions of this Act'. The Education Reform Act 1988 further added to governors responsibilities with the local management of schools.

See also: School Managers

GRADES OF SCHOOL

During the early years of the 1900s, the secondary school system was lacking in cohesion and organisation, and to bring more coordination the **Board of Education** (Report 1908–09 p. 68) attempted to classify the various schools and placed them in grades. 'In a typical borough where the scheme of

provision of **evening schools** reaches its highest degree of development and organisation, there are to be found the following grades of school:

- Grade 1; *Continuation Schools*, providing instruction for boys and girls leaving the Public **Elementary Schools** at the age of 13 or 14. The normal course extends over two years and prepares for entry to –
- Grade 2; *Branch, Technical, Commercial, and Domestic Schools*, providing instruction suitable for young people who have passed through the course given by the Evening Schools of Grade 1, or for boys and girls leaving Higher Elementary Schools or Secondary Schools at the age of 15 or 16. The courses in schools of this grade are for two or three years and prepare for –
- Grade 3; *Central, Technical, Commercial, and Domestic Schools*, providing instruction of a still higher grade for more advanced students.'

GRADUATE APPRENTICESHIPS

Graduate apprenticeships were announced in the 1998 Green Paper *The Learning Age*, and seven pilots ran between 1998 and 2000. They were expanded and the first began on 5 January 2002. Their purpose was to enhance the employability of higher education students and graduates by combining an honours or post-graduate degree with work-based learning that was supported by **national vocational qualifications**, or **national occupational standards** and **key skills** units. GAs developed from a pilot run by the University of Luton that was designed to increase employability through training in work-based skills and work placement. Frameworks for the programmes were developed through national training organisations and subsequently **sector skills councils** and the award is delivered by the university.

Further reading: Centre for Developing and Evaluating Lifelong Learning (1999)

GRADUATE DEVELOPMENT PROGRAMME

(September 1991) This Northern Ireland programme was launched in September 1991 and all 250 places were filled. The 32-week programme provided integrated training, development and practical management experience. Successful completion of the programme gave participants a postgraduate qualification from Henley Distance Learning. It was subsequently replaced by **INTRO**.

See also: Premiere Graduate Management Development Programme

Further reading: Training and Employment Agency Annual Report 1992)

GRADUATE ENTERPRISE PROGRAMME

(1983–93) Piloted in 1983 in Stirling and then went national in 1984. GEP was designed for recent graduates who had qualified less than two years earlier. It was delivered in 10 universities and provided up to 12 weeks training to promote self-employment. It ended up as a part of **Training for Work** and then Option 3 of **Business Growth Training**. In Northern Ireland GEP was run by the **Training and Employment Agency** and it began two years after the mainland and was delivered by the Northern Ireland Small Business Institute.

Further reading: Brown and Myers (1990); Brown (1995)

GRADUATE GATEWAY PROGRAMME

Encouraged graduates to develop skills for setting up their own business and provided work experience.

Further reading: MSC (1987c)

GRADUATE TEACHER PROGRAMME

(1998) This was a school-based teacher training programme where a graduate learned to teach and also received a salary. It was funded by the **Teacher Training Agency** and supervised by a higher education institution.

GRADUATE TEACHERS

Teachers who graduated from university were entitled to teach in schools and the 1883 **Code** stated: 'Graduates of any university in the United Kingdom, women over 18 years who have passed university examinations recognised by the department, and persons who have passed the examination for admission to a training college, may be recognised as assistant teachers' (Report 1882–83 p. 117).

GRAMMAR SCHOOLS

Grammar schools or 'scholae grammaticales' became generally recognised from the fourteenth century, although they were in existence before then, They originally had a strong focus on Latin, resulting in a number of them being called Latin schools and many of the scholars later followed a profession in the church. This narrow curriculum became too restrictive and the Grammar School Act 1840 enabled the schools to use their income to broaden the curriculum beyond the emphasis on classical languages. Later, the **Education Act 1944** enabled **local education authorities** to create the **tripartite system** of secondary **technical schools**, **secondary modern schools** and grammar schools, entry to the latter being achieved by passing the **11+ examination**. During this period there were two types of grammar schools: 'maintained grammar schools', which received full state funding; and direct grant grammar schools, which received some funding from the state for state pupils and the rest from fee-paying students. In the 1960s, Circular 10/65 and the Education Act 1976 were designed to provide only **comprehensive education** and end grammar schools; however, the Education Act 1979 repealed this and allowed local education authorities to apply selective education, which continues to operate in some areas.

GRANT-MAINTAINED SCHOOLS

The Education Reform Act 1988 enabled grant maintained schools to receive their funding directly from the state rather than local education authorities. In 2000, they were replaced by **foundation schools**.

GRANTS – DEVELOPMENT AREA

Designed to promote craft and technician training in development areas. These were capital grants towards the cost of providing additional off-the-job training places and per capita grants to employers who took on additional trainees.

Further reading: Heriot-Watt University (1974); Ministry of Labour Gazette 1966 p. 316

GRANTS FOR EDUCATIONAL SUPPORT AND TRAINING

(1993–1998/99) A schools-based support fund that enabled them to buy 'capital equipment' such as computers and sports equipment. The grants were first made in 1993 and were then superseded by other forms of funding, mainly the **Standards Fund**, in 1998/99.

Further reading: DES (1990)

GRANTS FOR NATIONAL VOLUNTARY YOUTH ORGANISATIONS

The **Department for Education and Employment** provided grants for NVYOs to support programmes of personal and social education for young people especially those aged 13–19.

See also: National Youth Agency

Further reading: DfEE Departmental Report, Plans 2001–02 to 2003–04, Cm 5102

GRANTS – LOCAL CONSULTANCY

To enable small firms to purchase professional analysis of training needs and to enable them to meet emerging skill needs. Together with **grants – local training**, these offered a package of grant aid to firms, particularly to small firms to promote training amongst local employers. Consultancy grants offered contributory financial help in identifying training needs and considering appropriate solutions – they were a discretionary payment made direct to firms. It was then finally absorbed as part of Option 3 of **Business Growth Training**.

See also: Adult Training Strategy

Further reading: MSC (1986c) (1988a)

GRANTS – LOCAL TRAINING

Designed to help employers in small firms to improve performance, to manage change by providing training for employees, and to train recruits for hard-to-fill vacancies. There were around 9,400 grants awarded in 1986/ 87 for around 50,000 people. The grants were for £25 per day, per employee, for up to 40 days, and were for small firms with under 200 employees. Employers used them to 'test skills', rather than have a job interview and then have to dismiss the employee because they were not suitable for the work that they had been employed to do.

Further reading: MSC (1985i); Training Commission Annual Report 1987/88 p. 38

GRANTS – SANDWICH COURSE

(1968) The **Department of Employment** paid grants to employers who provided the first 52 weeks of industrial training for students following sandwich courses. This scheme was for a limited period and, having been in operation for the previous five years, it was deemed to be closed at the end of the 1969 educational year.

Further reading: Employment & Productivity Gazette 1968 p. 564; Ministry of Labour Gazette 1966 p. 826

GRANTS TO EMPLOYERS SCHEME

(1978) Was part of the umbrella scheme of the **Job Training Programme**. It was designed to offer employers £60–£80 per week per employee sent on approved courses in programming and systems analysis.

Further reading: MSC (1986b) (1988a); MSC Annual Report 1981/82 p. 19

GRANTS – TRAINING OF INDUSTRIAL TRAINING OFFICERS

(1964) Arising from the Industrial Training Act 1964, the Government emphasised the important role of training officers by paying half the cost of fees incurred by organisations sending training officers to approved full-time courses of four to eight weeks at **colleges of advanced technology** and **technical colleges**.

Further reading: Ministry of Labour Gazette 1964 p. 453

GREAT EXHIBITION

(1851) 'The Great Exhibition of the Works of Industry of all Nations' was held at Crystal Palace and organised by the **Royal Society of Arts** under the patronage of Prince Albert. Its purpose was to display '"material aids" to education, in an Educational Exhibition' (Minutes 1854–55 p. 315).

GROUP CERTIFICATE

This was a certificate endorsed by the **Board of Education**, which was awarded to scholars who had successfully completed a minimum of three years technical education in technical schools having followed a **grouped course**.

Further reading: Laurie (1912a)

GROUP TRAINING ASSOCIATION SCHEMES

This initiative represented the option to amalgamate the training needs of a number of small firms and was run under the auspices of **industrial training boards**. This grouping enabled cohorts of trainees to be formed on an economical basis, and for employers to have a closer involvement with how the training levy was spent.

See also: National Association of Training Groups

Further reading: Spandler (1991)

GROUPED COURSE

In the early 1900s pupils were allowed to choose their technical subjects, but this proved unsatisfactory for many, and so in Lancashire and Yorkshire a system of coordinated grouped courses was introduced that the pupils followed as a whole. This was then adopted by the **Board of Education** in 1910 and sometimes a **group certificate** was awarded.

GROWTH PROGRAMME

(1992) This Northern Ireland initiative targeted small businesses that had a good growth potential and helped owners/managers to plan competitive strategies. Training was delivered in structured interactive workshops, with peer group learning, and by in-company counselling.

Further reading: Training and Employment Agency Annual Report (1992)

GRUNDTVIG

This is a European lifelong learning programme to encourage partnerships and training opportunities for people and organisations involved with non-vocational adult learning. The other European lifelong learning programmes include **Comenius**, **Erasmus**, **Leonardo da Vinci** and **Transversal**.

Further reading: www.grundtvig.org.uk/; http://ec.europa.eu/education/lifelong-learning-programme/doc78_en.htm

GUARANTEE LIAISON OFFICER

This role involved making **youth training** more accessible to young disadvantaged people including the homeless. The Guarantee Liaison Officer acted as a 'last resort' for those who found it difficult to obtain a training place and who wanted to take advantage of the Government's guarantee of one.

Further reading: Working Brief (1990)

H

HADOW REPORTS

There were three reports: The Education of the Adolescent (Hadow, 1926); Primary Education (Hadow, 1931) and, Infant and Nursery Schools. They were produced by a committee chaired by Sir (William) Henry Hadow, vice-chancellor of the University of Sheffield. They made numerous recommendations, in particular the development of secondary education and the separation of **primary education** from secondary education.

HALF-TIME CHILDREN

This group of children were so named because of the **Factory Act** (7 Victoria, c. 15 amended by 13 & 14 Victoria, c. 54), or Half-time Act, which required them to attend school for two-and-a-half or three hours per day. This regulation was sometimes interpreted as attending school every other day. The schools that they attended were often called half-time schools (Report 1864–65 p. 178). Children aged between 8 and 13 employed in cotton mills had to attend school half-time; and on reaching 13 they are considered 'whole time'. In silk mills 'whole time' was as early as 11 years old. A mill owner was not legally allowed to employ a child unless it had a certificate of having attended school (Minutes 1852–53 p. 358). In rural districts half-time attendance linked to capitation grants was addressed: 'The Minute of 29 April 1854 remits eighty-eight days (one half) from the minimum period of attendance, not, however, absolutely, but in order that labour and instruction may be combined together for some regular plan … The managers of schools should be referred to the Minutes of 1854–55, page 121, and it should be pointed out to them that a system of rural half-time may be greatly facilitated by inducing the employers of boy-labour to adopt the practice of resorting to the managers of the parish school in the first instance for the supply' (Minutes 1855–56 p. 35). This practice gradually extended into other areas, including farming, that operated in Acton, and from 1856 in Tatton where Lord Egerton divided his boys into two groups who alternated weekly between morning and afternoon classes (Report 1860–61 p. 105). Attendance of half-time scholars was kept in a half-time register, if the scholar had presented a **labour certificate** from the local authority (**school board** or **school attendance committee**) (Report 1889–90 p. 195). The 1899 Act raised the minimum school leaving age to 12 although the half time provision continue until 1921 when the provisions of the Education Act 1918 came into force.

See also: Compulsory Education

HAND AND EYE TRAINING

(*c.*1890s) Various manual skills, or 'occupations', were encouraged in **kindergarten** and the **Board of Education** (Report 1910–11 p. 18) retrospectively described the introduction of the compulsory requirement for 'one suitable occupation' in the 1895 **Code** at **Standard[s]** I, II, and III 'as an important landmark in the history of **Elementary School** Curriculum'. The board also quoted a circular: 'So also as regards hand and eye training, it is to be much regretted that the ingenious and progressive kindergarten exercises for training scholars in deftness of hand and correctness of eye should be almost entirely discontinued after children leave the infants' school; and the more so when it is remembered that the mind itself is most effectively trained by such exercises, whenever they are the expression of the child's own thought'. The Circular described how hand and eye skills were promoted in **elementary schools** through **manual instruction** classes that developed physical skills and dexterity. Mr Legard, HM Inspector, noted that '[b]rush work and clay modelling are perhaps the occupations that are likely to be the most valuable to scholars in our own senior schools. In brush work the child is introduced to colour, and brought into immediate contact at an early age with the beauties of nature, and in clay modelling a knowledge and appreciation of form is gained such as cannot be acquired in drawing from the flat. … The universal testimony of the instructors at Leeds and Bradford is that the preliminary hand and eye training is exceedingly valuable to boys who take up manual instruction at a later stage' (Board of Education 1900–01 Vol. 2, p. 70).

HEAD TEACHER

This is the schoolmaster or schoolmistress who is in charge of a school. In one of the earlier mentions of head teacher in the Minutes of the Committee of Council on Education the HMI, Mr Moncrieff, stated that ' … time will be turned to far better account, if spent in careful supervision, than if frittered away in many fragmentary lessons. Every class should know well the master's voice, and feel that (morally) it was under the master's eye, and guided by the master's hand. But the power of the guiding hand and eye should be felt in the very fact that *his* system is harmoniously worked throughout the school, by other agencies besides his own' (Report 1861–62 p. 116).

HEADLAMP

(September 1995) HEADLAMP was established by the **Teacher Training Agency** to fund the training and development of those head teachers taking up a first appointment. Up to £2,500 was available over a period of two years from the date of appointment. Most of the funds had to be spent with trainers registered with the TTA and subject to OFSTED (**Office for Standards in Education**) quality inspection. The training plan, which had to be agreed between governors and the head teacher, focused on leadership and management tasks and abilities defined by the Teacher Training Agency.

Further reading: Teacher Training Agency (1994)

HEALTH AND MORALS OF APPRENTICES ACT 1802

(1802) This factory act of 1802 was titled 'An Act for the preservation of the health and morals of apprentices and others employed in cotton and other mills and cotton and other factories'. It specified that they should not work more than 12 hours per day; prohibited working at night; and, required that they receive education for the first four years of their apprenticeship.

See also: Indenture; Statute of Artificers 1563

HEALTH AND SAFETY COMMISSION

(1 October 1974) The Health and Safety at Work Act 1974 enabled the introduction of the Health and Safety Commission as a statutory body whose duties were to: inform, stimulate, guide and secure compliance from those

responsible for the safety of workers and of the public from industrial risks. The commission was appointed by the Secretary of State and reported to a number of different departments. It had a full-time chairman and eight representatives from trade unions, employers and local authorities. Its primary function was to make arrangements to secure the health and safety welfare of people at work, protect the public from risks arising from work activities, and control the keeping and use of explosive, highly flammable and other dangerous substances.

See also: Industrial Safety Training Centres

Further reading: Annual Reports and Accounts of the Health and Safety Commission; Health and Safety Commission (1993)

HEALTH AND SAFETY EXECUTIVE

The HSE assists and advises the **Health and Safety Commission** and is responsible for the enforcement of the Health and Safety at Work Act 1974. It is a statutory body consisting of a Director General and two other people appointed by the Health and Safety Commission. It advises the commission, and its staff are the primary instruments for carrying out the commission's policies.

Further reading: Health and Safety Commission (1993); www.hse.gov.uk

HEALTH AND SAFETY IN WORK-BASED TRAINING

With the implementation of Health and Safety legislation in the field of work-based training the **Health and Safety Executive** asked for health and safety training as the data collected on training injuries was growing in the early 1990s.

Further reading: Annual Reports and Accounts of Health and Safety Commission; Health and Safety Commission (1993); www.hse.gov.uk

HEDGE SCHOOLS (IRELAND)

The Penal Laws prohibited teaching by a Roman Catholic, with the result that many Irish people sent their children to hedge schools, which were often held outdoors or in barns. In 1826 a commission of inquiry reported that there were more than 400,000 pupils enrolled in hedge schools out of a school population of 550,000.

Further reading: Dowling (1935)

HER MAJESTY'S INSPECTORATE OF EDUCATION SCOTLAND

(April 2001) HMIe was established as an executive agency to raise standards and improve the quality of education in schools and colleges for children, young people and adults in Scotland.

See also: Estyn (Wales); Office for Standards in Education, Children's Services and Skills (England); Education and Training Inspectorate (Northern Ireland)

HER MAJESTY'S INSPECTORATE OF SCHOOLS

(1839) The Committee of the Privy Council on Education was established in 1839 and, in order to ensure that the aid it provided for schools was spent properly, it introduced a system of inspection with the appointment, in December, of the first two inspectors, Reverend W. Allen and Mr Tremenheere. 'The Committee recommend that no further grant be made now or hereafter, for the establishment or support of **Normal Schools**, or any other Schools, unless the right of inspection be retained, in order to secure a conformity to the regulations and discipline established in the several Schools' (Minutes 1839–40 viii). Also, they stated, 'The Inspectors will not interfere with the religious instruction, or discipline, or management of the school, it being their object to collect facts and information, and to report the result of their inspections to the Committee of the Council (Minutes 1839–40 p. 4). This light touch approach did not last and the powers of inspectors were progressively widened. Although the first grants by the **Lords of the Treasury** were contributions to the cost of constructing school buildings, subsequently, '**annual grants**' were awarded for pupils' attendance and performance under the 1862 Revised **Code**. Under this 'Code', children were only examined in reading, writing and arithmetic, which meant that other subjects, for example geography, history and grammar, were largely disregarded. To address this, the minute of 20 February 1867 was introduced to provide a financial premium for instruction in these 'higher subjects' (Report 1868–69 p. 145). During the 1860s there was a form of 'simple inspection', which was not as detailed as that required under the Revised Code. Simple inspection was undertaken for a number of reasons in three main types of schools: 'by request of the managers' for schools that did not receive grants but considered that inspection would be beneficial for the school; sometimes inspection was 'sought as the first step towards making a school good and obtaining grants, and here the inspector's duty is rather to advise than to criticise'; also, there were schools that had received a grant for buildings or annual grants in the past (Report 1865–66 p. 217). The **Elementary Education Act 1870** changed the denominational inspection of schools to one of district inspection. The 1890 Code specified that '[t]he term "Inspector" means one of the Inspectors of Schools appointed by Her Majesty on the recommendation of the Department, or any person employed by the Department as acting inspector, sub-inspector, or inspector's assistant, or any other inspector or returns, appointed under the Elementary Education Act, 1870, sec. 71. The term "Chief Inspector" means one of Her Majesty's Inspectors appointed to superintend the work of the other Inspectors in a certain division of England and Wales, or to inspect **Training Colleges**' (Report 1889–90

p. 117). In 1896 an experiment of appointing women as sub-inspectors of schools was considered a success (Report 1896–97 p. xvii), although the first was in 1883 with a Directress of Needlework (Report 1922–23 p. 26). The Education (Schools) Act 1992 resulted in the **Office for Standards in Education (OFSTED)** having responsibility for school inspection.

Further reading: McClure (2001)

HERIOT HOSPITAL SCHOOL

(1659) George Heriot (1563–1624) bequeathed funds that led to the establishment in 1628 of a **hospital school** in Edinburgh based on the blue-coat school in London. Through an Act of Parliament in 1836, twelve out-schools were also built and known as Heriot Hospital Schools

Further reading: Minutes 1855–56 p. 556

HESELTINE INITIATIVES

Named after Michael Heseltine, who initiated a review of inner cities following the riots in Brixton, Moss Side, Southall, St Paul's, and Toxteth during the period April 1980 to July 1981. A number of initiatives and regeneration strategies were initiated to address issues in inner cities including **garden festivals**.

Further reading: MSC (1981e)

HIBERNIAN SOCIETY FOR SOLDIERS' CHILDREN

(1765) This was established through public subscription in the parish of St Paul's, Dublin. Through support from the Crown and the Irish Parliament a hospital was established in Phoenix Park and the children were transferred there in 1770. It later became known as the Hibernian School, in 1812 as the Hibernian Military School, and in 1846 as the Royal Hibernian Military School.

(THE) HIGHER CERTIFICATE

(1925) The Higher Certificate, originally called the Day School Certificate (Higher), was introduced in Scotland in 1925 to replace the **Intermediate Certificate**. The Higher Certificate was awarded originally for the successful completion of a two- or sometimes three-year advanced division course with pupils leaving at about fifteen or sixteen.

See also: (The) Lower Certificate

Further reading: Report of the Committee of Council on Education in Scotland 1924–25 p. 9

HIGHER CLASS PUBLIC SCHOOL

(1872) Arising from the Education (Scotland) Act 1872, schools in Scotland that provided education in subjects beyond the elementary subjects of reading, writing and arithmetic might be considered a higher class public school. These subjects included: 'Latin, Greek, modern languages, mathematics, natural science and generally in the higher branches of knowledge' (Minutes 1872–73 p. cxli).

HIGHER COMMERCIAL SCHOOL

This was a higher grade school that gave emphasis to the commercial subjects found in the **specific subjects**.

Further reading: Laurie (1912a p. 92)

HIGHER EDUCATION

This term is commonly used for **universities** and degree awarding institutions, although, previously, when there was little public education, it meant what we now understand as **secondary schools**.

HIGHER EDUCATION ACADEMY

Announced January 2003 in the White Paper *The Future of Higher Education* and originally described as the Teaching Quality Academy. The HEA was formally launched in October 2004 and was designed to encourage the development of learning and teaching in higher education and the development of nationally recognised standards for higher education teachers. It was intended to provide a unified body incorporating the work of the **Institute for Learning and Teaching in Higher Education** and the Learning and Teaching Support Network.

Further reading: www.heacademy.ac.uk/

HIGHER EDUCATION AND BUSINESS – STRENGTHENING LINKS

(1998) Arising from the Dearing Report, a suite of development projects were launched in 1998 to equip graduates with skills needed in work and that addressed: 'key skills in higher education; recording achievement; work experience; guidance for graduates; high level lifelong learning; labour market intelligence in higher education; graduate business start ups; and, creativity in the curriculum' (DfEE Departmental Report 1998–99 Cm3910 p. 70).

HIGHER EDUCATION FUNDING COUNCIL FOR ENGLAND

This body replaced the Universities Funding Council and the Polytechnics and Colleges Funding Council. HEFCE was empowered to deal with the financial institutions of the English university system and to ensure that allocated funding was used under the stipulated terms and conditions. Funding councils for Wales and Scotland were established at the same time under the Further and Higher Education Act 1992.

Further reading: PCFC/UFC (1992); www.hefce.ac.uk

HIGHER EDUCATION INNOVATION FUND

This scheme was jointly funded by the DfES and the Office for Science and Technology, and delivered by the **Higher Education**

Funding Council for England. It was to help higher education institutions encourage innovation in the economy through the development of skills and knowledge transfer. HEIF was a third stream of funding in addition to teaching and research.

Further reading: DfES Departmental Report 2003, Cm 5902, p. 128

HIGHER EDUCATION QUALITY COUNCIL

Established in May 1992, 'The HEQC is responsible for undertaking academic quality audits of institutions of higher education in the whole of the United Kingdom. The scope of audit is wide, covering activities which are privately or publicly funded and including postgraduate provision, as well as degree and diploma programmes' (HEFCE 1994). It replaced the Academic Audit Unit (1989) introduced by the **Committee of Vice-Chancellors and Principals**. It was replaced by the **Quality Assurance Agency for Higher Education**.

See also: Higher Education Funding Council

HIGHER EDUCATION REGIONAL DEVELOPMENT FUND

This fund was provided through Government offices. It was designed to help higher education connect with employers, **training and enterprise councils** and other key partners to enhance local and regional competitiveness.

Further reading: DfEE Departmental Report 1998–99 Cm 3910 p. 70

HIGHER ELEMENTARY SCHOOLS

(6 April 1900) The 1900 **Code** established higher elementary schools into which children, between the ages of ten and fifteen years, who had passed Standard IV might then attend for four years. 'The Board issued a Minute, which was approved by Parliament, enabling the Board to recognise a new class of public elementary school termed "Higher Elementary Schools". In these schools will be given elementary instruction of a more advanced kind than has hitherto been possible under the Code, and their curriculum will be such as to embrace in the higher classes the work of the elementary course prescribed for **Schools of Science**' (Report 1899–1900 Vol. 1, p. 11). During the early 1900s the title of some of these schools was changed to **central schools** in which similar studies were conducted.

HIGHER GRADE SCHOOLS

Following the Education Act 1870, higher grade schools emerged out of the elementary school system as a means to provide more advanced instruction in **special** or **specific subjects** for the more able pupils beyond the **elementary subjects** of reading, writing and arithmetic.

The education lasted for three years and was for pupils in **Standard[s]** V–VII. Many of these schools were located in the upper departments of larger elementary schools (sometimes known as higher grade elementary schools); alternatively, Upper Standard schools were established and brought together children from a number of elementary schools. Grants from the **Science and Art Department** helped advance the growth of these schools and the Science and Art Directory stated, 'The object of the grant is to promote instruction in science, especially among the industrial classes' (Forsyth 1912, p. 82). However, the Cockerton judgement of 1901 stopped their development (Vlaeminke 2000).

See also: Evening Continuation School Code; Higher Elementary Schools

HIGHER NATIONAL CERTIFICATE/ DIPLOMA

See: Business and Technology Education Council

HIGHER NATIONAL CERTIFICATES

Arising from the introduction of **national certificates** in 1921, the Institution of Mechanical Engineers promoted them widely to employers, workmen and apprentices. 'The Institution has also decided to recognise a connection between higher national certificates and diplomas in Mechanical Engineering and the associate membership examination of the Institution. Holders of certificates and diplomas who become candidates for election as Students, Graduates, or Associate Members of the Institution, and are otherwise qualified, are exempted from such subjects of the Associate Membership Examination as in the opinion of the Council correspond to the subjects of the Final Examination named on the applicant's Higher Certificates, or Higher Diplomas' (Report 1924–25 p. 118). The **Business and Technology Education Council**'s higher national certificates are now awarded by Edexcel in England, Northern Ireland and Wales; and in Scotland it is called a higher national and is accredited by the **Scottish Qualifications Authority**.

See also: Higher National Diplomas

HIGHER NATIONAL DIPLOMAS

These diplomas had a similar history to **higher national certificates**, originating with the Institution of Mechanical Engineers in about 1921. It is a higher education qualification approximately equivalent to two years of degree-level study and this **Business and Technology Education Council** qualification is awarded by Edexcel.

HIGHER SCHOOL CERTIFICATE

(1917–1951) The Higher School Certificate was introduced by the Secondary School Examinations Council in 1917. It was awarded for those pupils who had stayed on at school until 18 years of age and had successfully taken the **Second Certificate** in England and Wales (Report 1929 p. 21). It was

replaced by the General Certificate in Education **advanced levels** in 1951.

Further reading: Board of Education Report 1943

HIGHER STANDARD ELEMENTARY SCHOOLS

These constituted the upper departments of large elementary schools in which children could study **specific subjects** at a more advanced level.

See also: Higher Grade Schools

HIGHER TECHNICAL NATIONAL TRAINING

HTNT was targeted at the supply of highly qualified people at professional or near professional level. It aimed to help remedy national high-level skill shortages and foster the creation of training partnerships with and between **training and enterprise councils**, employers and Institutes of Higher Education to address national skill shortfalls. It was part of **Employment training** and ran over the same period. There were three strands to the programme:

- the national courses programme linked to academic programmes;
- the experimental programme, designed at post-graduate level for leading edge technologies; and,
- the special groups programme recognising special groups in the labour market, the greater majority being in IT and engineering.

About 6,000 people per annum took this course.

Further reading: Makrotest (1991)

HIGHER TECHNICIANS SCHEME

(1945) Training scheme operated in the UK for Indian University Graduates with at least 3 years industrial experience.

See also: Overseas Nationals – Industrial Training for.

Further reading: Ministry of Labour and National Service (1948 p. 99) Cmd 7559

HIGHLAND SOCIETY SCHOOL

This school was established in 1727 in Glasgow. The objective of the Highland Society of Glasgow Schools was 'to give education, clothing, and trades to the children of poor Highlanders residing in Glasgow and the neighbourhood' (Minutes 1844 Vol. 2, p. 332).

HIGHLANDS AND ISLANDS ENTERPRISE

(1990) Created, together with Scottish Enterprise, by Enterprise and New Towns (Scotland) Act 1990. Both bodies had overall responsibility for training and enterprise programmes, as well as other duties. It worked through a network of 22 **local enterprise companies** (LECs)

Further reading: Highlands and Islands Enterprise (1993)

HIGHLANDS AND ISLANDS ENTERPRISE JOINT TRAINING GROUP

In 1982/83 the group provided 22 one- to three-day courses at 14 locations throughout the highlands and islands. They were attended by 307 people and covered such subjects as finance, stock control, sales, management, employment legislation and staff recruitment. The courses were originally aimed at small farmers, foresters and crofters, but subsequently expanded. Initially, all work was done on what were known as correspondence or distance learning courses.

Further reading: MSC Annual Report 1982/83 p. 28

HINDU SCHOOL

A Hindu faith school, Krishna-Avanti school at Harrow, London, first received state funding from 15 September 2008.

HOME AND COLONIAL INFANT SCHOOL SOCIETY

(February 1836) It was established by Charles Mayo and his sister Elizabeth Mayo to encourage the methods of Johann **Pestalozzi**, the Swiss education reformer who was a follower of the principles expounded by Jean-Jacques Rousseau. This was one of a number of **educational societies**/groups whose purpose was to encourage education.

'II. That its object be the improvement and general extension of the Infant School System, on Christian principles, as such principles are set forth and embodied in the doctrinal articles of the Church of England.
III. That with this view it proceeds –
To obtain individuals of character and piety, "apt to teach", and to qualify them by appropriate instruction for masters and mistresses.
To afford existing teachers the means of improvement, and to recommend them to schools as occasions offer.
To appoint inspectors to visit existing schools, and also places where schools may be required.
To circulate information on the Infant School system; to correspond with the friends of infant tuition in different parts of the world; to print and publish proper lessons; provide school materials, etc.' (Minutes 1842–43 p. 596).

HOME EDUCATION

The **Education Act 1944** Section 36 decreed that '[i]t shall be the duty of the parent of every child of compulsory school age to cause him to receive efficient, full-time education suitable to his age, ability and aptitude, either by regular attendance at school or otherwise'. And, Section 76 continued, ' … pupils are to be educated in accordance with the wishes of their parents'. In effect, these stipulations provided an option for the education at home of children by parents or other people.

See also: Home Lessons

HOME LESSONS

This was a term used to describe homework given by the school teacher. The report by Mr Bellairs, HMI, stated: 'These as a rule are not sufficiently encouraged. In many schools all the work is done in school. No preparation of lessons or written exercises. A good system of home lessons would considerably increase the progress of the children' (Report 1868–69 p. 32). The report by Mr Bowstead, HMI, stated: 'Home lessons deserve a passing notice. They are of the greatest value in keeping up the interest not only of the children but of the parents in their work, in giving them employment during the winter evenings, and (if the subjects are judiciously selected) in imparting a varied knowledge of facts and facility of composition to be otherwise acquired. I may mention that in the Red Cross Street British School at Bristol this system is pursued by Mr Reed with excellent results' (Report 1872–73 p. 47). In later years, the instructions to inspectors stated: 'The best teachers use such lessons rather to illustrate, and to fix in the memory, lessons which have already been explained in school, than to break new ground or to call for new mental effort. This purpose is best served by lessons of a very simple and definite character – a sum, a short poetical extract, a list of names or dates, a letter, an outline map, a parsing exercise, such as may readily be prepared in half an hour, and may admit of very easy testing and correction on the following day. When these conditions are fulfilled the home task is found to have a very valuable effect, not only in helping the progress of the scholar, and in encouraging the habit if application, but also in awakening, on the part of the parents, an interest in the school work' (Report 1889–90 p. 182). The term 'home lessons' would appear to have been replaced with 'home work' by 1909 (Report 1908–09 p. 76).

See also: Home Education

HOME OCCUPATIONS AND INDUSTRIES

This was a classification of subjects or divisions within a range of principal subjects provided within **evening schools** at the beginning of the 1900s. 'Home Occupations and Industries. The objects aimed at in the instruction given under this Division are: (1) to render the home as far as possible self-contained by enabling its inmates to undertake work that would otherwise have to be done outside at greater expense. The leading subjects in this category have been Domestic Economy, Cookery, Laundry Work, Needlework, and Dressmaking; (2) to encourage small home industries and thus add to the resources of the home. Basket-making, Gardening, Bee-keeping, Poultry-keeping and similar rural industries have formed subjects of instruction under this head' (Report 1903–04 pp. 62–63).

HOME TRAINING CENTRES

The scheme began operations on 3 January 1928 (Report 1928 p. 89). The first home training centre was established in Market Harborough. The home training was conducted by the Central Committee on Women's Training and Employment and funded by grants under the Empire Settlement Act 1922. Their initial purpose was to train women for employment overseas, particularly Australia, but the Depression largely removed this option and the main intention then became to train women as housewives or domestic servants.

Further reading: Field, 2009

HOMEWORK

See: Home Lessons

HONOUR CERTIFICATES

(1876) Under the Elementary Education Act 1876 children who had passed in reading, writing and arithmetic and had 350 half-day

133

attendances each year for the two previous years, in no more than two public elementary schools during the year, would be awarded an Honour Certificate and might be entitled to have their fees paid for the next three years by the Education Department.

Further reading: Report 1876–77 p. 257

HORTICULTURE

The subject of horticulture was included in the 1892 **Code** as a **specific subject** for teaching to children in the upper classes of **elementary schools**. Details of the syllabus were described in the report.

See also: (Cottage) Gardening

Further reading: Report 1891–92 pp. 140/180; Report 1891–92 p. 205

HOSPITAL SCHOOLS

The word 'hospital' is derived from the Latin 'hospes' relating to a visitor or host and did not always mean a place for the sick. The Greenwich Hospital School was established as a result of William and Mary's Royal Charter of 1694 specifying the support of seamen, their widows and the education of the children of seamen. In 1712, the first pupils went to Weston's Academy in Greenwich and the first school opened in 1715. In 1798 another school, the Royal Naval Endeavour was founded in Paddington, London, for the children of seamen who had died or been killed and injured. This was renamed the Royal Naval Asylum in 1805 and subsequently moved to Greenwich. The two schools merged in 1821 with the Asylum being the lower school and the Greenwich Royal Hospital School being the upper school. The girls' school was discontinued in 1841. The upper school consisted of two divisions with the higher part being the nautical school and the lower called the upper school (Report 1858–59 p. 423). In 1933 the school moved to Holbrook, near Ipswich,

and became known as the Royal Hospital School. There were other hospital schools including Preston Hospital in Shropshire (Report 1861–62 p. 89) and the **Heriot Hospital School**. By the 1930s the term hospital school meant a school associated with a hospital and ill children. 'On 31st March, 1930, there were still 56 Poor Law Schools educating 9,625 children. Of these, 28 were ordinary schools for normal healthy children, and 28 were Hospital Schools for invalids and convalescents' (Report 1931 p. 19).

HOUSES OF INDUSTRY

(1858) Numerous schools of industry or **industrial schools** were established in the mid-1800s, one such being the Female School of Industry at Eglington Ironworks. It was termed a Culinary and Industrial School and to put this learning into practice a house was organised near the school to provide 'ample and costly accommodation'. This house of industry contained a kitchen, washing house, laundry, dining room and lodging for the housekeeper. Meals were prepared for unmarried workmen, 'the institution not being meant to interfere with the domestic habits of the married class' (Minutes 1858–59 pp. 234–35).

HOUSES OF OCCUPATIONS

These were schools providing accommodation and training; for example, the **Royal Philanthropic Society** was established in 1788 and one of its main objectives was to care for the children of convicted felons and also those children who had been convicted for offences. The society established a house of occupations that contained accommodation and workshops to provide support for the children and to give them the skills to provide a living (Minutes 1848/49/50 p. 300). The Bridewell Royal Hospital in London apprenticed children from the late 1500s and built a new house of occupations in 1632.

HOUSES OF REFUGE

This term was used in a report by Reverend F. C. Cook, HMI, (Minutes 1856–57 p. 242). These institutions existed alongside **ragged schools** in the mid-nineteenth century to support destitute children and Reverend Cook described houses of refuge in connection with industrial schools for destitute children and **schools of industry**.

HOUSEWIFERY

See: (Practical) Housewifery

(PRACTICAL) HOUSEWIFERY

(1897) This subject was recognised as a subject of instruction in the 1897 **Code**. 'As it is a wide subject, requiring a thorough knowledge of the practical work of a house and its management, together with Elementary Hygiene and Physiology, it is necessary that the teacher should be well grounded in all these subjects. A practical class of Housewifery should not consist of more than 14 girls; the instruction given should comprise the usual school syllabus of Domestic Economy, together with the practical teaching of House Management. Housewifery should not be taken as a school subject unless practical teaching in Cookery and **laundry work** is included in the school curriculum. It is not intended that this teaching should resolve itself into a class for training children for domestic service, but it is intended to be a course of instruction to fit them on leaving school for the various household duties which devolve more or less upon all women' (Report 1896–97 p. 511).

(JUNIOR) HOUSEWIFERY SCHOOLS

During the 1920s, junior housewifery schools were described as providing 'Domestic and (at least for those under exemption age) General [education], in full-time courses extending at least till exemption age' for those aged '13 or 14 on admission' (Report 1925–26 p. 57).

HUMAN RESOURCE DEVELOPMENT (HRD) STRATEGY

(1988) The **Employment Department Group** developed a Human Resource Development Strategy with the objective of sustaining and increasing the effectiveness of each part of the ED Group. Its intention was to optimise the existing talent and future potential of each employee. Progress was measured through attitude surveys and annual reviews. Staff agreed developmental objectives with their line managers and special development programmes were provided for selected groups of graduate entrants and middle managers who were expected to reach senior management positions. Part of this strategy involved achievement of **Investors in People**.

Further reading: Employment Gazette 1988 pp. 42–44

HYGIENE

This subject was officially included in the school curriculum in the 1907 **Code** and followed previous guidance for personal health about food, drink, cleanliness and fresh air, and an outline scheme proposed by the Board of Education for hygiene and temperance (Report 1906–07 p. 33).

I

IMPROVING THE TRAINING MARKET

(1997) The objective of ITM was to support activities that improved the quality, impact and cost-effectiveness of the national training and vocational education systems. It complemented and provided a focus for action directed at the department's priorities for vocational education and training. Development was largely carried out through individual projects that were competed for by a wide range of external organisations including **TECs** and **LECs**. The budget for 1997–98 was £7m.

See also: Measures to Make the Training Market Work Better

Further reading: Department of Employment Departmental Report 1994 Cm 2505 p. 16

INCENTIVE TRAINING GRANTS

(1978) A short-term measure to counter rising unemployment among young people. Incentives were given for young people to train for vacancies at higher skill levels and £46m was made available for this purpose.

Further reading: MSC Annual Report 1977–78, p. 10

(THE) INCORPORATED SOCIETY

(1733) This was founded to promote the establishment, in Ireland, of English Protestant Schools. The Royal Charter, by George II, described its objectives as to provide instruction in English in 'the principles of true religion' to 'children of Popish and other poor natives' in subjects such as: husbandry, housewifery, trades and manual occupations (Fletcher, 1912 p. 73). Until 1803 only Roman Catholic children were educated in these charter schools and from this date other denominations were accepted. In 1825 they became exclusive to Protestants.

Further reading: Fletcher (1912 pp. 71–103)

INCREASED FLEXIBILITY FOR 14- TO 16-YEAR-OLDS PROGRAMME

(September 2002) This was an initial two-year £38m initiative to 'raise the attainment in national qualifications of participating students; increase their skills and knowledge; improve social learning and development; and increase retention in education and training after 16' (DfES Departmental Report 2003, Cm 5902, p. 103).

Part of this initiative was the introduction of **Vocational GCSE**s. In addition, approximately 273 local partnerships were established involving more than 2,000 secondary schools and largely involving FE colleges. Financial and other support for the partnerships was routed through the **Learning and Skills Council**. Government regional offices provided funding to involve employers in the programme. Students could also choose to take extended work experience with an employer that was longer than the conventional two-week experience undertaken by most **Key Stage** 4 students.

INDENTURE

With some apprenticeships there was a payment made to the craftsman. This sometimes caused some unscrupulous employers to take on the apprentice and then dispense with their services and also caused some less-committed apprentices to resign. To reduce the difficulties the parties signed a contract or indenture.

See also: Health and Morals of Apprentices Act (1802); Statute of Artificers 1563

Further reading: Minutes 1844 Vol. 2, p. 415

INDEPENDENT SCHOOLS

These are schools that operate entirely without public support and that receive their funding from fees and sometimes charitable funds. They are sometimes known as **public school[s]** or private schools.

INDIVIDUAL DEFERMENT

(January 1942) Replaced **block reservation** and was the system where men were individually reviewed for military service. Deferment was only granted for important war work.

See also: National Service

Further reading: Slack (1942)

INDIVIDUAL LEARNER RECORDS

(2002) These provided learning records and statistics on learners and were collected by the **Learning and Skills Council**. The ILR replaced the **individualised student record**, which had been introduced by the **Further Education Funding Council** in 1994. Also subsumed within the ILR was the

national trainee database, which contained work-based learning records that were previously collected by the DfES. From 2001, schools have submitted the Pupil Level Annual Schools Census (PLASC). Records for higher education were compiled by the Higher Education Statistical Agency.

See also: Labour Force Survey

INDIVIDUAL LEARNING ACCOUNTS

(1999/2000) A national framework of learning accounts to encourage people to save and plan for their learning development. It was intended to continue for 3 years. Funding for the programme was set at £150m of the **Training and Enterprise Council** resources to allow for up to one million accounts to be opened, of which around 847,000 would be in England. There were three main target groups for applicants:

- areas of skills shortages;
- people with low or no qualifications (NVQ Level 2 and below);
- employees in firms with 50 or fewer employees, plus those returning to the labour market.

As an incentive, 20 per cent discount could be claimed for any learning and up to 80 per cent for specific courses, the latter with a ceiling of £500. There were tax incentives for employers who contributed to employees' learning. This scheme was discontinued in November 2001 following evidence of 'potential fraud and abuse'.

Further reading: DfEE (1998d); DfEE(1999c); Scottish Executive (2000)

INDIVIDUAL PARTICIPATION PLAN

Participants on **Learning for Work** have individual participation plans that describe the content and duration of the course, and support, guidance and job search arrangements.

Further reading: Department of Employment Departmental Report 1994 Cm 2505 p. 15; Employment Department (1994a)

INDIVIDUALISED STUDENT RECORDS

(1994–2002) These were records and statistics kept on students by the **Further Education Funding Council**. They were superseded by **individual learner records**.

INDOOR/OUTDOOR CHILDREN

There were two types of children educated in **ragged schools**. Indoor meant that they had accommodation within the ragged school, and outdoor meant they were impoverished but lived at home (Report 1861–62 p. 473).

INDUSTRIAL DEVELOPMENT ACT

(19 August 1966) An act covering the majority of Scotland, Wales, Ministry of Labour Northern Region, Merseyside, and most of Cornwall and North Devon, where funding was available to encourage employers to relocate and use local labour. This act ended the 10 per cent plant and machinery grants that had been available since 1963; they were superseded by a 40 per cent grant for those employers who chose to move.

See also: Development Districts

Further reading: Ministry of Labour Gazette 1966 p. 568

INDUSTRIAL GARDEN

Many schools and **industrial schools** had an attached garden in which pupils could develop their horticultural skills. An account of Elsecar School Garden, Rotherham, describes how the gardens 'create and foster habits of industry, neatness, and order, as well as serving as the basis of some little theoretical teaching in agricultural chemistry' (Minutes 1856–57, p. 315).

See also: Farm Schools; Agricultural Schools; (Cottage) Gardening; Horticulture

INDUSTRIAL LANGUAGE TRAINING SERVICE

(1974–88) This service was operated by local education authorities and funded by the **Manpower Services Commission** from 1978 on a partial fee-recovery basis. The initial aim of this service was to enable ethnic minorities to develop their skills by providing English language training in the workplace. Communication skills and awareness training for managers and trade union officials in a multi-racial workplace was also available. Replaced by English for Speakers of Other Languages (ESOL).

See also: The National Centre for Industrial Language Training

Further reading: MSC (1986a); Nicod and Jackson (1985)

INDUSTRIAL REHABILITATION UNITS

(1943–73) The courses provided at IRUs were designed for adults who had completed medical treatment or had been unemployed for a long period. The courses were designed to provide special help to allow people to adapt mentally and physically to re-employment, or to choose a new job. Participants arrived weekly and courses normally ran for a period of between eight and twelve weeks. There was no set syllabus and case conferences designed courses around individual needs. A rehabilitation officer, a part-time doctor, an occupational psychologist, a social worker, a technician in charge of the workshops, and a disablement resettlement officer were all involved. Each unit consisted of seven workshop sections: machine operating, bench engineering, woodwork, assembly and other light work, commercial and clerical work, gardening, and heavy work (for example, laying concrete). The IRUs were designed to reproduce actual working conditions so that both physical and mental abilities could be accurately assessed before a return to work. The first IRU was set up at Egham in Surrey in 1944. By 1964 more than 20,000 had been trained there and altogether 134,000 passed through the units. IRUs were replaced by **employment rehabilitation centres** in 1973.

See also: Employment Rehabilitation Service and Remploy

Further reading: Department of Employment (1959); Ministry of Labour Gazette 1963 p. 486

INDUSTRIAL RELATIONS AND EUROPE DIRECTORATE

(November 1990) Part of the Employment Department's reorganisation effective from November 1990. It was one of three directorates set up within the **Employment Department Group**, and was responsible for industrial relations, pay and equal opportunities, European and International work, statistics, tourism, liaison with the **Health and Safety Executive**, the Employment Agency Licensing, and the Overseas Labour Section. It was replaced by the **Industrial Relations and International Directorate**.

Further reading: Department of Employment Report 1991 Cm 1506 p. 7

INDUSTRIAL RELATIONS AND INTERNATIONAL DIRECTORATE

(1991) IRID was established in 1991 as part of the **Employment Department**, with a wide remit to promote a competitive and efficient labour market. It was responsible for the administration of the Redundancy Payments Service, the Wages Council System, the Work Permits System and the **industrial tribunals**, as well as international policies, promoting the tourism industry and statistical services.

See also: Training, Enterprise and Education Directorate; Resources and Strategy Directorate.

Further reading: Department of Employment Report 1992 Cm 1906 p. 11

INDUSTRIAL RELATIONS TRAINING RESOURCE CENTRE

(1977) Set up internally by the **Manpower Services Commission**. Its first major work in 1977 was to conduct a survey of the industrial relations training needs of managers within the commission. Its main purpose was to support organisations to provide improved industrial relations training for managers.

Further reading: Industrial Relations Training Resource Centre (1980); MSC Annual Report 1977/78, p. 25.

INDUSTRIAL RESEARCH ASSOCIATIONS

In 1916, the Committee of the Privy Council for Scientific and Industrial Research provided grants to support the establishment of industrial research associations.

See also: Joint Industrial Councils

INDUSTRIAL SAFETY TRAINING CENTRES

(1951) The oldest and largest industrial safety training centre was established in Birmingham in 1951. It originally provided courses in the safe use of power presses and the range of courses was gradually extended.

See also: Health and Safety Commission

Further reading: Ministry of Labour Gazette 1962 p. 455

INDUSTRIAL SCHOOLS

Schools of industry based on the experience of M. de Fellenberg at Hofwyl, Switzerland, were encouraged by the **Committee of**

Council on Education during the 1830s and 1840s. The committee suggested that schools of industry for pauper children, large orphan schools, or military schools might be converted into industrial schools. The schools would consist of day-rooms, exercise-grounds, workshops, and sleeping-rooms. The workshops for the boys and the older pupil teachers were not intended to train them in a specific trade or craft but in 'industrious application', which would be beneficial in whatever labour a person might enter and also be of value in their personal lives. 'Thus a labourer who could repair his cottage, cultivate his garden with skill, who could repair his shoes and clothes, would be able to support his family in greater comfort; and if he could execute any rough carpenter's or smith's work, he would be more valuable to his employer, and would secure better wages' (Minutes 1839–40, p. 80). Also, 'The cultivation of a garden would afford an opportunity of instructing the boys in the management of manures and composts, in the rotation of garden crops, in pruning and grafting, and in the general management of a kitchen garden, (81) for this purpose a garden of sufficient extent should be attached to this department of the school' (Minutes 1839–40, pp. 80–81).

'The Girls' School of Industry – The oldest girls and female **pupil-teachers** would be employed in the several departments of the kitchen, the washhouse, the laundry, and the needle room. In the kitchen the girls would cook for the infants, boys, girls, and pupil-teachers. In the washhouse and laundry the clothes of the entire establishment (excepting those belongings to the sick-wards) would be cleansed, chiefly by the girls. In the needle-room the requisite sewing would be executed' (Minutes 1839–40, p. 81).

The early schools of industry for pauper children were established in Norwood, Manchester, Liverpool and Sheffield (Minutes, 1842–43 p. 279). They were sometimes called Industrial Training Schools, or, for example, Moral and Industrial Training

Schools of the Manchester Poor Law Union (1845, Volume 2, p. 302). They were sometimes known as schools of industry or **day schools of industry**. These industrial schools were often, as in the case of Sutcliffe Industrial School in Bath, 'for the reformation of juvenile offenders and of youths in imminent danger of becoming criminal' (Minutes 1854–55, p. 469). This industrial principle was also applied in 1807 in the Free School of Whitechaple where pupils worked in printing and earned a wage (Minutes 1854–55, p. 415). The children attending these schools were sometimes known as industrial scholars (Report 1858–59 p. 76). The Industrial Schools Act 1860 transferred responsibility for industrial schools from the Education Department to the Home Department. The Reformatory School (Scotland) Act 1854 allowed similar provision with funding coming from the Home Office alone. The terms industrial school and **ragged schools** were often used interchangeably. 'One proper object of schools of industry is to enable children to earn as much money as will remove the difficulty occasioned by the poverty of their parents. By this means parents are enabled to keep their children at school until they have acquired habits of industry, which will follow them into future life' (Lancaster 1808 p. 120).

See also: Workhouse School; Reformatory School; Approved Schools; Elementary Education Act 1876

INDUSTRIAL SCHOOLS ACT (1857)

This was based on Scotland's first Industrial and Reformatory Schools Acts (Act 17 & 18 Vict. c. 74), which were passed in 1854. For England and Wales, the Act 20 & 21 Vict. c. 48 was fully titled, 'An Act to make better provision for the care and education of vagrant, destitute and disorderly children, and for the extension of industrial schools' (Minutes 1857–58, p. 15). It was intended to increase the number and use of industrial schools to educate and house impoverished and vagrant children. A further act was passed in 1861 that included additional categories of homeless children.

INDUSTRIAL TRAINING ACT 1964

'This Act was designed to ensure an improvement in both the quantity and quality of training, and to distribute the costs of training more equitably amongst employers. The Act gave the **Ministry of Labour** power to set up **Industrial Training Boards** for individual industries. The Boards were required to raise a levy on employers in their industry and paid grants to those firms which provided training of an approved standards'. The Act provided for a **Central Training Council** to be set up.

(Ministry of Labour Gazette March 1964, p. 104)

INDUSTRIAL TRAINING BOARDS

ITBs were established by the **Industrial Training Act 1964**, to apply the levy systems and manage grants. They were free to generate income from subscriptions and charge for services or products. Also, they had responsibility to secure the provision of sufficient training, while the responsibility of establishing an adequate standard for their own industry rested with the individual board. The first to be set up and approved were wool, engineering, iron and steel, and construction. The **Central Training Council** was responsible for recommending the suitability of an industry for an ITB and by 1981, there were 27 established. The only board wound up as inoperable was hairdressing (1971). Following a review, 16 boards were closed in 1982/83. Subsequently the **Training Services Agency** (TSA) funded the ITBs' operational costs and certain special initiatives. Later, only two ITBs (Construction Industry Training Board; Engineering Construction Industry Training Board) remained for construction and engineering that were

recognised by the Government as the **national training organisation** for their industries. The majority of ITBs were succeeded by **industry training organisations**. In 2008, a Film Industry Training Board was introduced.

See also: Sector Skills Councils

Further reading: Sheldrake and Vickerstaff (1987)

INDUSTRIAL TRAINING COUNCIL

(1958–64) A single national council, as recommended in the 1958 **Carr Report** 'Training for Skill', the ITC was established in 1958 as a tri-partite initiative of the British Employers Confederation, the Trades Union Congress, and the boards of the nationalised industries. Its purpose was to encourage the growth of training opportunities for young people, and raise the quality of industrial training. A government grant-in-aid of £75,000 funded training development officers together with a **Training Advisory Service** (renamed **Industrial Training Service** in 1964), offering support to industry. The ITC also encouraged the establishment of regional Industrial Training Committees – services facilitators with no executive powers.

Further reading: Industrial Training Council (1965); Ministry of Labour Gazette (October 1964 p. 418)

INDUSTRIAL TRAINING FOR OVERSEAS NATIONALS

See: Overseas Nationals – Industrial Training for

INDUSTRIAL TRAINING RESEARCH REGISTER

(1967) Introduced by **Ministry of Labour** and designed to provide information annually about current and recently completed research; identify gaps in research coverage; and minimise duplication of research in training areas. The register listed 250 research projects and was designed to help training specialists to identify research in their area of interest. It was one of four linked publications designed to encourage the application of new ideas and techniques by encouraging a wider audience, the others being the **Glossary of Training Terms**; **Training Abstracts Service**; and **Training Information Papers**.

See also: Training Research Register

Further reading: Ministry of Labour Gazette (1967 p. 956); (1968 p. 1010)

INDUSTRIAL TRAINING RESEARCH UNIT

Funded by **Manpower Services Commission**, the ITRU was one of the arms of the Industrial Relations Training Centre. Research was carried out at the request of the MSC, ITBs and independent employers on areas such as instructor effectiveness, team skills management, and trainability testing.

Further reading: MSC Annual Report (1978/79 p. 21)

INDUSTRIAL TRAINING SERVICE

(1964) Successor to the **Training Advisory Service,** it had a staff of **training development officers** based in Scotland, the North of England, the Midlands, South West England, Wales and London. Their duties involved identifying training needs in industries or individual companies, producing training schemes for workers at operative, semi-skilled, craft, and supervisory levels. It promoted **Group Training Association schemes**, organised conferences of senior executives and held courses for instructors.

Further reading: Ministry of Labour Gazette October 1964, p. 418

INDUSTRIAL TRIBUNALS

Were set up following the **Industrial Training Act** 1964 to adjudicate on appeals by employers against assessment to levy by **industrial training boards**. Their jurisdiction was widened to cover the hearing of appeals under the Redundancy Payments Act, 1965, The Contract of Employment Act, 1963, and the Selective Employment Payment Act, 1965. They also served to resolve Docks and Harbour Boards' disputes on the definition of dock work. Industrial tribunals' responsibilities were further expanded to workplace rights and they were renamed **employment tribunals** arising from the Employment Rights (Dispute Resolution) Act 1998.

See also: Advisory, Conciliation and Arbitration Service

Further reading: Incomes Data Services (1994); Ministry of Labour Gazette 1967 p. 291

INDUSTRY

(1840) The term industry was used for a range of manual activities used in schools. Among the questions that school inspectors were required to consider for infant schools was 'Industry. How many Children learn to sew?

To knit?
To plait straw?
To keep the garden-border free from weeds?
To sweep the School-floors
Minutes 1839–40, p. 44

Also, although most teachers were male their wives were encouraged to become involved. For example, 'The master's wife, if properly trained, might conduct the infant-school, and give industrial instruction in the girls' school' (Minutes 1839–40 p. 58).

INDUSTRY LEAD BODY

See: Lead Body

INDUSTRY TRAINING ORGANISATIONS

(1984–98) ITOs were statutory and non-statutory training organisations supported by the **MSC** with the purpose of developing the nation's training infrastructure by monitoring skill requirements and responding to them. They were set up in 1984 (succeeded **industrial training boards** for most professions) to encourage employer commitment to training with three main objectives:

- to deliver the **National Priorities Skills Scheme**;
- to assist with industrial placement of college-based sandwich course students under the **New Training Initiative**; and,
- to act as managing agents in the **Youth Training Scheme**. By 1988 there was a **National Council of Industry Training Organisations** established as a forum for information exchange, a collective response to national and international training initiatives and a channel for identifying and disseminating best practice. By 1993 there were 126 ITOs and two ITBs − construction and engineering. ITOs were replaced by **national training organisations**.

Further reading: Berry-Lound et al. (1991); MSC Annual Report (1984/85 p. 24); National Council for Industry Training Organisations (1990)

INFANTS SCHOOLS

These are schools for young children normally aged four to seven at which stage they enter the **junior school** and continue their education there until eleven. Infant and junior schools together are known as **primary schools**. Children normally enter the reception class of an infants school aged 4–5. Historically, the Minutes (1865–66 p. vii) defined infants as 'children under seven years of age'. However, children were often admitted much earlier. Mr Waddington, HMI, commented: 'To admit children thus, *as is often the case, at 15 months old*, is to turn the school into a *Crèche* or Babies' Home. The universal excuse is, of course, that an elder sister's attendance depends on the infant's admission also; that the parents say "you must take all, or none"; ... and two years old may, I think be fairly laid down as the very earliest age for admission'. During the 1850s and 1860s infants schools were often, in practice, separate from their associated elementary schools. The Hadow (1931) Report recommended that there be a separation in the primary school with an infants division and a junior division and subsequently Infants 1 and Infants 2 were for five and six year olds with the children then entering the junior school at about seven. These two years of education are now known as Years 1 and 2.

See also: Early Years Foundation Stage; Middle School; Division

INFORMATION ADVICE AND GUIDANCE

As part of the reorganisation of education and training arising from the Leitch Report it was acknowledged that an important component of the process was to ensure appropriate information, advice and guidance to young people to help them make the right learning decisions.

Further reading: DCFS (2009)

INFORMATION, ADVICE AND GUIDANCE FOR ADULTS

IAG services supply free information and advice to adults in England. The main objectives are to: ensure a coordinated local network of IAG on opportunities in work and learning; ensure that all members of the community have access to information and advice; make sure that IAG standards meet the matrix quality standard for learning and work; and, work with the **Learning and Skills Council** to achieve coherence between IAG services and other connected services.

Further reading: DfES Departmental Report 2002 Cm 5402 p. 120; Sadler (2002)

INFORMATION TECHNOLOGY CENTRES

(1981) A specialised one-year training workshop scheme started in 1981 as a joint venture between the **MSC** and the **DTI**. Training was focused on the application and production of information technology. The IteCs provided broad based **YTS** training in new technology, for example electronics, computing and electronic office skills. During 1985/86 there were 175 ITeCs offering 6,758 places at a cost of £26m.

Further reading: MSC (1983c); MSC Annual Report 1985/86, p. 15

INITIAL TEACHER TRAINING

In 1995 this scheme covered such areas as those beyond the curriculum specialism of the teacher. ITT was seen as a means of keeping new teachers and head teachers up to date on current best practice within the profession. Teachers who had been in the profession for up to ten years were able to return and get updated in their skills.

See also: In-Service Education and Training (INSET); Qualified Teacher Status

Further reading: Millett (1997); Teacher Training Agency (1997)

INITIAL TRAINING

(October 1989) IT combined two overlapping initiatives (**Extended Introduction** and **Further Assessment)** within **employment training** that were designed to cater for the long-term unemployed, who needed to develop the confidence and competence to cope with full-time training. Its aim was to prepare people for entry to training by helping them develop clear ideas, appropriate attitudes, motivation, and the basic skills needed to cope in a training environment. It offered an opportunity to train on a part-time basis while receiving benefit. For the first four weeks there was no minimum time commitment.

Those who chose to do so could convert from benefit to a training allowance and were then required to attend for a minimum 20 hours per week. This approach then allowed a smoother transition to employment training.

Further reading: Employment Gazette 1988 p. 513; Grubb Institute (1990)

INNER-CITY INITIATIVE

The **Employment Department Group** was involved with a number of initiatives for inner cities. For example, in 1991–92 **ES** and **Training Enterprise and Education Directorate** spent around £905m on inner cities through national programmes to help unemployed people and through focused inner city activity. The 1991–92 Employment Service Annual Performance Agreement required that 34 per cent of ES placements were to inner-city residents. Also 500 **job-clubs** covered inner cities and catered for people mainly with literacy, numeracy or English language difficulties and £3.95m was set aside during this period for special regional projects. 'Action for Cities', launched by the Government in 1998, was an interdepartmental initiative that was supported by the ED group. The ED group was also deeply involved with the development of '**City Challenge**' implemented by the Department of the Environment between 1992–93 and 1996–97.

Further reading: Department of Employment Departmental Report February 1992, Cm 1906, p. 31; Employment Gazette 1989 p. 154

INNER-CITY PARTNERSHIPS

Working groups in collaboration with local authorities set up to meet local concentration of special training needs. For example, in 1982 **MSC** field staff were involved in a number of initiatives set up by the Merseyside Task Force to train 1,424 young and long-term unemployed in basic work skills; £2.8m was funded by the MSC.

Further reading: MSC Annual Report 1982/83 p. 23

IN-SERVICE EDUCATION AND TRAINING

(1998) INSET applied to teachers and to head teachers to update skills and further their professional development. Funding from The **Teacher Training Agency** was allocated to **higher education** institutions, **local education authorities** and others to schoolteachers' award-bearing in-service training courses. This was aimed at raising standards of teaching in the key areas of literacy, numeracy, leadership and management, ICT and special needs.

Further reading: Department for Education and Employment Report March 1999 p. 31; Farrow (1990)

INSTITUTE FOR LEARNING

'The Institute for Learning (IfL) is the professional body for teachers, trainers and assessors across further education (FE), including adult and community learning, emergency and public services, FE colleges, the armed services, the voluntary sector and work-based learning' (http://www.ifl.ac.uk (accessed 21 March 2010)). Its aim is to build and promote a distinctive reputation for teachers and trainers in further education and skills.

See also: Institute for Learning and Teaching in Higher Education; Higher Education Academy; General Teaching Council

INSTITUTE FOR LEARNING AND TEACHING IN HIGHER EDUCATION

(1998–2004) The ILTHE was the professional body for those teaching and supporting teaching in higher education. It developed and maintained standards of professional practice. Its responsibilities were taken over by the **Higher Education Academy**.

Further reading: DfEE Departmental Report 2001–02 to 2003–04, Cm 5102, p. 93

INSTITUTE OF TRAINING AND DEVELOPMENT

Originally the Institute of Training Officers, which published the *Training Officer*, it joined with the Institute of Personnel Management to form the Institute of Personnel and Development, which later became the **Chartered Institute of Personnel and Development**.

INSTRUCTIONAL CENTRES

In 1929, instructional centres were established to support the employment of young people, the majority of whom had never had a job because of the Depression. They later became known as **employment rehabilitation centres**.

INSTRUCTIONAL FACTORIES

(1917–25) During the First World War, 'The Ministry of Munitions have recently established at convenient centres, Instructional Factories which afford more advanced and specialised courses of training, individual and collective, for intending munition workers, most of whom have received their preliminary training in **technical schools**. These factories also act as 'Clearing Houses' for the distribution of the skilled labour thus provided. In these factories 'production' work is carried on side by side with the instruction, but neither of the two types of work is permitted to prejudice the other. The system, which enables the learner to become accustomed to actual factory conditions, has proved very satisfactory. The Instructional Factories are largely staffed by men trained in the technical schools' (Report 1916–17 p. 38). After the First World War, these government instruction centres assumed responsibility for the training of people disabled in the war. When this finished they were renamed **government training centres**.

INSTRUCTOR TRAINING COLLEGES

ITCs provided two-week courses on instructional techniques at the **Ministry of Labour**'s Colleges in Letchworth (Herts) and Hillingdon (Glasgow). There were also a few Instructor Training Units attached to **government training centres**. The courses involved the intensive combination of theory and practice and each student had six practice periods involving: instruction on a manipulative job in his own trade to a fellow member or group; a trade talk - describing a manufacturing process, and; two half-hour lessons to a class of beginners. In 1967 the two colleges were doubled in size to be capable of producing 3,000 instructors per year. By 1970 an advanced ITC had been introduced, with a further period of project work and use of modern audio/visual aids.

Further reading: Ministry of Labour Gazettes (1966 pp. 215, 814) (1968 pp. 10–14, 111)

INSTRUCTOR TRAINING SCHEMES

(1964–80) Trainers were trained at the colleges mentioned above (and at training units attached to **government training centres** at Cardiff, Killingworth – Northumberland, Leicester, Liverpool, Perivale and Plymouth).

Further reading: Employment and Productivity Gazette (1970 pp. 280–82); MSC Annual Report (1977/78 p. 42)

INTERIM SCHEME FOR THE TRAINING AND RESETTLEMENT OF DISABLED PERSONS

(1941) This scheme was inaugurated to support those injured in the war, both civilians and service personnel. The **Ministry of Labour** worked with voluntary organisations who ran training centres for the disabled at Letchworth and Exeter and this was formalised by the **Disabled Persons (Employment) Act 1944** and later extended by the Disabled Persons (Employment) Act 1958.

Further reading: Ministry of Labour Gazette May 1964 p. 196

(THE) INTERMEDIATE CERTIFICATE

This was introduced by the Education Department in 1902 and the certificate was awarded in Scotland to any pupil, not under fifteen years old on 1 January following the examination, for satisfactory completion of three years of intermediate study. 'Candidates for this certificate were admitted for the last time at the **Leaving Certificate** Examination held in 1924' (Report of the Committee of Council on Education in Scotland 1924–25 p. 10) and it was replaced in 1925 by the Day School Certificate (**Higher Certificate**).

See also: (The) Lower Certificate

Further reading: Alison (1912 pp. 74–80)

INTERMEDIATE EDUCATION (IRELAND) ACT 1878

This act established an intermediate education board in Ireland to promote and oversee intermediate and secular education. Prior to this there had been no state system of secondary education and this provided secondary education on **payment by results**.

Further reading: Durcan (1972)

INTERNAL VERIFIERS

These people were appointed by an **approved centre** to ensure that the assessment within the centre has consistency and quality.

See also: External Verifier; Awarding Body

Further reading: The Monitor (1997)

INTERNATIONAL CENTRE FOR ADVANCED TRAINING

(1965) This centre was established by the **International Labour Organisation** in Turin in 1965. The various member states of the ILO provided subscriptions for the running of the ILO and the Centre.

See also: European Training Foundation

Further reading: Ministry of Labour Gazette April 1965, p. 164; International Centre for Advanced Technical and Vocational Training (1967)

INTERNATIONAL DIRECTORS PROGRAMME

(February 1992) A Northern Ireland initiative designed to develop people in leadership and organisational change. The programme was delivered in partnership with the Ulster Business School and it was intended to improve the participants' organisations and advance Northern Irish businesses.

Further reading: Training & Employment Agency (1992)

INTERNATIONAL LABOUR ORGANISATION

(1919) The ILO was created by the Peace Treaty of Versailles in 1919, alongside the League of Nations. Following the Second World War its basic goals and principles were restated and enlarged and it became the first specialised agency associated with the United Nations. It has a tripartite structure incorporating workers' and employers' representatives and those of governments. Minimum international labour standards and broad policies are set by the International Labour Conference. The budget and work programmes are set every two years by the Conference and it is financed by member states. It has its

headquarters and permanent secretariat based in Geneva and its four main strategic objectives are:

- 'to promote and realise standards and fundamental principles and rights at work;
- to create greater opportunities for women and men to secure decent employment;
- to enhance the coverage and effectiveness of social protection for all; and,
- to strengthen tripartism and social dialogue'.

It has its headquarters and permanent secretariat based in Geneva.

See also: International Centre for Advanced Training

Further reading: www.ilo.org (accessed 21 March 2010)

INTERRUPTED APPRENTICESHIP SCHEME

(12 April 1945 – 1952) Administered by the **Ministry of Labour and National Service**, the scheme came into operation on 12 April 1945 following consultation between the ministers, the British Employers Confederation and the TUC. It applied to those whose apprenticeship training had been interrupted due to the 1939–45 war. By the end of 1946, some 26,179 applications had been dealt with, and applications ceased to be accepted after June 1951 with 82,500 people being assisted by the end of 1952.

Further reading: Ministry of Labour and National Service Annual Report (1964 p. 160)

INTERWORK

This was a sheltered placement scheme developed by **Remploy** to enable severely disabled employees to work in locations outside the main Remploy factories.

Further reading: Hibbert (1991); The Government Expenditure Plans: Department of Employment Report 1991/92, p. 37

INTRO

(Northern Ireland) (2006) This was a management development programme that evolved from the **Premiere Graduate Management Development Programme**. It was designed to improve the management and leadership skills of graduates through a 24-week programme with 4 weeks classroom training and a 20-week business improvement project. Participants could achieve the Advanced Diploma in Management Practice. The **Department for Employment and Learning** provided a bursary support of up to £2,500 towards the training costs of each person.

INVESTING IN YOUNG PEOPLE

(Announced December 1997) This scheme was aimed at 16–18-year-olds, working alongside the Social Exclusion Unit and other agencies with the aim of valuing all young people and ensuring that they would leave school with some form of recognised qualification when they sought to enter the field of work. There were key criteria such as:

- Increasing the range of relevant options and aiming to raise attainment levels to NVQ2 of 16–19-year-olds;
- a single school leaving date set at the end of June of each year;
- A new **national record of achievement** to help young people plan and manage their own learning;
- a **learning card** to make young people more aware of their entitlement to learning; and,
- **national traineeships** offered as a work-based route to NVQ2.

Further reading: Employment News No. 260 p. 3; DfEE (1999f)

INVESTORS IN PEOPLE UK

(1990) Set up as a Non-Departmental Public Body (NDPB), Investors in People UK became a limited company in 1993. Its aims were to maintain, update and develop the Investors in People standard amongst employers in all three sectors and promote it across the UK. In April 2000, the company introduced a new standard that required the organisation to demonstrate their achievements. In 2010 responsibility for Investors in People passed to the **UK Commission for Employment and Skills**.

Further reading: Spilsbury et al. (1995); Taylor and Thackway (1995); www.investorsinpeople.com

INVESTORS IN YOUNG PEOPLE

As a result of a conference held in November 1999 for young people in Oldham, a group of them called Dream suggested that organisations providing services to young people should be assessed against a set of quality standards. IiYP was based on meeting a number of performance criteria in four key principles – that services should: be young person centred; be anti-oppressive in practice; provide appropriate environments; and, be accessible and transparent.

Further reading: Making Connexions Newsletter March 2001 Issue 1

INWARD INVESTMENT

Was seen as a crucial factor in economic regeneration by the creation of jobs and strengthening of the skills base. Training was seen to be an important part of any inward investment plan, helping to increase a local pool of skilled labour and directly helping poorly skilled people, as well as those unemployed. In 1998 inward investment had access to a £3m per annum budget to facilitate this option as part of the **Training and Enterprise Councils Discretionary Fund**.

Further reading: DfEE Departmental Report 1998–99 Cm 3910 p. 73

IRELAND – COMMISSIONERS OF NATIONAL EDUCATION IN

The commissioners' first report was in 1834.

IRELAND – NATIONAL SCHOOLS

(1831) The Irish national system of primary education was formed as a result of Lord Stanley requesting the Board of National Education to become involved in '[e]stablishing and maintaining a model school in Dublin and training teachers for country schools'. The first model school was opened in 1834 and district model schools were established throughout the country from 1849. Books written and published by the Irish Educational Society were used extensively in Ireland and Britain. Also the teaching methods used in a number of Catholic schools in England were described as being 'model school, Dublin' (Minutes, 1853–54, vol. 2, p. 911).

Further reading: Mangione (2003)

IRIS

(1988–92) A European network of vocational training schemes for women. Its purpose was to complement and support action by individual member states. Activities included a network of demonstration projects, inter-project visits, information exchange, conferences, seminars and research. There were 70 initial projects, which expanded to 250 in September 1990. Of these, 25 were UK projects, with another 14 waiting for membership of the network.

Further reading: Commission of the European Communities Task Force (undated)

ISLE OF MAN SCHOOLS

The schools in the Isle of Man received grants from the Committee of Council until 1862, following which funds were received from Island revenues (Minutes 1872–73 p. 205). In 1967 the Education Authority was replaced by a Board of Education. Major educational acts include: Education (Evening Schools) Act 1902; Educational Endowments Act 1907; Higher Education Act 1907; Education (Young People's Welfare) Act 1944.

ITINERANT INSTRUCTION

(early 1900s) In Ireland, a scheme of itinerant instruction in technical areas was introduced and subjects included: 'dairy work, poultry rearing, bee-keeping, horticulture and fruit growing, domestic economy, manual instruction, lace and crochet making, and many other forms of rural industries' (Fletcher 1912 p. 95).

J

JANUARY GUARANTEE

See: September Guarantee

JEWISH SCHOOLS

(1852) Arising from financial support for Church of England schools and also Roman Catholic schools, the Jewish Board of Deputies wrote to the Committee of Council of Education asking for similar consideration and this was granted on 7 February 1852 (Minutes 1851–52 Vol. 1 p. 36).

JOB CLUBS

(Piloted November 1984) They began slowly with only 36 in 1986, increasing to over 1,000 by the end of 1987. The aim of the job clubs was to support long-term unemployed and unemployed people with disabilities to find their own jobs through better job-hunting techniques and restoring confidence. Support and counselling were provided by improving CVs, as well as free use of facilities, for example telephones, stationery and stamps. Participants were normally expected to attend on four half-days per week for two weeks and retained their right to unemployed benefits. At the close, they still had access and ongoing support from the job club leader. Job clubs were succeeded by **programme centres**.

Further reading: Employment Service (1988b)

JOB CREATION PROGRAMME

(October 1975) Introduced to provide around 140,000 temporary jobs of up to 12 months duration (average duration 32 weeks) for people who otherwise would be unemployed. Priority was given to people between the ages of 16 and 24 and those who were 50 plus. Labour intensive projects were sponsored mainly by local authorities and sponsors were reimbursed for approved wages and employers' N.I. contributions. The actual cost of jobs created was estimated as £186m, but was reduced to £85m net after taking savings in unemployment benefit etc. into account. All projects finished by 31 December 1978, with around 15,000 projects accepted for funding and it was said to have created some 140,000 temporary jobs. It was succeeded by the **Special Temporary Employment Programme**.

Further reading: MSC (1978a); MSC Annual Report 1978–79 p. 4

JOB INTERVIEW GUARANTEE

(Piloted in 1989) Piloted in 20 inner-city areas and went national in April 1991. The stated purpose of the JIG was to alter employers' perceptions of the long-term unemployed and consider them for suitable vacancies. It was also designed to overcome demotivation arising as a result of long-term unemployment. JIG involved an arrangement between the employer and the ES where the

151

employer agreed to interview all applicants who were submitted through options including a screening and matching interview; a job preparation course (rather like **Restart** but designed to meet employers' specific needs); or a work trial of up to three weeks (during which the participant remained on benefit). Expenditure at its peak in 1993/94 was estimated at £3.3m and 124,000 were recorded as assisted.

Further reading: Employment Gazette March 1991, p. 105; Price (2000 pp. 91–92); British Market Research Bureau (1992)

JOB INTRODUCTION SCHEME

(July 1977) Initially experimental, with the aim of encouraging employers to provide a trial period for people with disabilities. For the first six weeks, £30 was paid weekly to employers who engaged people with disabilities on a part-time or full-time permanent job that was expected to last at least six months after the 6-weeks trial period. The scheme was still operative in 1997 and paying £45 weekly.

Further reading: MSC Annual Report (1997/98 p. 13); Employment Service (June 1997)

JOB LIBRARIES

(February 1978) Launched with an initial trial in three **jobcentres**: Eastbourne, Wrexham and Edinburgh. Job related information was available to the public with data supplied by **COIC (Careers and Occupational Information Centre)** listing careers/job vacancies/qualifications requirements etc. – predecessor of the self-help system that was to arrive in jobcentres whereby the seeker could use a touch screen system to access job vacancies. It was estimated that in the first year around 18,000 personal callers were helped. These libraries continued in an updated form as Infosearch.

See also: Worktrain; Jobpoints

Further reading: MSC Annual Report 1978/79, p. 9; Cameron et al. (1983); Hunn (1987)

JOB PREPARATION COURSES

These courses prepared clients for a guaranteed interview with a particular employer.

See also: Job Interview Guarantee

Further reading: British Market Research Bureau (1992)

JOB RELEASE SCHEME

(1977–84) This programme encouraged early retirement, thus opening up more jobs for the younger unemployed. It initially applied to men of 64 and women of 59 but was later changed to apply to men of 62. Numbers decreased in the early 1980s and the scheme was discontinued in 1984.

Further reading: Employment Gazette July 1980, pp. 720–26); Makeham (1980)

JOB REVIEW WORKSHOPS

(October 1991–October 1996) These workshops provided short courses, normally of two days duration. They were intended for professionals and executives who had been unemployed for 13 weeks to reassess their job options. In 1994/95, over 37,000 attended workshops at a cost of £2.2m. The 1995/96 estimate was £1.9m before being replaced by **job search plus**.

Further reading: Department of Employment Annual Report February 1992, p. 48; Heather and Kay (1995)

JOB SEARCH PLUS

(Introduced between April and October 1996) This had an estimated spending of £5.5m per annum, which combined the best of **job search seminars** and **job review workshops** and consisted of a three-day seminar designed to help those who had been unemployed for at least 13 weeks to explore their choice of job and improve their job seeking skills. People with disabilities; returners to the labour market; those who had been in prison; or those who had left the armed forces could join before 13 weeks. It did not totally expand to become a national scheme but was absorbed into the **job club** programme. It was funded to the sum of £6m, of which £2.7m came from the **European Social Fund**.

Further reading: DfEE Departmental Report March 1996, Cm 3210, p. 104

JOB SEARCH SCHEME

JSS helped unemployed people to travel to other areas for employment interviews; the scheme was temporarily modified in 1980 and was discontinued in June 1986. It was replaced by the **Travel to Interview Scheme.**

Further reading: MSC Annual Report 1980; Training Agency Annual Report 1985/86, p. 28

JOB SEARCH SEMINARS

(July 1991–October 1996) Aimed to assist people who had been unemployed for at least 13 weeks to improve their job search and to assist them with such skills as writing a job application, preparing a better CV, improving job interview skills. The seminars were for those not eligible for **job clubs** and were conducted by external providers. Expenditure of £4.4m in 1994/95 provided some 66,000 opportunities. The seminars were replaced by **job search plus.**

Further reading: DfEE Annual Report 1996, p. 105

JOB SPLITTING SCHEME

(January 1983–April 1987) In this scheme, employers received a grant (initially £750) if they split a job that previously had been full-time and placed two employees facing redundancy, or two unemployed people, in it. It was replaced by **jobshare**.

Further reading: Department of Employment (1986b)

JOB TRAINING PROGRAMME

Northern Ireland programme to provide skills training that was delivered by **recognised training organisations**. It was replaced by **jobskills** in April 1995.

Further reading: Training and Employment Authority 1991/92, p. 8

JOB TRAINING SCHEME

(July 1985–September 1988) JTS was an umbrella programme that succeeded **TOPS (Training Opportunities Scheme)** and provided unemployed adults with intensive vocational training of 3–6 months' duration to improve or convert their skills. **Skillcentre** courses were largely concentrated on engineering and construction. It was replaced by the **New Job Training Scheme** (NJTS) in November 1986 for the long-term unemployed, with the original Job Training Scheme becoming known as the Old Job Training Scheme; this change was applied nationally in April 1987. NJTS was superseded by **Employment training**.

Further reading: Thompson and Rosenberg (1987); Smith (1989)

JOB TRANSFER SCHEME

(September 1993–1995) The Job Transfer Scheme was part of a package of measures designed to help those in areas affected by pit closures. Its purpose was to enable people to take jobs outside their home area by providing assistance with fares, as well as a weekly allowance for a fixed period and grants towards the costs of moving home. It assisted some 670 people in 1993–94 and 190 in 1994–95.

Further reading: Department of Employment Departmental Report March 1994 p. 45.

JOBCENTRE

(1973) Replaced **employment exchanges** and was seen as a significant element in the modernisation of the employment service, with payment of benefits totally separated from job seeking. There were approximately 1,000 existing offices and some 80 per cent were scheduled for suitable re-housing, for which the Treasury allocated an extra £1.7m per year. Jobcentres introduced self-service of notified vacancies, with specially trained employment advisers and more sophisticated matching/circulation, notably through the **CAPITAL** project in London. Employment exchanges and jobcentres co-existed during the changeover period. The first jobcentre was opened in Reading in April 1973. By March 1982, some 800 jobcentres were operating, increasingly being seen as also the gateway to other services or special schemes. They were often located in high areas of pedestrian density. Payment of unemployment benefit was joined with the jobcentres' function in 1988 and integrated offices were introduced. They were progressively replaced by **Jobcentre Plus**, and this transfer was completed in early 2008.

Further reading: MSC (1978d); Price (2000)

JOBCENTRE PLUS

(Announced in March 2000) A **Department for Work and Pensions** initiative which began in 2001 to enhance the overall provision of support from **jobcentres**, with pathfinder offices being rebadged Jobcentre Plus. It was preceded by a series of 12 pilots – the ONE pilots – which began in April 1999. It was an approach that created an integrated one-stop shop for benefits and employment advice; a personal advisor service to help people to return to work; and work-focused interviews for all new benefit claimants.

154

Further reading: Department for Work and Pensions (2002)

JOBCENTRE PLUS SUPPORT CONTRACT

(December 2009) The support contract replaced **programme centres** provision and parts of the **New Deal for lone parents**, **New Deal for partners**, and Carers. This British scheme was delivered by supplier organisations and consisted of two elements: Improving Job Search modules – targeted at jobseeker's allowance customers and contracted customers with moderate needs to actively seek jobs; and Getting Ready for Working Modules – for carers, NDLP and NDP participants who needed substantial help to become active in effective job search.

Further reading: Department for Work and Pensions (2009)

JOBFINDER PLUS

Replaced the Jobfinder Programme in June 1998.

Further reading: DfEE Departmental Report 1998–99 Cm 3910 p. 105; Dickenson and Broome (1998)

JOBFINDER PROGRAMME

(April 1997–June 1998) A mandatory programme of up to seven intensive interviews with concentrated back-to-work help from the employment services, for all claimants who were over 25 and had been unemployed for two years or more. Benefits sanctions could be applied to those who failed to attend these interviews. Financial provision in 1997–98 was £15.5m and this provided around 192,000 job opportunities. Replaced in June 1998 by **Jobfinder Plus**.

Further reading: Boutall (1998); Employment Service (1998)

JOBFINDERS GRANT

(Piloted in 1994 in East and West Midlands and extended nationally on 18 April 1995) The scheme gave assistance to people who had been unemployed for two years or more (long-term unemployed). It was intended to encourage people to take jobs that they might not have considered, by helping with the initial costs of returning to employment. The national scheme gave a one-off payment of £200 to long-term unemployed people who found a permanent full-time job paying less than £250 weekly. There was no entitlement to those who had savings of over £2,800, and the grant was subject to repayment if the recipient left their employment in the first twelve weeks. It had the aim of reducing the long-term unemployed numbers by some 25,000 per annum. In 1997–98, some 15,800 grants were awarded, and it was intended to keep the total annual allocation to £4m.

See also: Jobfinders Programme

Further reading: Dickinson and Broome (1998)

JOBMATCH

(Piloted from April 1995 in four areas; a national scheme for 18- to 24-year-olds by April 1997) Jobmatch was designed to encourage people who had been unemployed for two years or more to take a part-time job of at least 16 hours but less than 30 hours per week as a route out of unemployment. A tax-exempt allowance was paid weekly for six months, together with training vouchers. Participants received an allowance of £50 per week for six months. The estimated cost of the pilot was £8m; forecast expenditure had been from £0.7m to £3m.

See also: Workstart; Jobfinders Grant

Further reading: Loyd and Hussey (1996); Lourie (1998 pp. 60–61)

JOBPLAN WORKSHOPS

(29 March 1993) These workshops were designed to help people aged 25 or over who had been unemployed for more than 12 months (**Restart**). The scheme provided an introduction to job and training options. The workshops were run by specialist external providers, involving intensive leader support, and normally lasted for a week. Attendance was mandatory for people who had been unemployed for over 12 months and had rejected other opportunities to get them back into work. Reported initial expenditure for 1993/94 was £27.8m. By 1998/99 it was planned to reduce this figure to £9.3m.

Further reading: Birtwhistle (1994); Lourie (1996 pp. 39–40)

JOBPOINTS

These are touch-screen terminals placed in **jobcentres** in 2001–02 to allow people to search for and find suitable jobs.

See also: Worktrain; Job Libraries

Further reading: Breen (2001); Employment Service Annual Report and Accounts 2000–01.

JOB-READY

(Northern Ireland) This initiative was designed to give a person the tools and confidence to get them back into work. It had no time limit for gaining the basic skills and qualifications to help advancement within **Training for Success**.

JOBS PLEDGE

(2007) This initiative, in Scotland, was to encourage major public and private employers to offer 250,000 job opportunities to those who were at a disadvantage in the labour market, for example lone parents, and those on incapacity benefit. It involved **Jobcentre Plus**, **Learning and Skills Council** and other providers to help employers meet the

155

Welfare to Work challenge. It built on the Leitch Review recommendations for a more integrated system for skills and employment. It complemented the **Skills Pledge** in England.

Further reading: Department for Work and Pensions (2008)

JOBSEEKER'S ALLOWANCE

(October 1996) It was introduced following The Jobseekers Act 1995 and replaced unemployment benefit and income support. It was intended to show a clear distinction with looking for work, rather than being unemployed. Official discussions centred around dual delivery, the DHSS (Benefits Agency) and the **Department of Employment** (Employment Service). The two agencies agreed a National Memorandum of Understanding, setting out their respective accountabilities 'side by side'.

Further reading: White Paper *Jobseeker's Allowance (Cm2687)*; DfEE Report (March 1997 p. 27)

JOBSEEKER'S CHARTER

(1991) It developed from the Citizen's Charter and applied throughout the **Employment Service**'s 1,400 offices. Its purpose was to provide a clear statement of the standards of service that could be expected by the public.

Further reading: Department of Employment Report February 1992, p. 9; Employment Service (1993)

JOBSEEKER'S GRANT

A limited trial programme in 1995 that enabled a potential employee to apply for a grant for clothing, fares to interview and any equipment that might be needed.

See also: National Development Programme

JOBSHARE

(September 1988–December 1991) This scheme replaced the **Job Splitting Scheme** and was designed to encourage employers to create more part-time job opportunities for unemployed people and introduce arrangements for more flexible working. A grant of £1,000 was provided towards the extra costs incurred. Take-up of this scheme was low and it was discontinued at the end of December 1991.

Further reading: Martin Hamblin Research (1991)

JOBSKILLS

(April 1995–August 2007) Northern Ireland programme that was originally piloted in Ballymena and Newry and replaced the **Youth Training Programme** and the **Job Training Programme** in April 1995. The training was designed to lead to qualifications at **NVQ** Level 2 and above. It was subsequently replaced by **Training for Success**.

Further reading: Training and Employment Agency Annual Report (1996)

JOBSTART ALLOWANCE

(July 1986–Feb. 1991) It was introduced to complement the **Restart** programme. People unemployed for 12 months or more who accepted a job paying less than £80 per week were 'topped up' with a payment of a further £20 per week, payable for 6 months. The allowance was taxable but did not affect receipt of Family Income Supplement or housing benefit.

Further reading: Smith et al. (1990)

JOBWISE

A Northern Ireland preliminary course designed as a stepping stone to **Bridge to Employment.** It aimed to help people who were wary of education and training to understand and value them and so progress to the next level of the programme.

Further reading: Training and Employment Agency Annual Report (1997)

JOINT INDUSTRIAL COUNCILS

These councils, consisting of employers and trade unions, were established *c*.1920 in a wide range of industries and also had regional and national councils for England and Wales, Northern Ireland and Scotland. **Her Majesty's Inspectorate** of **technical schools** was attached to the JICs to provide consultative advice. 'As a rule each of these officers has some knowledge, and in some instances an expert knowledge, of the industry with which he is dealing, and he is available to give information and, if desired, advice, when questions concerning technical education, apprenticeship, welfare of young workers, or other matters which have an educational aspect arise in the deliberations of the Joint Industrial Councils' (Report 1919–20 p. 42).

See also: Industrial Research Associations

JOINT INTERNATIONAL UNIT

The Joint International Unit was described in the DfES Departmental Report 2003 (p. 160) as representing the international business of the **Department for Education and Skills**, and the **Department for Work and Pensions**. It sought to promote:

- 'the Lisbon Agenda of employability, skills and qualifications in the European Union;
- international links and partnerships between schools, colleges and universities;
- UK educational exports;
- exchange of information on best practice; and
- the use of UK education expertise in Africa'.

JUNIOR ART SCHOOLS

These were schools equivalent to **junior commercial schools** and **junior technical schools** (Report 1930 p. 14).

See also: Schools of Art

JUNIOR COMMERCIAL SCHOOLS

These were schools similar to **Junior technical schools** and **Junior art schools**.

See also: Commercial Schools

JUNIOR EVENING INSTITUTES

During the 1920s junior evening institutes provided 'General, with or without Vocational, Domestic or Art instruction, in part-time courses, normally after 5 p.m'. for those students 'between exemption age and 15 on admission, and under 17 on leaving' (Report 1925–26 p. 57).

See also: Senior Evening Institutes

JUNIOR INSTRUCTION CENTRES

(1929) After the Armistice, **juvenile unemployment centres** were established for unemployed young people aged 15–19 years. They were required to attend as a condition for receiving a donation from the Out-of-Work Donation Scheme. The centres were organised by **local education authorities** and the cost was carried by the Exchequer through the **Board of Education** or **Scottish Education Department**. In 1929 their title was changed to Junior Instruction Centres. With the economic revival resulting from the Second World War, demand decreased and the last Juvenile Instruction Centre in Scotland closed on 17 December 1941.

Further reading: Scotland (1969); Bell (1934)

JUNIOR SCHOOL

This was sometimes known in the late 1800s and early 1900s as the juvenile department, which followed on from the infant school (or division) for approximately three years depending on the ability of the child – brighter scholars could sometimes compress this study into two years. The junior school was divided into a junior division (ages 7/8 to 9/10); and a senior division for children aged

10/11. The classes in the junior division were numbered Junior 1, 2, 3 and corresponded to the older classification of **Standard[s]** I, II, III. When they were 12/13 years old, pupils had the opportunity to take the **qualifying examination** (Scotland), which allowed them to take supplementary subjects (**specific subjects** in England and Wales). The **Hadow** (1931 p. iii) Report used ' ... the phrase "Junior School" in contradistinction to "Infant School" to describe self-contained schools for children between the ages of seven and eleven, i.e. the upper stage of primary education'.

Further reading: Robertson (1912)

JUNIOR SECONDARY SCHOOL (SCOTLAND)

This was a school that offered a three-year education at secondary level.

See also: Senior Secondary School

JUNIOR TECHNICAL SCHOOLS

These schools began in the 1900s and became fully recognised with the publication of 'Regulations for Junior Technical Schools', which came into force from 1st August 1913, and which were subsequently incorporated within the Regulations for Technical Schools (Cd. 6919). By 1914–15 there were 49 schools recognised under the Regulations for Junior Technical Schools (Report 1914–15 p. 3) for the education of children approximately aged 12–15 and offering courses of two and three years duration (Report 1922–23). The term 'junior technical school' included two separate categories: ' ... the junior technical schools proper and **trade schools**. The former prepare for entrance to industries, such as the engineering and building industries, without restriction to one particular branch of the industry. The latter prepare for such highly specific occupations as cabinet making, silversmithing, printing, trade tailoring, trade

embroidery, hairdressing and photography. Both types have this in common, that they set out definitely to prepare boys and girls for skilled occupations. ... The essential difference between the curricula of these two types of school lies in the proportion of time devoted to vocational work. In the junior technical school proper this is usually not much more than 20 per cent., but in the trade school it may be as much as 50 per cent. and even more if the term "vocational" is widely interpreted. ... In general, therefore, a school is not established unless the demand for a particular industry or trade is sufficiently great to absorb the output of the school, and the number of pupils annually admitted to the school is restricted to the absorptive power of the industry or trade for which it prepares' (Report 1934 p. 31).

JUVENILE ADVISORY COMMITTEES

The Labour Exchanges Act 1909 did not cater for those young people under the age of 17 years, and to address this shortcoming the **Board of Trade**, following consultation with the **Board of Education**, issued *Special Rules for the Registration of Juvenile Applicants*. Paragraphs 2 and 5 made provision for the establishment of juvenile advisory committees to advise young people about employment opportunities. Provision was also made for this advice to be provided by **local education authorities** (Report 1909–10 pp. 37–38).

See also: Juvenile Employment Bureaux

JUVENILE EMPLOYMENT BUREAUX

The Education (Choice of Employment) Act 1910 enabled **local education authorities** to provide advice, information and assistance through juvenile employment bureaux to young people under the age of seventeen; in 1918, this was subsequently extended to those under 18 years.

See also: Juvenile Advisory Committees

JUVENILE EMPLOYMENT SERVICE

(1909–1948) This service for young people had its origins in the 1909 Labour Exchange Act and the 1910 Education Act. It was replaced by the **Youth Employment Service** in 1948.

JUVENILE ORGANISATIONS COMMITTEE

(December 1916) This was appointed in 1916 as a standing committee of the Home Office, with local committees operating in many regions, and its duties were transferred to the **Board of Education** on 1 October 1919. 'The Committee was originally established to bring together those experienced in social and welfare work among young persons to assist in dealing with a specific emergency, the increase in juvenile delinquency noted in 1916, and was designed to co-ordinate, strengthen and extend the work of the various voluntary organisations which cater for the recreative and social interests of children and young persons' (Report 1918–19 p. 4). The activities provided by the local committees were supported by Section 17 of the **Education Act 1918**, which specified the need to support the social and recreative needs of young people. It declined due to the industrial depression in the early 1920s but was revived in 1924 when a grant was provided to help local authorities cooperate with voluntary agencies and particularly the Juvenile Organisations Committee 'with a view to extending the work of juvenile organisations, more especially among young persons between 14 and 16 years of age unable to find employment. This public recognition of the value of the contribution made by voluntary agencies working among juveniles towards the training and, in the widest sense, the education of young people, has, we believe, been a source of the greatest satisfaction to all the voluntary bodies concerned, and a considerable stimulus has been given to voluntary work of this character in a number of populous centres' (Report 1923–24 p. 5).

See also: Evening Play Centres

JUVENILE UNEMPLOYMENT CENTRES

(December 1918–1929) Before the First World War Armistice, there was concern about the number of young people who might be made unemployed as a result of the cessation of hostilities. In addition, it was believed that the early removal of children from school might have had an effect on their discipline. 'In order to minimise the mischief of this period, the Board suggested to Local Education Authorities that they should establish Juvenile Unemployment Centres, at which young persons might be brought under educational supervision, and receive some informal instruction until they obtained employment'. The first centres, funded for six months, opened in December 1918 and, 'By an arrangement with the **Ministry of Labour**, all young persons between 15 and 18 who claimed an out-of-work donation were required to attend a centre if instructed to do so' (Report 1918–19 p. 53).

JUVENILE WAR SCHOLARSHIPS

Following representations by the **Board of Education**, the National Relief Fund used some of their surplus funds to provide maintenance allowances to young people who had been in the **juvenile unemployment centres**. This enabled the young people to defer employment and continue free full-time education for one year and receive 15s., 17s. 6d., or 20s. per week (Report 1918–19 p. 49).

K

KEY SKILLS

(September 2000) Originally developed by the **National Council for Vocational Qualifications** for use in England, Wales and Northern Ireland (in Scotland they were called **core skills**) the key skills specifications describe skills that were important in adult and working life. To be flexible, adaptable and competitive as members of the workforce, there are generic skills or key skills that were required: communication; application of numbers (numeracy); information technology; working with others; improving one's own learning and performance; and problem solving (the latter three are also known as wider key skills). Communication, application of numbers, and information technology require evidence of actual application and the passing of external tests. Some **GCSE** and other qualifications act as 'proxies' to allow exemption from the tests or application elements, or both. Initially these skills were designed for 16–19-year-olds, but they were intended to be embedded in higher education and it was proposed to advance them to all employed and unemployed people.

See also: Functional Skills

Further reading: DfEE (1999h)

KEY STAGE 1, 2, 3, 4, 5

The key stages were defined originally in Section 3(3–6) of the Education Reform Act 1988, as amended by the Education Reform Act 1993. They represented specific stages in the **national curriculum**. In September 1998 regulations were amended to allow pupils to drop two national curriculum subjects out of science, design, technology, and a modern foreign language, and give more attention to work-related learning in place of the subjects that were no longer studied. This was with the intention of removing disaffection with learning, if the theoretical was replaced with more practical topics.

Key Stages 1–3 involve tests in specific subjects while Key Stage 4 represents GCSEs and Key Stage 5 is A level.

Further reading: Education Reform Act 1988

Table 3 Key stages

	Pupils' ages	Year Groups
Key Stage 1	5–7	1–2
Key Stage 2	7–11	3–6
Key Stage 3	11–14	7–9
Key Stage 4	14–16	10–11
Key Stage 5	17–18	12–13

KEY TRAINING GRANTS

Provided by the **Training Services Agency** for specific training activities within industries identified by the **industrial training boards** as needing extra assistance to meet the TSA training targets for increased productivity, or better use of labour. As an example, in 1976,

£204,000 from a total of £14.4m was granted for sandwich courses, whilst some £6m was allocated to the engineering industry. These same grants were also available to non–ITB sectors and an example in the same period was £5,650 awarded to the Merchant Navy Training Board for safety training.

Further reading: MSC Annual Report 1976/77, p. 21

KILDARE PLACE SOCIETY

(7 December 1811) This society, officially the Society for Promoting the Education of the Poor of Ireland, was established to provide non-sectarian education by Dublin philanthropists with support from Joseph Lancaster. In the schools the reading of the Bible was undertaken 'without note or comment', thus avoiding the conflict between Roman Catholic and Protestant faiths. In 1814–15 it established a model school in Kildare Place, Dublin and trained many teachers and published spelling and reading books, arithmetic, geometry, trigonometry, mechanics, geography and needlework and a schoolmaster's manual, many of which were used in Britain. It received grants of £6,980 in 1814, which subsequently increased to £30,000; however, resistance from Roman Catholics meant that its efforts failed and grants were withdrawn in 1833.

Further reading: Durcan (1972); Fletcher (1912)

KINDERGARTEN

(1837) Friedrich **Froebel** established the first kindergarten (children's garden) in Blankenberg, Germany, in 1837 and introduced the term 'kindergarten' in 1840. His philosophy was to provide an organised environment in which pre-school children could develop at their own speed through creative play. He developed a number of toys or Froebel gifts, which included blocks, sticks and drawing books (Minutes 1855–56 p. 314). Activities undertaken by the children were called 'occupations'. In 1851 the Prussian Government ordered the kindergartens to be closed because it felt threatened by the unrestricted development of children's abilities that might lead to radical democratic alternatives. As a result, many kindergarten teachers travelled abroad with some establishing a school in Tavistock Place, London, in September 1851. The school was established by Johannes and Bertha Ronge, who encouraged teachers and wrote 'The Practical Guide to the English Kinder Garten'. Circular 323 from the Education Department stated: 'In the Education Code of 1892, teachers holding either the Elementary or Advanced Certificate of the National Froebel Union are allowed to rank as assistant teachers in infant schools under inspection. And you will doubtless have rightly inferred from this concession that the Department are desirous of giving further encouragement to the employment of Kindergarten methods' (Report 1892–93 p. 475).

Further reading: Ronge and Ronge (1855)

KING'S NATIONAL ROLL

(1919–71) Set up by royal proclamation in 1919 to encourage the employment of disabled servicemen from the First World War. The scheme allowed employers who had at least 5 per cent of their workforce as disabled servicemen the privilege of having their names put on the roll and were allowed to display a badge. A provision was added in 1921 to give preferential treatment for contracts to those companies on the roll by government departments and some local authorities. The scheme was superseded by the **Disabled Persons (Employment) Act 1944**, which obliged organisations to employ a quota of disabled people. Since all ex-servicemen were over 70 the roll scheme was discontinued in 1971.

See also: Quota Scheme

Further reading: Department of Employment Gazette 1971 p. 264

KING'S SCHOLARS

See: Queen's Scholars

KNOW HOW FUND

This was assistance provided to Central and Eastern Europe and the former Soviet Union to support the transition of the countries to pluralist democracies and market economies. This included expertise in areas including employment services and vocational training.

Further reading: DfEE Report 1996 Cm 3210 p. 128

KNOWLEDGE EXCHANGES

Described in the DfES Departmental Report 2003, these were institutions or consortia that would demonstrate good practice in interactions between less research-intensive institutions and business. Emphasis was on knowledge transfer and skill development in the public and private sectors. They were part of a network within the **new technology institutes**.

Further reading: DfES Departmental Report 2003, Cm 5902, p. 128

KNOWLEDGE TRANSFER NETWORKS

'A Knowledge Transfer Network is a single over-arching national network in a specific field of technology or business application which brings together people from businesses, universities, research, finance, and technology organisations to stimulate innovation through knowledge transfer'. They are managed by the Technology Strategy Board.

http://www.innovateuk.org/deliveringinnovation/knowledgetransfernetworks.ashx (accessed 01 June 2010)

See also: Knowledge Transfer Partnerships

KNOWLEDGE TRANSFER PARTNERSHIPS

KTPs were officially launched in June 2003 and were the successor to the **Teaching Company Scheme**. The main differences between the two initiatives were that KTP projects could be of any duration from 12–36 months, and the TCS projects normally lasted 24 months with a few lasting 36 months. Secondly, FE colleges could be involved with a project, whereas formerly they were excluded. The KTP represented a merger of the TCS and the Colleges and Businesses in Partnership Scheme. The CPB ran as a pilot throughout the UK between 1996 and 1999, and then ran only in Northern Ireland and Wales. The KTPs involved the recruitment of a person (known as a KTP Associate) to work with a company on a business development project that might involve, for example, changing a manufacturing process, improving quality or introducing management information systems. The associate was a graduate, or post-graduate or someone with an HNC/HND or SNVQ Level 4 in a relevant subject to the project. The associate had the support of the company and also a Knowledge Base Partner – a university academic, further education college tutor, or researcher from a research-based organisation. There had to be a business need for a project and expertise that was not at the time available to the company and that might involve one or more associates. There was no direct financial support to the organisation; however, a grant was paid to the Knowledge Based Partner and the company was invoiced for the balance. The scheme was run by the **Technology Strategy Board**.

Further reading: www.ktponline.org.uk (accessed 01 June 2010)

L

LABOUR CERTIFICATES

The provisions of the Factory Act 1874 incorporated the periodic holding of labour certificate examinations by Her Majesty's Inspectors (Report 1878–79 p. 515). The certificates (sometimes called a **Certificate of Proficiency**) confirmed that a child between 13 and 14 had satisfactorily completed **Standard** IV and therefore could work full time. Prior to this act, children of the age of ten years might be awarded certificates according to previous labour acts. The use of labour certificates was continued under the Employment of Children Act 1903, which also stipulated that no child under the age of 14 years was allowed to work between the hours of 8pm and 6am, nor in excess of 9 hours per day, or on Sundays. Subsequent to the Education Act 1918 the term 'labour examination' was used (Report 1918–19 p. 26).

See also: Mines – Regulation and Inspection Act; Elementary Education Act 1876; (The) Agricultural Children Act 1873

LABOUR COLONIES

Labour colonies, or work camps, for the unemployed were introduced, often by **distress committees**, during the 1890s and 1900s to address the rising levels of unemployment especially in urban areas. The Salvation Army founded Hadleigh Farm Colony in 1891 and numerous others were also established for the purpose of working the land and developing the body and mind in residential centres.

See also: Farm Training Scheme

Further reading: Field (2009)

LABOUR DEPARTMENT

(20 January 1893–January 1917) In 1886, a motion was passed in the House of Commons: 'In the opinion of this House, immediate steps should be taken to ensure in this country the full and accurate collection and publication of Labour Statistics' (Parliamentary Debates, Vol. CCCII March 2nd, 1886, 1768–1804). This resulted in the abolition of the Commercial Department and the creation of a separate branch within the Department of Trade named the Commercial, Labour and Statistical Department in 1893. One of its main roles was to produce the *Labour Gazette*. Many of the responsibilities of the Labour Department were transferred to the **Ministry of Labour** during the First World War in order to support the war effort.

LABOUR EXCHANGES

(1 February 1910 – 10 October 1916) A labour exchange was defined in the **Labour Exchanges Act 1909** as 'any office or place used for the purpose of collecting and furnishing information, either by the keeping of registers or otherwise, respecting employers who desire to engage workpeople and

workpeople who seek engagement or employment'. The first British public employment exchange was established by a philanthropist in Egham in 1885 and others were subsequently provided by local **distress committees** until national provision was formally provided by the labour exchanges. In 1910, 62 labour exchanges were opened and they were renamed **employment exchanges** in 1916 to provide a clearer representation of their purpose.

Further reading: Crooks (1993); Price (2000)

LABOUR EXCHANGES ACT 1909

This act provided the **Board of Trade** with financial support to establish **labour exchanges**, although there was no demarcation of support for juvenile employment, which limited the scope of education authorities since they received no financial resources in this area.

LABOUR FORCE SURVEY

Originally this was conducted by the Office of Population Censuses and Surveys (later the Office for National Statistics) and was commissioned by the **Statistical Services Division**; it was quarterly from 1992. It is a continuous sample survey undertaken in the UK through interviews with people about their circumstances and work. The LFS allowed comparisons with other EU countries through a harmonised system of surveys.

See also: Labour Market Trends; Individual Learner Record

Further reading: Department of Employment Annual Report 1991/92, p. 26

LABOUR GAZETTE

In 1886, a motion was passed in the House of Commons that, 'In the opinion of this House, immediate steps should be taken to ensure in this country the full and accurate collection and publication of Labour Statistics'. Following this, a monthly journal was first published in May 1893 by the **Board of Trade**, which provided statistical information and reports about employment and the labour market. It was later called the *Ministry of Labour Gazette* 1920–67; the *Employment and Productivity Gazette* between 1968–70; the *Department of Employment Gazette* 1971–78; and *Employment Gazette* 1979–95; and subsequently from November 1995 *Labour Market Trends*.

Further reading: Parliamentary Debates, Vol. CCCII (March 2nd, 1886), 1768–1804

LABOUR HOARDING

Term from the National Joint Advisory Council Report of the Working Party on the Manpower Situation, January 1962, when there were low levels of unemployment. Some firms held on to employees even though they were under-employed, due to the cyclical nature of work production contracts, in order not to lose them to other employers, who might be at a different part of the 'work cycle', and then have insufficient workers when they were needed in the future.

Further reading: Ministry of Labour Gazette February 1962, p. 47

LABOUR MARKET TRENDS

(November 1995) Incorporated *Employment Gazette*. The title resulted from the transfer of responsibility for labour market statistics from the **Employment Department** to the Central Statistical Office (subsequently, in April 1996, the Office for National Statistics). The publication initially did not contain news of policy developments in employment, health and safety, training and other labour market elements that were published in the free newspaper *Employment News*. From January 2007 *Labour Market Trends* was merged with *Economic Trends* to become the *Economic and Labour Market Review*.

LABOUR MOBILITY

Considered in the same report as **labour hoarding**. Labour mobility was assessed in three main areas: geographical, industrial, and occupational. Inter-regional migration was measured on the basis of a count of insurance cards. Industrial mobility was based on the surveys of working population analysed by the main industry classifications. In 1962 little information was available about mobility between professions.

Further reading: Ministry of Labour Gazette February 1962, p. 46

LADS' AND GIRLS' CLUBS

These were voluntary organisations established around 1900 to support unskilled young people socially and into employment. Two examples were: Mr Charles Russell's Heyrod Street Lads' Club in Manchester, and Mr Hamilton Mexwell's Industrial Home for Lads in Edinburgh. 'The Lads' and Girls' Clubs owe their attractions for the boys and girls attending them mainly to the social, moral and recreative influences which the managers who conduct them are able to exercise. … The subjects of instruction which appeal most forcibly to the young members of these clubs are recreative handicrafts, such as Fretwork, Bent-metal work, Bookbinding, Chip carving, and simple woodwork and Carving with pocket knife in the case of boys, and Needlework, Rush-plaiting, and Paper flower making in the case of the girls. These subjects not infrequently lead to more systematic and educational work in properly organised classes in Woodwork, Dressmaking, Millinery, Cookery and Laundry work. Singing is also an attractive subject for girls, even of the roughest type, and is not infrequently the avenue by which such girls are brought into the sphere of further educational influences. Physical exercises, especially when associated with the free use of a gymnasium, are also among the means by which both boys and girls are most readily brought under systematic disciplinary restraints, and so influenced for good even when they are not immediately induced to take up other forms of educational work' (Report 1908–09 p. 75).

Further reading: Gordon (1911)

LANCASTERIAN SCHOOL

(1798) So named after Joseph Lancaster, a Quaker, who first set up a school in outbuildings belonging to his father in 1798. These soon became overcrowded and he moved to Borough Road, which subsequently became a teacher training institution and is now part of London South Bank University.

See also: British and Foreign School Society; Simultaneous Method

LANGUAGE COLLEGES

The Education Reform Act 1988 enabled the development of **city technology colleges** of which only a few were developed. In 1995, the Government expanded provision beyond technology and allowed the introduction of language colleges that had a foreign language emphasis. This development has continued with the growth of language **specialist schools**. Language colleges tended to avoid the use of '**language school**', which was more commonly used for private schools providing English language tuition for overseas students.

LANGUAGE EXPORT CENTRES

In 1987, Language export centres became part of a network of UK centres that were established to encourage the learning of languages and so support the international trade of goods and services, thus benefiting the economy. They provided language training, export advice, cultural briefings and consultancy services.

LANGUAGE SCHOOLS

These schools normally provide English language tuition to students for whom English is a foreign or second language. They are generally privately owned and often have accreditation from the Association of Recognised English Language Schools, **British Council** or other bodies.

LANGUAGES

Languages (Latin, French and German) were first recognised as **specific subjects** for the purpose of the award of grants in 1880. Foreign languages were first included in admission examinations for teaching students in 1874 and were included as part of study in all training colleges for men and some for women in 1882.

Further reading: Report 1882–83 pp. xxvii, xxvi

LATIN SCHOOLS

These were schools that emerged during the 1300–1600s in Europe and that were more commonly, but not exclusively, known as grammar schools in Britain.

See also: Trivium

LAUNDRY WORK

This subject is described in the 1890 **Code** as a specific subject for girls; 'where the Inspector reports that special and appropriate provision has been made for the practical teaching of Laundry-work by a teacher recognised by the Department as qualified to teach that subject, a grant of 2s is made on account of any girl presented for examination in elementary subjects in **Standard** IV, or any higher Standard, who has attended not less than 20 hours during the school year at a laundry class of not more than 14 scholars' (Report 1889–90 p. 135).

See also: Cookery – Training School of

LEAD BODY

The Government's Review of Vocational Qualifications in 1986 led to the creation of the **National Council for Vocational Qualifications**. Lead bodies were established on which were representatives of employers, employees and the MSC. They conducted a functional analysis of the job and developed occupational standards upon which **Scottish/National Vocational Qualifications** were based.

Further reading: Wolf (1995); The Monitor (1997); Mansfield and Mitchell (1996)

LEADERSHIP FOUNDATION FOR HIGHER EDUCATION

(24 March 2004) The Leadership Foundation (a company limited by guarantee) was established by Universities UK and GuildHE to provide 'a dedicated service of support and advice on leadership, governance and management for all the UK's universities and Higher Education colleges'. It took over some of the responsibilities of the Higher Education Staff Development Agency.

See also: National College for School Leadership

Further reading: Leadership Foundation for Higher Education (2004); http://www.lfhe.ac.uk

LEAGUE TABLES

The provision of school performance tables existed in the nineteenth century with Her Majesty's Inspectors publishing lists in their reports of inspections and examinations. This concept was developed with the Parents Charter in 1991, which promised an annual report. League tables describing schools' performances were extended to primary schools in 1997.

See also: Merit Table

LEARNDIRECT

Initially it was **learning direct**, a free national telephone helpline providing callers with impartial information and advice on learning. The cost in 1998 was £0.7m and in 1998–99 it rose to £3.1m, with one quarter of a million callers. Developed by **University for industry (UfI)** Limited, it was designated learndirect and officially launched in October 2000 to provide online learning materials and services available at home, in the workplace and learndirect learning centres. Funding for 2000–01 was £74m for the development and operation of UfI Ltd and £10m for the development and maintenance of the advice service.

Further reading: DfEE Departmental Report 2001–02 to 2003–04, Cm5102, p. 84; www. learndirect.co.uk

LEARNER SUPPORT FUNDS

These are for students aged 16+ in further education. There are four main areas: funding for hardship and general costs; childcare; transport; and residential/lodging funds for learners who have to travel beyond daily travel. Priority groups include: those with disabilities and learning disabilities; those leaving care; probationers; and students reaching 19 and losing benefits during their period of study. This support programme has reduced drop-out rates.

See also: Education Maintenance Allowance; Care to Learn

Further reading: DfES Departmental Report 2004, Cm 6202, pp. 77–78

LEARNING AGREEMENTS

(April 2006) These began as pilots in eight **Connexions service** partnerships. It was a training plan arranged by a Learning Agreement Broker between young people and their employers to gain an accredited training qualification while staying in employment. A maximum of £250 would be paid to those who progressed through milestones on the training programme(s). It was targeted at 16- to 17-year-olds currently employed in Jobs Without Training and priority was given to those who had not attained Level 2 qualifications. It built on the **Right to time off for study or training** legislation and aimed to raise the number of people participating in education and training.

See also: Education Maintenance Allowance

Further reading: Department for Education and Skills (2007) Departmental Report 2007, Cm 7092, p. 59

LEARNING AND DEVELOPMENT & ASSESSMENT AND VERIFICATION NATIONAL OCCUPATIONAL STANDARDS

(2002) These NOS were revised by the Employment National Training Organisation (formerly the Employment and Occupational Standards Council and originally the **Training and Development Lead Body**) in 2002. They addressed the main areas of learning and development, and assessment and verification. The assessment and verification units replaced the **D-units**.

Further reading: Employment NTO (2002); www.empnto.co.uk

LEARNING AND SKILLS ADVISORY BOARD

(1 January 2002–31 December 2003) (Northern Ireland) The LSAB succeeded the **Training and Employment Agency** Board and the Further Education Consultative Committee. It objectives were: 'to help secure strong collaboration and co-operation between the Department for Employment and Learning and the private sector, and to assist the Department, and provide advice on, the development of: training; the employment service; further education; and provision for 16–19 year olds'.

(http://archive.nics.gov.uk/el/031222d-el.htm (accessed 05 April 2010))

LEARNING AND SKILLS BEACON STATUS

Designed to encourage excellence in teaching and learning by providers. These were providers that also demonstrated strong leadership and management; shared good practice; developed curriculum specialisms; and used innovative methods for institutional improvement. By February 2004, 38 providers had received the award and they included further education colleges, tertiary colleges, sixth-form colleges, work-based learning providers, and one adult and community learning provider.

Further reading: DfES Departmental Report 2004, Cm 6202, p. 74

LEARNING AND SKILLS COUNCIL

(2001–31 March 2010) The National LSC was established in 2001 (following the Learning and Skills Act 2000) with its headquarters in Coventry, and represented a comprehensive reform of post-16 learning that integrated the planning and funding of all post-compulsory learning below higher education. Its purpose was to encourage local freedom and flexibility within a nationally determined set of standards for quality and outcomes. The key tasks were:

- to raise participation and achievement by young people;
- to increase the demand for learning by adults;
- to raise skills for national competitiveness;
- to raise the quality of education and training delivery;
- to equalise opportunities through better access to learning; and,
- to improve effectiveness and efficiency.

Its responsibilities were taken over by the **Skills Funding Agency** and the **Young People's Learning Agency** and **National Apprenticeship Service**.

See also: Local Learning and Skills Councils

Further reading: DfEE (1999e); Learning and Skills Council (2001); www.lsc.gov.uk

(LOCAL) LEARNING AND SKILLS COUNCILS

Launched in April 2001 the 47 Local Learning and Skills Councils were part of a national

chain and they had a budget of £6b to work with 6 million learners. By May 2002, each local council was to have developed a three-year strategic plan to ensure that education and training provision met local and economic needs. From April 2010 the responsibilities were transferred to the **National Apprenticeship Service**; **Skills Funding Agency**; and **Young People's Learning Agency**.

See also: Learning and Skills Council

Further reading: Learning and Skills Council (2001)

LEARNING AND SKILLS DEVELOPMENT AGENCY

(27 November 2000–March 2006) The LSDA was formerly the Further Education Development Agency (established in 1995), which itself was formed as a result of a merger of the **further education unit** (a policy body established in 1977) and the Further Education Staff College (involved with training and professional development). The LSDA addressed all provision funded by the **Learning and Skills Council** and focused on policy, research, and staff development. It was succeeded by the **Learning and Skills Network** (with responsibility for training, consultancy, research and service delivery) and the **Quality Improvement Agency for Lifelong Learning** (with responsibility for strategy and policy). A number of its functions were taken over by the **UK Commission for Employment and Skills**; in addition some advisory, research and training provision were continued by the Learning and Skills Network, an independent and not-for-profit organisation. The LSDA continued to operate in Northern Ireland after March 2006.

LEARNING AND SKILLS DEVELOPMENT AGENCY NORTHERN IRELAND

Delivers programmes, conducts research and supports government, further education and other training providers and stakeholders with information, advice and guidance. Among the training offered is governance training for FE governors. Although the LSDA was discontinued elsewhere it continued in Northern Ireland.

Further reading: www.lsdani.org.uk (accessed 30 May 2010)

LEARNING AND SKILLS IMPROVEMENT SERVICE

(announced in November 2007, officially named on 10 June 2008 and fully operational 1 October 2008) The responsibilities of the **Centre for Excellence in Leadership** and the **Quality Improvement Agency for Lifelong Learning** were combined within the Learning and Skills Improvement Service in 2008. The Learning and Skills Improvement Service was responsible for supporting further education and skills.

Further reading: www.lsis.org.uk (accessed 30 May 2010)

LEARNING AND SKILLS NETWORK

(April 2006) The LSN is one of the two successor organisations to the **Learning and Skills Development Agency** (the other being the **Quality Improvement Agency**). The 'LSN provides services to policy makers, to organisations that fund, manage and provide education, and to individual providers and practitioners across education and training'. It develops programmes, conducts research and offers training and consultancy. It works in partnership with numerous organisations including the **Department for Children, Schools and Families**; the **Learning and Skills Council**; the Scottish Funding Council, **CollegesWales**, and the **Learning and Skills Development Agency Northern Ireland**.

Further reading: www.lsneducation.org.uk/ (accessed 30 May 2010)

LEARNING AND SKILLS OBSERVATORY FOR WALES

This is 'a portal that provides users access to education, learning, skills and labour market news, information and research materials. The LSO is dedicated to the provision of up to date information in the field of education, learning and skills in Wales and encourages the development and exchange of evidence-based policy and improved decision-making across Wales'. Formerly called Future Skills Wales, the Learning and Skills Observatory (Porth yw'r Arsyllfa Dysgu a Sgiliau) was managed by the Department for Children, Education, Lifelong Learning and Skills and was guided by the LSO Strategy Group, which consisted of representatives from education, economic and training organisations.

See also: Future Skills Wales

Further reading: http://www.learningobservatory.com/ (accessed 30 May 2010)

LEARNING AND TEACHING SCOTLAND

(1 July 2000) LT Scotland was formed from the merger of the Scottish Council for Educational Technology and the Scottish Consultative Council on the Curriculum. Its purpose is to work in partnership to develop the curriculum, improve learning and teaching, and encourage the use of ICT in education and lifelong learning.

LEARNING AND TRAINING AT WORK

(1999) The LTW survey provides information on the provision of training and workforce development activities by employers in England. It covers all employers except schools and LEAs and in the survey, LTW 2001 included data for employers with 1–4 employees. It replaced the Skill Needs in Britain surveys that were undertaken during the 1990s.

LEARNING AND WORK BANK

This was a proposed project envisaging:

- a jobs bank with details of **Employment Service** and other job vacancies;
- a people bank, with CVs and jobs sought by individuals, which could be searched by employers;
- a careers bank containing information on careers choices; and,
- a directory of work-related learning opportunities.

It was subsequently named **worktrain**.

LEARNING AT WORK DAY

This initiative began in 1999 as part of Adult Learners Week and involves 'fun opportunities' to encourage learning in the workplace and to demonstrate that there can be, for example, informal learning in the lunch hour and not just in the classroom. It is organised by the Campaign for Learning and involved 2,500 firms in 2001.

See also: Adult Learners Week

Further reading: Hammond (2002)

LEARNING CARD

(1999) Formerly called the **youth card**, it was produced with specific aims:-

- to help reduce levels of disaffection and economic inactivity by encouraging more young people to consider learning as a viable post-16 option; and,
- to increase participation and attainment in post-16 learning, by helping young people to make better choices.

These aims were supported by the **national record of achievement** (NRA) and also by impartial careers guidance and advice in the final two years of compulsory education. The card is the size of a business card, using CD-ROM technology and can be played like a conventional CD-ROM. It was replaced by the **connexions card**.

Further reading: Newscheck (1998a)

LEARNING COMMUNITIES

Skills and learning were considered important elements in breaking the cycle of deprivation, underachievement and unemployment in some communities. To address this, 28 Learning Community Test-beds were set up. **Regional development agencies**, local **learning and skills councils**, and local strategic partnerships worked together to develop the learning communities.

See also: Learning Curve

Further reading: DfES (July 2003)

LEARNING CURVE

(2002) The learning curve is the learning and development strategy of the Skills and Knowledge Programme for neighbourhood renewal. It considers how learning can be used in supporting deprived areas, developing the skills of residents and supporting those involved with delivery including civil servants, practitioners, professionals and organisations. The strategy describes a range of actions at national, regional, and local neighbourhood levels. To achieve a situation where 'within 10 to 20 years no one should be seriously disadvantaged by where they live' (p. 4), the vision was for 'a step change in the levels of skills and knowledge of everyone involved with neighbourhood renewal'.

Office of the Deputy Prime Minister (October 2002 p. 4)

Further reading: www.communities.gov.uk/communities/neighbourhoodrenewal/ (accessed 30 May 2010)

LEARNING DIRECT

Launched in February 1998 this was a free national telephone helpline giving callers impartial information and advice on learning. It became **learndirect**.

Further reading: DfEE Departmental Report 1998–99 p. 56

LEARNING FOR WORK

(August 1993–September 1994) Provided vocational courses for the long-term unemployed. £55m was allocated to enable 25,000–30,000 starts. Participants studied full time on courses ranging from 2 to 42 weeks. 60 per cent were expected to gain a qualification and **individual participation plans** described the content and duration of the course, as well as the support, guidance and job search arrangements. Eligibility criteria were very strict (participants had to have been unemployed for 12 months, and had to stay unemployed till the start of their course). Started at the same time as **Training for Work (TfW)** but only lasted a year, due to poor take-up.

Further reading: Department of Employment 1994, Cm 2505, p. 15; Finn (1993)

LEARNING GATEWAY

(1996) This programme was designed to aid those who wished to return to the field of learning, and was a partnership between **further education colleges** and universities that had adult continuing education facilities. It was designed for young people who were not in work, education or training.

Further reading: Chatrik (1999)

LEARNING PARTNERSHIPS

They were set up in 1997 through a partnership fund of £10m and by 1999, there were 101 learning partnerships. The partnerships are non-statutory, voluntary groupings of local learning providers including employers, faith groups, connexions/career service, local government, trade unions, higher education institutions and the voluntary sector. Their purpose is to achieve more coherence and better coordination of lifelong learning strategies at the local level.

Further reading: DfES Departmental Report 2002 Cm 5402 p. 137

LEARNING REPRESENTATIVES

The Employment Act 2002 (amended the Trade Union and Labour Relations (Consolidation Act 1992) gave the right for recognised trade unions to appoint learning representatives. These representatives were entitled to 'reasonable' time off with paid leave to train for, and perform, their duties, which were set out as: analysing training needs; providing information and advice on training matters; arranging training; and promoting its value. Union members were entitled to unpaid leave in order to meet their learning representative.

Further reading: Employment Act 2002

LEARNING SUPPORT PRACTITIONER

A learning support practitioner is 'a person who performs a learning support role. Learning support practitioners work directly with the learner, with the learning process and under the direction of the person(s) leading the learning'. Also: 'Learning support contributes to the provision of inclusive learning opportunities. It enables identified learning needs to be met and learners' independence, achievement and progression to be promoted' (Lifelong Learning UK, December 2008 p. 3). The development of learning support practitioner **national occupational standards** in 2008 complemented the **teaching in the lifelong learning sector qualifications**.

See also: Lifelong Learning UK

Further reading: www.lluk.org (accessed 30 May 2010)

(THE) LEAVING CERTIFICATE

Leeds Educational Council encouraged evening classes through the use of a 'leaving certificate' designed to act as a 'passport' from day school to evening school. Pupils who left school after passing the 4th or higher **Standard** were urged to attend an evening class. When the winter session was finished, the evening school teacher completed the certificate and sent it to the Educational Council, which awarded prizes based on attendance and examination performance (Report 1879–80 p. 329). Leaving certificates continued to evolve and develop and in the early 1900s in Scotland could be gained through completion of two years post-intermediate instruction in not less than four subjects.

See also: (The) Intermediate Certificate

Further reading: Alison (1912)

LEAVING CERTIFICATE SCOTLAND

After the Education Act 1872 the Leaving Certificate examination was introduced for secondary schools and those pupils satisfying the requirements received a certificate. Pupils received certificates for each subject satisfactorily passed.

LECTURERS

In 1853, lecturers who passed an examination in one or at most two subjects (history, English literature, geography, physical science, applied mathematics) were paid an additional sum to instruct in **normal schools**: schools in which people learned to become teachers

Further reading: Report 1863–64, p. lvii

LECTURERS INTO INDUSTRY INITIATIVE

(Northern Ireland) This initiative was to encourage FE lecturers to return to undertake structured placements in industry to update their skills. It involves a placement – minimum 6 weeks, but up to 12 weeks – and includes completing a mutually beneficial project with the company. Technicians may also undertake a 4–6 week placement to update their knowledge and skills with equipment, technologies and software.

Further reading: Department for Employment and Learning Annual Report 2002–2003

LEEDS SEWING SCHOOL FOR FACTORY GIRLS

(*c.*1852) This was a twice-weekly sewing school held from 7pm–9pm. It originated from a Sunday school and it was designed to encourage females to develop sewing skills after work and break down social barriers between classes. During the sewing (mainly of clothing), hymns and other songs, and readings and conversation were encouraged among the 150–200 attendees (Minutes 1856–57, p. 313).

Further reading: Hyde (1862)

LEONARDO DA VINCI

This is a European lifelong learning programme that funds vocational training initiatives for learners, staff and organisations. Its purpose is to support and supplement the training policies of member states. There are six main areas: mobility projects; multilateral projects; networks; partnerships, preparatory visits, and transfer of innovation. The other European lifelong learning programmes include **Comenius**, **Erasmus**, **Grundtvig**, and **Transversal**.

See also: Lingua, Petra

Further reading: Commission of the European Communities (1993); www.leonardo.org.uk; www.leonardo.org.uk/; http://ec.europa.eu/ education/lifelong-learning-programme/doc78 _en.htm (accessed 30 May 2010)

LIBRARIES – SCHOOL

During the 1840s and 1850s the number of books in schools was few in number. Gradually this number increased beyond the Bible and a few other texts. Book-hawking, or travelling books, was also used to complement stationary libraries. Lending libraries were encouraged by Reverend W. J. Kennedy, HMI, who reported that a Mr Horner, Her Majesty's Inspector of Factories had made grants for books using mill-fines.

Further reading: Minutes 1855–56, p. 274; Minutes 1855–56, p.367

LICENCE TO COOK

(September 2008–) This initiative provided an entitlement for all pupils in maintained school to learn to cook, and to learn about nutrition and diet, food shopping, and health and safety. From September 2011, cooking is a compulsory element of **Key Stage** 3 Design and Technology.

See also: School Food Trust; (Practical) Housewifery

Further reading: www.licencetocook.org.uk (accessed 30 May 2010)

LIFE AND DUTIES OF THE CITIZEN

This was a subject first described in the 1893 **Evening Continuation School Code,** which addressed three main areas: representative government, the empire and industrial life, and social life and duties. The latter included a number of headings including: 'Selection for boys or girls of work in life. Loss to the nation when they are set to uncongenial labour. Corresponding gain of 'tools to the man who can use them'. What constitutes national wealth. Every capable and industrious and self-respecting citizen should add to the wealth of the community. Relation of skill and knowledge (a) to personal well-being and happiness; (b) to industrial success; (c) to the power of public usefulness'. The **Code** also addressed 'the importance to the nation of effective, honest, and intelligent management of all forms of business and industry. The disasters which result from mismanagement and fraud' (Report 1892–93 p. 404; Report 1892–93 p. 405).

See also: Citizenship Education

LIFELONG LEARNING NETWORKS

(2004) LLNs were concerned with the progression of vocational learners into and through higher education. The networks were concerned with curriculum development, new opportunities, and encouraging agreement across institutions about the value of qualifications and publicity.

Further reading: www.lifelonglearningnetworks.org.uk (accessed 01 June 2010)

LIFELONG LEARNING UK

(July 2004) LLUK is the independent employer-led **Sector Skills Council** responsible for the professional development of all those working in community learning and development, further education, higher education, libraries, archives and information services, and work-based learning. The goals of LLUK are:

- 'to reduce skills gaps and shortages;
- to improve productivity, business and public service performance;
- to increase opportunities to boost the skills and productivity of everyone in the sector;
- to improve learning supply; and,
- to improve LLUK's performance and delivery'.

See also: Teaching in the Lifelong Learning Sector Qualifications

Further reading: www.lluk.org/ (accessed 01 June 2010)

LINGUA

An EC programme aimed at promoting quantitative and qualitative improvement in European language competence. It covered the working languages of the EC. UK LIN-GUA was set up in 1990 in London, Belfast and Edinburgh, with EC funding set at £130m for the period 1990–95.

Further reading: Dickson et al. (1994)

LITERARY INSTITUTES

In 1918, London County Council encouraged the establishment of non-vocational adult education and provided support to literary institutes that opened in September 1919. Subjects included: literature, music, history and social science, psychology and philosophy, art, folk dancing, physical exercise and science (Report 1922–23 p. 103). One of the first was the City Literary Institute, which still continues to provide a wide range of classes.

LOAN GUARANTEE SCHEME

The Loan Guarantee Scheme helped small firms to obtain finance where conventional loans were unavailable due to lack of security or track record. This scheme enabled small firms to start up or expand. The Government guaranteed 75 per cent (85 per cent in Inner City Task Force Areas) of loans up to £100, 000 maximum in return for a premium payment of 2.5 per cent per year on the guaranteed amount. The procedure for loans up to £15,000 was simplified, in January 1988, increasing applications from 120 per month in 1987 to 300 in 1991/92. For Inner City Task Force Areas this premium was reduced to 2 per cent in April 1990.

See also: Inner-City Initiatives

Further reading: Barrett (1990)

LOCAL ACTION TEAMS

(1988) As part of the initiative for inner city redevelopment, teams were set up drawing on local **Department of Employment** and **Manpower Services Commission** staff, along with private sector involvement to tackle specific local problems. Part of the **Action for Cities** programme.

Further reading: Rebello (1991)

LOCAL AREA AGREEMENTS

(Piloted from 2005) The LAA '[i]s a three year agreement, based on Local Sustainable Community Strategies, that sets out the priorities for a local area agreed between Central Government, represented by Government Office (GO), and the local area, represented by the lead local authority and other key partners through Local Strategic Partnerships'. Skills levels, for example reducing the number of young people '**not in education, employment or training**' (NEET), are included within the agreement.

Further reading: Office of the Deputy Prime Minister 2006, p. 7.

LOCAL COLLABORATIVE PROJECTS

(1984–1988) A joint initiative between the **MSC** and **Education Department** where employers and education providers in both HE and FE got together to expand updating. A total of 126 projects were set up with 1,800 employers and training providers, and 25 per cent of the thrust was aimed at the SME sector of industry. These projects were designed as part of the **Department of Education and Science's Professional, Industrial and Commercial Updating** (PICKUP) programme. Over £8m was spent on LCPs – 'pump priming' for around 650 projects involving some 4,000 employers. They ended with the formation of **training and enterprise councils (TECs)**.

Further reading: HM Inspectors (1990); MSC (1985g); MSC Annual Report 1986–87, p. 27

LOCAL COMPETITIVENESS BUDGET

Combined **Department for Education and Employment** and **Department for Trade and Industry** support to business through **Training and Enterprise Councils** and **Business Link** Partnerships. It had a primary aim to improve business performance and was intended for SMEs. The DfEE involvement was with planning and workforce skills development and in 1997–98 the budget for England was £62.1m, rising to £65.2m in 1999–2000.

Further reading: DfEE (1999g)

LOCAL CONSULTANCY AND TRAINING GRANT SCHEMES

(1984) Grants were introduced to help small firms to improve business performance and manage change more effectively by providing more or better training for their employees and to train recruits for hard-to-fill vacancies.

See also: Grants – Local Consultancy; Grants – Local Training

Further reading: MSC (1985c)

LOCAL DEVELOPMENT PROJECTS

(1986) Ran along similar lines to **local collaborative projects**, and encouraged local organisations to look at and remedy training deficiencies and also to improve adult training. They ended with the introduction of **Training and Enterprise Councils**.

Further reading: MSC Annual Report 1986–87, p. 28

LOCAL EDUCATION AUTHORITIES

The **Education Act 1902** abolished the **school boards** and replaced them with 333 local education authorities operating with borough or county councils, urban districts etc. The earliest 'appointed day' for the operation of the act was 1 April 1903. Under

the act, LEAs were also responsible for the training and instruction of teachers, including **pupil-teachers**. Since that time LEAs responsibility for education and training has ebbed and flowed depending upon policies and governments. A major change occurred as a result of the Education and Skills Act 2008, which raised compulsory education and training from 16 to 18 years, and the Apprenticeships, Skills, Children and Learning Act 2009. Prior to April 2010 the **Learning and Skills Council** had responsibility for funding further education; this was then transferred to LEAs, giving them control of education and training from 5 to 19 years.

LOCAL EMPLOYER NETWORKS

LENs were set up as employers' self-help groups where assistance from departmental sources could be called upon. They were more appropriate for SMEs, so that economies of scale and best practice could be identified and achieved.

Further reading: Bennett et al. (1990)

LOCAL EMPLOYMENT ACTS 1960 AND 1963

Provided for training support in areas where new employment was needed – the beginnings of 'Development Area Status'. Financial assistance was in the form of grants to firms for the training they initiated to provide further jobs. This could also include the loan of the department's instructors to train semi-skilled engineering workers on employers' premises.

Further reading: Ministry of Labour Annual Report 1962, pp. 47, 66, 220

LOCAL EMPLOYMENT COMMITTEES

Were the main voluntary advisory bodies attached to employment exchanges and were originally set up in 1917 under the Labour Exchanges Act 1909. Their main purpose was to supply local knowledge on local industrial problems. They also kept the employment exchanges in close contact with local employers and workers and acted as monitors of local office activities. Their authority was subsequently based on the 1948 Industrial Training Act and in 1966 there were 364 committees. The 1973 Employment and Training Act, which established the **Manpower Services Commission (MSC)**, repealed the statutory authority of LECs, which were wound up in 1974 and replaced by District Manpower Committees in the autumn of 1975. In October 1982 the MSC replaced the DMCs with a new network of **Area Manpower Boards**.

Further reading: Price (2000)

LOCAL EMPLOYMENT PARTNERSHIPS

(Announced at Budget 21 March 2007) Led by **Jobcentre Plus** in England, Wales and Scotland and the **Employment Service** in Northern Ireland, LEPs were designed to encourage long-term unemployed people back into work. Initially, major retail employers such as Asda, B & Q, Marks and Spencer, Sainsbury's and Tesco agreed to encourage managers to support a number of initiatives:

- offering 2–4 week work trials;
- offering a target number of places to **New Deal** applicants;
- agreeing that the partners would work together and advise on pre-employment training, offering interviews to those who had completed the training;
- encouraging employees to provide one-to-one mentoring for long-term benefit claimants; and,
- reviewing the application process to ensure local benefit claimants were not unreasonably excluded due to lack of qualifications etc.

See also: Jobs Pledge

Further reading: Department for Work and Pensions (July 2007)

LOCAL ENTERPRISE COMPANIES

There were originally 22 LECs in Scotland responsible to **Scottish Enterprise** and **Highlands and Islands Enterprise**. The LECs developed flexible responses to support local labour market needs. They worked within a framework of plans agreed by the respective Secretaries of State for Employment and Scotland to organise delivery of national programmes to national standards and objectives. Their equivalent in England and Wales were **training and enterprise councils**.

Further reading: Price (2000); Wicks (1992)

LOCAL EXAMINATIONS

These were examinations instituted by the universities of Cambridge and Oxford and their purpose was to support schools. 'The Local Examinations instituted by the two ancient Universities more than half a century ago were devised with the sole purpose of helping the Schools at a time when no other guide or standard was available' (Report 1923–24 p. 28).

Further reading: www.cambridgeassessment. org.uk/ca/About_Us/Our_Heritage (accessed 31 May 2010)

LOCAL GRANTS TO EMPLOYERS

See: Grants to Employers Scheme

LOCAL INITIATIVE FUND

The Local Initiative Fund gave each **Training and Enterprise Council / Local Enterprise Company** the opportunity to support innovative solutions to local training and enterprise requirements. The fund consisted of several parts:

- an annual award – funds provided to TECs based on their working populations;
- matching funding – each £1 raised from private sources was matched by £1 from public sources; and,

- performance-related funding – based upon TECs achieving performance targets.

Examples of initiatives include: local training awards, and improving labour market information.

Further reading: Grubb Institute (1992)

LOCAL LEARNING AND SKILLS COUNCILS

See: (Local) Learning and Skills Councils

LOCAL LEARNING CENTRES

See: Neighbourhood Learning Centres

LOCAL STRATEGIC PARTNERSHIPS

(2001) LSPs are non-statutory bodies which bring together public, private, voluntary and community stakeholders at a local level to take a number of decisions about priorities and funding for their local area. Their purpose is to provide a single co-ordinating framework to develop community strategies targeted at economic, social and environmental wellbeing.

LOG BOOK OF SCHOOL

Schoolteachers were encouraged by HMIs to keep a record of events and this was eventually mandated in the **Revised Code of Regulations**: '56. The diary or log-book must be stoutly bound, and contain not less than 500 ruled pages. 57. The principal teacher must daily make in the log-book the briefest entry which will suffice to specify either ordinary progress, or whatever other fact concerning the school or its teachers, such as dates of withdrawals, commencements of duty, cautions, illness, may require to be referred to at a future time, or may otherwise deserve to be recorded'. (Report 1861–62 p. xxv)

LONDONDERRY REGENERATION INITIATIVE

A similar programme to **Making Belfast Work** and aimed at particularly disadvantaged areas. The **Training and Employment Agency** introduced the initiatives to provide access to local information about jobs and training opportunities, target training in growth sectors, and improve skill levels and innovation. The purpose was to involve local community organisations where possible. In 1991/92 £0.5m enabled 450 people to obtain jobs or training. Projects included a new open learning access centre and **Job Training Programme (JTP)** and **Youth Training Programme (YTP)** initiatives.

Further reading: Training and Employment Agency Annual Report (1992)

LORDS OF THE TREASURY

On 17 August 1833 Parliament resolved: 'That a sum not exceeding £20,000 be granted to His Majesty, to issue in aid of private subscriptions for the erection of school houses for the education of children of the poorer classes in Great Britain, to 31st March 1834' (Minutes 1844 Vol. 1, p. 126). Applications for aid were referred by the Lords of the Treasury to the National Society and the British and Foreign Schools Society, who issued a form of questions to the applicants and reported back to the Treasury. Among the conditions related to their Lordships' grants were:

1. 'That no portion of this sum be applied to any purpose whatever, except for the erection of new school-houses, and that in the definition of a school-house the residence for masters or attendants be not included.
2. That no application be entertained unless a sum be raised by private contribution equal at the least to one-half of the total estimated expenditure.
3. That the amount of private subscription be received, expended, and be accounted for,

179

before any issue of public money for such school be directed'.

For example, £10,000 pounds was granted by Parliament in 1835 for the erection of **normal** or **model schools**, and the Lords of the Committee recommended that it be equally divided between the National Society for Promoting the Education of the Poor in the Principles of the Established Church; and the **British and Foreign School Society'.** (Minutes 1844 Vol. 1, p. 126). This responsibility for disbursing grants was subsequently taken over by the **Committee of the Council of Education** in 1839.

(THE) LOWER CERTIFICATE

The Lower Certificate was awarded in Scotland and it was sometimes known as the Day School Certificate (Lower). This certificate, which replaced the Merit Certificate (Report Scotland 1925–26 p. 14) was awarded to pupils who had completed not less than one years study after the completion of elementary education, which used to be called the 'Qualifying' stage (Report of the Committee of Council on Education in Scotland 1924–25 p. 8).

See also: (The) Higher Certificate; (The) Intermediate Certificate

LOWER SCHOOL

This was a term often used, within the overall school, to describe that part of the school in which the younger children attended. It might include infants but more generally referred to marginally older children.

See also: Upper School

Further reading: Report 1860–61 p. 450

LYCEUMS

These were established in the 1800s for the adult education of the working classes. Examples of lyceums were found in Ancoats, Salford, Chorlton-on-Medlock and Oldham.

Further reading: Tylecote (1957 p. 79)

M

MACHINE CONSTRUCTION AND DRAWING

An examination for this subject was described in the report of the **Board of Education** (1899–1900 Vol. 1, p. 22).

MADRAS SYSTEM

This was developed by Andrew Bell (1753–1832), a Scottish Anglican priest, who was born in St Andrew's, Fife. In 1774 he travelled to Virginia and became tutor to the sons of a tobacco planter. Later, in 1789, he took charge of the East India Company's newly established Madras Male Orphan Asylum at Egmore, near Madras, which was for the sons of private soldiers and native Indian mothers. While in India (1787–91) he noticed, in a local native school in Malabar, children learning the alphabet by writing in sand. His attempt to introduce sand-boards in the asylum was resisted by the teachers and so he used an advanced pupil, Johnnie Frisken, to teach the other children, thus introducing **pupil-teachers** and **monitorial education**. Returning to Britain, he published a pamphlet in 1897 titled 'An experiment made at the Male Asylum, suggesting a system by which a school or family may teach itself under the superintendence of a master or parent'. First World War veteran Henry Allingham later described the sand-boards as smelling badly because the sand was not changed regularly. In 1798, he established his Madras System at St Botolph's school, Aldgate, London, and the following year in Kendal Industrial School. Also, while living in Swanage, Dorset, he introduced the Madras System to the Sunday school and day schools. In 1811, Bell was approached by supporters of education and formed the 'Metropolitan Society for Promoting the Education of the Poor in the Principles of the Established Church, according to the system invented and practised by the Reverend Doctor Bell'. This was then renamed 'National Society for Promoting the Education of the Poor in the Principles of the Established Church, throughout England and Wales' – **National School Society**. Bell's system was adopted and developed by Joseph Lancaster and it became known as the Bell-Lancaster method or **Lancasterian** method. This was a system of **mutual instruction** where the children taught each other, often through a system of pupil-monitors. Bell bequeathed funds to found a number of schools in Scotland. Madras College was opened in October 1833 in St Andrew's, Scotland. Other Madras schools were founded, including Edinburgh, Glasgow, Aberdeen, and Inverness (Minutes 1855–56, p. 560).

Further reading: Stephen (1982)

MAINTAINED SCHOOLS

These are schools operating in the public education system that are maintained, or funded, by public funds. They can be contrasted with **independent schools**, which are privately funded.

MAINTENANCE ALLOWANCE

(1962–65) Previously the **training allowance scheme**, this was support provided to those undergoing a course of training at a **government training centre**. Rates were based on sex, age, number of dependants, and whether the person was living at home (local), or in lodgings or a ministry hostel (non-local).

Further reading: Ministry of Labour Gazette 1962, p. 387

MAKE A DIFFERENCE

(April 2007–March 2010) This was a lifelong learning UK initiative designed to encourage high flying graduates to build a career in the sector. It is one of four programmes set out in the 2006 White Paper *Further Education: Raising Skills, Improving Life Chances*, the others being: **Give Something Back**; **Business Talent,** and **Business Interchange**.

Further reading: www.lluk.org.uk (accessed 31 May 2010)

MAKING BELFAST WORK

Together with the **Londonderry Regeneration Initiative**, these two schemes in Northern Ireland were aimed at particularly disadvantaged areas. The **Training and Employment Agency** introduced the initiatives to provide access to local information about jobs and training opportunities, target training in growth sectors, and improve skill levels and motivation. The purpose was to involve local community organisations where possible. In 1991/92, £4m was spent on MBW and almost 5,000 people were placed in jobs or training. The projects included **Job Training Programme** and **Youth Training Programme** and also helped create **jobcentres** and extra **Action for Community Employment** places.

Further reading: Training and Employment Agency Annual Report (1992)

MANAGEMENT ACTION PROGRAMME

(1980–84) Was developed in line with needs identified by the June 1978 **Manpower Services Commission** policy document. Its purpose was to work with managers to improve their effectiveness; bring managers together; and to make successful techniques and approaches known throughout the national network using support materials. It used an action learning approach to bring ten individuals together in an action group and with the aid of a professional advisor encourage them to learn from the experiences of each other. There were five contracts between **MSC** and EMAS consultants amounting to funding of £578K. It was superseded by the Action Learning Programme.

Further reading: EMAS Consultants Ltd (1984)

MANAGEMENT ANALYSIS AND PLANNING

(Northern Ireland) (2007) This was a business improvement tool using online technology and people development consultants to work with companies of 10–250 employees to produce customised business training and development reports. A maximum of three days consultancy was fully subsidised by the **Department for Employment and Learning** and it encouraged companies to progress to **Investors in People**.

Further reading: www.delni.gov.uk/index/ successthroughskills/skills-and-training-program mes-2/ (accessed 31 May 2010)

MANAGEMENT AND LEADERSHIP DEVELOPMENT PROGRAMME

(September 2002) (Northern Ireland) This series of programmes targeted 250 graduates and 165 undergraduates. Also 500 opportunities were provided for new and existing managers across seven key development themes. A Management and Leadership Network was also developed.

Further reading: Department for Employment and Learning Annual Report 2002–2003

MANAGEMENT CHARTER INITIATIVE

(1988) The initiative arose from a national debate on management education and development, and concern about British managers receiving less training and less systematic training. The **Training Commission** conducted a study in the area. The Council for Management Education and Development launched the Management Charter Initiative and proposed the establishment of a coherent set of management qualifications and a Chartered Institute of Management. Subsequently the MCI (a **lead body**) produced the Management Standards. It was superseded by the **Management Standards Centre**.

Further reading: Barker (1993)

MANAGEMENT COMMITTEE OF SCHOOLS

During the 1800s, schools generally had a committee of management that oversaw the establishment and overall operation of the school. Committee members often included members of the church and people supportive of these educational initiatives. The HMI Reverend F. C. Cook reported: 'As a rule, the committees of management in my district interfere very little with the internal organization of schools. They generally leave this to be settled by the teachers, or delegate their authority to the parochial clergy. Undoubtedly much harm might be done by frequent and in discreet [sic] meddling; but I am satisfied that it would be advantageous to all parties if the managers regularly called for school reports, formally investigated the condition of the school, made a point of attending the periodical examinations, and from time to time inspected the work in the several classes, especially in the lowest part of the school. Good teachers are much encouraged by such marks of sympathy and interest' (Report 1858–59, p. 18).

See also: (School) Governors

MANAGEMENT DEVELOPMENT INITIATIVE

Designed to improve quality and quantity of training for managers. During 1984/85, 57 projects were funded and 40 approved at the cost of £1m. The Management Development Initiative was part of a series of measures within the **Job Training Programme**.

Further reading: MSC Annual Report 1984/85, pp. 76, 98–99

MANAGEMENT DEVELOPMENT PROGRAMME

Delivered through the **Management Charter Initiative**.

Further reading: DfEE Departmental Report 1998/99, Cm 3910, p. 76

MANAGEMENT EXTENSION PROGRAMME

This programme was part of **Training for Enterprise** and the **Manpower Services Commission** funded secondments of redundant managers to small firms. The first stage involved the proposals and requirements of the host firm being carefully assessed. Second, participating managers received intensive training in special techniques and problems of small businesses. Next, the manager spent a week with the firm examining the problem; and then the formal secondment, normally for twelve weeks, began at the end of the first week.

Further reading: MSC (1985d)

MANAGEMENT STANDARDS CENTRE

This was originally the Management Charter Initiative and was formed in 2001 as the Standards Setting Body for the **National Occupational Standards** in Management. It is an independent unit of the Institute of Management.

Further reading: www.management-standards.org

MANAGERS DEVELOPMENT PROGRAMME

Designed to support small business owner/managers in Northern Ireland. It aimed to strengthen and expand business and personal skills of second tier managers.

See also: Managers Programmes

Further reading: Training and Employment Agency Annual Report (1992)

MANAGERS PROGRAMMES

These programmes were designed to support existing managers and future graduate managers through practical management training within Northern Ireland companies.

See also: Managers Development Programme

Further reading: Training and Employment Agency Annual Report (1994)

MANAGING AGENTS

Providers of training for **Youth Training Scheme** and **Job Training Scheme**

Further reading: Linell (1985)

MANAGING COMPANY EXPANSION

A hybrid scheme formed from Aiding Company Expansion, which was a pilot project in 1985, and the Management Development Demonstration Programme of 1984. MACE used a problem-centred approach to address issues that were hindering growth and was largely focused on smaller employers. Its purpose was to link the problem or opportunity to the training and development of staff, using a top down approach. Grants, for half the cost of successful applications up to £15k, were used to pump-prime initiatives over a period of a year. In the 1987 review there were 120 companies involved and the total cost was £3.085m (MSC £1.372m and firms £1.713m).

Further reading: Sheppard and Blakey (1987)

MANAGING THE GROWING TOURISM BUSINESS

This initiative was focused on senior managers within the tourism business in Northern Ireland. Its development reflected the importance attached to tourism for the development of the economy.

See also: Young Managers Development Programme; Opryland Hotel Project

Further reading: Training and Employment Agency Annual Report (1997)

MANCHESTER CITY MISSION

(1837) During the 1800s a number of cities established missions with Manchester being one of the first. They introduced a system of tracking down children who did not attend school as a result of poverty and/or neglect, and, through influence or paying part of the school fees, helped parents select a school for their children (Minutes 1855–56 p. 369).

See also: Manchester Education Aid Society; Owens College

MANCHESTER EDUCATION AID SOCIETY

(1864) This society was formed from the merger of the Manchester and Salford Committee on Education and the National Public School Association. Their research identified that 'in every fifteen children between the ages of three and 12, one was at work, six were at school, and the other eight neglected as regards education' (Report 1865–66 p. 129). This evidence and the arguments of others led to the **Education Act 1870**.

See also: Manchester City Mission

MANPOWER RESEARCH UNIT

(1963) Established within the **Employment Department** of the **Ministry of Labour**. Its purpose was to investigate future labour requirements in the various sectors of the economy. This included the effects of new technology. One of the main objectives was to supply information to the **industrial training boards** so that they could plan training, and also to **government training centres**.

MANPOWER SERVICES COMMISSION

(1 January 1974 – August 1988) Was set up under the **Employment and Training Act 1973** to run the public employment and training services previously provided by the **Department of Employment**. It had two agencies, the **Employment Service Agency** and the **Training Services Agency**, which were statutory corporations. The commission also advised the Government on manpower policies. The commission had ten members. The chairman was an official appointment, with three members from the CBI and three from the TUC, two from local authority associations and one with education sector interests. The main aims of the commission were to:

- contribute to efforts to raise employment and reduce unemployment;
- assist manpower resources to be developed and contribute fully to economic well-being;
- help secure for each worker the opportunities and services he or she needed in order to lead a satisfying working life; and,
- improve the quality of decisions affecting manpower.

In 1978 the commission was brought together as a single body under unified management, with three operating divisions: Employment Service, Training Service, Special Programmes. There were also two support divisions: Corporate Services and Manpower Intelligence and Planning. At the same time operations had been decentralised in Scotland and Wales and permanent **manpower services committees** established in both, under their own chairmen. In 1987 employment services and related programmes, including **jobcentres**, transferred back to the direct control of the Department of Employment, with subsequent reorganisation. As a consequence, and following the **Employment Act 1988** the name of the commission was changed on 26 May 1988 to the **Training Commission**, identified as the national training authority. Under the 1988 act, the Training Commission had the power to appoint up to six commissioners without consultation. During 1988 the work of the Training Commission was taken over by the **Training Agency** – a departmental agency within the **Employment Department Group**.

Further reading: Ainley (1990); MSC Annual Reports 1974/75–1986/87; Price (2000); Training Commission Annual Report 1987/88, pp. 1–2, p. 95; Thompson and Rosenberg (1987)

MANPOWER SERVICES COMMITTEE – SCOTLAND

(July 1977–1988) Responsibility for the operation of the Manpower Services Commission in Scotland, was transferred to the Secretary of State for Scotland on 1st July 1977 and an office set up in October 1977, headed by a director. A permanent Manpower Services Committee was appointed under its own chairman. Committee members consisted of three representatives nominated by the STUC, three nominated by the Scottish CBI, two local authority representatives, and one representative of professional education interests. On the inception of the **Training Agency** in 1988, the Committee and its 47 **area manpower boards** ceased to exist.

Further reading: Brown and Fairley (1989); MSC Annual Reports; Training Commission Report (1987/88)

MANPOWER SERVICES COMMITTEE – WALES

(1977–88) Responsibility for the operation of a Manpower Services Commission in Wales was transferred to the Secretary of State for Wales in November 1977, and an office set up headed by a director. A permanent Manpower Services Committee was appointed under its own chairman. The composition of this permanent Committee was along the same lines as those for Scotland – *see entry above*. On the inception of the **Training Agency** in 1988, the Committee and its five **area manpower boards** ceased to exist.

Further reading: MSC Annual Reports; Training Commission Annual Report (1987/88); Manpower Services Commission in Wales Annual Report 1986/87

MANUAL INSTRUCTION

The Technical Instruction Act 1889 stated: 'The expression "manual instruction" shall mean instruction in the use of tools, processes of agriculture, and modelling in clay, wood, or other material' (Report 1900–01 Vol. 3, p. 413). Article 12f of the 1890 **Code** made provision for other subjects including manual instruction and training (1889–90 p. 118). 'In some foreign schools manual exercises in continuation of the employments of the **kindergarten**, are graduated in difficulty, are carried onward through all the classes of the school, and are found to be not without a useful reflex influence on all the ordinary school studies. Such exercises sometimes consist of modelling, the cutting, fixing, and inventing of paper patterns, the forming of

geometrical solids in cardboard, and the use of tools and instruments' (Report 1889–90 p. 180). Guidelines for manual instruction stated: 'Instruction must – (a) be, as a rule, carried on continuously throughout the school year for two hours weekly; (b) be in the use of the ordinary tools used in handicrafts in wood or iron; (c) be given in a properly fitted workshop wholly devoted to manual instruction; and (d) be connected with the instruction in drawing, that is to say, the work must be from drawings to scale previously made by the scholars' (Report 1897–98 p. 532).

See also: Manual Instruction Centres, Manual Work

MANUAL INSTRUCTION CENTRES

Manual instruction received impetus as a result of the Technical Instruction Act 1889; however, some school sites were only approved for ordinary school activities, and some other schools were built on playgrounds violating building regulations. To address these circumstances rules were issued stating: '(1) Manual Instruction should not be given in the class-rooms of the school. (2) A room to be used for Manual Instruction need not be on the same site as the school to which it is attached. (3) A room to be used for Manual Instruction should not be built on a site already occupied by the playground of a school, unless it can be so built that the school continues fully to fulfil the conditions of Building Rule 15, as to uncovered space, and the supply of fresh air to the school is not impeded. (4) The plan, arrangements, construction, lighting, and ventilation of the room should be those suitable for a workshop rather than those suitable for a school' (Report 1896–97 p. 659).

See also: Manual Work

MANUAL WORK

Manual work was encouraged by many school boards including Sheffield School

Board where most schools provided training in carpentry, which proved very popular. Sheffield City Council also provided a yearly grant to support instruction of teachers in Slöyd and Mr Rooper, HMI, in the Bradford District, commented: 'Of all the schools of manual training with which I am acquainted I find Slöyd to be the most effective for developing delicacy of manipulation, thoroughness of workmanship, and truth in the senses of touch and sight' (Report 1892–93 p. 17).

See also: Educational Development Association

MARINE CLASS

(1853) Schools in the nineteenth century were established for a variety of occupational purposes including seafaring. A Marine class was established at Berwick Charity School to educate boys in the traditional subjects as well as training and instruction as seamen. After three years of instruction, the boys were morally bound to be placed on ships as apprentices for five years according to the customary terms of marine indentures (Minutes 1854–55 p. 559).

MARINE SCHOOLS

Children of non-commissioned officers and privates attended marine schools and, after examination, were issued with certificates of proficiency by the Inspector of Naval Schools (Report 1882–83 p. 182).

See also: Royal Dockyard Schools; Navigation Schools; Merchant Marine Training Ships

MATRIX QUALITY STANDARD

(1 April 2002) The standard was designed to help organisations identify and follow best practice in the provision of information, advice and guidance services. It detailed the quality of service outcomes that helped individuals to use the information, investigate opportunities and make action plans in connection with learning and work. The standard setting body for the matrix was the Guidance Council and the assessment and awarding body was the Guidance Accreditation Board. It replaced the existing quality standards for learning and work. It had a ten-point framework – five areas of service delivery and five areas of management of the service.

1 'People are made aware of and engage with the service.
2 People understand the nature of the service.
3 People's use of the service is agreed.
4 People are provided with access to information.
5 People are supported in exploring options and making choices.
6 Service delivery is planned and maintained.
7 Premises and equipment are sufficient to deliver the service.
8 Staff competence and the support they are given are sufficient to deliver the service.
9 Feedback on the quality of the service is obtained.
10 Continuous quality improvement is ensured through monitoring and action'.

www.matrixstandard.com/
(accessed 31 May 2010)

MEASURES TO MAKE THE TRAINING MARKET WORK BETTER

This was an umbrella term for a number of programmes including: **Adult Training Strategy**; **Open Tech Programme**; **Open Learning Programme**; **Open College**; **local collaborative projects**; **local employer networks**; **National Online Manpower Information System (NOMIS)**. The purpose of these initiatives was 'to increase the effectiveness of vocational education and training; to ensure that consumers and providers of training have adequate information on labour market issues; and to make relevant and cost-effective provision easily accessible to employers and individuals' (MSC Annual Report 1985–86, p. 19).

MECHANICS

Mechanics, engineering, physical geography, industrial work, chemistry, gardening and cookery were introduced in some schools as subjects during the 1840s and 1850s (Report 1870–71 p. 127) and there was even an examination paper in 'Mensuration and Industrial Mechanics' (Report 1854–55 p. 83). However, these subjects proved relatively unsuccessful and only two decades later were revived with mechanics being introduced as a **specific subject** in 1878–79; this allowed grants to be awarded for satisfactory provision of this subject. Mr Arnold, HMI, commented that: 'The excuse for putting most of these matters [mathematics, German, mechanics, animal physiology, physical geography, and botany] into our programme is that we are all coming to be agreed that an entire ignorance of the system of nature is as gross a defect in our children's education as not to know that there ever was such a person as Charles the First. Now our ordinary class-programme provides, or at any rates suggests, some remedy against the second kind of ignorance, for history is one of our class subjects it provides none against the second. This is a blot; we ought surely to provide that some knowledge of the system of nature should form part of the regular class course. ... And this is what the teaching of *Natur-kunde* or natural philosophy (to use the formerly received somewhat over-ambitious, English name for the kind of thing) should aim at' (Report 1878–79 p. 462).

See also: Mechanics Institutes

MECHANICS INSTITUTES

During the Industrial Revolution numerous societies were established to share knowledge and explore the links between mechanical experience and science. One of the earliest was the Spitalfields Mathematical Society founded by artisans, weavers and shopkeepers in 1717 (Cawthorne, 1929). In 1789, workmen in Birmingham established the Birmingham

Sunday Society, which delivered lectures and classes in the trades. Dr George Birkbeck extended this idea with free classes in the 'mechanical arts' between 1800 and 1804 and this led to the establishment of the first mechanics' institute in Glasgow in 1821. Birkbeck established the London Mechanics Institute (later becoming Birkbeck College) in 1823 and the model was swiftly copied in other towns and cities. 'The original object of the mechanics' institution was the professional instruction of operatives; they were never intended to supersede apprenticeship, but to afford such instruction in the branches of science applicable to each particular trade, that a workman might be in a position to reason about the work on which he was engaged, and be qualified to suggest improvements in the methods he was adopting' (Minutes 1853–54, Vol. 2, p. 580). The various societies such as mechanics institutes were exempted from taxation by the Scientific and Literary Societies Act 1843. The New **Code** of the Education Act 1870 allowed for the first time evening classes to be unconnected with day schools and many mechanics institutes allowed their elementary classes to be inspected and thus receive grants (Minutes 1874–75 p. 211).

See also: Mutual Instruction Societies; Society for the Diffusion of Useful Knowledge; Newsrooms

Further reading: Cawthorne, 1929; Tylecote, (1957)

MENTAL AND GENERAL CULTIVATION

In 1893 there appeared recognition of the importance of mental and general cultivation for **pupil–teachers** beyond that of academic study. 'Study and bookwork alone do not complete the education of these young persons for the work and the life which are before them. A natural history club, a cricket club, a little debating or literary society, a course of **university extension** lectures, a visit to a neighbouring factory or picture gallery or famous building, a well-planned holiday excursion may have no visible or immediate relation to the school duties; but anyone of these things is in its own way useful in its influence on the character and general power of the youthful teacher' (Report 1892–93 p. 474).

See also: Mental Science

MENTAL SCIENCE

In training colleges in the early 1880s it was felt that an understanding of mental science, that is, the operation of the brain and mind, would help an understanding of education. Mr Sharpe, HMI, presented a condensed syllabus of lectures by Mr Sully on this subject including: 'I. – Introductory – Mental Science and its relation to Education – How we know Mind – Observation of Children's Minds – Three-fold division of Mind: Knowing, Feeling, and Willing – Conditions of Mental Activity – Physical Conditions: Vigour and Freshness of Brain – Mental Conditions: Attention' (Report 1882–83 p. 549).

See also: Mental and General Cultivation

MERCHANT MARINE TRAINING SHIPS

(1859) The merchant training ship HMS Conway was founded by the Mercantile Marine Service Association in 1859. It was moored on the River Mersey at Liverpool and its purpose was to develop the skills of boys to become future officers in the mercantile marine. Three other training ships were to be found on the Mersey at this time, two of them **reformatory ships**: the Akbar (1865) for Protestant boys and the Clarence for Catholic boys. The fourth was the TS Indefatigable (1864), which was a charitable institution for pauper boys (Minutes 1859–60 p. 488). In 1937 a central board was established to coordinate the provision of officer training: 'The object of this Board is to initiate and conduct a training scheme for apprentices while at sea and, in addition to making the

scheme known as widely as possible among ship owners, they are concerned with the supervision of facilities for instruction, including a scheme of correspondence courses linked up with technical navigation schools on shore; the preparation and issue of suitable syllabuses of instruction; and the conduct of annual examinations to test the progress of apprentices pursuing the course leading to the Second Mate's Certificate of the Board of Trade and to accustom them to examination conditions' (Report 1937 p. 31).

See also: Marine Schools; Navigation Schools; Royal Dockyard Schools

Further reading: Cowan (1984)

MERIT GRANT

This was an award based on school performance in comparison to other schools and was described in the 1883 **Code of Regulations**: 'A merit code of 2s, 4s, or 6s., if the Inspector reports the school or class to be fair, good, or excellent, allowing for the special circumstances of the case, and having regard to the provision made for (1) suitable instruction in the **elementary subjects**, (2) simple lessons on objects and on the phenomena of nature and common life, and (3) appropriate and varied occupations. No merit grant is made unless the report on the instruction in the elementary subjects is satisfactory' (Report 1882–83 p. 123).

See also: Merit Table

MERIT TABLE

With the introduction of the Revised **Code of Regulations** in 1862, HMIs were expected to examine the school pupils during their inspection. This assessment of pupils against the standards meant that they were then able to compare the performance of schools. A number of HMIs began to produce merit tables. Mr Middleton, HMI, used four elements to construct a score: 'I. Marks for discipline; II. Proportion of marks gained for each child examined. III. Proportion of marks gained for each child present. IV. Proportion of marks gained in the three upper standards for each child examined' (Report 1864–65 pp. 265–66).

The HMI also remarked: 'I now add a Merit Table which shows the competitive standing of all the school, except one – a purely infant and sewing school, which, for obvious reasons, is omitted. The female schools are subjected to the same rigid ordeal of calculation as the others, though, in consideration of the greater prevalence of the infant and purely sewing elements in them, and the daily subtraction from their intellectual work of the time devoted to *industrial training* it would have been only just to have added to their marks say, one-eighth of the recorded numbers … But in a competitive Table the justice of such an addition might have been questioned by some' (Report, 1864–65 p. 265).

See also: League Tables; Merit Grant

METAL WORK

(1897) '**Manual instruction** in metal' was first described in the 1897 **Evening Continuation School Code** and it consisted either: '(i) Of elementary metal work, such as chipping, filing, and shaping metal, either by hand, or in the lathe, or by the use of machine tools; or (ii) Of metal embossing and chasing, in which case sheet-metal is either driven back from the face, or hammered out from the back into relief and finished on the front surface with fine punches and graving tools' (Report 1896–97 p. 631). It was expected that metal work would be associated with accurate scale drawings with a focus on accuracy rather than speed. The properties of metals and alloys were taught together with the use of tools.

See also: Manual Instruction; Woodwork

MIDDLE SCHOOL

This term was in use in 1852 (Minutes 1852–53, Vol. 1, p. 58) and it had two distinct uses.

The first referred to schools that began to emerge in 1850s/1860s and meant the class between the infant school and the upper **division** (Report 1860–61 p. 312). The second use related to social status with an HMI recommendation for middle schools to be built for the middle classes providing education that was different to that provided by 'religious zeal' for the poorer classes (Minutes, 1853–54, Vol. 2, p. 434). However, in later correspondence it was articulated: 'With regard to that class which, as small farmers, small shopkeepers, small tradesmen of what ever kind above the class of journeymen, or lastly, as foremen and highly skilled artisans, forms the stratum of society next above labourers, properly so called, The Lord President is not of opinion that the education of their children should be separated from that of the children of the labourers by any act on the part of the State' (Minutes 1857–58, p. 42).

Later, the **Hadow reports** and **Education Act 1944** encouraged the distinction between primary and secondary education. In 1964 the law was changed to allow middle schools, and a range of models emerged covering the ages of 8–12, 9–13 and also 9–14. Middle schools were viewed by some as smoothing the transition from primary to secondary education, which often resulted in a decline in performance; however, the continued restructuring of education led to a decline in their popularity.

See also: Primary Education

MILITARY DRILL

(1871) The **Code** of 1871 first recognised the teaching of military drill to boys attending school. A 'Manual of Elementary Military Exercises' used in army schools for the children of soldiers was included in a list of War Office publications by the Controller of the Stationery Office and made available for use in elementary schools (Report 1882–83 p. xviii). Before this official recognition, the drilling of school children, often combined with drum and fife **bands**, was successfully introduced into many schools improving discipline, patriotism and making them 'more fit for defenders of their country' (Report 1861–62 p. 27).

MILITARY TRAINING

During the First World War the **Board of Education** provided aid to local authorities who provided training 'for men serving with the Colours'. 'The instruction given tended to fall under one or the other of two types. The first type consisted of instruction in subjects which were likely to be of practical use to the soldiers, such as French, German, Map-reading, Telegraphy, or Field Cookery; the second included more recreative work, such as Singing or popular Lectures. The most common subject of instruction was French' (Report 1914–15 p. 52).

MILLENNIUM TRAINING PROGRAMME

This initiative in Northern Ireland was designed to provide training to enable employees to address the potential IT problems arising from the Year 2000 problem or the 'Millennium Bug'. In Britain it was called **Bug Buster Training**.

Further reading: Training and Employment Agency Annual Report (1999)

MILLENNIUM VOLUNTEERS

Launched in 1999 it offered an opportunity for people to develop initiative and communication skills. Volunteers signed up to a volunteer plan. After completing 100 hours they received a Millennium Volunteer Certificate. After 200 hours they were presented with a Millennium Award Certificate.

Further reading: DfEE Employment News February 2001, p. 8; DfEE (1999j)

MINES – REGULATION AND INSPECTION ACT

(1860) The Regulation and Inspection of Mines Act 1860 prevented females from working in mines and raised the minimum working age of boys from ten to twelve; ' … no boy under twelve years of age might be employed in a coal mine, unless he could produce a certificate from a competent schoolmaster that he could read and write, or, failing in this, that he was attending school for not less than three hours a day during two days in each week' (Report 1863–64 p. 87).

See also: Coal Mines Regulation Act, Colliery Schools

MINING PROPRIETORS IN MONMOUTHSHIRE

(1840) Arising from a massed march on the town of Newport in November 1839, a letter was written to the proprietors of mines in Monmouthshire asking them to establish a school or schools in the area in order to help improve education and thereby improve public behaviour etc. An offer was made to provide half of the cost of school buildings. 'These considerations are based on the comparatively low level of wise foresight concerning the interests of the industry and trade of the district, which will be prosperous in proportion as capital is secure, and as labourers are skilful, intelligent, steady and industrious' (Minutes 1839–40 p. 32).

MINING SCHOOLS

Mining schools would appear to have been established in the mid-1800s with Wigan Mining and Technical College (subsequently Wigan and Leigh College) being established in 1858. There is also evidence of a mining school in Cornwall in 1838 (Minutes 1851–52 Vol 2 p. 10). Further centres for instruction were established at later periods, for example the Mining Instruction Centre at West Stanley, Durham (Report 1928 p. 30).

191

See also: Colliery School; Government School of Mines

MINISTRY OF EDUCATION

(1944–64) The **Education Act 1944** replaced the **Board of Education** with the Ministry of Education. The ministry was then succeeded by the **Department of Education and Science**.

MINISTRY OF LABOUR

(January 1917) Its origin began in 1893 as a branch of the **Board of Trade**. It was called the Commercial, Labour and Statistical Department and was quickly renamed the **Labour Department**. It was created as a separate ministry in 1917 and the Labour Exchanges Division was given the title, **Employment Department**. In 1927 responsibility for youth employment was transferred from the **Board of Education** to the **Ministry of Labour** and the latter also acquired charge of training and employment for the disabled from the Ministry of Pensions. It changed to the **Ministry of Labour and National Service** in 1939 and reverted to the **Ministry of Labour** in 1959. In 1968 it became the **Department of Employment and Productivity**.

Further reading: Price (2000)

MINISTRY OF LABOUR AND NATIONAL SERVICE

(8 September 1939–1959) Previously known as the **Ministry of Labour** it was re-titled the **Ministry of Labour and National Service** in 1939 and reverted to the **Ministry of Labour** in 1959.

MINISTRY OF LABOUR TRAINING OFFICERS

These trainers provided training of supervisors in organisations. Prior to 1 April 1962 the provision of training was restricted to small firms and after that date charges were made for the training.

Further reading: Ministry of Labour Gazette (1962)

MINISTRY OF TECHNOLOGY

The Ministry of Technology was established by the Labour Government in October 1964 to support technological and economic development. It acquired the responsibilities of the Ministry of Aviation in 1967 and Ministry of Power in 1969. In October 1970 it was merged with the **Board of Trade** creating the **Department of Trade and Industry**.

MINUTES OF THE COMMITTEE OF COUNCIL OF EDUCATION

The minutes were published from 1839–40 to 1857–58 when the minutes became a report. It was directed that one copy of the minutes be supplied to each school under in inspection from 1855–56 and further copies could be purchased from Mr Hansard, Printer to the House of Commons (Minutes 1855–56, p. 21).

MIXED METHOD

This approach was a modification of **mutual instruction** in which better educated monitors or **pupil-teachers** instructed groups of pupils within the same classroom under the supervision of the schoolmaster. School designs in the 1840s were illustrated to show how the mixed method might be used.

Further reading: Minutes 1840–41, pp. 46/47

MIXED SCHOOLS

During the 1840s and 1850s many schools in small rural parishes had two separate rooms with a schoolmaster teaching boys in one and a schoolmistress teaching girls in the other. This structure was gradually replaced with mixed schools in which the master taught both sexes in the morning and the girls were taught needlework by a sewing mistress in the afternoon. The HMI Reverend J. J. Bland-ford reported: 'Without expressing an opinion as to the desirability and comparative efficiency of mixed schools ... I cannot report any bad consequences that have taken place from mixed schools'. And: 'Whether ... the girls exert a beneficial influence over the boys by softening their manners and making them less rough, is more than I can say; I sincerely hope for the sake of the softer sex, and for their future comfort as wives, that such may be the case' (Report 1858–59 p. 73).

See also: Municipal Dual Schools

MOBILE INSTRUCTOR SERVICES

The Mobile Instructor Service was part of the Training Services Agency **direct training services**. It trained 350 employees from 36 firms in 1977, compared with 250 in 1976. It provided instructors for workers in engineering, electronics and various allied skills. There were short courses between one and eight weeks in length, to unskilled workers, and additional skills to existing workers, for example in technological change and general safety procedures.

Further reading: MSC (1978b); Training Services Agency (1978)

MODEL SCHOOLS

(1840s–) These were sometimes called practising schools; however, the two were distinguished by the Reverend H. Moseley, HMI, who stated: 'The obvious conception of a model school attached to a training school is, that it should be a school presenting to the students the example of such schools as each might reasonably hope eventually to become the master of' (Minutes 1853–54, Vol. 1, p. 448). With reference to the Caermarthen

Training Institution, the history of the name 'model school' was described in the Minutes (1856–57, p. 517): '[it is] designed to serve not only the common purpose of instruction, but to provide some kind of training for schoolmasters employed by the trustees, and hence it receive the name of the "central" or "model" school.'

See also: Demonstration Schools; Normal Schools

MODERN APPRENTICESHIPS

These were prototyped in 40 **training and enterprise councils** in 1994 and then extended nationally in 1995. They were a new approach to apprenticeships offering young people aged 16–24 a programme of work-based training leading to technician, supervisor and similar level qualifications and typically taking three years. It was an upgrade of **youth training** and designed to qualify young people to at least NVQ Level 3 and a nationally recognised qualification considered equivalent to two A levels. One of the main features was a training agreement signed by the individual, the employer and the **TEC**, setting out the training in key skills to be given and a mutual commitment to see it through. Initial government funding for the first three years was £100m. In 1999, the **DfEE** reported that **NTOs**, together with **TECs** and employers had developed frameworks for 81 sectors of industry, business and commerce, attracting over 2,000,000 young people with modern apprenticeships recognised as a pathway for progression to higher levels of qualification within their chosen career.

A Report of the Modern Apprenticeship Advisory Committee, issued by the **Department for Education and Skills** in September 2001 made a number of recommendations for future delivery and further expansion. 'Modern apprenticeships' have become a generic term incorporating foundation modern apprenticeships and advanced modern apprenticeships. The original modern apprenticeships have been incorporated within advanced modern apprenticeships.

See also: National Apprenticeship Service

Further reading: DfES (September 2001); Ernst & Young (1995)

MODERN APPRENTICESHIPS – ACCELERATED

(Sept. 1995) Accelerated modern apprenticeships were announced in the White Paper *Competitiveness – Helping Business to Win.* Modern apprenticeships were to be extended to school and college leavers between the ages of 18 and 19. The training took less time because entrants were more mature and had prior qualifications and competencies. Take-up did not reach expected numbers and following a review, the decision was taken to merge accelerated modern apprenticeships with **modern apprenticeships** from April 1996.

Further reading: Bayliss (1998)

MODERN APPRENTICESHIPS – ADVANCED

The recommended age of entry to this qualification was normally 16–24 and participants were originally registered with **local learning and skills councils**. Entry requirements were originally set by the **National Training Organisation**, and the minimum duration was normally two years with the provision of an accelerated option of not less than one year for 18–24-year-olds who already had key skills in the occupation. The minimum standard for successful completion is **Scottish/ National Vocational Qualifications** Level 3 in the relevant occupation, as well as satisfactory off-the-job attainments: key skills at Level 2 in communication and numbers. On successful completion, the person was to receive the award of the advanced modern apprenticeship Diploma by the **Sector Skills Council (SSC)**. Both the **AMA** and **FMA** lead to **NVQs**, **key skills** qualifications, and

technical certificates. Advanced modern apprenticeships are not to be mistaken with **accelerated modern apprenticeships**.

Further reading: DfES (September 2001); Coleman & Williams (1998)

MODERN APPRENTICESHIPS FOR ADULTS

In response to industry's concern that the age limit on modern apprenticeships was a barrier to meeting skills needs the DfES' *Skills Strategy: 21st Century Skills – Realising Our Potential* recommended removing the age limit. From 1 August 2003 young people who started modern apprenticeships up to their 25th birthday could complete it.

See also: Apprenticeship

Further reading: DfES Departmental Report 2004, Cm 6202, p. 84

MODERN APPRENTICESHIPS – FOUNDATION

They were designed for young people aged 16 and upwards. Guidance on entry qualifications and duration, which should be at least one year, was originally decided by the **National Training Organisation**. The minimum standard of attainment should be **NVQ** Level 2 in the relevant occupation, together with satisfactory off-the-job attainments, that is **key skills** specified by the NTO. On successful completion of the FMA the person would receive the NVQ Level 2 award of the Foundation Modern Apprenticeship Diploma by the **Sector Skills Council**.

See also: National Traineeships

Further reading: DfES (September 2001)

MODERN SKILLS DIPLOMA FOR ADULTS

(29 June 2001) The Modern Skills Diploma for Adults was introduced, in Wales, to

provide over-25s with training similar to that of the **modern apprenticeship**. It developed further and could be progressed to be equivalent to a Level 4 **National Vocational Qualification** applicable to people in a management position.

MONITORIAL SYSTEMS

These began in approximately 1820 (Minutes 1847–48, Vol. 2, p. 329) and ended approximately 1859. Many schools used monitors (average age 11) to bring the ratio of instructors to pupils to a suitable level. Monitors were normally used where there were insufficient financial resources to employ master(s) or assistant teachers. Where this was the predominant approach it was sometimes called a monitorial school where a system of **mutual instruction** occurred. 'The monitors, who are young, act, as well as the **pupil teachers**, under the immediate guidance and superintendence of the assistant, chiefly in hearing the classes read over again the lesson read to the superior teacher; in questioning on a simultaneous lesson previously given by him to a class, in order to fix it in their memory; in hearing the spelling, and the arithmetic tables; in attending to the writing, and to various other points of the general routine and discipline. For such employments young monitors may be used without disadvantage, though in proportion to the skill and industry of the master and his teachers will the numbers of monitors be small, and the dependence on them diminished' (Minutes 1842–43: p. 440).

In addition: 'It seems that all monitors who are permanently employed in that capacity should be paid, trained and instructed' (Minutes 1844, Vol. 2, p. 184). As teaching became more professional it became recognised that the use of monitors was unsatisfactory. The inspector stated: 'The old monitorial system, which was introduced to meet this difficulty of overwhelming numbers, is now generally acknowledged to be a failure' (Minutes 1847–48, Vol. 2, p. 73).

Because of the limitations of the monitorial system the Minutes of 1846 provided for the creation of **pupil-teachers**. 'The monitorial system has in great measure passed away; but with it have not passed many monitorial traditions originally invented for maintaining attention in the absence of vigilant and practised teachers. Of these I will only mention, by way of instance, the habit of "taking places" – as it is called – or that of a child who answers a question correctly going above one higher in the class who had failed to do so' (Minutes 1859–60 p. 83).

See also: Mutual Instruction; Simultaneous Instruction; Madras System

MORAL INSTRUCTION

This subject was introduced to the curriculum in the 1906 **Code**. The Code explained that the instruction might be, 'either incidental, occasional and given as fitting opportunity arises. … or given systematically and as a course of graduated instruction … The teaching should be brought home to the children by reference to their actual surroundings in town and country, and should be illustrated as vividly as possible by stories, poems, quotations, proverbs, and examples drawn from history and geography. … The object of such instruction being the formation of character and habits of life and thought, an appeal should be made to the feelings and personalities of the children. Unless the natural moral responsiveness of the child is stirred, no moral instruction is likely to be fruitful' (Board of Education 1905–06 p. 25).

MOSAIC

The **Training Services Division** developed a course to help resettlement of redundant steelworkers from Ebbw Vale at the Blaenau Gwent Training Centre. Mosaic provided counselling and assessment, and basic line manufacturing disciplines. The success or otherwise of this programme depended on the future availability of manufacturing work.

Further reading: MSC Annual Report 1977/78, p. 28

MUNICIPAL DUAL SCHOOLS

This were **mixed schools** for both sexes and the **Board of Education** reported that '[t]he building in which the school (a Municipal Dual School) is conducted has to accommodate both the Secondary School and also boys' and girls' elementary departments, each of which comprises three **standards**' (Report 1905–06 p. 56).

MUNICIPAL SECONDARY SCHOOLS

In the early 1900s, the **Board of Education** described how these schools had largely developed out of older **technical institutes** or organised **schools of science** (Report 1905–06 p. 55), which had been supported by the **Science and Art Department**. For this reason they were often associated with technical education and were occasionally called **municipal technical schools**; however, as the secondary school system developed over the next two decades general education became more common and this interpretation declined.

MUNICIPAL TECHNICAL SCHOOLS

Municipal technical schools frequently developed as a result of local demands and support from the Science and Art Department as well as the Technical Instruction Act 1889. They were also known as **central technical schools** and in many boroughs contained, in one building, **technical, commercial, domestic** and **art schools** (Report 1908–09 p. 68).

MUNITIONS COURSES

In the early stages of the First World War there was a shortage of skilled people to support the development and manufacture of munitions, which impacted on **technical schools** in two ways. 'In the first place, a number of schools engaged in actual munition work, including specific researches on various points, the testing of materials, and the making of gauges, aeroplane parts, and other engineering details. In the second place, the rapid development of the munition supply created a large demand for munition workers, and a number of experimental courses for training unskilled persons for the purpose were established' (Report 1914–15 p. 50).

The courses varied from a few days to between six and eight weeks and including talks on tools, materials, operations, and testing and measuring instruments. Much of the instruction was practical with half of the courses being general in nature and including: bench-work, lathe-work and machine tool work; while other centres specialised and limited training to the use of a few machine tools. In addition to these activities, the workshops in three **municipal secondary schools** in Leeds were used during the 1915 summer vacation by staff, older pupils and friends to produce dummy cartridges for use in the training of troops (Report 1914–15 p. 38).

MUSLIM SCHOOLS

The first state funded Muslim school in Britain was the Islamia Primary School, Kilburn London, which received funding in 1998.

MUTUAL INSTRUCTION

This form of instruction was also known as Dr Bell's or the **Madras system** (or **monitorial system**/monitorial school) and was adopted in the **national schools**. 'The system of Dr Bell does not, indeed contemplate, as originally propounded by him, and as practically applied in many of our large schools, the intervention of a well-instructed master at all – otherwise than vicariously, and through his monitors' (Minutes 1845, Volume 1, p. 244).

Subsequently, it involved the pupils instructing each other following classes from the schoolmaster, where present. The method of mutual instruction was also modified through the use of monitors or **pupil-teachers** resulting in smaller groups – this was called the **mixed method**. The recommended design of schools in the 1840s allowed for these methods or the **simultaneous method**. The monitorial system was not considered very satisfactory because of the young age of the monitors and their limited knowledge. Mr Cook an Inspector stated: 'The fact that on the continent the system of mutual instruction was at first adopted with enthusiasm, tried under every favourable circumstance of high government patronage and popular favour, and after such trial, universally abandoned, needed the corroboration of home convictions. And I now, for the first time, entertain a hope that within a definite period, all the schools will demand an increase of duly-qualified teachers' (Minutes 1845, Volume 1, p. 149).

MUTUAL INSTRUCTION SOCIETIES

Also known as mutual improvement societies, they were particularly popular in the late 1700s and 1800s and involved the systematic sharing and communicating of knowledge. A number of them grew out of **Sunday schools** and they often included a library and encouraged reading. One of the earliest was Kings Lynn Religious Society for Mutual Improvement 1679. The Duckinfield Mutual Instruction Society focused on concrete matters and '"avoiding vain and curious disputations" should direct its discussions "to subjects of a useful and practical bearing"'. The **mechanics institutes** were examples of these societies (Tylecote 1957 p. 122).

N

NATIONAL ADVISORY COUNCIL FOR EDUCATION AND TRAINING TARGETS

(1991 – 31 March 2001) Established by industry and commerce to develop national targets for education and training and these were first published in 1991. Revised targets were set in 1995, and these were superseded by **national learning targets**. NACETT was replaced by the **Learning and Skills Council**, which took responsibility for setting and advising on post-16 targets.

Further reading: National Advisory Council for Education and Training Targets (1995; 2000)

NATIONAL ADVISORY COUNCIL ON EDUCATION FOR INDUSTRY AND COMMERCE

(1948–77) Advised on technical and vocational education including ONCs and HNDs in the 1960s.

See also: Scottish Technical Consultative Council

NATIONAL ADVISORY COUNCIL ON THE EMPLOYMENT OF PEOPLE WITH DISABILITIES

It was formerly the National Advisory Council on Employment of Disabled People and (NACEDP) was established under the **Disabled Persons (Employment) Act 1944**. Its statutory responsibility was to advise the Secretary of State on matters concerning the employment, self-employment, and training, of people with disabilities. This responsibility was enlarged under the Chronically Sick and Disabled Persons Act 1970 to include 'the duty of giving the Secretary of State such advice as appears to the Council to be necessary on the training of persons concerned with placing disabled persons in employment or training disabled persons for employment' (MSC Annual Report 1978–79, p. 11).

See also: Disability Rights Commission and National Disability Council

Further reading: National Advisory Council on the Employment of People with Disabilities (1992)

NATIONAL APPRENTICESHIP SERVICE

(27 April 2009) The NAS was launched to provide 'end to end' support to employers and learners wishing to become apprentices and to lead the World Class Apprenticeship programme. Other responsibilities included coordination of funding for apprenticeships; providing an online Apprenticeship Vacancies System; providing information to enable, for example, **Business Link** and employers' intermediary bodies to promote apprenticeships; improving the arrangements for certification; and, working with the **Department for Children, Schools and Families** to

establish apprenticeships within 14–19 provision. The National Apprenticeship Service had a national team and regional teams supporting the growth and development of apprenticeships and many of its objectives were given statutory support with the Apprenticeships, Skills, Children and Learning Act 2009. It replaced some of the responsibilities of the **Learning and Skills Council**.

See also: Apprenticeships; Modern Apprenticeships

Further reading: www.apprenticeships.org.uk (accessed 31 May 2010)

NATIONAL ASSESSMENT AGENCY

(April 2004 – December 2008) The NAA's purpose was to safeguard and modernise the delivery of exams, tests and assessment through schools, colleges, other exams centres and partners, including local authorities and awarding bodies. It was a part of the **Qualifications and Curriculum Authority** and was responsible for:

- 'The secure delivery of national curriculum tests.
- The secure delivery of public exams such as A levels and GCSE.
- Modernisation of the exam and testing system.
- Ensuring there is a pool of examiners that can be used for public exams.
- Implementing the exams office improvement programme.
- Establishing the Institute of Educational Assessors'

National Assessment Agency (2008)

It was subsequently absorbed into the **Qualifications and Curriculum Development Authority** following serious delays in the administration and delivery of SATs results by ETS.

See also: Office of the Qualifications and Examinations Regulator

NATIONAL ASSOCIATION FOR THE CARE AND RESETTLEMENT OF OFFENDERS

NACRO was established in 1966 and is the main voluntary body concerned with the welfare of offenders. Over the ensuing years it has been involved in a variety of training and development initiatives including **Youth Opportunities Programme** for young offenders and **Community Enterprise Programme** for those who were mature prisoners.

Further reading: MSC Annual Report (1989); NACRO Annual Reports

NATIONAL ASSOCIATION OF MANUAL TRAINING TEACHERS

(c.1900) When cookery and laundry work were introduced into the school syllabus, they were often taught by specialist teachers who did not have full teaching status. The association was established to represent them and achieve equality with certified teachers.

See also: Association of Teachers of Domestic Science

Further reading: Durcan 1972

NATIONAL ASSOCIATION OF TRAINING GROUPS

This was a separate grouping of employers who came together to form **group training associations**. GTAs were groups of companies which opted out of **industrial training boards** and pooled what would have been their training levy to provide training for organisations within their association. These GTAs generally consisted of small- to medium-sized enterprises which wanted to have more control over the training with economies of scale and choice that were less available to individual organisations.

Further reading: National Association of Training Groups (1991)

NATIONAL CENTRE FOR INDUSTRIAL LANGUAGE TRAINING

In 1975 the Government launched a scheme to encourage English language training in the workplace through the use of language training units set up and operated by local authorities. Included in the scheme, the Training Services Division financed the National Centre for Industrial Language Training, which had responsibility for staff training materials development and information. It was later known as the **Industrial Language Training Service** and as well as providing language training in the workplace for members of ethnic minorities, it also provided training in communications skills and awareness for the managers, supervisors and trade unions. The service worked on the basis of a partial fee recovery for the service. In 1984–85, 11,300 people received training at a cost of £1.9m.

See also: ESOL for Work Qualifications; English Language Training

Further reading: Hedge et al. (1975)

NATIONAL CERTIFICATES

(1921) These were first awarded to students in technical schools by the **Board of Education** in consultation with the Institution of Mechanical Engineers. Their success led to the establishment of national certificates for other professions, for example electrical engineering, chemistry and applied chemistry, gas engineering and gas supply (Report 1923–24 pp. 84–85). By 1926, in Wales, a small but increasing number of students were taking Ordinary Grade National Certificates and Diplomas (Report 1925–26 p. 124). A few years later the **Higher National Certificate** and **Higher National Diploma** were awarded.

NATIONAL CHALLENGE

Launched in June 2008, the National Challenge was a £400m initiative to raise standards in secondary schools so that at least 30 per cent of children in all schools achieved five A*-C grade GCSEs by 2011 (DCSF Departmental Report 2009 p. 63).

Further reading: http://www.dcsf.gov.uk/nationalchallenge/ (accessed 15 February 2010)

NATIONAL COLLEGE FOR SCHOOL LEADERSHIP

(September 2000) Introduced to provide a coherent national training framework for head teachers, aspiring heads and school leaders so that they might have access to high quality, practical and professional training at all stages of their careers. It developed the Leadership Programme for Serving Heads, which allowed heads to review their leadership style. The LPSH: uses *National Standards for Headteachers* and Hay/McBer's research into the characteristics of highly effective headteachers; allows heads to focus on personal development and insights into their leadership style and the impact of this on school performance; uses seven national providers at locations across England; and supports and challenges the heads in a neutral and confidential setting. Subsequently, a National Professional Qualification for Headship was made mandatory from 1 April 2004.

Further reading: DfEE (2001a); www.ncsl.org.uk

NATIONAL COLLEGE FOR THE TRAINING OF YOUTH LEADERS

The National College for the Training of Youth Leaders was set up as a result of recommendations made by the 1960 Albemarle Committee report on the youth service.

See also: Youth Service Development Council

Further reading: Ministry of Labour Gazette 1961, p. 332

NATIONAL COUNCIL FOR EDUCATION AND TRAINING FOR WALES

Under the Learning and Skills Act 2000, this national council was established on 10 October 2000 and replaced the **Further Education Funding Council for Wales**, also taking on the responsibilities of the local education authorities and the four **training and enterprise councils**. The national council had responsibility for planning and funding post-16 education and training although not higher education. In conjunction with the **Higher Education Funding Council** for Wales, and together known as **ELWa**, they had responsibility for all post-16 education and training in Wales. It had similar responsibilities to the **Learning and Skills Council**.

NATIONAL COUNCIL FOR EDUCATIONAL EXCELLENCE

(10 July 2007) The NCEE was established to promote excellence in children and young people's education. Its purpose was to mobilise all sectors of the community: business, schools, universities and the voluntary sectors to support the continuous raising of educational standards. The body also aimed at every secondary school having a business and university partner.

Further reading: www.dcsf.gov.uk/ncee/

NATIONAL COUNCIL FOR EDUCATIONAL TECHNOLOGY

The DfEE funded the NCET with an annual grant of approximately £5m to support, promote and evaluate the effective use of information and communications technology. In January 1998, following a review of its functions, it was renamed **British Educational Communications and Training Agency (BECTA)**.

Further reading: National Council for Educational Technology (1988)

NATIONAL COUNCIL FOR GRADUATE ENTREPRENEURSHIP

(13 September 2004) The council provides a central information source for students and graduates who are contemplating starting a business.

See also: Enterprise Advisor Pilots

Further reading: DfES Departmental Report 2003, Cm 5902, p. 27; http://www.ncge.com

NATIONAL COUNCIL FOR INDUSTRY TRAINING ORGANISATIONS

NCITO was established 1988 and was a voluntary organisation set up by the **ITOs** to maintain and develop the effectiveness of independent sector training arrangements. Arising from the Government's White Paper *Employment for the 1990s*, the NCITO published the Code of Good Practice for Industry Training Organisations in January 1990. This was a set of guidelines from which sector training organisations could identify the objectives they should be aiming to achieve, and so judge their progress. Superseded by the **National Training Organisation National Council**.

Further reading: Berry-Lound et al. (1991); National Council for Industry Training Organisations (1990)

NATIONAL COUNCIL FOR VOCATIONAL QUALIFICATIONS

(1986) Funded jointly by the **Department of Employment, Department of Education and Science**, The Northern Ireland Education Department and from 1992/93 the **Welsh Office**. The NCVQ's aim was to rationalise the vocational qualifications system by developing and implementing a new national framework of qualifications accreditation. It was succeeded by the **Qualifications and Curriculum Authority**.

Further reading: Gokulsing et al. (1996); Mansfield and Mitchell (1996); NCVQ (1989); Wolf (1995)

NATIONAL COUNCIL FOR WORK EXPERIENCE

(2002) The NCWE, a charity, and part of the Higher Education Career Services Unit, 'promotes, supports and develops quality work experience for the benefit of students, employers and the economy'. It disseminates information, encourages placement opportunities and good practice in work experience for students in FE and HE. The main aims of partnerships with employers are to:

- improve the quality and increase the quantity of work experience;
- raise the academic value of work experience;
- become recognised as independent and authoritative by the business and academic communities; and,
- become a one-stop shop of expertise and advice on all aspects of work experience.
(www.work-experience.org/ncwe.rd/ index.jsp (accessed 10 January 2010)

See also: Work Experience Quality Mark

NATIONAL COUNCIL OF TECHNOLOGICAL AWARDS

(announced 1955–1964) The purpose of the council was to coordinate and approve advanced technological courses. It was succeeded by the **Council for National Academic Awards**.

NATIONAL COUNCIL ON THE EMPLOYMENT OF DISABLED PEOPLE

See: National Advisory Council on Employment of People with Disabilities

NATIONAL CURRICULUM

A curriculum was specified by the Committee of the Privy Council on Education in the Code of 1862; however, by the early 1900s it was increasingly recognised that it was too restrictive and schools and teachers were given greater freedom to exercise their own judgement about the nature and content of teaching. The Educational Reform Act 1988 brought in a national curriculum of specified subjects that were to be taught in schools. Initially, there were three prioritised core subjects of English, mathematics and science, together with seven other subjects: art, geography, history, modern foreign language, music, physical education and technology. The national curriculum regularly undergoes changes to reflect policy and revised priorities.

NATIONAL CURRICULUM COUNCIL

(1988–93) The School Curriculum Committee was replaced by the National Curriculum Council in 1988, and the NCC was replaced by the **School Curriculum and Assessment Authority**.

NATIONAL DATABASE OF ACCREDITED QUALIFICATIONS

(Developed for public access in 2003) Previously the National Database of Vocational Qualifications, the NDAQ contains information on qualifications that are accredited by the regulators of external qualifications in England (**Office of the Qualifications and Examinations Regulator**), Wales (**Department for Children, Education, Lifelong Learning and Skills**) and Northern Ireland (**Council for the Curriculum, Examinations and Assessment**). It also lists the awarding bodies.

Further reading: www.accreditedqualifications. org.uk

NATIONAL DEVELOPMENT PROGRAMME

Consisted of a series of small-scale projects that were run at local and district level and were designed to test innovative approaches to labour market problems. The first round of projects ended in 1996 and from all of these there were three, **jobseeker's grant,** new ways of working and debt management, which were chosen to undergo more widespread testing. It was successful and was included in a package of help as part of **New Deal**. Expenditure in 1996–97 was £362K with plans for increased expansion in the following years.

Further reading: DfEE Departmental Report 1998–1999, Cm 3910, p. 97; Employment Service (June 1997)

NATIONAL DISABILITY COUNCIL

It was set up under the Disability Discrimination Act 1995. The NDC, consisting of a chairman and 17 members, was an independent body with statutory duties to advise the Government on initiatives to reduce or eliminate discrimination against disabled people and on the operation of the DDA. It was replaced by the **Disability Rights Commission**.

Further reading: National Disability Council (1996)

NATIONAL ECONOMIC DEVELOPMENT COUNCIL

(1962–1992) The council consisted of representatives from government, management and trades unions, and its purpose was to investigate and propose strategies to encourage economic development.

NATIONAL EDUCATION AND TRAINING TARGETS

NETTs were originally developed by the CBI and other partners in 1991 after wide consultation by the **National Advisory Council for Education and Training Targets**. The first targets were launched in 1991 and revised in 1995 in the White Paper: *Competitiveness: Forging Ahead*. They were also

known as National Targets for Education and Training (NTETs). Their purpose was to allow benchmarking and to raise standards to at least match those of other advanced nations. They were developed because research indicated that the average performance of education and training concealed good standards at one end but poor standards at the other. This underpinning tail needed to be addressed to achieve economic success and social inclusion. The targets consisted of Foundation Learning Targets and Lifetime Learning Targets. The NETTs were replaced by **national learning targets**.

Further reading: National Advisory Council for Education and Training Targets (1995); (2000); National Training Task Force (1992)

NATIONAL EDUCATION BOARD

(1831–1922) This was established in Ireland by the Irish Chief Secretary with funding from the Lord Lieutenant's School Fund (established in 1819) and from 1848 from the Exchequer. An initial seven commissioners were nominated to supervise a system of education that provided general instruction and separate religious education. Model schools were planned for the 32 counties and eventually 30 were built and used as examples for others to copy. In 1921 the Northern Ireland Ministry of Education took responsibility for education.

See also: Ireland – Commissioners of National Education in

Further reading: Durcan (1972)

NATIONAL EMPLOYER SERVICE

(c.2002) The NES (originally the National Contracts Service) was established to help the **Learning and Skills Council** interface with large companies and organisations of over 5,000 people and help them understand the Government skills strategy and the support available for workforce development. It aims 'to be the catalyst for large employers to take ownership of, and invest in, the skills of their workforce'. It became an agency of the **Skills Funding Agency**.

http://nationalemployerservice.org.uk/ (accessed 12 December 2009)

NATIONAL EMPLOYERS' SKILLS SURVEY

This was a survey of employers that was conducted by the **Learning and Skills Council**. Responsibility for the survey passed to the **UK Commission for Employment and Skills**.

Further reading: Learning and Skills Council 2004

NATIONAL EMPLOYMENT PANEL

(1997 – 31 March 2008) The National Employment Panel was originally the New Deal Task Force and the NEP was an advisory non-departmental public body of 20–24 people and a chair, representing various sectors of society whose aim was to:

- 'Increase the opportunities for disadvantaged and unemployed people to gain productive employment and economic sufficiency.
- Recommend effective and innovative ways of ensuring that the labour market programmes are responsive to the changing needs of the labour market'.
  (National Employment Panel Skills Advisory Board 2004 p. 28)

Its role was superseded by the **UK Commission for Employment and Skills** and **Working Ventures UK**'.

NATIONAL ENDOWMENT FOR SCIENCE TECHNOLOGY AND THE ARTS

(1998) The main purpose of NESTA is to make the UK more innovative through investment in early-stage companies, developing policy and providing programmes to stimulate a culture of innovation. It was established by an act of Parliament in 1998 and received an endowment of £250m from the National Lottery Fund, which has been supplemented with investment from other sources.

Further reading: www.nesta.org.uk (accessed 01 June 2010)

NATIONAL EXTENSION COLLEGE

(1963) The college was founded by Michael Young with the objective of providing alternative routes into education for adults through distance learning etc.

NATIONAL FOUNDATION FOR EDUCATIONAL RESEARCH

(1946) An independent body, the NFER undertakes research and development projects across the public education system with the intention of improving education and training.

Further reading: See Annual Reports; www. nfer.ac.uk (accessed 31 May 2010)

NATIONAL GRID FOR LEARNING

Launched in 1998, its purpose was to provide a national focus for using new technologies to raise educational standards. This would be achieved by linking all learning institutions and training providers including schools, colleges, universities, libraries, adult learning institutions, museums, galleries, etc. The lead agency for the NGfL was the **British Educational Communications and Technology Agency (BECTA)**.

Further reading: DfEE (1997b); National Grid for Learning (1997)

NATIONAL INFORMATION SYSTEM FOR VOCATIONAL QUALIFICATIONS

During the development of **youth training** and the setting up of **Training and**

Enterprise Councils and **Local Enterprise Companies**, the designers of **Youth Training** recognised that there was no source of reliable information on the vocational qualifications gained or held by young people at local level. The main aims of the NISVQ were to monitor the achievement of vocational qualifications, to monitor and evaluate the Standards Programme, as well as to evaluate the UK training market and Government training schemes. The system also served to provide indicators of **TEC** performance.

Further reading: NISVQ (1993)

NATIONAL INSTITUTE FOR HOUSEWORKERS

Was established in 1946 to train and place women in domestic service, specify minimum rates of pay and award efficiency certificates. In 1972 it was dissolved.

See also: Domestic Training

Further reading: Ministry of Labour Annual Report 1960 p. 49

NATIONAL INSTITUTE OF ADULT CONTINUING EDUCATION

Originally NIACE was the British Institute for Adult Education, which was founded in 1921 and which, itself, had roots in the 1918–19 World Association for Adult Education. NIACE is a registered charity and the national organisation for adult learning. Its aim is 'to promote the study and general advancement of adult continuing education'.

(DfEE Departmental Report 1999–00 to 2001–02, Cm 4202, p. 78; http://www.niace.org.uk)

NATIONAL INSURANCE ACT 1911

This act, which was passed in two parts, was the first national contributory insurance scheme to mitigate against illness and unemployment. In part 1, each worker contributed 4d per week with the employer paying 3d and the state 2d, which enabled the person to receive sickness benefit of 10 shillings per week for 13 weeks and 5 shillings for the following 13 weeks. The second part required the employee to pay 2.5d, the employer 2.5d and the state 3d per week, which entitled the unemployed person, after the first week, to receive 7 shillings per week for 15 weeks, which they got from the **labour exchange**.

NATIONAL INSURANCE CONTRIBUTION HOLIDAYS

The Jobseekers Act 1995 and the Employer's Contributions Re-imbursement Regulations 1996 SI No 195 detailed the opportunity for employers to claim a full national insurance rebate for up to one year for recruiting anyone who had been unemployed for two or more years, from April 1996.

Further reading: Lourie (1998)

NATIONAL JOINT ADVISORY COUNCIL REPORT OF THE COMMITTEE ON THE MANPOWER SITUATION

(1961) This committee was recommended in the **Carr Report** (1958) and consisted of three groupings: British Employers Confederation (now CBI), TUC and government. Among other recommendations, it advised that workers be made more versatile by broader training.

Further reading: Ministry of Labour Gazette February 1962, p. 45

NATIONAL LEARNER PANEL

(November 2006) This panel provided a learner's view of proposals, policies and initiatives in further or adult education. It provided a voice at national level to the Government, **learning and skills councils** etc.

See also: Adult Learners Week

Further reading: www.direct.gov.uk/en/Educa
tionAndLearning/AdultLearning/DG_068290
(accessed 28 May 2010)

NATIONAL LEARNING AT WORK DAY

This initiative was introduced to encourage
fun and business learning events and activities
in the workplace and was managed by the
Campaign for Learning.

Further reading: www.campaign-for-learning.
org.uk/cfl/workplacelearning/lawday/index.
asp (accessed 21 March 2010)

NATIONAL LEARNING DATABASE

(2001) This was formerly the National
Learning Directory and it provides details of
almost one million courses that can be
uploaded by learning and training providers
through the **learndirect** website. It is a service supported by the Careers Advice Service
and accessed through the Directgov website.

Further reading: http://careersadvice-findacour
se1.direct.gov.uk/pls/hot_ca/aff_page_pls_all_
homepage?a=260405 (accessed 10 May 2010)

NATIONAL LEARNING NETWORK

The network was established in 1999 to
improve the information technology infrastructure in further education. All FE colleges
are connected by broadband connection to
the Joint Academic Network (JANET).

Further reading: DfES Departmental Report
2002 Cm 5402 p. 140

NATIONAL LEARNING TARGETS

Were launched in October 1998 and succeeded **national education and training
targets**. Announced in *Learning and Working
Together for the Future: a Strategic Framework to
2002*, the targets cover a wide range of
education, skills and training activity. Targets
include those for 11-year-olds; 16-year-olds;
young people; adults; organisations; and the
participation in learning targets. Individual
targets were set for England, Wales, Scotland
and Northern Ireland. They underpinned the
Government's two main goals: an inclusive
society and a globally competitive economy.
They were replaced by departmental **public
service agreement** targets.

Further reading: DfEE (2000e); National
Advisory Council for Education and Training
Targets (2000)

NATIONAL OCCUPATIONAL STANDARDS

These were originally called **occupational
standards** and were developed by **lead
bodies**. The standards were developed to
represent the expected work requirements of
employees in a particular industry and specified the competences and outcomes, for example the **Management Charter Initiative**.

See also: Sector Skills Councils

Further reading: Mansfield and Mitchell
(1996)

NATIONAL OFFENDER MANAGEMENT SERVICE

The Offender Management Act 2007 enabled
the establishment of the National Offender
Management Service, whose aims were to
'deliver effective punishments; protect the
public from offenders and communities from
the impact of crime; reduce re-offending;
deliver the sentence plans in accordance with
the court's requirements; take account of the
needs, wishes and rights of the victims of
crime; rehabilitate offenders; make the best
use of resources'. The rehabilitation of offenders involved a range of training and development provision.

See also: National Association for the Care
and Resettlement of Offenders

Further reading: http://noms.justice.gov.uk/ (accessed 01 June 2010)

NATIONAL ONLINE MANPOWER INFORMATION SYSTEM

This was publicly available information about labour market, skills and training data. NOMIS was one computer database and the other was Quantime Ltd's database for the **Labour Force Survey**.

Further reading: Department of Employment Report 1991 Cm 1506 p. 26

NATIONAL PRIORITY SKILLS SCHEME

(1982–88) NPSS was a grant scheme to fund training provided by the Industry Bodies Branch of the **Training Agency**. It increased provision for training in **key skills** for national competitiveness, giving particular emphasis to small firms. It helped employers to train their employees in priority skills identified by their **industry training organisation**. Over 6,000 people were involved within the scheme and expenditure in 1984/85 was £7.3m.

Further reading: Mas Research, Marketing and Consultancy (1989)

NATIONAL QUALIFICATIONS FRAMEWORK

(2003/04) In 1996 Sir Ron Dearing recommended a national framework of qualifications in the Review of Qualifications for 16–19 Year Olds. The Education Act 1997 (Section 24) provided the legal structure for the framework that would provide more clarity for students, employers etc. into the wide and sometimes incomprehensible range of qualifications. In addition, a NQF was developed for higher education to articulate with that above. The purpose of this initiative was to provide a transparent lifelong learning ladder of progression that showed pathways and equivalence among qualifications. Initially,

the framework had five levels but this was then expanded, in 2004, to nine levels ranging from Entry Level to Level eight, which is the equivalent to a doctorate. The **Scottish Credit and Qualifications Framework** has twelve levels. In late 2008 the NQF was replaced by the **Qualifications and Credit Framework**.

See also: Credit and Qualifications Framework for Wales; Scottish Credit and Qualifications Framework; European Credit Transfer and Accumulation System

Further reading: www.qcda.org.uk (accessed 01 June 2010)

NATIONAL RECORD OF ACHIEVEMENT

Launched jointly in England, Wales and Scotland in February 1991 and shortly afterwards in Northern Ireland. The NRA is a record of a person's achievements throughout education, training and working life. The objective was to encourage people to be actively involved with their own training and development and to provide employers with a coherent record of their career and abilities. It consisted of a nationally recognised cover; personal details; summary of school achievement in the curriculum; summary of qualifications and credits; summary of other achievements and experiences; a personal statement and employment history. It was mandatory for all 16-year-old school leavers, and free to all school leavers, **youth training**, and **training for work** trainees. A charge was made to employers and post-16 school leavers. In 1993/94, 737,000 were issued free in England. Responsibility for production and distribution subsequently passed to the **NCVQ** and the **Scottish Vocational Education Council**.

See also: Progress Files; National Record of Vocational Achievement

Further reading: Employment Department (1991d); National Record of Achievement (1997)

NATIONAL RECORD OF VOCATIONAL ACHIEVEMENT

(June 1988) This was introduced for young people on the **Youth Training Scheme**. Its purpose was to record achievements in addition to examination successes.

See also: National Record of Achievement

NATIONAL SCHOOL SOCIETY

(1811) Originally titled 'National Society for Promoting the Education of the Poor in the Principles of the Established Church', the society was founded in 1811 to provide Church of England schools in contrast to the non-denominational **British and Foreign School Society**, or the **Central Society of Education**, which argued for no religious teaching. Similar schools were also developed in Scotland, Ireland and Wales with the latter being supported by the Welsh Education Fund of the National Society. The titles 'National School' and 'British School' were removed in 1906 because of the potential confusion with the provision of education nationally which arose from the **Elementary Education Act 1870**. 'The epithet "National" in the names of Schools was frequently misapplied. In its original and strict meaning the term indicated that the School to which it applied was in union with the **National Society**. It had, however, gradually come to be used loosely as synonymous with "Church of England", and it appeared to the Board that it was in any case somewhat misleading now that the maintenance of all Public Elementary schools has become a national charge. The epithet "British" originally applied to Schools in union with the **British and Foreign School Society** is open to similar objections' (Report 1906–07 p. 28).

NATIONAL SERVICE

(1939–60) The Military Training Act 1939 was superseded by the National Service (Armed Forces) Act 1939 on the outbreak of war and dealt with the enlistment of men aged 18–40 inclusive into the armed forces. The National Service Act 1941 (April) extended the coverage of these men for enrolment into civil defence forces (Police War Reserve and National Fire Service). The National Service (No. 2) Act 1941 (December) increased the liability for national service for men to 50 years and for women aged 18–30. The National Service Act 1942 (December) provided for registration and medical examination of men from the age of 17 years and 8 months but they were not liable for service until 18. The legislation included the possibility of registration as a conscientious objector and for the postponement of service due to hardship. Provision for deferment of military service was also made under the **block reservation**, **individual deferment**, and schedule of reserved occupations schemes. *Defence: Outline of Future Policy* (Cmnd 124) announced that call-up of men under the national service acts would cease at the end of 1960.

Further reading: Slack (1942)

NATIONAL SKILLS ACADEMY

(2005) The academy was part of the reform of further education described in the White Paper, *Further Education: Raising Skills, Improving Life Chances*. It was intended that all major sectors of the economy would have a NSA that would be employer-led world-class centre of excellence. **Centres of vocational excellence** were to be incorporated within the scope of the national skills academies. The Fashion Retail Academy was the first to open for students in September 2005, and by 2010 there were 14 academies. NSAs' priorities were drawn from **sector skills agreements**.

Further reading: www.nationalskillsacademy. co.uk (accessed 01 June 2010)

NATIONAL SKILLS AGENDA

(1998–2001) Developed by the **National Skills Task Force** to create a national

209

consensus about objectives and a shared sense of priorities. It was intended to:

- 'help to ensure that we get the best possible return on the large and growing investment the country is making in education and training;
- be built around the country's longer term overall skill needs and not focus solely on current skill shortages'

(DfEE 1998f p. 4)

Further reading: DfEE (1999b); DfEE (2000a); National Skills Task Force (2001)

NATIONAL SKILLS TASK FORCE

Announced in the Learning Age Green Paper. Its purpose was to assist the Secretary of State in developing a **National Skills Agenda** to 'ensure that Britain has the skills to sustain high levels of employment, compete in the global market place and provide opportunity for all'. The task force provided advice on the nature, extent and geography of industrial skill needs and shortages, and gave practical measures to ease skills and recruitment difficulties. It aimed to raise the level of sustainable employment, identify changes in long-term skill needs and consider how the education and training system might respond to the identified needs. The work of the task force was continued by the **Learning and Skills Council**.

Further reading: DfEE (1998f); DfEE (1999b); DfEE (2000a); National Skills Task Force (2001)

NATIONAL TEACHING FELLOWSHIP SCHEME

The NTFS was administered by the **Higher Education Academy** and funded from the **Teaching Quality Enhancement Fund**. It had two separate strands: individual awards and projects. In 2008 there were 50 individual awards of £10,000 for personal excel-

lence, which the winners might use for personal and professional development in learning, development and pedagogy. The projects had a value of up to £200,000, which, if awarded, might be used by higher education institutions to work with National Teaching Fellows to enhance student learning.

Further reading: www.heacademy.ac.uk/ourwork/supportingindividuals/ntfs (accessed 01 June 2010)

NATIONAL TRAINEE DATABASE

This was gathered by the DfES and from 2002 was subsumed within the **individual learner record**.

NATIONAL TRAINEESHIPS

Introduced in September 1997 they arose from the Dearing Review of 16–19 qualifications. **National training organisations** developed the traineeship frameworks in conjunction with **TECs** to provide framework-based opportunities at NVQ2 and SVQ2 level for school and college leavers. The traineeships were designed to replace **youth training** and aimed 'to provide a high quality work-based route for young people with skills and qualifications linked to the national qualifications framework'. Government funding was originally via TECs and **LECs**. Optional elements included training over and above the core, which would assist the young person to progress to a **modern apprenticeship** or otherwise in the sector, for example through additional GNVQ/NVQ units. Succeeded by **foundation modern apprenticeships**.

Further reading: Everett, Tu and Caughey (1999)

NATIONAL TRAINING AND FURTHER EDUCATION CONSULTATIVE GROUP

Established in 1976 by the **Manpower Services Commission** and the **Department of**

Education and Science as a result of the convergence of the training and vocational preparation fields with the education and careers services. The group's purpose was to provide a forum for discussing matters of common interest to training and education. This collaboration was also mirrored by long-term policies for young people with the education and careers services; special measures for young people where there was a reliance with the careers services; and the operation of training schemes where the **Training Services Agency** had close working relationships with various educational bodies.

Further reading: MSC Annual Report 1976/77

NATIONAL TRAINING AWARDS

Initiated in 1987 to recognise excellence in training by running a competition for employers. These awards celebrated and highlighted the contribution training could make to the success of an enterprise and their aim was to create a focus for excellence in training and thus they publicised examples of good practice among companies, individuals and training providers. Entrants were required to demonstrate the direct link between developing a targeted training solution and achieving measurable benefits. From 1997 greater emphasis was placed on the partnership of individuals and training providers working with and within companies to produce visible results. In 2000 they merged with **Investors in People** training awards. They were managed by **UK Skills**.

Further reading: Evans (1995); National Training Awards (1997); www.nationaltrain ingawards.com

NATIONAL TRAINING ORGANISATION NETWORK

(May 1998) This was an umbrella body representing **Industry Training Organisations**, **Lead Bodies** and **Occupational Standards Councils**. It was replaced by the **Skills for Business Network**.

See also: National Training Organisations National Council

NATIONAL TRAINING ORGANISATIONS

Instituted on 13 May 1998. The introduction of NTOs represented a rationalisation and development of **lead bodies, occupational standards councils**, and **industry training organisations**. NTOs were national experts on education and training for sectors and occupational groups. At a macro-economic level they collated comprehensive labour market information, analysed key levers of business competitiveness, identified critical skills shortages and developed systems to predict future skill needs and produce action plans. The NTOs own representative bodies were the **NTO National Council** and the **Scottish Council of NTOs** (SCONTO). NTOs were replaced by **sector skills councils** in April 2002.

Further reading: National Training Organisations (1998)

NATIONAL TRAINING ORGANISATIONS NATIONAL COUNCIL

Previously the **National Council for Industry Training Organisations**.

See also: Skills for Business Network; Sector Skills Councils

NATIONAL TRAINING TASK FORCE

The NTTF was established in 1989 partly in response to the demise of the **Manpower Services Commission** and it consisted of eight employers and four others.

See also: National Education and Training Targets

NATIONAL VOCATIONAL QUALIFICATIONS

The Government's Review of Vocational Qualifications in 1986 identified the need for a coherent qualification structure. It led to the establishment of the **National Council for Vocational Qualifications** whose remit was to establish the framework of NVQs/SVQs through which people could be assessed against nationally agreed standards of competence. A broad definition of the levels is:

- Level 1 – foundation and basic work activities;
- Level 2 – a broad range of skills and responsibilities;
- Level 3 – complex skills and/or supervisory work;
- Level 4 – managerial specialist; and,
- Level 5 – professional/senior management.

The NVQs were based on **occupational standards** identified by employers for the industry. The approach used to develop most UK standards was to:

- 'Establish the "key purpose" of the job or occupation.
- Gather information on what knowledge and skills are required using group and individual interviews, workshops, questionnaires etc.
- Set "performance criteria" for judging people's performance.'
  www.instant-news.co.uk/metco/viewitem ?newsno=3061&session=3528976856233
  (accessed 05 April 2010)

Further reading: British Vocational Qualifications (2001); DfEE (1998h); Mansfield and Mitchell (1996); Wolf (1995)

NATIONAL VOCATIONAL QUALIFICATIONS INFORMATION SYSTEM

The information system was established to collect information about the number of NVQs/SVQs awarded at local, regional and national levels. This allowed the monitoring of vocational qualifications in the workforce.

Further reading: Dept of Employment Departmental Report 1993/94, Cm 2205, p. 16

NATIONAL VOLUNTARY YOUTH ORGANISATIONS – GRANTS FOR

See: Grants for National Voluntary Youth Organisations

NATIONAL YOUTH AGENCY

The National Youth Agency worked with the local authority and voluntary sectors of the Youth Service to increase the quality, range and effectiveness of youth work. Its purpose was to assist in fulfilling government objectives targeted at social exclusion and in support of the lifelong learning agenda.

Further reading: DfEE (1996/97); www.nya. org.uk

NATIONAL YOUTH EMPLOYMENT COUNCIL

The council was set up to advise the Secretary of State on the performance of the **Youth Employment Service** operations and those of **local education authorities** under the 1948 Act; and also advise the **Ministry of Labour** on issues of policy affecting the development and administration of the Youth Employment Service. It was disbanded in 1974.

Further reading: Ministry of Labour Gazette 1962, p. 9

NATURE STUDY

The 1882 **Code** encouraged the introduction of **elementary science**; however, this was largely unsuccessful until the 1890 Code relaxed the rule requiring English to be the first choice of the 'class subjects', from which time science became very popular. The teaching of science was based on the principle that science should be taught according to the environment around the school, which encouraged nature study. In rural areas there were plenty of resources; in cities there were museums, parks etc. and for those schools which did not have access to resources the Schools Mutual Aid Society encouraged the exchange of specimens (Report 1910–11 p. 29). A nature study conference was held in 1902 and this encouraged major growth in the subject.

(SCHOOLS OF) NAUTICAL COOKERY

The Merchant Shipping Act 1906 introduced the requirement for ships over 1,000 tons to have a certificated cook who could receive a certificate as a result of long service or examination. The act resulted in a number of schools being established in port cities; however, they had existed prior to this time with the first being the London School of Nautical Cookery (1893-*c*.1985).

NAUTICAL SCHOOLS

See: Navigation Schools

(SCHOOLS OF) NAUTICAL TRAINING

Six schools were recognised in 1921–22 according the Regulations for Schools of Nautical Training. 'All the schools are residential and non-local, and some of them belong to institutions, the main purpose of which is to maintain and train for useful occupations boys who would otherwise be ill-cared for. The educational purpose of a School of Nautical Training is to give a two-years' course of training from the age of thirteen, which is designed to continue their general education and to give some practical training which will fit boys for employment either in the Mercantile marine or in the Royal Navy' (Report 1922–23 p. 92).

There were also non-residential schools which were defined by the Board of Education: 'A School of Nautical Training is a day school providing a continued full-time education under school conditions for pupils from elementary schools in preparation for employment at sea' (Report 1928 p. 217).

See also: Royal Dockyard Schools; Navigation Schools

NAVIGATION

The subject of navigation was included in the 1892 **Code** as a **specific subject** for teaching to children in the upper classes of **elementary schools**.

Further reading: Report (1891–92) pp. 140/180

NAVIGATION SCHOOLS

The Marine Department of the **Board of Trade** established two navigation schools in London and Liverpool, largely for use by apprentices, mates, masters and those intending to be seafarers 'for the purpose of obtaining such information as was necessary to enable them to pass their examinations for certificates of competency in seamanship' (Department of Science and Art 1854, p. xxxi).

The nautical school within the Greenwich Royal Hospital Schools was divided into three classes. 'Formerly the third class was a dunces class, consisting of those boys whom it was considered hopeless to attempt to teach anything beyond the merest rudiments of navigation and nautical astronomy. The consequence was, that all hope of rising higher in the school being taken away, there remained no inducement for exertion, and idleness and insubordination were the characteristics of the class. This restriction has been removed for about six years with the best effect and the boys circulate regularly through all the three classes of the nautical school'. (Report 1858–59 p. 435) Among the subjects taught were geometry, trigonometry, algebra and navigation and nautical astronomy.

See also: Admiralty Schools; Hospital Schools; Royal Dockyard Schools; (School of) Nautical Training; Sea Training

213

NEEDLEWORK

This subject was taught to girls in schools from the mid 1800s onward. Considerable detail was given to the levels of the syllabus and in instructions to HM Inspectors it was stated, 'It is essential, however, that children should be taught needlework according to this approximate standard [e.g. hemming Infants and Standard I., about 6 to 10 stitches to the inch] without counting threads (a habit which is most pernicious to the eyesight), and that their knowledge of it should be attained simply by training the hand to work with the eye' (Report 1890–91 p. 202).

See also: Sewing Classes

NEIGHBOURHOOD ENGINEERS

This scheme was established by the Engineering Council with initial funding of £612,000 from the **DTI**. It was intended that three or four engineers would be linked to each secondary school. They would work for a few hours each week on voluntary secondment, helping teachers and providing advice and practical support to pupils and parents.

Further reading: Employment Gazette 1990, p. 233

NEIGHBOURHOOD LEARNING CENTRES

These built upon the experience of Local Learning Centres, which made education and training accessible to individuals and communities excluded by barriers such as distance, culture etc. and which were linked to the **national grid for learning**. The national learning centres were described in the **learning curve** and were part of the strategy of supporting **learning communities**.

Further reading: Office of the Deputy Prime Minister (October 2002)

NEIGHBOURHOOD SUPPORT FUND

This fund was targeted at young people who had dropped out of training and education, or were likely to, in the most deprived English neighbourhoods. Its purpose was to develop new initiatives and support existing ones to encourage the young people to involve themselves with learning and training. To achieve this it supported the development of work-based learning in those areas; and secondly, it supported community-owned projects that reflected local education and training needs.

Further reading: DfEE Departmental Report 1999–00 to 2001–02, Cm 4202, p. 85

NEW CLIENT ADVISERS

(1988) NCAs were the first point of contact for clients attending **Employment Service** offices for the first time. They helped clients find alternatives to unemployment by giving practical advice on job seeking, training, enterprise opportunities, vacancies, **employment training** and the **Enterprise Allowance Scheme**. The NCAs identified those who were eligible for benefit and deterred those who were not or who were unavailable for work.

Further reading: Employment Gazette April 1991, p. 205

NEW CODE

See: Code of Regulations

NEW COMMUNITY SCHOOLS

See: (New) Community Schools

NEW DEAL

A range of New Deal programmes for unemployed people were developed from 1998 onwards and these all contained some common features including: a personal advisor; a focus on the needs of the individual; a partnership between the public, private and voluntary sectors; rights and responsibilities of the unemployed person; **Jobcentre Plus**; and working with employers (Department for Work and Pensions 2008). From 2009 **(Flexible) New Deal** gradually replaced the existing range of new deals for those on **job-seekers allowance**.

(FLEXIBLE) NEW DEAL

(October 2009) The Flexible New Deal replaced the New Deal 18–24 and New Deal 25+, and **Employment Zones** programmes. By January 2008, a number of the New Deal programmes had been in operation from a pilot stage for ten years and, as part of a reform of welfare, the introduction of the Flexible New Deal Programme was announced (Department for Work and Pensions 2008). This programme had five main principles:

- 'A stronger framework of rights and responsibilities to move benefit customers from being passive recipients to active job-seekers.
- A personalised and responsive approach to individual customer needs which will provide tailored employment and skills support to meet the needs of both customers and local employers.
- A partnership approach with public, private and third sector organisations working together to maximise innovation, leading to more and better outcomes.
- Devolving and empowering communities for future sustainable employment which will be at the heart of neighbourhood renewal.
- Not just jobs, but jobs that pay and offer opportunities for progression, with an emphasis on sustaining and progressing in work to ensure all customers who need help to develop their skills have access to the relevant pre-employment and in-work training'

www.dwp.gov.uk/supplying-dwp/
what-we-buy/welfare-to-work-services/
flexible-new-deal/
(accessed 28 May 2010)

The targets were ambitious and private sector agencies supporting the programme were financially rewarded for placing people in employment, which sometimes led to questionable practices.

NEW DEAL 25 PLUS/NEW DEAL FOR THE LONG-TERM UNEMPLOYED

This programme was for the long-term unemployed aged 25+ and was introduced on 29 June 1998. Its purpose was to help the long-term unemployed into jobs, enhance their employability and improve their prospects of staying in and progressing in employment. The programme lasted from several months to one year and consisted of: a series of individually tailored advisory interviews; a range of further provision; and a follow through period. In the period up to the end of April 2001 there were 357,000 starts and 70,740 obtained jobs.

Further reading: DfEE (1998a); Employment Service Operational Plan (2000–01); Hasluck (March 2000)

NEW DEAL 50 PLUS

The New Deal 50 plus was introduced in nine pathfinder areas in October 1999 and went national in April 2000. The programme was part of the Government's **Welfare to Work** initiative. It was directed at people aged 50+ who had been out of work for six months or more and participation was voluntary. The main components of the programme were one-to-one support with a New Deal personal advisor for job search; and a wage top-up (employment credit – £60 per week for full time and £40 per week for recipients on less than £15,000 per year) for one year; and a training grant (up to £750).

Further reading: Kodz and Eccles (2001)

NEW DEAL FOR COMMUNITIES

This initiative was targeted at deprived communities and had five main targets: poor job

215

prospects; high crime levels; educational under-achievement; poor health; and, problems with housing and the local environment. This focus was described in *A New Commitment to Neighbourhood Renewal* (Social Exclusion Unit 2001) with the overall aim that within 10–20 years no-one should be seriously disadvantaged as a result of where they live. **Local strategic partnerships** combining public, private, community and voluntary sectors were encouraged to work together to alleviate the problems faced by people living in these neighbourhoods.

NEW DEAL FOR DISABLED PEOPLE

(July 2001) This programme was originally a joint **Department for Education and Employment** and Department of Social Security programme to support those on incapacity benefits to return to work. It included a personal advisor service, innovation schemes, and an information campaign and a programme of research and evaluation.

Further reading: DfEE Departmental Report 2001–02 to 2003–04, Cm 5102, p. 107

NEW DEAL FOR LONE PARENTS

The NDLP began in eight pilot areas in July 1997 and went national on 26 October 1998. In the period from October 1998 until the end of April 2001, some 234,750 lone parents had attended an initial interview. Of these people, 86,500 had found employment and 22,150 had taken up education or training opportunities. Of the 97,370 lone parents participating on the NDLP 95 per cent were female.

Further reading: Hasluck (September 2000)

NEW DEAL FOR MUSICIANS

Started as a national programme in August 1999. It was aimed at young musicians who were eligible for the **New Deal for young**

people. It was intended to improve the participants' employability in skills, motivation, and experience. There were three main elements: advisory support from a music industry consultant; an open learning route with a music open learning provider; flexibility on the NDYP self-employment route to provide continuing access to open learning materials and to allow test trading within the music industry.

Further reading: Thomas et al. (2001)

NEW DEAL FOR PARTNERS OF UNEMPLOYED PEOPLE

Announced in March 1998, and launched nationally in April 1999 for partners of unemployed people who were also out of work. Previously, partners had been treated as dependants of the **jobseeker's allowance** claimant and had not received advice, support and guidance.

Further reading: Griffiths and Thomas (June 2001)

NEW DEAL FOR SKILLS

(2004) One of the objectives of New Deal for skills was to remove the financial inconsistencies that existed between young people in full-time education and those receiving unpaid training. Research indicated that 16–19-year-olds 'may be forced to leave courses before achieving their qualification because of the pressure on the family finances of losing financial support' (HM Treasury March 2004 p. 27). As a result, child benefit, income support and child tax credit would not end on the nineteenth birthday if a person was still in training. It also aimed to help all unemployed young people to get the equivalent of 5 **GCSEs**.

NEW DEAL FOR YOUNG PEOPLE

(6 April 1998) NDYP was mandatory for anyone aged 18–24 who had been claiming

the jobseeker's allowance for six months or more. NDYP provided a range of help:

- Gateway provision that included help with job search, careers advice and preparation for and submission of a range of options; and,
- four options: which each included an element of education or training: a subsidised job with an employer; full-time education or training; work on the Environment Task Force or with the voluntary sector; and a follow-through strategy to support clients throughout their participation on an option and assistance if they returned to unemployment.

Further reading: Tavistock (1999)

NEW ENTERPRISE PROGRAMME

(1977–1988) This was a form of **training opportunities scheme** for individuals who wished to launch businesses with potential for growth. Courses were initially piloted at the Manchester Business School and ran for four weeks with up to twelve weeks of funded research. A parallel programme was the Small Business Course, which was designed for people who wished to set up more modest ventures. Their purpose was to help people quickly get their businesses off the ground and increase the chances of survival and growth. Between 1977 and 1981/82, the two programmes created 800 new businesses that had survived more than a year and had employed 3,500 people.

Further reading: Johnson (1983); MSC Annual Report 1982/93

NEW FRAMEWORK FOR ADVISING CLIENTS

Launched in 1990, this programme was developed by the **Employment Service** to provide more coherent and targeted help to unemployed people. The framework included:

- a **Back to Work** plan giving individual guidance on how to find work;
- a thirteen week review of claimants and selective interviews for those in skill shortage areas;
- a unified advisory service allowing continuity of contact by skilled advisors;
- Systematic follow-up of those not taking jobs or places on programmes;
- an intensive burst for those unemployed for more than two years; and,
- more case loading of those with particular difficulties.

Further reading: Employment Gazette 1991

NEW FUTURES FUND

(May 1998) The New Futures Fund was established to assist the most disadvantaged unemployed 16- to 34-year-olds to re-engage with the labour market. These people may have experienced low confidence and motivation; alcohol and drug abuse; and homelessness. These people often did not match the more traditional strategies and three levels of progression were designed:

- community based training; **New Deal**; labour market returners' courses;
- **further education**; supported employment; vocational training; and,
- employment.

Further reading: McGregor et al. 2005

NEW HORIZONS

This programme began in Northern Ireland in 1983 and was originally called the **Management Extension Programme**. Its purpose was to match the skills and experience of unemployed managers with the needs of small- and medium-sized enterprises that wanted to improve their performance.

Further reading: Training and Employment Agency Annual Report (1997)

NEW JOB TRAINING SCHEME

(April 1987–September 1988) NJTS became a national training programme in April 1987, five months after it was introduced in pilot areas. It replaced the Old **Job Training Scheme** and was designed to provide training and practical work experience for people who had been unemployed for at least six months, with priority to those under 25 years old. It lasted up to 12 months and the main aim was to equip people with knowledge, skills, and relevant work experience to help them compete effectively in the labour market. It was delivered by local **managing agent**s who were contracted to the **Training Agency**. An allowance of £25 per week or the equivalent of the trainee's benefit was provided, whichever was the higher. In April 1988 a training premium of £10 per week was also added. It was succeeded by **Employment training** in September 1988.

Further reading: Smith (1989)

NEW MANAGER PROJECT

This pilot involved two stages. The first involved the design, implementation and evaluation of an intervention programme that provided a newly appointed manager with FE resources (a personal tutor and back-up services) to improve job performance. The second stage involved making recommendations that would enable a self-supporting service to be established. The average cost of providing the service to one manager was £950 (£700 tutorial costs and £250 for expenses and overheads).

Further reading: Kingston Regional Management Centre (1981); Thurbin and Hinton (1981)

NEW STANDARD

(2007) This was a voluntary assessment framework 'designed to recognise and celebrate the best organisations delivering training and development solutions to employers. The standard allowed organisations to explain their strategy, the approaches they deployed, and the results they achieved, and to submit this for robust assessment with the potential of accreditation for those meeting the high standards set for capability and performance'. The first awards were made in December 2007. It complements the Framework for Excellence, which sets standards for FE colleges and providers. The New Standard was linked to the re-accreditation of **centres of vocational excellence**. It became the **Training Quality Standard**.

Further reading: New Standard (June 2007)

NEW START STRATEGY

(1996) The purpose of New Start was to help 14- to 17-year-olds who had, or were at risk of, dropping out of education and training to be motivated and to re-engage in learning. It spanned compulsory schooling and post-16 learning. It provided funding to support local partnerships to coordinate existing local initiatives and develop new approaches to addressing disaffection. Between its start in 1997 and 1999, there were 17 projects involving the **careers service**, schools, **further education colleges**, **TECs**, local authorities, the **Youth Service** and voluntary organisations. In the autumn of 1998, 43 projects began and ran to the summer of 2000.

Further reading: West and Ciotti (1998)

NEW TECHNOLOGY INSTITUTES

Described in the DfES Departmental Report 2003, these consortia of HEIs, **further education colleges** and private sector partners to provide high-quality training to businesses and students in advanced technology skills, particularly ICT.

See also: Knowledge Exchanges

Further reading: DfES Departmental Report 2003, Cm 5902, p. 128

NEW TRAINING INITIATIVE

The New Training Initiative was implemented in 1984/85 and was divided into three objectives:

- 'Objective One – to develop occupational training, including apprenticeship, in such a way as to enable people entering at different ages and with different educational attainments to acquire the agreed standards of skill appropriate to the jobs available and to provide them with a basis for progression through further learning.
- Objective Two – to move towards a position where all young people under the age of 18 have the opportunity either to continue in full-time education or to enter training or a period of planned work experience combining work related training and education.
- Objective Three – to open up widespread opportunities for adults – whether employed or unemployed or returning to work – to acquire, increase or update their skills and knowledge during the course of their working lives'

MSC Annual Report 1984, p. 14

Further reading: MSC (1981b); MSC (1981c); MSC (1984a);

NEW WORKERS' SCHEME

(April 1986–January 1988) The NWS was designed to encourage the recruitment of young people into jobs where the wages were relatively low. This scheme was based on the view that youth unemployment was higher than necessary because the proportion of young people's pay was relatively high compared to adult pay levels. Employers received £15 per week subsidy for a year for every 18- to 19-year-old they employed at wages of £55 or under and for 20-year-olds at £65 per week. The NWS replaced the **Young Workers Scheme**.

Further reading: Chapman and Tooze (1987); IFF Research Ltd (1987)

NEWLY QUALIFIED TEACHER

When a person achieved **qualified teacher status**, they then spent a year as a newly qualified teacher and then the head notified the **General Teaching Council** that they had successfully, or otherwise, completed their probationary period.

See also: Probationary Teacher

NEWSROOMS

These were reading rooms containing newspapers etc. and were often found alongside libraries in the **mechanics institutes**. The provision of periodicals provided a cheaper access than purchasing them directly and was, therefore, a popular attraction for members. The success of the libraries and newsrooms in mechanics institutes and other institutes demonstrated the demand for reading and led to the Museums Act of 1845, which enabled local authorities to raise levies to establish museums and the first library funded in this way within the museum was Warrington. In 1850 this was followed by the Public Libraries and Museums Act.

Further reading: Tylecote (1957)

NEXTSTEP

The **Learning and Skills Council** funded information, advice and guidance about learning and work through discrete and embedded provision. Discrete IAG was delivered through nextstep, **learndirect** advice, and the **Skills Coaching Service**. Embedded **IAG** was incorporated within programmes of personal and community development learning; student support services; work based learning, etc.

Further reading: www.nextstepstakeholder. co.uk

NIGHT SCHOOLS

During the 1840s, Mr Watkins, an HMI in the northern district of England, noted an

219

increase in the number of night schools for those aged 13 and above. They were taught by a national schoolmaster, superintended by a clergyman and ran between 7 p.m. and 9 p.m. or 8 p.m. and 10 p.m. in the evenings. They were for males and females with different arrangements for each gender; sometimes they came on separate evenings; different rooms were used or sometimes different parts of the same room. There was a 'slight difference in the hours of entrance and departure, so that no mischievous consequences may arise from the circumstances' (Minutes 1845 vol. 2, p. 176). They were sometimes called **evening schools**. With the **New Code**, night schools no longer needed to be attached to day schools and many mechanics institutes invited inspection for elementary classes and the provision of grants (Report 1874–75 p. 211). In the early days, night schools were used by young people who had to leave school early. The subjects taught were the same as in elementary school: reading, writing and arithmetic, and as the range of **specific subjects** increased in the elementary schools this policy was adopted in the night schools (Report 1881–82 p. iv).

See also: Continuation Schools

NON-ADVANCED FURTHER EDUCATION

Under the 1984 White Paper, the MSC responsibility was extended to allow it to purchase a larger proportion of NAFE from **local education authority** maintained **further education colleges** and other providers.

Further reading: MSC Annual Report 1984/85, p. 24

NON-STATUTORY TRAINING ORGANISATIONS

In 1981 the MSC reviewed industrial training arrangements. Of the 42 sectors with training arrangements, 24 were covered by statutory **industrial training boards** set up under the 1964 Training Act. The Government decided that satisfactory training arrangements could be developed without the compulsion and bureaucracy that characterised the statutory system in many sectors. Seven ITBs were kept and the Employment and Training Act 1981 transferred the running costs of the ITBs back to industry. A total of 16 ITBs were wound up and major adjustments were made to three others. Some 90 independent boards were created and 12 further sectors had voluntary arrangements. These 102 were designated non-statutory training organisations and were commonly called **industry training organisations**.

Further reading: Anderson (1987); O'Connell (1990)

NORMAL COLLEGES

Training establishments for teachers in Scotland (Edinburgh and Glasgow) and in Wales (for example Bangor) were commonly called normal colleges; in England they were called **training colleges**. The Edinburgh normal school was founded in 1842 by the Church of Scotland, but following the Disruption (1843) and the establishment of the Free Church of Scotland, its normal and sessional school was opened at Moray House in 1848. The college subsequently became part of Edinburgh University (Minutes 1856–57, p. 669).

See also: Glasgow Educational Association; Normal Schools

NORMAL SCHOOLS

"Normal school" means a training establishment for teachers, such as Westminster, Battersea, Whitelands (Chelsea), etc; not a mere National or other school' (Minutes 1852–53, Vol. 2, p. 288). The **Committee of Council on Education** provided grants that contributed to the building of schools but not for their annual maintenance. They also insisted that normal schools be used for the training of masters and mistresses and that accommodation be provided onsite for the principal and masters. Normal schools began in Scotland in 1845. 'A normal school includes (a) A college, for boarding, lodging, and instructing candidates for the office of teacher in schools for the labouring classes; and (b) A practising department, in which such candidates may learn the exercise of their profession' (Revised Code of Regulations: Report 1863–64 p. xlviii). The term 'normal school' originated because rules of teaching or 'norms' were practised and people trained to be teachers or pupil teachers. The first École Normale or normal school was established in Reims in 1685 by Saint John Baptist de la Salle to train teachers practically in school (Minutes 1844 Vol. 1 p. 6). The person in charge of the school was called a normal master (Report 1865–66 p. 492).

NORTH NORFOLK ACTION

A local initiative based on **community action** for the Norfolk area. It was designed to provide work experience that was of benefit to the community and help people back into work.

Further reading: Department of Employment Departmental Report March 1994 p. 45 Cm 2505

NORTH STAFFORDSHIRE ADULT EDUCATION PRIZE SCHEME

(c1865) This prize was designed to encourage evening scholars to regularly attend classes that would help them appreciate lectures given in mechanics institutes.

See also: Prize Schemes

Further reading: Report 1865–66 p. 104

NORTHERN IRELAND COUNCIL FOR THE CURRICULUM, EXAMINATIONS AND ASSESSMENT

The Northern Irish equivalent of the **Qualifications and Curriculum Authority**.

Its remit is described in the Education (Northern Ireland) Order 1998 and it has responsibility to:

- 'keep under review all aspects of the curriculum, examinations and assessment;
- give advice to the **Department of Education** about the curriculum, assessment, examinations and external qualifications;
- publish and distribute information about the curriculum, assessment and examinations;
- carry out consultation with the educational community in Northern Ireland about proposed changes to legislation governing the curriculum, examinations and assessment;
- consult and moderate examinations and assessment, ensuring that standards are equivalent in these areas to other parts of the United Kingdom.'

www.ccea.org.uk (accessed 28 May 2010)

NORTHERN IRELAND MINISTRY OF EDUCATION

The ministry assumed overall responsibility for education in Northern Ireland following partition in 1921. **The Education Act (Northern Ireland) 1923** resulted in the establishment of county councils and county borough councils that had responsibility for the local provision of education. **The Education Act (Northern Ireland) 1947** provided for secondary education. Following devolution the **Department of Education Northern Ireland** was created in December 1999 with responsibility for primary and secondary education, and the **Department for Employment and Learning** having responsibility for **further** and **higher education**.

NORTHERN IRELAND OFFICE

Had responsibility for education and training in Northern Ireland through the **Department for Education and Learning**.

Further reading: www.delni.gov.uk

See also: Training and Employment Agency

NORTHERN IRELAND SKILLS TASK FORCE

The task force was formed in 1998 to advise on labour market research and monitoring, broad policy issues, and on strategies to address future skill needs. Membership included employers and trade union representatives as well as officials from government departments and agencies.

Further reading: Training and Employment Agency Annual Report (1999) Operating Plan 1999–2000 p. 20

NORTHERN IRELAND TRAINING AUTHORITY

The Department of Economic Development (DED) commissioned a review of the training system in Northern Ireland, which had remained unchanged for 20 years. It identified that there was no coordinated policy and that a new training organisation should be established. In 1988 spending on training was: DED £120m; industrial training boards £10.5m; and NITA £1.5m. It was succeeded by the **Training and Employment Agency**.

Further reading: Department of Economic Development (1988)

NOT IN EDUCATION, EMPLOYMENT OR TRAINING

Young people, aged 16–18, who were not in employment, education or training were considered to be socially and economically at risk. They were sometimes known as NEETs. This term came into prominence in the late 1990s.

Further reading: House of Commons; Children, Schools and Families Committee (2010)

NURSERY SCHOOLS

HM Inspector Mr Balmer presented a history of elementary education and referred to a publication about a nursery school established in Clerkenwell in 1686: *An Account of the General Nursery or Colledg [sic] of Infants Sat [sic] up by the Justices of Peace for the County of Middlesex* (Board of Education 1899–1900 Vol. 3 p. 322). Grants were paid for nurseries for the year ending 31 March 1918, and the **Board of Education** first issued *Regulations for Nursery Schools* in January 1919 (Report 1918–19 p. 20) and began more systematic provision of nursery schools. 'This is a small contribution to the urgent problem of the physical and educational welfare of the pre-school child … The Nursery School affords special advantages in providing a system of preparatory medical supervision before the child is admitted to the infants' department of the Public Elementary School. The necessity for such measures is revealed by the fact that about 35 per cent of entrants at five years of age require some form of medical treatment; by giving early advice and guidance to the mother a certain proportion of these defects need not occur. In fact, the aim of the Nursery School is preventative rather than remedial. The educational influence of the Nursery School is seen in the development of self-control, the formation of good habits, and the foundation of interest in different forms of handwork. The social effect has been clearly shown in the raising of standards of home life and increased parental co-operation' (Report 1923–24 p. 137). In September 2001, the Foundation Stage was introduced, which provided a curriculum for young children entering the nursery until completion of the reception class in the **infants school**.

See also: Early Years Foundation Stage

NURSING

'Nursing and Hygiene', and 'First Aid to the injured' were first included within the specific subject of 'Ambulance' in the 1895 **Code**. Areas within nursing included: the sick room, infection and disinfection, details of nursing; and application of local remedies (Report 1894–95 pp. 483–484).

OBJECT TEACHING

Teaching through the use of objects or items presented to learners has probably been in existence as long as humankind have interacted. An early recorded use was the **Pestalozzi method**, which used object lessons and Mayo (1831) wrote about its application in Cheam, Surrey. Later, Circular 369 by the **Education Department** brought clarification about the nature of object lessons. 'In schools in which Object Teaching has been introduced with most success the teachers have carefully distinguished between two kinds of instruction which in other schools are not seldom confused. These two kinds of instruction are – (1) observation of the Object itself, and (2) giving information about the Object. This distinction is of importance, because the scope and method of the lesson differ according to its nature. Object Teaching leads the scholar to acquire knowledge by observation and experiment; and no instruction is properly so-called unless an Object is presented to the learner so that the addition to his knowledge may be made through the senses' (Report 1894–95 p. 530). Object lessons were made compulsory by the 1895 **Code**.

OBLIGATORY SUBJECTS

(1883) In the 1883 **Code** the term 'obligatory subjects' was first used to mean reading, writing, arithmetic (and needlework for girls).

These subjects were more commonly known as **elementary subjects**. Other subjects described in the 1883 Code were optional subjects also called **class subjects** and **specific subjects** (Report 1882–83 p. 113). In 1900, '[t]he old classification of subjects as "obligatory", "class", "specific", was replaced by a twofold division into – (a) Subjects to be taken "as a rule" in all schools though not necessarily in every class – English; Arithmetic; Drawing (for boys); Needlework (for girls); Lessons, including Object Lessons, on Geography, History, Common Things; Singing and Physical exercises. (b) A list of subjects, one or more of which was to be taken when circumstances in the opinion of the Inspector made it desirable. These were the old "specific' subjects"' (Report 1910–11 p. 20).

OCCUPATIONAL GUIDANCE SERVICE

Started in an experimental form in 1966 within the public employment service and continued until 1980. In 1974 it became part of the **Employment Service Agency**, which was part of the **MSC**. The main purpose was to counsel individuals on their choice of occupation and their suitability, taking into account educational and training considerations. In 1978 there were 43 occupational guidance units with 185 guidance officers who provided guidance to 54,000 clients.

Further reading: MSC (1978e); Price (2000)

OCCUPATIONAL STANDARDS

These were precise competence descriptions for each occupational area of what a person should achieve in employment. The standards consisted of an element title, performance criteria, range statements and underpinning knowledge (the latter being added a few years later). The standards describe: what should happen; how it should happen; the range of applications; and the knowledge required to undertake the task.

See also: National Occupational Standards

Further reading: Mansfield and Mitchell (1996)

OCCUPATIONAL STANDARDS COUNCILS

These councils superseded the **lead bodies** and continued to develop the standards for specific occupational areas.

See also: National Training Organisations

Further reading: Mansfield and Mitchell (1996)

OFFENDERS LEARNING AND SKILLS SERVICE

(31 July 2006) Formerly the **Offenders Learning and Skills Unit**, OLASS built on the partnership between the National Probation Service and the **Learning and Skills Council**. It did not have an organisational structure or staff but was designed to coordinate services for offenders. Its vision is 'that offenders, in prisons and supervised in the community, according to need, should have access to learning and skills, which enables them to gain the skills and qualifications they need to hold down a job and have a positive role in society'.

Department for Innovation, Universities and Skills (2007); http://olass.skillsfundingagency.bis.gov.uk (accessed 28 May 2010)

OFFENDERS LEARNING AND SKILLS UNIT

(April 2004) Formerly the **Prisoners Learning and Skills Unit**, this a joint DfES/Home Office unit, which worked with stakeholders to address the educational and skills needs of offenders. From April 2004 the remit for the OLSU included the provision of learning to offenders under supervision in partnership with the probation service and the Learning and Skills Council. By 2004 the prison service had appointed more than 100 Heads of Learning and Skills in England and Wales. Subsequently became the **Offenders Learning and Skills Service**.

Further reading: DfES Departmental Report 2004, Cm 6202, p. 86

OFFICE FOR NATIONAL STATISTICS

(April 1996) The ONS was formed by the merger of the Central Statistical Office and the Office of Population Censuses and Surveys. Among its duties it publishes *Labour Market Trends* and *Labour Force Survey*, which became the *Economic and Labour Market Review*.

Further reading: www.statistics.gov.uk

OFFICE FOR STANDARDS IN EDUCATION (OFSTED)

(1 September 1992–1 April 2007) 'The aim of the Department is to help improve the quality and standards of education through independent inspection and advice to the Secretary of State … The Department works to:

- deliver high quality inspection of schools, funded nursery education, teacher training and local education authorities (**LEAs**), providing independent assessment to help them raise educational standards;
- provide high quality advice, based on inspection evidence, to the Secretary of

State to assist in the formulation and evaluation of Government policies.'

OFSTED (2001a)

It was subsequently reformed and retitled: **Office for Standards in Education, Children's Service and Skills**.

See also: School Assessment; League Tables

Further reading: www.ofsted.gov.uk (accessed 01 June 2010)

OFFICE FOR STANDARDS IN EDUCATION, CHILDREN'S SERVICE AND SKILLS

(1 April 2007) The Education and Inspections Act 2006 established the new OFSTED, which was created from four former inspectorates: the **Adult Learning Inspectorate;** the Commission for Social Care Inspection; Her Majesty's Inspectorate of Court Administration, and the previous **Office for Standards in Education**. Its purpose was to inspect and regulate care for children and young people, and education and training for all people of all ages.

Further reading: OFSTED (2007); http://www.ofsted.gov.uk (accessed 01 June 2010)

OFFICE OF THE MANPOWER SERVICES COMMISSION

This office serviced the commission and coordinated and supervised grant-in-aid.

Further reading: MSC Annual Report 1975/76

OFFICE OF THE QUALIFICATIONS AND EXAMINATIONS REGULATOR

(8 April 2008) Ofqual took over the regulatory functions of the **Qualifications and Curriculum Authority** and its purpose was to be an 'independent guardian of standards and quality across the exams system'. It achieves this by:

- 'Making sure that organisations that offer and deliver qualifications (awarding organisations) have good systems in place, and that they are held to account for their performance.
- Making sure that all qualifications offered by awarding organisations are fair and are comparable with other qualifications.
- Ensuring that there is fair access to qualifications for all candidates.
- Ensuring the quality of marking of exams, tests and other assessments to make sure that learners get the results they deserve.
- Making sure that the qualifications market provides value for money and meets the needs of learners and employers.
- Encouraging debate about important topics, such as standards of exams and qualifications.'

Office of the Qualifications and
Examinations Regulator (2008 p. 3)

Ofqual lists all accredited qualifications in the **National Database of Accredited Qualifications**.

Further reading: www.ofqual.org.uk (accessed 01 June 2010)

OFFICE OF THE SCHOOLS COMMISSIONER

(September 2006) The role of the schools commissioner, a non-departmental public body, was described in the White Paper, *Higher Standards: Better Schools for All*. One of the main responsibilities of the OSC was to identify under-performing schools and to challenge local authorities to improve the situation. Four main themes for the OSC were: promoting choice and diversity; championing fair access; parental involvement, choice and satisfaction; and local authority commissioning role.

Further reading: www.dcsf.gov.uk/schoolscommissioner/ (accessed 01 June 2010)

OLD JOB TRAINING SCHEME

See: Job Training Scheme

ONE PILOTS

See: Jobcentre Plus

OPEN AIR SCHOOLS

(1904) These schools were originally established in Charlottenburg, Germany, for those children who were diagnosed as being backward due to ill-health. It was estimated that between 3 per cent and 5 per cent of children fell into this category in urban areas, and to address these concerns the first open-air established in England by London County Council at Bostall Woods, Woolwich, was followed by schools in Bradford and Halifax. Children received education in a number of subjects and, '[t]he hygienic aims of such a school should be to strengthen and cure the children by simple hygienic measures, such as fresh air and sunshine, plentiful and suitable food, baths, exercise, and periods of absolute rest' (Laurie 1912a, p. 3).

OPEN COLLEGE

(1987) The Open College was launched in 1987 with the mission to raise vocational competence through the increased provision of open learning opportunities and thereby raise UK economic performance. It began with a range of programmes developed under the **Open Tech Programme**. Programmes were also broadcast under contract by Channel Four. It provides courses for young people and adults for whom traditional qualifications are inaccessible, inappropriate or not available. By 2000, 250,000 students had enrolled with the Open College Network.

Further reading: MSC (1987d); www.nonc.org.uk

226

OPEN COLLEGE OF THE ARTS

(1987) Founded by Michael Young, this college, in Barnsley, provided distance learning higher education in the arts.

OPEN FOR LEARNING

This was a three-year programme that provided support for libraries to give an open-learning service. In 1996–97, some 99 out of the 108 library authorities offered an open-learning service with, on average, 192 new open-learning users a year and 20,000 individuals.

Further reading: DfEE Departmental Report 1996, Cm3210, p. 95

OPEN LEARNING ACCESS CENTRES

Twelve OLACs were supported by the **Training and Employment Agency** during 1996/97 in Belfast, Londonderry, and Castledawson. They provided flexible training for those people who found traditional learning and training provision an unattractive option. Target groups included women returning to work, people with disabilities and the unemployed.

Further reading: Training and Employment Agency Annual Report (1997)

OPEN LEARNING CREDITS

(1993–95) Never went beyond a pilot programme that took place in 14 **TECs** in 1993/94 and funded the unemployed to undertake distance training. The concept was incorporated within **Training for Work** in 1995. The intention was to test out the open learning credits as a possible alternative to mainstream training provision for unemployed adults. Open learning would allow people to study at a time, place and pace that suited them and thus allowed them to continue their job search while learning. It also allowed the unemployed to take more responsibility for their own training and development. The pilots were delivered with a budget of £2.4m for England.

Further reading: Crowley-Bainton (1995)

OPEN TECH PROGRAMME

(August 1982–1987) This was a series of projects designed to increase open learning (OL) opportunities for technical and supervisory personnel. It was a precursor to later efforts to encourage lifelong learning. Initial work was to create OL programmes and work at creating a market for these.

Further reading: MSC (1982c); Open Tech (1982); Tavistock Institute of Human Relations (1987)

(THE) OPEN UNIVERSITY

The Open University was founded in 1969 and received its first students in 1971. It applied an open access policy with no, or limited, entry qualification requirements. It is based at Milton Keynes and has regional centres throughout the UK and overseas and provides a wide range of part-time open-learning programmes delivered through classes, summer schools, online learning, television, etc.

Further reading: www.open.ac.uk/ (accessed 01 June 2010)

OPPORTUNITY 2000

(1990) This was a scheme run by the **Business in the Community Scheme** with the aim of supporting women to rise into management and increase the number of women managers. It was launched in late 1990 by the then Prime Minister, John Major, with the backing of sixty-one leading employers. Each employer set its own goals and monitored progress made over the following years; for example, National Westminster Bank pledged to increase women managers from 16.3 per cent to 33 per cent by 2000. This initiative arose because research had shown that only one in five managers were women and fewer than two per cent were executives.

Further reading: Employment Gazette 1991 p. 637

OPRYLAND HOTEL PROJECT

This project placed 18 people in the Opryland Hotel in Nashville, USA, and participants had the opportunity to train at manager/supervisor level in various hotel operations. This initiative reflected the importance of tourism to the Northern Ireland economy.

See also: Young Managers Development Programme; Managing the Growing Tourism Business

Further reading: Training and Employment Agency Annual Report (1997)

OPTIONAL SUBJECTS

(1883) These were more commonly known, at the time, as **class subjects** and were: singing, English, geography, elementary science and history (Report 1882–83 p. 113).

See also: Elementary Subjects; Specific Subjects

OPTIONS PROGRAMME

See: Business Growth Training

ORDINARY LEVELS

See: General Certificate of Education

ORDINARY NATIONAL CERTIFICATE/ DIPLOMA

See: Business and Technology Education Council

ORGANISATION FOR ECONOMIC CO-OPERATION AND DEVELOPMENT

The OECD was established in Paris on 14 December 1960 to promote policies designed:

- 'to achieve the highest sustainable economic growth and employment and a rising standard of living in Member countries while maintaining financial stability, and thus to contribute to the development of the world economy;
- to contribute to sound economic expansion in Member as well as non-member countries in the process of economic development; and
- to contribute to the expansion of world trade on a multilateral, non-discriminatory basis in accordance with international obligations'.

www.oecd.org/document/7/0,3343, en_2649_201185_1915847_1_1_1_1,00. html (accessed 05 April 2010)

The UK's interests are represented at international organisations including **ILO**, OECD and the Council of Europe.

Further reading: Organisation for Economic Co-operation and Development (2001)

ORGANISED COURSES

In the early 1900s there was a considerable growth of vocational courses provided in **evening schools**, which had originally been for young people who had not completed their elementary education and which provided a route to **technical schools**. 'The provision of systematic courses of instruction as distinguished from detached classes is being rapidly extended in Evening Schools, especially in the northern part of the country. In a great many of the schools, organised courses based upon an attendance of three nights per week are now provided, and special work is laid down for those students who are following, or who are about to follow, industrial, commercial, or domestic occupations. Except in very special circumstances, students in these schools are required to take the whole course prescribed in order that they may get a comprehensive knowledge of the branch of study selected' (Report 1907–08 p. 85).

OUT-OF-SCHOOL CHILD CARE GRANT

(April 1993) The objective of this grant was to increase the quality and quantity of out-of-school provision and allow parents of school-age children the chance to participate more fully in the labour market. Grants were paid through **TECs/LECs** to employers, schools, voluntary organisations, local authorities or various combinations, to help set up childcare facilities outside of school hours and in school holidays. The grants were for initial start-ups and operating costs for up to 12 months. The proposals had to satisfy four criteria. They had to: meet statutory requirements and be of high quality; be capable of being self financing in a limited period; impact on the labour market; and add extra places to supply.

Further reading: Department of Employment Report 1993, Cm 2205, p. 24

OVERSEA TRAINING CENTRES

(1925–28) These were work camps developed by the **Ministry of Labour** with the first centre beginning operations in November 1925 at Claydon, East Anglia. Initially for ex-servicemen, they were designed to address the high levels of unemployment and train people for work in the dominions; however, with the decline in agriculture during the Depression and the consequent reduction in jobs, they were halted and some became **transfer instructional centres**.

Further reading: Field (2009)

OVERSEAS CAREER DEVELOPMENT PROGRAMME

(Northern Ireland) This provided young graduates with first-hand experience of management best practice through placement with companies throughout the world.

See also: Overseas Export Marketing Programme–Explorers; Business Education Initiative; American Management and Business Internship (AMBIT)

Further reading: Training and Employment Agency Annual Report (1992)

OVERSEAS EXPORT MARKETING PROGRAMME – EXPLORERS

This small Northern Irish programme took 33 graduates into an export environment in the United States and Europe in 1991/92. Its purpose was to enable them to acquire the skills of selling and attracting buyers.

See also: Overseas Career Development Programme

Further reading: Training and Employment Agency Annual Report (1992)

OVERSEAS NATIONALS – INDUSTRIAL TRAINING FOR

(1967) This scheme started in 1967 and was put in place as a joint venture led by the Ministry of Overseas Development and the **Ministry of Labour**, following consultation with the CBI and the TUC. It was part of Britain's programme of technical assistance to developing countries and was designed to increase the number of officially sponsored trainees to 500 over the ensuing two years. The provision of training opportunities was considered one of the most valuable forms of aid to developing countries. It was also believed that providing the training was in the long-term interests of British industry because it fostered good relationships with industries and potential customers in the developing countries. The scheme did not substitute for existing arrangements such as the CBI Scholarship Scheme, or private training initiatives: the Overseas Students Advisory Bureau.

Further reading: Ministry of Overseas Development/Ministry of Labour (1970); Ministry of Labour Gazette (1967)

OVERSEAS TRADE TRAINING

In the early 1980s the Training Services Division of the MSC provided courses in import and export procedures. This was part of the **MSC**'s programme to encourage British industry to improve the training of staff involved with international trade as a means of improving export efficiency.

Further reading: MSC Annual Report 1980/81, p. 18

OWENS COLLEGE

(1851–80) John Owens, a nonconformist cotton merchant in Manchester, left £96,942 in his will for the establishment of a college that did not require a test of religious knowledge. Other supporters raised additional funds and the college was inaugurated in 1851. Subsequently, a new college was erected in Oxford Street in 1873 and became the Victoria University of Manchester in 1880 when it received its Royal Charter. In 2004 it merged with the University of Manchester Institute of Science and Technology (UMIST) (whose origins were the Manchester Mechanics Institute – 1824) to form the University of Manchester.

OXFORD AND CAMBRIDGE SCHOOLS EXAMINATION BOARD

(1873) In 1857 the **Birmingham Educational Association**, not content with the irregular system of **prize schemes**, formally approached both universities to supervise examinations in Birmingham. Only boys could take the examinations but the certificates awarded exempted those holding them from taking university entrance examinations. This subsequently led to the formation of the Oxford and Cambridge Schools Examination Board in 1873.

See also: Oxford, Cambridge and RSA Examinations

OXFORD, CAMBRIDGE AND RSA EXAMINATIONS

(1998) OCR was created by the merger of the University of Cambridge Local Examination Syndicate, **Royal Society for the Encouragement of Arts, Manufactures and Commerce** (RSA), Oxford and Cambridge Examinations and Assessment Council and a number of other examinations boards. It is one of the three English unitary awarding bodies the other two being **Assessment and Qualifications Alliance**, and **Edexcel**. It is an **awarding body** for academic, vocational and occupational qualifications. OCR is a section of the Cambridge Assessment Group, itself being a department of the University of Cambridge.

Further reading: www.ocr.org.uk (accessed 01 June 2010)

P

PARENTS NATIONAL EDUCATIONAL UNION

In Wales, 'In one Council School a general scheme of instruction based upon the syllabuses of the Parents National Educational Union has been followed and developed in the boys' and girls' departments with commendable success. The courses in English are particularly good, introducing as they do a wide range of general reading in prose and poetry and the study of established classics in English literature and in translations from other languages. The works selected are intended to broaden the outlook of the children, to stimulate their interest and their imaginations, to increase their vocabularies and to lead them to utilise their extended vocabularies in oral and written composition' (Report 1923–24 p. 57).

PAROCHIAL BOARDS

(1845–94) Under the Poor Law (Scotland) Act 1845, parochial boards were established to 'pay for the instruction of pauper children, both at parish and other schools. The Kirk Sessions of the Established Church being relieved by the same Act, from the duty of providing for the maintenance of the poor, now educate needy, but not pauper children, from the funds produced by church collections. Individuals more frequently, from benevolence, educate children at their own cost. And bequests for educational purposes in a charitable manner receive occasional accessions' (Report 1858–59 p. 227). They were replaced by Parish Councils in 1894.

PAROCHIAL SCHOOLS

In Scotland, in 1663, the Legislature in Edinburgh passed an act that directed the establishment of a school in every Scottish parish to be maintained 'upon a sum to be stented upon every plough or husband land according to worth' (Minutes 1844, Volume 2, p. 353). Later, in 1696 another act made this assessment imperative and fixed the amount of the salary. Later the Act of 43 Geo.III., b.54, 1803 increased the amount and specified rules for the government of the schools. These developments were preceded by the recommendations made by the **Committee of Ministers of the Reformed Church**.

See also: Privately–Endowed Schools

PAROCHIAL UNION SCHOOLS

(1834) These were workhouses established under the Poor Law Amendment Act 1834, which required parishes to join together to build workhouses to house and educate pauper children.

See also: Poor Law Acts

Further reading: Report 1858–59 p. 480

PARTNERSHIPS FOR PROGRESSION

(2002) To achieve the target of 50 per cent participation in higher education by 2010 for those aged between 18 and 30, it was recognised that there was a need to strengthen partnerships between **higher education**, **further education** and schools in order to raise the attainment levels and aspirations of young people. As part of this P4P strategy, there was a need to increase participation particularly among lower socio-economic groups; raise attainment at NVQ levels 2 and 3; and increase work based learning and progression routes to HE.

Further reading: www.hefce.ac.uk

PATHWAYS TO WORK

(piloted from October 2007 and then rolled out 28 April 2008) The British Pathways to Work initiative was described in the 2002 Green Paper *Pathways to Work*, and was designed to provide employment, financial and health support to reduce the large number of people who received incapacity benefit, and employment and support allowance. People receiving this support were required to have a medical assessment or work capability assessment that determined whether a person was fit to return to work. Pathways to Work involved mandatory, work-focused interviews; support programmes to prepare for work; and, a return to work credit of £40 per week for the first year for those people earning under £15,000.

Further reading: www.dwp.gov.uk/policy/ welfare-reform/pathways-to-work/ (accessed 01 June 2010)

PAUPER SCHOOLS

See: Workhouse Schools; Schools of Industry; (The) Training of Pauper Children

PAYMENT BY RESULTS

(1862–95) The introduction of the 1862 **Revised Code** gave the state power to control directly the school curriculum, which it

did through a system of individual examinations conducted by **Her Majesty's Inspectors** who visited and tested the performance of scholars. Grants were awarded according to the success of the scholars.

PEACE PROGRAMME

(Northern Ireland)

See: European Union Special Support Programme for Peace and Reconciliation

PENNY DINNERS

The provision of school dinners (that is, at lunch time) first began in the Sunderland district from whence it expanded rapidly and was viewed as a valuable support to education. Mr Rooper, HMI, commented: 'The idea must not die out. Teachers have too often in the past had to generate steam without fuel. In future we may hope to stoke the little engines properly for the work they have to do' (Report 1884–85 p. 277).

See also: School Meals; Education (Provision of Meals) Act 1906

PENNY SAVINGS BANK

(1860s) The HMI Mr Pickard noted that in the night school established by the Farnley Iron Company, near Leeds, 'there is a cricket club, a reading room, and a lending library; and there is a penny savings bank connected with the schools and works in which upwards of £1,000 is deposited. There is also a Provident Society for affording help in the cases of sickness and death, the funds of which amount to nearly £200' (Report 1866–67 p. 172).

See also: School Savings Banks

PENSIONS – TEACHERS

(1857) A system of superannuation for teachers began to be progressively developed and this was described in a circular letter from

232

the Committee of Council on Education (12 June 1857). 'The pensioners must have served for fifteen years in school and their schools must have been, during seven of those years under inspection. Age or infirmity is a condition of every pension (£30 per annum being the maximum for an elementary teacher), and the pension may be withdrawn on proof of misconduct, or of sufficient means of livelihood from other sources' (Minutes 1958–59, p. xxxviii).

PEOPLE'S COLLEGES

(1842) One of the earliest of these was **Sheffield People's College**, which was established to support a wider education than that provided by the **mechanics institutes**. The long-lasting people's college in Nottingham (founded in 1846) merged with Broxtowe College in 2006 to create Castle College. A more recent people's college – Ulster People's College – was founded in 1982 with the purpose of using education and training to support economic and social development and address political and cultural divisions.

Further reading: Moore Smith (1912)

PERSONAL AND COMMUNITY DEVELOPMENT LEARNING

PCDL was defined by the **Learning and Skills Council** as 'learning for personal development, cultural enrichment, intellectual or creative stimulation, and enjoyment. It is also learning developed with local residents and others to build the skills, knowledge and understanding for social and community action. There is no requirement that learners must necessarily progress to other learning or achieve accreditation … This approach also recognises the wider benefits of learning in the community, including its contribution to broader government policies such as health (mental and physical well-being) and community cohesion' (Learning and Skills Council 2006 p. 3). It was very similar to traditional adult education provision.

PERSONAL, LEARNING AND THINKING SKILLS

The **Qualifications and Curriculum Authority** published its *Personal Learning and Thinking Skills Framework* in 2007 to support the new secondary curriculum aims of developing young people to become: successful learners, confident individuals and responsible citizens, which were based on the Every Child Matters policy. The six groups of skills were: independent enquirers; creative thinkers; reflective learners; team workers; self-managers; effective participators. Each group of skills had a focus statement that described the range of skills and qualities involved.

Further reading: www.qcda.gov.uk/libraryAssets /media/PLTS_framework.pdf

PERSONNEL MANAGEMENT ADVISORY SERVICE

PMAS was the predecessor of the advisory function of **Advisory, Conciliation and Arbitration Service (ACAS)**.

PESTALOZZI METHOD

This was a teaching/learning approach developed by Johann Heinrich Pestalozzi (1746–1827), a Swiss educator. Drawing on the work of Jean Jacques Rousseau he established a number of schools that encouraged children to learn through the use of their senses, practice and observation. These principles were adopted by the **Home and Colonial Infant School Society**.

Further reading: Green (1912)

PETRA

(1988–94) Petra was a European programme based on the council decisions of 1 December 1987 and 22 July 1991 and became operational in autumn 1988. It was enlarged and ran to 31 December 1994. The main objective was to support member states to ensure

233

that young people received one and preferably two years vocational training. Petra also encouraged transnational youth exchanges, cooperation and the development of networks in the area of vocational training.

Further reading: Commission of the European Communities (1993)

PHILOSOPHICAL SOCIETIES

These were a form of **mutual instruction society** that were widely established to encourage the understanding of science and industrial activities. The philosophical societies were sometimes known as philosophical and literary societies and were to be found in many towns and cities including Liverpool (1812), Leeds (1820), Sheffield and Hull (1822), Whitby (1823 and still operating), Bristol (1824), Halifax (1830), Leicester (1835), and Barnsley and Rochdale (1833).

Further reading: Kelly (1992)

PHYSICAL EDUCATION

Physical education or physical training became increasingly popular in the latter part of the 1800s and the Report for 1899–1900 stated that 'the higher grant for discipline and organisation is not paid to any School in which provision had not been made for instruction in Swedish or other drill or in suitable Physical Exercises' (Report 1906–07 p. 12).

It was first included in the Day School Code 1901, which stated, 'The course in Physical Training should be carried on continuously throughout the school year for not less than one hour in each week for each class, and for not more than one half-hour for each class on any one day ... It may be supplemented by further and more varied Physical training, including, where possible, systematic instruction in swimming, cricket, such further Physical training ... should always be conducted with due regard to the age, sex, and bodily constitution of the children. Thus, to

take one instance, fixed gymnastic apparatus is unsuitable for children under fourteen years of age' (Report 1900–01 Vol. 3, p. 143).

Mr Aldis, HM Inspector, stated, 'No account of school life in Birmingham, however incomplete otherwise, ought to fail to notice the provision for physical training, which is, I believe, unique. Apart from the regular and systematic exercises carried on in all the schools of the city, a very comprehensive scheme exists for the encouragement, promotion, and control of outdoor games, as well as drill and gymnastics. ... Cricket, football, swimming, running and gymnastics are systematically organised. Challenge shields are competed for annually, while medals and books are awarded to the individual boys of the winning teams (with free passes to the county cricket ground – for cricket), and medals to the teachers who have acted as "trainers". ... The football shield is played immediately before the final for the Birmingham and District and Counties Football Association Challenge Cup, with the same officials for both matches. The 100 yards inter-school race is decided at the Aston Villa ground – the best athletic ground in the city' (Board of Education 1899–1900 Vol. 3. p. 173).

In 1904 an Interdepartmental Committee on Physical Training and the **Scotch Education Department** issued a Syllabus of Physical Exercises (Board of Education 1903–04 p. 16). And in the 1906 Code they expressly allowed that 'a part of the afternoon period may be devoted to cricket, football, hockey and rounders for boys and similar appropriate games for girls' (Board of Education 1905–06 p. 24).

The Circular 1445 on Physical Education in (Report 1936 p. 5) recommended organised daily exercise in primary schools and the Physical Training and Recreation Act 1937 extended this provision.

PIT CLOSURE AREAS

(1994) This initiative was designed to alleviate the impact on communities by redundancies in pit closure areas. Funding that amounted to

£200m was provided to help restructure the areas, of which £75m was allocated to **TECs** and the **Employment Service** in England and Wales. Contingency plans were drawn up by TECs, the Employment Service, the **Department of Trade and Industry**, the Department of the Environment, English Estates, and British Coal Enterprise. Labour market plans included: guarantee of assessment and guidance for a period of twelve months; additional training and retraining opportunities; assistance in starting a new business; new opportunities for people seeking voluntary work; priority access for all people affected by the closure of the mines including mineworkers and other employed people. The TEC contingency plans offered an additional 20,000 places on labour market measures and assessment and guidance with provision for up to 100,000 people.

Further reading: Department of Employment Report 1994, Cm 2505, p. 26

PLACING, ASSESSMENT AND COUNSELLING TEAMS

PACTs provided more support to disabled people than could be provided by the **jobcentre**. PACTs provide special assessment of needs and access to special programmes to help people find and keep jobs. The priorities were to: ensure that the **ES** could deal with disabled clients; provide specialist help where mainstream services were unsuitable; provide support to employers; and monitor and ensure quality of externally delivered programmes. They provided support with ability assessment centres formerly known by their provisional name – disability resource centres.

See also: Employment Rehabilitation Service

Further reading: Johnson et al. (1993)

PLAY CENTRES

The **Education (Administrative Provisions) Act 1907** empowered local education authorities to provide play centres, and vacation schools and classes for children (Report 1906–07 p. 8). Evening play centres were further encouraged during the First World War in order to 'provide suitable occupation and amusement after school hours' in order to reduce offences being committed by children (Report 1915–16 p. 4).

POLICY ACTION TEAM FOR SKILLS

See: Skills for Neighbourhood Renewal

POLYTECHNIC

The term 'polytechnic' has existed in Britain since the Royal Polytechnic Institution opened in 1838. A building was acquired in Regent Street in 1881 by Quintin Hogg, and it subsequently became known as the Regent Street Polytechnic. The report of the **Board of Education** (1924–25 p. 70) described how a boy could obtain pre-employment training in sewing, through attending the three-year course in the **junior technical school** at the Regent Street Polytechnic. It later became the Polytechnic of Central London and, finally, the University of Westminster. Likewise, the Northern Polytechnic Institute was founded in 1892 with support from the London Parochial Charities funds and Clothworkers' Company of London and is now London Metropolitan University. A White Paper, *A Plan for Polytechnics and other Colleges,* in 1966 encouraged the development of polytechnics to interact with business and industry and 34 were established. The Further and Higher Education Act 1992 enabled polytechnics to award their own degrees and they subsequently changed their name to university, although one, Anglia Polytechnic University, adopted both terms before becoming Anglia Ruskin University in 2005.

Futher reading: Pratt (1997)

POOR LAW ACTS

These were a series of acts that were introduced to support the poor and destitute. The

Poor Law Act 1601 allowed parishes to distribute support to those in need. The Settlement Act 1622 enabled parishes to return poor people to their 'home' parish after 40 days unless they possessed a settlement certificate. Knatchbull's Act 1722 allowed the purchase of buildings for use as workhouses for the able-bodied poor who could be denied relief if they did not enter. This was repealed in 1796 in order that out relief could be provided. As the terms suggest, in(door) relief was provided for residents, and out (door) relief for those who had accommodation but insufficient funds for food etc. In 1834 the Poor Law Amendment Act required parishes to unite into unions and build a central union workhouse. The workhouses were supervised by the Poor Law commissioners and were replaced by a Poor Law board in 1847, which subsequently became the Local Government Board in 1871. The Local Government Act 1929 abolished workhouses and their responsibilities were transferred to county boroughs and county councils.

See also: Workhouse Schools Poor Law School

POOR LAW SCHOOL

This was a school established by the Poor Law authorities to educate the children of paupers who suffered from disability, illness, poverty and unemployment. The title poor school also carried negative connotations; Mr Stokes, HMI, stated: 'It has indeed been reported to me that children of artisans are kept from the schools, because they bear the name *poor* schools, and I have even heard of the case where a boy had a handsome bronze medal, which was awarded to him as a prize for proficiency in religious knowledge, thrown by his mother behind the fire, because it was inscribed, "Catholic Poor School Committee"' (Report 1860–61 p. 208).

Inspection of Poor Law schools was transferred to the **Board of Education** on 1 April 1904, following arrangement with the local government board. The number of Poor-Law schools progressively declined particularly following the **Elementary Education Act 1891**, which provided for free education, and by boards of guardians encouraging the children to attend **elementary schools**. By 1929 there were 56 remaining Poor Law schools, **district schools** and Schools of Metropolitan Asylums Board in England and none in Wales. The responsibilities for these schools transferred from the guardians to the county councils and county boroughs as a result of the Local Government Act 1929, and many of the councils transferred this provision on 1 April 1930 with the Poor Law schools becoming elementary schools (Report 1929 p. 16).

See also: Workhouse School, Poor Law Acts

POSITIVE ACTIVITIES FOR YOUNG PEOPLE

(15 July 2003) This was a three year cross-departmental government programme designed to provided diversionary activities for young people (aged 8–19) who were most at risk of community crime and social exclusion. It replaced a number of Summer Acitivity Programmes and ran throughout the year with a total budget of £ 124.5m.

Further reading: CRG Research (2006)

POSTGRADUATE CERTIFICATE OF/IN EDUCATION

The PGCE is a one-year programme that contains taught classes and supervised school teaching, which, on successful completion, leads to **qualified teacher status** in England and Wales, and 'eligibility to teach' in Northern Ireland. The programme contributes credits at masters level. Between 2005 and 2007 a Professional Graduate Certificate of/in Education was introduced, which was equivalent to a higher/professional level in the **Framework for Higher Education Qualifications**. In Scotland, the Post-Graduate Certificate in Education was replaced with the Post-Graduate Diploma in Education.

See also: Teaching Certificate

POSTGRADUATE DIPLOMA IN EDUCATION

See: Post-Graduate Certificate in Education

PRACTICAL INSTRUCTION

This subject replaced the term '**special subjects**' due to the removal of special grants for optional subjects as a result of the Education Act 1918. Section 48 of the act, defined practical instruction as '[i]nstruction in Cookery, Laundrywork, Housewifery, Dairywork, Handicraft and Gardening, and all such subjects as the Board declare to be subjects of practical instruction' (Report 1919–20 p. 19).

PRACTISING SCHOOL

This was a school connected to a training school where teachers and **pupil-teachers** were trained, observed teaching practices and taught. Many of the early teacher training colleges had their own practising or **model school** where the students were employed as assistant teachers. 'In the early history of **training schools** the special function of these elementary schools was, as the name given to them implies, to practise the students in the art of teaching, and give them experience in the management of a school' (Minutes 1853–54 Vol. 1, p. 447). For example, there was Worcester Diocesan practising school (Minutes 1859–60 p. 345).

See also: Demonstration Schools

PRELIMINARY EDUCATION CLASSES

(1954–56) The purpose of these classes was to support the industrial rehabilitation of lower age groups who were hindered in obtaining employment by a low standard of literacy. A teacher was seconded from Surrey Education Authority to the Egham **Industrial Rehabilitation Unit**.

Further reading: Ministry of Labour and National Service Report 1955 p. 80

PREMIERE GRADUATE MANAGEMENT DEVELOPMENT PROGRAMME

This Northern Ireland programme focused on the needs of industry and newly qualified graduates who wanted to work in industry. The main feature of Premiere was the placing of graduates with local employers to undertake projects that developed the graduate and assisted the business. It was subsequently replaced by **INTRO**.

See also: Overseas Career Development Programme

Further reading: Training and Employment Agency Annual Report (1996)

PREPARATORY SCHOOLS

A preparatory school, or 'prep' school, is an independent day or boarding school that is designed generally to prepare children for entry to an independent secondary school or public school. The 1917 Regulations of the Board of Education included, for the first time, preparatory schools, which were categorised within a list of 'efficient schools', and during 1917–18, ten schools were recognised (Report 1917–18 p. 26). More recently, the schools prepare most children to take the **Common Entrance Examination**, which facilitates entry to a fee-paying independent secondary school. The traditional age range for pupils is 8 to 13, at which time they may go to public school. Prior to this they may attend a pre-prep school from the ages of 4 or 5 to the age of 8. In more recent times many preparatory schools continued until pupils reached the age of 11, so matching the state school system.

PRESCHOOL EDUCATION

The compulsory attendance age for beginning school is five; however, many children begin well before that and from September 2010 all three- and four-year-old children were entitled to 15 hours of free early education.

See also: Infants Schools; Nursery Schools; Primary Education; Sure Start

PRIMARY EDUCATION

The **Board of Education** (Report 1908–09 p. 31) explained that the term 'primary' originated in France as a means of classifying the progressive stages of: primary, **secondary** and **tertiary education**. Originally, the term elementary education was commonly used; however, its use became 'misleading' due to its extension to include what are now called secondary schools and so the Hadow (1926) Report recommended that it be replaced with the term 'primary'. The report (p. 132) also stated that '[p]rimary education should be regarded as ending at about the age of 11+'.

See also: Infants Schools; Nursery Schools; Preschool Education; Sure Start

PRINCE'S SCOTTISH YOUTH BUSINESS TRUST

(1989) The Trust was originally established with support loans provided by the **Employment Department.** It provides business advice, counselling, and financial help to young people who intend to set up in business but cannot obtain financial backing.

Further reading: P-e International (1992)

PRINCE'S YOUTH BUSINESS TRUST

(1986) PYBT was formed by the merger of the Youth Business Trust and the Youth Enterprise Scheme in 1986. It was established as a charitable trust in 1986 to help young people to become self-employed through the provision of: 'financial assistance (test marketing grants, start-up grants, start-up loans, go and see grants and expansion loans) and, personal business advisors'. Applicants must: be 18–29 (30 if they have a disability); have been unemployed for six weeks; demonstrate that all other sources of finance have been approached without success; have suitable business experience or training and a viable business plan. Financial support for the trust came from the government, private sector contributions and voluntary contributions.

See also: Youth Enterprise Initiative

Further reading: P-e International (1992); Dalgleish (1993); www.princes-trust.org.uk

PRINCIPAL LEARNING

(July 2007) The core of the **diploma** was the main subject of study or 'line of learning' that could be studied in seventeen areas: engineering, travel and tourism, etc. 'Principal learning is the key constituent qualification in each Diploma and covers the essential curriculum relating to the sector title'. It was designed to encourage the development of knowledge and skills and a significant proportion of time was expected to be spent in a work-related or applied learning situation. Principal learning and project qualifications were accredited by the **Qualifications and Curriculum Authority** in 2007.

Further reading: www.qcda.gov.uk/ (accessed 31 May 2010)

PRINCIPAL SCHOOLROOM

Many schools during the 1800s had only one room in which all the pupils were instructed. In time, the room was divided or other rooms built or provided. 'The "principal schoolroom" is named because the school must for many purposes meet as one body, and 80 cubical feet of space per child is a minimum everywhere' (Report 1862–63 p. xxv).

PRIORITY SKILLS INITIATIVE

This Northern Ireland initiative was developed to identify and meet skill requirements on a short-term and flexible basis. Each **sectoral representative body** worked with the **Training and Employment Agency** to survey labour market and skill requirements and produced a strategic training plan for each sector.

Further reading: Training and Employment Agency Annual Report (1995)

PRISONERS' EDUCATION COMMITTEE OF THE HOME OFFICE

The Report of 1924–25 (p. 129) mentioned that '[t]he Committee continued to render assistance to the Prison commissioners in a scheme of adult education in Prisons, carried on by voluntary teachers, which was inaugurated by the Commissioners in co-operation with the Committee during their first term of office'.

PRISONERS LEARNING AND SKILLS UNIT

The unit was created to increase the quality and quantity of educational provision in prisons. In particular, objectives were to increase literacy and numeracy skills. It was subsequently renamed the **Offenders Learning and Skills Unit**.

See also: From Learning to Earning

Further reading: DfES Departmental Report 2003, Cm 5902, p. 147; www.dcsf.gov.uk/offenderlearning/

PRIVATE ENTERPRISE PROGRAMME

(April 1987) This programme was designed for owners of small businesses and those planning to start businesses. It involved the basic skills of business, including marketing, selling, bookkeeping etc. It was part of the **Training for Enterprise** programme.

Further reading: Kirkland (1986)

PRIVATELY-ENDOWED SCHOOLS

These schools were frequently established by bequests. The endowments were sometimes insufficient to fully cover the salary and this had to be supplemented in some cases by subscriptions from parents, or landowners and other proprietors. For example, in Scotland, '[t]he labour of the intelligent workman may be considered as somewhat more productive than that of others; and with many [landowners or proprietors] it may be a point of good ambition to establish on their possessions the ornament of an instructed and moral peasantry' (Minutes 1844 Vol. 2, p. 356).

See also: Endowed Schools; Parochial Schools

PRIZE SCHEMES

The Reverend J. P. Norris discussed the suitability of reward or prize schemes for encouraging pupils. Numerous schemes existed and were supported by a variety of organisations including London and North-Western Railway Company's Prize Scheme, and the South Staffordshire Iron and Coal Masters Prize Fund, which began in 1850 (Minutes 1854–55, pp. 747–763). These prizes had a number of purposes including to encourage excellence and sometimes to encourage pupils to stay at school and many of these received certificates of good conduct, for example the **school certificate**. Many districts offered prizes (frequently financial), for example the Worcester and Coventry archdeaconries; however a more systematic approach was developed by **Birmingham Educational Association**, which approached Oxford and Cambridge universities to supervise an examination system.

See also: Oxford and Cambridge Schools Examination Board

PROACT

(2009) This programme provided financial aid from the Welsh Assembly and the European Social Fund to support businesses to use periods of reduced activity during the recession to train employees and, thus, be prepared for improved times. ProAct also helped with employees on short-time working, and businesses trying to retain skilled people, who might otherwise have been made redundant. It provided a proactive initiative to complement the **Redundancy Action** (ReACT) programme operated for larger-scale redundancies.

Further reading: www.careerchangewales.co.uk/ReAct-and-ProAct-Funding.aspx

PROBATIONARY TEACHERS

(*c*.1860) Those teachers who had completed a course of study at a training college and then entered a school were considered to be on probation. They were also known as 'yearling' teachers (Report 1860–61 p. 143). This was a new class of teacher and was different to assistant teachers who had served a five-year apprenticeship as **pupil-teachers** (Report 1860–61 p. 46). The probationary period tended to last between one and two years (Report 1861–62 p. xxvii).

See also: Newly Qualified Teacher

PROFESSIONAL AND EXECUTIVE RECRUITMENT

(1973–88) The registration system originally set up as the **Professional and Executive Register** was computerised and then replaced in October 1980 by a self-selection system using a weekly jobs magazine *Executive Post*. This was sent off to all enrolled job seekers except those seeking first appointments, who were dealt with under separate arrangements. At its height, the distribution of *Executive Post* was around 150,000 copies. PER was run by the **MSC** and earned income from the placements service. After expenditure was taken into account, the financial position varied between profit and loss. For example, in the years 1977/78, 1979/80 and 1980/81 there were surpluses of £100K,

£275K and £92K. The following year there was an estimated loss of £977K. In September 1988 it was bought for £8m by Pergamon, part of Maxwell Communications Corporation.

Further reading: MSC Annual Report 1980/81, p. 29; Price (2000)

PROFESSIONAL AND EXECUTIVE REGISTER

(1957) Originally the Technical and Scientific Register, established in 1942 to aid the war effort, it was renamed Professional and Executive Register in 1957 as a specialised advertising and recruitment service for professional and executive level vacancies. The PER held a record of those professionals and executives who were seeking employment. It also carried out a matching service, identifying suitable jobs or candidates. The decision was then taken to charge employers for recruitment and the Government had to withdraw from an international labour office convention. In March 1973 a subsidiary of the **Employment Service Agency**, the **Professional and Executive Recruitment**, was set up.

See also: Appointments Service

Further reading: PER (1976); Price (2000)

PROFESSIONAL DEVELOPMENT PLACEMENTS

This was formerly called **teacher placements** and allowed teachers to get business and industrial experience in each of the 47 **LSC** areas.

Further reading: DfES Departmental Report 2002 Cm 5402 p. 138

PROFESSIONAL, INDUSTRIAL AND COMMERCIAL UPDATING

(1982) Pickup was launched in 1982 by the **Department of Education and Science** in

England in 1982, Wales in 1984, and Scotland in 1986/87. Its purpose was to encourage colleges, polytechnics and universities to produce self-financing vocational courses for people in employment. This was a pump-priming initiative to increase the involvement of educational institutions with industry and commerce.

See also: Local Collaborative Projects

Further reading: Department of Education and Science (1985); HM Inspectors (1990)

PROGRAMME CENTRES

(Piloted April 1997) Programme centres were piloted and delivered by external organisations under contract to the **Employment Service**. They subsequently succeeded **job clubs**. This represented a change of direction from traditional, fixed-length courses to the delivery of modules better tailored to the needs of the job seeker. District managers had the discretion to allow client referrals after thirteen weeks of unemployment but priority was given to those who had been unemployed for a longer period of time. The modules were adapted from existing programmes/sessions and included aspects of job search, advice and guidance.

Further reading: DfEE Departmental Report April 1998, Cm 3910, p. 97; Employment Service (December 1998)

PROGRAMME DEVELOPMENT FUNDS

(1989) PDFs were introduced by the **Employment Service** in June 1989; they were designed to help clients in inner cities and allowed local flexibility of funding to tailor responses to inner-city requirements. The funds enabled ES to be involved with collaborative projects with other agencies to provide individual support such as **Fares to Work**.

Further reading: CEI Consultants (1991)

PROGRAMMED INSTRUCTION IN INDUSTRIAL TRAINING

In 1965 the **Central Training Council** issued a memorandum on advantages and disadvantages of programmed instruction and summarised the principles: '(a) the training need must be clearly identified and precisely stated; (b) the learner should be actively involved in learning; (c) the units of information should be small enough to be readily assimilated by the learner; (d) instruction should normally be self-paced or matched to the learner's personal learning speed; (e) people learn best when their efforts are rewarded. The more immediate the acknowledgement, reward or correction ("feedback of results") the more effective the learning' (Ministry of Labour Gazette 1966 p. 67).

PROGRESS 2 WORK

The National 10 Year Drug Strategy identified that people with drug problems found difficulty with accessing employment, education and training. Beginning in 22 pathfinder areas in April 2002, this £40m UK-wide Progress 2 Work programme was targeted at unemployed people disadvantaged through alcohol or drug misuse, or who were ex-offenders or homeless people, with the aim of returning them to work or keeping them in work. The ability of **Jobcentre Plus** staff was enhanced to enable them to identify and support claimants with a history of drug misuse and then provide information, advice and guidance towards returning to the job market. The programme was delivered through a number of external providers or specialist support workers. Its remit was extended with Progress 2 Work Link-up.

PROGRESS FILES

Progress files were designed to replace the **national record of achievement** after the completion of demonstration projects in July 2002. The four national objectives were:

241

- 'to equip young people with the knowledge, understanding and skills to plan and manage their own learning, including making effective and sustained transitions within and between education, training and working life;
- to increase individual motivation and confidence to achieve, and promote a positive attitude to lifelong learning;
- to stimulate learning to gain knowledge and skills, including that not formally recognised in national qualifications;
- to assist people to best present those attributes they have relevant to future education, training and career goals.'

DfES (2003, p. iii)

Further reading: DfEE (1999i); DfES (2002b)

PROGRESSION PATHWAYS

(2008/2009) They were designed as frameworks for learning constructed from qualifications at Entry Level and Level 1 within the **Qualifications and Credit Framework**. A number of progression pathways were developed that allowed an individual to progress within or across pathways. A **functional skills** qualification was needed in English, maths, and ICT for a person on a progression pathway.

See also: Foundation Learning Tier

Further reading: Qualifications and Curriculum Authority/Learning and Skills Council (2007)

PROJECT-BASED WORK EXPERIENCE

PBWE was provided under the **Youth Opportunities Programme** to give unemployed (for at least six weeks) young people practical experience of a variety of working activities that could be presented as a positive asset to prospective employers. The projects varied in length, but were generally between 6 and 12 months. The projects were to be of benefit to the community and were not

intended to lead to private gain. Preference was given to those involving environmental improvement especially in inner cities. The projects had to include four elements common to other YOP schemes: induction, planned work experience, opportunities for training or further education as appropriate, and personal advice and support.

Further reading: MSC (1980a); (1980c)

PROJECT WORK

(1997) Project work was announced on 28 November 1995 and its purpose was to provide intensive job search and work experience to help the long-term unemployed (more than two years) aged from 18 to 50. It was compulsory.

Further reading: DfEE Departmental Report 1998–1999 Cm 3910 p. 96

PROPRIETARY SCHOOL

This was a system operated in the nineteenth century whereby funds to run a school were raised by a shareholding system in a joint-stock company. The parents bought the shares and so enabled the education of their child(ren).

See also: Adventure Schools; Commercial Schools

PUBLIC ELEMENTARY SCHOOLS

Before the arrival of universal public education, many schools were established by religious denominations and were called elementary schools. With the enactment of the **Elementary Education Act 1870** many **elementary schools** were provided by school boards and so, to distinguish them, they were called public elementary schools. There was pressure to ensure religious freedom and Section 7 of the act defined a public elementary school. 'Every elementary school which is conducted in accordance with the following regulations shall be a public elementary school within the meaning of this Act; and every public elementary school shall be conducted in accordance with the following regulations (a copy of which regulations shall be conspicuously put up in every such) school; namely,

1 It shall not be required, as a condition of any child being admitted into or continuing in the school, that he shall attend or abstain from attending any Sunday school or any place of religious worship, or that he shall attend any religious observance or any instruction in religious subjects in the school or elsewhere, from which observance or instruction he may be withdrawn by his parent, or that he shall, if withdrawn by his parent, attend the school on any day exclusively set apart for religious observance by the religious body to which his parent belongs;

2 The time or times during which any religious observance is practised, or the instruction in religious subjects is given at any meeting of the school shall be either at the beginning or at the end of such meeting, and shall be inserted in a timetable to be approved by the **Education Department**, and be kept permanently and conspicuously affixed in every school-room; and any scholar may be withdrawn by his parent from such observance or instruction without forfeiting any of the other benefits of the school;

3 The school shall be open at all times to the inspection of any of Her Majesty's Inspectors, so, however, that it shall be no part of the duties of such Inspector to inquire into any instruction in religious subjects given at such school, or to examine any scholar therein in religious knowledge, or in any religious subject or book;

4 The school shall be conducted in accordance with the conditions required to be fulfilled by an elementary school in order to obtain an annual parliamentary grant.

See also: Elementary Schools

PUBLIC SCHOOL

This term commonly refers to an **independent school** that does not receive state funding and instead relies on fees, endowments etc. The earliest mention of 'public school' was 1364 when the Bishop of Winchester referred to a public school in Kingston. Generally, a public school is a member of the Headmasters' and Headmistresses' Conference.

PUBLIC SERVICE AGREEMENTS

Public service agreements were first introduced in the 1998 Comprehensive Spending Review and they describe targets and how they are to be achieved and measured. In 2009, the **Department for Children, Schools and Families** had responsibility for five PSAs: PSA 10 – Raise the educational achievement of all children and young people. PSA 11 – Narrow the gap in educational achievement for children from disadvantaged backgrounds. PSA 12 – Improve the health and wellbeing of children and young people. PSA 13 – Improve children and young people's safety. PSA 14 – Increase the number of children and young people on the path to success.

Further reading: DCSF Departmental Report 2009 p. 10

PUNISHMENT

(ended in state schools in 1987 and in independent schools by 2003) Punishment was applied in most if not all schools during the 1800s but progressively this began to decrease with more experienced teachers and better teaching methods. 'If organisation and method be useful anywhere, surely they are in the conduct of a public school. This truth is becoming every year more apparently recognised by teachers. Of old the rule was, – *very* little method and very much *tawse*, the Scotch representative of English *birch*. The modern tendency is to invert this rule, and to minimise corporal punishment by the

243

substitution of constant and agreeable employment, by proper classification and skilful class-teaching. This modern tendency has by some old-fashioned people been called the **normal school** method, and loud regrets are occasionally heard that teachers are now trained and tied by government inspection to a servile uniformity' (Report 1861–62 p. 220).

PUNISHMENT BOOK

This book contained details of the punishments given to children. 'Full particulars of all punishments should be entered either in the "**log book**" or some other book provided for the purpose, and should be open to the inspection of the managers' (Report 1882–83 p. 466).

PUPIL-TEACHER SCHOOLS AND CENTRES

These were centres that were established in the 1880s to provide more advanced training for **pupil-teachers** than could be received within their own schools (Board of Education 1900–01 Vol. 2 p. 252). It was also known as the **centre system**. The **Education Act 1902** provided for pupil-teachers to spend half their time under systematic instruction in pupil-teacher centres. Grants were also made to preparatory classes connected with pupil-teacher centres for those between the ages of 14 and 16 years. Two types of educational institution developed in the early 1900s that were recognised by the term 'pupil-teacher centre'; some pupil teachers were educated in secondary schools, and others were educated in centres which did not have other pupils (Report 1906–07 p. 51).

PUPIL-TEACHERS

In schools with an average attendance of over 100 it was believed that a pupil-teacher was necessary. Pupil-teachers (not less than 13 years old nor more than 16 years old) were apprenticed within schools for five years during which time they were educated by the schoolmaster and in turn educated the pupils. Included in the indenture contract for the apprenticeship it was stated that the pupil-teacher '[w]ill not, except from illness, absent himself from the said school during school-hours, and will conduct himself with honesty, sobriety, and temperance, and will not be guilty of any profane or lewd conversation or conduct, or of gambling or any other immorality' (Minutes 1839–40 p. 111). Pupil-teachers were increased in number to replace the use of monitors because of the latters' lack of success and the 'Minutes of 1846 provided for the creation of Pupil-teachers' (Minutes 1854–55 p. 307). The Minute of 4 May 1859 limited a teacher to supervise a maximum of pupil-teachers (Report 1860–61 p. 152). On successful completion of the apprenticeship a pupil-teacher could become an **assistant teacher** in an **elementary school**; a Queen's Scholar in a **normal school**; or be provisionally certified to be in charge of a rural school (Report 1861–62 p. xxxii). In 1897, the age for pupil teachers was increased from 14 to 15 years. The **Education Act 1902** stipulated that pupil-teachers would not be recognised until the age of sixteen years and in rural districts fifteen years (Report 1896–97 p. 469). Also, they were not permitted to spend more than half their time in an elementary school, the remaining half was to be spent in development and instruction at pupil-teacher schools or centres. 'The new Regulations are designed to secure for Pupil Teachers a more complete and continuous education than they have hitherto received, and to make their period of service in the Elementary School a time of probation and training under supervision, rather than one of premature practice in teaching at the expense of the general education essential to their full effectiveness as teachers in after life' (Report 1902–03 p. 13). A bursary system was introduced in 1907 and recipient pupil teachers were known as Bursars (Report 1906–07 p. 53).

See also: Monitorial System; Madras System; Mutual Instruction; Queen's Scholars

Q

QUALIFICATIONS AND CREDIT FRAMEWORK

World Class Skills–The Leitch Review proposed that employer qualifications were accredited and to achieve this, the Qualifications and Credit Framework was developed. This replaced the **National Qualifications Framework**, which had proved unsatisfactory and which only dealt with full qualifications. The QCF allowed recognition of small units of learning and their transfer, that is credits that were equivalent to 10 hours of study. To simplify the system there were three sizes of qualification: Awards (1 to 12 credits); Certificates (13 to 36 credits); Diplomas (37 credits or more). Each qualification title describes:

- the level of the qualification (Entry Level to Level 8-PhD);
- the size of qualification (award/certificate/diploma); and
- details indicating the content of the qualification.

This also allowed the framework to be applicable to the European Qualifications Framework as proposed by the Copenhagen Declaration for Lifelong Learning and Mobility.

See also: European Credit Transfer and Accumulation System; European Credit System for Vocational Education and Training

Further reading: Qualifications and Curriculum Authority/Learning and Skills Council (March 2004)

QUALIFICATIONS AND CURRICULUM AUTHORITY

(1 October 1997–1 April 2010) Arising from the Education Act 1997 it replaced the **National Council for Vocational Qualifications** and prior to that the **School Curriculum and Assessment Authority**. The QCA had responsibility for standards in education and training. It 'works with others to maintain and develop the school curriculum and associated assessments, and to accredit and monitor qualifications in schools, colleges and at work. It is responsible for establishing a coherent and comprehensive national framework of qualifications in England, Wales and Northern Ireland. **NVQs, GNVQs** and **key skills** are approved by the QCA'. On 8 April 2008 its regulatory functions were taken over by the **Office of the Qualifications and Examinations Regulator**. As a result of the Apprenticeships, Skills, Children and Learning Act 2009, the Qualifications and Curriculum Authority became the **Qualifications and Curriculum Development Authority**.

Further reading: DfEE Departmental Report 2001–02 to 2003–04, Cm 5102, p. 138

QUALIFICATIONS AND CURRICULUM AUTHORITY NORTHERN IRELAND

(May 1996) The QCA Northern Ireland supervised national vocational qualifications.

See also: Qualifications and Curriculum Development Authority

QUALIFICATIONS AND CURRICULUM DEVELOPMENT AUTHORITY

(1 April 2010) This body took over from the **Qualifications and Curriculum Authority** following the Apprenticeships, Skills, Children and Learning Act 2009. It had responsibility for curriculum development, assessment and qualification reform in England.

QUALIFICATIONS, CURRICULUM AND ASSESSMENT AUTHORITY FOR WALES

ACCAC provided a similar service in Wales to that of the **Qualifications and Curriculum Authority** in England.

See also: Awdurdod Cymwysterau, Cwricwlwm ac Asesu Cymru

Further reading: Prys and Jones (1998); www. accac.org.uk

QUALIFIED TEACHER STATUS

A teacher who has successfully completed **initial teacher training** is awarded this status.

Further reading: Teacher Training Agency (1997)

QUALIFYING EXAMINATION

In the late 1800s passing this examination allowed scholars, aged 12–13, to progress in the senior division of the juvenile school to study supplementary subjects that were advanced disciplines.

See also: 11+ Examination

QUALITY ASSURANCE AGENCY FOR HIGHER EDUCATION

(1997) The main responsibility for the QAA is to maintain standards in higher education. It carries out academic audits of institutions' quality control systems; it advises the Secretary of State on applications for degree-awarding

powers and the university title. It also undertakes quality assessment of teaching provision on behalf of the **HEFCE**. It is an independent body that receives funding from UK universities and colleges of higher education, and UK higher education funding bodies. It took over responsibility from the **Higher Education Quality Council**.

Further reading: www.qaa.ac.uk (accessed 01 June 2010)

QUALITY IMPROVEMENT AGENCY FOR LIFELONG LEARNING

(1 April 2006–30 September 2008) The purpose of this non-departmental public body was to work across the **further education** sector and prisons to improve performance and skills. The Quality Improvement Agency for Lifelong Learning worked with colleges and providers to:

- 'support your action plans for improvement arising from self-assessment, enabling you to respond to strategic change, within the further education system;
- enhance the pursuit of excellence by researching what works best to drive improvement and translating this into action with colleges and providers;
- support colleges and providers in your efforts to respond to reforms in curriculum, skills provision and further education;
- identify effective practice, facilitate its dissemination, and promote a culture of self-improvement across the system;
- bring about rapid improvement where there are risks to provision for learners and employers and in the support of the **LSC**'s quality assurance role.'

Quality Improvement Agency
(2006 p. 14)

In 2008, the responsibilities of the QIA and **Centre for Excellence in Leadership** were combined within a new body, the **Learning and Skills Improvement Service**.

QUEEN'S COLLEGES

(1845) In Ireland, an act was passed by Sir Robert Peel for three Queen's colleges to be established in Belfast, Cork and Galway to provide non–denominational education.

QUEEN'S SCHOLARS

(1846) **Pupil–teachers** who had completed their apprenticeship and had good testimonials and examination results could be nominated by the Inspector of Schools for an award, or 'exhibition', of £20 or £25 and those who were successful would be called 'Queen's Scholars' (Minutes 1846, Vol. 1 p. 10). Subsequently, students in training colleges were called Queen's Scholars on passing, first or second class, for admission, the Queen's Scholarship Examination (Report 1894–95 p. 338). The Queen's Scholars became King's Scholars when Queen Victoria died in 1901.

QUOTA SCHEME

The Disabled Persons (Employment) Act 1944 required employers of 20 or more people to employ a quota of disabled people. This was fixed at 3 per cent in September 1946. A special percentage of 0.1 per cent was set for crews in the shipping and fishing industries. It was superseded by the **Disability Discrimination Act**.

See also: Designated Employment; King's National Roll

Further reading: Ministry of Labour and National Service Report for 1947, Cmd 7559, p. 108

R

RACE RELATIONS ACT 1976

This act replaced the 1968 Act and extended it, for example by making indirect discrimination illegal. Section 2 explained: 'A person ("the discriminator") discriminates against another person ("the person victimised") in any circumstances relevant for the purposes of any provision of this Act if he treats the person victimised less favourably than in those circumstances he treats or would treat other persons'. The act also enabled the setting up of the **Commission for Racial Equality**.

Further reading: *Race Relations Act 1976*, London, HMSO

RACE RELATIONS AND EMPLOYMENT FORUM

The Race Relations and Employment Forum investigates and advises ministers on the progress of people from ethnic minorities in education, training and employment.

See also: Race Relations Employment Advisory Service; Disability Rights Commission

Further reading: DfEE Departmental Report 2001–02 to 2003–04, Cm 5102, p. 138

RACE RELATIONS EMPLOYMENT ADVISORY SERVICE

In the early 1990s the **Department of Employment** had the role of promoting a labour market free of unlawful discrimination based on race. As part of this policy the RREAS consisted of 24 field advisors (1993/94) whose purpose was to act as a catalyst and source of expert advice to employers in developing and implementing equal opportunities policies.

See also: Race Relations and Employment Forum

Further reading: Dept of Employment Report February 1993, Cm 2205, p. 28

RACIAL DISTURBANCES – RESPONSES TO

During 2001 there were a number of race-related riots in Bradford, Oldham and Burnley. A number of reports were produced that contained recommendations to address these issues, including the Ousley Report (Bradford), the Oldham Report, and the Burnley Task Force Report. The Cantle Report provided a broader overview. A number of recommendations were made including strategies for regeneration that included training and development.

See also: Heseltine Initiatives

Further reading: Bradford Vision (2001); Home Office (2001a); Home Office (2001b); Oldham Independent Review (2001)

RAGGED SCHOOLS

During their travels in the 1840s, inspectors (**Her Majesty's Inspectorate of Schools**)

found that the children of the very poor did not attend school because of the cost; they had no suitable clothes and no regular family meals. Mr Watkins, HMI, acknowledged that the national schools could not alter their rules, and so suggested another group of schools '[i]n which little attention should be paid to wholeness or raggedness of dress – in which the scholars might come during certain hours without strict requirement of punctuality'. He continued: 'Nor need such be called "Ragged Schools". This name seems to imply that all who go there must needs be in tattered and untidy dress. They might be called more pleasantly, and as truly, "Half-day Schools", or "Second National Schools". The expenses attending their institution would not be great; they would be supported at small cost, and, independently of their other benefits, would act most beneficially as *filters* through which the stream of the most polluted humanity should pass before it was poured into the broad reservoir of our national schools' (Minutes 1845, vol. 2, p. 176). Ragged schools were also known as **free schools** and sometimes as industrial free day schools (for the destitute). The Ragged School Union began operations in 1844 under its president, Lord Shaftsbury (Minutes 1851–52, vol. 2, p. 512). A circular, 31 December 1857 (Minutes 1857–58 p. 14) stated that its purpose was 'to withdraw the Committee of Council as much as possible from the field occupied by the Home Office, in relation to reformatories, properly so called; to encourage the transformation of those ragged schools which are organised as asylums or refuges into certified **industrial schools**, and to extend a certain measure of assistance to ragged schools generally'. At this time destitute children were often mixed with those who had committed criminal acts and this circular was an attempt to clearly distinguish reformatories from other types of schooling. The circular also stated that 'the industrial classes of ragged schools and of common day schools are placed upon the same footing'. It also stated: 'Ragged schools

are to be regarded as provisional institutions, which are constantly tending to become either elementary schools of the ordinary kind, or industrial schools certified under Acts of Parliaments'. The terms ragged schools and industrial schools were often interchangeable (Report 1862–63 p. viii).

RAINER

See: Royal Philanthropic Society

RAPID RESPONSE SERVICE

(April 2002) The Rapid Response Service was created within **Jobcentre Plus** to provide swift action when there were major redundancies. There were two main responses: the first was rapid intervention to find new jobs for people before they became redundant; and, secondly, to provide enhanced support options that were not available to other job seekers.

See also: Redundancy Action

Further reading: www.jobcentreplus.gov.uk/ JCP/stellent/groups/jcp/documents/website content/dev_010594.doc

RECOGNISED TRAINING ORGANISATIONS

(Northern Ireland) These organisations were vetted by the **Training and Employment Agency** in Northern Ireland and delivered **jobskills** training. These were the equivalent of **managing agents** in Britain.

Further reading: Training and Employment Agency Annual Report (1996)

RECRUITMENT SUBSIDY FOR SCHOOL LEAVERS

(Piloted in October 1975, operational from September 1976) The RSSL was organised by the **Department of Employment** and was piloted in October 1975 at the same time as the **Job Creation Programme**. Employers were offered £5 per week for six months for recruiting a school leaver who had been unemployed since the summer. The high cost of the general recruitment subsidy and its limitations in addressing certain types of unemployed people encouraged the Government to focus the approach on disadvantaged groups. Consequently, in October 1976 a **youth employment subsidy** (YES) was introduced that paid £10 per week for recruits unemployed for six months or more.

Further reading: Casson (1979)

RED-BRICK UNIVERSITY

This term represented those universities created during the late-nineteenth and early-twentieth centuries, for example Birmingham, Bristol, Leeds, Liverpool, Manchester, Sheffield. The term derived from Bruce Truscot's book *Redbrick University* (1943). This term distinguished these universities from Oxbridge, that is Cambridge and Oxford; the 1960s universities; and the 'new universities' that were formed in 1992 largely from the **polytechnics**.

REDUNDANCY ACTION

(1 June 2004) The ReACT scheme in Wales was designed to support people who were facing unemployment; who had been unemployed for less than six months; or, who had not received any publicly funded training since being made unemployed. It contained three elements: recruitment and training support; a discretionary award for vocation training; and, a miscellaneous discretionary award. This European-funded scheme originally began as a one-off Rapid Response to Redundancy programme designed to address the closure of a large business and was then expanded into the Redundancy Action Fund. In 2004, it became Redundancy Action and ran to 30 September 2008 with a new round beginning on 1 October 2008.

See also: Rapid Response Service

Further reading: http://wales.gov.uk/topics/educationandskills/learners/worklearning/gettingbacktowork/redundancyaction/?lang=en

REDUNDANCY FUND

Redundancy payments made to employees whose employers had financial difficulty, and insolvency payments that cover debts to employees by insolvent employers – covers such areas as wage arrears and holiday pay. As a result of the Employment Act 1990 the Redundancy Fund and the National Insurance Fund merged on 1 February 1991.

Further reading: Department of Employment Report February 1991, Cm 1506, p. 26

REDUNDANCY PAYMENTS SERVICE

The service dealt with the payments from the **Redundancy Fund**.

REFORMATORY SCHOOL ACT (1854)

This act (Act 17 & 18 Vict., c. 86) enabled courts to send convicted children to reformatories rather than prison. A circular, 31 December 1857 (Minutes 1857–58 p. 14), stated that its purpose was 'to withdraw the Committee of Council as much as possible from the field occupied by the Home Office, in relation to reformatories, properly so called; to encourage the transformation of those **ragged schools** which are organised as asylums or refuges into certified **industrial schools**, and to extend a certain measure of assistance to ragged schools generally'. At this time destitute children were often mixed with those who had committed criminal acts and this circular was an attempt to clearly distinguish reformatories from other types of schooling. A subsequent act of 1866 stipulated that any child under the age of 16 who was sentenced for ten days or more might, on completion of the sentence, also be sentenced to a minimum of two years and a maximum of five years in a certified **reformatory school**. The reformatory school in Bath engaged the juvenile offenders in a wide range of activities including: shoemaking, gardening, washing, hair-picking, tailoring and wood-cutting. It then encouraged employment as apprentices in numerous areas including HM navy (Minutes 1855–56, p. 296).

See also: Houses of Refuge

REFORMATORY SCHOOLS

The **Royal Philanthropic Society** and private founders opened a number of voluntary reformatories in the early-nineteenth century, and the **Reformatory School Act (1854)** brought a public response to juvenile delinquency. A distinction was made between certified **industrial schools** and certified reformatories.

REFORMATORY SHIPS

See: Merchant Marine Training Ships

REGIONAL DEVELOPMENT AGENCIES

(1999) The RDAs were enabled through the Regional Development Agencies Act 1998 and eight agencies were launched in England in 1999, followed by the London Development Agency in 2000. Their purpose was to encourage focused economic development on regional priorities through a variety of strategies including the development of skills and other capabilities. Among the statutory areas of responsibility were: economic regeneration and development; promoting business efficiency; promoting employment and skills.

See also: Skills Development Fund

Further reading: www.englandsrdas.com

REGIONAL EMPLOYMENT AND SKILLS FORUM

See: Framework for Regional Employment and Skills Action

REGIONAL EMPLOYMENT PREMIUM

(4 September 1967–1977) Employers became eligible for payment of the increased premium authorised by the Finance Act 1967. The regional employment premium was an additional sum payable with the selective employment premium to employers within **development areas**. The full-time weekly rates were £1.50 for men over 18; £0.75 for women and 'boys' under 18; and £0.475 for 'girls' under 18. The purpose of the scheme was to reduce the labour market costs of manufacturing industry in the development areas to make it more competitive and over time to increase its share of manufacturing production in Britain. It also was set up to reduce the disparity of unemployment there and in the rest of Britain. The premium also could be used to reduce prices by financing investment, increasing training or improving markets. The Government also stressed that increasing dividends or wages would only frustrate the objective.

See also: Regional Selective Assistance

Further reading: Ministry of Labour Gazette 1967 p. 718; King (1990)

REGIONAL INDUSTRIAL TRAINING COMMITTEES

Regional Committees of the **Training Advisory Service** – set up by the **Industrial Training Council (ITC)**.

See also: Training Development Officers

REGIONAL MANPOWER INTELLIGENCE CENTRES

(1 July 1977) The centres were established by the **MSC** to identify labour needs and supply the agency's managers with information that they needed. It was also proposed that there should be regional representatives to coordinate the manpower services, to establish contact with leading employers, and to contribute to regional economic planning. It

was recognised that these plans might 'raise difficulties' in relation to existing agencies and the **Department of Employment**.

Further reading: MSC Annual Report 1976/77, p. 9

REGIONAL SELECTIVE ASSISTANCE

(1972) These were discretionary grants given by the **Department of Trade and Industry** and Scottish and Welsh Offices to protect employment in assisted areas. They were introduced via the 1972 Industry Act.

See also: Regional Employment Premium

Further reading: King (1990)

REGIONAL SKILLS PARTNERSHIPS

(April 2004) These RSPs were described in the skills strategy White Paper (2003) and were designed to integrate action on skills, training, business support and labour market services across a region. They are led by **regional development agencies**; **learning and skills councils**; **jobcentre plus**; the **Small Business Service**; and the **Sector Skills Development Agency**.

Further reading: DfES Departmental Report 2004, Cm 6202, p. 84

REGIONAL TRAINING ADVISORS

These people were part of the **MSC**'s **Training Services Division** who provided advice on the training within regions.

Further reading: MSC Annual Report 1977–78 p. 22

REGIONAL TRAINING CENTRES

See: National Skills Academy

REGISTERS

Many schools kept registers to record basic details about pupils' attendance. With the provision of annual grants to schools, which were based on minimum attendance levels, a school register was required to be kept. The conventional notation of this was not fully formulated in the early days and was subject to considerable discussion and potential abuse in order to receive the **capitation grant** (Report 1861–62 p. 159). Many registers were kept in public schools, for example at Sedburgh, and one was in use in the **sessional school** of St John's, Glasgow in the early years of the 1800s (Report 1861–62 p. 206).

See also: Logbook of School

REGULAR FORCES EMPLOYMENT ASSOCIATION

(1990) The RFEA received most of its income from the Ministry of Defence and was a registered charity. The headquarters were in London and there was a network of employment officers (ex-regulars) in the regions.

See also: Armed Forces Recruitment

Further reading: Employment Gazette 1990, p. 20–24

REGULAR FORCES RESETTLEMENT SERVICE

(1958) Employment exchanges formed part of the Regular Forces Resettlement Scheme and each exchange had a member of staff to help ex-regulars to get civilian employment. Regulars also received advice on employment prospects during the last few months of their service. It was renamed the Forces Resettlement Service, which brought together the Ministry of Defence, the **Employment Service**, the **Training Agency** and the **Regular Forces Employment Association**.

See also: Regular Forces Employment Association; Armed Forces Recruitment

Further reading: Ministry of Labour and National Service Report 1959, Cmnd 745, p. viii

RELAUNCH

Introduced in September 1997, this was a strategy to motivate disaffected young people and give them skills to take advantage of education and training opportunities. It drew upon action and innovation by local partnerships to increase participation in learning among 14–19-year-olds. Relaunch was designed to improve access provision post-16 and targeted year on year reductions in the number of 16- and 17-year-olds not in learning.

Further reading: DfEE (1997d)

REMPLOY

(1947) Began as Disabled Persons Employment Corporation in 1945. It was changed to Remploy in 1947. In 1951, it was running in 90 factories (its highest number). Remploy was designed to employ the disabled in **sheltered employment** (later renamed Supported Employment) and to give them work skills. Its mission is 'to transform the lives of disabled people and those experiencing complex barriers to work by providing sustainable employment opportunities' (Remploy 2009).

See also: Interwork; Industrial Rehabilitation Units

Further reading: www. remploy.co.uk

REORIENTATION COURSES

(April 1958) These were six-week orientation courses for services personnel. Their aims were to smooth the transition from service to business life and act as an introduction to industry and commerce.

Further reading: Ministry of Labour and National Service Report 1959, Cmnd 745, p. viii

REPEATER

(1855) In a letter to the Committee of Council about the **Bristol Diocesan Trade School**, the Reverend Henry Moseley described operations: 'If, as is probable, the Committee of Council consents to apprentice **pupil-teachers** in the school or to allow stipends to assistant-teachers, one of these should be employed by each lecturer or master as a *Repeater* (Repétiteur), as he is called in French schools. He is an officer whose business it is to assist at every lecture, to make himself thoroughly master of it, aided by the lecturer's explanations and notes, and to *reproduce* or *repeat* it to the class, giving them fuller explanations, impressing it more fully on their minds, and, as it were, *compelling* the *reception* of it' (Minutes 1855–56 p. 25).

RESEARCH COUNCIL UK

(1 May 2002) The Research Council UK heads the seven research councils that were established by Royal Charter: Arts and Humanities Research Council (AHRC); Biotechnology and Biological Sciences Research Council (BBSRC); Engineering & Physical Sciences Research Council (EPSRC); Economic & Social Research Council (ESRC); Medical Research Council (MRC); Natural Environment Research Council (NERC); and Science and Technology Facilities Council (STFC). The **Department for Business, Innovation and Skills** has responsibility for the research councils.

RESETTLEMENT TRANSFER SCHEME

This scheme enabled the permanent resettlement of unemployed persons away from areas of high unemployment. This scheme also included certain categories of ex-service personnel irrespective of the areas they came from.

See also: Free Forward Fares Scheme; Employed Key Workers Transfer Scheme; General Transfer Scheme

Further reading: Ministry of Labour and National Service Report 1953, Cmnd. 9207, p. 45

RESOURCES AND STRATEGY DIRECTORATE

One of three directorates within the **Employment Department**. Provided corporate services (finance and audit, personnel and staff development and business services) and economics, research, and evaluation support to all staff in **Employment Department Group**. The other two directorates were: **Industrial Relations and Europe Directorate**, and **Training, Enterprise and Education Directorate**.

Further reading: Department of Employment Report February 1991, Cm 1506, p. 7

RESPONSIVE COLLEGE PROJECT

(1985) Two-year programme to help improve the responsiveness and labour market relevance of **further education** provision. This was carried out in conjunction with local authorities and aimed to demonstrate how the **LEA**s and FE colleges could better meet the education and training needs of the labour market. Part of the project was the dissemination of lessons learned to enable LEA plans for work-related **non-advanced further education**.

Further reading: MSC Annual Report 1985/86, p. 20; Bilbrough (1988)

RESTART

(January 1986) Restart interviews began in January 1986 as part of the Stricter Benefit Regime and went national in July 1986. The interviews were given to all those who had been unemployed for more than a year and were given every six months. From September 1989 unemployment benefit claimants were required not only to be available for work but also to be actively seeking work. **Restart courses** ran in parallel with the interviews.

Further reading: Pearce and Neave (1989)

RESTART COURSES

(July 1986–March 1987) Established to provide a more positive approach to a person's search for work. A person needed to have been unemployed for more than twelve months. Restart courses targeted long-term unemployed people who had been severely affected by unemployment, and who were not, as a result, ready for a job, other employment or training programme. The courses were designed to rebuild confidence and motivation, identify skills, learn about available opportunities and plan the best way back to work.

See also: Restart; Jobplan Workshops

Further reading: Pearce and Neave (1989)

REVISED CODE OF REGULATIONS

See: Code of Regulations

RIGHT TO TIME OFF FOR STUDY OR TRAINING

(1 September 1999) The Employment Rights Act 1996 was amended by Part III of the Teaching and Higher Education Act 1998 and came into force on 1 September 1999. It ensured that young people aged 16 and 17 who had not achieved 5 GCSEs at grades A★–C, five SQA Standard Grades at grades 1–3, Intermediate Level GNVQ, GSVQ Level 2, NVQ/SVQ Level 2, or BTEC First, were entitled to study for a suitable qualification while they were at work. The young people must be paid at their normal rate for attending external courses.

See also: Day Release

Further reading: Highley (1999)

ROMAN CATHOLIC SCHOOLS

In 1847, Roman Catholic schools became eligible for funding from the Parliamentary grant. This was on condition that only their secular instruction was inspected and that inspectors were not appointed without the agreement of the Roman Catholic Poor School Committee (Minutes 1847–48 Vol. 1, p. xlvii). Following extensive correspondence regarding the terminology with Roman Catholic bishops, a Model Deed Trust was agreed in 1852 (Minutes 1851–52 vol. 1, pp. 45–53).

See also: Catholic Poor School Committee

ROYAL COLLEGE OF ART

'The chief purpose of the Royal College of Art is to give to advanced students a thorough technical training together with a general education through the practice and study of Art. The previous artistic education of the majority of the full-time students has been obtained in the Schools of Art maintained or directed by Local Education Authorities' (Report 1923–24 p. 98).

See also: Science and Art Department

ROYAL COLLEGE OF SCIENCE

The college began, in 1845, as the Royal College of Chemistry and in 1853 it merged with the **Government School of Mines** under the responsibility of the **Science and Art Department**. The combined institution was known as the Metropolitan School of Science applied to Mining and the Arts; and as the Government School of Mines and Science applied to the Arts. (Department of Science and Art Report 1854 p. xliv). In 1881, it was renamed the Normal School of Science and Royal School of Mines, and subsequently the Normal School of Science became the Royal School of Science in 1890. Later, in 1907, the Royal College of Science and the Royal School of Mines jointly merged with the **City and Guilds** Central Technical College to form the Imperial College of Science and Technology. 'The primary purpose of the Imperial College is to make provision for the most advanced

training and research in Science, especially in its application to industry' (Report 1906–07 p. 18).

ROYAL COMMISSION ON TRADES UNIONS AND EMPLOYERS ASSOCIATION

(1965–68) Known as the Donovan Report. The final report in 1968 para. 330 was critical of the traditional systems; recommendations included standardised training and formal qualifications.

ROYAL DOCKYARD SCHOOLS

The first naval dockyard was a drydock in Portsmouth established during the reign of Henry VII. Others dockyards followed and established schools to train the apprentice with the first dockyard school being opened in Chatham in 1842. By 1858 there were other schools in Deptford, Devonport, Pembroke, Portsmouth, Sheerness, and Woolwich (Minutes 1852–53 Vol. 1, p. 361). The ships included HMSs: Asia; Britannia; Cambridge; Excellent; Fisgard; Formidable; Illustrious; Impregnable; Queen Charlotte; Royal Adelaide; Victory; Wellesley; Wellington (Report 1860–61 pp. 465–70). A range of subjects were taught to the apprentices including English, mathematics, and physical sciences. The apprenticeships were respected and there was competition for places (Report 1858–59 p. 450).

See also: Admiralty Schools; Hospital Schools; Navigation Schools; Royal Marines Schools; Sea Training

Further reading: Robertson (1974)

ROYAL DUBLIN SOCIETY

(1731) Originally titled the Dublin Society for improving Husbandry, Manufactures and Useful Arts, it is now more commonly known as the Royal Dublin Society. Its objectives, since its charter, have been to develop and encourage agriculture and rural affairs, arts, industry and commerce, science and technology, and equestrianism. It inspired the establishment of the **Royal Society for the encouragement of Arts, Manufactures and Commerce**.

Further reading: www.rds.ie (accessed 01 June 2010)

ROYAL INSTITUTION OF GREAT BRITAIN

(1799) It was founded by a number of scientists including Henry Cavendish in 1799 and received its Royal Charter in 1800. A large source of its early funding came from the Society for Bettering the Conditions and Improving the Comforts of the Poor. The intention of the institution was the 'diffusing the knowledge, and facilitating the general introduction, of useful mechanical inventions and improvements; and for teaching, by courses of philosophical lectures and experiments, the application of science to the common purposes of life'. The institution continues to encourage research and deliver lectures including the Christmas Lectures, which were initiated by Michael Faraday.

See also: Philosophical Societies

Further reading: www.rigb.org (accessed 01 June 2010)

ROYAL MARINES ARTILLERY SCHOOLS

The Royal Marines Artillery schools at Woolwich consisted of a children's school and an adult school. 'Every gunner, at his enlistment, is sent to school until he can satisfy the commandant that he can read and write fairly and has some elementary knowledge of arithmetic. The non-commissioned officers are required also to attend school until they can pass a certain examination and are certified as qualified for the grade they occupy. The drummers also are required to attend daily when off duty' (Report 1859–60 p. 506).

See also: Royal Dockyard Schools

ROYAL MARINES SCHOOLS

In 1858 there were six boys, seven adults and four girls schools, with the boys and adults receiving instruction from masters (known as schoolmaster-serjeants [sic]) who were trained at the Military Training School in Chelsea. Schools were to be found in Chatham, Plymouth, Portsmouth and Woolwich (Report 1858–59 p. 461).

See also: Royal Marines Artillery Schools; Royal Dockyard Schools

ROYAL PHILANTHROPIC SOCIETY

(1788) The society originated from meetings held in St Paul's Coffee House to discuss the problems of begging and stealing associated with homeless children. The society opened homes where the children could be trained in cottage industries under the supervision of tradesmen. The **Reformatory School Act 1854** enabled courts to send convicted children to the society's reformatories rather than prison. The society is now called Rainer after a printer who made a donation to rescue children from the courts.

Further reading: www.raineronline.org (accessed 01 June 2010)

ROYAL SCHOOLS

(1608–) Five schools were established in Armagh, Cavan, Dungannon, Enniskillen, and Raphoe, under King James 1 as part of the plantation process in which English and Scottish settlers replaced many of the local people following the flight of the earls. A decree in 1608 stated that 'there should be one free school, at least, appointed in every county, for the education of youths in learning and religion'. In practice this meant that the schools were mainly sectarian due to the religion being that of the established church.

www.royalschoolarmagh.com/Portal.aspx?tab index=11& tabid=3021 (accessed 05 April 2010)

ROYAL SOCIETY FOR THE ENCOURAGEMENT OF ARTS, MANUFACTURES AND COMMERCE

(1754) It was originally founded by William Shipley, Viscount Folkestone and Lord Romney as the Society of Arts and received a Royal Charter in 1847. Its inspiration was the Dublin Society for improving Husbandry, Manufactures and Useful Arts or **Royal Dublin Society**. Among many initiatives the society encouraged the Great Exhibition (1851); organised the first educational exhibition (1854); founded the National Training School for Music, which subsequently became the Royal College of Music; and the RSA Examinations Board now **Oxford, Cambridge and RSA Examinations**. It also held examinations in technology that were taken over by the **City and Guilds of London Institute** in 1879.

Further reading: Report 1924–25 p. 10; www.thersa.org (accessed 01 June 2010)

RURAL SCHOOLS

These are schools found in country areas and to adapt the curriculum and make it more relevant 'specimen courses of object lessons connected with rural life and industries' were presented in 1901. 'The aim is that children who live in the country should, when they leave school, find themselves in sympathy with their surroundings, and should be able to take an intelligent interest in the pursuits and occupations which are open to those whose lives and homes are in the country. It is important however to notice that education of this kind, while necessary for country children, is of equal value to those whom necessity may require to spend much of their future lives in towns or large centres of industry'. It also specified that '[i]t is not desirable to attempt a definite course of instruction in the principles of agriculture or to teach the art of farming' (Board of Education 1900–01 Vol. 3, p. 185). The courses were not prescriptive and covered a wide range of areas including the theory and practice of bee-keeping.

RUSKIN COLLEGE

(1899) 'Until the beginning of 1925–26 the only Residential College (providing a full-time course of at least one year's duration for adult students of the working classes) which had been recognised by the Board was Ruskin College, Oxford. In that year recognition was extended to the Catholic Workers College, Oxford and to Fircroft College, Birmingham' (Report 1925–26 p. 83).

S

SAFETY TRAINING

Industrial training boards had a duty under the **Industrial Training Act 1964** to 'provide or secure the provision of such courses and other facilities … for the training of persons employed or intending to be employed in the industry'.

(Industrial Training Act 1964)

SANDWICH COURSE

This was a programme of study that provided alternating experience of formal education and industrial or commercial placement. It was commonly used in **polytechnic** courses and the sandwich could be thick, that is. a year in full-time employment, or 'thin', that is for a shorter period of time.

SCHEMES OF INSTRUCTION

As the curriculum became more detailed with the inclusion of **specific subjects** etc. the **Board of Education** presented specimen schemes of instruction for schools in different areas including for **rural schools**; a town school in a poor district; a large town boys' school in prosperous circumstances; a boys' school in seaside town; and a girls' school with average attendance of about 170 (Report 1900–01 Vol. 3, pp. 227–39).

SCHOLAR'S CERTIFICATE

(19 September 1855) It was recommended that a certificate be used in schools under inspection that would encourage attendance. 'Such a certificate should be given by the managers to any child, aged upwards of twelve years, who has been in the same school continuously for three years; who has reached the standard of attainment required of candidates for stipendiary monitorships; and who, during the time embraced by the certificate, has been regular and punctual in attendance, clean in person, and neat in dress, and has uniformly borne a good character' (Minutes 1855–56 p. 18). The certificate noted that the pupil could read, write, work sums, and had a knowledge of Holy Scripture, the church catechism, geography, grammar and English history. 'The Form of Certificate is surrounded by an ornamental border, designed and engraved under the superintendence of the **Department of Science and Art**. The border is composed of the rose, shamrock, and thistle, wreathed together, and is surmounted by a motto, "Well begun is half done"' (Minutes 1855–56 p. 19). These certificates were sometimes known as 'Good-conduct Certificates' and 'A combination on the part of employers of labour, to give a preference to all children possessed of these certificates, would give at once a marketable value to them, which would have, I doubt not, a very marked effect, independent of all other considerations, upon the retention of children at school' (Minutes 1855–56 p. 242). The Reverend F. Watkins made this recommendation in 1852 (Minutes 1855–56, p. 261).

See also: School Certificate

SCHOOL ASSESSMENT

During the 1870s and 1890s the **Education Department** awarded **merit grants** based on the quality of school performance. Originally this was based on the level of the pupils' attainments under examination; however, this subsequently changed to consider a wider range of factors including 'the skill and spirit of the teaching, the neatness of the registers, the behaviour of the children, especially their honesty under examination, and the interest they evince in their work'. Also consideration was given to other factors which might influence the quality: 'A shifting, scattered, very poor or ignorant population; any circumstance which makes regular attendance exceptionally difficult; failure of health, or unforeseen changes among the teaching staff, will necessarily and rightly affect your judgement'. In the Report of 1882–83 (p. 158) descriptions of fair, good and excellent schools were presented, and these continued to be revised with guidance to **HM Inspectors** suggesting that a bad or unsatisfactory school with 'faults of instruction or discipline' and 'a preponderance of indifferent passes, preventable disorder, dullness, or irregularity; or [with a] teacher [that] is satisfied with a low standard of duty', would receive no merit grant. Other grades of school were categorised: 'A school of humble aims which passes only a moderately successful examination, may properly be designated "Fair", if its work is conscientiously done, and is sound as far as it goes; and if the school is free of any conspicuous faults. … Generally, a school may be expected to receive the mark "Good" when both the number and quality of the passes are satisfactory; when the scholars pass well in such classes as are taken up; and when the organisation, discipline, tone, and general intelligence are such as to deserve commendation … The mark "Excellent" should be reserved for cases of distinguished merit. A thoroughly good school in favourable conditions is characterised by cheerful and yet exact discipline, maintained without harshness and without noisy demonstration of authority. Its premises are cleanly and well-ordered; its time-table provides a proper variety of mental employment and of physical exercise; its organisation is such as to distribute the teaching power judiciously, and to secure for every scholar – whether he is likely to bring credit to the school by examination or not – a fair share of instruction and attention. The teaching is animated and interesting, and yet thorough and of attention' (Report 1885–86 p. 160).

See also: OFSTED

SCHOOL ATTENDANCE COMMITTEE

The **Elementary Education Act 1876** enabled the appointment of a school attendance committee for boroughs and parishes where there was not a school board. The purpose of the committee was to ensure the attendance of children at school; reports of children failing to make a specific number of attendances were reported and the committee had the power to serve warnings and fine parents up to five shillings (Report 1877–78 p. 93).

SCHOOL AUTHORITY

The school authority was defined in the **Code** and was the body responsible for the provision of education in an area. 'The term "Local Authority" means the **school board** or **school attendance committee**, as the case may be (Elementary Education Act, 1876, secs. 7 and 33)' (Report 1893–94 p. 316).

SCHOOL BOARDS

(1870) School Boards were enabled by the **Education Act 1870** and their purpose was to establish non-denominational schools in their districts where there was insufficient or no provision. The board members were elected by local rate payers, under the Poor

Rate Assessment and Collection Tax 1869, and could include women even though emancipation had not been achieved. The schools were funded by a local rate or tax. The 1870 Education Act did not introduce **compulsory attendance** although it allowed the school boards to introduce bye-laws to require attendance; for example, Liverpool School Board passed a law 'requiring the parents of children of such age, not less than five years nor more than thirteen years ... to cause such children (unless there is some reasonable excuse) to attend school' (Minutes 1871–72 Appendix Part II, p. 1). The **Elementary Education Act 1876** stipulated that in school districts not served by a board, there was to be a school attendance committee in boroughs and parishes. In the Act, school boards and school attendance committees are 'referred to as the local authority' (Minutes 1876–77 p. 2). School boards were replaced by **Local Education Authorities** as a result of the **Education Act 1902**.

Further reading: Cunningham (1870)

SCHOOL CERTIFICATE

(1854–55) This was a certificate awarded to pupils on leaving school and originally was based on a prize scheme introduced in Staffordshire. Increasing widespread support for this grew and at a meeting of national school masters in Sheffield a resolution was made to support this (Minutes 1854–55 p. 450). The Reverend Watkins reported that 'I have, in a previous report, (1853–54), stated my belief that a school certificate of good conduct, given to children of a certain age when leaving school, might be productive of good effects – tending both to make the children stay longer at school, and attend there with more regularity. I have now expressed my satisfaction that the Lord President is willing to carry out my suggestion. I trust, in the course of the present year, to see it working beneficially in our schools' (Minutes 1854–55

p. 440). The influence of the certificate grew and was often related to satisfactory performance: achievement at Standard V. The certificate also was incorporated within the Factory Act 1873, which maintained that children in possession of a certificate could begin work at 13 years of age while those without a certificate would have to wait until 14 (Minutes 1874–75 p. 201). The establishment of the **Secondary Schools Examination Council** in 1917 resulted in a school certificate being awarded for passing the **first examination** and passing this examination coincided with the movement from the middle to the upper forms of the school. 'The School Certificate gained on the First Examination, exempt, under conditions, from Matriculation and from the preliminary examinations of the Professional Bodies. They are coming also to have considerable value to boys and girls seeking posts in the commercial world' (Report 1923–24 pp. 30–31). Pupils then had the possibility of staying on at school and taking the **second examination** for the award of the **Higher School Certificate**. This certificate was not the same as the one introduced by the **Secondary School Examinations Council** in the twentieth century, which is mentioned below.

See also: Scholar's Certificate

SCHOOL CERTIFICATE

(1917–51) It was introduced by the **Secondary School Examinations Council**. Pupils in fifth forms (Year 11) took examinations in 5 or more subjects from four groups and had to pass in groups 1, 2, and 3. Group 1: English subjects; Group 2: foreign languages; Group 3: science and mathematics; Group 4: domestic subjects. This qualification preceded the **General Certificate of Education** ordinary levels. The School Certificate was followed at 18 years of age by the **second examination** and the **Higher School Certificate**. This certificate is not the same as the nineteenth century certificate listed above.

Further reading: Secondary School Examinations Council (1932)

SCHOOL CURRICULUM AND ASSESSMENT AUTHORITY

(1993–97) The establishment of the Schools Curriculum and Assessment Authority represented the recombination of the responsibilities for curriculum and examinations previously held respectively by the **National Curriculum Council** and the **School Examinations and Assessment Council**. It was enabled through the Education Act 1993. The SCAA was merged with the **National Council for Vocational Qualifications** to form the **Qualifications and Curriculum Authority**.

SCHOOL DAY

The length of a school day may be determined by the governing body of a school under the Education Reform Act 1988.

See also: School Year; School Terms

SCHOOL DRILL

(c.1850s) Many schools operated a system of school drill that was designed to provide coordinated exercise and discipline for the pupils and a drill book was issued by the **Home and Colonial Infant School-Society**. The drilling was sometimes accompanied by singing as in the Roman Catholic schools in Kidderminster and Stourbridge and Mr Hernaman, **Her Majesty's Inspector**, wrote: 'I attach great importance to the ordinary class drill. **Military drill** can only be practised in a limited number of schools and under certain circumstances, but class drill can be practised in all schools, without disturbance of the ordinary arrangements. Class drill might consist of the military facings; the balance step; marking time; movements of

the arms and shoulders; body flexions; rising on the toes, and falling; getting in and out of desks; and as a change to all these, what I may venture to call rhythmical drill. This latter can be accompanied by songs, or instrumental playing, or the teacher may beat time with a wand. One of the most forward pupils should be put to lead the rest, and show when changes are to be made' (Report 1874–75 p. 105).

SCHOOL EMPLOYMENT BUREAUX

(1908) These were sometimes called **juvenile employment bureaux** or educational information and employment bureaux. They were championed by Mrs Ogilvie Gordon, who made a public address in March 1904 to the Glasgow Branch of the National Union of Women Workers about the need for expert guidance for young people about employment routes and opportunities. She was also concerned that most children did not attend **continuation school** and there were no serious efforts made to encourage attendance for unskilled young people. The main objects of the bureaux committee were: '(1) To lead all boys and girls who are physically fit towards some employment likely to bring them a livelihood, and to prove congenial to them. (2) To foster a fuller co-operation between schools and the workshops' (Gordon 1911 p. 168). The Education (Scotland) Act 1908 enabled the Edinburgh School Board to establish an Educational Information and Employment Bureau. In England there was no supporting legislation that enabled an extra charge on the rates; however, bureaux were established by the education committees in Nottingham, Wigan and Liverpool and under voluntary committees in Hull and Sheffield.

SCHOOL EXAMINATIONS AND ASSESSMENT COUNCIL

(1988–93) This body took over responsibility from the **Secondary Schools Examinations Council**; it was the first statutory regulatory body for examinations enabled by the Education Reform Act 1988. Its responsibilities were subsequently taken over by the **School Curriculum and Assessment Authority**.

SCHOOL FOOD TRUST

(2005) The School Food Trust, a non-departmental public body, was established by the **Department for Education and Skills** to 'transform school food and food skills, promote the education and health of children and young people and improve the quality of food in schools'. In September 2008 nutritional standards were introduced for primary schools and in 2009 for **secondary school**s.

See also: Penny Dinners; School Meals

Further reading: www.schoolfoodtrust.org.uk (accessed 01 June 2010)

SCHOOL FOR LABOURING POOR

These schools were for children and adults, or children alone, of the labouring, manufacturing, and other poorer classes in the area (Minutes 1839–40, p. 109).

SCHOOL FORMS

In the autumn of 1921, an experiment was begun in the upper departments of selected elementary schools. 'The senior departments were divided into two parts – the lower part up to and including **Standard** V., classed in "Standards": and the upper part all above that line, classed in "Forms". It was intended to take the entrants into secondary schools from Standard V., and to leave the rest of the children over 12 in the upper school. The teaching in the upper school was to be given by "specialists", as far as possible, and the most modern methods were to be used. In the second year of the experiment, Second Forms were organised without much difficulty, but in the third year, i.e., April, 1924, it was found difficult to keep enough pupils in the Third Form, since they were inclined to leave when they found employment, as, of course, they were entitled to do' (Report 1924–25 p. 91).

SCHOOL LEAVING AGE

See: Compulsory Schooling

SCHOOL MACHINERY

The Reverend Birley, HMI, used the term school machinery to describe the buildings, offices and playgrounds of schools (Report 1864–65 p. 24).

SCHOOL MANAGERS

During the 1800s the term 'school managers' meant those **trustees**, church ministers etc. who supervised the running of the school and to whom the master answered. For example, in Scotland, 'With few exceptions, the Minister and Deacons' Court constitute the managers of the school, though the direct management and control devolve, in most cases, on the minister alone. In the schools connected with iron or coal works, the manager of the work is naturally the manager of the school, while in the schools erected and supported by private persons, the management is, generally speaking, in the hands of the patron assisted by the clergyman. These systems of management seem to work well, and I rarely meet with cases either of officious interference, or of positive neglect on the part of the managers of schools in my district' (Report 1862–63 p. 171).

See also: (School) Governors

SCHOOL MEALS

(1905) Circulars were issued by the Local Government Board and the **Board of Education** concerning the undernourishment of children attending public elementary schools.

263

'It was therein pointed out that if a child in any Poor Law Union is in fact destitute of necessary food, and if application is made by the child or any responsible person on his behalf to the Guardians or Relieving Officer, it is the duty of the Guardians, or even (in cases of urgency) of the relieving Officer to afford relief, and this although the parent is able to provide food but has failed to do so. In this last case, however, the cost of relief will in general fall, not on the ratepayers, but on the parent. These special applications may be made, in the case of children attending school in a state of destitution for want of food, by any Manager of the school or by a teacher' (Report 1904–05 p. 29). As a result of the **Education (Provision of Meals) Act 1906** and particularly during severe stages of the Depression, school breakfasts, dinners and teas were provided to needy children. The **Education Act 1944** required local education authorities to provide school meals and this obligation was removed by the Education Act 1980.

See also: Penny Dinners; School Food Trust

SCHOOL MEDICAL SERVICE

The Ministry of Health Act 1919 transferred from the **Board of Education** '[a]ll the powers and duties of the Board of education with respect to the medical inspection and treatment of children and young people' (Report 1918–19 p. 7). Also, the Education Act 1921 extended these responsibilities and required **local education authorities** to provide for the medical inspection of pupils prior to their admission to **secondary school**s and other institutions of higher education (Report 1924–25 p. 167). School medical officers were required to examine children.

See also: Education (Administrative Provisions) Act 1907

SCHOOL MUSEUM

Some schools collected a range of objects that could be used for teaching in object lessons: lessons focused around a particular item that could be examined by the pupils; and when all these items were gathered together they were sometimes known as a school museum. Mr Sharpe, Her Majesty's Inspector maintained, 'The first condition of a good school museum seems to be a good local character, i.e., it should be illustrative chiefly of the natural features of the neighbourhood and of the principal manufacturers, or in agricultural neighbourhoods of the processes of gardening and farming. The second condition is, that it should be well suited for teaching object lessons in the lower classes, and the specific subjects selected for the higher classes. Every school could attempt at least as much as this, but besides this more definite collection, which may be obtained with little or no cost, a miscellaneous collection of articles could readily be formed very suitable for giving general object lessons. Actual specimens are more suitable for the purpose than diagrams, they are life size, can be handled by the class, and present varieties differing from the lithographed type' (Report 1882–83 p. 547).

SCHOOL OF DESIGN

(1 June 1837) In 1836 the Board of Trade contributed £1,600 for the establishment of a central school of design, which was established the following year. The Government School of Design was opened in Somerset House ' … the express purpose of which was to provide for the architect, the upholsterer, the weaver, the printer, the potter, and all manufacturers, artisans better educated to originate and execute their respective wares, and to invest them with greater symmetry of form, with increased harmony of colour, and with greater fitness of decoration, to render manufactures not less useful by ornamenting them, but more beautiful, and therefore more useful' (Minutes 1852–53 Vol. 1, p. 23).

In 1841, the Government provided aid for the establishment of provincial schools of design. However, it was recognised that because many pupils did not have the ability to draw, this skill had to be taught first before they could begin with design. As a consequence, it became recognised that the skills of drawing should be developed before students were able to study in schools of design. This situation led to the establishment of elementary classes or schools of drawing and modelling in 1852–53. The (Government) School of Design became know as the National Art Training School in 1853, and, lastly, the Royal College of Art in 1896. Many schools of design were replaced by schools of art by the **Science and Art Department**.

SCHOOL PENCE

This was the fee paid by parents for children to attend the school. This was sometimes paid by an employer when the children were 'withdrawn for field or other labour'. The amount paid sometimes varied depending on the financial standing of the parents. Where payment was not made the educational value was not as appreciated. 'The most serious complaint of irregularity which I found in any town of this class was that made against the freemen's children at Morpeth, who enjoy an old privilege of frequenting the schools free of any payment; which induces their parents lightly to avail themselves of this advantage, and as lightly to relinquish it' (Minutes 1844 Vol. 1, p. 124).

SCHOOL SAVINGS BANKS

School savings banks were to be found in the 1870s and increased rapidly in the early 1890s in response to provision of free school education and encouragement from the **Education Department** about thrift.

See also: Penny Savings Banks; Thrift-Lessons

Further reading: Report 1878–79 p. 558; Report 1892–93 p. ix

SCHOOL TERMS

(*c.*1918) Compulsory attendance at school was originally fixed to the age of a child, which meant that many children left on the day of their birthday upon reaching the end of compulsory attendance. The impact of this was that many were 'marking time' during the last year and classes were continuously losing members, thus reducing the benefits of education. To address this the Education Act 1918 stipulated that 'If a child who is attending, or is about to attend, a Public Elementary School … attains any year of age during the school term, the child shall not, for the purpose of any enactment or byelaw, whether made before or after the passing of this Act, relating to school attendance, be deemed to have attained that year of age until the end of term (Report 1922–23 p. 60).

In the act, the specification of a school term was left to the local education authority, and to provide clarity the **Board of Education** in Circular 1123, 31 July 1919, stated that, '[i]n the view of the Board, a school term must necessarily be a substantially continuous period of education beginning as a rule at the end of one school holiday, and ending at the beginning of another school holiday … Authorities who desire to have three terms can do so by making the terms begin with the first day on which the school meets after the Christmas, Easter, or summer holidays as the case may be, and end on the last day on which the school meets before the next of such holiday periods. If four terms are preferred, a convenient arrangement may be to adopt the practice already followed in some areas of making a break in the autumn term, e.g. about the end of October. Either arrangement need cause no alteration in the times of the ordinary school holidays, which in many places are determined by the date of harvest, or other local conditions' (Report 1922–23 p. 61).

The Board continued: 'To Authorities who proposed six terms in the year the Board felt bound to reply that from the educational point of view they were unable to agree that six divisions of the school year could be made which would not result in at least four of the so-called terms being too short to fit in with any plan which a teacher could frame for the due progress of his class' (Report 1922–23 p. 62).

See also: School Day; School Year

SCHOOL TRANSPORT

Possibly the first report of school transport, the Scrane End School van, is included in Mr Synge's, Her Majesty's Inspector, report from Lincolnshire. 'At Scrane End, a remote part of the Frieston parish, with a considerable population, a school was, I think, needed. But the governors of Butterwick Endowed Schools determined to meet the difficulty by conveying the Scrane End children to and from the Butterwick schools, between two and three miles distant. A suitable conveyance has been built, and has been for some time in use. The success of this experiment cannot well be determined until it has had a trial through the winter' (Report 1895–96 p. 111).

SCHOOL UNION

(*c.*1856) Many schools were established for social, religious and philanthropic reasons and often tended to operate independently of one another. Greater coordination provided a number of benefits as this example from Carlisle indicates. 'Its [the School Union] specific object was to check one principal cause of irregularity and relation of discipline – the causeless removal of children from school to school, at the caprice of the parent, or the mere fancy of the child. The Union includes *nearly* every public school for the labouring classes in or near Carlisle, with one or two large private establishments. The agreement is, that no child shall be received from one of these schools into another, without producing a certificate that a month's

notice has been given before its removal. The general testimony of teachers is very strongly in favour of the efficacy and beneficial working of this simple machinery' (Report 1858–59 pp. 134–35).

SCHOOL VISITS

The 1895 Code recognised that visits to museums, art galleries and other places of education value would be recognised, under specific conditions, as school attendance.

SCHOOL YEAR

(1897) The 1897 **Code** acknowledged the value of a uniform education school year and abolished Article 101f, the practice of individual examinations in **specific subjects**, which occurred close to the end of a school's financial year and which was normally based on the foundation date of the school (Report 1896–97 p. 485). In 1898 Mr Colvill and Mr Dibben, HM Inspectors, suggested a uniform instruction year of three terms in Guildford and Croydon (Board of Education 1899–1900 Vol. 3 p. 233). 'The suggestion made in the autumn of 1898 by my colleague (Mr Colvill) and myself to boards, managers, and teachers to adopt throughout our districts an uniform instruction year of three terms, ending on 31 March (or at Easter), was very cordially received and has been almost universally adopted with the happiest of results. The Division of the year into three terms ending at Easter, mid-summer holidays and Christmas gave the teachers an opportunity of holding their examinations on completed terms of work at dates immediately preceding the holidays, secured the promotion of children at regular intervals, and by uniformity in instruction year did away with the objection so often raised of children "marking time" when removing from one town or village to another in the same district. To the infants the advantage of the instruction year ending at Easter is particularly great, as it transfers the older children to the senior schools at a time when the large influx of new young children takes place, prevents to a certain extent over-crowding during the hottest months of the year, and secures greater equality in the average attendance' (Board of education 1899–1900 Vol. 3, p. 234).

See also: School Day; School Terms

SCHOOLS COUNCIL FOR CURRICULUM AND EXAMINATIONS

(1964–89) Control over the curriculum taught in schools during the first half of the twentieth century was largely the responsibility of the school and the local authority. This was reflected in the **Education Act 1944**, which specified that the only subject that should be taught in schools was religion. However, by the 1960s there was a concern about educational standards and that some schools were not providing a broad and balanced curriculum. To address this a Curriculum Study Group was established in the **Department of Education and Science** and in 1964 this, and the **Secondary Schools Examinations Council,** were replaced with the Schools Council for Curriculum and Examinations, which had representatives from government, local education authorities and teachers. It was replaced by the School Curriculum and Development Committee and the **Secondary Examinations Council**.

SCHOOLS FOR DRAWING AND MODELLING

See: Elementary Drawing Schools

SCHOOLS FOR MUSLIN WEAVING

(1853) These schools in Kells, Ireland, instructed girls in the sewing of muslin under the direction of the Sisters of Mercy. The funds that were raised were used to help educate the girls. 'Children must be fed before they can be taught, and it is a double

charity which enables them to earn their own food' (Minutes 1853–54, Vol. 2, p. 851).

SCHOOLS OF ART

These were schools encouraged by the **Science and Art Department** and in 1900 there were 263 art schools in England and Wales, and 12 in Ireland (Board of Education 1899–1900 Vol. 1, p. 48).

See also: Art Schools; Schools of Practical Art

SCHOOLS OF COMPASSION

These were industrial schools found in London that provided industrial training (Minutes 1853–54, Vol. 2, p. 850).

See also: Industrial Schools

SCHOOLS OF EASE

These were schools that were at some distance to, and managed by, an existing one. Mr Stokes, HMI, suggested that '[t]he prospect of grants upon practicable conditions might induce managers of existing central schools to open "schools of ease" where, in plain rooms and under homely teachers, the valuable experience already gained might be made to avail towards carrying the moral and intellectual benefits of education down to the classes not reached by established institutions'. (Report 1869–69 p. 323). An example of this type of school was Linden Road School of Ease in St Luke's Mission Hall, Clevedon. This was a type of auxiliary school.

See also: Branch Schools

SCHOOLS OF ELEMENTARY ART

See: Elementary Drawing Schools

SCHOOLS OF FEMALE INDUSTRY

(1850s) These schools in Scotland were predominantly elementary schools with an industrial element and concentrated almost exclusively on needlework and knitting. The Scottish Ladies Association (1854) was founded 'for promoting female industrial education in Scotland' and to 'combine with the usual branches of female industry sewing, knitting, spinning, laundry work, and household work' (Minutes 1855–56, p. 575).

Further reading: By a Lady (1849)

SCHOOLS OF INDUSTRIAL ART

These were developed along the lines of schools of practical art and could be found, among others, at Southwold and Keswick. Mr Fisher, HMI, stated '[t]he Keswick School of Industrial Art is an interesting example of the practical value of teaching some artistic handwork. Here during the slack winter months boatmen, drivers, and others work at articles of artistic furniture in wood, brass, and copper, under the direction of Mrs Rawnsley, who supplies them with most of the beautiful designs which have made the work of the school famous' (Report 1893–94 p. 18). The school was established in 1883/84 and survived until 1984.

See also: Schools of Practical Art; Schools of Ornamental Art

SCHOOLS OF INDUSTRY

See: Industrial Schools

SCHOOLS OF ORNAMENTAL ART

(c.1850s) The purpose of these schools was to 'afford an opportunity of acquiring a competent knowledge of the fine arts, *as far as the same are connected with manufactures*; to enable our designers and manufacturers, by the instruction therein obtained in the principles of beauty, and the skill to embody those principles, to add beauty to utility, – to adorn and decorate the useful' (Minutes 1852–53, Vol. 1, p. 29).

SCHOOLS OF PRACTICAL ART

(1852) Previously known as **schools of design**, schools of practical art received their name from the **Department of Practical Art**. They were also known as governmental schools of practical art. By 1852 there were 21 schools established in London (2), Belfast, Birmingham, Cork, Coventry, Dublin, Glasgow, Leeds, Limerick, Macclesfield, Manchester, Newcastle, Norwich, Nottingham, the Potteries, Paisley, Sheffield, Stourbridge, Worcester and York (Minutes 1852–53, Vol. 1, p. 31).

See also: Schools of Industrial Art; Schools of Ornamental Art

SCHOOLS OF SCIENCE

The **Department of Science and Art** Report 1854 (p. xxx) described the intention of large towns to advance their schools of science (sometimes schools of applied science (Minutes 1854–55 p. 763)) into higher institutions. The department recommended the establishment of an 'intermediate class of secondary schools' to encourage longer attendance at schools and impart the main principles of science. Science education progressively developed and was strongly encouraged by the **Technical Instruction Act 1889**. The education had to be provided in day classes and the instruction had to be approved by the board. 'A School of Science must provide a thorough and progressive course of education in Science combined with literary or commercial instruction adapted to the students whose education is such as would fit them to enter Standard VII. Of the English Code for a Public Elementary School. ... In order that a School may be eligible for recognition as a School of Science, (a) it must possess such properly equipped laboratories as are necessitated by the courses ... ' (Report 1900–01 Vol. 3, p. 342). In 1901 some science schools were reorganised into higher elementary schools (Report 1900–01 p. 6).

See also: Science Schools

SCIENCE AND ART DEPARTMENT

(1853–99) This was established by the Lords of the Committee of the Privy Council for Trade and represented an expansion of the previous **Department of Practical Art** and it also absorbed the Government **School of Design**. Its purpose was 'to extend a system of encouragement to local institutions for Practical Science, similar to that already commenced in the Department of Practical Art; to combine systems on an enlarged scale, and to furnish, through the instrumentality of one Department in connexion with the Executive Government, having the support and being subject to the control of Parliament, the means for mutual co-operation and correspondence to every district of the kingdom, where the local intelligence and energy of the inhabitants would create schools of Industrial Science and Art. Accordingly the Government School of Mines and Science applied to the Arts, the Museum of Practical Geology, the Geological Survey, the Museum of Irish Industry, the Royal Dublin Society, and the Department of Practical Art, including the provincial Schools of Design, were brought into mutual action and co-operation for the benefit of the whole of the United Kingdom … The object of a Metropolitan Establishment was to create, exhibit, and distribute the most improved illustrations, models and diagrams, both in Science and Art, which would be readily accessible to the public at large, but especially to all persons throughout the country interested in education, to managers and schoolmasters of training and national and other schools, and to masters in training, and students' (Department of Science and Art Report 1854 p. x).

The department supported education in art, design, science and technology in Britain and Ireland. In 1856 the newly formed **Education Department** took over responsibility for the Science and Art Department, which continued to maintain some autonomy in higher education for art, science and teacher training. In 1899 the Education Department and the Science and Art Department were merged into one **Board of Education** Department.

Further reading: Minutes (1855–56 p. 1; Macdonald (2004)

SCIENCE AND ENGINEERING CLUBS PILOT

(2006) The 2006 Budget announced funding for 250 schools to set up and run science and engineering clubs. Their purpose was to help supply the UK with people with science, technology, engineering and mathematics (STEM) skills and to increase the interest of young people in STEM. The aims of the clubs were to:

- enrich, enhance and extend the Key Stage 3 curriculum;
- improve attainment in, interactions with and experiences of science among those pupils already showing interest and ability in these subjects;
- encourage these individuals to consider continuing their education in STEM;
- improve collaboration between schools, and between schools and industry and the research base.

Further reading: HM Treasury (July 2004)

SCIENCE CLASSES

During the mid-1800s the subject of science gradually began to emerge in schools and this was supported by grants from the **Science and Art Department** in South Kensington (Report 1877–78 p. 435). Although popular, these classes were not universally welcomed and some HMIs were sceptical about their value. Mr Campbell, HMI, noted that night schools were declining due to the increase in teachers' salaries and ' … the too prevalent fashion of holding what are called "science classes". I am inclined to believe that the vague abstraction known to us now by the name of "science" is much more profitable to its teachers than useful to its learners' (Report

1876–77 p. 448). The 1882 Code attempted to encourage elementary science but this was not successful until the 1890 Code relaxed the regulation that required that English be the first choice as a '**class subject**'. The 1890 Code provided a description of the main areas of elementary science, which consisted of mechanics; animal physiology; botany; principles of agriculture; chemistry; sound, light and heat; magnetism and electricity; domestic economy. These disciplines could also be studied as **specific subjects** and the Code also emphasised the importance of practice upon learning and stated: 'It is intended that the instruction of elementary science shall be given mainly by experiment and illustration. If these subjects are taught by definition and verbal description, instead of by making the children exercise their own powers of observation, they will be worthless as means of education' (Report 1889–90 p. 152). Many lessons on **common things**, that is, descriptions of a key, egg, metals, senses, etc. could be regarded as science lessons and these were often previously known as **object lessons**. The 1892 Code added: lessons on common things in reference to the care of health and conduct of life (Report 1892–93 p. 174). The 1882 **Code** encouraged the introduction of **Elementary Science**; however, this was largely unsuccessful until the 1890 Code relaxed the rule requiring English to be the first choice of the 'class subjects', from which time it became very popular. The teaching of science was based on the principal that Science should be taught according to the environment around the school which encouraged mechanics and chemistry for urban areas and beekeeping, managing poultry, and agriculture in rural areas (Report 1910–11 p. 29).

(ORGANISED) SCIENCE SCHOOLS

These secondary schools were established by school boards with grant support from the **Science and Art Department**. Known as organised science schools, their curriculum placed emphasis on science and art, which was a requirement of the grant. These schools grew out of the **Technical Instruction Act 1889** and filled a temporary gap before the **Education Act 1902** gave greater power to **local education authorities** and most of these schools became secondary ones. In 1899 there were 169 **science schools** many of which were grammar schools. Regulations issued in 1895 specified that science be taught for 13 hours and literary subjects for 10 hours.

Further reading: Abbot (1933)

SCIENCE, TECHNOLOGY, ENGINEERING AND MATHEMATICS

Although science, technology, engineering and mathematics skills are considered vital to the economic future, fewer students are studying these subjects. The original STEM Mapping Review in 2004 identified 470 STEM initiatives run by the DfES, DTI and other agencies. To rationalise these and build on successful ones required coordination to provide a vision across all areas of education and to make recommendations to ministers about priorities. To support this a STEM Strategy Group met for the first time in October 2006.

Further reading: Department for Education and Skills (October 2006)

SCIENCE, TECHNOLOGY, ENGINEERING AND MATHEMATICS NETWORK

Funded by the **Department for Innovation, Universities and Skills** this is a strategic UK initiative designed to encourage interest and support in these areas. Through SETPOINT, professional support is provided to teachers, young people, schools and colleges. Among the initiatives are ambassadors consisting of professional people and graduates with backgrounds in these areas who use their knowledge and experience to encourage interest in these areas.

Further reading: HM Treasury (July 2004); www.stemnet.org.uk (accessed 01 June 2010)

SCOTCH EDUCATION DEPARTMENT

(1872) The Church of Scotland's Board of Education for Scotland was replaced by a new Board of Education for Scotland that consisted of five members appointed by Queen Victoria and that oversaw the Scotch Education Department. This was established through the Education (Scotland) Act 1872 and the '"Scotch Education Department" shall mean the Lords of any committee of the Privy Council appointed by Her Majesty on Education in Scotland' (Report 1872–73 p. cxxv). The offices were based in London and in 1885 the post of Secretary of Scotland was established with responsibility for the Scotch Education Department. The Department was moved to Edinburgh in 1918 and was renamed the **Scottish Education Department**.

SCOTTISH CERTIFICATE OF EDUCATION

The SCE consists of two grades: the Standard Grade (formerly Ordinary Grade) and Higher Grade. The Standard Grade is generally taken at 16 years old and is the equivalent of the **General Certificate of Secondary Education**. Between 1986 and 1994 the Ordinary and Standard Grades coexisted and were reported on a common scale. Ordinary Grades were classed at 1–5, while Standard Grades were classed at 1–7, with 1 being the highest.

The SCE Higher Grade is taken by pupils in schools, in further education and also by adults. Candidates may pass in bands A, B and C and those narrowly failing receive a band D, which was formerly a 'compensatory ordinary grade award'. These qualifications are used for access to university as well as admission criteria by some employers.

The Advanced Higher was introduced in 2000 and is equivalent to the first year of a four-year undergraduate programme in Scottish universities. The Advanced Higher is a one-year course with assessment through course work and examinations.

SCOTTISH COUNCIL OF NATIONAL TRAINING ORGANISATIONS

This network was a rationalisation and development of the work undertaken by **lead bodies**, **occupational standards councils**, and **industry training organisations**. Key elements of SCONTO were to:

- represent a defined sector or occupational group;
- promote investment in people by employers as an integral part of competitive business performance;
- assess and respond to the education, training and development needs of their sector and its employees;
- represent to government and others the sectors' education and training interests;
- cover the sectors response to national initiatives;
- ensure the development, review and implementation of national (UK) cccupational standards for the sector and occupations within it;
- demonstrate the strategic and operational involvement of employers and other key interests within the sector; and,
- develop and maintain effective national, sectoral and local partnerships on shared education and training issues.

Further reading: SCONTO (1998); (1999)

SCOTTISH CREDIT AND QUALIFICATIONS FRAMEWORK

(Launched December 2001) The purpose of the SCQF was to allow employers, learners and the public to understand how qualifications related to each other and to assist in developing learning pathways. In this way it was similar to the National Qualifications Framework; however, the SCQF had twelve levels.

Further reading: http://www.scqf.org.uk/ (accessed 01 June 2010)

271

SCOTTISH EDUCATION DEPARTMENT

(1918–91) This department officially replaced the **Scotch Education Department** in 1918 although the term Scottish Education Department was in use before then. Administration was also moved from London to Edinburgh in that year. In 1991, the department was renamed the Scottish Office Education Department; and its named changed again, in 1995, becoming the Scottish Office Education and Industry Department. Following the Scottish Parliament Act 1998 the Scottish Education Department's responsibilities were taken over by the **Scottish Executive Education Department**.

SCOTTISH ENTERPRISE

It was created together with **Highlands and Islands Enterprise** by the Enterprise and New Towns (Scotland) Act 1990. Both bodies had overall responsibility for training and enterprise programmes, as well as other duties. They operated through a network of 22 **local enterprise companies (LECs)**. Scottish Enterprise has responsibility for:

- 'furthering the development of Scotland's economy and in that connection providing, maintaining and safeguarding employment;
- enhancing skills and capacities relevant to employment in Scotland and assisting persons to establish themselves as self-employed persons there;
- promoting Scotland's industrial efficiency and international competitiveness; and
- furthering improvement of the environment of Scotland'.

Scottish Executive Enterprise and Lifelong Learning Department (2000a p. 9)

SCOTTISH EXECUTIVE EDUCATION DEPARTMENT

(1999 – May 2007) Scottish devolution enabled the Scottish Executive to establish the Scottish Executive Education Department which replaced the **Scottish Office Education and Industry Department**. In May 2007, the Scottish National Party abolished departments and replaced them with directorates forming: **Scottish Government Directorate for Children, Young People and Social Care; Scottish Government Directorate for Education**; and, **Scottish Government Directorate for Lifelong Learning**.

SCOTTISH EXECUTIVE ENTERPRISE AND LIFELONG LEARNING DEPARTMENT

(1999 – May 2003) SEELLD had responsibility for economic and industrial development, **further** and **higher education**, learndirect Scotland, student support, skills and lifelong learning, and tourism in Scotland; and coordination of the New Deal. In May 2003 its remit expanded and it was retitled the **Enterprise, Transport and Lifelong Learning Department**.

SCOTTISH FURTHER EDUCATION FUNDING COUNCIL

The purpose of the SFEFC was to develop 'flexible, accessible and relevant provision', which was cost effective in the college sector. The Council had 12 members, which decided on strategy and funding decisions, provided guidance to the colleges, and advised the First Minister. The staff of approximately 100 are shared with the Scottish Higher Education Funding Council.

SCOTTISH GOVERNMENT DIRECTORATE FOR CHILDREN, YOUNG PEOPLE AND SOCIAL CARE

Established in May 2007, the directorate has wide-ranging responsibilities including: childcare; child protection; parenting; and preschool education.

Further reading: www.scotland.gov.uk/Home (accessed 01 June 2010)

SCOTTISH GOVERNMENT DIRECTORATE FOR EDUCATION

Established in May 2007, the directorate oversees and supports schools' policies and workforce development as well as Learning and Teaching Scotland and the Scottish Qualifications Authority. The directorate also works to achieve Scottish Government's overall purpose, 'to focus Government and public services on creating a more successful country, with opportunities for all of Scotland to flourish, through increasing sustainable economic growth'.

(www.scotland.gov.uk/Home (accessed 26 February 2010))

See also: Scottish Executive Education Department

SCOTTISH GOVERNMENT DIRECTORATE FOR LIFELONG LEARNING

Established in May 2007, the directorate is responsible for all schooling after children leave school. It is divided into five divisions: Employability and Skills; Enterprise and Employability for Young People; Further and Adult Education; Higher Education and Learner Support; and, Learning Connections.

Further reading: www.scotland.gov.uk/Home (accessed 01 June 2010)

SCOTTISH HIGHERS

See: Scottish Certificate of Education

SCOTTISH OFFICE

The Scottish Office took over responsibility for training, enterprise, and education programmes in April 1991 from the **Employment Department**.

Further reading: www.scotland.gov.uk (accessed 01 June 2010)

SCOTTISH OFFICE EDUCATION AND INDUSTRY DEPARTMENT

(1995–99) **Scottish Office Education Department** was replaced by the Scottish Office Education and Industry Department in 1995 reflecting the prevailing views at the time of connecting education more closely with the needs of industry. After devolution, in 1999, the department became the **Scottish Executive Education Department**.

SCOTTISH OFFICE EDUCATION DEPARTMENT

(1991–95) The **Scottish Education Department** was replaced by the Scottish Office Education Department in 1991. The SED later became the **Scottish Office Education and Industry Department** in 1995.

SCOTTISH QUALIFICATIONS AUTHORITY

(1 April 1997) The SQA took over the functions of the Scottish Examination Board and the **Scottish Vocational Education Council** (SCOTVEC) in 1997. Among others, it had responsibility for Highers and Standards Grades, National Certificate modules, GSVQs, Higher National Certificates and Diplomas, Professional Development Awards and Scottish Vocational Qualifications: in other words, for all main qualifications other than degrees. It set and standardised the examinations and arranged for the marking of papers to ensure that a uniform standard was set and met.

See also: Scottish Credit and Qualifications Framework

Further reading: Newscheck (1998b); www.sqa.org.uk (accessed 01 June 2010)

SCOTTISH SOCIETY FOR PROPAGATING CHRISTIAN KNOWLEDGE

(1709) This was the earliest association formed in Scotland and within its Charter of Incorporation it stated that it would use funds to ' … erect and maintain schools, to teach to read, especially the Holy Scriptures and other good and pious books; as also to teach writing, arithmetic, and such like degrees of knowledge in the Highlands, Islands, and remote corners of Scotland'. In a second patent it added that the SSPCK should encourage those 'children as they shall think fit to be instructed and bred up to husbandry and housewifery, or in trades and manufactures, or in such like manual occupations as the Society shall think proper' (Parliamentary Papers 1880) (Minutes 1844, Vol. 2, p. 357). Other Scottish societies included the Gaelic School Society and the Ayrshire Educational Society: subsequently came known as Scottish Society for Promoting Christian Knowledge.

See also: Society for Promoting Christian Knowledge

Further reading: www.archive.org/stream/ parliamentarypa183commgoog/parliamentarypa 183commgoog_djvu.txt (accessed 02 April 2010)

SCOTTISH TECHNICAL CONSULTATIVE COUNCIL

Advised on **ONC**s and **HND**s.

See also: National Advisory Council on Education for Industry and Commerce

Further reading: Ministry of Labour Annual Report 1961, p. 49

SCOTTISH UNIVERSITY FOR INDUSTRY

(1998) SUfI operates through the brand name learndirect Scotland. It is a company limited by guarantee and has charitable status. It was established to support learning and to connect education and training (the providers) with business and the labour market (the customers). Its objectives include:

- stimulating increased demand for learning;
- simplifying access to learning;
- developing new business relationships;
- improving guidance on learning choices;
- developing a national network of customer-focused learning centres;

- identifying gaps in learning materials and approaches and commissioning new material;
- improving learning experiences, choice and management; and,
- minimising barriers to learning.

See also: UfI

SCOTTISH VOCATIONAL EDUCATION COUNCIL

(1985–97) SCOTVEC was formed by the merger of the Scottish Business Education Council and the Scottish Technical Education Council. SCOTVEC was responsible for vocational qualifications in Scotland and was superseded on 1 April 1997 by the **Scottish Qualifications Authority**.

Further reading: Newscheck (1998b)

SCOTTISH VOCATIONAL QUALIFICATIONS

Are based on occupational standards identified by employers to meet the needs of industry. They are similar to **national vocational qualifications**, but they are accredited and awarded by the **Scottish Qualifications Authority**.

Further reading: DfEE (1998h)

SEA TRAINING

The royal navy and **merchant marine** had a number of ships that were used for training. In addition, there were also training ships on land within schools, which were fully rigged out in the school yard: for example, the Central London School at Norwood and Stepney School (Minutes 1859–60 p. 521).

See also: Admiralty Schools; Hospital Schools; Navigation Schools; (School of) Nautical training; Royal Dockyard Schools

SECOND EXAMINATION

(1919–20) This examination, established in 1917 and first taken in 1919–20, was taken by pupils of about 18 years of age and led to the **Higher School Certificate** which was a predecessor to **advanced levels**. It was overseen by the **Secondary Schools Examination Council**, which was tasked with bringing order to an incomplete and wide range of qualifications. It was preceded by the **first examination** for those of about sixteen years (Report 1923–24 p. 30).

See also: Advanced Courses; School Certificate

SECONDARY EXAMINATIONS COUNCIL

(1982–88) The functions of the Schools Council for Curriculum and Examinations were separated in 1982 with the formation of the Secondary Examinations Council and the School Curriculum Development Committee. Section 14 of the Education Reform Act 1988 transferred the responsibilities of the Secondary Examinations Council and the School Curriculum Development Committee to the Curriculum Council for Wales, the **National Curriculum Council** and the **School Examinations and Assessment Council**.

SECONDARY INTERMEDIATE SCHOOLS

(Northern Ireland) These schools provided a lower general education that had an emphasis on practical subjects.

See also: Technical Intermediate Schools

SECONDARY MODERN SCHOOLS

The Hadow (1926) Report recommended the expansion of secondary education and its division into two main types: **grammar schools** and modern schools. The modern schools were to have a three- or four-year programme with a more limited curriculum than grammar schools, and were to provide an initial general education that was followed by a more practical focus in the last two years. The report also proposed that for able children there be an opportunity to transfer from the modern to the grammar school at the age of 12 or 13 and vice versa.

SECONDARY SCHOOLS

The term 'secondary schools' began to come into common usage in the 1850s. At the time, many **infant[s] schools** were separate from **elementary schools** although they gradually merged to form primary schools. A report by Mr Kennedy, HMI, stated: 'There is not a sufficiently high style of school for boys ranging from 10 to 14 years of age. We want at least three grades of schools, an infant or first school, a second school, and a third school' (Minutes 1855–56 p. 359). 'The Lord President thinks that a system of secondary schools might with great advantage be added to the present system of primary schools, in all those localities where schools of the latter kind are sufficiently large, or sufficiently numerous to afford a supply of children who have mastered the common elements of instruction, and are prepared to proceed with more specific studies. Schools of this secondary kind are beginning to be established in different parts of the country under the name of **trade schools**, the instruction being generally directed towards the application of science to productive industry' (Minutes 1856–57, p. 42). The Board of Education report incorrectly stated that the term 'secondary school' came from the 1860s and then explained that, 'It came from France, where it had been invented as part of a general classification of education throughout its stages, from the lowest to the highest, in the three successive grades of primary, secondary and tertiary. In this country the term "tertiary" has never come into use at all, and the term "primary" has been mostly replaced by the term "elementary". The Elementary Education Act of 1870 established this latter term in official usage, which popular usage has mainly followed and confirmed' (Report 1908–09 p. 31). In 1906, secondary school was defined for clearer understanding in the Regulations for Secondary Schools as a school, 'which offers to each of its scholars a general education of a wider scope and higher grade than that of an Elementary School, given through a complete progressive course of instruction continuing up to and beyond the age of 16.' (Board of Education 1905–06 p. 46). The Hadow (1926) Report recommended that secondary education should begin from the age of eleven.

See also: Primary Education

SECONDARY SCHOOLS BRANCH

(1903) A Secondary Schools Branch was formed within the Board of Education to support the development of secondary schools. The 1903 regulations of the board moved **pupil-teachers** from **elementary schools** into the **secondary school** system. These developments represented the development of higher grade schools into county council secondary schools and **municipal secondary schools**.

SECONDARY SCHOOLS DIVISION A & B

Following the **Board of Education Act 1899**, in which the **Education Department** and the **Science and Art Department** were combined, legacy grants and new entitlements were in operation at the same time. To manage this situation the **Board of Education** described two categories: Division A schools (formerly called **schools of science**) and Division B schools ('formerly called Secondary Day Schools simply'), the former getting a larger grant. 'This differentiation was a survival of the time when the sole form of higher education for which grants were paid from Government was that given in Science and Art classes' (Board of Education 1903–04 p. 19).

SECONDARY SCHOOLS EXAMINATION COUNCIL

(1917–64) In the early 1900s, the various professional bodies, universities, civil service, army, etc. set their own individual demands regarding the content and requirements of examinations and matriculation. The Report 1923–24 (p. 29) observed: 'These societies [professional bodies] have the right to lay down the conditions not only for the various technical examinations proper to their own requirements, but also for the initial general examination which lies at the entry to the profession. In effect, this created a great number of authorities, each of which was free to make its own rules for general school education ... The purpose was excellent but with a multitude of independent authorities, each actuated by its own theory as to what general education should be, chaos was inevitable'. For example, in 27 schools supported by the Lancashire Education Committee there were 26 different examinations taken in one year and a school pupil might take five or more different external examinations (Report 1935 p. 10). To address this lack of cohesion a consultative committee of the **Board of Education** considered the situation and reported in 1911. The First World War hindered progress, until on 12 September 1917 the Secondary Schools Examination Council was announced (Circular 1010) to bring some order and uniformity. It consisted of representatives of the recognised examining bodies, the Teachers Registration Council, the Associations of County Councils, municipal corporations, and education committees. Eight examining boards were recognised, which conducted **first** and **second examinations** and, 'The corresponding examinations of the various Bodies are roughly equivalent in standard and in general construction, though there is considerable variety in detail' (Report 1923–24 p. 30). Its responsibilities were taken over by the **Schools Council for Curriculum and Examinations** in 1964.

SECTOR SKILLS AGREEMENTS

(progressively put in place and all agreed by 2008) The SSAs map the skills employers need in their workforce and how those skills are to be supplied in order to provide a skilled and productive workforce. SSAs are facilitated by sector skills councils and involve employers, education and training providers, and key funding partners. It is a five stage process:

'Stage 1: A sophisticated assessment of each sectors' needs to cover the long-term, medium-term and short-term, mapping the drivers of change in the sector five to ten years down the track, and determining skill needs.

Stage 2: A review of the range, nature and employer relevance of current training provision across all the levels.

Stage 3: An analysis of the main gaps and weaknesses in workforce development leading to agreed priorities to be addressed.

Stage 4: A review of the scope for collaborative action – engaging employers to invest in skills development to support improved business performance – and an assessment of what employers are likely to sign up to.

Stage 5: A final agreement of how the SSC and employers will work with key funding partners to secure the necessary supply of training'.

Skills for Business (2004 p. 4)

See also: Sector Targets Challenge

SECTOR SKILLS ALMANAC

(May 2007) Provides an overview of the skills of the UK workforce sectors. It also describes the work of the **Skills for Business Network**, which consists of the 25 sector skills councils. In addition the **Sector Skills Matrix** draws upon official data sources to provide comparable information on 27 industry categories.

SECTOR SKILLS COUNCILS

(Announced 16 October 2001, some operational from April 2002) Designed to replace the 73 **national training organisations** in April 2002 when the NTOs were no longer funded or recognised by the Government.

They are independent organisations developed by groups of employers in sectors that have an employment base of economic or strategic significance. Their purpose is to lead the enhancement of skills and workforce development and their targets are based on four key goals: 'reducing skills gaps and shortages; improving productivity, business and public service performance; increasing opportunities to boost the skills and productivity of everyone in the sector's workforce, including action on equal opportunities; and improving learning supply, including **apprenticeships**, **higher education** and **national occupational standards**'. The Sector Skills Council Standard will set out the minimum requirements for a Sector Skills Council, which will then be licensed for five years. There are 25 SSCs that are overseen by the **UK Commission for Employment and Skills**, and represented by the Alliance of Sector Skills Councils.

Further reading: Sector Skills Development Agency (2001); www.sscalliance.org/ (accessed 01 June 2010)

SECTOR SKILLS DEVELOPMENT AGENCY

(2002–31 March 2008) The SSDA provided funding and support for the sector skills councils. It was headed by a chair and a chief executive appointed by the Secretary of State for Education and Skills and there was an employer-led board. It was a company limited by guarantee and a non-departmental public body. Its role was to:

- 'assist employers in sectors in bidding to become SSCs;
- fund, support and monitor the performance of SSCs across the UK;
- ensure quality and consistent standards across the network;
- provide minimum cover for essential functions in sectors without an SSC;
- ensure skills provision is designed to meet sector needs;

- ensure generic skills are effectively covered in the work of the SSCs;
- promote best practice sharing and benchmarking between sectors;
- provide a website portal for public bodies and individuals to access high quality sectoral labour market intelligence across the UK' Sector Skills Development Agency (2001 p. 3).

It was superseded by the **UK Commission for Employment and Skills**.

SECTOR SKILLS MATRIX

See: Sector Skills Almanac

SECTOR TARGETS CHALLENGE

The Sector Targets Challenge was described in the 1995 White Paper – *Competitiveness: Forging Ahead*. It was designed to encourage **industry training organisations** to work with companies to set targets for skills in their industry.

See also: Sector Skills Agreements

Further reading: DfEE Annual Report 1996/97

SECTOR TRAINING COUNCILS

In Northern Ireland the sector training councils were formerly **sectoral representative bodies.** Their purpose was to encourage companies in their respective sectors to invest in training and developing their employees and thereby improve their business.

Further reading: Training and Employment Agency Annual Report (1997)

SECTOR WORKING PARTIES

During the 1970s these sector working parties provided advice, including that on skill shortages, for example technician training

to support the Government's industrial strategy.

Further reading: MSC Annual Report 1977–78 p. 22

SECTORAL DEVELOPMENT PROGRAMME

In 1995 this Northern Ireland programme replaced part of the Company Development Programme that offered support for training needs analysis. The objectives of the SDP were to encourage companies in certain sectors outside the scope of the CDP to raise the competence of their workforce by developing a cost-effective training infrastructure and thereby help achieve **national education and training targets**. It was managed by **sectoral representative bodies**.

Further reading: Training and Employment Agency Annual Report (1995)

SECTORAL REPRESENTATIVE BODIES

During the early 1990s the **Training and Employment Agency** in Northern Ireland encouraged the development of sectoral representative bodies to provide an effective network that could voice training needs and help set standards in each of the main sectors. They subsequently became the **sector training councils**.

Further reading: Training and Employment Agency Annual Report (1992)

SECULAR SCHOOLS

(*c*.1850s) A number of schools existed in which there was no religious education, such as William's Secular School in Edinburgh and the **Birkbeck schools** found in Peckham, Manchester, Glasgow and Leith. These schools did not receive grants in the early days because they did not provide religious instruction (Minutes 1853–54, Vol. 1, pp. 43–44).

SENIOR EVENING INSTITUTES

During the 1920s the senior evening Institutes provided 'Vocational, Domestic, Art or General [education], in part-time courses, normally after 5p.m'. to older students (Report 1925–26 p. 57).

See also: Junior Evening Institutes

SENIOR SECONDARY SCHOOL (SCOTLAND)

This was a school that offered a five- or six-year education at secondary level.

See also: Junior Secondary School

SEPTEMBER GUARANTEE

(September 2007) This was designed to ensure that every 16-year-old, on completing compulsory education, was offered a guaranteed place in education or training by the end of September. The 14–19 Implementation Plan described this objective and, initially, the strategy was coordinated by the **Department for Education and Skills**, **learning and skills councils** and **Connexions**. It was designed to increase the number of young people staying in education and training and reduce the numbers **not in education, employment or training**. On 18 November 2009, an extension to the scheme was announced and called the January Guarantee. It was recognised that there was a significant demand for education and training in January after seasonal employment had ended and short courses had been completed. The objective was to support young people who were not in education, employment or training to re-engage and be positive about future learning options. An additional 10,000 places were made available on **entry to employment** courses, and funding was also made available to provide **education maintenance allowances**.

Further reading: Department for Education and Skills (2007) Departmental Report 2007, Cm 7092, p. 58

SERVICE CHILDRENS EDUCATION AGENCY

The mission of the Service Childrens Education Agency is, '[t]o provide an effective and efficient education service, from Foundation Stage through to sixth form, for dependent children residing with MOD personnel serving outside the United Kingdom, and to enable those children to benefit from their residence abroad'. It is an agency of the Ministry of Defence and provides education from Foundation Stage to **sixth form** (Years 12 and 13), following the national curriculum, assessments, and public examinations.

Further reading: www.mod.uk/DefenceInternet /DefenceFor/ServiceCommunity/Education/ sce/ (accessed 01 June 2010)

(EX)-SERVICE STUDENTS GRANT

A grant was made available from January 1919 after the First World War for officers and men of satisfactory educational attainment to follow full-time courses in universities, university colleges and other institutions of higher education. 'Almost every kind of training came within the scope of the Scheme', from short courses to the five-year study of medicine (Report 1921–22 p. 5). The grant closed to new applicants from the start of 1923 and at the end of the 1923–24 academic year 20, 980 students had completed courses with 235 students yet to complete (Report 1923–24 p. 127).

SESSIONAL SCHOOLS

Were so named because they fell under the responsibility of the kirk session, or church congregations, of the parish church in Scotland (Minutes 1842–43, p. 742).

SEVENTH-DAY ADVENTIST SCHOOL

The John Loughborough Seventh-Day Adventist School in Tottenham, London, was originally opened in April 1980 and was the first to be voluntary-aided from September 1998.

See also: Faith Schools

SEWING CLASSES

Many schools during the 1800s had sewing classes for the girls and female teachers were expected to have sewing skills, which were assessed in **training colleges**. Dr Cumming, HMI, commented that 'Few will deny that needlework should form an essential part of a girl's education, and that every exertion should be made to have this branch thoroughly engrafted in the previously existing system' (Report 1863–64 p. 261).

See also: Needlework

SEX DISCRIMINATION ACT 1975

This act promotes the equal treatment of men and women in employment and more widely. It also provided for the establishment of the **Equal Opportunities Commission**. The act came into force on 29 December 1975 at the same time as the Equal Pay Act 1970, whose delay was to allow employers to gradually achieve equal pay between men and women.

SHEFFIELD PEOPLE'S COLLEGE

(1842–78) This was established by Reverend R. S. Bayley, minister of Howard Street Congregational Church, for the wider education of working men and women than that provided for in mechanics institutes. It served as a model for Maurice's **working men's college**. The People's College in Nottingham was founded in 1846 and survives to the present day. More recently there has been the Ulster People's College.

Further reading: Moore Smith (1912)

SHELL TECHNOLOGY ENTERPRISE PROGRAMME

STEP was originally run by the Local Enterprise and Development Unit and was then transferred to the Northern Ireland's **Training and Employment Agency**. The programme enabled 30 graduates per year to experience small firm management.

Further reading: Training and Employment Agency Annual Report (1992)

SHELTERED EMPLOYMENT AND ADVISORY SERVICES LTD

(1964) This company was set up by the **Ministry of Labour** on the recommendations of a working party that looked at the operations of workshops for the blind. Its purpose was to provide an advisory service for the 67 workshops in which 3,500 blind people were employed. This initiative was to encourage the modernisation of production and the marketing of the output from the workshops. It was recognised that the traditional trades of basket and mat making were becoming uneconomic and that new trades were needed such as light engineering, plastic injection moulding, and soap making. A main aim of the company was to reduce running costs. The company also investigated new outlets for the produced goods and the subcontracting of work from industry.

Further reading: Ministry of Labour Gazette 1964, p. 104

SHELTERED EMPLOYMENT, PROCUREMENT AND CONSULTANCY SERVICES

(1979) SEPACS was a small unit that became operational in mid 1979 to help sheltered workshops find more public sector business and operate more efficiently. The Sheltered Employment and Consultative Group included members from trade unions, **Remploy**, local authorities and voluntary bodies.

Further reading: MSC Annual Report 1978–79, p. 11; MSC (1985a)

SHELTERED EMPLOYMENT SCHEME

(1944) This was a scheme for the disabled whereby, if they could not work within conventional industry due to their disability, they were given work that could be done at home. It was succeeded by **Remploy**. From 1995 the scheme has been called the **Supported Employment Programme**.

Further reading: Dutton et al. (1989)

SHELTERED PLACEMENT SCHEME

This scheme, developed in the mid-1980s, was introduced to provide employment opportunities for people with severe disabilities who had the ability to undertake productive work. The people undertook normal work but were not as productive as able-bodied people. The scheme involved a host firm that provided the work, the sponsor, a local authority, a voluntary organisation or **Remploy** as the employer of the disabled person, and was responsible for paying the wages and meeting employment legislation. Costs were met by a payment from the host firm for the work done and a contribution from the **MSC** towards the net costs. The scheme was restricted to voluntary organisations.

Further reading: Jones et al. (1988)

SHIP SCHOOLS

Instruction ship schools in the royal navy were run onboard the flagships Victory, Portsmouth, Impregnable, Devonport, and other harbour ships (Minutes: 1858–59 p. 465).

See also: Admiralty Schools; Royal Dockyard Schools; Royal Marines Artillery School; Sea Training

SHOE SCHOOL

(1858) This was a school established at St Giles, Northampton, to reduce the number of children leaving school early and to counteract the negative influences of the workplace on young children who worked in the shoe trade. This enabled the boys to learn a trade and also continue their education. They received a weekly payment that began at 9d (Report 1858–59 p. 76).

SHOPKEEPING

In the early 1900s numerous courses were being developed for industry and commercial education for clerks, accountants and administrative staff; however, a report noted that 'up to the present there has been very little done in the way of providing for those employed in the retail trades instruction as to the nature, qualities, and the supply of articles and commodities with which they deal. The difficulties in the way are no doubt very great but that they may be overcome is shown by the success that has attended classes of this kind specially intended for employees in the grocery trade, which were given in London and in other towns. The success obtained was largely due to the active help given by prominent members of that trade, and to the care taken to secure for each part of each course teachers who had expert knowledge of the matters to be discussed' (Report 1907–08 p. 88).

SHORT INDUSTRIAL TRAINING COURSES

This was a thirteen-week (approximately) **Youth Opportunities Programme** scheme for specific though broad occupational areas.

See also: Work Preparation Courses

Further reading: MSC (1980b)

SHORTHAND

This was described as a **specific subject** in the 1890 **Code** (Report 1889–90 p. 119).

SHORT-TIME WORK COMPENSATION SCHEME

(May 1978–March 1979) Brought in specifically for the textile, footwear and clothing industries to clear the foreseen redundancies.

Its purpose was to encourage employers to adopt short-time working instead of making employees redundant. There were 140 awards covering some 8,000 jobs. It was introduced when the EEC objected to the **temporary employment subsidy**.

See also: Temporary Short-Time Work Compensation Scheme

Further reading: MSC Annual Report 1978–79 p. 7

SIKH SCHOOL

(September 1999) Guru Nanak College in Hayes, Middlesex originally opened as an **independent school** in 1993 and from 1999 became the first Sikh school to become voluntary-aided and receive state funding. In addition to the national curriculum, it also offered classes in Punjabi and Sikh culture and history.

See also: Faith Schools

SIMULTANEOUS METHOD

This method of instruction involved the school master or mistress teaching all the pupils at the same time from a gallery leading to the term '**gallery lesson**'. The classroom was laid out with rows of parallel benches often rising to the back of the class. It was also named the **Lancasterian** method after Mr Joseph Lancaster (who originally set up a school in 1798 in Borough Road) and was adopted by the **British and Foreign School Society**. It contrasted with the **mutual instruction** method and sometimes the two approaches were combined under a mixed method. In the 1840s the designs of schools allowed for both methods to be used (Minutes 1839–40, pp. 46/47).

SINGING

The 1872 and 1874 codes included provisions intended to improve singing and used grants to encourage this activity. In a circular dated May 1872, Inspectors were required to request a minimum of six simple songs in **infants schools** and 12 in **elementary schools**. Singing was included as a class subject in the 1884 **Code** and grants were provided for satisfactory performance (Report 1883–84 pp. 105 and 116).

SINGLE REGENERATION BUDGET

(April 1993) The SRB was formed by the merger of 20 regeneration programmes from five government departments. A number of the **Department of Employment's** programmes were transferred to constitute this single budget including: **Business Start-Up, Compacts, Education Business Partnership, Local Initiative Fund,** The Programme Development Fund, Teacher Placement Service and TEC Challenge (**Training and Enterprise Councils Discretionary Fund**). Its purpose was to provide a coordinated multi-department funding mechanism that was appropriate for local requirements. The SRB later known as the SRB Challenge Fund was allocated through an annual competition. The funds were subsequently allocated through regional development agencies. It is based on a partnership approach that had an agreed delivery plan and the grant was dependent on delivery of specific outputs and achieving key indicators. Part of SRB funding was related to skills development, education and training.

Further reading: Department of Environment (1997); House of Commons Environment Committee (1995); Hall and Mawson (1999)

SIXTH FORM

The development of public secondary education in the early years of the 1900s tended to focus on what was known as the 'Four Years' Course', which was for those aged approximately 12–16 years. Increases in the number of schools and pupils, together with competition for scholarships to Cambridge and Oxford and to pass the London Intermediate Examination, combined with preparation for training colleges, created a demand for more advanced education in a sixth form. In 1913, the **Board of Education** issued a circular that investigated the curriculum in general and also for the sixth form. 'It laid down the principle that there should be specialisation, though not to the excessive degree often practised; it suggested that pupils should follow a course in a group of allied subjects, either in Classics or in Mathematics and Science or in Modern Languages, Literature and History; that, in any case, not the whole of the time should be given to the group, but that time should be reserved for some complementary subjects to be taken more lightly' (Report 1923–24 p. 26). The circular encouraged debate but the main impetus came in 1917 with Mr Fisher obtaining funds to encourage an '**advanced course**' in the sixth form and the proposals were incorporated into the regulations for 1917. A sixth form college was one that catered for pupils aged 16–19.

See also: Advanced Levels

SKILL BUILD

This Welsh initiative was established for all-age unemployed people who were unclear about which line of vocational training they wished to follow. The programme provided work taster placements, motivational training, **basic skills** training where required; and, occupational learning at **national vocational qualification** Levels 1, 2 & 3.

Further reading: http://wales.gov.uk/topics/educationandskills/learners/worklearning/gettingbacktowork/?lang=en (accessed 01 June 2010)

SKILL CHOICE

(April 1993) The Skill Choice initiative was introduced in April 1993 with 15 **TECs/LECs**

initially involved. The objective was to provide credits to 250,000 individuals (mainly in work) during 1993–94 and 1994–95. The Government contributed £25m (Great Britain) over this period with 30 per cent of costs in year one and 40 per cent of costs in year two met by individuals and/or employers. It was a pump-priming initiative to encourage employers to assess training needs by demonstrating the benefits to be gained. Various methods of delivery were studied and TECs/LECs issued vouchers to individuals that contributed towards the cost of assessment and guidance. The individuals could use the vouchers to purchase services from a local accredited supplier.

Further reading: Julie Janes Associates (1994)

SKILLCENTRES

Originally called **government training centres**. In 1980/81 there were 68 skillcentres and 24 annexes. In 1990 skillcentres were sold to Astra Training Services Ltd. Terms were agreed for the majority of STA's training businesses. A short time later Astra became insolvent.

See also: Skills Training Agency; Skillplus

Further reading: Berthoud (1978)

SKILLPLUS

The Skillplus Scheme offered short individually designed **skillcentre** training modules to update and upgrade the existing skills of unemployed people, especially in the field of engineering. In 1981–82, 1,400 unemployed 'craftsmen' were trained and this training marked a diversification of skillcentre training away from 'green labour' adults under **TOPs**.

Further reading: MSC Annual Report 1981/82

SKILLS

The term 'skills' has a broad range of meanings that tend to overlap and sometimes mean slightly different things. The Scottish Executive identified seven different groups: 'personal and learning skills that enable individuals to become effective lifelong learners; literacy and numeracy; the five core skills of communication, numeracy, problem solving, information technology and working with others; employability skills that prepare individuals for employment rather than for a specific occupation; essential skills that include all those above; and, vocational skills that are specific to a particular occupation or sector' (Scottish Government 2007 p. 8). The seventh area is soft skills, for example effective time management, planning and organising.

SKILLS ACCOUNTS

These were trialled in the same areas as **adult learner accounts** from late 2008. The purpose of skills accounts was to support learners to: identify the right course; identify how much financial support there might be; arrange an appointment with a careers advisor; and create an action plan based upon skills and achievements.

Further reading: https://skillsaccounts.direct. gov.uk/Pages/default.aspx (accessed 28 May 2010)

SKILLS ALLIANCE

(14 October 2003) The purpose of the Skills Alliance was to encourage key government departments, and employer and union representatives to join together in a social partnership. The key partners were the Confederation of British Industry, the Trades Union Congress and the Small Business Council. The objective was to work more closely at national, regional, and local levels in order to improve skills, business support and the labour market. It was designed to oversee the skills strategy described in the White Paper *21st Century Skills*. There was a hierarchy: National Skills Alliance, Regional Skills Alliance and Local Skills Alliance (which matched local **Learning and Skills Council** boundaries). Following the Leitch Review, the Skills Alliance was disbanded and replaced by the **UK Commission for Employment and Skills**.

Further reading: DfES (2003)

SKILLS BROKERS

(3 April 2006) Help employers to identify and agree training needs and broker an arrangement with one or more training providers. The skills brokerage service was provided by the **Learning and Skills Council** and is free for employers. It provided access to funding where applicable and monitored the quality of provision and satisfaction of the employer. Some parts of training provided through the **Train to Gain** service attracted subsidised funding. A five step process was used:

- identify the skills a business needs;
- identify the right training;
- agree a tailored training package;
- find available funding; and,
- review the progress that has been made.

A performance management framework was developed to assess the brokers. Performance was primarily measured on the number and engagement of 'hard to reach' employers; employer satisfaction levels; and the achievement of competency and quality standards. Competency standards for brokers were published in February 2006. National standards for brokerage were published in March 2006.

See also: Training Advisory Service

Further reading: www.traintogain.gov.uk/ (accessed 01 June 2010)

SKILLS CHALLENGE

Skills Challenge was described in the 1995 White Paper *Competitiveness: Forging Ahead*. It was designed to address the dis-economies of scale and encourage small firms to invest in skills by issuing a £5m Skills Challenge to groups of small firms to address their shared skill needs. It was a joint initiative between the Department for Education and Employment and the DTI. Groups of at least 10 small companies could bid for awards to develop innovative solutions to shared training needs. The emphasis was on firms employing under 50, but those with up to 200 hundred employees could apply. In 1995, 14 successful bids were announced and the target was for 100 awards to support over 1,000 companies.

See also: National Education and Training Targets

Further reading: DfEE (1996b); (1997a)

SKILLS COACHING SERVICE

This was part of the **New Deal for skills** initiative and was an intensive coaching service targeted at unemployed people who were inactive benefit recipients or **job seekers allowance** recipients. The **Learning and Skills Council** provided a Requirements Document for the coaching provision, which described the annual delivery specifications for nextstep contractors and training providers. Skills coaching was introduced in a number of tranches, the first beginning in April 2005.

SKILLS COMPETITIONS

See: Skills Olympics

SKILLS DEVELOPMENT FUND

(1999) The Skills Development Fund was announced in September 1998 and £39m was allocated to it. The funding package was designed to assist the **regional development agencies** working with **further** and **higher education**, **TECs** and other partners to develop and implement regional skills strategies, especially in priority areas, and to contribute to economic growth. £5m of the

£39m was set aside as a Rapid Response Fund to help in the retraining of those involved with large scale redundancies. It was subsequently integrated within the **Framework for Regional Employment and Skills Action**.

Further reading: GHK (2002); DfEE Departmental Report 2000, Cm 5102

SKILLS DEVELOPMENT SCOTLAND

(1 April 2008) The Scottish Government's (2007) Skills for Scotland: A Lifelong Skills Strategy led to the establishment of Skills Development Scotland, which combined Careers Scotland; **Scottish University for Industry** and **learndirect** Scotland; key skills areas from the Scottish Executive and **Highlands and Islands Enterprise**. The SDS provided advice through Careers Scotland; funding through ILA Scotland; and skills and training through initiatives such as: **Get Ready for Work**; **modern apprenticeships**; **skillseekers**; and, **Training for Work**.

Further reading: www.skillsdevelopmentscotland.co.uk

SKILLS ENTERPRISE NETWORK

The Skills Enterprise Network involved over 30,000 subscribers and provided decision makers with information on recent research and development reports into training, education and development.

Further reading: Department of Employment 1993–94 to 1995–99, Cm 2205, p. 15; DfEE (1999k)

SKILLS ENVOY

(Announced in pre-budget speech 6 December 2006) The Leitch Review argued for a strong coherent employer voice to be delivered through the **UK Commission for Employment and Skills**. As part of this strategy, Lord Digby Jones was appointed as the first skills envoy 'to help build a national consensus about the need to work together to improve the UK's skills'. He subsequently became Minister for Trade Promotion in July 2007 and was no longer eligible to be skills envoy because the two posts were incompatible.

(Pre-Budget Report 2006, *Investing in Britain's Potential: Building our Long-term Future*, Cm 6984, HM-Treasury, 3.92)

SKILLS FOR BUSINESS NETWORK

(October 2002) The Skills for Business Network replaced the **National Training Organisation Network**. The purpose of the SfB is to bring 'centre-stage' the skills needs of employers and to deliver skills-based productivity improvements. It consisted of **sector skills councils** and their regulatory body the **Sector Skills Development Agency**. From 1 April 2008 it was replaced by the **Alliance of Sector Skills Councils**, which was designed to support the network.

Further reading: www.improve-skills.co.uk (accessed 01 June 2010)

SKILLS FOR LIFE

(March 2001) This was the national strategy for raising adult literacy, language (English for speakers of other languages) and numeracy skills. It developed from the Moser Report *A Fresh Start – improving literacy and numeracy*, and its purpose was to improve basic skills and develop a society in which people were able to find and stay in work, thereby improving economic performance and social cohesion. In particular it catered for all those of working age, including those with learning difficulties or disabilities from pre-entry Level to Level 2 inclusive (DfES (2001b). Within the initiative there were: the Skills for Life Improvement Programme; Functional Skills Support Programme; and, Functional Skills for Adults.

Further reading: http://www.skillsforlifenetwork.com/ (accessed 01 June 2010)

SKILLS FOR LIFE QUALIFICATIONS

These qualifications were designed to help people develop the skills that were used in daily life. These were predominantly for people over 16 who had left full-time education, although some 14- to 16-year-old pupils studied them in schools. There were skills for life certificates in: adult literacy; adult numeracy; information and communication technology; and in English for Speakers of Other Languages (ESOL). The certificates could be taken at Entry Level, Level 1 and Level 2. Assessment at Entry Level involved tasks assessed by the learning centre, college or school. Levels 1 and 2 were assessed by 40, multiple choice questions on paper or computer. Skills for life is another term for basic skills.

See also: Basic Skills Agency

SKILLS FOR LIFE STRATEGY UNIT

(November 2000) It is responsible for promoting the national Skills for Life strategy that was launched in March 2001. It had partners in the Prison Service, **Qualifications and Curriculum Authority**, and the **Learning and Skills Development Agency**. The unit was originally located within the **Department for Education and Employment** and subsequently the **Department for Education and Skills**. it was later located in the **Department for Innovation, Universities and Skills**.

Further reading: www.skillsforlifenetwork.com/; http://rwp.excellencegateway.org.uk/readwriteplus/ (accessed 01 June 2010)

SKILLS FOR NEIGHBOURHOOD RENEWAL

Report published by the Policy Action Team on Skills, which was one of 18 teams established to examine issues identified in the Social Exclusion Unit's report on neighbourhood renewal. In particular the Policy Action Team considered the skills gap in poor neighbourhoods; how well institutions such as **TECs/LECs**, **FE** colleges, adult education services, etc. met these needs; how well alternative methods, for example informal learning, outreach units, IT and distance learning motivated adults to be involved with learning; and assessed the number of adults who did not have essential skills.

Further reading: Policy Action Team on Skills (1999)

SKILLS FOR SMALL BUSINESSES

(April 1995) Designed as a three-year programme to assist development of supervisors and others in firms with less than 50 employees, it was intended to address the training problems facing small businesses: they could not spread cost over a larger number of employees, so costs were higher; small firms have higher labour turnover than large firms and thus employers were more reluctant to invest in training; releasing key staff for training was more difficult; and many lacked knowledge to gain access to the training market. The initiative was intended to develop training and assessment skills of 24,000 employees so that they could lead training in their organisations. **TECs** worked with small companies to: identify one key worker per firm to develop their skills as a trainer and assessor; identify which NVQ Level 3 units or above the person should work towards; produce a company training plan; and develop consortia approaches to sharing key worker experience between small firms. There was a low take-up on this programme.

Further reading: GHK Economics and Management (1996)

SKILLS FOR WORK

Skills for Work pilots began in Scotland in August 2005 to provide 14- to 16-year-olds

with knowledge and skills in vocational areas, combined with practical experiences. The courses, which lasted for two years, were not graded and there was no external examination.

Further reading: www.sqa.org.uk/sqa/5951. html

SKILLS FORESIGHT

This research report was completed in April 2000 by **NTO**s. They addressed a sector's current and future skill needs, recruitment difficulties and their causes. It also included regional and national breakdowns, with a strong emphasis on practical actions.

Further reading: DfEE (2000a)

SKILLS FUNDING AGENCY

(1 April 2010) The establishment of the Skills Funding Agency was enabled by the Apprenticeships, Skills, Children and Learning Act 2009. It was one of two bodies that took over from the **Learning and Skills Council**, the other being the **Young People's Learning Agency**. The agency has responsibility for post-19 learning in England with the exception of **higher education**. It is an agency of the **Department of Business, Innovation and Skills** and provides funds to **further education colleges** and other providers through three main gateways: national apprenticeship services (responsible for apprenticeships); employer skills services (**Train to Gain** and **National Employer Service**); and, learner skills services (adult and careers services; **skills accounts**; funding of FE colleges and other providers).

SKILLS OLYMPICS

The skills olympics are a bi-annual event in which competitors compete in 40 skills areas. They were first held in Portugal in 1950, and in 2001 were held in South Korea. They are organised by World Skills, formerly the

International Vocational Training Organisation. Winning competitors of national competitions go forward to the skills olympics.

See also: UK Skills

Further reading: Wilson (2000, pp. 201–08)

SKILLS PLEDGE

(14 June 2007) This initiative encouraged a voluntary public commitment by chief executive officers in England to support employees to gain literacy and numeracy skills and qualifications up to Level 2. The Government committed to providing funding through **Train to Gain** to help employees gain these skills and qualifications. Although employers could commit beyond the basic pledge, the basic wording was:

'On behalf of (company/organisation name), I, as Chief Executive/Chief Operating Officer (or other board member), make a commitment that we shall:

- Actively encourage and support our employees to gain the skills and qualifications that will support their future employability and meet the needs of our business/organisation.
- Actively encourage and support our employees to acquire basic literacy and numeracy skills, and with government support work towards their first level 2 qualification in an area that is relevant to our business/organisation.
- Demonstrably raise our employees' skills and competencies to improve company/organisation performance through investing in economically valuable training and development.

Signed ... '

Department for Work and Pensions (2007); HM Government (2007) *Skills Pledge: A Leaflet for Employers*

See also: Basic Skills Employers Pledge

SKILLS TRAINING AGENCY

(1983) The Skills Training Agency was established as part of the **Manpower Services Commission**; it provided training in craft, technical and supervisory skills, mainly to unemployed people through a network of 60 **skillcentres** (originally called **government training centres**). The agency had a history of making losses and in May 1990 the Government sold 45 centres to Astra Training Services Ltd. Nine centres were closed and the others were sold separately.

Further reading: National Audit Office (1991)

SKILLSEEKERS

(1991) Skillseekers began on a trial basis in 1991 and was delivered across the **local enterprise companies'** network by 1996. It replaced **youth training** in Scotland and was available to young people aged 16–24. It provided financial support for young people involved in work-based learning that led to a nationally recognised qualification. Its aims were to:

- 'Increase the commitment of employers to training and development of young people, thereby ensuring that both the quality and quantity of training available was sufficient;
- Increase the level and volume of skills achieved by young people; and
- Ensure that opportunities were available equally for all young people including those with special needs' (Scottish Executive Enterprise and Lifelong Learning Department 2000a, p. 13).

The *Skills for Scotland* document (Scottish Government 2007 p. 35) announced the phased withdrawal of skillseekers in favour of the **modern apprenticeships**.

SKOPE – CENTRE ON SKILLS, KNOWLEDGE AND ORGANISATIONAL PERFORMANCE

The Centre on Skills, Knowledge and Organisational Performance was established as a result of the 1996–97 Economic and Social Research Council research competition and this multi-disciplinary centre was designed to research the links between knowledge and skills and economic performance. It was originally based at Oxford and Warwick universities and in 2006 the Warwick University centre moved to Cardiff University.

Further reading: www.skope.ox.ac.uk (accessed 21 March 2010)

S LEVEL EXAMINATION

This was a type of higher advanced level examination sometimes used by candidates who wished to enter **higher education**.

SMALL BUSINESS SERVICE

(2000–2007) The SBS was established by the **Department of Trade and Industry** to champion the interests of small businesses and work across government departments and with the **Business Link** network throughout the UK. It purpose was ' ... to build an enterprise society in which all small businesses thrive and achieve their potential'. It had the following aims:

- 'help all small businesses realise their potential, especially by minimising the burden of regulation;
- promote world class business support services to enhance the performance of small businesses;
- promote enterprise across society and particularly in under-represented and disadvantaged groups;
- achieve the highest standards of service delivery and provide value for money'.

www.sbs.gov.uk
(accessed 11 August 2004)

In 2007 the SBS was replaced by Enterprise and Business Support.

See also: Enterprise Directorate

SMALL FIRMS EMPLOYMENT SUBSIDY

(July 1977–Mar 1980) This was a subsidy of £20 per week for 6 months for each full-time job created by small manufacturing firms. Began as a pilot in 1977/78 and then expanded into firms in assisted areas and inner cities. To begin with, the subsidy was available for firms with less than 50 employees, but the limit was raised to firms with less than 200 employees.

Further reading: Department of Employment (1978a)

SMALL FIRMS INFORMATION SERVICE

Designed to provide small firms with a comprehensive information service. The service was transferred to the **training and enterprise councils** in 1991/92.

See also: Business Link

Further reading: Training Agency (1989b)

SMALL FIRMS TRAINING LOANS PROGRAMME

(June 1994) The objective of this initiative was to help small firms, which often under-invested in training, to increase the skills of their employees and increase productivity and growth. The programme was based on the model of the **career development loan** and was run using the same banks. Loans of £500 to £125,000 were available for firms of up to 50 employees.

Further reading: Employment Department Group Departmental Report 1995 Cm 2805 p. 55

SOCIETY FOR PROMOTING CHRISTIAN KNOWLEDGE

(1698) It was originally called the Society for the Propagation of Christian Knowledge and was founded by Reverend Thomas Bray. The **Board of Education** stated that the earliest

289

record of adult education was a circular recommending the establishment of adult evening schools by the Society for Promoting Christian Knowledge in 1711.

See also: Scottish Society for Propagating Christian Knowledge

Further reading: Report 1922–23 p. 102

SOCIETY FOR PROMOTING THE EDUCATION OF THE POOR OF IRELAND

See: Kildare Place Society

SOCIETY FOR THE DIFFUSION OF USEFUL KNOWLEDGE

(1826–48) It was established with support from Lord Brougham to publish inexpensive texts for people attending **mechanics institutes** and **mutual instruction societies**, or for self-education. Among its publications were: *Manual for Mechanics Institutes, Library of Entertaining Knowledge, Library for the Young, Penny Cyclopaedia*, and, *Quarterly Journal of Education*. The University of Central Lancashire traces its origins back to 1828 and the Preston Institution for the Diffusion of Knowledge.

Further reading: Percival (1978)

SOCIETY OF FRIENDS' SCHOOLS

In 1667, the founder of the Society of Friends, George Fox, encouraged the establishment of schools to educate boys and girls 'in all things civil and useful in creation' (Stansfield 1912, p. 129). Voluntary establishment of schools was insufficient, with the result that public boarding schools were begun with the first being at Ackworth near Pontefract.

Further reading: Stansfield (1912)

SOCRATES

A programme run by the European Commission whereby research funding could be obtained by consortia of universities and industry within the EU to carry out work in the field of education and youth. Projects could last up to three years and involved partners carrying out similar work within their own countries, and the production of a report, plus any other form of dissemination, that might be deemed suitable, such as conference papers, papers in journals or even published books based on the results.

Further reading: House of Commons European Standing Committee (1994)

SOUTH WALES BRITISH SCHOOL ASSOCIATION

(1850s) This was established by nonconformists or dissenters for 'promoting education in South Wales according to the unsectarian principles of the **British and Foreign School Society,** with the aid of the Committee of Council on Education' (Minutes 1854–55, p. 641).

SPADE HUSBANDRY

This was the use of spades used by boys in agriculture in **parochial union schools**. The HMI Mr Bowyer, in the Eastern and Midland District commented: 'Spade husbandry still continues to be the principal means of industrial training for boys, though many of the schools, during several years, so dwindled in numbers that the land hired for that purpose by the guardians has been necessarily given up; while, in other instances the greater part of the work is performed by old men. At the Warwick, Stoke-on-Trent, and Boston workhouses, and the Hartismere **House of Industry** (an establishment exclusively for children) the cultivation of the land is directed by an industrial trainer, whose salary is repaid to the union from the Parliamentary grant' (Report 1862–63 pp. 347–48).

SPECIAL AIDS TO EMPLOYMENT

(1944) The **Disablement Advisory Service** (DAS), whose purpose was to encourage employers to adopt progressive policies and practices in the recruitment, retention and career development of people with disabilities, provided assistance to people with disabilities including: special aids (supportive equipment), **adaptions to premises and equipment**, and the **Fares to Work** Scheme.

Further reading: Parker (1990)

SPECIAL APTITUDES SCHEME

(September 1947–31 August 1956) This scheme applied to young people who were unable to find suitable training in their home area and were assisted to undertake training away from home. It operated from September 1947 until 31 August 1956 when it was retitled **Training Allowance Scheme**.

Further reading: Ministry of Labour and National Service Report 1956 Cmnd 242 p. 60

SPECIAL CERTIFICATE

(Scotland) This certificate was awarded by the Secretary of State for Scotland to graduates and recognised them as qualified to teach in **secondary school**s in the subject(s) in which they had received their degree.

SPECIAL EDUCATIONAL NEEDS

Provision for those children requiring special support has been required by statute since the **Elementary Education (Blind and Deaf Children) Act 1893** and the **Elementary Education (Defective and Epileptic Children) Act 1899**. The **1944 Education Act** also recognised the needs of such children and the 1996 Educational Act required **local education authorities** to respond to parents wishes and undertake an assessment of special needs. The Special Educational Needs and Disability Act 2001 provided for SEN children to have mainstream school access and also gave the right to school heads to request that children be assessed. A Special Educational

Needs Coordinator is required in all schools to enable appropriate support for SEN children and to coordinate with parents and school staff.

SPECIAL EMPLOYMENT MEASURES

This was a collective term used during the 1980s to describe some of the **MSC**'s programmes including: **Community Programme; Enterprise Allowance Scheme; Youth Training Scheme; New/Young Workers Scheme; Community Industry Scheme; Job Release Scheme; Jobshare/ Job Splitting Scheme; Job Training Scheme**; and the **jobstart allowance**.

Further reading: Unemployment Unit (1987); Gregg (1990)

SPECIAL EMPLOYMENT NEEDS

(1977) The special employment needs experiment was designed for those who had difficulty in obtaining work because of social, personal or other problems. It was introduced in autumn 1977 to provide special interviewing and intensive placing action. In the first ten months more than 8,500 people were assisted with a 37 per cent success rate into employment and 7 per cent entering or awaiting training.

See also: Special Employment News

Further reading: MSC Annual Report 1978/ 79, p. 8

SPECIAL EMPLOYMENT NEWS

(1977–80) Newspaper - experiment for the long-term unemployed containing adverts for jobs.

See also: Professional and Executive Recruitment

SPECIAL SCHOOLS

Special schools were provided by **local education authorities** and this provision has been available since the **Elementary**

Education (Blind and Deaf Children) Act 1893 and the **Elementary Education (Defective and Epileptic Children) Act 1899**. A special school was one that provided education suitable to those children who had special educational needs and who were not catered for in mainstream school provision. The Education Act 1981 classified children into different categories and special schools catered for different requirements.

See also: Special Educational Needs

SPECIAL SUBJECTS

The term 'special subjects' in elementary schools generally meant additional subjects to the **elementary subjects** of reading, writing and arithmetic; however, the precise meaning tended to change as education developed and they became predominantly known as **specific subjects**. In the 1860s it meant 'The plan for establishing higher departments where higher fees might be charged for learning special subjects, e.g. drawing, grammar for girls, mechanics, mensuration, book-keeping, French' (Report 1866–67 p. 200). Around 1911–12 (Report 1911–12 p. 53) 'Instruction in Special Subjects' was used to describe the main areas of domestic subjects, handicraft and gardening until, 'The effect of the Education Act, 1918, and of the revised system of grants, [was] to abolish the category of "Special Subjects" (at all events in the sense of optional subjects for which special grants were payable), and Local Education Authorities [were then] required to make adequate provision in their areas, as part of the ordinary provision of elementary education, for **practical instruction** appropriate to the needs of the pupils and circumstances of the Schools'. (Report 1919–20 p. 19).

See also: National Curriculum

SPECIAL TEMPORARY EMPLOYMENT PROGRAMME

(April 1979–March 1981) STEP was introduced on 1 April 1979 and was designed to provide 25,000 jobs in its first year to people aged 19 and over, with priority being given to those in the 19–24 age range. A further 8,000 jobs in supervisory and similar posts were created for unemployed adults. Sponsors were encouraged to come forward with projects that provided worthwhile work that would not otherwise be done. It was a successor to the **Job Creation Programme** and **Work Experience Programme**. The long-term unemployed were given work of community benefit for up to one year. It was withdrawn because targets were not met and was replaced by the **Community Enterprise Programme**.

Further reading: MSC (1978c); MSC Annual Report 1978–79, p. 23

SPECIAL TRAINING MEASURES

(1975–79) Special training measures were run between 1975 and 1979 during which 30- to 40,000 young people per year were helped to obtain apprenticeships or long-term training. **MSC** funding was channelled through **industrial training boards** and other industry training organisations. These were counter-cyclical measures designed to reduce unemployment and increase skills.

Further reading: Chapman and Tooze (1987)

SPECIALIST SCHOOLS

(1994–) The purpose of specialist schools was to develop secondary schools through the encouragement of specialisation and collaboration. The aim was for 'all secondary schools to develop a distinct ethos and, through the focus on a curriculum specialism, bring about whole school improvements for pupils across the ability range'. Originally there were ten specialisms: arts, business and enterprise, engineering, humanities, language, mathematics and computing, music, science, sports and technology. It is possible for schools to combine two specialisms. The original emphasis on specialisation in technology, that is, in **city technology colleges**, changed to one that envisaged the 'specialist school' status improving overall performance. In December 2004, 12 trailblazer schools were invited to begin pilots during 2005 in a new Specialist Schools Programme strand – Special Educational Needs. This allowed them to specialise in one of the areas of the SEN Code of Practice: communication and interaction; cognition and learning; behavioural, emotional and social development; and sensory and/or physical needs (OFSTED 2001c). In 2007–08, 208 of the strongest schools were given high performing specialist school status, which also involved helping other schools.

See also: Beacon Schools; City Technology Colleges; Specialist Schools and Academies Trust

SPECIALIST SCHOOLS AND ACADEMIES TRUST

(2005) This originally began as the **city technology colleges** Trust in 1987. In 2003, it changed its name to better reflect its involvement with **specialist schools**, and from 29 September 2005 was known as the Specialist Schools and Academies Trust.

See also: Trust Schools

Further reading: www.ssatrust.org.uk (accessed 26 July 2009)

SPECIFIC SUBJECTS

(1880) Specific subjects i.e. English, mathematics (algebra and Euclid), Latin, French, German, mechanics, animal physiology, physical geography, botany and domestic economy were increasingly taught in schools as the curriculum was loosened in order to build upon the **elementary subjects** of reading, writing and arithmetic; they stretched the more-able pupils; and they encouraged pupils to stay longer at school after the age of ten

when they could leave having passed the elementary subjects at **Standard** IV. Although other subjects had been taught previously they were not eligible for grants but this situation altered with a change in the **Code** for 1880, which then allowed school managers to 'extend to any others which can be reasonably accepted as special branches of elementary instruction, and properly treated in reading books, graded so as to suit the capacities of the children of various ages, in whose hands they are placed' (Report 1879–80 pp. xvii–xviii). Specific subjects differed from **class subjects** in that 'grants are paid (Article 21) in respect of the proficiency of the scholars as tested by individual examination', which differed from class subjects where grants were awarded for the 'general proficiency of the class' (Report 1882–83 p. xvii). Students were not expected to take more than two specific subjects. The range of subjects taught in schools increased and the 1883 Code allowed for this expanded provision by stating that '[a]ny other subject, other than those mentioned in the Article, may, if sanctioned by the Department, be taken as a specific subject, provided that a graduated scheme of teaching it be submitted to, and approved by, the Inspector' (Report 1882–83 p. 113). In 1900, '[t]he old classification of subjects as "obligatory", "class", "specific", was replaced by a twofold division into – (a) Subjects to be taken "as a rule" in all schools though not necessarily in every class – English; Arithmetic; Drawing (for boys); Needlework (for girls); Lessons, including Object Lessons, on Geography, History, Common Things; Singing and Physical exercises. (b) A list of subjects, one or more of which was to be taken when circumstances in the opinion of the Inspector made it desirable. These were the old "specific" subjects' (Report 1910–11 p. 20).

See also: Elementary Subjects; National Curriculum; Obligatory Subjects; Optional Subjects

SPINNING SCHOOLS

These were schools in which the spinning of yarn was taught and one of the earliest was introduced by the **Scottish Society for Promoting Christian Knowledge** in Stornaway in 1763.

STANDARD

(1862) Schools receiving grants from the Committee of Council on Education were required to educate children up to a certain specified level. Six standards (I-VI) were specified in the **Revised Code of Regulations** detailing the expected attainments in reading, writing and arithmetic. For example, Standard V stated: 'Reading: A few lines of poetry from a reading book used in the first class of the school. Writing: A sentence slowly dictated once, by a few words at a time, from a reading book used in the **first class** of the school. Arithmetic: A sum in compound rules, common weights and measures' (Report 1861–62 p. xxiii). There was a general correspondence between the standards and the ages of children: children of 10, 11 and 12 were expected to be able to respectively pass Standards IV, V and VI (Report 1861–62 p. xi). As the children progressively stayed longer at school, the **New Code** of 1882 introduced a Standard VII for elementary subjects of reading, writing and arithmetic, and **specific subjects/class subjects** of English, geography and elementary science (Report 1881–82 pp. 133–35).

STANDARD SUBJECTS

In the 1880s the term 'standard subjects' meant **elementary subjects** (Report 1885–86 pp. 131–32).

STANDARDS FUND

(1998/99) Launched to replace **grants for educational support and training**. This work-related programme of learning for 14- to 16-year-olds was one of a number of initiatives (including **action research** and **Key Stage** 4 demonstration projects) launched to support locally derived and delivered work-related learning projects. This was part of the government's commitment to extending the range and quality of vocational and work-related opportunities for pupils at Key Stage 4. The programme was targeted at the disaffected and under-achievers, but also provided opportunities for 14–16-year-olds. It encouraged schools to collaborate with other partners, including **LEA**s, **FE** colleges and **TECs**, to develop innovative approaches to vocational and work-related education that help pupils make a successful transition into adult and working life. Expenditure in 1997–98 was £3.1m and in 1998–99 it was £5.1m.

Further reading: DfEE Departmental Report, Expenditure Plans 1998–99, Cm 3910, p. 15; DfEE (2000f)

STANDARDS PROGRAMME – THE

The Standards Programme was developed to provide advice, guidance and help to employers to establish occupational standards of competence at all levels across all industry and commerce. These standards formed the basis for **NVQs** accredited by the **National Council for Vocational Qualifications** and **SVQs** in Scotland by the **Scottish Vocational Education Council** (SCOT-VEC).

See also: Occupational Standards Councils

Further reading: Department of Employment Report February 1993, Cm 2205, p. 16; Harrison (1989)

STANDARDS UNIT

(2002–05) This was a short-lived body responsible for teaching standards in the **further education** and skills sector and some of its responsibilities were taken over by the **Quality Improvement Agency for Lifelong Learning**. The Standards Unit, overseen by the **Department for Education and Skills**, worked with partners and practitioners to support the learning of best practice in classrooms, workshops, workplaces or through e-learning. It also examined assessment and the curriculum and introduced subject learning coaches to provide peer-to-peer coaching of colleagues in the areas of business education; construction; **entry to employment**; science; mathematics; ICT; health and social care; and, land based studies.

STANDARDS VERIFICATION AGENCY

(January 2005) The Standards Verification Agency replaced the **Further Education National Training Organisation** and took responsibility for qualifications in the **Initial Teacher Training** scheme and post-16 teaching; adult literacy and numeracy teachers; and teachers of English for speakers of other languages. It became a fully owned subsidiary of **Lifelong Learning UK** and was known as Standards Verification UK.

See also: Teaching in the Lifelong Learning Sector Qualifications

Further reading: www.lluk.org (accessed 18 December 2009)

STARNET PROJECT

(1989–91) The Starnet Project used the European Space Agency's communications satellite 'Olympus' to deliver training courses. The project designed by the Polytechnic of the South West, Plymouth, attempted to transmit 60 hours of interactive programmes to 1,000 UK trainees, who would be able to talk by telephone to the presenter and other trainees.

Further reading: Employment Gazette 1989 p. 279

STATE BOARDING SCHOOLS

These are schools which receive funding from the state for educational costs, and parents or guardians pay for the boarding expenses; in 2010 there were 35 such schools in England and Wales. Attendance eligibility is for UK nationals, EU nationals and those who have a right to UK residence.

STATISTICAL SERVICES DIVISION

The division produced monthly, quarterly, and annual statistics on employment, unemployment, vacancies, redundancies, industrial disputes, earnings, skill shortages, training and tourism. The Statistical Services Division also carried out the New Earnings Survey and Census of Employment, and also commissioned the Office of Population Censuses and Surveys to research the **Labour Force Survey**. Data collection was subsequently transferred to the **Office for National Statistics**.

Further reading: Department of Employment Report 1991, Cm 1506, p. 26; Employment Gazette 1991 pp. 285–86

STATUTE OF ARTIFICERS 1563

This act was introduced to address the legal relationships between masters and servants; if there was a dispute, it could be brought before a Justice of the Peace or mayor. The act was also designed to manage the disturbances and crime caused by the increasing number of vagrants and vagabonds who had been outcast by the dissolution of the monasteries and displaced as a result of the land enclosures. In brief, the act required all unmarried people under the age of thirty who had served an apprenticeship to serve a master if requested; those aged between 12 and 60 to look after land and animals when directed; and women aged between 12 and 40 to serve if requested. It also enabled wages to be set annually by justices, with the amount to be paid to the workers dependent on circumstances such as demand and labour supply.

STEPS TO WORK

(2009) This **Department for Employment and Learning** Northern Ireland initiative was designed for unemployed people over 18 and consisted of three steps: first, one-to-one guidance and short courses; second, from three to fifty-two weeks training or work experience and support with an additional £15.38 per week; third, an additional six weeks of support from an advisor to help find a job.

STOW, DAVID

(1793–1864) Stow was a Scottish educationalist who established a Sabbath school in 1816 and subsequently a 'Local School' (his term). Later, on 31 October 1837, he went on to help establish, through the Glasgow Educational Association, a normal seminary for the training of teachers. He published eleven editions of his **Glasgow training system**, which focused on intellectual, physical and moral education and the 1845 edition contained a chapter on moral school training with areas including: calling names, charity, half-lie, honesty, lying, and obstinacy. Some editions of the training system had chapters on Book-keeping and Female Schools of Industry. He advocated that 'teaching was not training' (by teaching he meant lecturing) and stressed that pupils should not only be instructed but trained to behave morally. He also used a system of criticism lessons for the trainee teachers, where each of them taught a lesson to pupils and were later criticised by the others and an accompanying teacher.

Further reading: Wood (1987)

STRAW PLAITING SCHOOLS

(1860s) Dealers cut and prepared straw, which was then sold or let to cottagers and the plaited straw bought back or paid for on completion. Children began plaiting in their homes as early as four years old, 'for the flexibility and tenderness of their fingers is best preserved by beginning early' (Report 1865–66 p. 170). In addition, plaiting schools were established largely in the cottage living rooms in Hertfordshire and Buckinghamshire where groups of children were supervised. 'These schools, or workshops, seldom profess to teach anything besides "a little reading", which is commonly found to be "a mere mechanical pronunciation of words, to which little or no meaning is attached, and the art is sometimes lost after the children leave school"' (Report 1865–66 p. 179). These schools were eventually forced to close by the Factory Act (Report 1874–75 p. 90).

STUDENT LOANS COMPANY

The UK Student Loans Company, a non-departmental public body, was established to provide loans and grants to students.

See also: Career Development Loan

Further reading: www.slc.co.uk (accessed 26 July 2009)

STUDENT TEACHERS

(1907) The *Report on the Instruction and Training of Pupil Teachers 1903–07 (Cd.3582)* considered whether the traditional method of instruction and teaching of children was a suitable means for developing future teachers. To provide an alternative pathway a 'bursary system' was introduced in which intending teachers did not need to have practical experience of **elementary school** and could defer this until training college, thereby allowing them to continue their education until 17 or 18 years of age. The **Board of Education** provided grants to **local education authorities**, which enabled young people who intended to become teachers to continue their education for an additional year, and they were titled '**bursars**'. Bursars who had satisfactorily completed their Leaving Examination were entitled to enter training colleges one year earlier, at 17, than former **pupil-teachers**. If an ex-bursar wished to get practical teaching experience before entering training college, they were called 'student teachers' (Report 1906–07 p. 53). This system of grants to LEAs for individual Bursars was discontinued after the Act of 1918.

STUDIO SCHOOLS

In September 2007, small trials began with 23 14-year-olds at Barnfield College and Barnfield Academy West in Luton in collaboration with the **Department for Education and Skills**' Innovation Unit. It was intended that the trials would be scaled up to **secondary school**s containing around 300 pupils that would teach the national curriculum using interdisciplinary, enterprise themes that had an emphasis on practical work and enterprise. There would be mixed-aged teams and each pupil would have a coach. The schools were designed to provide an alternative option, especially for those pupils alienated by traditional schooling.

Further reading: http://launchpad.youngfound ation.org/fund/learning-launchpad/portfolio/ project/studio-schools (accessed 01 June 2010)

SUBSCRIPTION SCHOOLS

These were schools which were funded from several sources. People might gather together and each pay a sum of money, a subscription, for the establishment of a school. Parents might also pay a subscription for the school so that their children might attend; the parents might also pay additional **school pence** or fees. Landowners and proprietors might also contribute. Subscriptions were also collected by **educational societies**. In many cases the very impoverished did not pay to attend school, or paid a reduced amount.

Further reading: Minutes 1844, Vol. 2 pp. 213/330

SUCCESS THROUGH SKILLS

(2006) The draft consultation document in 2004 was the first to consider overall skills strategy. It consisted of four broad themes:

understanding the demand for skills; improving the skills levels of the workforce; improving the quality and relevance of education and training; and, tackling the skills barriers to employment and employability. Three types of skills were defined: essential skills – literacy, numeracy and ICT; employability skills – the key skills of team working, problem solving and flexibility; and, work-based skills – those skills specific to an occupation or sector. An essential skills programme was developed.

Further reading: Department for Employment and Learning (March 2005)

SUMMER SCHOOLS

The Government increasingly encouraged vacation courses for teachers and in the summer of 1924 there were six in England, organised by bodies other than local education authorities, compared with four in the summer of 1923. Two of the courses were under the direction of the Educational Handwork Association and one of the courses was specially arranged for teachers of the deaf.

Further reading: Report 1924–25

SUNDAY SCHOOLS

(1780) The Sunday school movement was begun by Robert Raikes, who started a school for boys from the slums in Gloucester. Teaching was held on a Sunday because many of the boys were working on the other days of the week and instruction was largely learning to read from the Bible. The schools expanded rapidly and by 1830 were educating more than one million people. The schools were run by a number of churches and taught Scripture and other areas of religion. In addition, many of them taught other subjects such as reading, writing, arithmetic, grammar, secular history and elocution. Those scholars who attended were not only of school age but there were also many young men and women and some of an older age.

Some of these Sunday schools then began to offer week-day evening meetings of the Sunday schools and then progressed to offering day-schools free for the poorest children (Minutes 1848/49/50 Vol. 2, p. 296). Established at a time when there was little education for the poor, the Sunday schools had a major influence on the development of state school provision (Minutes 1840–41, p. 164–65).

SUPERVACS

An automated system for the distribution of vacancy details run by the **Employment Service**.

Further reading: Cameron and Robinson (1983); Employment Department (1991/92)

SUPPORT FOR PEOPLE AT A DISADVANTAGE IN THE LABOUR MARKET

Support was provided to ensure equality of opportunity for individuals disadvantaged as a result of:

- discrimination;
- disability;
- age;
- lack of basic skills including language skills; and,
- where they live.

Further reading: DfEE Departmental Report 2001–02 to 2003–04, Cm 5102

SUPPORTED EMPLOYMENT PROGRAMME

The Supported Employment Programme enabled 22,000 people with severe disabilities to get and keep jobs. These people, who could work, were unlikely to do so because of limited productivity capability. Research into the programme revealed a high degree of satisfaction amongst participants and providers. From April 2001 it was known as **Workstep**.

See also: Sheltered Employment Scheme

Further reading: Employment Service (1999)

SURE START

(1998) The Sure Start initiative had the objective of providing children with the best start in life by integrating early years education, child care and family support. It began in 1998 and was rolled out in waves, with the first being targeted at deprived areas in 1999. A significant driver for this initiative was that investment in early child support might have a greater lifetime impact and be more economically effective than interventions later in life.

See also: Early Years Foundation Stage

Further reading: www.dcsf.gov.uk/everychild matters/earlyyears/surestart/whatsurestartdoes/ (accessed 01 June 2010)

SWEDISH DRILL

In the 1895 **Code** a school would only earn the highest grant for discipline and organisation if there was instruction in physical exercises, for example Swedish drill. This introduction of exercise into the curriculum formally recognised a trend that had been developing for a number of years; a school inspector noted that it had been used in several girls' schools (Report 1883–84 p. 314).

T

TALENTMAP

(7 July 2009) The **UK Commission for Employment and Skills** developed talentmap as an online tool and framework to provide a simple, 'jargon free', overview of education, employment and skills for employers, partners, brokers and providers. It was also designed to help organisations find and access funds to develop talent and skills. There were five main routes within talentmap: develop your people; find new people; improve performance; engage with education; and, support your industry.

Further reading: www.talentmap.ukces.org.uk (accessed 01 June 2010)

TAX RELIEF FOR VOCATIONAL TRAINING

See: Vocational Training Tax Relief

TEACHER PLACEMENT SERVICE

Originally funded by the **Department of Trade and Industry** and then by the **Employment Department**. The service allowed all teachers to undertake work placements and, thereby, broaden their understanding of the needs of industry and commerce. This was designed to relate teaching closer to the world of work. The service was later managed by **education business partnerships**. It was subsequently renamed **Professional development placements**.

Further reading: National Curriculum Council (1991); DfES Departmental Report 2002 Cm 5402 p. 138

TEACHER TRAINING

In September 1960, the training of teachers was increased to a three-year course.

See also: Initial Teacher Training

Further reading: Ministry of Labour Gazette 1961, p. 332

TEACHER TRAINING AGENCY

(Autumn 1994–31 August 2005) The Council for the Accreditation of Teacher Education was succeeded by the Teacher Training Agency, which was responsible for the funding and quality control of **initial teacher training** (ITT); for supporting continuous professional development of serving teachers; for promoting teaching as a profession; and for commissioning research. It was superseded by the **Training and Development Agency for Schools**.

See also: Initial Teacher Training; In-service Education and Training

Further reading: Teacher Training Agency (1997)

TEACHER TRAINING DAYS

Originally known as 'Baker days' after the proposal of Kenneth Baker, Secretary of

State, who suggested and then implemented the system whereby teachers would have a day when there were no pupils in the schools and could concentrate solely on training needs within their establishment.

TEACHERS ASSOCIATIONS

These developed in the 1850s to support the professional and practical development of teachers. Associations were found in most towns and cities, including Halifax and Sheffield, with lectures at Leeds Church Schoolmasters' Association on many subjects including: 'The progress of maritime commerce; The causes of unpunctuality and irregularity of attendance in children, and the remedies; The advantages of teaching music from notes' (Minutes 1855–56, p. 280). These local associations then reported to national associations, for example the General Association of Church Schoolmasters (Minutes 1855–56, p. 276).

See also: General Teaching Council

TEACHERS REGISTRATION COUNCIL

(1902–49) This registration authority was established by an Order of Council under Section 4 of the **Board of Education Act 1899**. Its purpose was to establish and keep a register of teachers and the posts that they occupied or had occupied. The order for this was presented on 6 March 1902 and stated: 'For the purpose of forming and keeping such a register of teachers, there shall be established a registration authority, called the Teachers' Registration Council, and in this Order referred to as the council, which shall consist provisionally of twelve members, of whom six shall be appointed by the President of the **Board of Education**, and of the remaining six one member shall be appointed by each of the following bodies: The Conference of Headmasters, The Incorporated Association of Head Mistresses, The Association of Head Mistresses, The College of Preceptors, The Teachers' Guild of Great Britain and Ireland, The National Union of Teachers' (Board of Education 1901–02 p. 112). There were two parts. Column A included teachers defined by the Board of Education: 'All certified teachers known to the Board of Education to have been employed since January 1, 1901, in **elementary schools**, training colleges, or **pupil-teacher** centres under inspection by the Board of Education, or in Poor Law schools or certified reformatory schools or **industrial schools**. Column B was composed of secondary school teachers who had paid one guinea and had a university degree or similar qualification, and after a probationary period who had received a teachers' diploma' (Willis 2005 p. 23). The cost to teachers and the Board of Education; the failure to keep it up to date; its lack of comprehensive coverage; no authority to remove the names of deceased teachers; and no records of additional experience and qualifications, were considered unsatisfactory and the council ceased operations in March 1908. It was re-established in 1912, with registrations commencing in 1914 and continuing until 1948; the council ended in 1949.

Further reading: Report 1907–08 p. 121

See also: General Teaching Council

TEACHERS SERVICE BOOK

(1926) This was introduced in 1926 to reduce the administrative load with regard to salary and pensions. 'The need has long been felt of an authoritative record of a teacher's service which would serve for the purposes of both salary and superannuation and would render it unnecessary for local authorities, on appointing a teacher, to obtain certified records of his service from his previous employers' (Report 1925–26 p. 5).

TEACHERS TV

(8 February 2005) Funded by the **Department for Children, Schools and Families**,

this television channel was designed to support teaching staff and school professions.

Further reading: www.teachers.tv (accessed 01 June 2010)

TEACHING CERTIFICATES

In 1846 the Committee of Council on Education resolved to introduce a system of examination papers and oral examinations and award Certificates of Character and Conduct for school masters and mistresses, **pupil-teachers** and stipendiary monitors in order to raise teaching standards. The examinations were held at Easter. The committee also resolved to issue pensions to those teachers who were unable to teach due to age or infirmity, provided they had taught for at least 15 years. The most successful at the examinations might become **Queen's Scholars**. It was also called a Certificate of Merit divided into 1st, 2nd and 3rd class (Minutes 1846, vol. 1 p. 2). Subsequently, the 'Minutes' (1851 vol 1 p. 20) describe four levels for teachers in workhouses: certificate: permission/probation/competency/efficiency. With the **New Code**, Article 59 allowed for HMIs to certify teachers' efficiency if they had been teaching for ten years or more and this clause helped overcome the shortage of qualified teachers, who were needed as a result of the universal provision of schooling provided for in the Education Act 1870 (Minutes 1873–74 p. cliii).

See also: Postgraduate Certificate of Education

TEACHING COMPANY SCHEME

The TCS involved the participating company initiating action to improve its performance, profitability and management. It did this in partnership with a university that had the relevant knowledge and its main purpose was to encourage lasting partnerships between higher education and industry. Governmental grants were provided to support this scheme and graduates who were appointed to work on the project were called teaching company associates. The TCS was replaced in June 2003 with **knowledge transfer partnerships**.

Further reading: Humble (1989)

TEACHING IN THE LIFELONG LEARNING SECTOR QUALIFICATIONS

The **Department for Education and Skills** (2004) policy paper *Equipping Our Teachers for the Future* described the reform of **initial teacher training** in the lifelong learning and skills sector. From 1 September 2007, teachers entering the post-16 and **further education** sector were required to take the 30-hour Preparing to Teach in the Lifelong Learning Sector (PTTLS or 'Petals') Course. The course had to be completed during the first year of teaching and it provided a license to practice. Teachers were then expected to achieve the Certificate in Teaching in the Lifelong Learning Sector (CTTLS or 'kettles') or the Diploma in Teaching in the Lifelong Learning Sector (DTTLS or 'Detols'). When the qualifications were completed, the teacher would then complete an induction year called a 'period of professional formation' and, following successful completion, a full licence to practice would be awarded giving the title Qualified Teacher, Learning and Skills (QTLS). Associate teachers or instructors, trainers or technicians with fewer teaching responsibilities were expected to achieve Associate Teacher, Learning and Skills (ATLS). Those teachers who only taught higher education level in a **further education** setting were exempt from needing these qualifications.

See also: Learning Support Practitioner; Lifelong Learning UK

Further reading: www.lluk.org (accessed 01 June 2010)

TEACHING QUALITY ENHANCEMENT FUND

(1999) This fund was established by the **Higher Education Funding Council for**

England to support learning through a number of initiatives: the **Higher Education Academy**, National Teaching Fellowship Scheme, 74 Centres for Excellence in Teaching and Learning.

Further reading: Higher Education Consultancy Group (2005)

TECHNICAL AND SCIENTIFIC REGISTER

(1955) This was a register of all those out of work who had a technical or scientific background. It also listed job vacancies. It was discontinued in the early 1970s and succeeded by the **Professional and Executive Register**.

Further reading: PER (1976); Price (2000)

TECHNICAL AND VOCATIONAL EDUCATION INITIATIVE

(September 1983) The purpose of the **MSC**'s TVEI was to increase the influence on curriculum design in schools and colleges to prepare 14–18-year-olds for work, particularly in the areas of science, technology, information technology and languages, and help them be more effective and enterprising. It encouraged them to improve skills and qualifications in these areas. In addition, it provided guidance and counselling, records of achievement and action plans. TVEI resulted in increased numbers of students taking balanced science- and technology-based courses. Funding for TVEI was still detailed on page nine of the **Department for Children, Schools and Families** Departmental Report in 2008.

Further reading: Atkins (1986); Chitty (1986); Dale (1985); Dale et al. (1990)

TECHNICAL AND VOCATIONAL EDUCATIONAL INITIATIVE RELATED IN-SERVICE TRAINING FOR TEACHERS

(April 1985–1998) In-service training for secondary school and **further education**

teachers, especially those teaching students aged 14–18. In 1985/86, 119 authorities applied for TRIST funding from the **MSC** (which was allowed for all but two), and £6.9m was spent that year. An emphasis was placed on the development links with industry.

Further reading: University of Exeter (1988)

TECHNICAL CERTIFICATES

In November 2001, the DfES announced plans for the development of knowledge-focused technical certificates for **modern apprenticeships**. This involved **national training organisations** and **sector skills councils** consulting on how wider employment skills might be incorporated within modern apprenticeships. The technical certificates are the vocationally related qualifications that provide the underpinning knowledge of the **NVQ**.

Further reading: Davey (2002)

(PRELIMINARY) TECHNICAL CERTIFICATES

(early 1900s) Preliminary technical certificates and junior commercial certificates were awarded by various institutes, particularly in the industrial centre of the north of England. The West Riding of Yorkshire County Council held examinations and awarded certificates and the Midland Union of Educational Institutes held examinations and awarded technical, commercial and general certificates in Lincolnshire, Staffordshire, Warwickshire and Worcestershire. The largest institute was the Lancashire and Cheshire Union of Institutes, which examined 12,996 male students in 1909.

See also: (Preliminary) Commercial Certificates

Further reading: Laurie (1912a)

TECHNICAL CERTIFICATES (SCOTLAND)

The Secretary of State for Scotland granted these certificates to recognise a person as being qualified to teach applied science, domestic science, music, and other technical subjects.

Further reading: Benge (1958)

TECHNICAL COLLEGES

Circular 305, 21 June 1956, *The Organisation of Technical Colleges*, '[d]escribes how the three existing types of college can contribute to the policy laid down in the White Paper on Technical Education (Cmd. 9703)'.

Benge (1958)

See also: Technical Schools; Technical Institution

TECHNICAL DAY CLASSES

During the 1920s, technical day classes were described as providing 'mainly Vocational or Domestic and normally in part-time or short full-time courses' to those students 'over exemption age' (Report 1925–26 p. 57).

TECHNICAL EDUCATION COMMITTEES

See: Technical Instruction Act 1889

TECHNICAL INSTITUTION

This was a term used by the **Board of Education** to encompass institutions that provided technical courses and that were not always separately distinguishable due to the development of provision. Technical institution courses included those in technical schools, **technical day classes** and universities (Report 1911–12 p. 95) A departmental committee on the organisation of the **Royal College of Science** also considered technical and technological education and concluded that ' ... the position of this country makes further provision for advanced technological education essential. The Committee lay down, as a first principle in this matter, that an essential condition of a food

technical education of whatever grade is a good general education of a corresponding preliminary grade. In view of this, it is satisfactory to note the development of the "Technical Institutions", in respect of which, since 1903, we have made grants under Chapter 3 of the Regulations. These institutions, among which are included Technical Departments more or less closely associated with Universities and University Colleges, provide courses of technical and technological instruction extending over two, three, or, four years for students qualified by their previous general education to profit by it. They may fairly be considered as being to some extent non-local in character, and the cost of their provision and maintenance is necessarily high' (Report 1906–07 p. 74).

TECHNICAL INSTRUCTION

The **Technical Instruction Act 1889** stated that '[t]he expression "technical instruction" shall mean instruction in the principles of science and art applicable to industries, and in the application of special branches of science and art to specific industries or employments. It shall not include teaching the practice of any trade or industry or employment but, save as aforesaid, shall include instruction in the branches of science and art with respect to which grants are for the time being made by the Department of Science and Art' (Report 1900–01 Vol. 3, p. 413).

See also: Science and Art Department

TECHNICAL INSTRUCTION ACT 1889

This act enabled local authorities to levy rates to support technical and manual instruction with funding managed by technical instruction committees or technical education committees within county councils or borough councils. The act stated: 'A local authority may from time to time out of the local rate supply or aid the supply of technical or manual instruction, to such extent and on such terms as the authority think expedient, subject to ... restrictions' (Report 1900–01 Vol. 3 p. 411). This technical instruction was not to be delivered in elementary schools, and involved science and art but not industrial practices and trades. 'The expression "Technical Instruction" shall mean instruction in the principles of science and art applicable to industries and in the application of special branches of science and art to specific industries and employments. It shall not include the practice of any trade or industry or employment, but, save as aforesaid, shall include instruction in the branches of science and art with respect to which grants are for the time being made by the Department of Science and Art'. Also, whisky money raised from publicans through the Local Taxation (Customs and Excise) Act 1890 could be used by local authorities for technical education and was distributed initially from the **Science and Art Department**. In 1900 a list of subjects sanctioned since the Technical Instruction Acts of 1889 and 1891 and the Technical Instruction Amendment (Scotland) Act 1892 was extensive and included: agriculture, boat building, bread making, coal tar products, design for textiles, electrical engineering, glass manufacture, insurance, mechanical engineering, paper manufacture, road making, tailors' work, veterinary science, and watch and clock making (Report 1899–1900 pp. 6–7).

TECHNICAL INTERMEDIATE SCHOOL (NORTHERN IRELAND)

This type of school provided a pre-vocational programme lasting 2–4 years and was associated with a **further education** institution which many of the pupils subsequently attended.

See also: Secondary Intermediate Schools

TECHNICAL SCHOOLS

A technical school was founded in Bradford in 1878 and, following the Technical Instruction Act 1889 (also Technical Schools

(Scotland) Act 1887), technical schools were of two main types: day technical schools and evening technical schools. Mr Pallinger, HMI, commented: 'It is very gratifying to be able to report that the Day Technical Schools are increasing in number and importance. There can be no doubt whatever that it is to these schools to which we must look for the provision of technical instruction if the industries of the country are to be improved and foreign competition checked. Evening classes, though useful in their own way, cannot be expected to have much effect in this direction. In a day school the students come fresh to their work and are occupied all day long in the study of science, art and technology' (Board of Education 1900–01 Vol. 2, p. 284).

The 1905 Code dispensed with the time of day during which technical education was received and day and evening classes were treated equally (Report 1906–07 p. 73). During the early 1900s, the technical day schools were considered to provide the highest level of technical instruction and '[i]n such Technical Institutions the instruction is to a large extent of University standard, and several of the technological and professional departments of our modern Universities have been included among them' (Report 1908–09 p. 88).

The courses were for students above sixteen years old and lasted for two, three or four years full-time and, while predominantly in areas of 'engineering – mechanical, electrical, civil, structural, sanitary, and mining', might also include 'architecture, carriage building, chemical trades, metallurgy, textile industries, leather manufacture, the boot trades, technical optics, photography, agriculture, and horticulture' (Report 1908–09 p. 89). Technical schools were also known as **technical institutions**.

See also: Colleges of Advanced Technology

(JUNIOR) TECHNICAL SCHOOLS

These were technical schools that were sometimes integrated with technical schools and were sometimes independent. The age range was generally up to sixteen years, for example Stanley Trade School, Croydon (Report 1924–25 p. 27). In the 1920s junior technical schools were described as providing 'Preparation for industrial, commercial or domestic employment, with continued general education, in full-time courses of two or three years' for students 'aged 13 or 14 on admission' (Report 1925–26 p. 57).

TECHNICIAN EDUCATION COUNCIL

See: Business and Technology Education Council

TECHNOLOGY SCHOOLS

The Education Reform Act 1988 enabled the introduction of 15 **city technology colleges** in the period to 1993; however, the need to partially fund these schools and the reluctance by some **local education authorities** hindered their development. A further number of grant-maintained and voluntary-aided schools were then designated as technology colleges with the Government matching £100,000 in private sponsorship, and also providing additional continuing support. Other specialisms were added with languages in 1995, and arts and sport in 1996. The School Standards and Framework Act allowed the schools to select 10 per cent of their intake and the 2001 White Paper *Schools Achieving Success* expanded the provision to encourage secondary schools to become **specialist schools**.

TECHNOLOGY SCHOOLS INITIATIVE

(1992–93) The objective of this **Department for Education** initiative was to support capital expenditure in schools that were committed to specialising in the teaching of technology and its vocational applications. Schools bid competitively for a grant and were chosen based on the quality of the plans for technology teaching. More than 200 schools received grants in the first two years of the initiative. In 1992–93, £25m was allocated and £23m in 1993–94.

Further reading: OFSTED (1994)

TECHNOLOGY STRATEGY BOARD

The Technology Strategy Board was originally established in October 2004 to manage the **Department of Trade and Industry**'s technology programmes. Its vision was '[f]or the UK to be seen as a global leader in innovation and a magnet for technology-intensive companies, where new technology is applied rapidly and effectively to wealth creation' (Sainsbury 2007 p. 47). In July 2007, a newly enlarged, non-departmental public body, the Technology Strategy Board, was established with a mission 'to promote and support research into, and development and exploitation of, science and technology and new ideas for the development of business, in order to increase sustainable economic growth and improve the quality of life' www.innovateuk.org/aboutus/faqs.ashx (accessed 14 April 2010). The TSB manages a number of programmes and delivers strategies including: collaborative research and development **knowledge transfer networks**; **knowledge transfer partnerships**; micro and nano-technology centres; and, international programmes.

TEMPERANCE

Concern about the abuse of alcohol resulted in Command 4746, issued 3 July 1909, which described a syllabus of lessons on 'temperance' for scholars attending **public elementary schools**.

Further reading: Report 1908–09 p. 196

TEMPORARY EMPLOYMENT SUBSIDY

(18 August 1975–31 March 79) Firms were offered £20 per week for 12 months for each full-time job maintained when there was a

threat of redundancy. This was ended because it was in contravention of EEC regulations.

See: Temporary Short-time Work Compensation Scheme

Further reading: Deakin and Pratten (1982)

TEMPORARY SHORT-TIME WORK COMPENSATION SCHEME

(April 1979–March 1984) Replaced **temporary employment subsidy** and the **Short-time Work Compensation Scheme**. Unlike the other schemes, which paid 75 per cent of wages for six months, this scheme paid 50 per cent of wages for nine months. By the end of 1981 it was effectively supporting nearly a million jobs.

Further reading: British Market Research Bureau (1981)

TERTIARY COLLEGES

Tertiary colleges provided full-time and part-time education for 16- to 19-year-olds in academic and vocational subjects, matching that available in **sixth forms** and **further education** colleges.

THE BIG PLUS

Launched in Scotland in January 2004 The Big Plus campaign was designed to assist people's reading, writing and numeracy skills. It was funded by the Scottish Government's Learning Connections.

Further reading: www.thebigplus.com (accessed 01 June 2010)

THE INDUSTRIAL SOCIETY

See: (The) Work Foundation

THRESHOLD SCHEME

(1980) This was run by the National Computing Centre, which providing training in computer programming and operating for unemployed school leavers, aged 16–19.

Further reading: Courtney and England (1982)

THRIFT – LESSONS

Circular 308 from the **Education Department** (12 October 1891) strongly encouraged the practice of thrift and economic prudence for school managers, teachers and children. It drew attention to the value of **school savings banks** in schools and the fact that good schools were not restricted by the **Code** and should seek 'by many subsidiary expedients to render service to the children, and a right to influence on their characters and their aims in life'. The circular continued: 'To learn how to economise slender resources, how to resist temptation to needless expense, and how to make reasonable provision for future contingencies, is an important part of education. Such knowledge is calculated to protect its possessor from much trouble and humiliation, and to help him greatly in leading an honourable and independent life … In a school much may be done to render its acquisition easy to children, and to show them the advantages of economy and foresight. Simple lessons on money, on the conditions which affect the rate of wages, on the relations of skill, prudence, and knowledge to industrial success, and on right ways of spending and saving, may be made very intelligible and interesting to the young' (Report 1891–92 p. 250).

See also: Schools Savings Banks

TOURISM – PROMOTION OF

Tourism is an important creator of wealth and jobs in the UK and the objectives of this programme were to promote the development, growth and international competitiveness of tourism. The **Employment Department** provided grant-in-aid to the British Tourist Authority and the English Tourist Board.

See: Tourism Training Initiative

Further reading: Employment Gazette 1989 pp. 8–88; Training Agency (1989a)

TOURISM TRAINING INITIATIVE

The TTI was developed to support improvements in the quality and quantity of training in the tourism industry. The initiative involved was encouraged by Employment Ministers and the **Training Agency**. Developments occurred in five main areas: occupational standards, vocational qualifications and common skills; training provision and skill needs; employer commitment; commitment to customer care; and Career Image.

Further reading: Employment Gazette 1989 pp. 8–88; Training Agency (1989a)

TOWARDS ENTERPRISE AND MANAGEMENT

(1986) This Northern Ireland initiative began in 1986 and encouraged self-employment and careers in management. In 1991/92 seven TEAM conferences were held involving 450 A level and BTEC students.

Further reading: Training and Employment Agency Annual Report (1992)

TRADE PREPARATORY SCHOOLS

During the early 1900s children often left school at the age of 14 and admission to apprenticeships was around the age of 16. To develop foundation skills and discourage casual labour, these schools provided instruction for those who wished to enter skilled trades. Boys were required to have succeeded at **Standard** VII and pass an entrance examination. Some scholarships were provided and, for others, a fee was charged.

Further reading: Laurie (1912a) pp. 90–111

TRADE SCHOOL

The Bristol Trade School (which subsequently became the University of Bath School of Management) was involved with building, mechanical, chemical and navigational teaching. 'The trade school is not one in which it is proposed to teach trades, but the knowledge applicable to trades. It is a school for boys before they go to work or are apprenticed, to enable them to follow their trades intelligently' (Minutes 1853–54, p. 487).

During the 1850s the term 'trade school' was a more common term for a **secondary school** since the education was delivered after **elementary school**. As state secondary schools emerged around 1900, the term trade school gradually reassumed a meaning closer to its purpose of training people in specific trade occupations and, by the 1930s, was closely incorporated with **junior technical schools**, the difference being the greater amount of time spent on vocational education in the trade schools (Report 1934 p. 31).

TRAIN TO GAIN

(3 April 2006) This service was originally provided by the **Learning and Skills Council** to help businesses get the training they needed to be successful. It was designed to address skills shortages and reduce the 40 per cent of people in the workforce who did not have Level 2 qualifications. Using a free skills brokerage service, **skills brokers** worked with employers to identify training needs, find training providers and evaluate the effectiveness of the training. A performance management framework was developed to assess the brokers. Performance was primarily measured on the number and engagement of 'hard to reach' employers; employer satisfaction levels; and the achievement of competency and quality standards. Competency standards for brokers were published in February 2006. National standards for brokerage were published in March 2006. Train to Gain developed from **employer training pilots**.

Further reading: www.traintogain.gov.uk/ (accessed 01 June 2010)

TRAINING ABSTRACTS SERVICE

First published in 1967 the *Training Abstracts Service* was one of four linked publications (The *Glossary of Training Terms*, *Training Information Papers*, and *Industrial Training Research Register* – later named the *Annual Register of Training Research*) that were designed to encourage the application of new ideas and techniques in training and also increase the audience. It was a recognition of the substantial body of articles, research and reports etc. Approximately 80 abstracts were circulated each month and provided bibliographical details and so on. It brought together material from a dozen abstracting sources that was not generally available, together with information from ministry staff. It did not abstract sources summarised elsewhere.

Further reading: Ministry of Labour Gazette 1971, pp. 78–79; Price (2000)

TRAINING ADVISORY SERVICE

(1960–64) The Training Advisory Service was set up by the **Industrial Training Council** to provide practical assistance to employers' associations, joint councils, and individual companies. It was run by a non-profit making limited company and the directors were appointed by the ITC. With the **Industrial Training Act of 1964**, the ITC was replaced by the **Central Training Council**, which appointed new directors to the Training Advisory Service and which was renamed the **Industrial Training Service**.

Further reading: Ministry of Labour Gazette 1964, Vol. LXXII, p. 418

TRAINING AGENCY

(1988–90) In 1988 the Training Agency succeeded the **Training Commission**. It was integrated into the **Employment Department** in November 1990 as the **Training Enterprise and Employment Directorate** (TEED), and the Employment Department was reorganised into three directorates.

Further reading: Price (2000)

TRAINING ALLOWANCE SCHEME

(September 1947) This was an allowance, instituted in 1947, paid to people attending courses at **government training centres**. It was previously called the **Special Aptitudes Scheme** and subsequently renamed **maintenance allowance**.

Further reading: Ministry of Labour Gazette October 1962, p. 387; Ministry of Labour Annual Report 1959, p. 41

TRAINING AND ACCESS POINTS

(*c.* 1987) Training and access points were terminals throughout the UK that provided a gateway to databases containing information on education and training opportunities and were located in public places to allow easy access.

See also: Learndirect; Jobpoints; Supervacs; Worktrain

TRAINING AND DEVELOPMENT AGENCY FOR SCHOOLS

(1 September 2005) It was established under the Education Act 2005 and replaced the **Teacher Training Agency** and had a wider remit. The main purpose of the TDA is to ensure an effective workforce to support the successful development of children. This is achieved through the supply of the workforce, in-service training and development, and supporting wider workforce modernisation.

Further reading: Training and Development Agency for Schools (2007); www.tda.gov.uk (accessed 01 June 2010)

TRAINING AND DEVELOPMENT LEAD BODY

This lead body developed training standards of which the **D-units** were used for assessment. It subsequently was known as the Employment and Occupational Standards Council; then as the Employment **National Training Organisation**; and, finally, as the **Sector Skills Council – Lifelong Learning UK**.

Further reading: Training and Development Lead Body (1995); Mansfield and Mitchell (1996)

TRAINING AND EDUCATION SUPPORT PROGRAMME

This programme aimed to improve the working of the training market by undertaking development work 'to tackle market failures' and provide support to **TECs** and **ITOs**. Support was targeted to give most effect with regard to a framework of national development priorities (Department of Employment Report 1992/93, p. 24). The TESP work included: **improving the training market**; the **Standards Programme**; the **Open College**; and **work-related further education**.

Further reading: DES (1990)

TRAINING AND EMPLOYMENT AGENCY

(2 April 1990–31 December 2001) The T& EA was established by the Secretary of State for Northern Ireland on 2 April 1990. It was responsible for the development and implementation of training and employment functions, originally within the Department of Economic Development, but, subsequently, within the **Department of Higher and Further Education Training and Employment**, and in 2001 the **Department for Employment and Learning**. With the restoration of the devolved government on 2 December 1999, the T&EA stopped being a Next Steps agency. Subsequently the Board of the Training and Employment Agency and the Further Education Consultative Committee were

replaced by one advisory body – the **Learning and Skills Advisory Board** (LSAB), which began operations on 1 January 2002. The T&EA's responsibilities were subsumed within the **Department of Higher and Further Education, Training and Employment** (DFHETE), subsequently the **Department for Employment and Learning**.

TRAINING AND EMPLOYMENT GRANTS SCHEME

(1989) TEGS operated in Scotland and its purpose was to allow employers to increase their workforce while receiving financial support. It also enabled individuals to take up jobs they might not have applied for because of a lack of skills. All individuals involved in TEGS had to live within specific postal code areas and be between 25 and 64 years old. In addition, they had to have been unemployed for at least 26 weeks or fit other categories including being unemployed with a disability; being ex-services people or being a participant on the **Training for Work** programme. If a new permanent job of at least 25 hours per week was created an employer would receive a 60 per cent wage subsidy for up to 26 weeks; 100 per cent of approved training costs; recruitment assistance; and, after-care support. Where there was a threat of redundancy, TEGS might also be used to retrain existing employees.

Further reading: www.scottish-enterprise.com (accessed 01 June 2010)

TRAINING AND ENTERPRISE COUNCILS

(1990–2001) TECs, and **local enterprise companies** in Scotland, were announced in December 1988 and were private, employer-led companies that had local responsibility for running government training programmes and stimulating training. TECs were funded from three main sources:

- an annual grant – This was based on the working population of TEC area.
- matching funding – For each £1 a TEC raised from private sources it was matched by £1 from public funds. This was restricted to £125k in the first year and then was subject to a national limit of £10m.
- performance related funding – On achieving specific performance targets, further funding was earned. This was equivalent to 2 per cent of programme funds.

By 1994, in the 82 TECs, over 1,000 directors were from business and community. In 1990 the maximum number of TECs and LECs existed: 82 TECs and 22 LECs. The amalgamated Income and Expenditure Account for 1997–98 detailed that total expenditure was £1.322b. Of this, the two largest beneficiaries were – Work Based Training for Young People £721m, and the **Training for Work** programme £210m. They were superseded by (local) learning and skills councils.

Further reading: House of Commons (2000); Price (2000)

TRAINING AND ENTERPRISE COUNCILS DISCRETIONARY FUND

(1996–97) Its objective was to help **TEC**s achieve the strategies detailed in their corporate and business plans and was worth £20m per year. The fund operated on a challenge principle and priority was given to those attracting the highest level of private funding.

Further reading: DfEE Departmental Report 1998–1999, Cm 3910, p. 73

TRAINING AND ENTERPRISE COUNCILS MANAGEMENT FEE

The management fee covered the cost of running the **TEC**s. Although each TEC was responsible for deciding how to manage resources, the TEC network was subject to

the same targets and minimum 2 per cent efficiency gains each year.

Further reading: Department of Employment Report 1992 Cm 1906 p. 13

TRAINING AND REHABILITATION ALLOWANCE

(Announced and implemented in 1961) It was designed for people receiving training under the General, Ex-Regular or Disabled Vocational Training Schemes who were entitled to an allowance. The amount varied and depended on a variety of factors including their age, and whether they were living locally or in lodgings whilst receiving the training.

See also: Training Allowance Scheme; Maintenance Allowance

Further reading: Ministry of Labour Gazette 1961, Vol. LXIX, p. 195

TRAINING CENTRES

(1945) Previously called **government training centres**, the first was established in 1945 at Felden in Northern Ireland. In 1992 there were 12 centres, which were run by the **Training and Employment Agency**. They were subsequently absorbed by **further education colleges**.

Further reading: Training and Employment Agency Annual Report (1992)

TRAINING COLLEGES

Mr W. Scot Howard, HMI, provided a brief history of teacher training colleges and stated: 'At the dawn of the nineteenth century there were few primary schools, and, as far as I can discover, no colleges for training teachers. It is only in 1805 that there is mention of such an institution. It is, I believe, the privilege of the **British and Foreign School Society** to claim as its child a small and obscure school, in which, under the direction of Joseph Lancaster, persons were in some way prepared to become teachers – it would seem to have been the first cell – the primordial germ – of the Borough Road Training Colleges' (Board of Education 1899–1900 Vol. 3, p. 332–33).

A number of colleges were established in the 1840s and 1850s to train schoolmasters, for example Borough Road, St Mark's College, Chester Diocesan Training College. These were in addition to the training that occurred in **normal schools**. With increased understanding of teaching, clearer expectations of the nature of training colleges began to appear; Mr Moseley, an HMI, stated: 'A course of education specially directed to the formation of the character of the schoolmaster, and having throughout a technical bearing and a professional development, whilst on the one hand it results in great earnestness of purpose, a deep sense of the sacredness of the teacher's office, and entire self-dedication, is on the other hand compatible with all the qualities of an accomplished mind and an elevated character' (Minutes 1845, Vol. 1, p. 331).

During the 1840s, the duration of training was one to three years, and two years was recommended. Article 120 of the 1894 Code formalised practices that enabled students of special merit to take an extra year's training either in the college or elsewhere including study overseas (Report 1893–94 p. 339). The terms '**training colleges**' and '**training schools**' were, to some extent, interchangeable (Minutes 1854, p. 26).

See also: (Day) Training Colleges; Normal Schools; Model Schools

(DAY) TRAINING COLLEGES

(1890) Teachers' training colleges were single-sex, two-year residential programmes that, although successful, did not provide a sufficient number of trained teachers. To supplement this provision, universities were encouraged, as an experiment, to establish mixed day training colleges to train teachers and award them degrees. Early established colleges included: one for men at The Victoria University of Manchester (Report 1891–92 p. 360); one for female students in Birmingham (Report 1891–92 p. 390); King's College, London in October 1890 (Report 1891–92 p. 442); Cambridge University Day Training College; Liverpool University College, Day Training College; The Yorkshire College (Leeds) Day Training College; and, Firth College, Sheffield (Report 1891–92 p. 443). The London Day Training College founded by the London County Council in 1902 subsequently became The Institute of Education, University of London. Mr Harrison, HMI, stated: 'The attraction of a degree will probably induce many students to prolong their studies for three years. The addition to the ranks of teachers with the advantages and prestige of a university training will be a clear gain to elementary education, and the influence of such teachers will in the future act as a stimulus to the existing colleges, but there is ample room for all, and a healthy rivalry is always a wholesome incentive to good work. Trained teachers must be more largely in demand. The untrained teacher of the future will find himself weighted in the race' (Report 1891–92 p. 361).

See also: Training Colleges

Further reading: Thomas (1978)

TRAINING COMMISSION

(1988) Formerly the **Manpower Services Commission**, the Training Commission was established by the Employment Act 1988 and it included a greater representation from employers. The reduced trades union influence created disagreement and eventually the TUC, after calling upon the Government to make amendments to **employment training** and being ignored, boycotted it. The Training Commission, which came into operation at the beginning of September was abolished ten days later by the government and was replaced by the **Training Agency**.

Further reading: Price (2000)

TRAINING CREDITS

(27 March 1990) Secretaries of State for Employment and Education launched a pilot Training Credits scheme on 27 March 1990. Training credits were designed to enable young people to 'buy' training from a specialist training provider or an employer. Training credits became **youth credits**.

Further reading: Employment Department Report February 1992, Cm 1906, p. 16; Employment Department (1992a)

TRAINING DEVELOPMENT INFORMATION SERVICE

TDIS provided a range of information on training areas including local and national quality initiatives, effective practice in training, research projects and development work. It also provided information about vocational qualifications, educational initiatives and publications. It was developed by the **Employment Department** and was available to those professionally involved with training provision through **TECs**, **LECs** and vocational education and training organisations.

Further reading: Employment Gazette January 1991, p. 49

TRAINING DEVELOPMENT OFFICERS

During the 1960s government grants of up to 50 per cent were made available to help non-profit making bodies with the initial costs in developing new, or expanding existing, schemes involved with training development officers. The grants were paid until an industrial training board was established, or for a period of three years, after which the sponsoring body became responsible. The TDOs' role was to advise the parent organisation on the planning of training arrangements at industry level and to assist implementation at company level. The officer acted as a consultant to companies in the industry and was a

specialist in training techniques and methods, and encouraged the setting-up of systematic training schemes.

Further reading: Ministry of Labour Gazette January 1967, p. 125

TRAINING DEVELOPMENT SERVICE

This was a programme run by the **Department of Employment and Productivity** in the late 1960s and early 1970s and provided training for operator instructors. Selected operatives were trained in the techniques of giving good instructions to other operatives during in-plant training. The 4- to 5-day course was preceded by an information session for managers and a briefing session for the operatives.

Further reading: Employment and Productivity Gazette 1970, Vol. XXVIII, pp. 280–82 and 856–61

TRAINING, ENTERPRISE AND EDUCATION DIRECTORATE

The Training Enterprise and Education Directorate was one of three directorates within the **Employment Department**. Its responsibilities included: training, enterprise and education policy; contract management for **TECs**, local education authorities and other bodies; training standards and systems; and, direct delivery of some programmes including **career development loans** and **Loan Guarantee Scheme**.

Further reading: Price (2000)

TRAINING FOR ENTERPRISE

(1985–88) Designed to help build wealth and job-creating small businesses by giving potential and existing entrepreneurs the skills and knowledge needed to launch, manage and ultimately expand the small business. Programmes could be as short as one day or last for several weeks, with the majority being of one week duration. There were three objectives: 'to increase the volume of training undertaken in the small business field; to develop a more effective training system; and, to encourage the spirit of enterprise in Britain'. It was succeeded by the **Business Enterprise Programme**.

MSC (1986e)

TRAINING FOR OFFSHORE OIL OCCUPATIONS

During the 1970s and early 1980s support was provided to oil and oil-related industries. For example, in 1977–78 the engineering, construction and other related industries in Scotland and the North East of England assisted the **MSC** in monitoring the demand for and supply of skills in oil rig and module fabrication, and the construction of on-shore terminal facilities etc. Training was given to more than 3,600 trainees, including helicopter pilots, rig crews, divers, and drilling and production personnel.

Further reading: MSC Annual Reports 1977/78, p. 39 and 1978–79, p. 31

TRAINING FOR OVERSEAS TRADE

See: Overseas Trade Training

TRAINING FOR SKILLS PROGRAMME FOR ACTION

(1979/80) TSPA was an **MSC** initiative to provide grants to sponsor first year apprenticeship training. It was a long-term programme intended to support training in important skills. From 1979/80 it replaced **special training measures** with a permanent system of marginal funding.

Further reading: MSC (1977a); MSC Annual Report 1979–80, p. 19

TRAINING FOR SUCCESS

(Northern Ireland) (3 September 2007) This initiative uses work-based apprenticeships to offer a range of professional and technical training opportunities to young people aged 16–24. It replaced **jobskills**.

Further reading: www.nidirect.gov.uk/training for success (accessed 01 June 2010)

TRAINING FOR TRAINERS

(May 1992) This Northern Ireland programme was designed to increase and enhance training provision in small businesses. It began in May 1992 and operated in partnership with the Northern Ireland Small Business Institute. On successful completion of the programme, participants were given the status of approved trainers/organisers.

Further reading: Training and Employment Agency Annual Report (1992)

TRAINING FOR WORK

(1993 – April 1998) It replaced **employment training** and **employment action**. The criteria for eligibility were the same as ET and were administered via **TEC**s: the person had to be between 18 and 63 years old and have been unemployed for 6 months or longer. On TfW courses 86 per cent had been unemployed for 6 or more months, compared to 75 per cent on the former employment training programme. TfW had a special emphasis on getting people into jobs or into self-employment, rather than solely acquiring qualifications. Training for Work was replaced by **work-based learning for adults** in 1998.

Further reading: Atkinson (1994); CRG (1996); Payne et al. (1999)

TRAINING FOR WORK (SCOTLAND)

In Scotland, the Training for Work programme was designed for people who had been unemployed for 13 weeks and were actively seeking work. It was run by **Skills Development Scotland** through training providers and involved vocational training.

Further reading: www.skillsdevelopmentscot-land.co.uk (accessed 01 June 2010)

TRAINING IN PERSONNEL MANAGEMENT

(1958) This was a special course to train ex-officers in the personnel management area of business or industry. The course consisted of one month's unpaid practical training in a personnel department and two month's theoretical study in the Department of Management Studies in the Regent Street Polytechnic in London.

Further reading: Ministry of Labour and National Service Report 1958, p. 60

TRAINING INFORMATION FRAMEWORK

(1981) Established to support connections between occupational structure and training provision in local labour markets. This involved an index of computer-based establishments that contained information for all employing establishments on the structure of their employment and on the training they provided. The second part of TIF was a system for estimating the numbers of young people making themselves available for training. This contributed to the arrangements for the **Youth Training Scheme**.

Further reading: MSC (1983b)

TRAINING INFORMATION PAPERS

Training Information Papers were one of four linked publications (The **Glossary of Training Terms**, **Industrial Training Research Register**, and **Training Abstracts Service**) designed to encourage the application of new ideas and techniques in training. They were specifically designed to encourage and speed up the practical application of research findings concerning realistic training situations. Each booklet presented briefly and simply the findings of the project and the practical implications and applications.

Further reading: Employment and Productivity Gazette 1968, Vol. LXXVI, pp. 1010–11

TRAINING INSPECTORATE

(1 April 1998) The **Department for Education and Employment** supported a programme to strengthen self-assessment and introduce external inspection in government-funded training in England only. The inspection of work-based training was guided by the same principles as those for colleges and schools. The intention was to avoid duplication of effort by the various inspection agencies involved in quality assurance. The proposals for the Inspectorate were developed by the **Training and Enterprise Council** National Council and involved a **Training Standards Council** and a training inspectorate representative. The main focus of the Inspectorate was **modern apprenticeships**, **national traineeships**, **work-based training for adults** and other youth and adult training programmes. The responsibilities of the training inspectorate were subsequently absorbed by the **adult learning inspectorate**.

Further reading: Adult Learning Inspectorate (2001); DfEE Annual Report (1998/99)

TRAINING MASTER

Sometimes called the **drill-master**. At the **school of industry** at Norwood there was a training-master who would ring the bell for classes, meals etc. The boys would be marched to classes. The military nature of this school is illustrated as follows: 'From ten to twelve o'clock the training-master will drill a class of mariners in seamen's duties, gymnastic exercises, naval gunnery, and military drill, whenever the weather will permit out-door work: whenever prevented by the state of the weather, the mariner's class will be taught to make netting, to knot, and splice ropes; and will be instructed on a model-mast to be provided for that purpose'.

Minutes of the Committee of Council of Education with Appendices 1844, Volume 2, (1845) London, William Clowes and Sons for HMSO, p. 393

TRAINING OF MIDWIVES AND HEALTH VISITORS

The Midwives Act 1902 introduced the requirement for the training, certification and registration of midwives by the Central Midwives Board. There was a two-year course that was devoted to theoretical instruction for half of the time and to practical training for the rest of it; and, there was a one-year course for fully trained nurses. The **Board of Education** had responsibility for the training of midwives and health visitors before this was transferred to the Ministry of Health on 1 April 1925.

Further reading: Report 1923–24 p. 138

(THE) TRAINING OF PAUPER CHILDREN

The volume *The Training of Pauper Children* published by the Poor Law Commissioners in 1841 described the main features. Between 500 and 1,000 children were gathered from a number of parishes and placed under the care of 'contractors', who received a certain sum of money per child per week to board, clothe and instruct them. A HMI report of a contractor, Mr Aubin, and his school of industry described how pupils were sometimes engaged in 'sorting bristles, making hooks and eyes, and picking oakum – [and this] prepared them for none of the ordinary callings of life, and disgusted them with labour of every kind' (Minutes 1842–43, p. 599).

TRAINING OF SERVICE RESETTLEMENT OFFICERS

(1945) This was training in career development for people involved with the resettlement of the military forces on return from the Second World War.

See also: Regular Forces Resettlement Service; Vocational Training Scheme

Further reading: Ministry of Labour and National Service Report 1939–1946, Cmd 7225, p. 154

TRAINING OF TRAINERS COMMITTEE

This committee operated within the **MSC**'s Training Services Division and advised on a variety of training matters.

Further reading: MSC Annual Report 1977/78, p. 25

TRAINING OPPORTUNITIES – FOR WOMEN

During 1979 and 1980, some 27,452 women completed courses under the **TOP**s scheme. This was predominantly in clerical and commercial subjects, but also included a significant number in what were seen as traditionally male-dominated jobs such as engineering, motor vehicle repair and electronic wiring. About 25 per cent of trainees on computer programming or operating courses were women and there were also increasing numbers of women taking higher level courses in management, science and technology, education and welfare. **Wider opportunities for women** (WOW) was provided under this initiative.

Further reading: MSC Annual Report 1979/80, p. 16; Commonwealth Secretariat (1984)

TRAINING OPPORTUNITIES SCHEME

(7 August 1972–July 1985) TOPs was run by the **Department of Employment** and was one of the longer running programmes as it did not end until July 1985. TOPs replaced the **Vocational Training Scheme** and extended the range of courses, including those of up to twelve months duration provided by **FE** colleges. It was designed to meet a variety of national and locally defined needs, train people for self-employment, and meet the training needs of people by offering wider opportunities to those who had not acquired skills after leaving school. The target was to increase the number of people in training from 18,000 in 1971 to between 60,000 and 70,000 in 1975 and as many as 100,000 soon

afterwards. Courses were free and training allowances were available. Training was full-time and open to those who wished to acquire new skills, whether they had a job or not. It was not generally available to those under 19 or those who were within three years of leaving full-time employment. It was replaced by the **Job Training Scheme**.

Further reading: Department of Employment Gazette 1972, pp. 701–02; Dunne and Elias (1986); McGill (1981); MSC (1978f)

TRAINING PROVIDERS

These were found in a variety of forms including: colleges of further education, local education authorities, chambers of commerce, private training companies, national and local charities, and voluntary organisations: **National Association for the Care and Resettlement of Offenders** (NACRO). They contracted with the local **Training and Enterprise Council (local enterprise companies** in Scotland) to provide training for young people and unemployed adults.

See also: Managing Agents

Further reading: Harris Research Centre (1987); Linell (1985)

TRAINING QUALITY STANDARD

(June 2007) The Training Quality Standard is a framework and an assessment and certification process through which organisations demonstrate the quality of their training and development to potential trainees and employers. A further purpose of the standard was to raise quality performance. The 2006 the **FE** Reform White Paper: *Raising Skills, Improving Life Chances* recommended that the Quality Mark be combined with the re-accreditation of **centres of vocational excellence** to create what was initially called the **New Standard** for Employer Responsiveness and Vocational Excellence and then renamed, Training Quality Standard. The

assessment framework consists of two parts: Part A addresses responsiveness in providing training and development to employers; and Part B examines sector expertise. Accreditation was funded by fees charged to organisations applying to be assessed against the Standard.

Further reading: www.trainingqualitystandard. co.uk

TRAINING RESEARCH REGISTER

First published in 1967.

See also: Industrial Training Research Register; Training Information Papers; Glossary of Training Terms

Further reading: Employment and Productivity Gazette 1968, Vol. LXXVI, p. 1010

TRAINING SCHEME FOR SCHOOL LEAVERS

The **Department of Employment** paid £1m to cover half the cost of a special scheme for first-year craft or technician training provided by the Engineering Industry Training Board. This was for up to 2,500 school leavers who would otherwise be unable to obtain an apprenticeship. The scheme covered the cost of training and an allowance of £5.50 per week. This sum represented about half of the estimated shortfall in the industry's recruitment in 1971–72 and helped to alleviate the shortages resulting from the raising of the school leaving age in September 1972.

Further reading: Department of Employment Gazette 1971, Vol. LXXIX, p. 733

TRAINING SCHOOLS

In the 1840s the training of teachers was achieved in a number of ways. In **normal schools** it was often expected that masters and mistresses received their training in the teaching profession through practice. In other schools young **pupil-teachers** (normally aged 16–18 who are apprenticed to the school) learned about teaching. There were also training schools established and one of the first, 'The Battersea Training Schools had been founded with two distinguishing objects:

1 To give an example of normal education for school-masters, comprising the formation of character, the development of intelligence, appropriate technical instruction, and the acquisition of method and practical skill in conducting an elementary school.
2 To illustrate the truth that, without violating the rights of conscience, masters trained in a spirit of Christian charity, and instructed in the disciplines and doctrines of the Church, might be employed in the mixed schools necessarily connected with public establishments, and in which children of persons of all shades of religious opinion are assembled' (Minutes 1842–43 p. 279).

The terms 'training colleges' and 'training schools' were generally coterminous during the 1860s and 1870s and the **New Code** (1873) explained that '[a] training school includes – (a) A college, for boarding, lodging, and instructing candidates for the office of teacher in elementary schools; and (b) A practising department, in which such candidates may learn the exercise of their profession' (Minutes 1872–73 p. xcv).

See also: Training Colleges

TRAINING SERVICES AGENCY

(1 April 1974) The **Employment and Training Act 1973** established three statutory bodies. The **Manpower Services Commission** and its two agencies: The TSA, and the **Employment Service Agency**. The MSC's executive agency and statutory body was responsible for training and had three aims:

- to increase the efficiency and effective performance of manpower;
- to help people to fulfil their needs and aspirations in their jobs; and,
- to increase the effectiveness and efficiency of training.

MSC (1974)

TRAINING SERVICES AND DESIGN CONSULTANCY

This Northern Ireland service was provided by the **Training and Employment Agency** to provide customised training plans, to assist with the design of training manuals and materials to support training activities, and to deliver training in a number of training and presentational techniques. This service was offered to potential inward investment companies and also provided expert advice on the local training infrastructure and the development of programmes of pre-employment training for local start-ups.

Further reading: Training and Employment Agency Annual Report (1995)

TRAINING SERVICES DIVISION

This was a division of the **MSC** whose purpose was to support the development of a national training system to meet the economy's manpower needs. Its purpose was also to 'offer training to individuals consistent with their abilities and wishes in skills for which there is a demand and to promote the efficiency and effectiveness of training in general' (MSC Annual Report 1977–78, p. 17).

TRAINING SHIPS

See: Merchant Marine Training Ships

TRAINING STANDARDS ADVISORY SERVICE

(September 1986) TSAS was originally formed to provide independent assessment of

317

the quality of **youth training** and provide guidance for further development. Its remit was expanded to include a range of initiatives within the **Employment Department**'s **Training Enterprise and Education Directorate**. Inspection was carried out by training standards inspectors (TSI). It also was designed to:

- 'carry out short surveys, thematic studies and fact finding visits to meet specific customer needs;
- increase TSI involvement in the spread of effective practice identified during inspections;
- develop regional advisory and consultancy services on all aspects of training quality;
- provide specialist advice and guidance to training development projects funded or managed locally;
- produce regular summaries of the quality of training across programmes and sectors in ED regions;
- and enable TSIs to become involved with national and sector working groups'.

Training Standards Advisory Service (1991: 3)

TRAINING STANDARDS COUNCIL

(1 April 1998) The TSC and its operational arm the **Training Inspectorate** were formed on 1 April 1998. The TSC is responsible for the independent inspection of government-funded, work-based training delivered through English **TEC**s/CCTEs and subsequently **LSC**s. The TSCs publication, *Raising the Standard*, described the national framework for self-assessment and external inspection. The TSC carried out 400 inspections during its first year. Expenditure on training inspections was estimated at £4.9m in 1998–99 and £6.9m in 1999–2000. Under the Learning and Skills Act 2000, the TSC's responsibilities were transferred to the **Adult Learning Inspectorate**.

Further reading: Training Standards Council (2000)

TRAINING WITHIN INDUSTRY FOR SUPERVISORS

(1944–84) In the early days this consisted of three courses, each having a duration of ten hours: Job Instruction, Job Relations and Job Methods. By 1962 Job Safety (ten hours); Office Supervision (thirty hours) and Union Job Relations (ten hours) had been added. The **Training Within Industry Job Safety Course** was introduced in 1957 by the **Ministry of Labour** as greater emphasis was given to reducing the number of deaths and injuries in the working environment. This programme was discontinued from 1984 because the areas covered by TWI were also addressed by alternative provision, thus freeing other staff to be more effectively deployed elsewhere.

Further reading: MSC Annual Report 1983/84, p. 26

TRAINING WITHIN INDUSTRY JOB SAFETY COURSE

(1957) Job safety courses were introduced by the **Ministry of Labour** in 1957. They were designed for those supervisors who had responsibility for safety in their firms. The general aim was to demonstrate that safety was an integral part of good supervision. In particular, the course sought to: '(1) improve a supervisor's knowledge of special or technical aspects of safety appropriate to his firm; (2) show him how to take action to prevent accidents; and (3) give him the basic information to co-operate effectively with safety specialists in his field' (Ministry of Labour Gazette 1962 p. 454).

See also: Health and Safety

Further reading: (Gent, 1983)

TRANS-EUROPEAN MOBILITY SCHEME FOR UNIVERSITY STUDIES

(1990) TEMPUS was one of a number of European Community measures to support

Eastern and Central European countries. It allowed individuals to participate in education and training programmes similar to existing European programmes such as **Leonardo da Vinci** and **Socrates**. It initially ran from 1990 to 1995 and was renewed for a third time in 1999 to run until 2006. It focused on management and business administration, science and technology, modern European languages, agriculture and environmental protection. It also covered finance for projects linking universities and enterprises from Eastern Europe with those within the European Community.

Further reading: Employment Gazette 1991 p. 358

TRANSFER INSTRUCTIONAL CENTRES

(1929–39) Introduced by the **Ministry of Labour**, these centres provided three-month long courses designed to address the high levels of unemployment particularly found in the 'distressed areas', and 'recondition' demoralised young men believed to be reluctant to work and who might become long-term unemployed. Participants were threatened with the withdrawal of benefit if they did not attend and activities involved the men in road building, forestry work, digging ditches, for example, as a means to increasing employability. These transfer instructional centres, previously known as 'testing centres', were renamed 'instructional centres' in 1931 and the annual admission reached over 17,000 in 1938 before finally closing in 1939.

See also: Labour Colony; Oversea Training Centres

Further reading: Field (2009)

TRANSVERSAL PROGRAMME

This is a European lifelong learning programme to encourage languages, policy cooperation, ICT, and study visits. The other lifelong learning programmes include **Comenius**, **Erasmus**, **Grundtvig** and **Leonardo da Vinci**.

Further reading: www.transversal.org.uk; http://ec.europa.eu/education/lifelong-learning-programme/doc78_en.htm

TRAVEL TO INTERVIEW SCHEME

From May 1985 the **MSC** piloted the TIS scheme in the northern region. Following the successful pilot, it was announced on 13 June 1986 that it would become a national scheme. It replaced the **Employment Transfer Scheme**, **Free Forward Fares Scheme** and **Job Search Scheme**.

Further reading: Bryson (1996)

TRIPARTITE PLAN

(1845) Traditionally schools consisted of one room, large or small, in which all the instruction occurred either through the **simultaneous method**, the **mutual instruction/monitorial system**, or the **mixed method**. This inevitably made it very difficult to communicate because of the large numbers and noise involved, not to mention the differing abilities. Furthermore, if the schoolmaster did teach each group, of which there might be 15 or so, this would mean that the pupils would receive little direct and influential attention. Mr Moseley, an HMI, suggested an organisational structure that he called the tripartite plan. This was based on his observation of the former **sessional school** in Edinburgh where its master, Mr Olifant, had taken over a number of rooms to enable separate elements of instruction. Mr Moseley suggested that **elementary school** instruction be divided into subjects of oral instruction (delivered by the schoolmaster); reading (supervised by monitors); and writing (slate arithmetic, drawing, committing to memory – that is silent occupations – supervised by a **pupil-teacher** or assistant master) (Minutes 1845, Vol. 1 p. 249).

TRIPARTITE SYSTEM

The tripartite system emerged after the **Education Act 1944** with three main types of state maintained school: **grammar schools**, **secondary technical schools**, and **secondary modern schools**. An insufficient number of secondary technical schools were built and so the education system tended to be divided between grammar schools and secondary modern schools. It largely ended with the introduction of **comprehensive education**.

TRIPLE SCHOOL

This was a school found in Winchester that had 'an educational machinery of three triple and six mixed schools, all of them above average in efficiency' (Report 1863–64 p. 159). The term has also been used in connection with Birmingham's Holte Mayfield Lozells schools, which are co-located and incorporate Holte secondary school; Mayfield special school; and, Lozells primary school – all of which were rebuilt as part of Building Schools for the Future in 2010.

See also: Bilateral School; Municipal Dual School

TRIVIUM

In the Middle Ages, education consisted of the trivium, the three subjects of grammar, logic and rhetoric. These were sometimes followed by the quadrivium: arithmetic, astronomy, geometry and music.

TRUANTS' SCHOOLS

The **Elementary Education Act 1880** made it the duty of the local authority to enforce compulsory attendance in schools and persistent offenders were sent to truants' schools or industrial schools. In Plymouth, Mr Cowie, HMI, reported: 'The operation of the truants' school has been notably successful. Up to the end of 1882 102 boys had been committed to the school, 80 of whom, after a detention of eight weeks or more, were allowed out on license. These boys, who before their committal were the most incorrigible truants, making 15 per cent of possible attendances, were transformed into the most regular attenders in their schools, making 99.13 per cent of attendance. Only four of them had to be returned to the truants' school for a second detention' (Report 1883–84 p. 280). Since 1880 and **compulsory education** there has been a problem with truancy that has exercised the minds of parents, schools, local education authorities and the state.

TRUST SCHOOLS

These were described in the Education and Inspections Act 2006 and the Early Adopters programme was launched in December 2006 and 30 Trust schools opened in September 2007. The purpose of Trust schools was to provide opportunities for new and different ways for schools to operate and work with partners. Schools or groups of schools are self-governing and are supported by a charitable trust. They are supported by the **Specialist Schools and Academies Trust**. They are a form of foundation school supported by a charitable trust and they are encouraged to develop sustainable relationships with business, **further** and **higher education** and the voluntary sector.

See also: Academies

Further reading: Department for Education and Skills (2007) Departmental Report 2007, Cm 7092, p. 54; www.ssatrust.org.uk/about/historyofthetrust/default.aspa (accessed 01 June 2010)

TRUSTEES – SCHOOL

During the 1800s when schools were established there was usually a board of trustees who oversaw the school but who did not manage day-to-day operations. Trustees were drawn from churches and respected people including heritors (Scotland). The Minutes (1857–58 p. 43) stated: 'Trustees and managers should not be confounded. The legal estate of the premises should always be vested in some corporate body having perpetual succession, so as to avoid the expense and trouble of renewing the number of trustees'. Specifications for the trust deed were made in the **Revised Code of Regulations**: 'The trust deed must declare the premises to be granted in trust for the education of the poor, and for no other purpose whatever. It must also provide for the legal ownership of the premises, and for the inspection and management of the school, according to one or other of the precedents settled for: Church of England Schools; British schools … ' (Report 1861–62 p. xx).

See also: School Managers

U

UfI – UNIVERSITY FOR INDUSTRY

(1998) The University for Industry was the original title for the organisation but it had not received a Royal Charter nor assent from the Privy Council and therefore was not entitled to use the term 'university' and so it became known as UfI. The pathfinder prospectus was published in spring 1998 and funding of £5m from the Windfall Tax was provided for start-up costs in 1998–99 and an additional £10m (including £0.9m for Scotland) was allocated in the March 1998 budget. UfI operates in England, Wales and Northern Ireland, and in Scotland the title is 'SUfI', originally called the 'Scottish University for Industry'. UfI is responsible for the operations of **Learndirect** and the latter's mission 'is to transform skills, productivity and individual lives by providing the best of online learning' (www.ufi.com/home2/default.asp [accessed 09 April 2010]).

Further reading: DfEE (1998b); UfI (1999)

UK COMMISSION FOR EMPLOYMENT AND SKILLS

(1 April 2008) The commission was one of the recommendations made in the Leitch Review and it took over a number of the functions of the **Sector Skills Development Agency** and the **National Employment Panel**. Its purpose was to '[r]aise UK prosperity and opportunity by improving employment and skills' through research and by giving advice to the four UK governments.

www.ukces.org.uk/
(accessed 01 June 2010)

UK e-UNIVERSITY

(February 2000 – March 2004) The UK e-University was established to provide a wider provision of **higher education** and to counter the potential challenge from institutions such as the US University of Phoenix Online. Approximately 20 universities and other institutions were listed and only 900 students recruited at a cost of £62m. As a result, the **Higher Education Funding Council for England** announced it would be restructured and it closed.

UK ONLINE

(2000) This initiative was launched in 2000 with an aim of establishing 6,000 centres by 2002. The purpose of the online centres was to narrow the gap between those who had access to the Internet and those who didn't. Each centre was designed to create a friendly environment where people could discover the Internet in their local communities. The centres were designed to attract people who might feel that technology was not for them, such as people with basic skill needs, lone parents, the over-60s, those with disabilities, people from minority ethnic groups and unemployed people. This was in support of the Government's commitment to provide Internet access to all who want it by 2005. Funding of £259m was made available from the Capital Modernisation Fund. The first annual report for UK Online stated: 'Electronic commerce and the Internet are transforming economies and societies across the world. The Government is committed to giving every individual, business and community in the UK the opportunity to participate fully in the benefits flowing from these changes – in short, getting the UK online' (UK Online 2001 p. 4).

See also: UK Online for Business; Neighbourhood Learning Centres

Further reading: DfES Departmental Report 2002 Cm 5402 p. 118; http://www.ukonline centres.com (accessed 01 June 2010)

UK ONLINE FOR BUSINESS

This initiative was developed to promote e-commerce uptake among small and medium- sized businesses. It was supported by the **Department of Trade and Industry** until 2004 and it helped UK companies to use information and communications technologies to build their businesses, grow sales and increase profitability. The initiative included: advisers who provided effective, jargon-free advice; the distribution of literature on various aspects of the technology; and, a programme of events around the UK to demonstrate the benefits of using new computer technology.

See also: UK Online

UK SKILLS

(1989) UK Skills was founded to 'encourage and promote the development of skills competitions as an effective means of raising and maintaining standards of vocational skills and contributing to the achievement of **National Education and Training Targets**' (Wilson 1999 p. 201) The skills competitions at local,

regional, national and international levels (**skill olympics**) are designed to reflect current practice, and to include problem solving, design and innovation where appropriate; they are judged according to commercial criteria and test key skills. UK Skills also manage the **national training awards**.

Further reading: www.ukskills.org.uk (accessed 01 June 2010)

UK VOCATIONAL EDUCATION AND TRAINING EXPORT CENTRE

(November 1997) Established in 1997, the centre coordinated marketing activities for organisations seeking to export vocational qualifications, occupational standards and related training services.

See also: British Training International

UNDERWATER TRAINING CENTRE

(1980–82 April 1982) During 1981–82 the **MSC** provided support for the Underwater Training Centre at Fort William through **TOP**s and trained 111 divers for North Sea operations. Discussions for the industry to take a major financial interest in the centre did not come to any positive conclusion and the Government withdrew the training scheme.

Further reading: MSC Annual Report 1981/ 82, p. 22

(CLASSES FOR) UNEMPLOYED ADULTS

In the 1920s and 1930s the Depression caused high levels of unemployment and, to partially counter this, **local education authorities** were required to provide day-time courses in addition to the free access to evening classes. There were three main groups of provision: practical subjects; commercial and academic subjects; and, physical training, first aid and hygiene (Report 1937 p. 33).

See also: Labour Colony

UNEMPLOYED INSURANCE ACT 1935

This act required education committees to provide training courses for young people under eighteen years of age.

Further reading: Scotland (1969)

UNEMPLOYED WORKMEN ACT 1905

This act enabled the establishment of distress committees to provide grants to businesses or local authorities to employ more people, thus reducing the level of unemployment.

UNEMPLOYMENT ACT 1934

This act, in addition to lowering the age of entry into unemployment insurance, required local authorities to provide courses for unemployed young people up to the age of 18, and obliged the unemployed young people to attend these courses of instruction (Report 1934 pp. 4–5).

UNEMPLOYMENT BENEFIT

On 19 May 1909 Winston Churchill announced that labour exchanges would also include a system of unemployment insurance that would operate under certain conditions. The first benefits were paid on 15 January 1913. A non-contributory 'out of work donation' was planned for returning ex-servicemen at the end of the First World War and this was then amended at the end of the war to include unemployed civilians. Payment was made through **employment exchanges** and branch employment offices. The cost of unemployment benefit was carried by the Unemployment Assistance Fund and from 5 July 1948 it was met from the National Insurance Fund, which was set out in the National Insurance Act 1946. When the National Assistance Act 1948 (which was designed to replace the existing **Poor Law** provision) came into effect on 5 July 1948 the payment of unemployment allowances ended. Instead, the **Ministry of Labour and National Service** local offices paid national assistance to people conditional upon registering for employment. Unemployment benefit was subsequently replaced by **jobseeker's allowance** in 1996.

Further reading: Price (2000)

UNIFIED VOCATIONAL PREPARATION

(1976–83) This was a five-year pilot begun in 1976 and jointly organised by the **Training Services Division** of the **MSC** and education departments. It was designed to test a variety of vocational preparation approaches for young people who left school and entered jobs in which they received little or no training or further education. In 1980/81, 300 schemes were run that involved 3,500 trainees, and in 1981/82 there were 481 schemes. UVPs were run in a number of industries including: local government, construction, printing and publishing, agriculture, distribution, hotel and catering, rubber and plastics processing, air transport and travel, and food, drink and tobacco industries. It ran until 1983.

Further reading: MSC (1981a); Wray et al. (1980)

UNION LEARNING FUND

(May 1998) This was announced in the White Paper *The Learning Age* and built on the experience unions had gained through the Bargaining for Skills initiative. The purpose of the fund was to encourage the unions to support members and, through them other people, to investigate learning opportunities and successfully complete them. The criteria for bids were that they had to be innovative, sustainable, and that they contained one or more elements of advice/guidance, equality/access, young workers, or organisation and development. Funding of £6m was announced at the TUC conference in September 1998. Unions involved included the AEEU, GMB, Unison, National Union of Journalists and the Musician's Union. The Scottish Union Learning Fund was established in 2000 and the Northern Ireland Union Learning Fund was established in late 2002.

See also: Union Learning Representatives; Unionlearn

Further reading: DfEE (1998b); Shaw (1999)

UNION LEARNING REPRESENTATIVES

Under the Employment Act 2002, which came into effect in April 2003, ULRs have statutory recognition. Their role is to promote training and development in the workplace; identify sources of training and development, and work with employers to address skill needs of individuals and the organisation.

See also: Union Learning Fund; Unionlearn

Further reading: www.unionlearn.org.uk/about/index.cfm?mins=109

UNION SCHOOLS

See: Parochial Union Schools

UNIONLEARN

(May 2006) Building on the work of the union learning representatives the **Department for Education and Skills** supported the establishment of a union academy known as Unionlearn. Its purpose was to offer guidance on training to employees and employers.

Further reading: www.unionlearn.org.uk (accessed 01 June 2010)

UNITED SCHOOLS

(c.1860s) These were groupings of small rural schools of not less than two or more than six that had insufficient pupils and resources to

satisfactorily sustain themselves. They had a resident teacher and 'may be united under the superintendence of one certified master or mistress, who must spend two clear hours at the least in each week at each school during its ordinary time of meeting, or, if the number of united schools be less than *six* such longer time per week as 12 hours divided among the united schools will give to each' (Report 1866–67 p. lxxxvi). The precise specifications for united schools were to be found in the **Revised Code** Articles 135–41 (Report 1866–67 p. xxxiii).

See also: Parochial Union Schools

UNIVERSITIES AND COLLEGES ADMISSIONS SERVICE

In 1992/93 the **Universities Central Council on Admissions** and the Polytechnics Central Admissions System were merged to form UCAS following the Further and Higher Education Act 1992. UCAS is responsible for advising and managing the applications of students wishing to enter **higher education**. It also incorporates the Graduate Teacher Training Registry. Applications for postgraduate and part-time study are normally made directly to the university or college.

UNIVERSITIES CENTRAL COUNCIL ON ADMISSIONS

(1961–1992/93) Prior to the establishment of UCCA, potential students applied to as many universities as they wished, which created a significant logistical and administrative load. To address this, the Committee of Vice-Chancellors and Principals recommended the creation of a central clearing house to which students could make six, and later, five, choices of university. These were then forwarded to the universities, which made unconditional offers, conditional offers or rejected certain applications. The students could then hold two of the offers they received, with one being a first choice and the second being a reserve if they did not achieve the required grades for the first choice. After the publication of **advanced level** examination results, students would receive a confirmed offer and those who were unsuccessful could then apply to 'clearing', where remaining university places were notified. The responsibilities of UCCA, the Polytechnics Central Admissions Council and the Standing Conference on University Entrance were taken over by the **Universities and Colleges Admissions Service** in 1993.

Further reading: Kay (1985)

UNIVERSITIES FUNDING COUNCIL

The purpose of the Universities Funding Council was to support teaching and research in UK universities. It was established as a result of the Education Reform Act 1988 and replaced the **University Grants Committee**. The Further and Higher Education Act 1992 separated its responsibilities into national components: **Higher Education Funding Council for England**; Higher Education Funding Council for Wales; and, the Scottish Higher Education Funding Council.

UNIVERSITIES UK

In 2000, this representative body of the heads of universities replaced the Committee of Vice-Chancellors and Principals that had been established in 1918. Together with Universities Scotland and Higher Education Wales the representatives promote the interests of higher education.

UNIVERSITY

The word university comes from the Latin. Oxford University (*c.*1096) and Cambridge University (1209) both received their charters from Henry III in 1231. In Scotland, three universities were established in the fifteenth century, with Edinburgh following a century later. Other universities followed and particularly the wave of **red-brick universities** promoted by the university extension movement. In the 1960s another wave followed with the **colleges of advanced technology** converting to university status. In 1992 most of the **polytechnic**s became universities.

UNIVERSITY DEGREE FOR TEACHING

A university degree was considered sufficient qualification for teaching in schools instead of acquiring a **teaching certificate** or training as a **pupil-teacher**. The **Education (Scotland) Act 1872** stated: 'When a degree in arts or science of any university in the United Kingdom conferred after an examination in all or any of the subjects specified by the Department as subjects for the examination of candidates for a certificate of competency is held by any such candidate, the examiners may lawfully dispense with his examination in such of the said subjects as he has already been examined in on obtaining the degree' (Minutes 1872–73 p. cxl).

See also: Colleges of Education

UNIVERSITY EXTENSION MOVEMENT

University extension movement grew in the second half of the nineteenth century and involved lecturers, predominantly from Oxford and Cambridge, travelling to large towns and cities to give public lectures. These classes provided a platform for the establishment of university colleges and universities.

UNIVERSITY FOR INDUSTRY

See: UfI

UNIVERSITY GRANTS COMMITTEE

(1918–1 April 1989) It was established to provide funds for universities and after the Second World War expanded its role to address the provision of **higher education**. The Treasury relinquished control of the UGC in 1964 when it came under the responsibility of the **Department of Education and Science**.

UNIVERSITY OF THE THIRD AGE

(1982) Originally founded in Toulouse in 1972 this initiative began in Britain in 1982. 'U3As are self-help, self-managed lifelong learning co-operatives for older people no longer in full time work, providing opportunities for their members to share learning experiences in a wide range of interest groups and to pursue learning not for qualifications, but for fun'.

www.u3a.org.uk/home.html (accessed 28 November 2009)

UNIVERSITY SCHOLARSHIPS

This scheme for the provision of state scholarships to support scholars from grant-aided secondary schools attend university began in 1920. It stopped during 1922 and 1923 due to economic conditions and resumed in 1924.

Further reading: Report 1923–24 p. 127

UNIVERSITY TUTORIAL CLASSES

University tutorial classes were largely established as a result of a conference at Oxford in 1907, and in 1913 special regulations for tutorial classes were introduced. By 1914–15 there were 131 university tutorial classes provided by the new universities and university colleges, with the most popular class being economics, which included industrial history (Report 1914–15 p. 55). They were provided by joint-committees of the universities and the **Workers' Educational Association** and study continued over three years (Report 1922–23 p. 103).

UNIVERSITY VOCATIONAL AWARDS COUNCIL

UVAC was established in 1999 to support higher education institutions and **further education** colleges in areas connected with vocational learning. The University Vocational Awards Council's mission was to champion vocational learning.

Further reading: www.uvac.ac.uk (accessed 01 June 2010)

UNNECESSARY SCHOOLS

To prevent schools being in local competition for pupils, clause 91 of the 1883 Code stated: 'The school must not be unnecessary. In a district not under a school board a school is not deemed to be unnecessary if at the date of its application for an annual grant it is recognised as a certified efficient school, and has had during the 12 months preceding such application an average attendance of not less than 30 scholars. A school will not be allowed the benefit of this provision if within two miles of it by the nearest road there is another school receiving a special grant under Art. 111' (Report 1882–83 p. 120).

UPPER SCHOOL

(1800s) This was a term sometimes used for schools that children attended after they had left **infants school** at the age of seven. They could then continue until the age of fourteen (Minutes 1855–56, p. 243).

See also: Lower School

URBAN PROGRAMME AREAS

See: Inner-City Initiatives

V

VACATION SCHOOLS

In the early 1900s it was recognised that the skills of practising teachers needed to be refreshed and enhanced. To achieve these ends, Saturday courses were held and some education authorities also provided vacation courses during the summer ranging in length from one to four weeks; for example, the West Riding LEA ran a summer school in Scarborough and made grants for fees, travelling and maintenance.

Further reading: Report 1908–09 pp. 64–65

VILLAGE COLLEGES

With the expansion of secondary education in the 1920s, Henry Morris, Chief Education Officer for Cambridgeshire, developed the concept of rural secondary schools into village colleges or **community schools** or colleges that would provide for the education and life of local children and adults and provide a central point for the whole community. The first was opened at Sawston in 1930.

Further reading: Rée (1985)

VILLAGE SCHOOLS

These were schools largely found in villages, although some were found in towns; for example, Surrey Street School, Sheffield, 'may be considered as a village school in the midst of a town' (Minutes 1844, Vol. 2, p. 428).

The main system used in these schools was individual instruction. The master set lessons for each child and then considered them individually. The Inspector of Schools maintained that this system was unsatisfactory because if one child was being instructed in a class of sixty the others would be wasting their time idly. 'For such schools it is evident there can no longer be any room. Either they must become entirely remodelled or sink into annihilation before the more systematic efforts of an advancing age' (Minutes 1847–48, Vol. II, p. 333).

VOCATIONAL A-LEVELS

See: Advanced Vocational Certificate of Education

VOCATIONAL GCSE

See: (Vocational) General Certificate of Secondary Education

VOCATIONAL TRAINING SCHEME

(July 1945–1972) Began as the Vocational Training Scheme for Men and Women Released from War Service. It rapidly expanded to 65 **government training centres** nationwide, but was reduced to 17 GTCs in 1952. Training was almost exclusively engineering, construction and vehicle repair. GTC expanded again in 1962 to facilitate conversion and refresher courses to meet skills shortages. It finished up with 52 centres in 1972. It was replaced by the **Training Opportunities Scheme**.

See also: Government Vocational Training Scheme

Further reading: Employment and Productivity Gazette 1970, Vol. LXXVIII, pp. 280–82; Ministry of Education (1953)

VOCATIONAL TRAINING TAX RELIEF

The inland revenue defined vocational training as 'training done to get the skills needed for an occupation, trade or profession'. Tax relief on payments for training counted towards an **NVQ/SVQ/GNVQ/GSVQ**. Tax relief first became available for payments made on or after 1 January 1994. Payments for **GCSE** or A level (Standard Grades and Highers in Scotland) did not qualify.

Further reading: Inland Revenue (1995)

VOLUNTARY-AIDED SCHOOL

Voluntary-aided schools are generally **faith schools** in which the governing body employs the school staff and controls admission policy. Empowered by the Schools Standards and Framework Act 1998, the school's building and land are owned by the charity or religious body and these contribute a small proportion to the capital costs of the school with the state paying the remainder. The **local education authority** maintains the school and pays teachers' salaries. Previously, many of these schools were aided schools.

See also: Voluntary Schools; Voluntary-Controlled Schools

VOLUNTARY-CONTROLLED SCHOOLS

Voluntary-controlled schools are under the responsibility of the **local education authority** that employs staff, maintains the school buildings and land, controls admissions, and appoints two-thirds of the governing body. These schools are generally faith schools and the buildings and land are owned by the church or charitable foundation.

See also: Voluntary Schools; Voluntary-Aided Schools

VOLUNTARY DAY SCHOOLS

The term 'voluntary day schools' was sometimes used in the late 1800s to distinguish the **elementary schools** from the growing number of **evening schools** and **night schools**.

VOLUNTARY PROJECTS PROGRAMME

(August 1982–September 1988) The aim of this programme was to set up projects creating opportunities for unemployed people to take up on a voluntary basis without affecting their benefit entitlement. Clients included: lone parents, people with basic literacy and numeracy needs, people with severe disabilities or with medical or drug-related problems. It was succeeded by **employment training** where an element of the programme was the Community Opportunities Programme (COP) and **initial training**.

See also: Community Programme

Further reading: MSC (1986d); Smith (1988)

VOLUNTARY SCHOOLS

A voluntary school was defined in the **Voluntary Schools Act 1897**: 'The expression "voluntary school" means a **public elementary day school** not provided by a **school board**' (Report 1896–97 p. 385). In practice, a voluntary school was one connected to a particular religious denomination. Under the act, voluntary schools were expected to organise themselves into groups under 'governing bodies representative of the Managers' (ibid). The **Education Act 1944** distinguished between **voluntary-controlled** schools fully funded by the state and controlled by the local education authorities; and **voluntary–aided schools** that partly contributed to capital costs and retained more control and self-governance. The Roman Catholic Church retained control of its schools, and more than half of Church of England schools became voluntary controlled.

VOLUNTARY SCHOOLS ACT 1897

Prior to this act, **board schools** received statutory funding, raised by local rates, under the **Elementary Education Act 1891**; however, funding for voluntary schools (church schools) came from pupil fees and other sources. To provide a more balanced educational system the 1897 Act was, 'An Act to provide for a Grant out of the Exchequer in Aid of Voluntary Elementary Schools, and for the Exemption from Rates of those Schools, and to repeal part of Section Nineteen of the Elementary Education Act 1876 … For aiding voluntary schools there shall be annually paid out of moneys provided by Parliament an aid grant, not exceeding in the aggregate five shillings per scholar for the whole number of scholars in those schools. The aid grant shall be distributed by the **Education Department** to such voluntary schools and in such manner and amounts as the Department thinks best for the purposes of helping necessitous schools and increasing their efficiency, due regard being had to the maintenance of voluntary subscriptions' (Report 1896–97 p. 384). It was not applicable to Scotland and Ireland.

W

WAGES COUNCILS

These bodies set a statutory minimum level of pay in certain industries and guided the **wages inspectorate**, which enforced these council orders. The councils were ended in 1989.

Further reading: Employment Department (1991e)

WAGES INSPECTORATE

These were the men and women who had power to visit employers and to ensure that they were paying statutory minimum wages in certain industries.

See also: Wages Councils

Further reading: Employment Department (1991e)

WALES EMPLOYMENT AND SKILLS BOARD

The Wales Employment and Skills Board was established in 2008 to 'strengthen the employer voice on skills in Wales; give expert advice to Welsh Ministers; and help Wales to develop a high-skills economy with opportunities for everyone' (Department for Children, Education, Lifelong Learning and Skills 2008 p. 66). The WESB replaced the Wales Employment Advisory Panel and Joint Skills Advisory Panel.

See also: Skills Development Scotland; UK Commission for Employment and Skills

Further reading: wales.gov.uk/topics/education andskills/foremployers/employmentskillsboard/ ?lang=en (accessed 01 June 2010)

WANT2WORK

This Welsh programme jointly developed between the Welsh Assembly and **Jobcentre Plus** was aimed at economically inactive people claiming health-related benefits. The initial phase ran between 2004 and 2008 and this was then extended with support from European convergence funding, a successor to Objective 1.

Further reading: http://wales.gov.uk/docs// dfm/research/090914want2worken.pdf (accessed 01 June 2010)

WARD SCHOOLS

A ward is an electoral area and schools were sometimes within these boundaries. In a description of the schools in the City of London, Mr King, HM Inspector, described 'the old City Ward Schools which link us with the past of elementary education' (Board of Education 1899–1900 Vol. 3, p. 326).

WELFARE TO WORK

The Chancellor of the Exchequer announced in 1998 that £3.5 billion from the windfall tax would fund a **New Deal** for the young and for the long-term unemployed. This was part of the Government's commitment to achieving high and stable levels of employment and also addressing the social disaffection and unemployment arising from the effects of poverty.

Further reading: DfEE Report April 1998, Cm 3910, p. 99

WELSH

The Welsh language was recognised as a **specific subject** for scholars in Wales in the 1890 **Code** (Report 1889–90 p. 119). Details of the syllabus were described in Report 1891–92 (p. 205). Also, in the 1893 Code there was explicit recognition that reading books, copybooks, arithmetic problems might be bi-lingual in Welsh districts (Report 1892–93 p. 331).

WELSH BACCALAUREATE

The Welsh Baccalaureate began pilots in September 2003 in 18 schools and colleges, six more followed a year later and a further seven in 2005. Its aims were to address inclusion, retention, completion and achievement and, following generally positive reviews, it was expanded and the Welsh Assembly set a target of one quarter of Welsh pupils to take the qualification by 2010. The 'Welsh Bac' is for pupils aged 14–19 and consists of three levels: Foundation Diploma, Intermediate Diploma and Advanced Diploma, with the Advanced Diploma being equivalent to an **A-level, that is** 120 points. It consists of two parts: options, which can be traditional qualifications such as **GCSEs**, **AS/A levels**, **BTEC** and **NVQs**; and, a 'core programme' in which **key skills** are developed.

WELSH CENTRAL BOARD

(1896) Under the **Welsh Intermediate Education Act 1889**, joint education committees were established for each county and these, in turn, established the Welsh Central Board (or Central Welsh Board) to coordinate, advise, and examine and inspect intermediate schools.

WELSH CIRCULATING SCHOOLS

See: Circulating Schools

WELSH DEPARTMENT

(1907) In February 1907 the Board of Education established a Welsh department, which administered education in Wales.

WELSH EDUCATION COMMITTEE

The Welsh Education Committee of the **National School Society** held a meeting on 6 May 1848 at which requests were made for inspectors with a knowledge of Welsh and for awards to be made to young men in order that they might attend the training institution at Carmarthen. The Committee of the Council on Education agreed to these requests (Minutes, 1847–48, Vol. 1, p. li).

WELSH EMPLOYMENT AND SKILLS BOARD

(May 2008) This was established to advise and support the Welsh Assembly to raise skills, employment, and business performance. Among its responsibilities were: supporting the monitoring, development and implementation of skills strategies and action plans; providing advice on business support, skills and employment priorities; and, overseeing the roles of **sector skills councils**, **sector skills agreements** and sector qualification strategies.

See also: UK Commission for Employment and Skills

Further reading: wales.gov.uk/topics/education andskills/foremployers/employmentskillsboard/?lang=en

WELSH INDUSTRIES ASSOCIATION

Classes in cookery, laundry work, dressmaking, woodcarving and horticulture were introduced in Anglesey in 1911–12 by the local branch of the Welsh Industries Association (Report 1911–12 p. 99).

WELSH INTERMEDIATE EDUCATION ACT 1889

The Local Government Act 1888 enabled elected county councils and county boroughs and endowed powers to support higher level education in England. To enable similar provision, the Welsh Intermediate Education Act was passed for intermediate and technical education for the people of Wales and the County of Monmouth, through county joint education committees.

WELSH JOINT EDUCATION COMMITTEE

(1948) Known in Welsh as Cyd-Bwyllgor Addysg Cymru, it was originally founded by **local education authorities** in Wales to replace the **Welsh Central Board**. It was an **examination board** that developed examinations and provided other educational services. Since 2007 it has been known as WJEC.

Further reading: www.wjec.co.uk (accessed 01 June 2010)

WELSH OFFICE

In 1970, the Welsh Office took over responsibility for **primary** and secondary **education** from the **Department for Education and Science**. Later, in 1978, it acquired responsibility for **further** and **higher education** (non-university functions), adult education, youth and community services and public libraries. In April 1992, the Welsh Office took over responsibility for training, enterprise and vocational educational programmes from the **Employment Department**. The Government of Wales Act 1998 replaced the Welsh Office with the National

Assembly for Wales in 1999. It became the **Department for Education, Lifelong Learning and Skills** and later the **Department for Children, Education, Lifelong Learning and Skills**.

Further reading: Department of Employment Report 1992 Cm 1906 p. 13

WESLEYAN SCHOOLS

These were schools established by the Wesleyan Church and were based upon a **Glasgow training system** developed by David Stow and used in the training schools connected with the Free Church of Scotland. 'Training, as opposed to instruction, was the object mainly kept in view; and the system was undoubtedly successful in its effects upon the moral and general intelligence of the children' (Minutes 1853–54, Vol. 2, pp. 764–65).

WHITWORTH SCHOLARSHIPS

(1868) These scholarships were founded and endowed by Sir Joseph Whitworth, an engineer, 'for the purpose of promoting the mechanical industry of this country by aiding young men in acquiring proficiency in Engineering' (Report 1907–08 p. 93). The scholarships are still awarded and the Whitworth Society continues to promote excellence in engineering.

WIDER HORIZONS PROGRAMME

This was a cross-border programme operated on a partnership basis between the **Training and Employment Agency** in Northern Ireland and FÁS in the Irish Republic. The Wider Horizons Programme was part of the International Fund for Northern Ireland. Its purpose was to provide vocational preparation and training overseas for disadvantaged or unemployed young people, and managers/entrepreneurs, particularly those from small and medium-sized enterprises (aged 16–28).

It was also designed to support the reconciliation process by helping individuals understand the diversity of views existing within the island of Ireland and by involving cross-community participation. During 1991/92, some 62 projects at a cost of £4.82m were approved.

See also: European Employment Service Cross Border Partnership

Further reading: Training and Employment Agency Annual Report (1992)

WIDER OPPORTUNITIES FOR WOMEN

WOW was provided under the **Training Opportunities Scheme**. Part of WOW provision was to help women return to the labour market, and this included part-time training for those unable to attend full-time courses.

Further reading: Fairburns (1979)

WIDER OPPORTUNITIES TRAINING PROGRAMME

(July 1985–September 1988) Designed to improve work-related skills, retain employability and cope with changing contents and patterns of work. There were two parts to the programme:

- The first part built upon existing work preparation schemes and aimed to give unemployed people training related to their individual needs and also to take advantage of local labour market opportunities; for example, in 1984–85, 1,600 people began training on pilot projects which cost £900K.
- The second part of the WOTP provided additional training involving participation on the **Community Programme**, which provided people temporary work with various training opportunities. In total, in 1984–85, 3,100 people were involved with the scheme costing £1.4m.

Further reading: Pascoe (1986)

WINNING WAYS

These were a series of seminars run in Northern Ireland during the early 1990s at which leading business speakers gave advice on best practice in areas such as teamwork, communication, customer care and managing change.

Further reading: Training and Employment Agency Annual Report (1994)

WOMEN AND TRAINING

(1979) Women and Training was a national body established to encourage organisations, employers and individuals to consider training needs for women of all ages, ethnic backgrounds and skills. In 1989 it was relaunched as a limited company and was part-funded by the **Training Agency** until mid-1992. Originally, it had been fully funded by the Training Agency.

Further reading: Employment Gazette 1989 pp. 662–64

WOMEN AND WORK COMMISSION

The Women and Work Commission was established in September 2004 to investigate ways of closing the gender pay and opportunities gap.

Further reading: www.equalities.gov.uk/what_ we_do/women_and_work/women_and_ work_commission.aspx (accessed 01 June 2010)

WOMEN AND WORK SECTOR PATHWAYS INITIATIVE

The two-year Women and Work Sector Pathways Initiative was introduced in 2007 to develop and test new recruitment, retainment and career pathways for women in sectors where they were under-represented. Funding of £10m was made available to be matched by employer funding and was overseen by the **Sector Skills Development Agency**.

Further reading: Women and Work Commission (2006 p. 9)

WOMEN'S TECHNICAL SERVICE REGISTER

This was a register devoted solely to women and their qualifications in the period between the two world wars. It was discontinued in 1945.

Further reading: Ministry of Labour and National Service 1939–1946, Cmd 7225, p. 105

WOODWORK

(1897) '**Manual instruction** in woodwork' was first described as a subject in the 1897 **Evening Continuation School Code** and it was insisted that it be associated with drawing. 'Each member of the class must make a measured working drawing (plan and elevation or isometric view) of each exercise before proceeding to the work at the bench, and must work as far as possible from his own drawing, not from a diagram or model, which may only be used so far as necessary to elucidate the drawing … The aim of the teacher, in all the exercises, should be to secure accuracy rather than quickness of work' (Report 1896–97 p. 628). **Object lessons** included timber and tools, and practical lessons included joints, models and carving.

See also: Metal Work

WORK-BASED LEARNING FOR ADULTS

In April 1998 Work-based learning for adults (previously called work-based training for adults) replaced **Training for Work**. It was designed for unemployed people aged 25+ to help them move into sustained employment and the key objectives were: tackling poor employability, and providing occupational skills. It consisted of a number of programmes including: **advanced modern apprenticeships**; **foundation modern apprenticeships**; life skills/life build; and, other training for young people that was previously known as **youth training**.

See also: Work-based Learning for Young People

Further reading: Employment Service Operational Plan (2001)

WORK-BASED LEARNING FOR YOUNG PEOPLE

WBLYP is a generic title that was delivered through the **Learning and Skills Council** and consists of **advanced modern apprenticeships** (AMA), **foundation modern apprenticeships** (FMA), life skills (LS) and other training (OT).

See also: Work-Based Learning for Adults

WORK CAMPS

See: Labour Colonies

WORK EXPERIENCE

Work experience was considered to be the main activity that provided young people with an insight into the world of work. Almost all pre-16 pupils undergo two weeks of work experience. The **Qualifications and Curriculum Authority** issued national quality standards for placements and a good practice guide addressing how to integrate work experience into the curriculum. Funding to support work experience was delivered through **TEC**s and subsequently through **local learning and skills councils**.

See also: Work Experience Quality Mark

Further reading: Hillage et al. (2001)

WORK EXPERIENCE ON EMPLOYERS' PREMISES

(1977) WEEP for unemployed young people was part of the **Youth Opportunities Programme** and was designed to:

- 'provide realistic introduction to the requirements, disciplines and satisfactions of working life;
- help them acquire basic skills in a variety of tasks;
- enable young people to find out what kind of work they are best able to do;
- help young people to make the transition from school to work;
- foster or restore motivation to learn and give young people confidence in their abilities;
- provide opportunities for further education and training in basic social and life skills'.

MSC (1982e)

WEEP programmes consisted of four parts: an induction; planned work experience; training and further education; and, personal advice and support. The young people were called trainees, worked a normal week, and were paid a weekly allowance by the sponsoring organisation that was reimbursed from the **MSC** area office.

WORK EXPERIENCE PROGRAMME

(September 1976–April 1978) WEP provided £18 per week that was paid by employers, who were reimbursed. The records for 1981 show that 461,500 people participated in the programme. Participants were accepted until December 1977 with projects continuing until its replacement, in April 1978, by the **Youth Opportunities Programme**.

See also: Work Experience on Employers' Premises

Further reading: Lasko (1978); O'Connor (1981); Smith (1977)

WORK EXPERIENCE QUALITY MARK

The Quality Mark was an accreditation awarded by the National Council for Work Experience, which recognised employers who provided a minimum standard of work experience, placements, and internships provision, thereby preparing students for work and raising the skill levels of the future workforce. It was part of a strategy to encourage workforce development and consisted of eight criteria: commitment, recruitment, induction, learning and development, assessment, resources and support, partnerships, programme evaluation and monitoring.

See also: Work Experience on Employers' Premises

Further reading: National Council for Work Experience (2006)

(THE) WORK FOUNDATION

On 3 April 1918, Reverend Robert Hyde, a campaigner for improvements in working conditions and an organiser of boys clubs, established The Boys Welfare Association in London. In 1919 it became known as The Industrial Welfare Society and gradually extended its range of services to include consultancy, research and training. In 1965, it became known as The Industrial Society and received a Royal Charter in 1984. In 2002, it sold its training arm and became known as The Work Foundation, which campaigns for good work for all.

Further reading: www.theworkfoundation.com (accessed 01 June 2010)

WORK INTRODUCTION COURSES

WICs or short industrial courses were developed under the **Youth Opportunities Programme** to provide courses of practical training and work-related remedial instruction in communication and numeracy. The courses were designed to support unemployed young people who had poor standards of numeracy and communication, and often low self-confidence, which prevented them from satisfying the minimum selection criteria of employers even for routine un-skilled jobs. The syllabus of the courses was flexible but largely consisted of an induction, assessment, training in basic work skills, social and life skills instructions, numeracy and communication.

Further reading: MSC Annual Report 1980–81, p. 22; MSC (1982a)

WORK-LIFE BALANCE ADVISORY COMMITTEE

Arising out of changes in the economy and customers expecting to access services outside of normal working hours, working patterns were changing. The result of this was that many workers regularly worked longer than their basic working hours. As part of good human resource management there was a recognition that employees should balance their work and their life outside work. A discussion document *Changing Patterns in a Changing World* explored the areas and produced a checklist for employers that included good working practices.

Further reading: DfEE 2000h

WORK PREPARATION

The Work Preparation programme was an individually designed programme to support disabled people to identify suitable work, get work experience, develop skills and increase confidence. The programme generally lasted between six and thirteen weeks and was delivered by a provider in a workplace or residential centre. It was one of three **Work-path** programmes, the others being **Access to Work**, and **Workstep**.

Further reading: www.direct.gov.uk/en/Disab ledPeople/Employmentsupport/WorkSchemes AndProgrammes/DG_4001970 (accessed 01 June 2010)

WORK PREPARATION COURSES

Work preparation courses were part of the **Youth Opportunities Programme**. They were usually held at educational centres, although many included placements with an employer. They lasted 13 weeks and were predominantly of two types: **short industrial training courses**, which focused on enabling young people to work at semi-skilled or operator level and **work introduction courses** aimed at helping low achievers to gain basic work, communication and numeracy skills.

Further reading: Maddocks (1981); MSC Annual Report 1980–81, p. 22

WORK-RELATED FURTHER EDUCATION

WRFE was for 16- to 19-year-old and older students involved in full- and part-time study. **Training and Enterprise Councils** took over responsibility from the **Employment Department** on 1 April 1991. Evaluation showed that employers benefited from greater responsiveness to their needs in relation to courses offered, higher quality products, and more efficient use of resources. In 1984 only 4 per cent of LEAs had a marketing strategy; by 1989 it was 61 per cent for WRFE. Also, 65 per cent of LEAs found that WRFE agreements had influenced new, redesigned or discontinued courses.

Further reading: Training Agency (1989b); Blamire (1990)

WORK TRIALS

(September 1989) Work trials allowed participants (who had been unemployed for six months or more) the opportunity to try a job for 3 weeks while continuing on benefits that were topped up with travel costs. This allowed the participants to demonstrate their ability, and also enabled employers to satisfy themselves of the abilities of the potential recruits. Employers guaranteed to interview each participant for a permanent job by the end of the work trial period. This originally started as part of the **job interview guarantee** and became a separate programme in April 1993. It involved up to 150,000 placements in 1995.

Further reading: Berry et al. (1993); Smith (1993)

WORKERS' EDUCATIONAL ASSOCIATION

(1903) The Association for the Higher Education of Working Men was founded in 1903 and this became the Workers' Educational Association in 1905. The WEA was founded to support the educational needs of working men and women and in the beginning the most popular subjects were economics and industrial and social history. The **Board of Education** acknowledged this success, which was due to three main factors: 'In the first place, while full liberty is left to the local branches of the Association in matters of management, the classes are usually in touch on the one hand with Local Education Authorities who co-operate with and in some cases aid or maintain them, and on the other hand with the Universities through the agency of joint committees consisting of representatives of the various Universities and of the workers' associations, which control the general arrangements for instruction. In the second place, the students usually undertake to attend the course regularly for three years, 24 meetings being held as a rule in each year, one hour at each meeting being devoted to a lecture, and one to class-work on questions arising out of the lecture; the regular writing of essays fortnightly is also a feature of the scheme. In the third place, the teachers are usually men of exceptionally high qualifications' (Report 1908–09 pp. 79–80). As a charity, it has continued this commitment to provide access to education and learning for adults from all backgrounds, especially those who had previously missed out on education.

WORKFORCE DEVELOPMENT CONFEDERATIONS

WDCs consist of representatives from various areas of healthcare including: NHS Trusts, Health Authorities, Primary Care Groups/Trusts, Social Services Departments, Higher Education institutions, the voluntary sector, the private sector, the Ministry of Defence, the Prison Service and the National Blood Authority. The WDC has responsibility for the planning and development of the whole healthcare staff across sectors; there were 24 WDCs across England.

Further reading: Simmons (2002)

WORKFORCE DEVELOPMENT PLANS

This scheme developed from the **National Training Organisation**'s **Skills Foresight**, whose purpose was to ensure that national training organisations' workforce development plans were based on a strategic assessment of skills needs. This allowed NTOs the ability to influence local and national workforce development in their sector.

Further reading: DfEE Report 2001–02 to 2003–04, Cm 5102, p. 84

WORKFORCE DEVELOPMENT PROGRAMME

This Welsh programme was designed to encourage and support employers to provide information, advice and guidance to their employees about publicly funded education and training, for example apprenticeships and discretionary funding. Human resource development advisors provided independent advice to employers about skill requirements, appropriate learning and how to access funding. The Workforce Development Programme was expanded in April 2008 to include **Flexible Support for Business**.

Further reading: Department for Children, Education, Lifelong Learning and Skills (2008 p. 56)

WORKHOUSE SCHOOLS

In the 1840s there were more than 700 workhouse schools, which were often called pauper schools. Prior to the Poor Law Amendment Act 1834 (which replaced the Poor Law Act 1601) many workhouses had a pauper-schoolmaster to instruct the children and sometimes adults. The minutes of the **Committee of Council on Education** (1846, First Volume, p. 15) noted the resolution, 'That it is desirable to train the pauper children now in workhouses in habits of industry', and funding was made available for the workhouse schools. Some workhouses were converted into **schools of industry**. In Scotland, workhouses were called poorhouses. The Local Government Act 1929 provided for the abolition of workhouses.

See also: Poor Law Acts

WORKING AGE AGENCY

This was the working title before becoming the **Department for Work and Pensions** created by the merger of the Department for Social Security and parts of the **Department for Education and Employment** including the **Employment Service**. The local offices were subsequently named **Jobcentre Plus** and were an integrated benefit and employment service with the first 50 pathfinder offices opened in October 2001.

Further reading: DfEE Report 2001–02 to 2003–04, Cm 5102

WORKING MAN'S EDUCATIONAL INSTITUTE

(1850s) This society, which was supported through voluntary contributions, encouraged education and produced educational diagrams for use in geography and history (Minutes 1854–55, p. 317).

WORKING MEN'S COLLEGE

(1854) This college in London is said to be Europe's oldest surviving adult education institution and was modelled on the **Sheffield People's College**. The Christian Socialists, including F. D. Maurice, Charles Kingsley and the Cooperative Movement were instrumental in its establishment, and in that of other colleges, including one in Halifax. Maurice also founded the **Working Women's College**, which merged with the Working Men's College in 1964. The college receives public funding and also maintains independence through investment incomes.

Further reading: Harrison (1954); www.wmcollege.ac.uk

WORKING VENTURES UK

National Employment Panel. The intention of WVUK was to engage with employers, and employment and skills providers to increase opportunities for disadvantaged communities. It was a **Department for Work and Pensions** sponsored, non-departmental public body and the umbrella agency for **Employer Coalitions**. Its purpose was 'To unlock employers' expertise, energy and resource to:

- meet employers' needs;
- up skill and recruit individuals, particularly people disadvantaged in the labour market; and
- enhance the employment and skills systems'.

Working Ventures UK (2009) p. 5

WORKING WOMEN'S COLLEGE

(1874–1964) It was established by F. D. Maurice and others as a residential community to educate women and focused on literature and the arts. It became the Frances Martin College and merged with the **Working Men's College** in 1964.

WORKLINK

See: Workwise

WORKPATH

This was an umbrella term incorporating three programmes for disabled people: **Access to Work**; **Work Preparation** and **Workstep**.

Further reading: www.direct.gov.uk/en/ Enployment/Jobseekers/programmesandservi ces/DG_173711 (accessed 01 June 2010)

WORKS' SCHOOLS

These were schools attached to industrial works and were of different types. Some were for the benefit of the children of the workers, while others were part of the **Factories Act 1961**, which required that children of a certain age were required to attend school for a part of the day. In Wales, there were works' schools connected to the iron works at Dowlais and Blana, and the copper works at Hafod and Llanelly (Report 1858–59 p. 156).

See also: Factory Schools

WORKSCHEME

(April 1984) In Northern Ireland, second-year full-time training places on the **Youth Training Programme** did not attract 17-year-olds in the numbers anticipated, which, apparently, was due to the young people wanting a job and not training. In response to this situation Workscheme was introduced in 1984, which encouraged employers to train 17-year-old employees – both existing and new employees. It offered the employer 'help by qualified staff to plan training; free further education at local colleges; free off-the-job training at **government training centres** and **community workshops**; monitoring the training and progress of employees; and £25 per week grant for up to 52 weeks. In the first year of operation 2,552 applications were approved.

342

Further reading: Dept of Manpower Services (1985)

WORKSKILL

(Piloted April 1997) Under the **jobseeker's allowance** regulations, jobseekers could undertake part-time education and training courses, provided this did not interfere with their availability and search for work. For the **Further Education Funding Council** (FEFC), part-time was considered to be a maximum of 16 guided hours per week in England and Wales (21 hours in Scotland) and was decided on a case by case basis for other programmes. Workskill was a relaxation of the rules and an initiative to encourage people to undertake education and training.

Further reading: Thomas et al. (1998)

WORKSTART

(Piloted July 1993) This was a long-term programme for those out of work for more than 2 years. The scheme paid £60 per week for the first 6 months and then £30 per week for the next 6 months. It was a subsidy paid to employers for the above periods and its purpose was to overcome the financial risk of employing someone who had been unemployed for a long time and also to overcome prejudice towards this client group.

Further reading: Coopers and Lybrand (1994); Atkinson and Meager (1994); Stern et al. (1996)

WORKSTEP

(April 2001) Originally called the **Supported Employment Programme**, it was intended to improve the opportunities for disabled people who need supported employment. Changes included the use of individual development plans, and a new range of support models to replace the subsidy approach. It was one of three elements of the **Workpath** initiative the other two being: **Access to Work** and **Work Preparation**.

Further reading: Employment Service Operational Plan (2001)

WORKTRACK

(August 1999) This Northern Ireland programme replaced **Action for Community Employment** in 1999/2000. Introduced by the **Training and Employment Agency**, it targeted women returners and the long-term unemployed who were not eligible for the **New Deal**. Its objective was to improve the employability of participants through work experience and training. Participation was for a maximum of 26 weeks.

Further reading: Training and Employment Agency Annual Report (1999); Department for Employment and Learning (May 2003)

WORKTRAIN

(March 2001) This was a website provided by the **Employment Service** and the **Department for Education and Employment** to supply information on jobs and training opportunities. It was designed to offer 500,000 learning opportunities and included 300,000 jobs held on the ES jobcentre network.

See also: Jobpoints; Supervacs; Training and Access Points; Learndirect

Further reading: MSC Annual Report 1985/86, p. 26

WORKWISE

(April 1994) Called **Worklink** in Scotland. This scheme was for people aged 18–24 who had been unemployed for at least a year and who had declined all other offers of help at their 12 month **Restart** interview. They were required to attend a course of assessment, guidance and practical job search lasting for four weeks. Workwise and **1-2-1** were introduced as separate pilots in April 1994, and from April 1995 the two schemes were combined and implemented throughout the **Employment Service**. The Workwise pilot had a target of 10,000 places in 1994/95 at a cost of £2.5m. In 1995/96 the programme had a target of 130,000 places (95,000 on **1-2-1** and 35,000 on Workwise) at a cost of £10m. Actual attendances were 67,557 on 1-2-1 and 24,762 on Workwise.

Further reading: Kay and Fletcher (1996); Kay et al. (1995a)

WORLD CLASS SKILLS

The World Class Skills – Delivering Employer Responsiveness initiative was introduced in 2008 in response to the Leitch Report (2006) *Prosperity for all in the Global Economy – World Class Skills*. WCS was introduced by the **Learning and Skills Improvement Service** to provide fully funded programmes to encourage **further education** providers to increase their responsiveness to the needs of employers and the development of skills leading to increased UK competitiveness.

Further reading: wcs.excellencegateway.org.uk/new-to-this-site (accessed 01 June 2010)

Y

YEAR IN INDUSTRY

This scheme was designed for pre-graduate engineers to spend a period of time working in a company and so increase their understanding of the needs of industry.

Further reading: Helsby (1992)

YOUNG APPRENTICES

(September 2004) This scheme was for 14- to 16-year-olds who spent a minimum of two days per week in work and the rest in school or college. The first cohort of 1,000 YAs began in September 2004 in three sectors: engineering, business and administration, and arts and media.

See also: Apprenticeships

YOUNG ENTERPRISE

(1962) It began operating in 1962 and was based on the American Junior Achievement, which began in the 1920s. Young Enterprise allowed students between the ages of 15 and 19 the chance to set up and run a company for one year.

See also: Youth Enterprise Initiative

Further reading: Hitchcock (1988); www. young-enterprise.org.uk (accessed 01 June 2010)

YOUNG MANAGERS DEVELOPMENT PROGRAMME

This Northern Ireland initiative was targeted at managers new to the tourism industry. It was specifically developed because of the importance of tourism to the Northern Irish economy.

See also: Managing the Growing Tourism Business; Opryland Hotel Project

Further reading: Training and Employment Agency Annual Report (1997)

YOUNG PEOPLE'S LEARNING AGENCY

(1 April 2010) This was one of the successor organisations to replace the **Learning and Skills Council**, the others being the **Skills Funding Agency** and the **National Apprenticeship Service**. Enabled by the Apprenticeships, Skills, Children and Learning Act 2009, its main priorities were to support and enable **local education authorities** to achieve their objectives; provide a national commissioning framework; provide a national statement of priorities and funding formula; provide strategic analysis and data; work with regional development agencies; and, fund and performance manage **academies**.

YOUNG PERSON'S GUARANTEE

(January 2010) The 2009 White Paper *Building Britain's Recovery: Achieving Full Employment* described the young person's guarantee, which specified that any person, aged 18–24 years, approaching the 12-months stage of receiving **job seekers allowance** would be guaranteed a job, work focused training, or a place on a community task force. From April 2010, young people approaching ten months on the job seekers allowance were required to take up the Young Person's Guarantee, the six-month offer or the **Backing Young Britain** scheme.

YOUNG PERSONS' WORK PREPARATION COURSES

YPWPCs were a forerunner of the **Work Experience Programme**. They ran during the 1960s and 1970s and were focused on disabled young people.

Further reading: Speke and Whelan (1979)

YOUNG WORKERS' EXCHANGE PROGRAMME

(1964–91) It was designed to enable young workers to experience work and life in other European countries through placements of between three and six months. YWEP was open to groups of young people aged between 18 and 28 who had completed basic vocational training. Organisations could apply for funding for group exchanges in a wide range of occupations including youth work, community care, computing and engineering. Projects had to focus on vocational rather than cultural activities. In 1989 there were 12 projects involving 300 people from the UK, and the community budget for the programme in 1990 was £3.5m. This programme merged with **PETRA** at the end of 1991.

Further reading: Commission of the European Communities Task Force (1992)

YOUNG WORKERS SCHEME

(January 1982–31 March 1986) The YWS provided a subsidy of £15 per week paid to firms employing young people under the age of 18 who were earning less than £50 per week. Its purpose was to encourage organisations to pay wages to the young person that took into account their age and lack of training and experience. A total of 436,700 successful applications were made by employers and the net cost per person was estimated to be £1,400 per year at 1985/86 prices. It was replaced by the **New Workers' Scheme**.

Further reading: Bushell (1986); Hedges (1985); Hedges (1986)

YOUTH ACCESS

The Youth Access initiative was targeted at young people who might not have achieved their full potential at school and who, as a result, were unable to gain access to higher level skills and qualifications. It added a fifth route for young people in addition to the four existing ones of: A levels, **YTS**, employment, and vocational courses: **BTEC**, **City and Guilds** and **RSA**. It was developed by the **Training Agency**'s Further Education and Partnerships Branch jointly with four **local education authorities**.

Further reading: Employment Gazette 1989, p. 649

YOUTH ACTION SCHEME

(1992) The **Department of Education and Science** introduced the **Grants for Education Support and Training Programme**. The fund supported short-term schemes to devise new methods of working in education. In 1993 the Youth Action Scheme was developed under GEST for the Youth Service. Its purpose was to enable youth workers to experiment with new approaches and **LEA**s were funded for 1993–95 (with a possible third year) at 60 per cent of running costs. The main aim was to support the Youth Service work with young people and reduce the risk of them becoming involved with crime. A total of 60 projects were developed.

Further reading: France and Wiles (1996)

YOUTH ADVOCATES

(Pilot project in 1999–2000) Youth advocates (personal advisers) were dedicated, named case workers who provided continuous one-to-one help and support to disaffected 16- to 17-year-olds. Funding of £200K from the Invest to Save Budget was used to encourage the development of innovative, local cross-agency approaches to promoting social inclusion and the take-up of existing education, training and employment opportunities.

See also: New Start; Neighbourhood Support Fund

Further reading: DfEE Departmental Report 1999–00 to 2001–02, Cm 4202, p. 85

YOUTH CARD

(Feasibility study in 1998) This scheme was set up to contribute to the DfEE objective of increasing the levels of participation and attainment in post-16 learning. This was attempted by:

- helping young people to make considered choices in the options open to them (There was to be a web site that could be accessed via the card.);
- offering a range of discounts via the card, and the possibility of attaching financial support to the card;
- using the card to track young people's attendance in learning; and,
- using the card to reward participation and attainment in learning.

The card resembled a business card but had CD-Rom technology. There were trials at eight discrete geographical areas as a result of the feasibility study carried out in 1998. It was renamed **learning card** and later became **connexions card**.

Further reading: DfEE Departmental Report 2001–02 to 2003–04 Cm 5102, p. 40

YOUTH COHORT STUDY

(1984-) The England and Wales Youth Cohort Study (YCS) tracks young people during their first few years after compulsory full-time education and provides the DfES with information on youth transitions. It is done every two years and uses a random sample of Year 11 pupils and then follows up on them in the spring after the end of compulsory education.

See also: Labour Force Survey; Individual Learner Record

YOUTH CREDITS

(April 1995) Youth credits was a method of helping young people choose and buy training from employers or other providers of training such as colleges, with the funding provided by **training and enterprise councils**. The credits were offered to young people of 16 or 17 and sometimes 18. The aim of youth credits was to 'encourage more school and college leavers to continue their education and training to reach higher levels of skills and qualifications, and, help more employers to provide good quality training for their young employees' (Callear 1994 p. 21). Each credit had a financial value that varied according to the level and type of training. When the initiative began in April 1991, youth credits had been known previously as **training credits**.

Further reading: Croxford et al. (1996); Hodkinson and Hodkinson (1999)

YOUTH EMPLOYMENT OFFICERS

Visited schools to give advice, talks and interviews. During 1963 more than 708,000

347

children received individual vocational guidance by the officers.

Further reading: Ministry of Labour Gazette 1963, Vol. LXXXI, p. 486

YOUTH EMPLOYMENT SERVICE

(1948–73) It was established as a result of the **Employment and Training Act 1948** and replaced the **Juvenile Employment Service**. The aim of the Youth Employment Service was to help young people during the transition from school to work and during the early years of employment up to the age of 18. The main tasks in 1967 were to:

- collect and provide information about careers and employment and assist teachers in career projects;
- give vocational guidance;
- provide assistance to those not continuing in further education; and,
- keep in touch with young people during the early years of employment so that advice could be provided.

The Central Youth Employment Executive provided direction to the service and was staffed by officers from the **Ministry of Labour**, the **Department of Education and Science** and the **Scottish Education Department**. The Minister of Labour appointed a **National Youth Employment Council** and separate advisory committees for Scotland and Wales to advise him. Locally, the service was delivered through youth employment offices established by **local education authorities** (in Scotland by education authorities). Where schemes were not in operation, this facility was delivered by Ministry of Labour offices. Each youth employment office had a **youth employment officer** or careers advisory officer. Youth employment committees consisted of teachers, employers and workers representatives, and others with special interest in young people. It was replaced by the **careers service**.

Further reading: Central Youth Employment Executive (1953); Ministry of Labour Gazette 1963, Vol. LXXXI, p. 486; Roberts (1971)

YOUTH EMPLOYMENT SUBSIDY

(October 1976–March 1978) YES paid £10 per week for recruits unemployed for six months or more. It replaced the **recruitment subsidy for school leavers**, but, unlike RSSL, all young people below 20, whether they had recently left school or not, were entitled to apply.

Further reading: Casson (1979)

YOUTH ENTERPRISE INITIATIVE

The Youth Enterprise Initiative is administered by the **Prince's Youth Business Trust**. It provides business advice, counselling, and financial help to young people (originally 18–25) who lack the financial backing to start a small business. The objective of the trust is to stimulate employment through the creation and development of viable businesses.

Further reading: British Market Research Bureau International (1997); www.young-enterprise.org.uk/pub

YOUTH FOR EUROPE

This was a project-based exchange programme between young people aged 15–25. Its intention was to bring together young people from different social, cultural and economic backgrounds to gain a greater awareness of European issues. The **British Council**'s Youth Exchange Centre was the UK's national agency co-ordinating the YFE programme. In 1988–89 more than 20,000 young people took part in exchanges. The visits were planned and organised by the young people and the upper limit for grants was 50 per cent of the costs involved.

Further reading: Employment Gazette 1991, p. 335

YOUTH OPPORTUNITIES PROGRAMME

(1 April 1978–September 1983) The YOP was introduced in 1978 together with the **Special Temporary Employment Programme**, and replaced the **Work Experience Programme** and **Job Creation Programme**. They were both designed to provide a constructive alternative to unemployment for young people. There were two main streams to YOP:

- work preparation involving courses to train and prepare young people for work (sponsored by **LEA**s in local workshops); and,
- work experience: there were three types. **work experience on employers premises (WEEP)**, **project-based work experience (PBWE)** and **community service**.

Trainee allowances for YOP were: April 1978 – £19.50; November 1978 – £20.55; November 1979 – £23.50; January 1982 – £25.00. YOP was succeeded by the **Youth Training Scheme**.

Further reading: Bedeman and Harvey (1981); Bedeman and Courtney (1983); Main (1985)

YOUTH SERVICE DEVELOPMENT COUNCIL

The Youth Service Development Council was set up as a result of the Albemarle Committee on the Youth Service, which published its findings in February 1960.

Further reading: Ministry of Labour Gazettes 1961, Vol. LXIX, p. 332; 1963, Vol. LXXI, p. 486

YOUTH TASK GROUP

A New Training Initiative: An Agenda for Action proposed the establishment of a 'high level task group' to involve the CBI, TUC, education interests and others and became known as the Youth Task Group (YTG). Its purpose was to encourage training beyond the immediate needs of specific job requirements and training that companies were unlikely to pay for. The YTG reported in April 1982 and its broad proposals were accepted by the Government and became the basis of the **Youth Training Scheme**.

Further reading: Chapman and Tooze (1987); MSC (1982b)

YOUTH TRAINING

(29 April 1990) YT replaced the **Youth Training Scheme** and aimed to: 'provide help for eligible young people to acquire the broad based skills necessary for a flexible and self reliant workforce; meet the skill needs of the local and national economy, including in particular the need for technician and craft level training; provide participants with training leading to **national vocational qualifications** (NVQs or equivalent qualifications as laid down by the Secretary of State) at or above Level 2 standard'. Trainee Allowances were: 29 May 1990 – £29.50 (aged 16) and £35 (aged 17+); 7 April 1997 – £30 (aged 16) and £35 (aged 17+); 1 September 1999 – £44 flat rate. Youth Training was succeeded by Other Training for young people.

Further reading: Gleeson (1900)

YOUTH TRAINING GUARANTEE

A guaranteed offer of a suitable training place for all 16- and 17-year-olds not in full-time education or a job was made by the Government. This guarantee included those who had lost or left a previous YT place and also included some 18-year-old people. The young person was due an immediate offer after 1 January if they had left full-time education the previous summer; and after 1 July if they had left after Easter.

Further reading: Chatrik and De Sousa (1993)

YOUTH TRAINING PROGRAMME

(September 1982–April 1995) This was Northern Ireland's equivalent of the **Youth Training Scheme**. It began in September 1982 (one year ahead of YTS) and involved vocational preparation for young people aged 16 and 17. It succeeded the **Youth Opportunities Programme** and was based on the **MSC**'s **New Training Initiative**, which set the objective of moving 'towards a position where all young people under the age of 18 have the opportunity either of continuing in full-time education or of entering training or period of planned work experience combining work-related training and education'. It was delivered through **community workshops**, **FE colleges**, employer led schemes and the **Training and Employment Agency**'s own **training centres**. In the first six months, 113 full-time courses offering 3,660 places were made available. Some of the features of the YTP were: young people could attend for up to two years; it was voluntary; it guaranteed 12 months full-time training to every minimum-age school leaver; it offered certification; and, it offered courses that combined training, further education and work experience. It was replaced by **jobskills** in April 1995.

See also: September Guarantee

Further reading: Department of Manpower Services (1985)

YOUTH TRAINING PROGRAMME FOR APPRENTICES

Under the YTP, in Northern Ireland, grants were only paid for the first year of vocational study. This had implications for those who were employed as apprentices and up to April 1984 firms could get a one-year grant to recruit and run apprenticeships. During 1982 and 1983 the apprenticeship training grant was criticised because: grants were only paid for one year and employers had no incentive to retain the apprentice; it reinforced the

concept of timeserving that was being replaced by training to recognised standards; and, many firms maintained their levels of apprentices and therefore did not qualify for grants which were only paid for additional places. From April 1984 the **Northern Ireland Training Authority** and the **ITB**s administered a new Skill Training Scheme in which an employer in a key economic sector could obtain grants up to £3,000 for each apprentice who achieved a series of recognised standards on the way to craft status.

See also: Youth Training Programme

Further reading: Department of Manpower Services (1985)

YOUTH TRAINING SCHEME

(September 1983–March 1986) This replaced **UVP**, **TOP** and **TSPA**, and the **Youth Opportunities Programme**. It started as a one-year programme of work experience integrated with work-related training or **further education** and became a two-year programme in 1986. Payments were made to providers of places, from which trainees received an allowance – £1,850 per year in 1983. A target of 460,000 places was set for the first year of operation. YTS provided training places for 16-year-olds and some 17-year-old unemployed young people (plus young people with disabilities who had left school/college aged 18–21). Each programme included an induction period; an assessment of the individual's needs and aspirations; planned work experience of up to 39 weeks; a minimum of 13 weeks relevant off-the-job training; guidance and support; training based on one or more broad areas of related occupations such as office work or construction; training in basic skills; and a record of achievement. Trainee allowances were: 1 September 1984 – £26.25; September 1985 – £27.30.

See also: Youth Training Scheme 2-Year; Youth Training

Further reading: Linell (1985); Government White Paper Cmnd 8445 (1981); MSC (1984b); Chapman and Tooze (1986)

YOUTH TRAINING SCHEME 2-YEAR

(April 1986–March 1990) 2-Year YTS as it was more commonly known was introduced as a response to requests from providers, trainees and employers for more detailed and comprehensive training for young people. The objectives were: make available to 16–17-year-olds leaving full-time education a broad foundation training that would provide the basis for job specific training; enable familiarity with the world of work and thus increase employability; add occupational competencies that are required by employers and supported by vocational qualifications; have places available for all young people up to the age of 18 who want one and do not have a job; improve the access to higher skills, jobs, and training for those under-represented in the training market; increase a training culture among young people and employers; and, increase the total share of training costs borne by employers. Trainee allowances were: 1 April 1986 – £27.30 and 2nd year £35; 6 April 1987 – £28.50 and 2nd year £35; 4 July 1988 – £29.50 and 2nd year £35.

See also: Youth Training Scheme and Youth Training

Further reading: Cockburn (1987); Finn (1987); Raffe (1990)

YOUTHWAYS

This Northern Ireland scheme was designed for less-motivated young people, many of whom had special educational needs. The purpose of the courses was to improve the young person's self-confidence; help them to relate better to society; and, help them to be more attractive to employers.

Further reading: Department of Manpower Services (1985)

Bibliography and References

References using the term '*Minutes*' refer to the Minutes of the Committee of the Privy Council on Education (1839–1857/58). References using the term '*Report*' refer to the Report of the Committee of Council on Education (1858/59–1899), and subsequently to the Report of the Board of Education (1900–38).

Abbot, A. (1933) *Education for Industry and Commerce in England*, London, Oxford University Press.

Adult Learning Inspectorate (February 2001) *The Common Inspection Framework: For Inspecting Post-16 Education and Training*, Coventry, Adult Learning Inspectorate and OFSTED.

Adult Literacy and Basic Skills Unit (1985) *Adult Literacy: The First Decade*, London, ALBSU.

——(1989) *After the Act: Developing Basic Skills Work*, London, ALBSU.

Ahier, J. and Esland, G. (1999) *Education, Training and the Future of Work I: Social, Political and Economic Contexts of Policy Development*, London, Routledge and the Open University.

Ainley, P. (1988) *From School to YTS: Education and Training in England and Wales, 1944–1987*, Milton Keynes, Open University Press.

——(1990) *Vocational Education and Training*, London, Cassell Educational.

Ainley, P. and Corney, M. (1990) *Training for the Future: The Rise and Fall of the MSC*, Oxford, Cassell.

Alison, J. (1912) 'The organisation of a typical Scottish secondary school,' in A. P. Laurie, *The Teacher's Encyclopaedia*, London, Caxton Publishing Company, Vol. 5, pp. 74–80.

Anderson, A. (1987) *Non-Statutory Training Organisations: Their Activities and Effectiveness: A Case Study Approach*, Brighton, Manpower Research for the MSC.

Anderson, R. D. (1995) *Education and the Scottish People 1750–1918*, Oxford, Clarendon Press.

Argles, M. and Vaughan, J. E. (1982) *British Government Publications Concerning Education During the 20th Century*, Leicester, History of Education Society.

Armytage, W. H. G. (1964) *Four Hundred Years of English Education*, Cambridge, University Press.

ASCETT (1995) *Education and Training Intelligence Gathering: Final Report*, Edinburgh, Profiles International Consulting.

Ashworth, K. (2001) *Education Maintenance Allowance: The First Year: A Qualitative Evaluation*, London, DfEE Research Report 257.

Atkins, P. (1986) 'MSC, TVEI and Education in Perspective', *Political Quarterly*, Summer.

Atkinson, J. (1994) 'Manpower Strategies for Flexible Organisations', *Personnel Management*, August, pp. 28–31.

Atkinson, J. and Meager, N. (1994) *Evaluation of Workstart Pilots*, Brighton, Institute for Employment Studies.

Barker, D. (1993) 'The Management Charter Initiative: An Interim Assessment', *Assessment and Evaluation in Higher Education*, Vol. 18, No. 2, pp. 125–34.

Barlow, H. (1995) *How to Pass A Levels and GNVQs*, London, Kogan Page.

Barrett, S. (1990) *An Evaluation of the Loan Guarantee Scheme*, London, Employment Department Research Paper 74.

Basic Skills Agency (2001) *Adult Literacy Core Curriculum Including Spoken Communication*, London, Basic Skills Agency.

Baumgratz-Gangl, G. and Deyson, N. (1990) *Mobility of Students in Europe: Linguistic and Socio-Cultural Conditions*, Brussels, Commission of the European Communities.

Bayliss, V. (1991) 'Doing Good by Stealth', *Employment Gazette*, July, pp. 393–96.

——(1998) *Redefining Work*, London, Royal Society of Arts.

Beard, C. and Wilson, J. P. (2002) *The Power of Experiential Learning: A Handbook for Trainers and Educators*, London, Kogan Page.

Beattie, A. (1997) *Working People and Lifelong Learning: A Study of the Impact of an Employee Development Scheme*, Leicester, NIACE.

Beattie, C. (1990) *Evaluation of ES Special Schemes for People with Disabilities: Report on Group Discussions with Disablement Resettlement Service Staff*, Sheffield, Employment Department Group.

Beaumont, G. (1996) *Review of 100 NVQs and SVQs*, London, NCVQ Evaluation and Advisory Group.

Bedeman, T. and Courtenay, G. (1983) *One in Three: The Second National Survey of Young People on YOP*, Sheffield, MSC Special Programmes Research and Development Series, No. 13.

Bedeman, T. and Harvey, J. (1981) *Young People on YOP, A National Survey of Entrants to the Youth Opportunities Programme*, Sheffield, MSC Special Programmes Research and Development Series, No. 3.

Bedford, T. (1982) *Vocational Guidance Interviews: A Survey by the Careers Service Inspectorate*, London, Department of Employment.

Beinart, S. (1996) *The Access to Work Programme: a Survey of Recipients, Employers, Employment Service Managers and Staff*, London, Social and Community Planning Research.

Bell, V. A. (1934) *Junior Instruction Centres and Their Future: A Report to the Carnegie United Kingdom Trust*, Edinburgh, T. and A. Constable Ltd.

Benge, R. C. (1958) *Technical and Vocational Education in the UK: a Bibliographical Survey*, Paris, UNESCO.

Benn, C. and Fairley, J. (eds) (1986) *Challenging the MSC on Jobs, Education and Training*, London, Pluto Press.

Bennett, R. J., McCoshan, A. and Sellgren, J. (1990) *Local Employer Networks (LENs): Their Experience and Lessons for TECs*, London, LSE.

Berry, C., Harrison, J. and Radley, C. (1993) *Evaluation of the Work Trials Pilots: Main Report*, Sheffield, ES Research and Evaluation Branch Report No. 85, October.

Berry-Lound, D., Chaplin, M. and O'Connell, Bill (1991) 'Review of Industry Training Organisations', *Employment Gazette*, October, pp. 535–42.

Berthoud, R. (1978) *Training Adults for Skilled Jobs: Skillcentre Training and Local Labour Markets*, Policy Studies Institute, April, No. 575 (Vol. 44).

Bilbrough, B. (1988) *Developing the Responsive College*, Bristol, Coombe Lodge Report, Vol. 20, No. 10.

Birtwhistle, A. (1994) *Jobplan Evaluation: Summary of Findings*, Sheffield, ES Research and Evaluation Branch Report No. 100.

Birtwhistle, A., Gawn, J., Jones, S. and Harrison, J. (1993) *Evaluation of 13 Week Review*, Sheffield, ES Research and Evaluation Branch Report No. 87.

Blamire, J. (September 1990) *Work Related Education in London 1990–93: A Summary of WRFE Plans*, London, Training Agency London Office.

Board of Education (1943) *Curriculum and Examinations in Secondary Schools*, HMSO, (Norwood Report).

Bolton, J. E. (1971) *Small Firms: Report of the Committee of Inquiry on Small Firms*, Cmd 4811, London, HMSO.

Boutall, S. (1998) *Evaluation of Jobfinder: Tracking Study*, Sheffield, ES.

Bradford Vision (2001) *Community Pride Not Prejudice: Making Diversity Work in Bradford*, Bradford, Bradford Vision, known as Ousley Report or Bradford Report.

Bramley, P. (1996) *Evaluating Training*, London, IPD.

Breen, E. (2001) *Early Evaluations of Jobpoint in Pathfinder Offices*, Sheffield, Employment Services.

British Educational Communications and Technology Agency (1999) *Corporate Plan 1999–2002*, Coventry, BECTA.

British Market Research Bureau (1981) *Temporary Short Time Working Compensation Scheme: Report on a Survey Prepared for the Department of Employment*, London, British Market Research Bureau.

——(1992) *Job Interview Guarantee Evaluation: Report on a Survey of JIG Employers*, London, British Market Research Bureau.

British Market Research Bureau International (1997) *Youth Enterprise Initiative Output Related Funding Scheme: A Research Report*, Sheffield, DfEE.

British Vocational Qualifications (2001) *British Vocational Qualifications: A Directory of Vocational Qualifications Available in the UK*, London, Kogan Page.

Brown, A. and Fairley, J. (eds) (1989) *The Manpower Services Commission in Scotland*, Edinburgh, Edinburgh University Press.

Brown, R. (1995) 'The Graduate Enterprise Programme: Attempts to Measure the Effectiveness of Small Business Training', *British Journal of Education and Work*, Vol. 8 (1), pp. 23–27.

Brown, R. and Myers, A. (1990) 'Encouraging Enterprise: Britain's Graduate Enterprise Programme', *Journal of Small Business Management*, October, pp. 71–77.

Bryson, C. (1996) *Evaluation of the Travel to Interview Scheme*, Public Attitude Surveys Ltd.

Bryson, J. R., Daniels, P. W. and Ingram, D. R. (1999) 'Evaluating the Impact of Business Link on the Performance and Profitability of SMEs in the United Kingdom', *Policy Studies*, Vol. 20, No. 2, pp. 95–105.

Bushell, R. (1986) 'Evaluation of the Young Workers Scheme', *Employment Gazette*, May.

Business and Technician Education Council (1985) *Review of BTEC Awards in Business and Related Studies*, London, BTEC.

Business in the Community (1989) *Putting the Enterprise into TECs: A Guide for TEC Boards*, London, Business in the Community.

——(1990) *Customised Training: A Guide for Employers*, London, BIC.

By a Lady (1849) *Lessons on Industrial Education*, London, Longman, Brown, Green and Longmans.

Callear, L. (1994) 'Youth Credits: Their Impact on Young People and Employers', *Employment Gazette*, March.

Cameron, A. P. and Robinson, D. (1983) *SUPERVACS User Interface: Staff Views of Self-Service and Order Input First-Cut Screen Format Designs*, Sheffield, MSC.

Cameron, A. P., Kelly, R. and Robinson, D. (1983) *Gateshead Jobcentre Library Link: Jobseekers' Views and Experience*, Sheffield, MSC.

Carr Report (1958) *Training for Skill: Recruitment and Training of Young Workers in Industry*, London, HMSO.

Carter, R., and Kirkup, G. (1990) *Women in Engineering: A Good Place to be?* MacMillan, London.

Casson, M. (1979) *Youth Unemployment*, London, Macmillan.

Cawthorne, H. H. (1929) 'The Spitalfields Mathematical Society (1717–1845)', *The Journal of Adult Education*, April, pp. 156–58.

CEDEFOP (1995a) *Teachers and Trainers in Vocational Education: Germany, France, Spain and the United Kingdom*, Luxembourg, Office for Official Publications of the European Communities.

——(1995b) *Teachers and Trainers in Vocational Education: Italy, Ireland and Portugal*, Luxembourg, Office for Official Publications of the European Communities.

——(1997) *Teachers and Trainers in Vocational Education: Austria, Belgium, Greece, Luxembourg and the Netherlands*, Luxembourg, Office for Official Publications of the European Communities.

——(1998) *Teachers and Trainers in Vocational Education: Denmark, Finland, Iceland, Norway and Sweden*, Luxembourg, Office for Official Publications of the European Communities.

CEI Consultants (1991) *Evaluation of Programme Development Funds: Main Report*, Sheffield, Employment Service.

Central Youth Employment Executive (1953) *Report of the National Youth Employment Council on the Work of the Youth Employment Service, 1950–1953*, London, HMSO.

Centre for Developing and Evaluating Lifelong Learning (1999) *The Graduate Apprenticeship Pilot Projects 2nd Stage Evaluation Report*, Nottingham, University of Nottingham.

CERI (Centre for Educational Research and Innovation) (1997) *Education at a Glance: OECD Indicators, 1997*, Paris, OECD.

Chapman, P. G. and Tooze, M. J. (1986) *The Youth Training Scheme in the United Kingdom*, Aldershot, Avebury.

——(1987) *Some Economic Implications of the Youth Training Scheme*, Royal Bank of Scotland Review, September.

Chapman, R. J. and Wilson, J. P. (1999) 'Total Quality Training and Human Resource Development', pp. 393–415, in Wilson, John P., *Human Resource Development: Learning and Training for Individuals and Organisations*, London, Kogan Page.

Chatrik, B. (1999) *Learning Gateway for 16 and 17 Year Olds*, Working Brief, April, pp. 18–19.

Chatrik, B. and De Sousa, E. (1993) *Where Are They Now? Black Young People and the Youth Training Guarantee*, Nottingham, Black Employment and Training Forum.

Chitty, C. (1986) 'TVEI: The MSC's Trojan Horse' in Benn, C., and Fairley, J., op.cit.

Clemens, S., Gray. R. and Smith, P. (1991) *Employment Training: A Survey of Ex-Participants: Report on Phase 1*, Social and Community Planning Research P1167.

Cockburn, C. (1987) *Two Track Training: Sex Inequalities and the Youth Training Scheme*, MacMillan, London.

COIC (1988) *Which Way Now: Options '88*, Sheffield, MSC.

Coleman, N. and Williams, J. (1998) *Evaluation of Modern Apprenticeships: 1998 Survey of Young People*, London, DfEE Research Report RR93, December.

Commission of the European Communities (1990a) *Eurotecnet: Action Programme to Promote Innovation in the Field of Vocational Training Resulting From Technological Change in the European Community*, Brussels, Eurotecnet.

——(1990b) *Proposal for a Council Regulation Establishing a European Training Foundation*, Luxembourg, Office for Official Publications of the European Community.

——(1991) *Structures of the Education and Initial Training systems, EURIDICE and CEDEFOP project*, Luxembourg, Office for Official Publications of the European Communities.

——(1993) *Establishing an Action Programme for the Implementation of a European Community*

Vocational Training Policy: Leonardo da Vinci, Brussels, Office for Official Publications of the EC.

Commission of the European Communities Task Force (1992) *Comett 1 Catalogue of Outputs: Final Version*, Brussels, Comett Technical Assistance Office.

——(undated) *Guide to the European Community Programmes in the Fields of Education, Training, and Youth*, Luxembourg, Commission of the European Communities Task Force: Human Resources, Education Training, Youth.

Coolahan, J. (1981) *Irish Education: Its History and Structure*, Dublin, Institute of Public Administration.

Coopers and Lybrand (1994) *Workstart Pilots. Qualitative Study Final Report to the ED and ES*, January.

Coopers and Lybrand Associates (1987) *Evaluation of the National Priority Skills Scheme: Final Report*, MSC, Sheffield

Cornes, P., Alderman, J., Cumella, S., Harradence, J., Horton, D. and Tebbutt, A. G. (1982) *Employment Rehabilitation: The aims and achievement of a service for disabled people*, MSC Employment Service, February.

Council of Military Education (1860) *The Council of Military Education on Army Schools: First Report*, London, HMSO.

Courtney, G. and England, J. (1982) *Study of the Threshold Scheme*, London, Social and Community Planning Research.

Cowan, I. D. (1984) 'Certified industrial Training Ships c.1860 – 1913', *Journal of Educational Administration and History*, 16(1), pp. 1–9.

CRG (1996) *Evaluation of the Self Employment Option within Training for Work*, DfEE Research Series RS 35.

CRG Research (2006) *Positive Activities for Young People: National Evaluation Final Report*, Sheffield, DFES.

Crook, J. (1991) *Eight Week Review Evaluation*, ES Research and Evaluation Branch Report No. 74. October.

Crooks, C. (1993) *100 Not Out: The Centenary of the Employment Department 1893–1993*, London, Employment Department.

Crowley-Bainton, T. (1995) *Evaluation of the Open Learning Credits Pilot Programme. Summary Report*, ED Research Series No. 45.

Croxford, L., Raffe, D. and Surridge, P. (1996) *The Impact of Youth Credits: The Round One Credit TECs in Their First Year of Operation*, DfEE, Sheffield, February.

Cunningham, G. W. (1870) *The Elementary Education Act 1870*, London, Shaw and Sons.

Dadzie, S. (1993) *Working with Black Adult Learners*, Leicester, NIACE.

Dale, R. (1985) 'The Background and Inception of the Technical and Vocational Initiative' in Dale, R., (ed.) *Education, Training and Employment*, Oxford, Pergamon Press.

Dale, R., Bowe, R., Harris, D., Loveys, M., Moore, R., Shilling, C., Sikes, P. J., Trevitt, J. and Valsecchi, V. (1990) *The TVEI Story*, Milton Keynes, Open University Press.

Dalgleish, M. (1993) 'Evaluation of the Prince's Youth Business Trust', *Employment Gazette*, January, pp. 661–66.

Davey, R. (2002) 'Technical Certificates and Modern Apprenticeship reforms', *Newscheck*, April, p. 7.

Deakin, B. M. and Pratten, C. F. (1982) *Effects of the Temporary Employment Subsidy*, University of Cambridge, Department of Applied Economics Occasional Paper 53, Cambridge University Press.

Department for Children, Education, Lifelong Learning and Skills (2008) *Skills That Work for Wales: A Skills and Employment Strategy and Action Plan*, Cardiff, DCELLS.

——, http://wales.gov.uk/about/civilservice/departments/dcells/;jsessionid=QpnmLfPhn2q TrH6xT0YhkYQ07y25wKzhfxyhnGWyKkY N9kN1nJps!1733788102?lang=en, (accessed 26 January, 2010).

Department for Children, Schools and Families (2007a) *Faith in the System: The Role of Schools with a Religious Character in English Education and Society*, London, DCSF.

——(2007b) *14–19 Partnerships and Plans: Emerging Findings from the Work of a Group of Volunteer Partnerships*, London, DCSF.

——(2009) *Quality, Choice and Aspiration: A Strategy for Young People's Information, Advice and Guidance*, London, DCSF. http://publications. dcsf.gov.uk/eOrderingDownload/IAG-Report-v2.pdf (accessed 15 February 2010).

Department for Employment and Learning (May 2003) *Worktrack: Equality Impact Assessment*, Belfast, Department for Employment and Learning.

——(March 2005) *Success Through Skills: The Skills Strategy for Northern Ireland: A Programme for Implementation*, Cm 6483, Belfast, DELNI

Department for Innovation, Universities and Skills (2007) *The Offenders Learning and Skills Service (OLASS) in England: A Brief Guide*, London, DIUS.

Department for Work and Pensions (2002) *Report on the One Pilots: Lessons for Jobcentre Plus: Reply by the Government to the First Report of the Work and Pensions Select Committee*, Cm 5505, London.

——(July 2007) *In Work, Better Off: Next Steps to Full Employment*, London, The Stationery Office.

——(2008) *Transforming Britain's Labour Market: Ten Years of the New Deal*, London, DWP.

——(2009) *Jobcentre Plus Support Contract: Specification and Supporting Information Invitation to Tender*, London, DWP.

Department of Economic Development (1988) *The Organisation of Training in Northern Ireland: Proposals for the Future*, Belfast, Department of Economic Development.

Department of Education and Science (1985) *The DES PICKUP Programme. Progress Report 1982–1985*, London, HMSO.

——(1990) *Public Education in England 150th Anniversary*, London, DES and HM Inspectorate.

Department of Employment (1959) *Industrial Rehabilitation: A Handbook for the Use of Rehabilitation Units*, London, Department of Employment.

——(1976) *Training for Vital Skills*, London, Department of Employment/Manpower Services Commission.

——(1978a) 'The Small Firms Employment Subsidy – an Evaluation of its Effectiveness', *Employment Gazette*, May.

——(1986a) *Working Together, Education and Training*, White Paper, Cmnd 9823, London, Department of Employment, HMSO.

——(1986b) *Job Splitting Scheme*, London, Department of Employment.

——(1988a) *Training for Employment*, White Paper, Cm 316, London, Department of Employment.

——(1988b) *Employment for the 1990s*, White Paper Cm 540, London, Department of Employment.

Department of Environment (1997) *Effective Partnerships: A Handbook for Members of SRB Challenge Fund Partnerships*, London, Department of Environment.

Department of Manpower Services (1985) *Youth Training Programme: A Step in the Right Direction*, Belfast, Department of Manpower Services.

DES (1990) *Grants for Education Support and Training 1991–92*, London, DES.

——(1992) *A Survey of the Enterprise in Higher Education Initiative in Fifteen Polytechnics and Colleges of Higher Education: A Report by HMI*, London, DES.

DES/DE (1985) *Education and Training for Young People*, Cmnd 9482, London, HMSO.

DES/ED (1991) *Education and Training for the 21st Century*, Cmnd 1536, London, HMSO.

DfEE (1995) *Career Development Loans Annual Report 1994–1995*, London, HMSO.

——(1996a) 'Part One GNVQ Pilots Take Off in 200 New Schools', *DfEE News*, 431/96.

——(1996b) *Meeting the National Skills Challenge: A Summary of Labour Market and Skill Trends*, London, DfEE.

——(1997a) *Evaluation of Skills Challenge*, London, DfEE/York Consulting.

——(1997b) *Connecting the Learning Society: National Grid for Learning – The Government's Consultation Paper*, Sheffield, DfEE.

——(1997c) *Education Action Zones: An Introduction*, London, DfEE.

——(1997d) *The Relaunch Strategy: Partnership Projects: Prospectus*, London, DfEE.

——(1997e) *Welfare to Work Employment Zones: Local Solutions to Individual Needs*, London, DfEE.

——(1997f) *Investing in Young People: a Strategy for the Education and Training of 16–18 Year-Olds*, Sheffield, DfEE.

——(1998a) *Design of the New Deal for Long-Term Unemployed People Aged 25 Plus*, London, DfEE.

——(1998b) *Union Learning Fund: A Partnership in Lifelong Learning – Prospectus*, London, DfEE.

——(1998c) *University for Industry: Engaging People in Learning for Life – Pathfinder Prospectus*, London, DfEE.

——(1998d) *Individual Learning Accounts, (Ref. ILA1 and ILA2)*, London, DfEE.

——(1998e) *The Learning Age: a Renaissance for a New Britain. (The Government Green Paper on Lifelong Learning)*, Cm 3790, London, HMSO.

——(1998f) *Towards a National Skills Agenda: First Report of the National Skills Task Force, (SKT1)*, London, DfEE.

——(1998g) *Promoting Disabled People's Rights: Creating a Disability Rights Commission Fit for the 21st Century*, Cm 3977, London, HMSO.

——(1998h) *NVQs and SVQs at a Glance*, London, DfEE.

——(1999a) *Adult and Community Fund: Prospectus*, Revised March 1999, London, DfEE.

——(1999b) *Delivering Skills for all: Second Report of the National Skills Task Force, (SKT5)*, London, DfEE.

——(1999c) *Individual Learning Accounts: A Summary of Progress, (ILA Prog)*, London, DfEE.

——(1999d) *Learning to Succeed: A New Framework for post-16 Learning, (White Paper Cm 4392)*, London, TSO.

——(1999e) *The Learning and Skills Council Prospectus: Learning to succeed*, London DfEE

——(1999f) *Excellence in Cities*, London, DfEE.

——(1999g) *Evaluation for the Use of the Local Competitiveness Budget*, London, DfEE Research Report 171.

——(1999h) *Key Skills Explained*, London, DfEE.

——(1999i) *Evaluation of the Trial of the Progress File*, Research Report RR107, London, DfEE, GHK Economics and Management.

——(1999j) *Early Lessons from Millennium Volunteers Demonstration Projects*, London, DfEE Research Report 180.

——(1999k) *Developing Tomorrow's Workforce, Skills and Enterprise Annual Conference Report 1999*, Sheffield, DfEE.

——(2000a) *Tackling the Adult Skills Gap: Third Report of the National Skills Task Force*, London, DfEE.

——(2000b) *Action Teams for Jobs*, London, DfEE.

——(2000c) *Connexions: A Strategy and a Service*, London, DfEE.

——(2000d) *Foundation Degrees: Consultation Paper*, London, DfEE.

——(2000e) *National Learning Targets for England for 2002: Annual Report*, London, DfEE.

——(2000f) *Changes to the Operation of the Standards Fund 2001–02*, Sheffield, DfEE.

——(2000g) *Colleges for Excellence and Innovation: Statement by the Secretary of State for Education and Employment on the Future of Further Education in England*, London, DfEE.

——(2000h) *Changing Patterns in a Changing World: Work-Life Balance: A Discussion Document*, London, DfEE.

——(2000i) (April) *Inspecting Post-16 Education and Training: Informal Consultation on the Common Inspection Framework for Use by OFSTED and ALI*, London, DfEE.

——(2001a) *Leadership Programme for Serving Head-teachers: Information and Application 2001–2002*, London, DfEE.

——(2001b) *Centres of Vocational Excellence: Heralding a New Era for Further Education*, London, DfEE.

DfES (2001a) *Evaluating the Connexions Card Demonstration and Pathfinder Projects*, London, DfES Report Paper 318.

——(2001b) *Skills for Life: A Guide to Funding Adult Literacy and Numeracy Learning Programmes*, London, DfES.

——(September 2001) *Modern Apprenticeships: The Way to Work, The Report of the Modern Apprenticeship Advisory Committee*, VET 4, London, DfES.

——(2002a) *Green Paper: 14–19: Extending Opportunities, Raising Standards*, Cm 5342.

——(2002b) *Progress Files: Best Practice Case Studies*, London, DfES.

——(2002c) *Evaluation of Education Maintenance Allowance Pilots: Leeds and London: First Year Evidence*, Research Report 353, London, DfES.

——(2002d) *Excellence in Cities: Schools Extending Excellence*, London, DfES.

——(2002e) *Academies: Schools to Make a Difference*, London, DfES.

——(November 2002) *Success For All: Reforming Further Education and Training – Our Vision for the Future*, London, DFES;

——(2003) *21st Century Skills: Realising Our Potential: Individuals, Employers, Nation*, Cm 5810, London, HMSO.

——(October 2006) *The Science, Technology, Engineering and Mathematics (STEM) Programme Report*. HM Treasury (July 2004) Science and Innovation Investment Framework 2004–2014, London, HMSO.

——(2007) *Raising Expectations: Staying in Education and Training Post-16*, Cm 7065 Green Paper, London, HMSO.

DfES Innovation Unit (undated) *All-Age Schooling: A Resource*, London, HMSO.

Dickenson, P. and Broome, S. (1998) *Jobfinders Grant Evaluation Study: Final Report*, Sheffield, ES.

Dickson, P., Moys, A. and Wightwick, C. (1994) *LINGUA: The UK Perspective*, National Foundation for Educational Research in England and Wales.

Dowling, P. J. (1935) *The Hedge Schools of Ireland*, London, Longmans Green.

Dunne, P. and Elias, P. (1986) *Jobs after TOPS: An Analysis of Survey Data from the Training Opportunities Scheme*, Institute for Employment Research, University of Warwick Research Report.

Durcan, T. J. (1972) *History of Irish Education from 1800*, Bala, North Wales, Dragon Books.

Dutton, P., Mansell, S. and Mooney, P. (1989) *The Net Exchequer Cost of Sheltered Employment*, ED Research Paper No. 69.

Edwards, A. D., Fitz, J. and Whitty, G. (1990) *The State and Private Education: An Evaluation of the Assisted Places Scheme*, Brighton, Falmer Press.

Ely, R. (1982) *In Search of the Central Society of Education*, Leeds: Museum of the History of Education, University of Leeds.

EMAS Consultants Ltd (1984) *Final Report on The Management Action Programme 1980–1984 for the Manpower Services Commission*, Sheffield, MSC.

Employment Department (1991a) *City Action: Business, Skills, and Jobs*, London, Employment Department.

——(1991b) *Flexible Learning: A Framework for Education and Training in the Skills Decade: A Guide to Developing Flexible Learning in Schools and Colleges of Further Education*, Sheffield, Employment Department.

——(1991c) *The Partnership Primer: An Introduction to the Management of an Education Business Partnership*, Sheffield, Employment Department.

——(1991d) *Recording Achievement and Planning Individual Development: Guidance on Summarising the Record and Completing the National Record of Achievement*, Sheffield, Employment Department.

——(1991e) *Wages Councils and Statutory Pay Rates*, London, Employment Department.

——(1992a) *Training Credits Progress Report: A Report on the First Twelve Months*, June. London, Employment Department.

——(1992b) *People, Jobs and Opportunity*, London, HMSO.

——(1992c) *Gateways To Learning Briefings Number 1, Statements of Service*, Sheffield, Information and Advice Services Unit.

——(1992d) *The European Social Fund: A Community at Work*, Sheffield, Employment Department.

——(1993a) *Career Development Loans: Annual Report 1991–1992*, London, HMSO.

——(1993b) *Access to Assessment: training and development NVQ Resource Pack*, Sheffield, Employment Department.

——(1994a) *Fair Play for Women: Government Initiatives*, Sheffield, Employment Department.

——(1994b) *The Relevance and Application of Individual Training Plans in Adult and Youth Training*, Sheffield, Employment Department.

——(1995) 'Career Development Loans', *Labour Market Quarterly Report*, Special feature, May.

Employment NTO (2002) *Learning and Development, and Assessment and Verification National Occupational Standards*, Leicester, Employment NTO.

Employment Policy Institute (1993) *Making Workstart Work*, EPI Economic Report, Vol. 7.

Employment Service (1988a) *Code of Good Practice on the Employment of Disabled People*, Sheffield, Employment Service.

——(1988b) *Job Club Annual Report*, Sheffield, ES.

——(1993) *Jobseeker's Charter*, London, Employment Service.

——(1994) *Community Action: Annual Review*, Sheffield, Employment Service.

——(June 1997) leaflet *The Job Introduction Scheme – Information for Employers*, Sheffield, ES.

——(1997a) *Evaluation of the National Development Programme Final Report*, Sheffield, Employment Service.

——(September 1998) *A Final Report on the Evaluation of Programme Centres*, Martin Hamblin Research, Employment Service

——(December 1998) *Research and Development Report: Evaluation of Jobfinder: Tracking Study*, Sheffield, Employment Service.

——(1999) *The Supported Employment Programme: A Consultation on Future Development*, Sheffield, ES.

Employment Service Operational Plan (2001) *Employment Service Operational Plan 2001–2002*, Sheffield, Employment Service.

England, J. (1983) *The Employment Transfer Scheme Study: the Interview Survey of Return Migration*, London, SCPR.

Equality and Human Rights Commission (2010) www.equalityhumanrights.com/ (accessed 12 February 2010).

Ernst and Young (1995) *The Evaluation of Modern Apprenticeships: Final Report*, October, Sheffield, DfEE.

Esp, D. (1990) 'City Technology Colleges: Fringe Benefit or Leading Edge?', *Education Today*, Vol. 40, No. 1, pp. 12–14.

European Commission (1995) *Towards the Learning Society, White Paper on Education and Training, Teaching and Learning*, Brussels, Office for Official Publications of the European Communities.

——(1996) *White Paper on Education and Training: Teaching and Learning: Towards the Learning society*, Luxembourg, Office for Official Publications of the European Communities.

Evans, K. (1980) *Day Release: A Desk Study: The Nature, Aims and Quality of the Education and Training Undertaken by Young People Following Day Release Courses Leading to Recognised Qualifications*, University of Surrey, Department of Adult Education.

Evans, N. (1995) *The Evaluation of the National Training Awards*, DfEE Research Series No. 56. Sheffield, DfEE.

Everett, M., Tu, T. and Caughey, A. (1999) *National Traineeships: An Evaluation of the Development and Implementation Phase*, A Mori Research Report RR122, London, DfEE.

Fairbairns, J. (1979) *Evaluation of Wider Opportunities for Women (WOW) Courses: Final Report*, London, Psychological Services, MSC.

Fairclough, M. (1992) *Working for Benefit? The Action Credit Pilot Scheme*, London, Low Pay Unit.

Farrow, S. (1990) 'Making INSET Work', *Head Teachers Review*, Spring, pp. 28–29.

FEFC (December 1994) *General Certificate of Education Advanced Level and Advanced Supplementary Qualifications: National Survey Report*, Coventry, FEFC.

——(April 2000) *Inspecting Post-16 Education and Training: Informal Consultation on the Common Inspection Framework for Use by the Office for Standards in Education and the Adult Learning Inspectorate*, London, DfEE.

Field, J. (2009) 'Able Bodies: Work Camps and the Training of the Unemployed in Britain before 1939', paper presented at the Institute of Continuing Education, University of Cambridge, 6 July.

Field, J. (1985) *The Disablement Advisory Service: Survey of Effectiveness Among Employers*, London, Social and Community Planning Research.

Findley, J. J. (ed.) (1908) *The Demonstration School Records: Being Contributions to the Study of Education by the Department of Education in the University of Manchester*, Vol. 1, Manchester, University Press.

Finn, D. (1987) *Training Without Jobs: New deals and Broken Promises. From Raising the School Leaving Age to the YTS*, London, Macmillan.

Finn, D. (1993) 'Learning for Work', *Working Brief*, No. 45, June, p. 6.

Fletcher, G. (1912) 'Education in Ireland', in Laurie, A. P. *The Teacher's Encyclopaedia*, London, Caxton Publishing Company, pp. 71–103.

Flude, M. and Sieminski, S. (1999) *Education, Training and the Future of Work II: Developments in Vocational Education and Training*, London, Routledge and The Open University.

Foreign and Commonwealth Office (1992) *Convention Revising the Convention Setting Up a European University Institute*, London, HMSO.

Forsyth, D. (1912) 'The Higher Grade School Movement', in A. P. Laurie *The Teacher's Encyclopaedia*, London, Caxton Publishing Company, Vol. 5, pp. 81–89.

France, A. and Wiles, P. (1996) *The Youth Action Scheme: A Report of the National Evaluation*, London, DfEE.

Frost, J. (ed.) (1857) *Lessons on Common Things for the Use of Schools and Families on the Basis of Dr Mayo's Lessons on Objects*, Philadelphia, J.B. Lippincott and Co.

Further Education Funding Council (1993) *Funding Learning*, Coventry, FEFC.

Gent, R. (1983) *Analysis of the Training Within Industry National Supervisory Questionnaire stage II Final Report*, Sheffield, MSC.

GHK (2002) *Evaluation of the Skills Development Fund*, DfES Research Report 364.

GHK Economics and Management (1996) *Early Evaluation of Skills for Small Businesses. Final Report*, February, Sheffield, DfEE.

Glazier, J. (1979) *CAPITAL Evaluation Report*, London, MSC.

Gleeson, D. (1990) *Training and its Alternatives*, Milton Keynes, Open University Press.

Gokulsing, K. (Moti), Ainley, P. and Tysome, T. (1996) *Beyond Competence: The National Council for Vocational Qualifications Framework and the Challenge to Higher Education in the New Millennium*, Aldershot, Avebury.

Gordon, O. (1911) 'School employment bureaux', in Laurie, A.P. *The Teacher's Encyclopaedia*, London, Caxton Publishing Company, Vol. 3, pp. 158–189.

Green, J. A. (1912) *Pestalozzi's Educational Writings*, London, Edward Arnold.

Green, J. R. (1883) *The Conquest of England*, London, Macmillan and Co. cited in De Montmorency, J. (1902) *State Intervention in English Education: A Short History from the Earliest Times Down to 1813*, Cambridge, University Press.

Gregg, P. (1990) 'The Evolution of Special Employment Measures', *National Institute Economic Review*, May, pp. 49–58.

Griffiths, R. and Thomas, A. (June 2001) *New Deal for Partners of Unemployed People: Case Studies on Delivery: Phase 1*, Sheffield, Employment Service.

Grubb Institute (1990) *Initial Training in YTS: The First Year: Report of an Evaluation Report*, London, Grubb Institute.

——(1992) *The Use of Local Initiative Funds by TECs: An Evaluation*, London, Grubb Institute.

Hackworth, C. (1988) *Education and Business Partnership*, Sheffield, MSC.

Hadow, W. H. (1926) *Board of Education: Report of the Consultative Committee on the Education of the Adolescent*, London, HMSO.

——(1931) *Board of Education: Report of the Consultative Committee on Primary Education*, London, HMSO.

Hall, K. (1972) *Study of Government Training Centres in Scotland*, Edinburgh, Heriot-Watt University.

Hall, S. and Mawson, J. (1999) *Challenge Funding, Contracts and Area Regeneration: A Decade of Innovation in Policy Management and Coordination*, Bristol, University of Bristol, Policy Press.

Hamblin, M. (1991) *The Evaluation of Jobshare*, London, Martin Hamblin Research.

Hammond, D. (2002) '"Back to the floor" for learners', *People Management*, 16 May, p. 12.

Harris Research Centre (1987) *MSC Training Providers Survey*, Sheffield, MSC.

Harrison, J. F. C. (1954) *A History of the Working Men's College 1854–1954*, London, Routledge and Kegan Paul.

Harrison, J. (1989) 'Standards for Success', *Training and Development*, Vol. 7, No. 17, October, pp. 22–24.

Hasluck, C. (March 2000) *The New Deal for the Long Term Unemployed – A Summary of Progress*, Sheffield, Employment Service.

——(September 2000) *The New Deal for Lone Parents: A Review of Evaluation Evidence*, Sheffield, Employment Service.

Health and Safety Commission (1993) *Health and Safety Commission: Health and Safety Executive: Accounts 1991–92*, London, HMSO.

Heather, P. and Kay, J. (1995) *Job Review Workshop Evaluation*, London, ES Research and Evaluation Branch Report No. 106.

Hedge, A., Roberts, C. and Cheetham, B. (1975) *Communications for Employment and Training: An Evaluation*, Southall, National Centre for Industrial Language Training.

Hedges, B. (1985) *Young Workers Scheme Survey 1985*, London, Social and Community Planning Research P.842, Employment Department Group.

——(1986) *Young Workers Scheme Follow-up Survey 1986*, London, Social and Community Planning Research P.870, Employment Department Group.

Helsby, G. (1992) 'The Year in Industry Scheme: a Partnership That Works', *Education and Training*, Vol. 34, No. 2, pp. 22–24.

Heriot-Watt University (1974) *Survey of Government Assistance with Industrial Training in Development Areas*, Edinburgh, Heriot-Watt University.

Hibbert, V. (1991) 'Matching Jobs to Disabled People the Interwork Way', *Recruitment and Development* Report, No. 22, Vol. 18, October, pp. 9–12.

Higher Education Consultancy Group (2005) *Summative Evaluation of the Teaching Quality Enhancement Fund: A Report to HEFCE by the Higher Education Consultancy Group and CHEMS Consulting*, Bristol, HEFCE.www.hefce.ac.uk/Pubs/rdreports/2005/rd23_05/rd23_05.pdf (accessed 7 April 2008).

Higher Education Funding Council for England (1994) *M1/94 HEQC/HEFCE Joint Statement on Quality Assurance*, Bristol, HEFCE.www.hefce.ac.uk/Pubs/hefce/1994/m1_94.htm, accessed 25 January 2010.

Highlands and Islands Enterprise (1993) *Highlands and Islands Enterprise Accounts 1992–93*, HC series (1992–93) 865.

Highley, H. (1999) 'The Right to Time Off for Study and Training', *Croner Training and Development Briefing*, No. 41, 9 December, pp. 9–11.

Hillage, J. and Mitchell, H. (2003) *Employer Training Pilots: First Year Evaluation Report*, London, DfES.

Hillage, J. and Wilson, A. (1992) *Employers' Requirements of the Careers Service*, Brighton, Institute of Manpower Studies.

Hillage, J., Kodz, J. and Pike, G. (2001) *Pre-16 Work Experience Practice in England: An Evaluation*, London, DfEE Research Report RR263.

Hitchcock, G. (1988) *Education and Training 14–18*, London, Longman.

HM Inspectors (1990) *Pickup in Scotland: A Report by HM Inspectors of Schools*, March, Edinburgh, HMSO/Scottish Education Department.

HM Treasury (March 2004) *Supporting Young People to Achieve: Towards a New Deal for Skills*, London, HM Treasury, Department for Work and Pensions, Department for Education and Skills.

——(July 2004) *Science and Innovation Investment Framework 2004–2014*, London, HMSO.

——(March 2007) *Supporting Young People to Achieve: The Government's Response to the Consultation*, London, HM Treasury.

HMI (2003) *Excellence in Cities: City Learning Centres: An Evaluation of the First Year*, HMI 1655, London, HMI.

Hodkinson, P. and Hodkinson, H. (1999) 'Markets, Outcomes and the Quality of Vocational Education and Training: Some Lessons from a Youth Credits Pilot Scheme', in Flude, M. and Sieminski, S. *Education, Training and the Future of Work II: Developments in Vocational Education and Training*, Routledge/Open University Press.

Home Office (2001a) *Ministerial Group on Public Order and Community Cohesion, Building Cohesive Communities: The Report of the Ministerial Group on Public Order and Community Cohesion*, London, Home Office.

——(2001b) *Community Cohesion Review Team, Community Cohesion: A Report of the Independent Review Team*, (Ted Cantel), London, Home Office.

House of Commons (2000) *Training and Enterprise Councils and Chambers of Commerce, Training and Enterprise in England, Income and Expenditure Account 1997–98*, London, The Stationery Office.

House of Commons: Children, Schools and Families Committee (2010) Young People Not in Education, Employment or Training, Eighth Report of Session 2009–10 Volume 1, London, The Stationery Office.

House of Commons Education and Skills Committee (2005) *UK e-University Third Report of Session 2004–05*, London, The Stationery Office.

House of Commons Environment Committee (1995) *Single Regeneration Budget: First Report: Vol. II Minutes of Evidence and Appendices*, London, HMSO.

House of Commons European Standing Committee (1994) *Education and Training: SOCRATES Programme*, London, HMSO.

House of Commons Work and Pensions Committee (2002) '"ONE" Pilots: Lessons for Jobcentre Plus, Report, Together with Proceedings of the Committee, Minutes of Evidence and Appendices', HC 426, London, The Stationery Office.

Hughes, M. (1996) *Competing for Business: Colleges and the Competitiveness Fund*, London, Further Education and Development Agency.

Humble, S. (1989) 'The UK Teaching Company Scheme: Graduate Employment in Industry', *Industry and Higher Education*, Vol. 3, No. 2, June, pp. 96–98.

Hunn, A. (1984) *The Employment Transfer Scheme Cohort Study*, London, MSC, March.

——(1987) *Trials of Infosearch, A Public Access Database in Eight Jobcentres and Two Libraries*, Sheffield, MSC.

Hyde, Mrs (1862) *How to Win Our Workers: A Short Account of the Leeds Sewing School for Factory Girls*, London, Macmillan and Co.

IFF Research Ltd (1979) *The Adult Employment Subsidy: Research Report*. London, IFF.

——, (1987) *New Workers Scheme*, London, IFF.

ILO (1984) *ILO and the World of Work*, Geneva, ILO.

Incomes Data Services (1994) *Industrial Tribunal: Practice and Procedure*, London, IDS.

Industrial Relations Training Resource Centre (1980) *Analysing Industrial Relations for Effective Training and Other Initiatives*, Berkhampstead, Herts, IRTRC.

Industrial Training Council (1965) *Industrial Training Council: Final Report*, London, ITC.

Inland Revenue (1995) *Tax Relief for Vocational Training*, Personal Taxpayer Series, April.

Institute of Manpower Studies (1991) *Basic Skills at Work: A Report on the Norfolk and Waveney Labour Market*, London, IMS.

——(1992) *Employers' Requirements of the Careers Service*, IMS, University of Sussex, Brighton.

International Centre for Advanced Technical and Vocational Training (1967) *The International Centre for Advanced Technical and Vocational Training*, Turin, ILO.

Jessop, R. (1989) 'Garden festival jobs scheme', *Training and Development*, Vol. 7, No. 10, pp. 11–12.

Jobcentre Plus (undated) *Condition Management Programmes: What They Are, What is the Evidence Base, What do They Currently Look Like?* www.jobcentreplus.gov.uk/JCP/stellent/groups/jcp/documents/websitecontent/dev_012591.doc (accessed 19 February 2010).

Johnson, P. (1983) *A Cost-Benefit Analysis of the New Enterprise Programme, Report for the MSC*, Durham, Dept. of Economics.

Johnson, S., Leffman, J., Moreton, T. and Murphy, L. (August 1993) *An Interim Examination of PACTs and ADCs*, Sheffield, Employment Service.

Jones, G. E. and Roderick, G. W. (2003) *A History of Education in Wales*, Cardiff, University of Wales Press.

Jones, M. G. (1938) *The Charity School Movement*, Cambridge, University Press.

Jones, T., Minns, A. and Wright, C. (1988) *An Evaluation of the Sheltered Employment Scheme*, London, Department of Employment.

Julie Janes Associates (1994) *Skill Choice Quality Workshop Report*, Sheffield, Employment Department.

Kay, J. and Fletcher, J. (October 1996) *Evaluation of 1-2-1 / Workwise for 18–24 Year-Olds: Tracking Study*, RED 109, Sheffield, Employment Service.

Kay, J., Gibbins, C. and Birtwhistle, A. (1995a) *Evaluation of Workwise/Worklink Pilots for 18–24 Year Olds. Tracking Study and Analysis of Register of Flows*, Sheffield ESREB Report 104.

Kay, J., Gibbins, C. and Birtwhistle, A. (1995b) *Evaluation of 1-2-1 Supportive Caseload Pilots for 18–24 Year Olds. Tracking Study and Analysis of Register of Flows*, Sheffield, ESREB 105.

Kay, R. (1985) *UCCA: Its Origins and Development*, Cheltenham, UCCA.

Kelly, T. (1992) *A History of Adult Education in Great Britain*, Liverpool, Liverpool University Press.

Keogh, J. E. (1999) 'Workplace Diversity and Training – More Than Fine Words', pp. 241–59, in Wilson, John P. (ed.) *Human Resource Development: Learning and Training for Individuals and Organisations*, London, Kogan Page.

King, J. (1990) *Regional Selective Assistance, 1980–84. An Evaluation by DTI, IDS and WOID*, London, HMSO.

Kingston Regional Management Centre (1981) *The New Manager Project Research Report: An Innovation in Manager Development*, Sheffield, MSC.

Kirkland, K. (1986) *Basic Accounting, Private Enterprise Programme Publication*, Sheffield, MSC.

Kodz, J. and Eccles, J. (2001) *Evaluation of the New Deal 50 Plus: Qualitative Evidence From Clients: Second Phase*, Sheffield, Employment Service/Institute for Employment Studies.

Lancaster, J. (1808) *Improvement in Education; Abridged. Containing a Complete Epitome of the System of Education Invented and Practised by the Author*, London, Lancaster, J., Free School, Borough Road, Southwark.

Lasko, R. (1978) 'The Work Experience Programme', *Employment Gazette*, March.

Laurie, A. P. (1912a) 'Continuation and Technical Schools in England', *The Teacher's Encyclopaedia*, London, Caxton Publishing Company, pp. 90–111.

——(1912b) 'Open-Air Schools', *The Teacher's Encyclopaedia*, London, Caxton Publishing Company, pp. 1–6.

Leadership Foundation for Higher Education (2004) *Introducing the Leadership Foundation for Higher Education*, London, LFHE

Learning and Skills Council (2001) *Learning and Skills Council: Strategic Framework to 2004, Draft Corporate Plan for Consultation*, Coventry, LSC.

——(2004) *The National Employers Skills Survey 2003: Key Findings*, Warwick, Learning and Skills Council/Institute for Employment Research, University of Warwick.

——(2006) *Our Single Statement of Requirements*, Coventry, LSC.

——(December 2009) *Evaluation of Adult Learner Account Trials: Synthesis Report*, Coventry, Learning and Skills Council.

Lehmann, H. (1993) *The Effectiveness of the Restart Programme and the Enterprise Allowance Scheme*, Centre for Economic Performance Discussion Paper No. 139.

362

Leitch, S. (December 2006) *Leitch Review of Skills: Prosperity for all in the Global Economy – World Class Skills*, London, TSO.

Levy, M. (February 1987) *The Core Skills Project and Work Based Learning*, Bristol, Further Education Staff College.

Lifelong Learning UK (December 2008) *Learning Support Practitioners in the Lifelong Learning Sector: Guidance for Awarding Institutions on Learning Support Practitioner Roles and Initial Training Qualifications*, London, LLUK.

Linell, J. (1985) *Staff Development Handbook for Youth Training Scheme*, Leicester, National Youth Bureau.

Lourie, J. (1998) *Employment and Training Schemes*, House of Commons Library Research Paper 97/98.

Loy, A. (1990) 'Helping the Unemployed Back to Work: Some Developments in the Employment Service', *Employment Gazette*, August, pp. 400–402.

Loyd, R. and Hussey, D. (1996) Evaluation of Jobmatch, Department for Education and Employment Research Studies, RS 26.

Macdonald, S. (2004) *The History and Philosophy of Art Education*, Cambridge, Lutterworth Press.

MacLeod, R. M. and Collins, P. (1981) *The Parliament of Science: the British Association for the Advancement of Science 1831–1981*, Northwood, Middlesex, Science Reviews.

Maddocks, A. J. (1981) 'An Industrial Simulation on a Work Preparation Course (for Students with Moderate Learning Difficulties) at Trowbridge College', *Educare*, No. 25, June, pp. 24–26.

Main, B. (1985) 'School-Leaver Unemployment and the Youth Opportunities Programme in Scotland', *Oxford Economic Papers*, Vol. 37, pp. 426–47.

Makeham, P. (1980) *Evaluation of the Job Release Scheme*, London, Department of Employment.

Makrotest (1991) *Report on Evaluation of HTNT*, Tunbridge Wells, Makrotest.

Mangione, T. (2003) 'The Establishment of the Model School System in Ireland 1834–1854', *New Hibernia Review*, Vol. 7.4, pp. 103–22.

Mansfield, R. and Mitchell, L. (1996) *Towards a Competent Workforce*, Aldershot, Gower.

Marshall, J. N., Alderman, N., Wong, C. and Thwaites, A. (1993) *BGT Option 3 Evaluation Project*, Employment Department Research Series No. 11, May.

Martin Hamblin Research (1991) *The Evaluation of Jobshare*, London, MHR. April.

Mas Research, Marketing and Consultancy (1989) *Final Report NPSS Evaluation* Autumn 1988.

Mayo, E. (1831) *Lessons on Objects, as Given in a Pestalozzian School, at Cheam, Surrey*, London, R. B. Seeley.

McClean, D. (1999) *Education and Empire: Naval Tradition and England's Elite Schooling*, London, I. B. Taurus and Co.

McClure, S. (2001) *The Inspectors' Calling: HMI and the Shaping of Educational Policy*, London, Hodder and Stoughton.

McCreath, D. and Naylor, A. (1992) 'Enterprise Awareness in Teacher Education: An Evaluation of the Relationship Between Institutional Policy Making and Implementation', *Assessment and Evaluation in Higher Education*, Vol. 17, No. 2.

McGill, P. R. (1981) 'Post Training Experience of TOPS Trainees', *Employment Gazette*, July, pp. 325–28.

McGregor, A., MacDougall, L., Taylor, K., Hirst, A., Rinne, S. and Clark, S. (2005) *Evaluation of the New Futures Fund Initiative*, Glasgow, Scottish Enterprise. www.scottish-enterprise.com/publications/new-futures-fund-evaluation-summary.pdf (accessed 19 February 2010).

Millett, A. (1997) 'Bringing a New Professionalism Into Teaching', *Education Journal*, Issue 10, March, pp. 12–13.

Ministry of Education (1953) *Training under the Government Vocational Training Scheme*, London, Administrative Memorandum (Ministry of Education) No. 449.

Ministry of Labour (1964) 'Industrial Training Act: A General Guide', cited in Ziderman, A. (1978) *Manpower Training and Policy*, London, MacMillan.

——(1968) *Training for Office Supervision: A Report by the Commercial and Clerical Training Committee of the Central Training Council*, London, HMSO.

Ministry of Labour and National Service (1948) *Report on the Business Training Scheme 1946–47*, London, MLNS.

Ministry of Overseas Development/Ministry of Labour (1970) *Industrial Training for Overseas Nationals*, London, HMSO. 'Minutes' refers to the Minutes of the Committee of the Privy Council on Education (1839–1857/58).

Montmorency, J. (1902) *State Intervention in English Education: A Short History From the Earliest Times Down to 1813*, Cambridge, University Press.

Moore Smith, G. C. (1912) *The Story of the People's College, Sheffield, 1842–1878*, Sheffield, Northend.

Morning, J. (1988) *CPVE: Evaluation Report*, London, Business and Technician Education Council City and Guilds.

Morris, M., Saunders, L. and Schagen, I. (1992) *The Impact of Compact 1991*, Slough, National Foundation for Educational Research.

MSC (1974) *Training Services Agency: A Five Year Plan*, London, HMSO.

——(1977a) *Training for Skills: A Programme for Action*, London, MSC.

——(1977b) *Young People at Work*, London, MSC.

——(1978a) *JCP Has Helped a Lot of People Face the Future: Here's the Next STEP*, London, MSC Special Programmes Division.

——(1978b) *Mobile Instructor Service: A Training Service for Industry*, London, MSC.

——(1978c) *Review of the Special Temporary Employment Programme*, London, MSC.

——(1978d) *Jobcentres: An Evaluation*, Sheffield, MSC.

——(1978e) *Review of Occupational Guidance: Report of the Occupational Guidance Review Group*, July, Sheffield, MSC, Employment Service Agency.

——(1978f) *TOPS Review 1978*, Sheffield, MSC Training Services Division.

——(1980a) *Project Based Work Experience: Sponsors Handbook*, Sheffield, MSC.

——(1980b) *Short Industrial Courses: Trainers Handbook: Youth Opportunities Programme*, London, MSC.

——(1980c) *Guide to Project Based Work Experience*, Sheffield, MSC.

——(1981a) *Unified Vocational Preparation*, Sheffield, MSC.

——(1981b) *A New Training Initiative: A Consultative Document*, Sheffield, MSC.

——(1981c) *A New Training Initiative: An Agenda for Action*, (Cmnd 8455), MSC, Sheffield.

——(1981d) *Direct Training Services*, Sheffield, MSC.

——(1981e) *Implications for DE and MSC of the Riots*, Sheffield, MSC, typescript document.

——(1982a) *Guide to Work Introduction Courses: Youth Opportunities Programme*, London, MSC Special Programmes Division.

——(1982b) *Youth Task Group Report*, Sheffield, MSC.

——(1982c) *Open-Tech Task Group Report*, Sheffield, MSC.

——(1982d) *Employment Induction Courses: Youth Opportunities Programme*, Sheffield, MSC.

——(1982e) *Guide to Work Experience on Employer's Premises: Youth Opportunities Programme*, London, MSC.

——(1983a) *Towards an Adult Training Strategy*, Sheffield, MSC.

——(1983b) *Training Information Framework (TIF): Second Progress Report*, April, Sheffield, MSC.

——(1983c) *A Handbook for Information Technology Centres: Youth Training Scheme*, Sheffield, MSC.

——(March 1983) *Guide to the Work of Area Manpower Boards*, Sheffield, MSC.

——(1984a) *A New Training Initiative: Modernisation of Occupational Training: a Position Statement*, Sheffield, MSC.

——(1984b) *Report on YTS Leavers Survey*, Sheffield, MSC.

——(1985a) *Priority Suppliers Directory 1985*, Sheffield, MSC.

——(1985b) *The Adult Training Strategy*, Sheffield, MSC.

——(1985c) *Local Consultancy Grants to Employers: Professional Assistance in Analysing Training Needs*, Sheffield, MSC.

——(1985d) *Management Extension Programme: An Exciting Opportunity for Unemployed Managers*, Sheffield, MSC.

——(1985e) *Adult Training Campaign: A Guide*, Sheffield, MSC.

——(1985f) *A Glossary of Terms Used in Education and Training*, Sheffield, Training Division, MSC.

——(1985g) *The Local Collaborative Projects Programme*, Sheffield, MSC.

——(1985h) *Access to Information Technology Scheme: Guide for Training Providers*, 5pp, Sheffield, MSC.

——(1985i) *Local Training Grants: Handbook for employers*, Sheffield, MSC.

——(1986a) *The Future of the Industrial Language Training Service*, Sheffield, MSC.

——(1986b) *Approved Training Organisations*, Sheffield, MSC.

——(1986c) *Local Grants to Employers: Planning for Change – Training Your Workforce*, Sheffield, MSC.

——(1986d) *Voluntary Projects Programme*, Sheffield, MSC.

——(1986e) *Get on Course for Success with Training for Enterprise*, Sheffield, MSC.

——(1987a) *ASSET Vocational Assessment Teams: An Evaluation of a New Approach to Employment Rehabilitation*, Sheffield, MSC.

——(1987b) *The Business Enterprise Programme: Free New Business Training*, Sheffield, MSC.

——(1987c) *Practical Vision Beyond Theory: The MSC Graduate Gateway Programme*, Sheffield, MSC.

——(1987d) *The Open College: Course Development Study Group Report*, January, Sheffield, MSC.

——(1988a) *Local Grants to Employers: Guide for Employers*, Sheffield, MSC.

National Advisory Council for Education and Training Targets (1995) *Review of the National Targets for Education and Training: Report on the Outcomes of the Consultation to Update the National Targets*, London, NACETT.

——(2000) *Aiming Higher: NACETT's Report on the National Learning Targets for England and Advice on Targets Beyond 2002*, November, London, NACETT.

National Advisory Council on Employment of People with Disabilities (1992) *NACEPD – Report January 1991 to June 1992*, NACEPD.

National Audit Office (1991) *Sale of the Skills Training Agency*, London, HMSO.

National Council for Educational Technology (1988) *Supported Self-Study: The State of the Art*, Sheffield, Training Commission.

National Council for Industry Training Organisations (1990) *Code of Practice for Industry Training Organisations*, Shepreth, Royston, Herts, NCITO.

National Council for Vocational Qualifications (1989) *Annual Report for the Period Ended 31 March 1989*, London, NCVQ.

National Council for Work Experience (2006) *NCWE Work Experience Quality Mark*, Manchester, NCWE.

National Curriculum Council (1991) *Teacher Placements and the National Curriculum*, York, National Curriculum Council.

National Disability Council (1996) *National Disability Council Annual Report 1995–1996*, London, HMSO.

National Employment Panel Skills Advisory Board (2004) *Welfare to Workforce Development*, http://www.dwp.gov.uk/docs/skillswelfaretoworkforcedevelopment.pdf (accessed 5 April 2010).

National Grid for Learning (1997) *Connecting the Learning Society: National Grid for Learning: The Government's Consultation Paper*, London, DfEE.

National Record of Achievement (1997) *National Record of Achievement: Report of the Steering Group*, London, DfEE.

National Skills Task Force (2001) *Opportunity and Skills in the Knowledge-Driven Economy: A Final Statement on the Work of the National Skills Task Force From the Secretary of State for Education and Employment*, London, DfEE.

National Training Awards (1997) *National Training Awards 1996*, London, DfEE.

National Training Organisations (1998) *National Training Organisations: Prospectus 1999–2000: Strategic Guidance*, London, DfEE.

National Training Task Force (1992) *National Targets for Education and Training*, London, NTTF.

New Standard (June 2007) *Introducing the New Standard: Developed by CFE for the Learning and Skills Council*, Leicester.

Newby, A. (1992) *Cost Effective Training: A Manager's Guide*, London, Kogan Page.

Newscheck (1998a) 'The Learning Card', *Newscheck*, Vol. 8, No. 6, April, pp. 5–6. Sheffield, COIC.

——(1998b) 'The Scottish Qualifications Authority', *Newscheck*, Vol. 8, No. 7, May, pp. 14–15, Sheffield, COIC.

Nicod, M. and Jackson, A. (1985) *Review of Industrial Language Training Service: Final Report*, MSC, Sheffield.

NISVQ (1993) *National Information System for Vocational Qualifications: First Report on Evaluation of Pilot (January 1992 – August 1993)*, Sheffield, Employment Department.

Normington, D., Brodie, H. and Munro, J. (1986) *Value for Money in the Community Programme*, Sheffield, MSC.

Northern Ireland Office (1990) *Religious and Political Discrimination and Equality of Opportunity in Northern Ireland*, Standing Advisory Commission on Human Rights presented to Parliament by the Secretary of State for Northern Ireland, Northern Ireland Office.

O'Connell, B. (1990) 'Training Infrastructure – The Industry Level', *Employment Gazette*, pp. 353–59.

O'Connor, D. (1981) *Probabilities of Employment on Leaving Work Experience Schemes*, Government Economic Service Working Paper, No. 53.

Office for National Statistics (1993) *Census of Employment Statistics*, London, Office for National Statistics.

Office of the Deputy Prime Minister (October 2002) *The Learning Curve: Developing Skills and Knowledge for Neighbourhood Renewal, Main report*, London, Neighbourhood Renewal Unit.

——(2006) *Local Area Agreements: Guidance for Round 3 and Refresh of Rounds 1 and 2*, London, ODPM.

OFSTED (1994) *The Technology Schools Initiative 1992–1993: A Report from the Office of Her Majesty's Chief Inspector of Schools*, London, HMSO.

——(2000) *Family Learning: A Survey of Current Practice*, London, OFSTED.

——(2001a) *Office of Her Majesty's Chief Inspector of Schools in England: Resource Accounts 1999–2000*, London, HMSO.

——(2001b) *Handbook for Inspecting Colleges*, London, OFSTED.

——(2001c) *Specialist Schools: A Evaluation of Progress*, London, OFSTED.

——(2001d) *Advanced Skills Teachers: Appointment, Deployment and Impact, HMI 273*, London, Office for Standards in Education.

——(2003) *College and Area-Wide Inspections*, London, OFSTED.

——(2007) *The Annual Report of Her Majesty's Chief Inspector of Education, Children's Services and Skills 2006/07*, The Stationery Office.

Office of the Qualifications and Examinations Regulator (2008) *Introducing the New Regulator of Qualifications, Exams and Tests*, London, The Stationery Office.

Oldham Independent Review (2001) *One Oldham One Future*, Panel Report 11 December 2001, Oldham, Oldham Independent Review.

Ollin, R. and Tucker, J. (1994) *The NVQ and GNVQ Assessor Handbook*, London, Kogan Page.

Open Tech (June 1982) *Open Tech Task Group Report*, Sheffield, MSC.

Organisation for Economic Co-operation and Development (December 2001) *OECD Economic Outlook 70*, Paris, OECD.

Owens, A. (1989) *General Research and Evaluation of the Enterprise Allowance Scheme (EAS) and EAS and the Long-Term Unemployed*, Sheffield, ES Research and Evaluation Branch Report No. 23.

Parker, G. (1990) *Who is Being Helped by the Special Schemes for People With Disabilities? An Analysis of Statistical Returns on the Fares to Work (FTW) Special Aids to Employment (SAE) and Adaptations to Premises and Equipment (APE) Schemes: (April 1987 – March 1988)*, Sheffield, Research and Evaluation Branch Report No. 57.

Parliamentary Papers (1880) Volume 15, Christian Knowledge Society (Scotland) 9 July 1880, London, HMSO.

Pascoe, K. (1986) *The Delivery of Restart Provision Taking Account of the Wider Opportunities Training Programme*, Sheffield, MSC.

Payne, J., Payne, C., Lissenburgh, S. and Range, M. (1999) *Work Based Training and Job Prospects for the Unemployed: An Evaluation of Training for Work*, DfEE Research Report RR96, London, DfEE.

PCFC/UFC (1992) *First Report on the Action Plan for the Creation of a Single Funding Council for Higher Education in England*, London, PCFC/UFC.

P-e International (1992) *Evaluation of the Prince's Youth Business Trust: Revised Draft*, Sheffield, Employment Service.

Pearce, S. and Neave, A. (February 1989) *Restart Courses – Follow-up Survey*, Sheffield, ES Research and Evaluation Branch Report No. 12.

PER (1976) *PER: The First Three Years*, London, Central Office of Information.

Percival, J. (1978) *The Society for the Diffusion of Useful Knowledge, 1826–1848: A Handlist of the Society's Correspondence and Papers*, London, The Library of University College London, Occasional Papers, No. 5.

Policy Action Team on Skills (1999) *Skills for Neighbourhood Renewal*, London, DfEE.

Powell, B. (1995) *Support for Adult Learning From City Challenge Schemes and Economic Initiatives*, Leicester, NIACE.

Pratt, J. (1997) The Polytechnic Experiment 1965–1992, Buckingham, Society for Research in Higher Education and Open University Press.

Pratten, C. and Ryan, P. (1995) *The Effects of Employment Action*, Cambridge, University of Cambridge Department of Applied Economics Working Paper No. 9530.

Price, D. (2000) *Office of Hope: A History of the Employment Service*, London, Policy Studies Institute.

Prys, D. and Jones, J. P. M. (1998) *Standardised Welsh Terminology for the Schools of Wales: English-Welsh, Welsh-English*, Cardiff, ACCAC.

Qualifications and Curriculum Authority (September 1998) *Education for Citizenship and the Teaching of Democracy in Schools*, London, QCA.

——(1999) *Qualifications 16–19: A Guide to the Changes Resulting From the Qualifying for Success Consultation*, London, QCA.

——(2001) *GCSE, GCSE in Vocational Subjects, GCE, VCE and GNVQ Code of Practice*, London, QCA.

——(2002) *GCSE, GCSE in Vocational Subjects, GCE, VCE and GNVQ Code of Practice 2002/3*, London, QCA.

Qualifications and Curriculum Authority/Learning and Skills Council (March 2004) *Principles for a Credit Framework for England*, London, QCA.

——(2007) *The Prospectus for Progression Pathways*, Draft Working Version for 2007/08, December 2007.

Quality Improvement Agency (2006) *Pursuing Excellence: An Outline Improvement Strategy for Consultation*, Coventry, QIA.

Raffe, D. (1990) 'The context of the Youth Training Scheme: An Analysis of its Strategy and Development', in Gleeson, D. (ed.) *Training and its Alternatives*, Oxford, Oxford University Press.

Rebello, S. (1991) 'Reviving the Inner Cities – the CAT Way', *Employment Gazette*, June, pp. 344–46.

Rée, H. (1985) *Educator Extraordinary. The life and achievement of Henry Morris 1889–1961*, London: Peter Owen.

Regional Development Agency National Coordination Unit (2002) *The Framework for Regional Employment and Skills Action*, Birmingham, RDA National Coordination Unit.

Remploy (2009) *Annual Report and Financial Statements 2009*, Leicester, Remploy Ltd.

Report of the Bristol Diocesan School Society (1855) London, Department of Science and Art, printed at the Mirror Office by John Flower containing the *Rules and Regulations of the Trade School*.

Roberts, K. (1971) *From School to Work: A Study of the Youth Employment Service*, Newton Abbot, David and Charles.

Robertson, P. L. (1974) 'Technical education in the British Shipbuilding and Marine Engineering Industries 1863–1914', *The Economic History Review* 27, pp. 222–35.

Robertson, T. J. (1912) 'Primary Schools (Scotland)', in Laurie, A. P. *The Teacher's Encyclopaedia*, London, Caxton Publishing company, Vol. 5, pp. 68–73.

Roebuck, M. (1985) *The 16+ Action Plan in Scotland*, Bristol, Coombe Lodge Report, Vol. 18, No. 2.

366

Ronge, J. and Ronge, B. (1855) *The Practical Guide to the English Kinder Garten: for the Use of Mothers, Nursery Governesses, and Infant Teachers*, London, J. S. Hodson.

Rowley, M. (1983) *Fit for Work Award Scheme Evaluation: Survey of Disablement Resettlement Officers*, Sheffield, MSC.

Rowntree, J. W. and Binns, H. B. (1903) *A History of the Adult School Movement*, London, Headley Brothers.

RSGB (1991) *Business Enterprise Programme Evaluation: Final Report*, Sheffield, Research Strategies of Great Britain Ltd.

Rudd, P., Jamison, J., Saunders, L., Davies, D., Johnson, F. and Ashby, P. (2000) *Evaluation of Pilot Beacon Schools*, London, DfEE Research Report RR223.

Sadler, J. (2002) *Making the Best Match: Improving the Quality of Pre-Course Information, Advice and Guidance*, London, Learning and Skills Development Agency.

Sadler, M. (1907) *Continuation Schools in England and Elsewhere: Their Place in the Educational System of an Industrial and Commercial State*, Manchester, Victoria University.

Sainsbury, Lord (October 2007) *Race to the Top: A Review of Government's Science and Innovation Policies*, London, HM Treasury.

School Examinations and Assessment Council (1990) *GCSE: A Guide to the General Certificate of Secondary Education*, London, SEAC.

SCONTO (1998) *National Training Organisations: A Guide to Effective Operation in Scotland*, Edinburgh, The Scottish Office.

——(1999) *National Training Organisations: A Practical Approach in Scotland*, Edinburgh, The Scottish Office.

Scotland, J. (1969) *The History of Scottish Education*, Volume 2, London, University of London Press.

Scottish Affairs Committee (1995) *The Operation of the Enterprise Agencies and the LECs*, HC 339, HMSO.

Scottish Executive (2000) *Introducing Learning Accounts in Scotland*, Edinburgh, Tactical Solutions.

——(2002) *Standard for Chartered Teacher*, Edinburgh, Scottish Executive.

Scottish Executive Enterprise and Lifelong Learning Department (2000a) *Scottish Enterprise: Skillseekers Training for Young People*, SE/2000/19, Edinburgh, The Stationery Office.

Scottish Government (2007) *Skills for Scotland: A Lifelong Learning Strategy*, Edinburgh, Scottish Government.

Scottish Office (1998) *Opportunity Scotland: A Paper on Lifelong Learning, Cm4048*, Edinburgh, The Stationery Office.

Scottish Office (1999) *New Community Schools Prospectus*, www.scotland.gov.uk/library/documents-w3/ncsp-01.htm (accessed 12 February 2010).

Secondary School Examinations Council (1932) *Curriculum and Examinations in Secondary Schools*, London, HMSO.

Sector Skills Development Agency (2001) *Skills for Business*, Wath upon Dearne, SSDA.

Senker, P. J. (1992) *Industrial Training in a Cold Climate*, Aldershot, Avebury.

Sexton, A. H. (1994) *The First Technical College: A Sketch of 'the Andersonian' and the Institutions Descended From it 1796–1894*, London, Chapman Hall.

Shanks, K. and Courtenay, G. (1982) *Young People, Work and Community Industry*, London, CI Research and Planning Paper No.3.

Shaw, J. (1999) *An Early Evaluation of the Union Learning Fund*, York Consulting Ltd.

Sheldrake, J. and Vickerstaff, S. (1987) *A History of Industrial Training*, London, Abbeystrand.

Sheppard, W. and Blakey, L. (1987) *An Evaluation of the Managing Company Expansion Scheme*, Sheffield, MSC, Evaluation and Research Branch.

Short, C., Sawdon, A. and Tucker, S. (1982) *CEP is Working: The Report of a Study of the Community Enterprise Programme by Youthaid*, MSC, Sheffield.

Simmons, A. (2002) 'NHS Workforce Development Confederations', *Newscheck*, April, p. 8.

Skills for Business (2004) *Sector Skills Agreements*, Wath upon Dearne, Sector Skills Development Agency.

Slack, G. G. (1942) *Liability for National Service*, London, Butterworth and Co.

Smith, A. (1776) *An Inquiry into the Nature and Causes of the Wealth of Nations*, Book V, London, W. Strahan and T. Cadell.

Smith, C. (1989) *The New Job Training Scheme in Retrospect*, Sheffield, Training Agency.

Smith, D. (1977) *A Small Scale Study of the Work Experience Programme*, Oxford, Birkbeck College.

Smith, D. V. L. (November 1993) *Evaluation of Worktrials: Employer Survey*, Sheffield, Employment Service.

Smith, P. (November 1988) *Survey of Voluntary Projects Programme Participants*, Sheffield, Employment Service.

Smith, P., Hamilton, L. and Clemens, S. (1990) *Jobstart: Survey of Employers*, London, Social and Community Planning Research P1015.

Smithers, A. and Robinson, P. (eds) (2000) *Further Education Reformed*, London, Falmer Press.

Social Exclusion Unit (2001) *A New Commitment to Neighbourhood Renewal: National Strategy Action Plan*, London, Social Exclusion Unit, Cabinet Office.

Spandler, P. (1991) *Report into Continued Development of Group Training Associations Without Support from the Statutory Levy-Grant Systems: Final Report*, Grimsby, National Association of Training Groups Ltd.

Speke, B. and Whelan, E. (1979) *Report of the Study Team on the Training Needs of YPWPC Occupational Supervisors*, Manchester, University of Manchester.

Spilsbury, M., Moralee, J., Hillage, J. and Frost, D. (1995) *Evaluation of Investors in People in England and Wales 1994–1995*, Institute for Employment Studies Report No. 289, Brighton, University of Sussex.

Stansfield, C. E. (1912) 'The boarding schools of the Society of Friends', in Laurie, A. P. *The Teacher's Encyclopaedia*, London, Caxton Publishing Company, pp. 129–35.

Stephen, K. (1982) *Andrew Bell*, Edinburgh, History of Medicine and Science Unit, University of Edinburgh.

Stern, J., Willis, C., Francis, N. and Goodyear, R. (1996) *OECD Wage Subsidy Evaluations: Lessons for Workstart*, London, Report for the DfEE by NERA.

Task Force Human Resources Education, Training, Youth (1990) *FORCE Continuing Vocational Training in Europe*, Brussels, Official Journal of the European Communities, 21.6.1990.

Tavistock Institute of Human Relations (1987) *The Open Tech Programme Development Review: Final Report*, London, Tavistock Institute of Human Relations Employment Policy and Vocational Training Research.

——(1999) *A Review of 30 New Deal Partnerships: Part of the Case Study Evaluation of New Deal for Young Unemployed People*, Sheffield, Employment Service.

Taylor, P. and Thackwray, B. (1995) *Investors in People Explained*, Kogan Page, London.

Teacher Training Agency (1994) *New Heads and Headteachers: Teacher Training Agency Consultations*, News 3/94, London, TTA.

——(1997) *Training Curriculum and Standards for New Teachers: Consultation*, London, TTA.

Teasdale, P. (1996) *Evaluation of Active Labour Market Policies: A Bibliography*, Sheffield, DfEE.

The Monitor (1997) 'Awarding an NVQ: The Key Players', *The Monitor*, Issue 5, p. 10, London, Qualifications and Curriculum Authority.

Thomas, A., Griffith, S. and Pettigrew, N. (1998) *Education and Training Whilst Claiming Jobseeker's Allowance: Workskill Pilots*, London, DfEE Research Report RR61.

Thomas, A., Williams, J. and Griffiths, R. (2001) *New Deal for Musicians: Qualitative evaluation phase II*, Sheffield, Employment Service.

Thomas, J. B. (1978) 'The day training college; a Victorian innovation in teacher training', *Journal of Education for Teaching*, 4.3. pp. 249–61.

Thomson, A. and Rosenberg, H. (1987) *A Users Guide to the Manpower Services Commission*, London, Kogan Page.

Thurbin, P. J. and Hinton, I. H. (1981) *The New Manager Project: A Research Programme Carried Out by the Kingston Regional Management Centre for the Manpower Services Commission: Final Report*, Sheffield, MSC.

Training Agency (1989a) *Inner Cities: Training in the cities, Series: Action for Cities Building on Initiative*, Sheffield, Training Agency.

——(1989b) *Business Plan Small Firms Service*, Sheffield, Training Agency.

——(1990) April, *Training Agency Research, Annual Report 1990*, Sheffield, Training Agency.

——(1989) *Tourism Training Initiative: TTI: Final Report*, Sheffield, Training Agency Industry Bodies Branch.

——(1989a) *Work Related Further Education: A Guidance Handbook*, Sheffield, Training Agency.

Training and Development Agency for Schools (2007) *2007–10 Corporate Plan: Developing People, Improving Young Lives*, TDA.

Training and Development Lead Body (1995) *National Standards for Training and Development*, Leicester, TDLB.

Training and Employment Agency (1991–2001), *Training and Employment Agency Annual Reports*, part of Department for Education and Learning, Belfast.

Training Services Agency (1978) *Mobile Instructor Service: a Training Service for Industry*, Sheffield, MSC, Training Services Agency.

Training Standards Advisory Service (1991) *TSAS: Review of Activity September 1989 – 31 March 1991*, Sheffield, Employment Department.

Training Standards Council (2000) *Annual Report of the Training Standards Council (1998–1999)*, Oxford, TSC.

Tremlett, N. (1995) *The Business Start Up Scheme Cohort Survey Second Stage*, London, SCPR, February.

Tremlett, N., Park, A. and Dundon-Smith, D. (1995) *Individual Commitment to Learning: Further Findings from the Individuals Survey*, London, SCPR.

Tucker, S. (1993) *The Report of a Study of Education and Training on the Community Enterprise Programme*, Sheffield, MSC.

Turner, P. (1985) 'After the Community Programme – Results of the First Follow Up Survey', *Employment Gazette*, January, pp. 9–14.

Tylecote, M. (1957) *The Mechanics' Institutes of Lancashire and Yorkshire Before 1851*, Manchester, Manchester University Press, p. 74.

Ufl (1999) *A New Way of Learning: The Ufl Network: Developing the University for Industry Concept*, Sheffield, Ufl.

UK Online (2001) *UK Online Annual Report 2001*, London, Office of the e-Envoy, Cabinet Office.

Unemployment Unit (1987) *Half Measures: A Review of MSC Special Employment and Training Programmes*, London, Unemployment Unit.

——(1988) *The Community Programme and the Long Term Unemployed*, London, Unemployment Unit.

University of Exeter (1988) *The Directory of TRIST Practice: An Analysis of the Project: Its Use and Impact*, Exeter, School of Education.

Vlaeminke, M. (2000) *The English Higher Grade Schools: A Lost Opportunity*, London, Woburn.

West, A. and Ciotti, M. (1998) *The New Start Strategy: Engaging the Community*, London, DfEE.

Weston, P. (2000) *Friedrich Froebel: His Life, Times and Significance*, London, Roehampton Institute.

——(2002) *The Froebel Educational Institute: The Origins and History of the College*, London, Roehampton, University of Surrey.

Whitear, G. (1995) *The NVQ and GNVQ Handbook and Guide to Career Success*, London, Pitman.

Wicks, P. (1992) *Scotland's Local Enterprise Companies (LECs): An Assessment*, London, London School of Economics.

Wilkin, A., White, R. and Kinder, K. (2003) *Towards Extended Schools: A Literature Review*, London, DfES Research Report 432.

Williamson, D. (1990) 'Filling the Breach in "Civvy Street"', *Employment Gazette,* May, pp. 20–24.

Willis, R. (2005) *The Struggle for the General Teaching Council*, London, RoutledgeFalmer.

Wilson, J. P. (ed.) (1999) *Human Resource Development: Learning and Training for Individuals and Organisations*, London, Kogan Page.

Wilson, J. P. (2000) 'Citius, Altius, Fortius: The Skills Olympics and Skills Competitions', *Industrial and Commercial Training*, Vol. 32, No. 6

Wolf, A. (1995) *Competence Based Assessment*, Buckingham, Open University Press.

Women and Work Commission (September 2006) *Government Action Plan: Implementing the Women and Work Commission Recommendations*, London, Department for Communities and Local Government.

Wood, H. P. (1987) *David Stow and the Glasgow Normal Seminary*, Glasgow, Jordan Hill College of Education.

Working Brief (1990) 'Failing the guarantee', *Working Brief*, December, p. 13.

Working Ventures UK (2009) *Working Ventures UK Limited Financial Statements for the Year Ended 31 March 2009*, London, HMSO.

Wray, M. J., Moor, C., and Hill, S., (1980) *Unified Vocational Preparation: An Evaluation of the Pilot*, Slough, National Foundation for Educational Research.

Youth Training Scheme (1984) *Youth Training Scheme: Guidance for Schemes – Accredited Centres*, London, YTS.

eBooks – at www.eBookstore.tandf.co.uk

A library at your fingertips!

eBooks are electronic versions of printed books. You can store them on your PC/laptop or browse them online.

They have advantages for anyone needing rapid access to a wide variety of published, copyright information.

eBooks can help your research by enabling you to bookmark chapters, annotate text and use instant searches to find specific words or phrases. Several eBook files would fit on even a small laptop or PDA.

NEW: Save money by eSubscribing: cheap, online access to any eBook for as long as you need it.

Annual subscription packages

We now offer special low-cost bulk subscriptions to packages of eBooks in certain subject areas. These are available to libraries or to individuals.

For more information please contact webmaster.ebooks@tandf.co.uk

We're continually developing the eBook concept, so keep up to date by visiting the website.

www.eBookstore.tandf.co.uk